T0265297

CONTEMPORARY CHINESE POLITICAL ECONOMY

www.royalcollins.com

CONTEMPORARY CHINESE POLITICAL ECONOMY

Jianxun Shi

Translated by Boying Li

RC

Books Beyond Boundaries

ROYAL COLLINS

Contemporary Chinese Political Economy

Jianxun Shi
Translated by Boying Li

First published in 2024 by Royal Collins Publishing Group Inc.
Groupe Publication Royal Collins Inc.
BKM Royalcollins Publishers Private Limited

Headquarters: 550-555 boul. René-Lévesque O Montréal (Québec) H2Z1B1 Canada
India office: 805 Hemkunt House, 8th Floor, Rajendra Place, New Delhi 110008

Original Edition © Tsinghua University Press
This English edition is authorized by Tsinghua University Press.

This book is published with financial support from the Chinese Fund for the
Humanities and Social Sciences.

ISBN: 978-1-4878-1211-9

To find out more about our publications, please visit www.royalcollins.com.

Contents

CHAPTER FOUR

CHAPTER FIVE

PART THREE   DEVELOPMENT CONCEPTS AND BUILDING A MODERN ECONOMIC SYSTEM

CHAPTER SIX

CHAPTER SEVEN

PART FOUR   THE DEVELOPMENT PATH AND DEVELOPMENT STRATEGY

CHAPTER EIGHT

PART FIVE PROMOTING HEALTHY DEVELOPMENT OF MARKET ENTITIES

PART SIX MACROECONOMIC REGULATION

PART SEVEN   BUILDING A COMMUNITY WITH A SHARED FUTURE FOR MANKIND ALONGSIDE AN OPEN ECONOMY

An Introduction to Contemporary Chinese Political Economy

Since the 18th National Congress of the Communist Party of China (CPC) in 2012, Chinese President Xi Jinping has further developed the Marxist political economy by combining its basic principles with "socialism with Chinese characteristics"; proposed a series of new ideas and assertions; innovated and enriched the theory of Chinese socialist political economy; introduced new concepts and theories of economic development to China and the world; and formed Xi Jinping Thought on Socialism with Chinese Characteristics for a New Era. Guided by these achievements, this book provides a systemic study of contemporary Chinese political economy and includes the following aspects.

I. The Formation and Development of Contemporary Chinese Political Economy

Contemporary Chinese political economy is China's latest achievement, incorporating basic principles of Marxist political economy with actual economic development in China. Spanning more than 150 years—including the pioneering economic theories of Marx and Engels and the establishment of the Soviet political system—the development of contemporary Chinese political economy is deemed to be an ideological instrument that guides the economic construction of socialism with Chinese characteristics.

1. The emergence of socialist political economy

Socialist political economy expands on the socialist mode of production and the laws of its development. It is an important part of Marxist political economy. Marx and Engels were the founders of both scientific socialism and socialist political economy. Through in-depth analysis of the contradictions and motive laws that underpin the capitalist mode of production, Marx and Engels formed the blueprint for future communist and socialist economic relations.

This blueprint includes realizing the free and comprehensive development of man and the establishment of a free human association; the elimination of private ownership and establishment of the social ownership of the means of production; the implementation of demand-based distribution in the higher stage of communism and labor-based distribution in the lower stage; the elimination of commodity production and the establishment of planned regulation of social production; the elimination of the distinction between urban and rural areas, and between workers and peasants, and the integration of urban and rural areas; the demise of classes and the state with the rule over people to be replaced by the management of things and the leadership of the production process; the disappearance of ethnic divisions and antagonisms between peoples of different countries; and the prolonged transition to socialism, during which various forms of intermediation—such as cooperative systems and commodity production—can be adopted. This theory is the origin, basis, and genesis of socialist political economy and an important guide for socialist revolution and construction. However, these theories only mark the starting point of a socialist political economy—not its finished form nor its end. The theories need continuous testing, enrichment, and development.

Socialist political economy burgeoned in the Union of Soviet Socialist Republics (USSR). With the continuous development of a socialist economy, there was an urgent need for a socialist political economy. In 1936, the Central Committee of the Communist Party of the Soviet Union (CPSU, or Bolsheviks) formed a resolution on Reforming the Instruction on Political Economy, formally proposing "Socialist Political Economy" as an independent course offered at universities. In 1937, the Central Committee organized a group of prominent economists to prepare a textbook on political economy, which included a section on socialist political economy. By the end of 1940, a draft form was completed, and under Stalin's leadership, it was effectively completed in 1951. After several revisions by the Central Committee, the textbook was officially published in August 1954, marking the birth of socialist political economy as an independent science.

2. The formation and development of contemporary Chinese political economy

With Marxism as the guiding ideology for its founding, the CPC has always attached great importance to its research and application. After the founding of the People's Republic of China (PRC) in 1949, the Chinese Communists, represented by Mao Zedong, led the nation in its transformation from a new democracy to a socialist system and strove to build a socialist economy suitable for China. Mao came up with a series of original theoretical views on socialist economic development—for example, regarding agriculture as the foundation of the economy and industry as playing the main role; approaching state planning of every sector as a whole; attaching equal weight to both central and local authorities; properly handling the relationships among the state, the collective, and the individual so that each party could get its share; establishing independent and relatively complete industrial and national economic systems, and fully modernizing agriculture, industry, national defense, and science and technology (S&T); and seeking self-reliance first and foreign aid only as a supplement. These perspectives were innovations in Marxist political economy. Mao paid great attention to the development of socialist political economy and repeatedly called on Party officials to study it and conduct in-depth studies of the Soviet textbook, recognize its valuable contents, point out its shortcomings and errors, and propose insights. This helped blaze the trail for a socialist political economy with Chinese characteristics.

Since the Third Plenary Session of the 11th CPC Central Committee, convened in December 1978, the CPC has incorporated the basic principles of Marxist political economy into the new practice of reform and opening-up. This has continuously enriched the Marxist political economy. After the adoption of the Decision of the CPC Central Committee on Reform of the Economic Structure in October 1984, Deng Xiaoping stated that the Decision represented a "first draft" of political economy that fused the basic principles of Marxism with the practice of Chinese socialism. Since China's reform and opening-up more than 40 years ago, Chinese socialism has evolved, making several important theoretical achievements, including theories on the essence of socialism; scientific development; development of a moderately prosperous society in all aspects; the three-step development strategy; the basic economic system of the primary stage of socialism; economic structural reform; the basic socialist distribution system; socialist market economy; opening up; new forms of industrialization, independent innovation, new-type urbanization and agricultural modernization; development of a new socialist countryside; deepening of supply-side reform; and development of a modernized economy, high-quality development, and a development paradigm in which "internal circulation" is the mainstay and the internal and external circulations reinforce each other. These achievements constitute a political economy adapted to contemporary China's national conditions and the characteristics of the times—they have not only guided China's economic development effectively but also enriched and developed Marxist political economy.

3. Contemporary Chinese political economy guided by Xi's socialist economic thought

Xi Jinping Thought on Socialism with Chinese Characteristics for a New Era is based on China's economic development entering a new era and new changes in the principal contradiction facing Chinese society. Not only does it profoundly reflect major shifts in the world's political and economic landscape in the new era, but it also addresses the essential question of how to assess and develop China's economy. Since the 18th National Congress, the CPC Central Committee, with Xi at its core, has put forward a series of major strategic ideas and perspectives on developing the modern socialist Chinese economy, including: firmly supporting innovative, coordinated, green, open and shared development; adhering to a people-centered philosophy of development; recognizing the market's decisive role in resource allocation; establishing an economic system with public ownership at the center and multiple forms of ownership surrounding it; making state-owned enterprises bigger and stronger (as they are an important force in driving modernization and safeguarding the common interests of the people); improving the integration of urban and rural development, and promoting the equal exchange and rational allocation of urban and rural factors and equalization of basic public services; expediting the establishment of a new system for open economy to further higher-level opening up and develop a more advanced open economy; fostering a broad community of interests; understanding, adapting to, and guiding, the new normal; strengthening supply-side structural reform; developing a modern economy and promoting high-quality development; developing a "dual circulation" economic pattern to ensure that China can eradicate poverty and build a moderately prosperous society in all respects; and building a modern socialist country, etc. These strategic ideas and theoretical perspectives have enriched the Chinese economy, established a new framework, and built on traditional Marxist theory.

Contemporary Chinese political economy, guided by Xi's socialist economic thought, draws deeply on previous Chinese socialist theories. It not only incorporates much of Mao Zedong Thought but also builds on the Deng Xiaoping Theory, the Theory of Three Represents, and the Scientific Outlook on Development. Additionally, Xi's socialist economic thought not only adheres to traditional Marxist political economy but also incorporates lessons drawn from contemporary capitalist economic development and rational components of Western economic theories.

This has formed an unprecedented "closed-loop" theoretical system which can be best summarized by the following seven points:

First, China insists on strengthening the centralized and unified leadership of the CPC on economic policies to ensure the Chinese economy continues to develop in the right direction. This statement captures the essence that "the leadership of the CPC is the essential feature and the greatest advantage of socialism with Chinese characteristics on the economic front."

Second, China adheres to a people-centered philosophy of development that promotes balanced economic, political, cultural, social, and ecological progress and coordinated implementation of the five-pronged comprehensive strategy. This philosophy of development answers the question of "development for whom"—i.e., the purposes of development and the orientation of values.

Third, the top leadership adapts to and steers the new normal of economic development based on the overall situation and development laws. This is a new approach to effectively anticipate and react to the economic situation. This new vision of innovative, coordinated, green, open, and shared development reflects a deepening of the CPC's understanding of economic and social development in China.

Fourth, China shall give the market a decisive role in the allocation of resources, improve the role of the government, and resolutely remove institutional obstacles to economic development. This answers the question of what kind of institutional mechanism is needed for economic development.

Fifth, China insists on adapting to changes in the principal contradiction in economic development by improving macro-control, making well-timed choices, and focusing on supply-side structural reform as the main line of economic work.

Sixth, China adheres to a solution-oriented strategy to develop its economy, which has far-reaching effects on economic and social transformation in China. This is a novel idea for solving major strategic issues concerning the long-term development of China.

Seventh, China maintains a conscientious working strategy and method, pursuing progress while ensuring stability, maintaining strategic focus, and moving forward step by step. This reflects the methodology and strategy of economic work—pursuing progress while ensuring stability is an important principle of national governance.

II. Content and Characteristics

1. The main contents of contemporary Chinese political economy

(1) The fundamental position of Chinese socialism

Taking a people-centered approach is key in the new era. Improving people's well-being, promoting well-rounded human development, and making steady progress toward common prosperity have always underpinned economic development, reflecting the values of a socialist political economy with Chinese characteristics.

(2) Fundamental tasks of Chinese socialism

Traditional socialist political economy takes production relations as the main object of study, while the principal objective of Chinese socialism is to develop productive forces and prioritize development. From this perspective, Chinese socialism gives greater prominence to the promotion of productive forces.

(3) The motive law and characteristics of the principal contradiction facing Chinese society in the new era

Research on this concept is the task of the Chinese socialist political economy. It strives to summarize China's practical experience into a systematic doctrine and extract universal principles from China's experience, providing a compelling alternative for nations across the world that wish to expedite development while maintaining their independence and contributing Chinese wisdom and solutions to common problems of mankind.

(4) Basic economic system of Chinese socialism in the primary stage

Along with the evolution of the principal contradiction of Chinese society, this forms the logical starting point of the Chinese socialist political economy today. The basic economic system (with public ownership at the core and multiple forms of ownership developing together) is the foundation, determining all aspects and interconnections of the socialist economy with Chinese characteristics. A mixed economy with a blend of state-owned, collective, and non-public capital is important for China's economic development.

(5) Distribution system

A diversified income distribution system with work at the center. China will improve efficiency, allow the income gap to widen to a reasonable degree, and mobilize the enthusiasm of all parties to create wealth. Meanwhile, it will make efforts to prevent polarization, maintain social equity, and gradually achieve common prosperity. Thus, people can share the fruits of reform and development. Both primary distribution and redistribution should give due consideration to efficiency and equity.

(6) Reform

Reform is the self-improvement of the socialist system and a powerful driving force for development. In accordance with the overarching goal of developing socialism with Chinese characteristics and modernizing national governance, China shall deepen economic structural reform across the board, balance the relations of production with the productive forces, as well as those of the superstructure with the economic base, and form a more mature economic system.

(7) Market economy of socialism with Chinese characteristics

Integrating the socialist system with the market economy, which makes full use of the advantages of socialism and the strengths of the market economy, is the theoretical core and distinctive feature of the Chinese socialist political economy. A series of original ideas have been put forward in the new era. Exploring the organic combination of public and private ownership, government and market, freedom and centralization, efficiency and equity, openness and autonomy, stability and change, and tradition and modernization has produced remarkable results.

(8) The state policy of opening up

China takes a holistic approach to the situation both at home and abroad and makes better use of both international and domestic markets and resources to develop an open economy of higher standards. It takes an active part in global economic governance to make the international economic order more just, equitable, and mutually beneficial. Also, it adheres to independence, stands firm in safeguarding its development interests, and guards against every risk to keep its economy safe.

(9) The development outlook

China is committed to innovative, coordinated, green, open, and shared development. Innovation is the primary driving force for development. Coordination is an inherent requirement for sustained and healthy development. Green development is a prerequisite for sustainable development and underscores people's expectations for a better life. Openness is a certain path to national development and prosperity. Sharing is an essential requirement for socialism with Chinese characteristics.

(10) The path of new industrialization, IT application, urbanization, and agricultural modernization

China advances the integration of IT application and industrialization, the interaction between industrialization and urbanization, and the coordination between urbanization, and agricultural modernization, thus promoting harmonized development. China also endeavors to improve the institutions and mechanisms of integrated urban-rural development to form new relations between industry and agriculture and between urban and rural areas. As a result, the overwhelming majority of farmers can participate in the modernization process on an equal footing.

The principal contradiction facing Chinese society in the new era has evolved, and China remains in the primary stage of socialism. This sets the backdrop for contemporary Chinese political economy and constitutes the basic foundation for the Chinese socialist economic system.

2. The significance of studying contemporary Chinese political economy

(1) Expanding the interpretation of the socialist economic system

The development of economic theory and practice of Chinese socialism has fused the socialist system and the market economy, creating a new form or model of socialism. First, China adopts an ownership structure in which public ownership is the foundation, and economic entities under diverse forms of ownership develop alongside it. Second, China adheres to an income distribution system centered on work. Third, it combines the decisive role of market forces with strong government regulations on economic operations. Fourth, it combines active participation in economic globalization with independence during the course of opening up. Fifth, it puts forward a systematic philosophy of development to promote economic growth. Finally, it remains dedicated to public ownership and distribution according to work, a system suited to the socialist market economy. These profound changes reflect the requirements of the times and inject the system with new life, invigorating Chinese socialism and playing to its strengths.

(2) Expanding the interpretation of a market economy

A market economy is a necessary stage in the development of human society. However, for a long period, the understanding of a market economy in both socialist and capitalist countries was extremely narrow. The perceived wisdom claimed that a market economy was exclusive to capitalism and could not exist within a socialist system. Thus, the development of a market economy under socialist conditions is a great achievement of the CPC and a major contribution to society.

The traditional market economy served a capitalist system that was bound to unleash severe deficiencies and drawbacks, including herd mentality, unpredictability, hysteria, economic crises, and wealth inequality. However, China's socialist market economy incorporates elements of socialism; it has features and strengths that differ from the traditional market economy. On the one hand, it has encouraged market dynamism, such as information responsiveness, high efficiency, effective incentives, and flexible regulation, thus improving the vitality of the economy. On the other hand, it has leveraged the creations of the socialist system, such as public ownership of the means of production, distribution according to labor, planned regulation, overall coordination, independence, and common prosperity. At all times, the CPC commands the entire situation and coordinates the efforts of all quarters from its core position of leadership. Therefore, the socialist market economy—embodying the general principles of a market economy and the inherent requirements of a socialist system—strives for efficiency and equity, independence and openness, and vitality and coordination, thus creating a brighter future for the development of a market economy.

(3) Expanding the understanding of reform methods

The success of China's economic reform shows the world that socialism and a market economy can be combined. The main features of this path are as follows: First, it respects the people's pioneering spirit and advances this cause under CPC leadership. Second, it ensures that reform, development, and stability proceed in tandem—taking into full consideration the momentum of reform, the speed of development, and the capacity of the general public to sustain change. Third, it promotes the improvement and progress of socialism with Chinese characteristics by means of transition from dual-track pricing to a market system, prioritizing steady growth, and making breakthroughs in key areas. Fourth, it focuses on improving the scientific nature of reform decisions and the coordination of reform measures.

China's progressive reforms offer a significant methodological principle test: Any reform or transformation aiming to improve rather than overturn the basic system is bound to follow a progressive approach, in which there is a clear continuity between the old and new systems instead of the two being distinct and opposed, and the transition must undergo many stages, including intermediate phases and steps. By following this methodological principle, China has avoided the institutional breakdowns, disorder, and economic destruction resulting from the radical reforms in the Soviet Union and Eastern Europe, thus maintaining economic stability, promoting economic growth, and delivering successful reforms.

(4) Expanding the understanding of economic development

Development is a pillar of contemporary China, and the CPC considers it to be a top priority in governance. The success of China's economic development has led to new development philosophies. The first relates to economic development strategy. China shows firm resolve in implementing the following strategies: three-step development, innovation-driven development, development of a quality workforce, sustainable development, and coordinated regional development. The second involves the economic development path. China pursues a new type of industrialization featuring advanced production, higher living standards, and healthy ecosystems. The third concerns the economic development mode, including the adjustment of economic speed, the improvement of economic structure, and the enhancement of economic quality and efficiency. These are not only theoretical summaries of China's real-world economic development, but they also represent a deepened understanding of the laws of social and economic development.

(5) Improving the relationship between government and market

The proper handling of the relationship between the government and the market is quintessential to the modern economic system. Features of this relationship vary under different social systems. The role of government in a socialist market economy is different in essence from that of government in a capitalist market economy, mainly in the following ways: first, the government is not only the creator of market rules and regulator of the macro-economy but is also the general representative of the ownership of the means of production owned by the whole people and public interests. Thus, the government is able to amass more resources to regulate economic operations. Second, the role of government is not limited to maintaining market order but also includes maintaining macroeconomic stability, strengthening and optimizing public services and market regulation, ensuring fair competition, promoting sustainable development and common prosperity, and making up for market failures. Third, the government's role is not limited to short-term demand adjustments but includes total adjustment and targeted policy implementation, supply and demand management, and coordination of domestic and international markets. Fourth, the government addresses issues not limited to fiscal and monetary policy but also those involving planning, holistic coordination, market regulation, state-owned asset management, industrial policies, etc. These have greatly surpassed the theoretical framework and experience of Western market economies and improved the understanding of the relationship between government and market.

(6) Greater insight into economic globalization

Economic globalization is partly a result of growing social productivity. However, economic globalization has been a product of the global expansion of capitalism over a long period of time, leading to the continuous global development of its basic contradictions. Therefore, how to integrate economic globalization with the common interests of people all over the world and promote the common development of all countries is a major issue. The discipline of Chinese socialist political economy explores this issue deeply and has formed a systematic understanding as follows: First, there is a loosening of restrictions and a move toward "going global," taking both the domestic and international situations into account and making full use of their markets to optimize resource allocation. Second, economic globalization, as an objective process, can have two development trends—on the one hand, economic globalization promotes a balanced allocation of world resources for the benefit of all peoples; on the other hand, it intensifies the imbalance of world economic development and exacerbates the basic contradictions of capitalism. China should encourage the former trend and be wary of the latter. Third, the nation implements the open strategy of win-win cooperation to help create a more equal and just economic global order and to form a community with a shared future. Fourth, while opening up to the outside world, China catalyzes its own strength and combines adherence to independence with active participation in economic globalization.

III. Building a People-Centered Political Economy in Contemporary China

Contemporary Chinese political economy is a theory dedicated to working for the happiness and well-being of the people. Meeting people's ever-growing needs for a better life is its fundamental purpose, and it explores the laws of "achieving common prosperity and the free and well-rounded development of human beings." A people-centered philosophy is its most fundamental theory and a prominent feature that distinguishes contemporary Chinese political economy from other economic theories.

1. The major principles to be followed in building a people-centered political economy in contemporary China

(1) Adhering to the guiding philosophy of Marxism

Marxism is a socioeconomic theory and the most important achievement in human history. The CPC has consciously integrated it with China's realities, creatively solving a series of major problems throughout the Chinese revolution, and made great achievements that have attracted worldwide attention. Therefore, to construct a socialist political economy with Chinese characteristics, the CPC must adhere to the guiding philosophy of Marxism and inherit the tradition of Marxist political economy. This tradition adopts the methodology of historical and dialectical materialism to scientifically analyze the principal contradictions, relations of production, and modes of production in the primary stage of socialism. This is done in an attempt to reveal the law of development of socialism with Chinese characteristics.

(2) Adhering to the fundamental goal of putting people at the center

It is a must for the CPC to build a socialist political economy with Chinese characteristics from China's actual national conditions and step outside of the set pattern of a capital-centered economic theory system. Solving the principal contradiction in the primary stage of socialism and releasing and developing the productive forces are the starting points. And improving people's welfare and promoting their free and well-rounded development are the ultimate goals. The CPC should summarize and refine the practices and valuable experience of reform and opening-up, reflect the interests and demands of the people, and provide scientific guidance to achieve the Two Centenary Goals that the CPC set forth in 2012. These two goals were to complete a moderately prosperous society by 2021 (the centenary of the CPC's founding) and to build China into a modern socialist country that is prosperous, strong, democratic, culturally advanced, and harmonious by 2049 (the centenary of the PRC's founding).

(3) Fully reflecting the theoretical innovations of the CPC in leading the economic construction of socialism with Chinese characteristics

While adhering to the guiding philosophy of Marxist political economics, the CPC has continuously refined and summarized the achievements of China's economic development. It has turned the practical experience into a systematic theory and put forward many original ideas. During reform and opening-up, for instance, it has developed theories on the basic economic system in the primary stage of socialism, the essence of socialism, socialist reform and opening-up, the socialist market economy, the Scientific Outlook on Development, and so on. Further, the CPC has introduced many additional concepts since the 18th National Congress, including the idea of the new normal for economic development; innovative, coordinated, green, open, and shared development; the theory of developing a socialist market economy (allowing the market to play a decisive role in resource allocation and facilitating the government's ability to play its role effectively); coordinated development of the new-type industrialization; IT application, urbanization and agricultural modernization; the effective utilization of international and domestic markets and resources; promotion of social justice and the gradual realization of common prosperity for all people, etc. All of these concepts have provided rich practical materials and theoretical guidance for the construction of a socialist political economy with Chinese characteristics.

(4) Drawing on Western economic theories

Western economics is "rigid" in its unchanging adherence to the capitalist system. However, it is also reasonable in its long-term exploration of the laws underpinning the operation and development of the market economy. To develop a socialist political economy with Chinese characteristics, the CPC should boldly absorb those theories of Western economics that reasonably expound on the general rules of market economy operation. These include the basic principles of supply and demand, competition and pricing in a market economy, theories on consumer and producer behavior, management of effective demand and effective supply, "market failure" and micro-regulation, modern economic growth and total factor productivity, "dual economic structure," modern property rights and transaction costs, etc. These are all worth learning. However, this does not suggest simply accepting all of the principles of Western economics but rather taking a discerning approach.

2. The major propositions to be studied in people-centered political economy in contemporary China

To study the people-centered political economy in contemporary China, one must adhere to the dialectical unity of logic and history, the abstract and the concrete. Not only is it necessary to systematically summarize the successful experience and theoretical evolution of economic development since the founding of the PRC, but one also should look to the future and examine the development concepts and laws that should be followed in the pursuit of the Two Centenary Goals. Achieving common prosperity and well-rounded development of the people, an essential requirement and development goal of socialism is the ultimate goal and theoretical pursuit of a people-centered socialist political economy with Chinese characteristics. Eliminating poverty, improving living standards, and achieving common prosperity are also fundamental and important missions of the CPC. To build a people-centered socialist political economy with Chinese characteristics, China must face up to and summarize the lessons learned so far. While it is true that the overall "pie" of development is growing larger, it is also the case that the portions are not being shared evenly. There are growing disparities in income levels and in urban and rural public services. Thus, it is imperative that the government systematically study the dynamic distribution law related to "synchronizing the growth of residents' income with economic growth and the increase of labor remuneration with labor productivity," as well as the "redistribution law" whereby national income is aimed at realizing fairness and justice. Moreover, the nation should proactively explore effective systems that uphold the principle that "development is for the people and by the people, and its benefits are shared by the people."

China's National Conditions and Stages of Development

PART ONE

China's National Conditions
and Stages of Development

CHAPTER ONE

China's Development Path and Stages of Advancement

The Historical Inevitability of Socialism with Chinese Characteristics

The foremost questions to be addressed when assessing the Chinese socialist political economy in the new era are as follows: From where does socialism with Chinese characteristics emanate? What paths has it taken? Where is it heading? And what is the historical status of its current development stage?

I. The Course of China's Development Path

For 170 years, China has been exploring its own unique developmental path, from constitutional monarchy to a democratic republic, from the incessant infighting between warlords to Japanese aggression and occupation, from the dictatorship of the Chiang family to the independence of socialist new China, and from the early exploration of socialism to the current practice of socialism with Chinese characteristics. This journey has been marked by three crucial historical events.

The outbreak of the first Opium War in 1839,[1] the first event, interrupted China's feudal society, forced open its closed doors, and compelled its integration into the modern globalized system of industrialization and capitalism. China was thereby reduced to a semi-colonial, semi-feudal society and began to explore the possibility of capitalism in the forms of constitutional monarchy and a fleeting democratic republic. Following the Revolution of 1911, which overthrew the feudal autocratic monarchy, China found itself at a crossroads, struggling to find a way forward. Why did China opt for Marxism and socialism rather than constitutional monarchy or a national bourgeois revolution at this crucial juncture? As will be discussed, its direction was determined by its specific national conditions at that time. As Mao Zedong once pointed out, "Everything else has been tried and failed," a sentiment echoed by General Secretary Xi Jinping during a visit to Europe when he stated, "Constitutional monarchy, imperial restoration, parliamentary system, multi-party system, and presidential government were all considered and tried, but none worked."[2] Both domestic bourgeois revolutionaries and reformists made various efforts to rejuvenate China after the 1911 revolution but to no avail. Events have repeatedly demonstrated that in semi-colonial and semi-feudal China, where Western powers and domestic feudal forces were extremely powerful, it became no longer feasible to attempt to establish bourgeois democracy. Since then, it has become a matter of historical necessity for the country to blaze a novel path under new leadership.

The October Revolution of 1917 in Russia, the second event, eventually brought to China Marxism-Leninism and the new model of Soviet socialism, through which less developed countries, such as China, could establish socialism first in order to shake off the semi-colonial and semi-feudal states they found themselves mired in. The new model of Soviet socialism catalyzed China's revolution. It illuminated the road in the dark night of the Chinese Revolution. As written in *On the People's Democratic Dictatorship* by Mao in 1949,

> The salvoes of the October Revolution brought us Marxism-Leninism. The October Revolution helped progressives in China, as throughout the world, to adopt the proletarian world outlook as the instrument for studying a nation's destiny and considering anew their own problems. Follow the path of the Russians—that was their conclusion.[3]

The fact that Russia, an economically backward state, could be built up into a socialist country through the efforts of a worker-peasant revolution thereby provided a strong precedent for China to emulate. The victory of the Bolshevik Revolution exerted a profound influence on the Chinese revolution in terms of direction, method, and spirit. It accelerated the realization of its Chinese equivalent, prompting the Chinese to finally choose Marxism, establish the CPC, and embark upon the road of winning national independence and the new-democratic revolution through armed struggle. It is no accident that the CPC, born in the early 1920s, has since grown in both strength and size. Seeing its solemn duty to transform the tragic fate of modern China from its poor and weak state, the CPC's stated mission was therefore to achieve national independence, liberation of the people, and prosperity of the country, all incorporated within its goal of striving for the lofty ideal of communism. Embarking on a journey of unremitting struggle, it has united and led the people of all ethnic groups nationwide to overcome a century of humiliation, thereby writing a glorious chapter of Chinese history in rescuing it from subjugation.

The salvoes heard at the founding ceremony of the PRC at Tiananmen Square on October 1, 1949, the third event, commenced a new path of exploration of China's socialist construction, heralding that the Chinese people had stood up and that the nation had entered a new historical stage featuring state independence, national self-determination alongside socialist development.

The first-generation central collective leadership of the CPC, with Mao at its core, led the entire party and all ethnic groups across the country to carry through to completion the new democratic revolution, socialist transformation, and establishment of the basic socialist system, laying the political and institutional foundations for all further development and progress within contemporary China. The establishment of the socialist system has completely put an end to internecine war and threats of secession, paving the way for the realization of the great rejuvenation of the nation. The original theoretical conceptual basis enabled great achievements in such fields as industry, agriculture, national defense, science & technology, and culture, and the many twists and turns during this journey have all amalgamated in providing invaluable experience and a material foundation for the creation of socialism with Chinese characteristics.

After the Third Plenary Session of the 11th CPC Central Committee in 1978, the central collective leadership, with Deng at its core, conducted a thorough review of China's past experiences and lessons in constructing socialism, including socialist transformation, the Great Leap Forward and the "Cultural Revolution," over the preceding 30 years. On this basis, it grasped the general trend of global development, brought order out of chaos through analysis of the truth test standard, decisively abandoned the slogan of "class struggle is the key link,"[4] and made the historically strategic decision to shift the focus of the Party and the government's efforts toward socialist modernization and pursuit of the policy of reform and opening-up. Moreover, it also put forward theses on the underlying goal of socialism and established the Party's basic line for the primary stage of socialism. As such, the great initiative of building socialism with Chinese characteristics was successfully launched. Afterwards, this socialist road was advanced and developed through decades of continuous exploration, reaching its final state in conforming to China's unique cultural tradition, national conditions, and historical destiny.

On the threshold of the second decade of the 21st century, China was faced with the difficult task of further upholding and developing socialism with Chinese characteristics in the new era. Since the 18th National Congress of the CPC, with a complicated environment both at home and abroad and facing challenges in terms of social development and the economy, the CPC Central Committee, with Xi at the core, concluded that only the road to socialism with Chinese characteristics that could result in continual national progress and the elevation of the people's happiness. Building on past achievements and striving for further progress, the leadership united and led the Party, the army, and the people in comprehensively promoting economic, political, cultural, social, and ecological progress while continuously enhancing the country's national strength, international competitiveness, and influence, thereby laying a more solid foundation for strengthening socialism with Chinese characteristics within a new historical context.

From an assessment of China's economic and social development since the 18th National Congress, it is clear that the analysis of changes in both the domestic and foreign environments and subsequent major decisions and strategic adjustments on economic and social development made by the CPC Central Committee under the helm of Xi has withstood the test of implementation. They have conformed to reality and made impressive theoretical and practical contributions in consolidating the foundation for the ongoing development of Chinese socialism, thus enhancing the sense of purposefulness and confidence of the Chinese people in taking this unique path.

II. The Historical Inevitability of China's Development Path

Observable reality demonstrates that it was a historical choice of the Chinese people to opt for the path of socialism under the CPC's leadership and that it has proven to be in line with China's reality and the evolution of human society.[5] If China is to continue a trajectory of development progress and achieve its full potential in contemporary China, it is imperative that the government continue to pursue this model of socialism with Chinese characteristics.

The road traveled by the Chinese is a summary of hands-on experience wedded to theoretical application. It is an empirical route the Party and people have explored through hardships and setbacks, reaching its conclusion during the establishment and construction of the New China. As Xi once pointed out, "Socialism with Chinese characteristics did not emerge out of the void. It is a fundamental accomplishment made by the Party and the people through untold hardships and at great expense."[6] In the 1950s, in order to completely ameliorate the state of poverty and weakness modern China found itself in, the CCP led the people to explore socialism, expecting to find a correct path in line with the reality facing the country. It firstly proposed "taking Russia as a teacher" and following the path of the Soviets, and then put forward "take(ing) the Soviet Union as a mirror" to ascertain the correct way to build socialism by combining Marxism with China's specific reality.

After the Third Plenary Session of the 11th CPC Central Committee, the Party reviewed and drew upon its previous 30 years' experience in exploring the socialist road, extricated itself from ideological chaos, and made the strategic decision to shift the focus of the Party and the country's work to socialist modernization and pursuit of the policy of reform and opening-up. In the 1980s, adhering to the idea of "crossing the river by feeling the stones,"[7] the Party led its people to push ahead against all odds in actively exploring new practices. The Party became keenly aware that China was still at a low level of economic and social development, with undertakings in all respects far from perfect. Recognizing that China's development differed from that envisaged by Marx and Engels and other classic communist writers, it concluded that the nation was still in the primary stage of socialism. Based on this judgment, the CPC profoundly elaborated upon the basic principles to be followed in the process of developing socialism with Chinese characteristics and successfully navigated a route suitable to local conditions. Therefore, the Chinese Road has been the result of continuous efforts made by generations of Chinese since 1978 to embody the wisdom and strength of its people, thus reflecting their interests and will, and is widely recognized by all levels of society.

III. The Historic Significance of China's Developmental Path

The Chinese Road follows the law of the development of historical materialism. It is a scientific and historical choice of the Chinese people, and in the process of exploration, the Chinese communists are committed to studying and revealing its true nature.

The Chinese direction is led by the CPC, the representative of advanced productive forces within the country. During its long tenure, the Party has gained invaluable experience in governance, endowing it with a unique political charm and an ability to lead and organize unequaled by any other political power. Due to the Party's painstaking efforts for almost a century, along with its great historical contributions to the nation, the Chinese people have truly come to realize that not only is its leadership the core force behind China's social progress and development but also the backbone in ensuring the Chinese people are masters of their own country, and the cornerstone for narrowing the gap between the rich and poor and ultimately achieving common prosperity amongst the population at large.

Thanks to the great victory achieved by the Chinese people under the leadership of the CPC, the Chinese nation with over 5,000 years of history has become moderately modernized and revitalized; the proposition of socialism raised several hundred years ago[8] has radiated with renewed vigor in the 21st century and the construction of New China spanning more than 60 years has made impressive gains. As the world's largest developing country, China has lifted itself from poverty, becoming the world's second-largest economy in just over 40 years, which not only rids itself of the danger of being sidelined on the international stage but represents a significant achievement in the history of human development.

The Chinese Road has effectively consolidated the material foundation of contemporary global society, as it took a mere four decades to propel China to the world's No. 2 position in terms of total economic volume. The Chinese population, counting for one-fifth of the world's total, has not only resolved the problem of food and clothing but also gradually embarked on the path toward common prosperity. This has laid a strong and solid foundation for ongoing national material abundance and people's well-being alongside social harmony and stability. More than just a huge change in the living conditions of the Chinese people, it is also an important contribution to the cause of world peace and material development. The great accomplishments of the Chinese Road, as well as the enormous economic energy and vitality it nurtures, have made it a powerhouse for the economic and social development of the entire world today. As a driver of global economic growth, China has created ongoing opportunities for other countries and shared, especially with developing countries, the fruits of economic development while promoting the steady growth of global GDP (gross domestic product).

The Chinese Road demonstrates the diversified developments of human civilization. The world is a multicolored one, where cultural diversity is a basic feature of human society. Countries across various continents experience different natural environments, historical conditions, and cultural traditions. Hence, there is a wide spectrum of civilizations across the globe. Over a long period, however, some Western countries have been self-centered in that they have interpreted Western civilization as the ideal form of human civilization[9] and advocated their road to modernization as an "exemplar" that all nations must follow. While blazing a new path of its own, China also acknowledges the necessity of absorbing and drawing upon the excellent achievements of all human civilizations, including those contributed by Western capitalist countries. However, one must soberly realize that absorption does not mean rigid duplication, and modernization does not mean Westernization. There is no way for nations with varied conditions to embark on exactly the same road to modernization. As the proverb states, "All roads lead to Rome." "There cannot be only one civilization, one social system, one development model and one value"[10] for the development of human society. The successful opening of China to the world refutes and deconstructs the myths of Western Centrism and notions of the "End of History," thus proving the diversity of developmental paths of human civilization with demonstrably opposing facts.

The Chinese Road provides a positive model for other developing countries to shake off poverty, becoming richer and stronger in the process. Compared with the modernization path provided by the West, the Chinese Road is distinctive in terms of the modes of economic and social development, values, and intellectual insights and has its own unique standards for ideas, policies, and actions when it comes to foreign relations. Despite this, there are some Western scholars who question or even vilify the Chinese Road out of deep-rooted ideological bias or unstated political intentions of various sorts. They wantonly deny the achievements of the Chinese Road, its relationship with the success of reform and opening-up, and its socialist nature, exaggerate the challenges facing it, and hold that a huge social crisis lurks underneath its "superficial" glories. Yet these schemes and ploys have all come to nothing. Modernization is the historical trend of the evolution of human society and the common goal pursued by many countries. Whenever the Western capitalist development system encounters severe challenges, China's path to modernization shakes the world with its strong, sustained, and rapid growth momentum and impressive successes. China's reform practices can be viewed as offering valuable experience and spiritual wealth, therefore serving as a model and reference for developing countries.

The Chinese Road remains not only the sole way to create a better life for the people but also to realize the great rejuvenation of the Chinese nation. Upholding and developing socialism with Chinese characteristics is the clear historical choice of its people, with the path taken providing a deeper understanding of the laws of governance, laws of building socialism, and laws of the development of human society, all under the auspices of the Communist Party. There is none other than the path of socialism with Chinese characteristics that can lead China's progress, promote national prosperity and improve the well-being of its people. Only by strengthening confidence in this road and unswervingly following it can China ensure that the people obtain further benefits and a greater sense of gain, happiness, and security; and only by doing so can China build a moderately prosperous society in all respects, accelerate socialist modernization, continue to win new victories for socialism with Chinese characteristics, and ultimately realize the Chinese Dream of national rejuvenation.

SECTION 2
The Essence and the Economic Laws of Socialism

I. The Essence of Socialism

In 1992, Deng Xiaoping said in his talks delivered during his tour of South China: "The essence of socialism is to liberate productive forces, develop productive forces, eliminate exploitation, eliminate polarization, and finally achieve common prosperity." The remarkable characteristics of this scientific generalization are: First, it defines the essence of socialism on the level of goals and distinguishes socialism from capitalism. Socialism is not immutable. One must consider the specific reality of a country to develop socialism; otherwise, the political system will encounter setbacks. Second, it highlights the foundational role of productive forces, the development of which penetrates socialist society, as it is an inevitable trend for socialism to replace capitalism in the development of said forces, and furthermore, the ongoing promotion of their development demonstrates the superiority of socialism. Third, it highlights the value of the goals of socialism, which is to eliminate exploitation and polarization to finally achieve common prosperity, as well as highlighting the essential difference between socialism and capitalism. Fourth, it describes the essence of socialist dynamics. Socialism is a process, and there is also a process of gradual realization in the essence of its application.

In December 2012, when Xi went to Fuping County, Hebei Province, to visit people in need and inspect the work of poverty alleviation and development, he emphasized eliminating poverty, improving living standards, and achieving common prosperity to be the essential requirements of socialism. Since the 18th National Congress, the CPC Central Committee, under Xi's direction, has elaborated upon the significance, scientific implications, and practical requirements of shared development, further strengthening adherence to the development of socialism with Chinese characteristics. The concept of sharing thus reflects the requirements and basic value orientation of gradually realizing common prosperity attachment, which remains the basic requirement of China's political philosophy. Holding steadfastly to these principles also reflects the inevitable requirement of building a moderately prosperous society in all respects and the superiority of the socialist system. Now is a period of interpretation of the essential requirements of socialism, which requires a long historical process to realize its stated goals. China remains in, and will do so for the foreseeable future, the primary stage of socialism. While China cannot get ahead of itself, this does not entail that the government has nothing to do in gradually realizing common prosperity. Rather, China should strive to achieve all it can according to the existing conditions, accumulating small accomplishments in place of larger ones while keeping sight of the goal of common prosperity for the masses.

II. A General Understanding of the Economic Laws of Socialism

1. The Meaning of Economic Law

Economic law is the inherent, essential, and inevitable relations between economic phenomena. In the process of social production and reproduction, as an objective force, it determines the inevitable development trend of economic phenomena. It is not only demonstrated by but also covered by economic phenomena. Therefore, to understand and discover economic law, one should commence with economic phenomena.

2. The Characteristics of Economic Law

Economic law is distinct from the laws of natural science in that it largely plays a role within only a certain historical period. It comes into being based on certain economic conditions mainly composed of social relations of production and is thereby impermanent. With the disappearance of old economic conditions, the veteran economic law will lose its function, withdrawing from the historical stage and giving way to its successor, the new economic law. The historicity of economic law is determined by the historicity of economic conditions. The withdrawal of the old economic law from prominence does not mean that it is eliminated, but that it becomes ineffective due to the emergence of new economic conditions, thereby demonstrating that it is not created by people's will, but rather an outcome of historical inevitability.

3. Types of Economic Law

Economic phenomena are various and complicated, and the economic laws that reflect the essential relations of these phenomena are also diverse. Economic laws can be divided into four types according to the length of the historical period during which they function:

(1) Common economic laws that work in all social economic forms and reflect some common essential relations of economic phenomena in the development of those forms. For example, the law that production relations correspond to the character and level of development of the productive forces emanated from and subsequently developed with the emergence and advancement of human society. The law of the correspondence between production relations and the character and level of development of the productive forces is a fundamental and universal law pertaining to the development of human society. This law reveals the fundamental cause and basic trend of social and historical development, highlighting the decisive role of productive forces in the contradictory movement of modes of production, thus revealing that productive forces are the final decisive factors in promoting the existence and development of society as a whole. It reflects the essential relationship between productive forces and the development of production relations existing across all periods of human social development. The interaction between the base and the superstructure constitutes their contradictory movement and runs through the whole process of social development. This contradiction between the base and the superstructure is restricted by the discrepancy between the productive forces and production relations. The solution to this conundrum depends on the resolution of the contradiction between the base and the superstructure. The contradictory movements between productive forces and production relations, and between base and superstructure, promote the change of social forms in turn. The superstructure of socialism comes into being before its own base and becomes the political premise for establishing the socialist economic footing. That is a special form of the law that the superstructure corresponds to the base. Within a socialist society, the contradiction between the base and the superstructure is generally manifested by the non-antagonistic contradiction among the people, which can be adjusted and overcome by the strength of the socialist system itself, instead of being resolved by fundamentally altering the social system as in a private ownership society. In all social economic forms, the existence of common economic laws shows that various social economic forms are interrelated.

(2) Common economic laws that work in several social economic forms and reflect common essential relations of certain economic phenomena which exist in several social economic modes. For example, the law of value is the basic economic law of commodity production and exchange in a market economy. The values of commodities are determined by the necessity of social labor time, with commodities being exchanged at equal values. In the process of commodity production and exchange, comparisons of commodity production technology occur, with the survival of the fittest reigning so as to continuously promote the development of productive forces. Whether in a private or public ownership society, as long as there is a commodity or market economy, this law plays a role. The fluctuation of price around value is the manifestation of the law of value. In a private ownership society, the law of value spontaneously regulates production, stimulates the improvement of production technology, and accelerates the differentiation of commodity producers. However, as the socialist economy is a market economy based on public ownership, it must consciously rely on and apply the law of value to promote its own development.

(3) Special economic laws that work in a certain social form and reflect some unique essential relations of economic phenomena in the development process of these social modes. For example, the law of anarchy of production and competition is one of the special economic laws of capitalist social economic forms, while the law of planned and proportional development is one pertaining to socialist and Communist societies.

(4) Special economic laws that work in a certain stage of a certain social form. For example, distribution according to work is the special economic law in the first stage of a Communist society, namely the socialist society, and distribution according to need is the special economic law in its second stage.

4. The Objectivity of Economic Law

Economic law, like natural law, is the internal relation of objective processes, which are inevitable and independent of human will. Whether people are aware of the economic law subjectively or not, it always exists objectively and functions inevitably. People can only discover, understand, and use economic laws but cannot create, transform or eliminate them. For example, when the law of the correspondence between production relations and the character and level of development of the productive forces conflicts with the narrow class interests of the decaying exploiting class, said class will employ all means to resist the advanced class's use of this economic law. However, no matter what their subjective will is, this economic law exists and functions and will ultimately achieve its requirements.

Under socialist conditions, objective economic laws cannot be violated either. Even a small violation will cause chaos, thus causing damage to the social and economic development and the economic interests of the working class. Although a socialist state plays a great role in intervening in the economy, it cannot create, transform, or eliminate economic laws. On the contrary, only by relying on objective economic laws can it give play to the special role of a socialist country and successfully accomplish the mission of eliminating exploitative systems and building a socialist economy. If the government denies the objectivity of the economic laws of socialism, it will be at the mercy of voluntarism and economic adventurism until it is punished by these immutable laws, thus bringing disaster upon the people.

5. The Correct Understanding and Use of Economic Law

The objectivity of economic laws does not mean that people are passive and powerless in the face of them. On the contrary, people can understand and utilize economic laws for the benefit of society at large. It is a gross error to idolize economic laws and become slaves to them. The understanding and use of natural laws is more or less smooth, while that of economic laws involves the interests of all classes in society. Therefore, in a class society, economic laws are understood and used under a class background.

Although the productive forces of capitalist society have been highly developed, due to the existence of private ownership of means of production, economic laws still work spontaneously, and people's conscious role is limited to a very narrow range. The situation is different in a socialist society. The establishment of socialist public ownership of the means of production and the consistency between the class interests of the proletariat and the interests of the overwhelming majority of the people in society make it possible to consciously use economic laws to serve the socialist revolution and socialist construction. Accordingly, instead of being powerless in the face of economic laws, the government can leverage and apply the laws to achieve benefits for society overall.

III. Basic Economic Laws of Socialism

Marxist-Leninist works have repeatedly pointed out that after the establishment of the public ownership of means of production, social production has a fundamentally different nature and purpose from that found in capitalism. The fruits of production are directly controlled and enjoyed by the producers, and there is a direct link between production and consumption. The purpose of social production is to fully meet people's needs and ensure people's all-around development. To achieve such purpose of social production, two conditions need to be met: first, there must be highly developed productive forces that can provide sufficient products, and second, there must be a perfect economic structure that can coordinate the various relations between supply and demand. As distinct from the basic economic law of socialism of developing production to meet people's needs, the essence of capitalist economic law is the law of surplus value, according to which all economic activities should be subject to the purpose of pursuing maximum profit. As long as it is not conducive to the realization of this purpose, it will be difficult to carry out innovation.

1. A basic definition of the economic laws of socialism

The content of the basic economic law of socialism includes the purpose of socialist production and the means of realizing such a purpose.

2. The purpose of socialist production and its objectivity

The purpose of socialist production is to meet the needs of all members of society for a better life, including the needs for survival and development. This shows that there is a direct relation between production and consumption in the process of socialist reproduction. The direct purpose of developing production is people's needs, and the fruits of this are directly controlled and enjoyed by the producers. Under the capitalist system, the workers themselves are only a personal production condition, not the purpose itself. Their personal consumption is required by capitalism only within the limits of the task of ensuring the capitalists accrue profits. Except for that, people and their needs remain out of sight.

The objectivity of the purpose of socialist production is determined by the public ownership of the means of production. Since the means of production have become the public property of all members of society, and the workers have become its owners, they can unite to use them for production. Naturally, the fruits of their labors belong to them and are used to meet their needs, and to this, there can be no exception. In the practice of socialist economic development, there may be some behaviors that deviate from the purpose of socialist production, but as they do not conform to the fundamental interests of the majority of workers, they will be corrected sooner or later. As an objective force, the purpose of socialist production will be enforced as part of the whole process of the socialist economic movement.

3. Means to achieve the goal of socialist production

The purpose of socialist production and the means to achieve it are unified. Only by developing and improving socialist production and increasing social products and services can the growing needs of society writ large be met. The general way in which to develop production is to increase the quantity of labor and levels of productivity. The development of socialist production simply by increasing the amount of labor is limited by the number of workers, the length of working days, and the intensity of labor. Increasing labor productivity however has infinite potential to expand production and is in line with the essence of socialist practices. With the continuous increase of labor productivity, society expends less labor time to produce an increasing quantity of colorful products, thereby providing further and better services, which can not only fully meet people's growing needs but also gradually shorten their labor time, increasing workers' free time, and help in achieving the gradual realization of people's all-around development. Therefore, increasing labor productivity is the fundamental means to achieve the purpose of socialist production.

Increasing labor productivity depends on many factors, the most important of which is the development of S&T and its application to the production process. The establishment of socialist public ownership allows the development of S&T to shed the shackles of capital and organize in a planned way across the whole of society, speeding up the process of transforming it into direct productive forces so that the greatest possibility is provided for making full use of such advanced technology in social production and allowing social labor productivity to grow at a comparatively high speed.

Under the socialist system, the purpose of production and the means to achieve it depend on and promote one another. There is no antagonistic contradiction between the unlimited expansion of production and a relative reduction of the consumption base under the capitalist system. The purpose of socialist production determines the possibility of unlimited development of production. The growing needs of workers provide the most powerful driving force for the development of socialist production and promote its continuous growth and improvement. On the other hand, the development of socialist production not only meets the needs but also creates new ones, promoting the development of consumption and making it possible for unlimited development to meet them. However, under the socialist system, there is some contradiction between social production and the needs of workers, but this does not contain any measure of confrontation and can be resolved continuously through the socialist system itself. This dialectical relationship between socialist production and needs promotes the continuous development of socialist production and fully demonstrates the superiority of the socialist system.

4. The basic economic law determines the essence of socialist production

In the system of economic laws of socialism, as the law determining the essence of socialist production, the basic economic law is placed at the central position, reflecting the essential connection between production and needs in the socialist economic movement. This then determines all the main aspects and processes of the development of socialist production and also determines the direction of socialist economic advancement. It is an economic law that has always existed and worked throughout the entire historical stages of socialism. All aspects of socialist production, distribution, exchange, and consumption, in addition to following their own inherent economic law, should be restricted by the basic economic law of socialism and meet the requirements of this law. All economic activities of socialism should be subject to the organic unification between the purpose of socialist production and the means of achieving such an end. Regardless of the adjustment of economic structures, the direction and layout of industrial development, the depth, breadth, and mode of exchange, the formation and change of prices, the distribution of national income and personal consumer goods, or the determination of consumption level and consumption structure, these should all be conducive to the development of socialist production and the satisfaction of the growing needs of all members of the society for a better life. The direction of socialist economic development is also determined by the basic economic law of socialism. The continuous growth and improvement of socialist production on the bedrock of high technology, the continuous strengthening of the material basis of socialism, and the increasing improvement and development of socialist relations of production will provide material and social conditions for the gradual development of socialism toward communism in the future.

Over the past 40 years of reform and opening-up, the CPC has followed the requirements of the basic economic law of socialism, correctly handled the contradiction between developing production and meeting the needs of the people, prioritized the development of production, and continued exploring effective ways of development. Since the 18th National Congress, Xi has summarized the experiences and lessons of China's development and place in the world, followed the basic economic law of socialism, putting forward a "people-centered" development doctrine and new development philosophy to keep pace with the times, whilst simultaneously achieving spectacular achievements in terms of China's reform & opening up and deepening structural reform of the supply side. The great practice of the past five years suggests that if the CPC follows the basic economic law of socialism, it will be able to win the broad support of the people and achieve the actual effect of economic development and social progress. The lesson of the disintegration of the former Soviet Union also demonstrates that if the government goes against Stalin's basic economic law of socialism and deviates from the essence of socialism, the ruling party will be rejected by the people, and socialism will become unsustainable.

SECTION 3
The Long-Term and Phase-Based Primary Stage of Socialism

To absorb the realities of China, one must, above all, figure out the nature and development stage of the society and understand the principal contradiction within it as well as its evolution. Under a new development pattern where China is faced with a complex international political and economic environment, it should base its work on the primary stage of socialism while striving to understand and grasp the new development laws that suit the basic dimension within the Chinese context.

I. An Exploration of the Development Stage of Chinese Socialism

Since the establishment of the Chinese socialist system, Mao repeatedly raised the issue about the development stage of Chinese socialism. At the Conference on Intellectuals held in January 1956, he put forward that China's socialist society had been initiated but not yet completed. Later on, he reiterated this idea, explicitly stating that it would take time to build the foundations of modern industry and agriculture, and only when the productive forces had been fairly developed to the point of providing a relatively sufficient material basis for the country's socialist economic and political systems could one say that the construction of a socialist society has been completed. However, because of China's new transition to socialism and lack of experience, the Party leadership did not possess a clear understanding of the laws of socialist construction and development and failed to maintain and develop this idea to its fullest extent. During the Great Leap Forward and the People's Commune Movement in 1958, the false hope materialized that "the realization of communism in China is not a matter for the distant future,"[11] which was entirely due to the unscientific understanding of the stage of socialist development and a serious miscalculation of the growth rate of social productivity. It was in the late 1950s and early 1960s when Mao realized that socialist construction in China was an arduous, complex, and long-term task after reviewing recent experiences and lessons in this regard. When reading the Soviet text *Political Economy*, he made an important point:

Socialism in this phase may be divided into two stages. The first is undeveloped socialism, with the second being relatively developed socialism. And the latter stage may be more time-consuming than the former." "In a country like ours, completing socialist construction is an arduous task. Don't talk too early about the completion of it.[12]

While examining the errors of the Great Leap Forward, he criticized those so eager to make the transition to communism that they misidentified not only socialism for communism but also the concepts of "distribution according to work" for "distribution according to needs" and "collective ownership" for "ownership by the people as a whole." Meanwhile, he was also critical of the tendency toward mistaken ideas, such as denial of the law of value and equivalent exchange. Mao's criticism was inspiring and helpful to later explorations of the developmental stage of China's socialist society. However, with the ever-increasing leftist deviation in the guiding ideology within the Party in the 1960s, socialism was regarded as "a period of revolutionary transformation from a capitalist society to a communist society."[13] The correct way in which to explore the development stage of Chinese socialism was thus interrupted.

At the end of 1978, shortly after the Third Plenary Session of the 11th CPC Central Committee, Deng pointed out that the reality of China was that it was still a country with a weak economic foundation, a large population, and underdeveloped productivity. And he emphasized that the modernization drive of the country was bound to be long-term. In the Resolution on Certain Historical Issues of the Party since the Founding of the People's Republic passed at the Sixth Plenary Session of the 11th CPC Central Committee in 1981, the Party leadership proposed for the first time that China's socialist system was still in its infancy. In September 1986, the Party passed the Resolution on the Guiding Principles of the Construction of a Socialist Spiritual Civilization at the Sixth Plenary Session of the 12th CPC Central Committee, in which it analyzed contents regarding cultural and ideological construction in this primary stage. But in general, when discussing the initial stage of a socialist society in the above three scenarios, the Party did not treat it as an issue of overall importance in building socialism with Chinese characteristics, nor did it further develop it into a fundamental basis on which to formulate the Party's guidelines and policies.

On the eve of the 13th National Congress of the CPC in 1987, Deng stressed,

The Thirteen[th] National Party Congress will explain what stage China is in the primary stage of socialism. Socialism itself is the first stage of communism, and here in China, we are still in the primary stage of socialism—that is, the underdeveloped stage. In everything we do, we must proceed from this reality, and all planning must be consistent with it.[14]

In this argument, the notion of China being in the primary stage of socialism was first defined as a fundamental reality that concerned the overall situation of the country and confirmed as the starting point and fundamental basis for the Party to formulate its line, principles, and policies. The systematic explanation of the primary stage of socialism and the Party's basic lines at this

Congress represented a leap forward in the Party's understanding of socialism and China's particular reality.

In September 1997, the Party placed further emphasis on the question regarding the primary stage of socialism at the 15th National Congress of the CPC and explained that in the face of the arduous tasks of tackling hard issues in the process of reform and creating a new dynamic, the key to resolving various contradictions, dispelling doubts and understanding why the country must carry out the existing line and policies lay in its unified, correct understanding of the basic conditions in China today in the primary stage of socialism. Based on this basic understanding— China is currently in the primary stage of socialism and will remain so for a long time to come, the 15th National Congress formulated the Party's basic program for the primary stage of socialism, decisively answering the questions of what the socialist economy, politics, and culture with Chinese characteristics in the primary stage are and how to build them, while further unifying the mindset of the entire party and the people.

In November 2002, the 16th National Congress of the CPC reiterated that China was now in the primary stage of socialism and would remain so for a long time to come; the higher standard of living the populace was enjoying remained at a comparatively low level, was not all-inclusive and very uneven so that the Party needed to make strenuous efforts over a long period of time to consolidate and uplift the quality of life further still. In October 2007, the 17th National Congress of the CPC further pointed out that after the unremitting efforts undertaken since the founding of the New China, especially since the reform and opening-up, the nation had made remarkable achievements in its development, with great and far-reaching changes having taken place from productive forces to production relations, from strengthening the economic foundation to enhancing the superstructure. However, the basic national condition had not changed, and the principal contradiction in Chinese society, that between the people's ever-growing material and cultural needs and the low level of production, had not changed either. In October 2020, the Fifth Plenary Session of the 19th CPC Central Committee remarked that in the face of the new contradictions and challenges brought about by the increasingly complex international environment, the Party should: enhance the awareness of opportunities and risks; base its work on its particular reality of being in the primary stage of socialism; maintain strategic focus; conduct its own affairs well; understand and grasp the law of development; accurately recognize periods of transition, responding to them scientifically and make changes using their initiative; learn to create opportunities during crises and blaze new innovative trails; seize opportunities and meet challenges; seek advantages and mitigate disadvantages, and move forward courageously with the requisite fighting spirit. In essence, act and react with dynamism.

In short, at each successive Party Congress following the Third Plenary Session of the 11th CPC Central Committee, the CPC has conducted deeper explorations into the historic stages of Chinese socialism and accurately identified the basic national conditions of the nation; that it is now in the first stage of socialism and will remain so for a long time to come, on the basis of summarizing the historical experience since the founding of the New China and more recent practical experience gained since the reform and opening-up era began. As such, the Chinese people under its leadership are able to successfully embark on a new path of building socialism with Chinese characteristics, bringing life to socialism and making great achievements in socialist modernization.

II. The Long-Term Primary Stage of Socialism

In the first stage of socialism, the basic realization of socialist modernization in China will take at least 100 years from the starting line of 1956, by which point the socialist transformation of the private ownership of the means of production was essentially completed. This is determined altogether by the historical premise, actual national conditions, and trends in world global economic development.

1. The historical premise of China's entry into socialism

China's productivity is underdeveloped, a situation mainly caused by the poverty and backwardness of old China (pre-1949), which had remained in the semi-colonial, semi-feudal era for an extended duration. Accordingly, the stage was not set for capitalism to obtain a real foothold in China and become fully developed. On the eve of the founding of New China, the modern industrial economy only accounted for 90%[15] of the entire national economy, which mainly relied on manual labor and was not much different from ancient times. Undoubtedly, when it entered socialism through the new democratic revolution, China lagged far behind the developed capitalist countries in terms of productivity and the degree of economic modernization. Therefore, this required the country to spend a long historical period developing advanced productive forces required by socialism, improving human modernization, and achieving industrialization. This historical period is the primary stage of socialism in China.

2. China's actual national conditions

With nearly 70 years of development after the founding of the PRC, and especially after 40 years of reform and opening-up, China's productivity has dramatically improved. Its GDP ranks second in the world. And the total output of some important products, including grain, cotton, coal, petroleum, steel, and electricity, is among the highest in the world. However, due to its large population, the per capita indicators of the country are much lower than the global average. The reality of a large population, weak foundation, uneven development, and underdeveloped productivity has not been fundamentally altered. As a result, China is still faced with many challenges: the economic quality and efficiency are of a low level; the socialist system is not perfect; the socialist market economy system is immature; socialist democracy and the legal system are not sound enough; and decadent ideas inherent to feudalism and capitalism alongside the force of habit of the small producer still generate an extensive influence over society. It is a reminder that there is still a long way to go before China can achieve full modernization and build itself into a prosperous, democratic, civilized, harmonious, and beautiful modernized socialist power. China's socialism will remain underdeveloped for a long time to come.

3. Global economic trends

With the rapid development of the scientific and technological revolution around the world following World War II, some advanced countries have enjoyed great increases in productivity. New economic growth methods have continuously emerged. From a global perspective, a new round of technological revolution and industrial transformation is in the making, and some disruptive technological innovations are bringing about new types of business. Innovations in industry and within institutions, combined with social governance driven by the rapid development of the technological revolution, have begun to profoundly affect the reshuffling of countries in terms of their comprehensive national strength and competitiveness. From a domestic perspective, despite the remarkable progress of scientific and technological developments in recent years, China remains a country whose overall level of science & technology, education, and culture is insufficient. Additionally, China's capacity for innovation and technological support for economic and social development is inadequate, and its contribution to economic growth is far lower than that of developed countries. Therefore, building a modernized China is clearly an arduous and complex challenge. It will take a long period of time before the country can truly establish the material and technological foundation required by mature socialism. In the meantime, China can only exist within the primary stage of socialism.

To sum up, the primary stage of socialism is the reality as well as part of the overall historical development process of Chinese socialism. It will take at least a century to navigate a series of transitions to see this process through to completion. The stark reality today is that China, the world's largest developing country, is still in the primary stage of socialism. And the key to solving all problems in China is further development along the lines that have been highlighted so far.

CHAPTER TWO

China's Economic Development Enters a New Stage

Conducting an analysis and judgment of what is regarded as the "principal contradiction" is a logical starting point for better understanding the theories that underlie the socialist political economy with Chinese characteristics. Only by scientifically comprehending the principal social contradiction can one accurately understand the basic national conditions and deduce a series of other economic principles and economic laws at play.

SECTION 1
The Evolution of the Principal Contradiction Facing Contemporary China

Socialism with Chinese characteristics has entered a new era, as stated by Xi Jinping in October 2017 at the opening of the 19th National Congress of the CPC. The idea of the "principal contradiction" facing Chinese society has evolved over time and today centers on the tension between the people's ever-growing needs for a better life on the one hand and unbalanced and inadequate development on the other. This judgment is a historical political judgment, theoretical judgment, and major theoretical innovation related to the overall situation.

I. The Historical Rationale behind the Evolution of the Principal Contradiction

According to historical materialism, the principle of social contradiction is not rigid and invariable. Rather, it develops and evolves with the changes in social and historical conditions and contradictions. Quantitative changes have given rise to qualitative change. After 40 years of rapid development of reform and opening-up, China's productivity has improved, comprehensive national strength has increased, social wealth has become more abundant, and the material foundation for meeting the various needs of the people has strengthened. China has steadily solved the problem of food and clothing for more than 1 billion people, has realized a well-off society on the whole, and will soon build a moderately prosperous society in all respects.

However, people's needs for a better life are becoming more and more extensive. They not only have higher requirements for material and cultural life but also increasing demands for democracy, rule of law, fairness, justice, security, and environment. People's ever-growing needs for a better life cannot be measured solely in quantities, but rather by continuous improvements in terms of quality and degree, frequent replacement of the old with the new, and expectations for personalization. From the perspective of production relations, profound changes have taken place in China's ownership structure, income distribution system, and economic system since the start of its reforms and opening up. The changes in production relations will inevitably promote productivity and the development of distribution and consumption and will influence people's consumption demands and the structure of their demands. It is clear that China's current social production, both productivity and production relations, has undergone major changes. Due to significant improvements in the level of social productivity, the social production capacity has risen to the forefront of the world in many respects. However, a persistent problem is one of unbalanced and inadequate development. The supply capacity of some traditional industries greatly exceeds demand and the relative surplus, and structural imbalance will become a major problem over the long term.

In the new era, the historic shifts that have occurred in China's understanding of the principal contradiction facing Chinese society are not accidental. They are rooted in historical reasons and logic, including changes in how China measures progress (shifting from quantitative to qualitative measures) as well as changes in and direction from the Party leadership since the 18th National Congress of the CPC.

Another historical logic that must be clearly understood and accurately grasped is what has remained "unchanged." Although the notion of the principal contradiction facing Chinese society has changed, the basic national condition of China—that it is still, and will remain, in the primary stage of socialism for some time yet—has not changed, nor has China's international status as the world's largest developing country. Although China's level of economic and social development has improved significantly, its productivity development is still at a mid-level when compared with developed countries, per capita national income has still not exceeded $10,000, and China's unbalanced and inadequate development has not fundamentally changed. These shortcomings are reflected in the inadequate development of under-developed areas and rural areas, the disparity in development progress between rural and urban areas, and the gap between the rich and the poor. They are also reflected in the insufficient supply of high-quality medical, educational, and elderly care resources and services in some developed areas and some big cities. There still remain many underdeveloped communities within some cities. In addition, the development of ecological environment, spiritual culture, democracy and the rule of law, and social progress lags behind economic development. This problem of unbalanced and inadequate development has become the main barrier to meeting people's ever-growing needs for a better life. Solving this problem will require a long process as part of the primary stage of socialism with Chinese characteristics.

The so-called "change" is such because the primary stage of socialism is characterized by constant change and in itself comprises several stages, including the time when the socialist system is initially established with "poverty and blankness"; the time when an independent industrial system and national economic system are built in socialist construction; the time when the problem of food and clothing has been resolved; and the time when a moderately prosperous society in all respects is built. To accurately understand the historical logic of the principal contradictions facing Chinese society in the new era, one must not only deeply understand the historical inevitability, continuity, and gradualness of the change in the principal contradiction but also the "two unchanged things" as well as the dialectical relationship between "change" and the "unchanged." Only then can the "basic national conditions" and "biggest reality" be fully grasped, and the historical logic of the change in the principal contradiction facing Chinese society be fully understood.

II. The Practical Rationale behind the Evolution of the Principal Contradiction

The evolution of the principal contradiction facing Chinese society in the new era is not only the inevitable result of the rapid economic and social development in the past 40 years of China's reform and opening-up but also the development of human social civilization, scientific and technological progress, and economic globalization, with distinct new characteristics such as timeliness, internationalization, and modernization.

1. Important changes in people's needs for a better life

Significant improvement of effective demand capacity. China's per capita GDP was little more than $220 in 1978 but reached more than $8,020 in 2016. In 1978, the disposable income of urban residents and the net income of rural residents were only 343 yuan and 133 yuan, respectively; by 2016, the per capita disposable income of urban and rural residents had reached 33,616 yuan and 12,363 yuan, respectively. The per capita savings deposit was only 22 yuan in 1978; by 2016, it was 44,000 yuan. The continuous upgrading of the demand structure is an inevitable requirement for the improvement of demand capacity. In 1978, China's urban and rural Engel coefficients were up to 57.5% and 67.7%, respectively; in 2016, they decreased to 29.3% and 32.2%, respectively. During the same period, service consumption also grew rapidly.

Richer connotation of demand. The ever-growing needs for a better life for the Chinese people include not only material and cultural needs but also needs for social security services, such as belief and spiritual pursuit, improvement of the living environment, elderly care, and medical treatment. People hope to enjoy more dignity and happiness, yearn for more fairness, freedom, and justice in society, and hope to face their complex world without unnecessary stress and anxiety. All of these diverse needs reflect people's growing expectations for a better life and the profound changes that have taken place on the demand side in the relationship between supply and demand. Since the reform and opening-up of China's economy, people's living standards have generally improved significantly, but a key reason for the decline in happiness and the increase in dissatisfaction is that social needs have become richer and more diversified. Many of people's needs go beyond material and culture, such as the demand for ecological environment improvement and social security. The spiritual pursuits and political demands—such as social fairness and justice, yearning for freedom and equality, participating in social governance, and gaining a sense of respect, security, belonging, achievement, and gain—have involved the superstructure, as understood according to Marxist theory, and ideology. That is the inevitable result of social progress and is also the logical result of the change in the understanding of the principal contradiction facing Chinese society in the new era reflected on the demand side.

From the perspective of demand, in the new era, *the ever-growing needs of the Chinese people for a better life reflect the characteristics of rapid development*, such as frequent replacement of the old with the new; increasing diversification of goods horizontally; increasing demand, vertically, in terms of consuming higher-end goods; unbalanced development; and so on. In the past, the pattern of China's consumer demand was characterized by a wave. The stage of wave-style consumption has since ended, and personalized, diversified, and multi-level consumption has gradually become mainstream. The demand is not a simple increase in quantity but a continuous improvement in quality and degree, and the superposition of high-, middle-, and low-level demand is prominent. From the perspective of the evolution and development characteristics of demand, the demand changes very quickly, and the development imbalance is prominent. It can be seen that with the rapid development of social production and the gradual renewal of people's ideas, significant changes have taken place in the structure, level, content, form, and connotation of China's social needs and will continue to evolve at a faster speed and deeper level.

2. The enhanced capacity to meet people's needs

After nearly 40 years of rapid development, China has strengthened its capacity to better meet people's needs for a better life and built an institutional system that can give full play to such capacity. First, in terms of capacity, China has relatively powerful financial and material resources to solve some deep-seated problems in people's needs, such as establishing better and higher-quality education, medical, and social security systems. Second, its international competitiveness and global resource allocation capacity have been significantly enhanced. In 2012, among the world's 500 major industrial products, China ranked first in the world with an output of more than 220 products. According to the research results of Deloitte and the United States (US) Council on Competitiveness on the global manufacturing competitiveness index, China, the US, and Germany ranked as the top three most competitive manufacturing economies in the world in 2016. Third, the trend of scientific and technological innovation has commenced and can inject new momentum into China's capacity to continuously meet people's needs. Statistics show that in 2015, China's innovation index nearly tripled since 2005, and in 2017, China's national innovation index ranked 17th, one place higher than the previous year. In terms of an institutional security system, China has not only formed a sound poverty alleviation system but also established a social security system covering urban and rural residents to meet basic needs, such as education, medical care, and employment, with a significant increase in relevant investment. All of these developments have prepared a good foundation for solving the principal contradiction facing Chinese society in the new era and created conditions for further improving such capacity.

3. The prominent problem of unbalanced and inadequate development

Compared with the more extensive, richer, higher-level, and higher-standard demands arising after people have realized a decent standard of living, China is facing the sustained problem of unbalanced and inadequate development, which has caused two problems. On the one hand, the development is unbalanced, and on the other hand, the development is inadequate. "Inadequacy" is the objective basis of "imbalance." In terms of unbalanced development, the gap between urban and rural areas, among different regions, and between the rich and the poor is still stark, and access to education, medical care, culture, and other public goods is also very unbalanced across different regions, classes, and urban and rural areas. In terms of inadequate development, the quality and efficiency of development are not high, and the medium- and high-end material products made in China are far from meeting people's needs.

III. The Theoretical Rationale behind the Evolution of the Principal Contradiction

The major historical judgment on the evolution of the principal contradiction facing Chinese society is a historical political judgment, major theoretical judgment, and theoretical innovation related to the overall situation. Contradiction is a philosophical category that reflects the unity of opposites of things. This method of contradiction analysis will help facilitate an understanding of the theoretical implications of the evolution of the principal contradiction facing Chinese society. It will also enable an understanding that people's ever-growing needs for a better life and the unbalanced and inadequate development are the two parts of the unity of opposites in the principal contradiction facing Chinese society. Only by grasping the principal contradiction can the fundamental content of the universal connection of things and the internal driving force of eternal development be understood. With a deep understanding of the above two parts of the unity of opposites, one can see the direction of history and the requirements of the times and grasp the difficulties and problems in upholding and developing socialism with Chinese characteristics. The world is changing all the time, and China is also changing all the time. China must keep up with the times in theory, continue learning the laws, identify new characteristics in the changed principal social contradiction, and continue promoting theoretical innovation, practical innovation, system innovation, cultural innovation, and other innovations. A clear understanding of the principal contradiction facing Chinese society is important to an accurate understanding of the basic national conditions, to the scientific formulation of the major policies and long-term strategies of the Party and the state, and to the long-term development of socialism with Chinese characteristics.

The new judgment on the principal social contradiction constitutes an important part of Xi Jinping Thought on Socialism with Chinese Characteristics for a New Era. The thought is a major theoretical innovation that combines Marxist theory with China's practice. It answers scientifically the major questions of the era, e.g., what kind of socialism with Chinese characteristics the government should uphold and develop under the conditions of the new era and how to uphold and develop this model of socialism. The nation should start by answering the question, "What is the principal social contradiction in this era?" The answer to this question is important to the future and destiny of the cause of socialism with Chinese characteristics and to the fundamental interests of the people. Therefore, the new judgment on the principal social contradiction is an important basis for the development of socialism with Chinese characteristics in the new era. It promotes theoretical innovation on the basis of practice, accurately positions the new era in theoretical innovation, and identifies from this position the next step of China's development path. Such evolution reflects the valuable character of the CPC, i.e., being innovative, never ossified, and never stagnant.

The new judgment on the principal social contradiction highlights the people-centered approach of Party leaders and reflects the Party's responsibility of "Remaining true to our original aspiration and keeping our mission firmly in mind" all along. The brief words of the new judgment capture the "people-centered" thinking and highlight the ideological essence of taking the interests of the people as the core. According to President Xi's report at the 19th National Congress of the CPC in 2017, "The aspiration of the people to live a better life must always be the focus of our effort, and we should rely on the people to create great historical undertakings." The new judgment meets the people's expectations and the requirements of the era for socialism with Chinese characteristics for a new era and reflects the superiority of the socialist system and the fundamental purpose of the CPC to serve the people wholeheartedly. The judgment on the principal social contradiction starts with people's needs, which is at the core of all undertakings of the Party. The aspiration of the people to live a better life is the focus of China's efforts. People's ever-growing needs for a better life are continuous, dynamic, changing, and open. The main factor restricting the fulfillment of people's needs for a better life is unbalanced and inadequate development.

The historic judgment on the evolution of the principal contradiction facing Chinese society is the basis for the CPC to formulate guidelines, lines, policies, and strategies in the new era. As President Xi Jinping states, "The era is the test maker, we are the respondents, and the people are the examiner." Accurately judging and grasping the principal social contradiction and its evolution is crucial to establishing the theoretical basis for the Party and the state to formulate the right policies; the theoretical premise for resolving contradictions and realizing comprehensive, coordinated, and sustainable economic and social development; and a major event concerning the future and destiny of the country. The history and reality of the CPC, which united and led the people of all ethnic groups in revolution and in the construction of a socialist country, demonstrates that in order to make a significant adjustment to the socialist development strategy and economic policy, the government must make an accurate theoretical judgment on the principal contradiction facing China's socialist society. For a long time, the Party has scientifically formulated its guiding principles and roadmap in various periods in history by revealing the principal social contradiction from complex social phenomena and analyzing and grasping the phased characteristics of social development. The judgment on the evolution of the principal contradiction facing Chinese society provides a strong theoretical basis for the thought of socialism with Chinese characteristics for a new era and a theoretical basis for formulating the Party's lines, principles, policies, and strategies.

Meeting people's needs for a better life and solving the principal contradiction are the focus, starting point, and foothold of the government's work. The aspiration of the people to live a better life is the focus of China's efforts. The problem of development will ultimately be solved with development. Emancipating and developing social productive forces is the essential requirement of socialism. The new changes in the principal contradiction facing Chinese society determine that the fundamental task in the new era is to vigorously emancipate and develop social productive forces so as to achieve higher-quality, more efficient, more equitable, and more sustainable development. One should grasp the phased characteristics of China's development in the new era, grasp the main aspects of the principal contradiction, grasp the aspiration of the people to live a better life, take "uniting and leading the people to continuously solve the principal contradiction facing Chinese society" as the focus, starting point, and foothold, guide development with new development concepts, and solve the problems of unbalanced and inadequate development.

SECTION 2
A New Stage for Socialism with Chinese Characteristics

Fully grasping the new development stage and incorporating its new characteristics requires understanding its significance in the process of rejuvenating the Chinese nation.

I. A Comprehensive Response to Changes in the Principal Contradiction

The principal contradiction facing Chinese society has evolved, and people are pursuing higher-quality life. The aspiration of the people to live a better life is the focus of China's efforts. For the economic and social development of the 14th Five-Year Plan period, the country must follow the people-centered principle, adhere to the dominant position of the people, adhere to the direction of common prosperity, always achieve development for the people, rely on the people and share the development achievements by the people, safeguard the fundamental interests of the people, stimulate the enthusiasm, initiative, and creativity of all the people, promote social fairness, improve the well-being of the people, and realize people's aspiration for a better life.

The proposal of the 14th Five-Year Plan firmly grasps the principal contradiction facing Chinese society, responds to the demands and expectations of the people, takes "meeting people's growing needs for a better life" as the fundamental purpose, implements the people-centered development thought, and puts forward a series of new tasks and measures to improve people's livelihoods and the level of social construction. The proposal of the 14th Five-Year Plan takes "solidly promoting common prosperity" and "reaching a new level of people's well-being" as one of the main objectives of economic and social development during the Plan period, and puts forward the long-range objective of realizing socialist modernization in people's livelihoods by

2035, i.e., "People live a better life, and more obvious substantive progress is made in the all-around development of people and the common prosperity of all people."

II. A High-Quality Development Stage with Continuous, Balanced, and Adequate Development

Development in this new stage must implement new development concepts, must be high-quality development, and must be more balanced and adequate development. At present and for a long time to come, the contradictions and problems in China's economic development are mainly reflected in the quality of development. This requires the government to put the quality of development in a more prominent position and strive to improve quality and efficiency. To comprehensively promote high-quality development during the 14th Five-Year Plan period, China should comprehensively grasp the new tasks and requirements in the new development stage, unswervingly implement new development concepts, build a new development pattern, uphold the underlying principle of pursuing progress while ensuring stability, comprehensively promote the five-sphere integrated plan and the four-pronged comprehensive strategy, coordinate development and security, elevate scientific and technological innovation, promote high-quality and sustainable economic and social development, and strive to make significant progress in reform and innovation and promote high-quality development. China should focus on supply-side structural reform, adhere to the principle of quality and efficiency first, effectively change the development model, and promote quality change, efficiency change, and power change so that development achievements can benefit all people, more balanced and adequate development can be achieved, and people's aspirations for a better life can be met.

III. A Development Stage in Which China Marches toward the Second Centenary Goal

The "new" in the new development stage is reflected in advance of the time node for the realization of strategic objectives—that is, realizing socialist modernization by 2035 and building China into a great modern socialist country that is prosperous, strong, democratic, culturally advanced, harmonious, and modernized by the middle of this century. The "new" in the new development stage is also reflected in the enrichment and expansion of the connotation of the strategic goal of building a modern power. For example, the overall goal of a modern country proposed in the planning proposal emphasizes that "China's economic strength, scientific and technological strength, and comprehensive national strength will rise sharply, and the total economic output and per capita income of urban and rural residents will rise to a new level." It takes the total economic output and per capita income of residents as the two major measurement indicators of a modern country, reflecting a high degree of unity between strengthening the country and enriching the people and between economic development and people's livelihoods. As another example, in terms of political construction, while further clarifying that "basically realizing the modernization of the national governance system and governance capacity," the planning proposal emphasizes that "people's right to equal participation and equal development should be fully guaranteed." In terms of cultural construction, it emphasizes "building a strong cultural country, a strong educational country, a strong talent country, a strong sports country and a healthy China, and achieving a new level of national quality and social civilization." In terms of social construction, while clarifying the "equalization of basic public services," it emphasizes that "the per capita GDP should reach the level of moderately developed countries, the middle-income group should expand significantly, and the gap in regional development and residents' living standards between urban and rural areas should narrow significantly." In terms of construction of ecological civilization, it emphasizes "widely forming a green production and life style" and "basically realizing the goal of building a beautiful China." In terms of security guarantees, it emphasizes that "the construction of [a] safe China should reach a higher level and the modernization of national defense and the army should be realized basically."

IV. A Development Stage that Comprehensively Responds to World Changes

The domestic and foreign situations are undergoing profound and complex changes. China's development is still in an important period of strategic opportunities, with bright prospects and severe challenges. The coexistence of an important opportunity period and a major risk period, and the coexistence of bright prospects and severe challenges, constitute the remarkable characteristics of the new development stage of socialism with Chinese characteristics. The world is now undergoing profound and complicated changes, with a new round of technological revolution and industrial transformation as well as profound adjustment in relative international forces, but peace and development remain the call of the day. The concept of community with a shared future for mankind is deeply rooted among the people. At the same time, the international environment is becoming increasingly complex, with a significant increase in instability and uncertainty. The impact of the COVID-19 pandemic is wide and deep, and economic globalization is facing headwinds. In a complex and changeable international economic and political situation, the world has entered a period of turbulence and change. Unilateralism, protectionism, and hegemonism pose a threat to world peace and development.

China is still in an important period of strategic opportunity for development, but both opportunities and challenges have new development and changes. China's overall development trend is good and has the foundation, conditions, and ability to achieve new milestones. At present, many contradictions are also superimposed, and risks and challenges have significantly increased. China is facing an unprecedentedly severe and complex development environment. The nation must grasp the strategic background of the coexistence of opportunities and challenges, bear in mind the overall strategic situation of the great rejuvenation of the Chinese nation and the great changes in the world, understand the new contradictions and challenges brought about by the complex international environment, enhance the awareness of opportunities and risks, base its decision-making on the basic national conditions of the primary stage of socialism, maintain strategic determination, strategic confidence, and strategic patience, and do its own things well. China should understand and grasp the development law of the new era and the new characteristics and trends in the external environment, be ready to fight, establish bottom-line thinking, accurately recognize change, respond scientifically, take the initiative to seek change, try to cultivate opportunities in crisis, open up a new situation within changing situations, forge ahead, meet challenges, seek advantages and avoid disadvantages, and advance bravely.

SECTION 3

China's Economic Development in a High-Quality Development Stage

Socialism with Chinese characteristics has entered a new era. China's social and economic development has also entered a new era, characterized by a shift in economic development from a rapid growth stage to a high-quality development stage. High-quality development is the inevitable means for solving the principal social contradiction. Only by understanding the strategic significance of promoting high-quality development can China firmly grasp the fundamental requirements of high-quality development, accelerate the transformation of development ideas and working methods, and promote high-quality development.

I. The Basic Characteristics of a High-Quality Development Stage

The high-quality development stage is a new stage in which China adapts to the change in the principal contradiction facing Chinese society, continuously meets people's ever-growing needs for a better life, and creates a better life for the people. In the new era, the Chinese people look forward to better education, more stable work, more satisfactory income, more reliable social security, higher levels of medical and health services, more comfortable living conditions, and a more beautiful environment. They look forward to better development of their children, better work, and better life. The aspiration of the people to live a better life is the focus of the effort of the CPC. High-quality development is to turn people's expectations for a better life into reality, seek more benefits for people's livelihoods, solve more worries about people's livelihoods, and keep improving people's sense of gain, happiness, and achievement.

The high-quality development stage is a new stage in which China solves the problem of unbalanced and inadequate development, deepens supply-side structural reforms, and builds a modern economic system. In reality, the main aspect of the principal contradiction facing Chinese society is the unbalanced and inadequate development, which is mainly manifested in the relative shortage of supply and the structural imbalance of supply. To solve the principal contradiction, China must adhere to Xi Jinping Thought on Socialism with Chinese Characteristics for a New Era; strengthen the Party's leadership in economic work; accelerate the formation of an index system, a policy system, a standard system, a statistical system, a performance evaluation, and an achievement assessment system to promote the high-quality development; create and perfect the institutional environment; and help China's economy to continuously make new progress in achieving high-quality development. China should start with the main aspects of the principal contradiction and take supply-side structural reforms as the main task. With the main direction of improving the supply structure and supply quality, the government should reduce ineffective supply, expand effective supply, improve the adaptability of the supply structure to the demand structure, and eliminate the institutional and mechanism obstacles to the optimal allocation of resources and the rational flow of factors by means of reform. China should improve the system and mechanism in which the market plays a decisive role in resource allocation, improve total factor productivity, and strive to achieve higher-quality development. Additionally, China should make overall plans to promote steady growth, promote reform, adjust structure, benefit people's livelihoods, and prevent risks. The government should vigorously promote reform and opening-up, innovate and improve macro-control, advance quality change, efficiency change, and power change, and improve total factor productivity. Relying on innovative development, China will accelerate the construction of a modern industrial system with high scientific and technological content, low resource consumption, less environmental pollution, and coordinated development of real economy, scientific and technological innovation, modern finance, and human resources. China should strengthen the organic integration of the industrial chain and innovation chain, cultivate new growth drivers and competitive advantages, and accelerate the formation of a modern economic system and development model, with innovation as the main guide and support. Only by eliminating the institutional obstacles to the optimal allocation of resources and the rational flow of factors, improving the system and mechanism in which the market plays a decisive role in the allocation of resources, and improving total factor productivity, can the nation achieve high-quality development.

The high-quality development stage is a new stage in which the development concepts of innovation, coordination, green, opening, and sharing are fully implemented. In other words, innovation becomes the first driving force, coordination becomes an endogenous feature, green becomes a universal form, opening becomes the inevitable way, and sharing becomes the fundamental purpose. High-quality development means that the supply side will provide more high-end products and high-quality services to meet the needs of the people. The constantly improved quality standards can ensure consumer safety and assure people of their daily necessities. High-quality development means that energy consumption per unit of GDP is reduced, there is less pollution, the sky becomes bluer, water is clearer, air quality is continuously improved, and the quality of life and health of urban and rural residents are improved. High-quality development means more balanced and coordinated development. The development gap among regions, fields, and groups, and between urban and rural areas, continues to be narrowed or eliminated. The people share the fruits of reform and development, and common prosperity and social fairness for all people will be realized. Only by achieving high-quality development can China form a development pattern of economic prosperity, political democracy, cultural prosperity, social fairness, and good ecology and build a prosperous, strong, democratic, culturally advanced, harmonious, and beautiful modern socialist country by the middle of this century.

II. Opening Up with Higher Standards: The Basic Path to High-Quality Development

With higher standard opening up to the outside world, China will accelerate the improvement of its industrial chain and supply chain level, integrate domestic and international industrial links, and keep improving the international growth and modernization level of China's industrial chain. Opening up is the inevitable means of promoting national prosperity and development. Since the reform and opening-up, China's position in the global economy has been rising and growing more connected. In the future, economic globalization, the international links of industrial chains, supply chains, and value chains, and international economic cooperation will still be the objective requirements and inevitable trends of global economic development. Under this major background and trend, the new development pattern the government wants to build is the "dual circulation" development pattern in which the domestic economic cycle plays a leading role while the international economic cycle remains its extension and supplement. It is by no means a closed domestic cycle but a dual domestic and international cycle of high-level open development. Expanding domestic demand as the strategic basis, it gives full play to the domestic demand potential of China's large-scale market, attracting foreign capital and multinational enterprises to participate in domestic economic cycle activities, and continue improving the internationalization and modernization level of China's industrial chain. Only under the general pattern of open development can the country improve the internationalization and modernization level of its industrial chain. Only by integrating domestic and international dual cycles can China give better play to the huge domestic demand potential of its population of 1.4 billion, continue improving the domestic market system, supplement, expand, and strengthen the innovation chain, supply chain, industrial chain, and value chain, and promote high-quality economic development.

In open cooperation, it is easier to form an industrial chain with stronger innovation and higher added value and enhance the toughness of the industrial chain. The competition and cooperation brought about by opening up are crucial for realizing the leading role of the domestic cycle and maintaining the vitality and competitiveness of the entities in the domestic cycle. Only in this way can the leading role of the domestic economic cycle be more stable and China's industrial chain, supply chain, and value chain be organically embedded in the global innovation chain, industrial chain, supply chain, value chain, and market chain, to turn it into an indispensable part of the global industrial chain and supply chain and make it more irreplaceable. To this end, China should accelerate the construction of the new development pattern, more actively participate in the international division of labor and cooperation, focus on both imports and exports, coordinate the use of foreign capital and overseas investments, enhance the adhesion between international and domestic markets and resources, accelerate the transformation from opening up based on flows of goods and factors of production to opening up based on rules and related institutions, improve the level of investment and trade facilitation, continue optimizing the business environment, promote the exchange and cooperation in capital, technology, talents, management, and other production factors with relevant countries, and strive to build an open, stable, and internationally competitive industrial chain, supply chain, and value chain.

China should deepen international scientific and technological cooperation, promote the in-depth integration of the industrial chain and the global scientific and technological innovation chain, and accelerate the improvement of innovation levels of China's industrial chain. Innovation is the first driving force leading development. In today's world, scientific and technological innovation has become an important driving force for countries to promote economic growth and sustainable development. At present, a new round of scientific and technological revolution and industrial change is ready to start. 5G technology has rapidly popularized, and information industry technologies such as big data, cloud computing, artificial intelligence (AI), the Internet of Things, and the industrial Internet are developing rapidly. The rise of these scientific and technological innovations and industrial changes will keep on providing a strong driving force for economic development. The new round of scientific and technological revolution and industrial change is the product of the effective integration and superposition of the innovation chain and industrial chain. To improve the level of the industrial chain, China should first improve the innovation ability of the industrial chain and systematically build an innovation chain to support industrial development. The reality suggests that core and key technologies cannot be fetched, bought, or otherwise obtained, but independent innovation is innovation in an open environment, and the country must not engage in scientific and technological innovation behind closed doors. The higher-standard open development will effectively promote the in-depth integration of a series of chains in scientific and technological innovation and industrial development. The links, such as scientific research, investment, design, and production, will bring the breeding and maturity of new technologies, new industries, and new formats into the process of open development more easily.

The innovation chain should be deployed around the industrial chain, and conversely the industrial chain should be deployed around the innovation chain. To improve the level of the industrial chain, China should always promote scientific and technological innovation from a global perspective, strengthen international scientific and technological innovation cooperation in a comprehensive way, actively integrate into the global scientific and technological innovation network, and improve its scientific and technological innovation ability in open cooperation. The more the nation faces blockade and repression, the less it should be self-isolated. Instead, China should implement a more open, inclusive, mutually beneficial, and shared international S&T cooperation strategy, actively promote the flow and optimal allocation of various innovative elements around the world, and form a new pattern of S&T cooperation with complementary advantages and win-win cooperation. This will help accelerate the upgrading of China's industrial chain. The country should strengthen international industrial security cooperation; focus on upgrading various industrial bases; promote the internationalization of scientific and technological innovation and the modernization of industrial chains; focus on new scientific discoveries, technological inventions, industrial directions, and development ideas; comprehensively deploy international industrial security cooperation with innovation from the source; and promote the deep integration of innovation chains and industrial chains so as to realize the reconstruction of the industrial chain and the promotion of value chain.

China will accelerate the construction of a new open economic system at a higher standard and attract the inflow of production factors from the global industrial chain. The flow of production factors determines the transfer and layout of the industrial chain. The establishment, maturity, and transfer of the industrial chain are accompanied by the flow of productive factors, such as capital, talents, technology, labor force, and big data. To stabilize the supply chain of the industrial chain and improve the level of the industrial chain, China must first have a new high-standard open economic system that can attract a steady flow of production factors in the global industrial chain. At the beginning of reform and opening-up, China implemented a series of preferential policies for opening to the outside world to attract foreign investment, made full use of the comparative advantages of low-price land, resources, and labor, attracted the inflow of international production factors, and drove the rapid economic development of China. In the new era, the price advantage of China's supply of factors, such as labor, land, and resources, is not clear. The government needs to accelerate the construction of a new open economic system at a higher standard, open wider to the outside world, promote trade and investment liberalization and facilitation, give full play to the comprehensive cost advantage and significant market advantage, open the market to a greater extent, optimize the business environment at a higher level, provide investors with a fairer, safer, more open, and convenient business environment, attract continuous inflow of international advanced production factors, such as capital, talent, logistics, brand, information, and data all over the world, and continue optimizing the transnational configuration or transregional flow of production factors so as to improve the internationalization and modernization level of the industrial chain.

To improve the level of the industrial chain, the government should give full play to the industrial agglomeration advantages of free trade zones (FTZs) (ports) and industrial parks and create a large number of economies with a new height of openness to attract the inflow of production factors in the global industrial chain. In FTZs (ports), in accordance with international practices and rules, China should accelerate the realization of freedom of trade, investment, capital flow, transportation, personnel residence, employment, and data flow; attract production factors of international high-end industrial chain into the zones; build an advanced manufacturing cluster, strategic emerging industrial base, production factors, and bulk commodity trading service platform and international trade and shipping hub; and strive to expand the height, depth, and breadth of China's economic opening up to the outside world. On the other hand, the government should reasonably guide the specialization and centralization of industrial parks, integrate industrial clusters, and give full play to the output scale effect and the superposition effect of industrial supporting facilities. China should also build a number of modern international industrial parks with high-level opening up and high-standard services according to the technical distribution principle and geographical location distribution characteristics of the supply chain of industrial chain to turn them into industrial cluster platforms to attract high-tech and cutting-edge elements in the world. At the same time, China should give full play to the advantages of its complete industrial system, accelerate the development of related industrial clusters, effectively improve the competitiveness of industrial clusters, and maximize the regional distribution advantages of industrial chain networking, collectivization, and modernization.

From the perspective of globalization, China should accelerate the implementation of industrial foundation reconstruction and industrial chain upgrading and strive to promote the upgrading of the industrial foundation and the modernization of the industrial chain. The global spread of COVID-19 has made the world aware of the importance of the industrial chain layout to national economic security. Some developed countries have tried to adjust the supply chain of the industrial chain in proximity, diversification, and localization. Therefore, China should plan ahead from the perspective of globalization, actively respond to the dynamics of the layout adjustments for the supply chain of the international industrial chain, and speed up the implementation of industrial foundation reconstruction and industrial chain upgrading. Fundamentally, the task of improving the level of the industrial chain and enhancing the toughness of the industrial chain will be borne by various large, small, and medium-sized enterprises and other market subjects. Therefore, China should further deepen enterprise reform and optimize the business environment. The government should make good use of the policy mix, further release the vitality of market subjects, and allow the creativity of market subjects to flourish. This is a long-term and fundamental policy to improve the level of the industrial chain. To this end, China should give full play to the institutional advantages and large-scale market advantages of concentrating resources on major areas, consolidate the basic industrial capacity, focus on self-control, safety, and efficiency, be based on enterprises and entrepreneurs, and be guaranteed by policy coordination. The government should be pulled by application and oriented by problem, combine government guidance with market mechanisms, focus on both independence and open cooperation, and win the battle for the upgrading of the industrial foundation and the modernization of the industrial chain.

The key to and focus of the implementation of the industrial foundation reconstruction and industrial chain upgrading project is to make up for the weakness and extend the strength of the industrial chain. On the one hand, China should speed up making up for the weakness in the supply chain of the industrial chain. Based on the principles of "consolidated, enhanced, improved and unimpeded," the government should support upstream and downstream enterprises to strengthen industrial coordination and technical cooperation, break through the technologies that others use to contain us, increase investment in and research and development (R&D) of basic science, establish a common technology platform, and solve key generic technology problems across industries and fields. China should improve the level of basic education and basic research with the strength of the whole country and build a strategic and overall industrial chain. On the other hand, the government should try its best to forge strengths. China should take effective measures and policy support to develop and expand its leading enterprises and core enterprises in the global industrial chain, expand its global market share, and stabilize and enhance the position of Chinese enterprises in the global industrial chain. China should give full play to the spirit of entrepreneurship and craftsmanship and cultivate a number of "specialized and novel" small and medium enterprises (SMEs). The nation will strive to build specialized and novel "trump" products into best-in-class in the world, organically combine enterprise cultivation with ecological construction of the industrial chain, and form a unique competitive advantage that is deeply embedded in the global value chain and will not be easily replaced.

III. Promoting Common Prosperity: A Requirement for High-Quality Development

Common prosperity is the essential requirement of socialism and the common expectation of the people. In the final analysis, China promotes economic and social development to achieve common prosperity for all people. The government will work to achieve fuller and higher-quality employment, synchronize the growth of residents' income with economic growth, improve the distribution structure, promote the equalization of basic public services, continuously strengthen education levels of all people, bolster the multi-level social security system, improve the health system, consolidate and expand achievements in poverty alleviation, and advance the Rural Revitalization Strategy (RRS). China will adhere to the principle of distribution according to work as the mainstay with the coexistence of multiple distribution methods, increase the proportion of labor remuneration in the primary distribution, improve the wage system, strengthen the mechanism for reasonable wage growth, and strive to increase the income of low-income groups and expand middle-income groups. The government will strive to increase the property income of urban and rural residents through multiple channels. It will also look to improve the redistribution mechanism, strengthen the adjustment and accuracy of taxes, social security, and transfer payments, reasonably adjust excessive income, and ban illegal income. China will give play to the role of tertiary distribution, develop charity, and improve the distribution pattern of income and wealth.

The goal of enabling people to live a better life, promoting people's well-rounded development, and realizing the common prosperity of all people would be achieved gradually with the accumulation of several objectives from stage to stage. China must keep realizing people's aspirations for a better life and moving toward the goal of common prosperity for all people, step by step, with clear demand orientation, problem orientation, effect orientation, detailed institutional arrangements, and pragmatic concrete measures. The government should grasp the new characteristics of the evolution of the principal contradiction facing Chinese society, adhere to demand orientation, problem orientation, and effect orientation, adhere to the people-centered development thought, work hard practically, promote common prosperity, continue improving the people's quality of life, and take more reform and innovation measures to solve the problems that the people raise.

To be demand-oriented is to aim at the people's livelihood demand goal of "good care for children, excellent education for students, substantial pay for workers, good doctors for patients, proper care for the elderly, livable housing and public support for the weak," set a standard for people's happiness, and explore a new path of high-quality development. China should always take the people's well-being and safety and their needs for a better life as the starting point and foothold for the work of the Party and government at all levels and find the development focus, direction, and goal from people's needs for a better life.

Problem orientation means identifying the expectations of the people according to the reality of unbalanced and inadequate development and the current situation of work and aiming to solve the overall problems affecting economic and social development, the prominent contradictions restricting the improvement of quality of life, and the people's strong demands for people's livelihoods—especially the obstacles and bottlenecks in the work of the region, the unit, and the field. Problem orientation also means ascertaining the problems accurately and thoroughly to solve them, break through bottlenecks, and make up for weaknesses and vulnerabilities to create a quality life. The people's sense of gain and happiness is the touchstone for testing the quality of life and the effect of life improvement.

To be effect-oriented, China should always pay attention to the safety and well-being of the people, take the benefit of the people as the greatest political achievement, concern itself with the needs of the people, start from the small challenges faced by the people, assess the cadres of CPC and government leaders according to the practical results of their work and the happiness of the people, strive for practical results and enhance the people's sense of gain so as to keep improving people's satisfaction.

A better life is achieved through struggle. To promote common prosperity in high-quality development and improve people's quality of life, China needs the labor and creation of the general population. Relying on the people to promote common prosperity and improve the quality of life reflects the people's dominant position and the ideological line of "everything for the people and everything depends on the people." If "everything for the people" answers the question of the value orientation of development, then "everything depends on the people" answers the question of the source of strength. In fact, people's need for a better life is not only a need to enjoy a better life but also a need to create a better life. China should adhere to the people-centered development concept. In particular, the government should respect people's creativity and keep absorbing the vitality of innovation and creativity for development from the people.

SECTION 4

Embarking on a New Journey to Fully Build a Modern Socialist China

After China has built a moderately prosperous society in all aspects by 2020, the second goal is to build a prosperous, strong, democratic, culturally advanced, and harmonious modern socialist country by 2049, when the country celebrates the centenary of the PRC. The year 2021 marks the start of the new journey to fully build a modern socialist China as launched by the 14th Five-Year Plan and happens to be at the intersection of those two goals, with the special significance of connecting the two goals.

I. The Significance of the New Journey to Build a Modern Socialist China

The new journey to build a modern socialist China began in 2021. It is not only a new journey in the sense of historical alternation and continuous promotion of the Two Centenary Goals but also in that "the world has entered a period of turbulence and change" triggered by the headwinds encountered by China in the "important strategic opportunity period" for development at the beginning of the 14th Five-Year Plan. From the perspective of the Chinese nation realizing a path from standing up to becoming rich and strong, this new journey entails sprinting toward the final goal outlined in the three-step strategic deployment as part of the primary stage of socialism formulated by the Party and successfully realizing the Chinese dream of national rejuvenation through three stages—the 14th Five-Year Plan to 2025, 2035 to 2049, and finally the 100th anniversary of the founding of new China.

II. China's Economic Development at a New Stage

China's economic development has entered a new stage. In this stage, China's development model should be transformed from one of "promoting the domestic cycle with the international cycle" to one of "driving the international cycle with the domestic cycle." This transformation is necessary for the "dual circulation" development pattern in which the domestic economic cycle plays a leading role, while the international economic cycle remains its extension and supplement so as to promote the coordinated development of marketization, industrialization, urbanization, informatization, greenization, and internationalization. In the new stage of development, marketization is to advance in depth, and various systems become mature and finalized. China should uphold and improve the basic socialist economic system, give full play to the decisive role of the market in the allocation of resources, give better play to the role of government, and promote a better combination of an efficient market and a promising government. Industrialization is turning to the middle and late stage, and the country should "cross the middle-income trap." China should accelerate the development of a modern industrial system, promote the optimization and upgrading of the economic system, put the focus of economic development on the real economy, unswervingly build a manufacturing power, a quality power, a network power, and a digital China, promote the upgrading of the industrial foundation and the modernization of the industrial chain, and improve the economic quality, efficiency, and core competitiveness. As urbanization moves into the second half of its process, the government should uphold the people-centered development concept. China will develop network urban agglomeration, promote urban clustering development, and form a multi-center, multi-level, and multi-node network urban agglomeration structure. The government should attach importance to county-level economic development and fully implement the RRS. Informatization has entered a comprehensive integration period, and China should vigorously develop 5G, AI, and digital economy, promote digital industrialization and industrial digitization, promote the integration of the digital economy with the real economy, and build a digital industry cluster with the international capital flow. China should strengthen the construction of a digital society and government, build a digital China, and create an intelligent digital platform. Green development has entered a comprehensive transformation period and crossed the inflection point of the Environmental Kuznets Curve. The government should uphold the concept of green development, promote the comprehensive green transformation of economic and social development, and build a modern country with harmonious coexistence between man and nature. China will strive to peak carbon dioxide emissions by 2030 and achieve carbon neutrality by 2060. The government will coordinate the integrated protection and restoration of mountains, rivers, forests, fields, lakes, and grasses and strengthen the ecological protection and systematic governance of major rivers, such as the Yangtze River and the Yellow River. Internationalization turns into rule guidance, and the country will cross the Thucydides Trap and the Samuelson Trap. China will continue wider and deeper opening up, build a new open economic system at a higher standard, promote high-quality development with joint construction of the Belt and Road, build economies with a new height of openness, and make new ground in opening China further through links running eastward and westward, across land and over sea. The nation should establish an international perspective, explore the common problems faced by mankind from the connection and interaction between China and the world, and contribute Chinese wisdom to the construction of a community with a shared future for mankind.

III. The Long-Range Objective of a Realizing Socialist Modernization by 2035

The second centenary goal will be realized in two stages: realizing socialist modernization by 2035 and building China into a modern socialist country that is prosperous, strong, democratic, culturally advanced, harmonious, and beautiful by the middle of this century. Based on the Outline of the People's Republic of China 14th Five-Year Plan for National Economic and Social Development and Long-Range Objectives for 2035, by 2035, China's economic strength, scientific and technological strength, and comprehensive national strength will rise by a large margin, the GDP and the per capita income of urban and rural residents will increase by a large margin, major breakthroughs will be made in key and core technologies, and China will be in the forefront of innovative countries. China will realize new industrialization, informatization, urbanization, and agricultural modernization and build a modern economic system. The modernization of national governance capacity and governance system will be realized. The ecological environment will fundamentally improve, and the goal of building a modernized China will be basically achieved. A new pattern of opening up to the outside world will come into being, and the international competitiveness will be significantly enhanced. China's per capita GDP will reach the level of moderately developed countries, basic public services will be equalized, and the development gap between urban and rural areas will be narrowed significantly. The modernization of national defense and the army will be basically realized. People will live a better life, and clearer substantive progress will be made in the well-rounded development of the people and the common prosperity of all people.

The long-range objective of socialist modernization will be realized for the most part by 2035, consistent with the Party's people-centered development thought, the new development concepts of innovation, coordination, green, openness and sharing, the historical logic, theoretical logic, practical logic, and goal orientation of promoting social fairness and justice and gradually realizing common prosperity for all people. Moreover, in the highly uncertain external environment that China will face at present and in the future, it has given the people of the whole country a highly certain expectation of a sense of gain, happiness, and security with a high degree of self-confidence and determination.

The Basic Economic System and the Market Economy System

CHAPTER THREE

The Form and Structure of Socialist Ownership with Chinese Characteristics

The form and structure of ownership serve as the fundamental standard for determining the nature of the socialist economy with Chinese characteristics, the basic decisive factor for regulating the economic interest relationships between people, and an important decisive factor for the development of productive forces.

SECTION 1
The Structure and Evolution of Socialist Ownership with Chinese Characteristics

Ownership structure refers to the composition of different types of ownership in the national economy, reflecting the composition and mutual relationships between the subjects of economic development. There is no fixed ownership form or structure in any social form. Ownership reform is the most fundamental part of China's economic system reform.

I. Ownership Structure and its Evolution Prior to China's Period of Reform and Opening-Up

Since the founding of the PRC in 1949, the CPC has combined the Marxist ownership theory with the reality of China and explored the nation's ownership structure. As of 1978, the following major changes had taken place in China's ownership structure.

First, in the early days after the PRC's founding, by depriving imperialists of their privileges in China, confiscating bureaucratic capital, and abolishing feudal land ownership, China formed an ownership structure in which the public and state-owned economy played a leading role, and multiple sectors coexisted within the individual and private economy. Data show that by 1952, the public and state-owned economy accounted for 19.1% of the national income, the collective economy 1.5%, public-private partnerships 0.7%, the private capitalist economy 6.9%, and the individual economy of agricultural and handicraft workers 71.8%.

Second, from 1952 to 1956, after the socialist transformation of agriculture, the handicraft industry, and capitalist industry and commerce, the ownership structure of China went through fundamental changes, with public ownership as the mainstay of the ownership structure, the state-owned economy in the leading role, and multiple sectors coexisting. Data show that by 1956, the state-owned economy accounted for 32.2% of the national income, the collective economy 53.4%, public-private partnerships 7.3%, the private economy 1%, and the individual economy 7.1%. The socialist transformation of means of production had essentially been completed, and the socialist economic system was established.

Third, from 1958 to 1978, there was a rapid transition from collective ownership to ownership by the whole people, forming a single form of public ownership. Although some local adjustments were made, no fundamental changes were made to the single public ownership structure until China's period of reform and opening-up began. Data show that by 1978, the state-owned economy accounted for 56% of the national income, the collective economy for 43%, and the individual economy less than 1%. By this point, there was essentially no longer a private economy.

The main reason for such an evolution is that under the past planned economy system, there were two misunderstandings about Marxist views on ownership: first, China prioritized the ownership standard over the standard of productivity and simply equated socialism with public ownership, and capitalism with private ownership; second, it treated the concept of public ownership in an inflexible way and considered a certain form of public ownership to be the only form. These misconceptions led to the continuous revolution of ownership relations in practice. In cities, enterprises operating under ownership by the whole people were developed vigorously, and collective enterprises were required to transition toward this model; in rural areas, movements such as "equalitarianism and free allocation" and "cutting the tail of capitalism" were carried out, and people mistakenly believed that the greater, the more public, and the purer the ownership, the better, regardless of the level of productive forces. The practice has proven that an exclusively public ownership structure does not align with China's actual productivity and is not conducive to the development of social productivity.

II. Ownership Structure and its Evolution since Reform and Opening-Up

At the Third Plenary Session of the 11th CPC Central Committee held at the end of 1978, the Party Central Committee made the decision to reform the single public economy. With deepened understanding, reforms to China's ownership structure took place in the following stages.

In the first stage, after the Third Plenary Session of the 11th CPC Central Committee, rural ownership reforms began. The reform of the Household Responsibility System began in China's rural areas, allowing the main means of production, namely land, to be collectively owned by the laborers, and for individual farmers to directly control the use of land and receive part of the ownership of income. Based on the Household Responsibility System adopted in agriculture in 1979, "except what is to be handed over to the state and what is to be left over to the collective, all will be their own." This new model of public ownership, combined with collective ownership and individual management, was adapted to the level of rural productivity at the time. It greatly motivated farmers in production and increased rural social productivity unprecedentedly. In the short period of five years from 1979 to 1984, the problem of food and clothing had essentially been solved in the vast rural areas of China. The fundamental reason for the success of rural reform lies in the breakthrough of traditional public ownership.

In the second stage, at the Third Plenary Session of the 12th CPC Central Committee, the focus of China's reform shifted from rural to urban areas, and the individual, private, and foreign-funded sectors of the economy grew rapidly. At the same time, rural township enterprises were booming. In the four years from 1984 to 1988, China's national economy reached a new stage.

In the third stage, since the 14th National Congress of the CPC, according to the require-ments of the socialist market economy, the public economy and non-public economy had been repositioned, promoting the rapid development of various sectors, including the public economy. In particular, a series of new breakthroughs in the theory of ownership was made in the 15th National Congress of the CPC, which raised the understanding of ownership structure in the primary stage of socialism to new heights and served as a milestone for ownership reform.

(1) It established that the basic economic system in the primary stage of socialism should entail positioning public ownership as the mainstay of the economy while allowing diverse sectors to develop side by side.

(2) New explanations were made on the understanding of the public economy. The public economy includes not only the state-owned and collective economy but also the state-owned and collective components of the mixed economy.

(3) Positioning public ownership as the mainstay of the ownership structure means that public assets are dominant in the composition of total social assets.

(4) The leading role of the state-owned economy is mainly reflected in its influence and control over the economy.

(5) The forms of public ownership can and should be diversified, and all the management and organizational forms reflecting the law of socialized production can be used boldly.

(6) The joint-stock system is a form of property organization in modern enterprises. One cannot just say that the joint-stock system is public or private. The key lies in who retains a dominant stake.

(7) The stock cooperative system is a new concept in reforms and should be actively supported and guided. In particular, the stock cooperative system based on the labor union and the capital union of laborers is a new type of collective economy and should be encouraged and advocated.

(8) The non-public economy is also an important part of the socialist market economy.

In November 2002, the "two unshakable policies" on ownership reform were raised in the 16th National Congress of the CPC, namely "to consolidate and develop the public sector of economy unshakably"; and "to encourage, support, and guide the development of the non-public sector of economy unshakably." With the public sector as the mainstay of the economy, China should promote the development of the non-public sector and unify the two sectors in the process of socialist modernization to jointly serve the development of socialist productive forces, as they are both indispensable in the market economy. They reflected the continuity and stability of the Party's policies on the non-public economy and paved the way for the development of the non-public economy at the basic system level, and then the non-public economy entered a new period of development.

In October 2003, the Third Plenary Session of the 16th CPC Central Committee broke through the traditional concept of realizing public ownership and put forward the joint-stock system as the main form for realizing public ownership, leading to the trend of integration of various forms of ownership, namely mixed ownership. In 2004, the "inviolability of private property" was written into the Constitution. In 2005, the 36 Articles on Non-public Economy was issued, showing China's confidence in the development of the non-public economy. In October 2007, the 17th National Congress of the CPC proposed to continue deepening reforms of China's ownership structure, adhere to the equal protection of property rights, and form a new pattern of equal competition and mutual promotion of various sectors of the economy. These two "equalities" were the highlights in the ownership theory of the 17th National Congress, along with another leap in the theory of the non-public economy and another breakthrough in the ownership theory. In November 2012, the report to the 18th National Congress put forward the theory that different market players can compete fairly with the core content of "three equalities." In November 2013, the Third Plenary Session of the 18th CPC Central Committee proposed that both the public economy and the non-public economy are important components of the socialist market economy and provide an important foundation for China's economic and social development. This specific statement on the fair development of various sectors of the economy represents another leap in the theory of ownership economy and a major innovation in the economic theory of socialism with Chinese characteristics. It also provides guidance for further deepening the reform.

Since the 18th National Congress, the Third, Fourth, and Fifth Plenary Sessions of the 18th CPC Central Committee launched several reform measures to expand market access and the equal development of non-public enterprises. The government has issued several relevant policies and measures, forming a policy system to encourage, support, and guide the development of the non-public economy. The development of the non-public economy is facing an unprecedented positive policy environment and social atmosphere. The report to the 19th National Congress emphasized the need to deepen the reform of state-owned enterprises, develop a mixed ownership economy, and cultivate world-class enterprises with global competitiveness.

III. Improving the Ownership Structure of Socialism with Chinese Characteristics

1. Improving the understanding of the ownership structure of socialism with Chinese characteristics

Over nearly 40 years of practice and exploration, China's understanding of ownership reform has continuously improved, providing a theoretical basis for the further improvement of the ownership structure with common development of the public and non-public economy.

In terms of its way of thinking, China has embraced a scientific methodology of seeking truth from facts and proceeding from practical reality while moving away from a dogmatic methodology of constructing a socialist ownership structure based on classical writers' prediction of future society. When Engels talked about the development of socialism from Utopia to science, he said that in order to turn socialism into science, one must base it on reality. Similarly, the socialist ownership structure, which is the basis of the socialist economic system with Chinese characteristics, must also be applied based on China's actual productivity level and economic form.

China has also challenged and improved on the idealistic standard of measuring and choosing only according to the abstract principles of socialism and established a realistic standard of "three benefits," that is, "whether it is conducive to the development of the productivity of socialist society, whether it is conducive to the enhancement of the comprehensive national strength of socialist countries, and whether it is conducive to improving people's living standards," as proposed by Deng Xiaoping during his 1992 Southern Tour. Any effective system of ownership must conform to the standard of "three benefits." There is no other standard. The most important of the "three benefits" is the productivity standard. This attitude of thinking about ownership reform from the demand of productivity development is the concentrated reflection of adhering to Marxist ownership theory and a sober judgment based on a deep understanding of China's current stage.

China, moreover, has challenged the traditional opposition to the relationship between public and non-public ownership, and the non-public economy is now considered to be an important part of a socialist market economy rather than an "alien" power. The government has been clear about the common development and integrated growth of the non-public and public economy and established the basic economic system of keeping public ownership as the mainstay of the economy while allowing diverse sectors to develop side by side. The establishment of this basic economic system has not only been a successful practice in the development of socialism with Chinese characteristics, it has also been an innovative achievement in the Sinicization of Marxist ownership theory.

In a nutshell, China's ownership structure and forms of public ownership have become increasingly diversified. The evolution from a unary static closed ownership structure to a diversified and dynamic open structure has essentially been realized. Adhering to and improving the basic economic system of keeping public ownership as the mainstay of the economy while allowing diverse sectors to develop side by side is the basic experience summed up through China's long-term practice. This is the institutional guarantee for avoiding wealth gaps and moving toward common prosperity. To a certain extent, this is also a safety line and warning line for controlling China's reform. China needs to maintain some bottom lines, which are also the edge of life and death related to the fate of socialism with Chinese characteristics and the fate of the Chinese nation.

2. Thoughts on improving the ownership structure of socialism with Chinese characteristics

The reform of state-owned enterprises should be deepened, striving to improve the control and competitiveness of the state-owned economy. China should continue to deepen reforms, promote the strategic adjustment of state-owned capital, and optimize the layout and structure of the state-owned economy. China should also build large enterprises with outstanding competitive ability, accelerate the restructuring of state-owned assets with the same market orientation and asset quality, and continuously strengthen state-owned enterprises' comprehensive strength, innovation ability, influence, driving force, and ability to control the lifeline of the national economy. The government should promote mixed ownership, encourage the entry of external investors, promote the integration of different ownership enterprises with capital as the link, ensure the smooth progress of equity diversification, and improve the operation efficiency and competitiveness of state-owned assets.

Relevant systems and policies should continue to improve, stimulating the vitality and creativity of the non-public economy. China should continue to support the healthy development of the non-public sector of the economy; adhere to equal rights, equal opportunities, and equal rules; and ensure that all sectors of the economy can participate in market competition fairly and use production factors equally in accordance with the law. The government should abolish unreasonable regulations on various forms of the non-public economy, eliminate various hidden barriers, and break administrative and economic monopolies. It is necessary to effectively relax the fields and conditions for entry to the non-public economy and accelerate relevant supporting policies on industry access to be standardized, procedure-based, and fair. China should improve the system of laws and regulations, improve the management system of impartial law enforcement, allow the non-public sector to have a truly equal position as other sectors, guide the legal operation of non-public enterprises, and support the healthy development of non-public enterprises. The government should increase the support for the financing of the non-public sector, solve the financing problem in the fundamental transformation of the mode of economic growth, and improve the independent innovation ability.

SECTION 2
The Dominant Position of Public Ownership and the Non-public Economy

To comprehensively deepen the reform of China's economic system and improve the socialist ownership structure with Chinese characteristics, China must keep pace with the times in how it addresses the relationship between the modern public economy and the non-public economy. It must also uphold the basic economic system of keeping public ownership as the mainstay of the economy while allowing diverse sectors to develop side by side.

I. The Definition of the Modern Public Economy and Its Dominant Position

"Public ownership as the mainstay of the economy" refers to the entire public economy in various forms rather than a single public ownership in the traditional sense. Since China's reform and opening-up, great changes have taken place in its ownership structure, and various forms of public ownership have emerged, including both the state-owned economy and the collective economy, as well as the state-owned and collective elements in the mixed economy. Public ownership is no longer realized through a single form, and public capital may exist in different forms of enterprises. The modern public ownership system can manage the economic interest relationship between people. It is in line with the objective requirements of social development, suitable for capital operation, and has greater potential to exert its control, influence, and driving force. Moreover, the production and operation of the modern public ownership system are closely aligned with its own economic interests, thereby overcoming the weakness of the traditional public economy to a great extent.

When talking about public ownership as the mainstay of the economy, it is with regard to the entire national economy rather than a requirement that every sector, every region, and every enterprise of the national economy take public ownership as the mainstay. At the present stage and for a long time to come in China, due to the great differences in the level of productivity development among various sectors, regions, and enterprises, the proportion of various ownership forms in different sectors, regions, and enterprises should be allowed to vary.

Public ownership as the mainstay of the economy is mainly reflected in the dominance of public assets in the total social assets, and public assets can control the national economic lifeline. The quantity of public assets is required, but the guarantee of "quantity" and proportion is required even more because the nature of socialist society is determined by the quantity and proportion of public ownership and the fields controlled by it. However, the dominant position of public ownership and the leading role of the state-owned economy does not simply depend on the large quantity and high proportion. The most important leading role is shown by the control of the lifeline of the national economy. Once the lifeline of the national economy is controlled, it can lead to the main development direction of the national economy. Therefore, the economic lifeline must not be controlled by private capital or foreign capital. At present, China's state-owned economy and state-owned capital are gradually concentrated in the important industries and key fields related to the lifeline of the national economy. Great progress has been made in the reform of state-owned enterprises' corporate and shareholding systems. Many large companies and enterprise groups with strong competitive power have emerged and begun to grow bigger and stronger in their operation quality, significantly improve their economic efficiency and competitiveness, and further enhance their control, influence, and driving force. Therefore, with the development of other economic sectors, although the proportion of the public sector continues to decline, social productive forces develop rapidly, national economic strength grows rapidly, and people's living standards quickly improve.

Public ownership as the mainstay of the economy must be connected with the leading role of the state-owned economy. The dominant position of the state-owned economy is the basis and guarantee of the dominant position of the public economy. Based on the current situation and development trend of China's economy, it is a difficult task that one must always face and complete to give better play to the leading role of the state-owned economy. In the new era, in addition to finance, railway, and postal service, the state-owned economy of China should maintain absolute control over the important industries and key fields related to national security and the lifeline of the national economy, including the military, power grid, petroleum and petrochemical, telecommunications, coal, civil aviation, and shipping. At the same time, the state-owned economy should also maintain strong control over key enterprises in basic and pillar industries, including equipment manufacturing, automobile, electronic information, construction, iron and steel, non-ferrous metals, chemical industry, survey and design, S&T, and other industries, in which the state-owned capital should hold the controlling position.

Public ownership, as the mainstay of the economy, is realized in market competition. To maintain public ownership as the mainstay of the economy, the public economy must rely on its own comparative advantages. In market competition, the public economy, like the non-public economy, faces two choices: to adapt to the market competition and grow more competitive through its own advantages; or not to adapt to the market competition and gradually be eliminated by market competition. To a large extent, the reform of state-owned enterprises in the public economy is carried out in accordance with the basic law of market economy operation. A modern enterprise system and a modern property rights system are established so that state-owned enterprises can truly become independent legal entities and dynamic market subjects, with economic efficiency and operating efficiency significantly improved. The public economy should not grow by relying on special policies of the state over the long run. Only by continuously enhancing its vitality through competition can it truly maintain a dominant position and have sufficient competitive power among other economic sectors.

The emphasis on consolidating and developing the public economy is not opposed to encouraging, supporting, and guiding the development of the non-public economy. Instead, they are organically unified. The public and non-public economies should complement rather than exclude and counteract one other.

II. Correctly Understanding the Status and Development of the Non-public Economy

1. An important part of China's socialist market economy
The understanding of the non-public economy should keep pace with the times. With the rapid development of the world's economy, the organizational form of non-public enterprises has been highly socialized. Enterprise capital mainly comes from the whole society rather than an individual. Social capital has become the main source of enterprise capital, and the degree of socialization has steadily increased. At the same time, the development of the modern non-public economy

should be guided and standardized. In allowing the existence and development of the non-public economy, one must not ignore its inferiority and negative effects. At present, the market system is not mature, and the market mechanism and legal system are not perfect, which can lead to the development of an inferior non-public economy. While gaining more profits, the foreign-funded economy controls key industries and leading enterprises through M&A or sole proprietorship; some foreign-funded economies gradually control important sectors and industries of China's economy for economic and even political purposes. Therefore, while continuing to create good conditions for the development of the non-public economy, China should guide and regulate its positive role while restraining its negative role to ensure the economic security and socially harmonious development of socialism with Chinese characteristics.

There is a natural connection between the non-public and market economies. The non-public economy has clear property rights relationships, independent management decision-making, and a flexible operation mechanism, which are consistent with the requirements of a market economy. The existence and development of the non-public economy are not only conducive to the optimal allocation and utilization of resources but also to the formation of market transaction order and the market competition system.

Because the private and foreign-funded economies are spontaneous and utilitarian in nature and are characterized by capitalist modes of production in which the owning class exploits surplus value (i.e., workers' unpaid work), it is necessary to strengthen the guidance and management of their development. However, their existence and development will not affect the nature of the socialist economy but rather will be conducive to the full exchange and equal competition of the market, the internal incentive mechanism and vitality of the public economy, the enhancement of the overall strength of the national economy, and the prosperity and development of the socialist market economy.

The non-public economy provides necessary conditions for the normal operation and development of China's market economy. It adapts to the internal management mechanism of the market and provides a reference for the reform of the public economy; it has opened up a broad area of employment for absorbing workers who have been laid off from the state-owned economy as well as a large number of surplus labor forces in society; and it has provided financial support and new impetus for the development of the national economy and made outstanding contributions. From this perspective, the existence and development of the non-public economy is an indispensable part of the development of China's socialist market economy.

The non-public economy has long-lasting vitality. First, the non-public economy has strong compatibility with the market economy. It not only grows in the environment of the market economy but is also an important institutional condition for the existence and development of the market economy. In a sense, there is no socialism without public ownership, and it is difficult to build a socialist economy with Chinese characteristics without non-public ownership. Second, China's economy has been integrated into the world economic system. The public and non-public economies do not only coexist among enterprises. They are also integrated within enterprises, while such integration is increasingly international. Foreign-funded enterprises, as a type of non-public economy, will play an increasingly important role in international competition. With the backdrop of economic globalization, the rapid flow of information, capital, and technology in the world, the mutual integration of capital in various countries, and the optimal allocation and sharing of resources worldwide are inevitable trends of economic development in various countries. The integration of foreign capital and technology with domestic capital and technology is a necessary condition for China's market economy to integrate into the world economic market and for its development to accelerate. Finally, economic development itself has two parallel tendencies: centralization and decentralization. On the one hand, the scale of production keeps expanding; on the other hand, the social division of labor is deepening. The division of labor between production departments is expanding, and the production of various products and even all links of production of a single product have become specialized. This characteristic of the development of social productive forces leads to the possibility and inevitability of the coexistence of enterprises with different scales and different ownership relations.

2. Implementing policies and measures to promote the healthy development of the non-public economy

Currently, a policy system to encourage, support, and guide the development of the non-public economy has been formed in China. The development of the non-public economy is facing an unprecedentedly favorable policy environment and social atmosphere. These policies include: encouraging non-public enterprises to participate in the reform of state-owned enterprises, encouraging the development of mixed-ownership enterprises controlled by non-public capital, allowing various market players to enter the areas beyond the negative list equally according to law, allowing more state-owned economies and other ownership economies to develop into mixed-ownership economies, allowing non-state-owned capital to participate in state-owned capital investment projects, allowing qualified private capital to initiate the establishment of small and medium-sized banks and other financial institutions in accordance with the law, allowing social capital to participate in the investment and operation of urban infrastructure through franchising, encouraging social capital to invest in rural construction, and allowing enterprises and social organizations to set up various undertakings in rural areas, and so on.

The current priority is to solve the following problems: First, efforts should be made to solve the financing problems of small and medium-sized enterprises (SMEs), improve the financial system, and provide reliable, efficient, and convenient services for SMEs. Second, efforts should be made to liberalize market access. Private capital should be encouraged to enter any industries and fields that are not explicitly prohibited by laws and regulations, and all fields that the Chinese government has opened or promised to open to foreign investment should be opened to domestic private capital. Third, efforts should be made to speed up the construction of the public service system, support the establishment of a generic technology service platform for private enterprises, actively develop a technology market, and provide technical support and professional services for the independent innovation of private enterprises. Fourth, efforts should be made to guide private enterprises to use the property rights market to combine private capital, carry out cross-regional and cross-industry mergers and reorganizations, and cultivate several large enterprise groups with outstanding characteristics and strong market competitiveness. Fifth, China should further clean up and simplify the administrative approval matters and enterprise-related fees involving private investment management, standardize the intermediate links and intermediary organizations, and reduce the burden and cost of enterprises.

SECTION 3

Collective Ownership of Rural Land and Its Improvement

Collective ownership of rural land is a major institutional advantage in China. Adhering to the collective ownership of rural land is a bottom line that must be held to promote work related to agriculture, rural areas, and farmers after socialism with Chinese characteristics enters the new era, and is a basic logic that must be followed in the implementation of the RRS.

I. The Evolution of Rural Collective Ownership since the Republic's Founding

As the embodiment of specific social production relations, a nation's land system has a significant impact on the development of social productive forces. After the founding of the PRC, the Party and the government attached great importance to the role of the land system in political stability, economic development, and social harmony and actively carried out land system reform in different stages of the new democratic revolution and socialist construction. In June 1950, the Chinese People's Political Consultative Conference passed the Land Reform Law of the PRC, launching the nationwide land reform movement, which was completed by October 1952. The land reform movement met farmers' urgent demands for land in the "Liberated Areas," also known as the Revolutionary Base Area of the CPC, and changed the feudal private ownership of land into a system of land ownership by farmers. During the socialist transformation from 1953 to 1958, agricultural production in the rural land system evolved through mutual aid and cooperation to become an elementary cooperative, to ultimately becoming a people's commune. This process realized the transformation from the separation of land ownership and use rights (land pooling, unified management mode) to a people's commune that is large in size and collective in nature. That is, land, agricultural tools, and other means of production and agricultural and animal husbandry products were all owned by the commune, single-level accounting was implemented, and equalitarian distribution was carried out within the whole commune. Since then, although the people's commune has been adjusted to a "three-level ownership, team-based" system, the collective ownership of land has not changed.

In 1978, Chinese farmers began spontaneously to explore and form the Household Contracted Management System. This marked not only an important turning point in the rural land system of contemporary China but in the basic economic system of rural areas as well. Under the principle of "collective ownership" of rural land, rural land property rights are divided into "rights of ownership" and "contracted management rights" in the Household Contracted

Management System. The right of ownership belongs to the collective, and the contracted management right is allocated evenly among the farmers by the collective economic organizations based on the registered residence population. The collective economic organization is responsible for supervising the performance of contracts, the unified arrangement, the use and dispatch of public facilities, and the adjustment and allocation of land so that the Household Contracted Management System forms a two-tier management system with integration of unification and division. With the trial and development of the Household Contracted Management System in rural areas, the original system of the people's commune was abolished in 1983, and the township or town was re-established as a rural grassroots administrative unit. The Household Contracted Management System replaced the people's commune system, not only giving play to the advantages of collective unified management but also motivating farmers in production. It took into account the efficiency of agricultural production under the principle of fairness and was a good economic system adapted to China's national conditions. Under the premise of adhering to socialist public ownership, the rural household contract management system aroused farmers' enthusiasm for production and developed market economy. It played a great role in liberating rural productivity, promoting rural economic development, and promoting social progress.

Since the beginning of the new century, with the deepening of industrialization and urbanization, a large part of the Chinese agricultural population migrated to cities and towns, while the scale of rural land circulation also expanded. It is more and more common that the subject of land "contracting rights" is separated from the subject of "management rights." To comply with the wishes of farmers to retain the land "contracting rights" while circulating the "management rights" of land, the CPC Central Committee and the State Council issued and implemented the "Opinions on Improving the Separation of Rural Land Ownership, Contracting Right and Management Right" on October 30, 2016. In other words, on the basis of collective ownership of land, the "contracted management rights" were divided into "contracting rights" and "management rights." This created a pattern in which there is a separation between "ownership," "contracting rights," and "management rights" so that the circulation of "management rights" could be formed. The separation of the three rights of rural land is helpful to promote the orderly circulation of land "management right" according to law, optimize the allocation in a wider range, and improve the efficiency of land use. The reform of the "separation of three rights" in the new era resulted from the continuous innovation of the Household Contracted Management System to meet the requirements of economic and social development. It is another major innovation and example of progress in the reform of the rural land system with Chinese characteristics and is in line with China's unique situation.

II. The Theoretical Source of Collective Ownership of Rural Land and Its Development

At present, China's rural land is under collective ownership, which is fundamentally different from the previous system of private land ownership in China's rural areas. It has been proven in practice that collective ownership is a new type of production relation adapted to the development of China's rural productivity.

1. An important part of the Marxist theory of public ownership

Marx and Engels repeatedly mentioned "state ownership," "collective ownership," and "cooperative economy" in a series of works. Marx interpreted the concept of "collective ownership" as follows: socialism is "a collective society based on the common possession of the means of production" and uses "collective ownership" as public ownership or social public ownership in parallel. Obviously, Marx and Engels used the term "collective ownership" to refer to the idea of single public ownership. In Volume 43 of his *Collected Works*, Lenin furthered the theory of collective ownership in the socialist practice of the Soviet Union and proposed that:

> Cooperative enterprises are different from private capitalist enterprises because cooperative enterprises are collective enterprises. They are not different from socialist enterprises, if the land they occupied and the productive materials they used belong to the state, namely belong to the working class.[16]

The concept of collective ownership developed by Marx, Engels, and Lenin refers to the community of producers as free persons, while collective economy refers to collective ownership economy. Collective ownership is a union of free people in society and a new type of public ownership production relation based on common possession and individual ownership, in which workers "work for themselves."

2. The inheritance and development of the theory of collective ownership in China

Since the founding of the PRC, the CPC has actively explored the practical development of Marxist "collective ownership." At the beginning of the founding of the PRC, Mao Zedong put forward that China's "collective ownership" is a system of collective economic organization of the working people under the state administration led by the proletariat; a "cooperative" is the realized form of "collective ownership"; the "public economy" is socialistic; a "cooperative" is semi-socialistic. These are all important components of the new democratic economy. In the early exploration of reform and opening-up, "collective ownership" was characterized by "two unions," namely a "collective ownership economy of labor union and capital union of laborers." The stock cooperative system and employee stock ownership were new forms of the "collective ownership" economy. Now, China's public ownership economy has developed into two forms: one is the state-owned economy, namely the socialist economy of "ownership by the whole people," which is the leading force in the development of the national economy; the other is the "collective ownership" economy, which is an important part of the public ownership economy. "Collective ownership" has successfully developed in China's rural areas. Under the principle of "collective ownership," the ownership of the means of production is separate from the right of contracted management in agricultural production. It is the unity of fairness and efficiency and is an advanced economic system in line with China's national conditions.

China's authoritative definition of "collective ownership" comes from the Constitution. Article 6 of the Constitution states: "The foundation of the socialist economic system of the PRC is the socialist public ownership of the means of production, namely the ownership by the whole people and collective ownership by the working people. Socialist public ownership is a system of eliminating human exploitation and implementing the principle of distribution according to one's ability and according to one's work. In the primary stage of socialism, China adheres to the basic economic system of keeping public ownership as the mainstay of the economy while allowing diverse sectors to develop side by side and keeping the distribution system according to work as the mainstay with multiple distribution modes coexisting." Article 8 of the Constitution states that:

> Rural collective economic organizations shall implement a two-tier management system based on household contracted management with integration of unification and decentralization. All forms of cooperative economy in rural areas, such as production, supply & marketing, credit, and consumption, are socialist economy of collective ownership by the working masses.[17]

The above articles of the Constitution define the nature and content of China's "collective ownership" and clearly show the development direction of China's "collective ownership" economy.

III. Collective Ownership of Rural Land as a Major Institutional Advantage

As the most basic system in China's rural areas, the collective ownership of rural land, with its strong adaptability and development, has become the fundamental institutional advantage in liberating, developing, and protecting China's agricultural productivity. This approach has not only overcome the development dilemma that some countries face with private land ownership in the process of agricultural modernization but also promoted the overall leap in China's agricultural productivity, showing confidence in China's path to developing socialism with Chinese characteristics. The report to the 19th National Congress of the CPC put forward the RRS for the first time and stressed the need to consolidate and improve the basic rural management system, deepen reform of the rural land system, and improve the "three rights" separation system of contracted land. The land contracting relationship should be kept stable and unchanged for the long run and should be renewed for another 30 years upon the expiration of the second round of land contracting. The reform of the rural collective property rights system should be deepened, farmers' property rights and interests should be protected, and the collective economy should be expanded. The following are the decisive reasons for upholding the collective ownership of rural land.

Collective ownership of rural land is a basic system that is required by Chinese law. It also represents the main realized form of socialist public ownership in rural areas. The collective ownership of rural land is clearly stipulated in the Constitution of the PRC, and there are clear institutional arrangements at the legal level in the Villagers' Committee Organization Law and the Rural Land Contracting Law. These are all the institutional designs at the level of social security oriented by fair value. The collective ownership of rural land is what has guided the path and direction of China's rural development and reform and has become the soul of China's rural basic management system and the fundamental economic system in China's rural areas. It can effectively solve the agricultural problems and farmers' problems in the process of agricultural modernization by facilitating the advantages of the system. Therefore, any reform involving the land system must take a clear stand to uphold and preserve the collective ownership of rural land and to promote development-oriented reform on the premise of keeping this most fundamental system unchanged.

The collective ownership of rural land can also meet the needs of current agricultural development and rural revitalization. Practice shows that in different stages of agricultural development, through the adaptive adjustment of the realized form of rural land ownership, the development level of agricultural productivity in China will be greatly improved, and the income level of farmers will be significantly increased. The two-tier management system combining household contracted management with collective unified management represents the biggest institutional achievement. At present, China's agricultural development faces new challenges, mainly in the transformation of agricultural production mode from human and animal power to mechanization, the wide use of biochemical technology, which reduces land differences, and the labor flow, which brings about changes in agricultural management subjects. Due to the above changes, the problem of land fragmentation becomes a bottleneck in restricting the development of agricultural modernization. As the sum of rural production relations, rural land ownership should respond to such changes in agricultural productivity. Therefore, the changes in agricultural production mode, production conditions, and production subject must be fully considered in the adjustment of land ownership to widely adapt to the development level of agricultural productivity. By upholding the collective ownership of rural land, on the one hand, China can solve the problem of land fragmentation through the integration of unification and decentralization, namely the "decentralization" of family management and the "unification" of collective economic organizations; on the other hand, on the premise that the land is owned by the collective, China should reconstruct the structure of property rights, actively explore new realization forms, and obtain the greatest common divisor of interests with the participation of farmers and the mobilization of collective economic organizations. Practice shows that in the new stage of China's agricultural development, the collective ownership of rural land can achieve the organic unity of improving agricultural production capacity, protecting farmers' rights and interests, and enhancing the strength of collective economic organizations with its strong institutional flexibility and advantages.

IV. Measures to Improve the Collective Ownership of Rural Land

1. Giving full play to the role of grassroots party organizations as a fortress

The ability and quality of rural cadres are important for the consolidation of the Party's ruling position in rural areas. In order to implement the collective ownership of rural land, release the potential energy of collective ownership of land, and give full play to the overall planning role of rural collective economic organizations, China must strengthen the development of rural grassroots party organizations so that they can become strong leaders in promoting agricultural prosperity, lead farmers to become more prosperous, and maintain rural stability.

2. Establishing the thinking of agricultural development based on farmers

By basing its thinking of agricultural development on farmers, China should fully consider the rights of each farmer and the overall interests of the majority of farmers in the process of rural collective economic organizations playing the role of overall planning. China should also seek to achieve the unity of individual interests and overall interests and avoid the opposition between farmers and the collective. Moreover, the government should correctly treat the role of capital in the process of agricultural and rural modernization, build a close interest connection mechanism between farmers and modern agricultural leading enterprises, and realize the organic connection between small farmers and the development of modern agriculture.

3. Enhancing the innovation space of collective ownership of land

Provided that the collective ownership of land remains unchanged, China should divide the farmers' land contracted management right into contracting rights and management rights, realize their separation and parallel importance, and truly stabilize contracting rights and liberalize management rights. To liberalize the right of land management, China should grant farmers the right of choice on the basis of respecting their will and safeguarding their rights and interests. The government should promote the orderly transfer of land management right, carry out the transfer, concentration, and scale management to an appropriate extent, adapt to the urbanization process and scale of rural labor transfer, adapt to the progress of agricultural S&T and the improvement of production means, and adapt to the improvement of agricultural socialized service level.

4. Building a scientific and reasonable relationship between the government and the market

A key problem in upholding the collective ownership of rural land involves managing the relationship between the government and the market, not only to give play to the decisive role of the market but also to the role of the government. First, the new agricultural development stage, in which land management is increasingly fragmented and agricultural infrastructure construction is insufficient, requires relevant departments to fully play the role of overall planning and coordination and to formulate and implement systematic rules to better reflect the role of the government with the overall planning function of the collective. Secondly, China should give full play to the role of farmers as economic subjects, uphold the rights of farmers and agricultural operators to speak on agricultural production and land rights disposal, and enhance their ability to implement property rights with the power of the market. Therefore, it is necessary to clarify the boundaries in behavior between the government and the market. The government should not be absent, act beyond authority, or be dislocated in regulation, and the market should be fair, orderly, and perfect so as to release the joint effect of the "visible hand" and the "invisible hand." Therefore, in matters related to the division and transfer of rural land rights, the government should only play a matchmaking role while giving full play to the enthusiasm and creativity of farmers and other stakeholders.

CHAPTER FOUR

The Socialist Income Distribution System and Social Security System

The income distribution system and social security system, as the fundamental institutional arrangements in economic and social development, make up the cornerstone of the socialist market economy system. Income distribution and social security are important institutional arrangements that help meet the needs of urban and rural residents for a better life and maintain common prosperity for all people. Building a moderately prosperous society in a comprehensive way requires continuing to deepen the reform of the income distribution system, establishing a multi-tiered social security system, vigorously promoting the equalization of public services, and allowing the people to share in development achievements.

SECTION 1
The Personal Income Distribution System in the Primary Stage of Socialism

The income distribution system depends on the development level of productive forces and the ownership structure. China must implement the income distribution system, with distribution according to work as the main focus and various forms of distribution coexisting. More attention should be paid to fairness in national income redistribution, and fairness and efficiency should be unified in the primary distribution. Only in this way can the growth of residents' income be synchronized with economic development, and the growth of labor remuneration be synchronized with the improvement of labor productivity to improve people's sense of gain and enhance development.

I. The Primary Distribution and Redistribution of National Income

National income distribution is divided into primary distribution and redistribution. Primary distribution means that in production activities, the enterprises distribute income among the state, enterprises, and individuals. Under a market economy, the market mechanism forms (or determines) the primary distribution relation, market supply and demand decides the price of factors of production, and the government adjusts and regulates it with laws, regulations, and taxes without direct intervention.

Redistribution of national income refers to a process by which the government readjusts the factor income based on the results of primary distribution. It focuses on adjusting the income relationships among regions, urban and rural areas, sectors, and between in-service personnel and retirees. These adjustments occur by means of taxation, social security and welfare, and transfer payments to prevent excessive income gaps and ensure a basic standard of living for low-income people. The gap in income distribution under market adjustment is readjusted under the guidance of the government to ensure a more reasonable gap and that "the shortfalls of primary distribution can be made up by secondary distribution."

The redistribution of national income is an important means of promoting social fairness. First, it can correct the income gap caused by the inequality of opportunities and by rules in the primary distribution. Second, it can correct the income inequality caused by the excessive difference between individual ability and factors of production in the primary distribution. Third, it can promote the equality of conditions and opportunities for people to participate in the primary distribution. It can narrow these gaps through the implementation of progressive income taxes, inheritance taxes, and gift taxes. It can also promote the equality of conditions and opportunities for people in the primary distribution by developing education and social security. Fourth, it can promote economic development. It can enhance people's sense of fairness by correcting unfairness in the primary distribution, improve the quality and mobility of workers through education and social security, and promote consumption growth by increasing the incomes of low-income residents and providing basic living security. Fifth, it can promote social stability. The redistribution of national income can provide the necessary economic base for social stability, help correct unfairness in the primary distribution, and develop education and social security.

In terms of the relationship between primary distribution and the redistribution of national income, ownership serves as the basis of the distribution system, primary distribution is the main part of the distribution, and redistribution is the auxiliary part of the distribution system. Whether one observes circumstances abroad or the current situation in China, the primary distribution is the primary basis of people's income relationship, accounting for 80-90% of residents' income, while redistribution only accounts for 10–20%. Even in the distribution of the welfare state, redistribution accounts for no more than 30%. If the problem of income inequality in the primary distribution is not solved, it will be difficult to solve the problem of poverty through redistribution alone, let alone expand the ranks of the middle-income population. In this sense, to deepen the reform of the income distribution system, China must highlight the reform of the primary distribution system, including solving the sharp contradictions in the primary distribution.

II. The Income Distribution System with Distribution according to Work as the Mainstay

1. The inevitability of implementing the income distribution system with distribution according to work as the main focus and various forms of distribution coexisting

The method of income distribution depends on the ownership and mode of production. Marx pointed out that "any type of distribution of the means of consumption is just the result of the distribution of the production conditions themselves, and the distribution of the production conditions shows the nature of the mode of production itself." The distribution of the means of production decides the distribution of the means of consumption. The ownership form of the means of production corresponds to the distribution form of the means of consumption. China is still in the primary stage of socialism. It implements the socialist market economy and establishes the basic economic system of keeping public ownership as the mainstay of the economy while allowing diverse sectors to develop side by side. Therefore, China implements the system with distribution according to work as the main focus and multiple distribution modes coexisting in the distribution of individual income. To be specific, China's implementation of this system is determined by the following factors.

(1) The ownership structure with the common development of various ownership systems in China at the present stage. As mentioned above, production determines distribution, ownership is the basis of production relations, and ownership structure determines the distribution structure. In the primary stage of socialism, the common development of various economic forms under the premise of public ownership will inevitably require the use of a variety of distribution methods in the distribution system. In addition to distribution according to work, there are various other distribution methods suitable for the non-public economy. The factors of production of various ownership economies need to be compensated by different methods of distribution. Therefore, the coexistence of multiple methods of distribution guarantees the existence of multiple forms of ownership and is the basis for the common development of multiple forms of ownership.

(2) Requirements for diversified realization forms of public ownership. The joint-stock system, joint-stock cooperative system, cooperative system, contracting system, and lease system have become the general operating models of public ownership at present. For different operating models, different distribution methods are needed to meet the economic interests of the owners, operators, and workers. This way, the owners, operators, and workers can perform their own duties, and their responsibilities, rights, and interests can be consistent. For example, the joint-stock system needs a distribution method of dividends according to shares; the joint-stock cooperative system needs to combine the distribution according to work with the distribution of dividends according to shares; and it is necessary to establish an annual salary system for managers to carry out the responsibilities of factory directors and managers.

(3) The need to improve the socialist market economy system. Under a market economy, the investment, arrangement, and use of all social resources or factors of production are carried out in accordance with the market mechanism. The market mechanism here refers to price, supply and demand, and competition, and its core lies in the economic interests of each owner. When the investment of these resources or factors of production can bring reasonable income to their owners, it is an affirmation of the value of the investment. On the contrary, if the investments do not result in reasonable income for the owners, they will be disappointed, and the situation is not conducive to the improvement of the socialist economy system. Therefore, the more fully the market mechanism functions and the better the market system is, the more one should recognize the rationality of distribution according to factors of production and insist on the coexistence of multiple methods of distribution.

(4) The need to improve the efficiency of resource allocation and change the mode of economic growth. Capital, technology, and natural resources are relatively scarce in China, so the government should implement a variety of distribution methods and combine distribution according to work with distribution according to factors of production. On the one hand, China can mobilize more investment in capital, technology, information, and other factors of production to expand reproduction and improve the quality of economic growth; on the other hand, only when the users of all factors of production use them with compensation according to the law of value, can China improve the efficiency of the use and allocation of scarce resources, avoid arbitrariness in the selection of and waste of resources, and realize intensive economic growth.

(5) The essential way to realize the goal of socialist development. To achieve the goal of socialism and achieve common prosperity, all must activate their full energy and creativity. China must adhere to the CPC's policy of "respecting labor, knowledge, talents, and creation," respect and protect all labor that is beneficial to the people and society, whether it is physical or mental labor, or simple or complex labor; and recognize and respect all labor that contributes to China's modernization construction. The coexistence of various ways of distribution and the distribution according to factors of production are the embodiments of this policy and an effective way to motivate the masses and achieve the goal of common prosperity.

2. "Two Synchronizations" transmitting the new signal of income distribution reform in the new era

China should adhere to the principle of distribution according to work, improve the system and mechanism of distribution according to factors, and promote more reasonable and orderly income distribution. At the same time, the nation should achieve growth of residents' income in synchronization with economic growth and achieve growth of labor remuneration in synchronization with an increase of labor productivity. The "Two Synchronizations" means the organic combination of improving economic development and individual income so that the increase of labor productivity can effectively benefit workers. Meanwhile, the "Two Synchronizations" does not take the relationship between efficiency and fairness as the relationship within the distribution system, but as an innovative adjustment to the relationship between efficiency and fairness.

The efficiency includes labor efficiency and production efficiency and is within the range of the production field, while the distribution field is about fairness and rationality, with nothing to do with distribution efficiency. Production focuses on efficiency, while distribution focuses on fairness. "Two Synchronizations" means that when building a prosperous and strong country, efforts should be made to allow the people to have more wealth and a greater share in the fruits of development. This has become an important direction for China's economic and social development and income distribution reform in the new era.

3. The significance of "Two Synchronizations" to social and economic development

First, the "Two Synchronizations" approach is conducive to expanding domestic demand supported by residents' consumption levels. The steady growth of income, simultaneous and synchronous with economic growth, and the continuous improvement of social security are the basic guarantees for continuously improving people's living standards and expanding consumer demand. On the one hand, it is helpful to cultivate the driving force of new demand for economic growth so as to realize the dynamic balance of supply and demand at a higher level; on the other hand, it is helpful to give play to the basic role of residents' consumption, reduce excessive dependence of economic growth on export and investment demands, and realize the internal benign balance of the three major demand factors.

Second, the approach is conducive to the transformation of China's economy from one of high-speed growth to one of high-quality development. The consumption demand formed by continuously increasing income can provide market signals and driving forces for improving the quality of the supply system and expanding high-quality supply. To build a modern economic system, the government should let the market play a decisive role in the allocation of resources and give better play to the role of the government. With an increase in people's income, diverse consumer demand can only be reflected through specific price signals and then transformed into market power for industrial structure adjustments and product quality improvement on the supply side.

Third, it is conducive to building income growth and remuneration improvement on a more solid and sustainable basis. Unit labor cost is one indicator reflecting a country's industrial competitiveness and is directly proportional to the wage level and inversely proportional to labor productivity. In other words, if wages rise too quickly beyond what labor productivity can support, unit labor costs will also rise, thus reducing the international competitiveness of the industry. As a result, the wage increase will be restricted by a rapid decline in economic growth and employment opportunities, making the momentum of income growth unsustainable.

The "Two Synchronizations" make clear the following specific means for increasing residents' income.

(1) Taking employment as the most important measure for people's livelihoods. As stated by President Xi Jinping, economic development in China entered a new normal during the period of the 13th Five-Year Plan (2016–2020), in which the economic growth rate shifted from high to medium-high, and the emphasis shifted from scale and growth rate to quality

and efficiency. As a result of this shift, the new characteristics of the employment problem are becoming increasingly apparent. That is, as the overall contradiction of limited hiring eases, the frictional and structural employment contradiction is becoming more prominent, and the task of improving the quality of employment is more challenging. The key to solving the frictional employment contradiction is to improve the labor market mechanism and enhance the matching between labor supply and demand. The key to solving the structural employment contradiction is to improve the skills of workers and enhance the adaptability of the human capital endowment to the transformation of the economic development mode and the optimization and upgrading of industrial structure. The key to improving the quality of employment lies in establishing and improving the labor market system and forming harmonious labor relations. The government should shift from policy measures of promoting economic growth and creating jobs to improving the balance of the labor market and the quality of employment and providing a full range of public employment services.

(2) Taking the improvement of labor productivity as the fundamental means to increase income. After a period in which the growth rate of urban and rural residents' wages exceeded that of labor productivity, this growth in wages began to slow down slightly in the past one or two years. In order to achieve its goals, such as the goal to double income by 2020 and the goal to sustain income increases, it is necessary to further improve labor productivity. There are typically three ways to improve labor productivity. The first is to replace labor with capital, that is, replacing manual labor with machines or robots. The pace of this process needs to match parallel improvements in the quality of workers, or it will lead to the decline of capital returns and the exclusion of employment. The second is to improve the total factor productivity as a part of labor productivity. And the third is to improve the level of human capital. This is a prerequisite and an important guarantee in order for capital to replace labor and improve total factor productivity.

(3) Taking the expansion of the middle-income group as a way to increase people's income. The key to maintaining rising incomes is to ensure such increases for the rural poor, who were lifted out of poverty in 2020.

(4) Taking the redistribution function as the way in which the government promotes the increase of income. Both international and Chinese experience has shown that distributing income is just as important as raising people's income levels. In the process of distribution, primary distribution and redistribution are equally important, and both require the government to perform a series of indispensable functions. In the primary distribution, the government should focus on creating a policy environment in which everyone can enjoy fair opportunities to cultivate human capital, get a job, start a business, and obtain public services. In redistribution, with reform measures and legal means, through public policy channels such as tax, labor legislation, law enforcement, transfer payments, social security, and other basic public services supply, the government should reasonably standardize the order of income distribution, adjust the results of primary distribution, undertake the transformation costs in system reform and structural adjustment, and protect the rights and interests of vulnerable groups in the labor market.

SECTION 2
Distribution according to Work and Factors of Production

"Distribution according to work" is the basic principle when it comes to the distribution of individual consumer goods within the socialist public ownership economy. While China's income distribution system has been adjusted many times since the start of reform and opening-up, the principle of distribution according to work has never changed. Distribution according to factors of production is a major innovation in the income distribution system under the socialist market economy.

I. The System of Distribution according to Work in the Primary Stage of Socialism

1. Distribution according to work in the socialist market economy with Chinese characteristics

There are different meanings and realization forms of distribution according to work under different conditions. In a planned economy, although China adhered to the principle of distribution according to work, it also tended toward egalitarianism in practice, due to the lack of timely and flexible performance evaluations and reward mechanisms. This affected the motivation and creativity of workers and the development of social productivity. Since the reform and opening-up, China has effectively explored distribution according to work in the process of market economy reform, enriching the practice of Marx's thought on distribution according to work. The distribution according to work under the condition of a socialist market economy has the following characteristics that differ from Marx's assumptions on the matter.

(1) The relation of distribution according to work in the socialist market economy with Chinese characteristics is distinct from the relation of direct deduction and direct collection among individuals in the society envisaged by Marx; however, it is represented by the distribution relations among the state, enterprises, and individuals. Distribution according to work does not happen through direct distribution by the social and economic management department, but rather through the intermediate link of enterprises, which is indirect. In a socialist market economy, enterprises are relatively independent commodity producers and operators. Under the "three-in-one" organizational form of the state, enterprises, and individuals, the state first makes various deductions according to the total value created and realized by the total social labor, including deducting the social funds provided by workers for society through enterprises. Enterprises leave part of the production development fund in the social deduction, and the remainder represents a personal consumption fund for workers to distribute according to work, thus forming the distribution relations among the state, enterprises, and individuals.

(2) The distribution according to work of socialism with Chinese characteristics is carried out within enterprises, which serve as the subjects of distribution according to work. Socialist public ownership of the means of production entails a separation between ownership and

management; that is, the means of production are owned by the state and managed by the enterprises. An enterprise is a relatively independent producer and operator of goods with independent accounting and self-financing. Although workers—as the individuals who make up the state—own the means of production, their labor force can only be combined with the means of production operated by the enterprises so that the workers only provide labor for the enterprises and then use the labor results of the enterprise as commodities and sell them in the market before the individual labor can be transformed into social labor. When a worker participates in the work of an enterprise, his remuneration is paid by the enterprise from its operating results. The state is the owner of the state-owned enterprises, but it is not the direct operator. It cannot bypass the enterprises and directly distribute income to the workers according to their work. It cannot directly interfere with the distribution of the enterprises. However, as the owner of the whole people, the state will regulate the distribution according to work within enterprises as necessary. It not only recognizes and protects the reasonable gap between different enterprise income levels but also ensures that the gap does not become too large. The state has the key responsibility for macro-control of income distribution and the maintenance of social fairness.

(3) In distribution according to work in socialism with Chinese characteristics, "work" refers to social labor instead of individual labor. Distribution according to work cannot be calculated according to the actual labor provided by workers but only according to the amount of labor recognized by society. Under the condition of a socialist market economy, there is a process of exchange between production and distribution. The individual labor condensed in the collective labor products must be exchanged via enterprises, and its value can be realized only after the commodities are sold. That is, individual labor should be transformed into social labor before the distribution according to work can be carried out within enterprises.

(4) Under the condition of the socialist market economy with Chinese characteristics, distribution according to work is realized through monetary wage. Marx's idea of distribution according to work is realized in the form of a "labor voucher." After workers provide labor to society and to enterprises, they receive monetary wages, which they use to buy consumer goods from the market. As distribution according to work is realized in the form of value, changes in price will inevitably affect the actual income level of workers and how the distribution according to work is realized.

2. Continuing to adhere to and develop the theory of distribution according to work in the new era

The dominant position of China's public ownership system determines that China must adhere to the principle of distribution according to work. At the same time, through its application in China's socialist market economy, Marx's theory of distribution according to work is developing with the evolution of socialist practice and is keeping pace with the times. Under the condition of the socialist market economy with Chinese characteristics, China needs to continuously promote and deepen the understanding of Marx's theory of distribution according to work so that the theory can reflect high efficiency in market economy operations so as to promote the high efficiency of socialist market economy operation and promote the healthy and rapid development of China's economy. However, the development of the theory of distribution according to work will not change its essence. The theory is a fundamental negation of the exploitation system. Only by following the principle of distribution according to work and matching income with labor can China maximally motivate the entire society.

II. Distribution according to Factors of Production in a Socialist Market Economy

Distribution according to factors of production is the theoretical extension and realization form of various distribution modes. Distribution according to factors of production refers to the economic behavior in which the owners of factors of production, by virtue of owning them, obtain rewards from the users of these factors. It includes three meanings: First, the subject participating in the distribution is the factor owner, and the basis is the factor ownership. Second, the object of distribution is the value created by various factors of production. Third, the measuring standard of distribution involves the quality, quantity, and contribution of the factors of production. Therefore, the internal basis of distribution according to factors of production is the ownership of the factors, and its direct performance and standard are the quantity and quality of, and the contribution of, the factors of production. Distribution according to factors of production has become an important part of China's income distribution system, mainly for the following four reasons. First, factors of production are the necessary conditions for the formation of value. Second, the different ownership of these factors determines their participation in distribution. Third, the importance and scarcity of factors of production determine the universality of factor distribution law. Fourth, distribution according to factors of production is a requirement for the development of a market economy.

Distribution according to factors of production is conducive to promoting the development and improvement of the production factor market, further promoting the adjustment and improvement of the ownership structure, and optimizing the allocation of factors of production of enterprises. It is also a prerequisite for building a moderately prosperous society in all respects and realizing common prosperity. Therefore, it is of great significance to the economic construction of socialism with Chinese characteristics. The participation of factors of production in distribution according to their contribution is based on the market mechanism and targets the pursuit of benefits. Therefore, it is bound to promote the optimal allocation of resources, stimulate the motivation of owners of different factors of production to maximize efficiency, and mobilize the incentives of all parties. This, in turn, will create more wealth in a shorter period of time and provide a solid foundation for building a moderately prosperous society in a comprehensive way and realizing common prosperity.

The participation of factors of production in distribution according to their contribution means that social contribution will be used as the unified standard of distribution for the participation of the production factors, such as labor, capital, technology, and management. This not only provides theoretical support for the combination of distribution according to work and distribution according to factors of production but also provides a fair and reasonable distribution standard for their organic combination in practice. The principle of factors of production participating in distribution according to contribution is a great innovation in the theory of income distribution.

First, the participation of factors of production in distribution according to their contribution injects new elements of the market economy into distribution according to work, increases the practicality of distribution according to work, and transforms distribution according to work into distribution according to the social contribution of labor. The traditional distribution according to work takes social labor as the only distribution scale. However, the realistic conditions required by the implementation of distribution are not fully met. In a socialist market economy, the specific forms of distribution according to work include distribution according to workability, work time, work products, etc., thus resulting in unfair phenomena such as the mismatch between work and remuneration—in other words, different remuneration for the same work and equalitarianism. This is of great significance for scientific correction and the implementation of distribution according to work. With the contribution of labor to society, distribution according to the contribution of labor unifies the standard of distribution according to work.

Second, the participation of factors of production in distribution according to their contribution reduces the ambiguity of the specific standard of distribution and makes it more operable in practice. Distribution according to factors of production is based on the ownership of the factors. This kind of distribution based on broad ownership in the legal sense cannot quantify the ownership or fully mobilize the enthusiasm of the factor subjects in the market economy. The participation of factor subjects in income distribution is the realization of factor ownership in the economy, but it does not mean that factor ownership contributes to income creation. The ultimate reason for factors to participate in income distribution is that their use value contributes to the formation of value. At the same time, distribution according to factors of production cannot be simply attributed to the quality and quantity of their distribution. Although the quality and quantity of factors of production are important conditions for forming value with the potential for making a contribution, they cannot accurately measure the contribution of these factors in the production process. In the process of creating distribution objects, various factors of production interact with one another, and their quality and quantity are not necessarily proportional to their contribution. Therefore, distribution according to factors of production can be realized only according to the contribution of factors of production rather than on the basis of ownership or quality and quantity.

SECTION 3
Allowing All People to Benefit from Reform and Development

It is the unswerving goal of the CPC to lead the people in creating a better life and allow all people to benefit from the gains of reform and development in a fairer way. Based on the major political judgments made by the Party's 19th National Congress on the major social contradictions in the new era, the CPC set new and higher requirements for improving people's livelihoods, grasped issues that most concern the Chinese, and established an overall plan for improving people's livelihood, including new ideas and measures.

I. Developing to Ensure and Improve People's Livelihoods

Improving people's livelihoods is the fundamental purpose of development. Since the 18th National Congress of the CPC, several measures to benefit the people have been implemented, people's lives have significantly improved, and people's sense of gain in reform and development has been enhanced. Decisive progress has been made in the fight against poverty. The income growth of low-income groups has accelerated, and the middle-income group has continued to expand. The pace of income growth for rural residents has exceeded that of urban residents, and the income growth of urban and rural residents is outperforming economic growth. The employment situation continued to improve, the synchronization of wage growth and labor productivity increase was enhanced, the pattern of income distribution changed, and the Gini coefficient of residents' income and the income gap between urban and rural residents continued to narrow. The level of equalization of basic public services has significantly improved, the social security system covering urban and rural residents has been largely established, the level of people's health and medical care has greatly improved, and the construction of affordable housing has been steadily promoted.

To protect and improve people's livelihoods, China must grasp the issues that most concern people and regard people's support, approval, satisfaction, and consent as the fundamental criteria for measuring the gains and losses of all work. Therefore, the key to improving people's livelihoods and well-being lies in action and implementation. The country should unify goal orientation, problem orientation, and effect orientation in an organic way, continuously improve the quality of employment and the income level of citizens, prioritize the development of education, promote the construction of a healthy Shanghai, and strengthen elderly care services and social security. China should focus on medical care, elder care, childcare, ecological environment improvement, and other key tasks. Its strategic goal should focus not only on meeting the basic living needs of its people but also on enhancing their overall quality of life. In accordance with the requirements of high-quality development, China should regard the achievements of practical work as the measures for assessing CPC and government leaders, seek practical results in enhancing the people's sense of gain, aim to meet the diversified needs of people's livelihoods, be more meticulous, committed, and effective in promoting people's livelihoods, strive to create a high-quality life, and bring a stronger sense of gain, happiness, and security to the people.

II. Winning the Battle against Poverty and Improving People's Living Standards

It is a solemn commitment of the CPC to the people and the world to help raise the living standards of the poor to a basic level of moderate prosperity, together with the rest of the country. One of the people's top concerns in recent years was to ensure that poverty-stricken people in rural areas and all poverty-stricken counties would be lifted out of poverty, that the overall problem of regional poverty would be solved, and that the income level would be raised when a prosperous society, in all respects, was established by 2020. It is also the key to ensuring the long-term sustainability of poverty alleviation and the effects of social policy support.

Employment provides not only the foundation for people's livelihoods but also the fundamental guarantee for the continuous improvement of people's income levels. China should adhere to the employment priority strategy and active employment policy and solve the structural and frictional employment contradictions. The way to guarantee and improve people's livelihoods is for all to do their best according to their abilities. The basic policy is that everybody performs their responsibilities and enjoys their rights, and all should be vigilant and prepared for challenges that arise, highlight the key points, improve the system, and guide expectations. The key task is to improve the public service system and guarantee the basic livelihood of the people. The goal of the work is to continuously meet the people's growing needs for a better life, promote social fairness and justice, and form effective social governance and good social order.

III. Narrowing the Income Gap and Increasing the Proportion of the Middle-Income Group

The focus when it comes to income levels is to increase the income of low-income groups, adjust excessive income, expand middle-income groups, and form a stable "olive-shaped" social structure. The social mobility of labor and talents with equal opportunities and smooth channels is the driving force of economic development, the embodiment of social progress, the essence of social policies, and the way to improve income distribution. With China building a moderately prosperous society in all respects and embarking on a new journey to build a great modern socialist country, the poor populations in rural areas will rise from poverty, those in need will receive better support from social policies, and the income of low-income groups will also significantly increase, which means that more people will join the middle-income group. In recent years, with the negative growth of the working-age population, the growth of migrant workers has slowed down, and the resulting effect of resource reallocation to improve labor productivity has weakened. There are major challenges to maintaining the continuous momentum behind the growth of farmers' income. Therefore, China must take more measures to reform the registered residence system so as to maintain the momentum of labor force transfer and the people-oriented new urbanization and provide sustained impetus for the economy to maintain high- and medium-speed growth. Secondly, the government strives to build a ladder of vertical social mobility and encourage everyone to move up. These efforts include eliminating institutional barriers formed by registered residence, industry, region, and ownership, enhancing fairness of the human capital cultivation system such as education and health, encouraging everyone to increase income and accumulate wealth while participating in social wealth creation, forming a joint effort, blocking the intergenerational transmission of poverty, and widening the channels for residents' labor income and property income, to allow low-income people to move into the middle-income group so that everyone has the opportunity to realize their own development through hard work.

IV. Improving the Public Service System and Promoting Social Fairness

To achieve social fairness and justice, China must focus on creating equal opportunities in the primary distribution, continue improving the labor remuneration of front-line workers, and improve the market allocation of factors of production and distribution according to contribution. The government must also give greater prominence to the adjusting role of the government in redistribution and improve the redistribution mechanism through taxation, social security, transfer payments, and equalization of basic public services. Historical and international experience shows that the primary distribution cannot on its own solve the problem of income gap and that the redistribution function of government is indispensable. In some developed countries with a small income distribution gap, the Gini coefficient after the primary distribution is not small. It is usually through redistribution that the Gini coefficient is reduced to a more reasonable level. In addition, China should encourage and support the development of charity and fully leverage its tertiary distribution function to give back to society and help the poor.

To allow all people to benefit from the gains of reform and development in a fairer way, China needs to increase the intensity of redistribution, improve its efficiency, and enhance coordination between redistribution and primary distribution. To continue to deepen the reform of the income distribution system, the government must focus on protecting legitimate income, regulating hidden income, containing income from non-market factors such as power and administrative monopoly, and banning illegal income with legal means and reform measures. This is the source of social fairness and justice. China should ensure people's livelihoods through the equalization of basic public services, support for social policies, and the protection of vulnerable groups so as to allow the fruits of development to benefit all social groups. Great efforts should be made to improve the public service system. In order to give priority to the development of education, the government should pay special attention to promoting educational equity and the integrated development of urban and rural compulsory education and strive for every child to enjoy fair and quality education. To strengthen the social security system, it is necessary to build a sustainable multi-tiered social security system that encompasses the whole people and balances urban and rural areas, with clear rights and responsibilities and moderate security. It is also necessary to build a tightly woven safety net and develop the necessary institutions. China should implement the Healthy China strategy, provide comprehensive health services for the people, deepen reform of the medical and health system, and actively tackle the challenge of an aging population.

SECTION 4

Building a Social Security System with Chinese Characteristics

Social security is a safety net for people's livelihoods and a social stabilizer. It relates closely to people's happiness and well-being and to the long-term stability of the country. Adhering to the people-centered development orientation and promoting the construction of social security system is related to not only the basic livelihoods of urban and rural residents but also a major institutional arrangement for meeting the needs of urban and rural residents for a better life and for maintaining the common prosperity of all people.

I. The Significance of Building a Comprehensive Multi-Tiered Social Security System

Building a multi-tiered social security system in a comprehensive way is a key approach taken by the CPC. This approach is based on the Party's scientific judgment of the world's conditions and firmly grasps the phased characteristics of China's development and the people's yearning for a better life. The approach is of great practical and far-reaching historical significance and is necessary for ensuring and improving people's livelihoods. It is also essential for promoting the modernization of a national governance system and its governance capacity, as well as driving economic and social development toward a higher-quality, fairer, more efficient, and more sustainable direction.

To build a multi-tiered social security system in a comprehensive way, China must adhere to the basic policy of full coverage, ensuring basic security and multi-level and sustainable development. The government must develop the system according to the requirements for maintaining readiness and agility to overcome potential difficulties that arise. This is done by building a tightly woven safety net and strengthening the necessary institutions. Additionally, the multi-tiered social security system should cover the entire population in both urban and rural areas, with clearly defined rights and responsibilities and appropriate security, to better reflect social fairness and justice and meet the differentiated needs of the people. It is an inevitable requirement for the self-development and perfection of the social security system, which is in line with the goal of building a moderately prosperous society in a comprehensive way.

To build a multi-tiered social security system in a comprehensive way, China should uphold social insurance, with social assistance for low-income people, and actively improve social welfare, charity, preferential care, and resettlement. In terms of organizational mode, China should adhere to the dominant position of the government, give active play to the role of the market, and promote the connections among social, supplementary, and commercial insurance. It should actively build an endowment insurance system that links basic endowment insurance and occupational (enterprise) annuity with personal savings endowment insurance and commercial insurance. The government should also promote the development of basic medical insurance, serious disease insurance, supplementary medical insurance, and commercial health insurance so as to meet the diversified and multi-level security needs of the people.

As described above, to build a multi-level social security system in a comprehensive way, the basic requirement is "to keep the bottom line, to build a tightly woven safety net, and to build the necessary institutions." "Keeping the bottom line" means that China should give full play to the function of social policy, effectively guaranteeing the basic needs of the people and placing people's livelihoods and social stability as the top priority. "Building a tightly woven safety net" means that China should achieve the widest coverage of the system so that everyone can enjoy basic social security. "Building the necessary institutions" means that the government should continue to deepen reform, establish and improve the institution and mechanism, and continuously improve the level of legalization and institutionalization of social security. As stated by President Xi Jinping at the 19th National Congress of the CPC on October 18, 2017, the goal of the government/Party is to achieve "a sustainable multi-tiered social security system that covers the entire population in both urban and rural areas, with clearly defined rights and responsibilities and appropriate security." "Covering the entire population" means that China should continue expanding the coverage of social security and realize the full coverage of legal personnel. "In both urban and rural areas" means that the country should promote the construction of a social security system for urban and rural residents as a whole, and reasonably narrow the differences between urban and rural areas in social security. "With clearly defined rights and responsibilities" means that China should clearly define the social security rights, obligations, and responsibilities of governments at all levels, employers, individuals, and society. "Appropriate security" means that it should determine the level of security benefits and reasonably guide people's security expectations according to the development of the economy. "Sustainable" means that China should ensure the balance of income and expenditure of various social insurance funds and the long-term stable operation of the system.

II. The Urgency of Building a Comprehensive Multi-Tiered Social Security System

At present, the yearning of urban and rural residents in China for a better life is relatively concentrated on the demand for social security. The current imbalance and inadequate development in the field of social security is an objective fact. Social security reform, which started in the 1980s, represents a comprehensive and profound institutional change. It has altered the original pattern of social security and benefit distribution and is inevitably affected by domestic economic, social, political, cultural, and other factors, as well as the process of globalization. In order to avoid social crises caused by drastic changes and to serve economic growth at the same time, a progressive approach similar to that used in economic reform is adopted for social security reform in China. In different stages, China's social security reform has experienced a change process from passive change to active change, from bottom-up to top-down, from pilot first and gradual promotion to top-level design and comprehensive promotion by the central government, from serving and submitting to the economic reform as a governance tool to maintaining and promoting the economic and social development independently. After entering the 21st century, the transformation from the state-work unit security system to the state-society security system was realized. That is to say, the social security system in the era of a "planned economy under state responsibility with work unit arrangement, comprehensive security, segmented structure, and closed operation" has been transformed into a new multi-tiered social security system that is dominated by the government, with responsibilities shared between enterprises and individuals. This system has also changed from an exclusive application for urban people to an institutional arrangement benefiting the whole people. For example, the basic endowment insurance system achieved full coverage in 2012, and all elderly people can receive different amounts of pension each month. The participation rate of the medical insurance system is stable at about 97%, covering more than 1.3 billion people. The comprehensive social assistance system with the subsistence allowance system as the core has covered as many people as possible, and so on. Moreover, social security reform has created a relatively stable social environment for economic reform and development, removed the obstacles to the free flow of labor through relevant institutional arrangements, and directly promoted China's economic growth through new financing methods. Therefore, the achievements of China's social security reform are enormous. They not only greatly improve the welfare level and quality of life of the Chinese people but also make an important contribution to the development of social security in the world. Excluding China, the coverage of social security in the world is only 50%; including China, it is 61%. In 2016, the International Social Security Association presented its Award for Outstanding Achievements in Social Security to the government of the PRC.

Now, great achievements have been made in China's social security reform. Although the framework of China's social security system has taken shape, the unbalanced and inadequate development pattern of this system has not changed. Problems such as system segmentation, unclear rights and responsibilities, lack of multiple tiers, and short supply of resources for social services still directly restrict the healthy development of the whole social security system. Even the pattern of regional and group interests has been rigid to a certain extent. Structural imbalance and insufficient development are still the main contradictions. This system has preliminarily achieved the goal of universality but not yet the goal of fairness. In practice, it highlights the responsibility of the government, but the boundary of the government's responsibility, including the division of responsibilities shared between the central and local governments, is not clear; the social security responsibility, financial system, and tax system have not been effectively matched, and the sharing of responsibilities by other subjects is very limited. Although the level of social security continues to improve, there is a lack of overall consideration and normal growth mechanisms. Pension, medical insurance, subsistence allowance, disaster relief, and various welfare services are basically separate from each other, and there is a lack of linkage with prices, wages, and other social security items, making the improvement of social security application unpredictable. In addition, the current social security system still has inherent defects or deficiencies and lacks the self-regulating function to keep pace with the times. All of these show that the current system lacks the function of self-correction, and the adverse consequences become more and more obvious and bring great problems to national governance.

III. The Requirements for Building a Comprehensive Multi-Tiered Social Security System

1. Basic requirements for building a multi-tiered social security system in a comprehensive way

(1) With sharing as the cornerstone, upholding the leading role of the government and implementing co-construction and co-governance by multiple subjects

As a new concept established at the Fifth Plenary Session of the 18th CPC Central Committee, shared development was reflected in the 13th Five-Year Plan. The 19th National Congress of the CPC once again strengthened this concept and highlighted that everyone should perform their responsibilities and enjoy their rights to progress along the road to common prosperity. That is determined by the socialist nature of China, and social security is the institutional arrangement that should respond directly to that. As modern social security is designed to reconcile individual risks with collective strength, mutual aid, and collectivism are its inherent qualities. Therefore, in deepening social security reform, the nation must adhere to sharing as the cornerstone and safeguard the foundation of mutual assistance. At present, it is particularly necessary to guard against the deconstruction of the social security system by individualism, egoism, or market worship, to prevent the social security policy from being hijacked by commercial forces or interest groups.

When the social security system with Chinese characteristics matures, it is particularly necessary to upgrade from the previous local innovation to a national-level one as soon as possible. Therefore, it is necessary to strengthen the decision-making responsibility of the central government to ensure that it has firm control over the basic security system. Local governments can choose the way and proportions of responsibility sharing, but they should not have the right to create or operate the system independently according to a "contracting system" approach. Under the condition of unbalanced regional development, the government can allow gaps for a certain period of time, but at no time should it shake the goal of a unified system or distort the path to the goal. In deepening reforms, China should not yield to regional gaps or divisions and should strive to promote a more equitable allocation of public resources through the unification of the social security system. Accordingly, social security can really become an important means to narrow regional gaps and realize fair and coordinated development among regions. The central government should shoulder the great responsibility of the top-level design, promoting social security legislation, rationally allocating resources, and maintaining the unity of the system. At the same time, China must clearly divide social security responsibilities between the central and local governments and match the financial resources reasonably. It should also fully motivate enterprises, social organizations, individuals, and families, and not only let them bear corresponding responsibilities and obligations such as payments but also allow trade unions, employers' organizations, and disabled persons' federations to represent the interests of different groups to participate in the system design and supervision. Only in this way can the government ensure the effective participation of all parties in co-construction and co-governance, which is an important condition for maintaining the rational development of the system.

(2) Achieving a top-level design for social security system construction

The current social security system is not yet mature, and almost all social security rules have internal defects or deficiencies. China must optimize these rules and consider them in a holistic way before the system can become mature. However, given the traditional institutional obstacles, the historical limitations of progressive reform, the formation of an interest imbalance pattern, and the complex social ecology that affect the whole situation, in order to deepen social security reform, China must firmly establish the concept of overall planning and coordination. Scientific top-level design should be made first to build a comprehensive social security system with Chinese characteristics.

At the macro level, there should be a special organization responsible for overall planning to incorporate the overall design of the social security system construction into the overall design of the central government. Such an organization will comprehensively deepen the reform and modernization of the national governance system so as to realize the scientific positioning of the social security system and its functions. In particular, that includes: planning the social security system rationally based on national development goals and processes; clearly defining the original intention, development goals, and functional positioning of the system; and clarifying the path of system development. At the macro level, the design also needs to solve the problems in the overall division and coordination of labor for the three basic systems of social assistance, social insurance, and social welfare, as well as the overall arrangement and positioning of the legal basic security level and other levels such as marketization, socialization, and family security.

At the meso level, China should solve the problems of structure, functional positioning, and resource allocation of different social security categories, as well as the relationships of relevant institutional arrangements, to avoid confusion about what considerations are the priority or remain incomplete. For example, all of the following require an overall optimization plan—the structural optimization of the medical security system and its collaborative promotion with the medical and pharmaceutical systems, the collaborative promotion and structural optimization of economic security and service security in the elderly security system, the collaborative promotion and structural optimization of social assistance and poverty alleviation and development, and the collaborative promotion and structural optimization between basic endowment insurance and enterprise (occupational) annuity and commercial pension.

At the micro level, China should refine the top-level design of specific security items, focusing on optimizing the institutional structure, reasonably distributing responsibilities, and ensuring the fairness, effectiveness, and sustainability of the system. Take the top-level design of medical insurance as an example. In effectively promoting the tripartite system (health care, medical insurance, and pharmaceutical) reform, it is necessary not only to integrate the current system but also to optimize the financing mechanism and reasonably share the responsibility, and make specific and clear institutional arrangements for hierarchical diagnosis and treatment, payment method, information system, and intelligent supervision, etc. It is also necessary, at the same time, to clearly draw the boundary between social medical insurance and commercial health insurance and finally move toward a health insurance system covering all people.

(3) Building a complete social security system with Chinese characteristics

China should establish the legal basic security system as soon as possible, increase or adjust the relevant institutional arrangements according to the needs, and truly achieve full coverage. This is the cornerstone of building a complete social security system. First, all uninsured people left out of the social insurance system should be included. For example, the government should implement the concept of Social Security for All in the medical insurance system, to ensure that all people can participate in and enjoy medical insurance in their permanent places of work or living. For the basic endowment insurance system, the government should assess the employment situation and occupational characteristics of the population of the eligible age as soon as possible and ensure that they all participate in the basic endowment insurance. The top priority is to include more than 100 million industrial workers (mainly migrant workers) in the basic endowment insurance system for workers and take effective remedial measures for cases where insurance is omitted or withdrawn due to various reasons. Doing this will help ensure that all people of the eligible age are insured and that they can enjoy a pension when they retire. The second priority is to ensure that the security system for a specific group can truly cover all members of the group. In particular, work-related injury and unemployment insurance should cover all occupational workers, social assistance should include and provide assistance to all urban and rural residents below the poverty line and in need of emergency assistance, and the social welfare and related service system for the elderly, children, and the disabled should cover those populations in need. Affordable housing should be able to meet the needs of those who can neither afford to buy nor rent. At the same time, it is necessary to meet people's welfare demands and the requirements of social justice and to increase or adjust legal security items— such as establishing the long-term care insurance system for the aging population, adjusting and increasing the birth or child allowance system according to the population policy, and so on. A complete social security system must and can only be established on the basis of a complete legal basic security system.

On the other hand, China should vigorously develop various types of supplementary security established through market and social mechanisms and build a multi-tiered social security system in a comprehensive way. Building a multi-tiered social security system is the common orientation of social security reform in various countries. In essence, it is intended to further divide the responsibilities of different subjects and allocate social security resources more reasonably through a multi-tiered framework. Take endowment insurance as an example: the responsibility of basic endowment insurance is shared by the employer, the worker, and the government; the occupational or enterprise annuity is usually shared by the employer and the worker; and commercial life insurance or pension is purely the individual responsibility of the insured. These examples reflect three different levels of insurance and, accordingly, three ways of sharing the responsibility. In the context of an aging society, it is difficult for a single level of pension to maintain sustainable development, so it is necessary to develop a second and third level of endowment insurance. As an example, with medical insurance, in order to comprehensively manage disease treatment and provide more convenient and efficient medical services, it is not enough to have only a basic medical insurance system—the system must also be supplemented by commercial health insurance. Only in this way can the government, enterprises, society, individuals, and families reasonably share the social security responsibility, and the material basis of social security be continuously strengthened. Strengthening commercial health insurance is the prerequisite for the continuous growth of national welfare. Therefore, accelerating the development of commercial insurance and charity, using relevant policies to maintain the tradition of family security and private mutual assistance, promoting the normal development of institutional welfare, and encouraging urban and rural residents to improve their capacity for risk prevention and self-protection should be an important direction for the comprehensive construction of a social security system with Chinese characteristics.

In the development of a complete social security system, it is particularly necessary to make up for the shortcomings as soon as possible, including by vigorously developing community-based and home-based elderly care services, increasing the investment in children's welfare, including prioritizing a "children first" strategy in the construction of the social security system, and accelerating the development of welfare for the disabled.

In summary, China needs to build a solid foundation for various levels of legal security, combine the formal and informal systems in an organic way, adopt a double-tiered framework of inclusive and preferential systems, and integrate government with market, society, family, and individual forces so as to truly build an orderly and flexible multi-tiered social security system.

(4) Optimizing the key institutional arrangements and reshaping the efficient operation mechanism

The main contents include, first, realizing the nationwide overall planning of basic endowment insurance as soon as possible and promoting the real unification of the endowment insurance system. Second, actively promoting the integration of the medical insurance system for residents and workers, as part of integrating the system for urban and rural residents, to cover all people with a system as soon as possible. This second action entails canceling individual accounts, balancing the burden of financing responsibility, building a mature system of national health insurance, effectively relieving people's concerns about disease and medical care, and improving the health of the whole people. Third, improving the subsistence allowance system as soon as possible. This includes implementing certain income exemptions to encourage low-income targets to increase their incomes and improve their lives through labor; establishing a standardized family survey system to ensure that qualified objects are insured as possible; promoting the orderly connection between low-income and poverty alleviation so as to truly ensure that the basic living needs of low-income and disadvantaged groups are met; and launching the legislative procedures of the Law of Social Relief as soon as possible so that all relief projects, including the subsistence allowance system, can operate on the legal track. Fourth, speeding up the optimization of the elderly care service system by basing more public investment in the community, combining the modern social elderly care service with the traditional family security of filial piety and respect for the elderly, and truly liberalizing the control over private as well as foreign investment so as to fully mobilize the market and social resources, and expand the material basis to support the development of the elderly care service industry. Fifth, China should implement the "children first" strategy; adopt a strategy of combining the public and private sectors, combining government and people, and making rational distribution; and vigorously develop nurseries so as to reduce the burden of family parenting, improve the welfare of residents, and achieve the goal of balanced population growth.

At the same time, in order to maintain the healthy and sustainable development of the whole social security system, it is imperative to reshape the efficient operating mechanism of social security. First, the government should establish a unified public service platform for social insurance as soon as possible, fully implement the initiative of Social Security for All, and provide technical support for improving the overall planning levels of social insurance. Doing this would effectively promote the integration of the system and improve the fairness of the system. Second, China should make full use of social forces and use the Internet, big data, and other information technology to improve the prediction, early warning, and monitoring capabilities of system operation. Third, it should enhance the flexibility of the handling mechanism. In terms of social insurance benefits, China should implement the parallel operation of local and remote benefits and the combination of continuous and segmented calculation. Fourth, the government should develop a scientific evaluation mechanism, including a social security policy evaluation mechanism, system operation risk assessment mechanism, and project implementation effect evaluation mechanism, and accept social supervision.

2. The main tasks of building a multi-tiered social security system in a comprehensive way
(1) Fully implementing the initiative of Social Security for All
The full implementation of the initiative of Social Security for All is the most important measure for enabling everyone to enjoy basic social security. The number of insured people in China has continued to grow. The number of people covered by basic endowment insurance has exceeded 900 million, the number of people covered by basic medical insurance has exceeded 1.3 billion, and medical insurance for all has essentially been realized. At present, the focus for expanding insurance coverage is on SMEs, micro-enterprises, migrant workers, flexible employees, new forms of workers, uninsured residents, and other groups. Through the implementation of the initiative of Social Security for All, China will improve the participation of various personnel in social insurance and develop a complete and accurate database of social insurance participation that allows for nationwide interconnection and dynamic updates. Effective measures should be taken to promote active participation in insurance and continuous payment of premiums by SMEs, micro-enterprises, and other key groups and to promote and guide the long-term continuous participation of various organizations and qualified individuals.

(2) Improving the basic endowment insurance system for urban workers and urban and rural residents and realizing the national overall planning of endowment insurance as soon as possible
China should comprehensively promote the reform of the endowment insurance system. The government should continue to improve the basic endowment insurance system for urban workers, which combines social pooling with individual accounts. It should further standardize the payment policies of basic endowment insurance for workers and urban and rural residents and improve the incentive and restraint mechanism for insurance payments. China should promote the investment and operation of endowment insurance funds and strive to maintain and increase their value. It should actively and steadily transfer part of the state-owned capital to replenish the social security fund and further consolidate the material basis for the sustainable operation of the system. Additionally, it should gradually establish a mechanism for normal adjustment of benefits and raise the basic pension standards for retirees and urban and rural residents in a comprehensive and orderly manner. The government should speed up the development of occupational (enterprise) annuities and encourage the development of personal savings endowment insurance

and commercial endowment insurance. In view of the accelerated development of the aging population, the government should study and introduce countermeasures, such as gradually postponing the retirement age. The national overall planning of endowment insurance is an important measure for improving the efficiency of fund use, balancing the burden of different regions, enterprises, and individuals, and promoting the rational flow of the labor force. To further consolidate provincial overall planning, China should start by establishing the central adjustment system of the basic endowment insurance fund for enterprise employees and provide subsidies and adjust nationwide through transfer payments and the central adjustment fund. On this basis, the country will realize the national overall planning as soon as possible and gradually form a fund management system with clear responsibilities of the central and provincial governments and tiered responsibilities.

(3) Improving the unified basic medical insurance system for urban and rural residents and the serious disease insurance system

China should continue deepening the reform of the medical insurance system. It will comprehensively unify the basic medical insurance and management systems for urban and rural residents, including integrating the services provided under the systems. The country must deepen the reform of payment methods and establish and improve the diversified composite payment methods that adapt to the characteristics of different groups, diseases, and services. It should improve the national remote medical management and cost settlement platform to provide efficient and convenient services for the people. The government should also look to establish a long-term care insurance system to reduce the family financial burden of long-term disabled people. It should encourage the development of supplementary medical and commercial health insurance and strive to meet the diversified medical security needs of the people. The full implementation of the serious disease insurance system for urban and rural residents is conducive to expanding the function of basic medical insurance, amplifying the security effect, and consolidating the foundation of medical insurance support and targeted poverty alleviation. China should continue consolidating and improving the serious disease insurance system and implement accurate payments for the poor by lowering the deductibles and increasing both the proportion of reimbursement and the yearly cap on insurance payments. By strengthening the interconnections among basic medical insurance, serious disease insurance, and medical assistance, the nation will implement comprehensive security, effectively improve the level of medical security, and alleviate the risk of serious diseases of people in need.

(4) Improving the unemployment and work injury insurance system

China should establish and improve the linkage mechanism between unemployment insurance premium rates and economic and social development; improve the mechanism for adjusting the unemployment insurance premium standard; relax the application conditions; and implement the allowance policies for stabilizing jobs and improving skills. The government should actively implement the provincial-level coordination of the work-related injury insurance fund, comprehensively promote efforts on work-related injury prevention, and promote the scientific and standardized treatment adjustment mechanism.

(5) Building a national unified social insurance public service platform

With the gradual improvement of the social security system, people will have higher expectations for high-quality and efficient public services. China must establish a unified national public service platform for various social insurances, rely on the national integrated social insurance agency service system and information system, including the use of social security cards, and make use of physical windows, Internet platforms, telephone consultations, self-service inquiries, and other means, to provide full-process convenient and fast services covering the whole network for insured units and personnel. The government will continue to consolidate and improve the five-level national social insurance management and service system and actively implement the "Internet Plus Social Security" action to achieve unified management, business collaboration, and data sharing of public service matters in cross-regional, cross-sectoral, and cross-level social insurance. It will also build a national integrated public service information platform for social insurance, implement a comprehensive teller system to provide "one-stop" service, fully apply Internet, big data, mobile applications, and other technical means, and gradually realize the organic connection of online and offline service channels. China should accelerate the application of social security cards, improve the basic information database function of social security cards for cardholders, and realize a "one card for all" system for social security. The nation should adopt a unified public service list and business processes of social insurance to standardize the basic public services of social insurance.

(6) Coordinating the urban and rural social assistance system, improving the minimum living standard security system, and improving the social assistance, social welfare, charity, preferential care, and resettlement system

These are the important institutional arrangements for relieving the challenges facing disadvantaged groups and maintaining basic social fairness. As a next step, China should strengthen the security of people's livelihoods and maintain readiness to address potential challenges that may arise and affect people's livelihoods. It should improve the minimum living standard security system, promote the overall development of urban and rural minimum living standard security, and ensure that the minimum living standard security should be guaranteed as possible under dynamic management. The government should develop and improve the basic welfare system for the disabled, improve the service system for helping the disabled, and comprehensively improve the level of children's welfare services. It should stimulate the vitality of the charity sector, standardize the behavior within the charity sector, and improve the regulatory system. The government should also improve the basic systems of preferential treatment, pension, and resettlement.

CHAPTER FIVE

The Market Economy System alongside Socialism with Chinese Characteristics

Exploring the organic combination of the superiority of the socialist system with the effectiveness of the market in the allocation of resources, along with speeding up the improvement of the socialist market economy system, is the only way to build socialism with Chinese characteristics and realize the great rejuvenation of the Chinese nation.

SECTION 1
The Socialist Market Economy with Chinese Characteristics

First, the market economy develops rapidly in a capitalist society. Can China implement a market economy in a socialist society with the goal of eliminating capitalist exploitation? Is socialism compatible with a market economy? Can it combine them organically, and if so, how does the nation do that? There have been many debates about these issues. With great courage in theory, Comrade Deng Xiaoping proposed organically combining socialism with a market economy. It was not only a momentous initiative in the history of scientific socialism but also initiated a revolutionary shift in the socialist political economy.

I. The Birth of the Socialist Market Economy in China

The market economy is a means of resource allocation. It came into being in Western capitalist countries and was once regarded as a proprietary and exclusive system for capitalist countries.

Over a long period of history, people have held this narrow and one-sided understanding of the market economy in both socialist and capitalist countries. However, under the leadership of the CPC, this understanding has been challenged, not only in theory but also in practice.

Deng Xiaoping was the founder of the theory of the socialist market economy. When meeting with foreign guests in 1979, he said: "The market economy is not just a capitalist thing. Socialism can also have a market economy." During his Southern Tour Speeches in 1992, he stressed that reforms should show that planning and markets are not mutually exclusive and that socialism can also develop a market economy. Deng established that the essential difference between socialism and capitalism lies not in the proportions of planning and the market. The planned economy is not exclusive to socialism, as capitalism also has elements of planning. Likewise, the market economy is not exclusive to capitalism, as socialism also has elements of markets. Both planning and markets are economic means. The market economy is a way to develop production and adjust the economy. Both capitalism and socialism can use it. This scientific conclusion of Deng set the tone for the 14th National Congress of the CPC to take "building a socialist market economy system" as the goal of China's economic system reform. Moreover, the economic system reforms undertaken since the Southern Tour Speeches have always been carried out based on the right treatment of the "relationship between the government and the market."

The socialist market economy system embodies the organic combination of a socialist basic system with a market economy. Deng's theory of the market economy has guided the Chinese people in the practice of combining the market economy with socialism. To develop a market economy under socialist conditions, China should give full play to the advantages of the socialist system while also giving full play to the basic role of the market in allocating resources, that is, to combine the advantages of the system with the effectiveness of the market economy. China has made impressive achievements in economic development, and its path has attracted worldwide attention.

II. The Logic of the Organic Combination of Socialism with a Market Economy

The organic combination of socialism with a market economy not only enriches and develops Marxist economic theory but also provides strong theoretical support and scientific guidance for the practice of building socialism with Chinese characteristics.

1. The essence of socialism as the theoretical basis of such a combination

There is a dialectical unity between socialism and the market economy, which are highly integrated with each other. A socialist economy is a mode of production in which productive forces and relations of production are dialectically unified. Highly developed productive forces are the content and decisive factor of socialism, while relations of production based on public ownership are the form of a socialist economy, namely the socialist economic system, which is determined by productive forces. Emancipating and developing productive forces is the fundamental task of socialism. To uphold the socialist system, the most fundamental thing is to develop productive forces. The ultimate purpose of socialism is to meet the people's material and cultural needs. Only by developing productive forces can China achieve this goal and promote common prosperity. The market economy is the method and means of developing productive forces and the mode of economic operation without institutional attributes. Either planning or market can be adopted as long as it is beneficial to the development of productive forces. Therefore, the organic combination of socialism with the market is the fundamental task of socialism of developing productive forces with better methods and means of developing productive forces. The development of productive forces is the goal, and the market economy is the means to achieve the goal. Therefore, their combination is a blending of the goal and the means in essence.

2. Streamlining resource allocation as the inevitable choice of such a combination

In order to develop productive forces and achieve the fundamental task of socialism, China must improve the allocation efficiency of social resources. There are four main criteria for measuring the rationality and efficiency of social resource allocation: first, whether the limited human, material, and financial resources can be fully utilized to promote economic development; second, whether social production and social demand can be balanced; third, whether the industrial structure is reasonable and whether the national economy can develop harmoniously; and fourth, whether the people's material and cultural living standards can be rapidly improved. By observing the development practice of various countries around the world, the outstanding advantages of the market economy are sensitive information and self-coordination, independence and vitality of enterprises, survival of the fittest and optimization of allocation, and innovation and vigor. From the perspective of the social system, a socialist system is superior to a capitalist system, so China must adhere to the socialist road. It can be seen that the combination of socialism with a market economy is the inevitable way to optimize the allocation of resources.

3. Deepening reform as the key to combining socialism with a market economy

Socialism itself requires common prosperity and the elimination of poverty. An ethical orientation or ethical principle of the market economy is subjective egoism and indirect altruism. A completely competitive market economy system can effectively ensure the interests of multiple stakeholders in the process of competition. Under the principle of a market economy, every economic subject engages in economic activities for the purpose of maximizing their own interests. However, such an economic behavior based on the principle of subjective egoism may eventually lead to the imbalance of the interests of the whole of society and the individuals within it. Therefore, in order to realize the deep integration of socialism and a market economy, China must deepen the reform of the economic system. On the whole, China's socialist economic system is moving in the direction of marketization, with the goal of meeting the requirements of the market economy and developing a socialist market economy system combining public ownership with a market economy.

The effort to combine socialism with a market economy is a pioneering initiative in the history of political economy. There has been no parallel experience in the world from which to learn. Only through tough economic system reforms and empirical learning can China achieve real integration. The miracle of the country's economic development has proved that the means of a market economy can be adopted under the socialist system. The socialist market economy is sensitive to market signals and efficient in resource allocation. It is an effective means to liberate and develop productive forces.

III. Characteristics of the Socialist Market Economy with Chinese Characteristics

A socialist market economy combines the market economic system with the basic socialist system. As such, it bears not only the general characteristics of a market economy but its own distinctive characteristics as well.

The organic combination of the basic socialist system with a market economy and the market economic system formed by this combination will inevitably reflect the institutional characteristics of socialism, as well as the general characteristics of the market economy. The institutional characteristics of socialism are mainly reflected in the following aspects. First, in terms of the ownership structure, as the basic economic system is "keeping public ownership as the mainstay of the economy and allowing diverse sectors to develop side by side," all forms of ownership that meet the standard of "three benefits" can and should be used to serve socialism. Based on the dominance of public ownership, public enterprises and other enterprises compete equally and develop together in the market economy, and the state-owned economy plays a leading role in the national economy. Second, in terms of the distribution system, distribution according to work is dominant, and multiple distribution modes coexist. Various regulatory means, including the market, are used to encourage and promote both advancement and efficiency and reasonably widen the income gap but also prevent polarization, pay attention to social fairness, and gradually realize common prosperity. Third, in terms of macro-control, to realize the interests of the working people, socialist countries can combine the people's current interests with long-term interests and local interests with global interests. This way, the market plays a fundamental role in resource allocation under the macro-control of socialist countries, the advantages of planning and market can be better exerted, and the advantages of socialism and market economy can be brought into full play.

Closely combining the market economy with the socialist system and developing the market economy under socialist conditions is not only a pioneering initiative of the CPC, but it is also a major contribution of socialism with Chinese characteristics to the development of human civilization. The socialist market economy means carrying forward advantages and abandoning the disadvantages of the capitalist market economy. It reflects not only the general principles of the market economy but also the basic characteristics of the socialist system, considers both efficiency and fairness and gives better play to the advantages of the socialist system and the advantages of the market economy. In this sense, the socialist market economy introduces new characteristics and advantages over the capitalist market economy. It will be an initiative of historical significance, not only to China but also to the world.

The Relationship between Government and Market in a Market Economy

The core issue of economic system reform is to properly handle the relationship between the government and the market so that the market plays a decisive role in resource allocation and the role of the government can be better played. This is a major development of the socialist market economy theory and socialist reform theory under the new historical conditions.

I. The Relationship between Government and Market in the Context of System Reform

After the establishment of the socialist system, what kind of economic system should be chosen has become a major theoretical and practical concern. The key is to understand the relationship between the government and the market.

Handling the relationship between the government and the market is the main task of economic system reform. The traditional highly centralized planned economy system is characterized by the exclusion of the role of the market. After the Third Plenary Session of the 11th CPC Central Committee, the CPC began to explore the system and mechanism of organically combining planning with the market. The 14th National Congress of the CPC proposed that the goal of China's economic system reform is to establish a socialist market economy system so that the market plays a fundamental role in resource allocation under national macro-control. This theoretical breakthrough has played an extremely important role in China's reform and opening-up and in economic and social development. Since the 14th National Congress of the CPC, the CPC has been looking for a new scientific positioning for the relationship between the government and the market according to the expansion of practice and the deepening of understanding. The Third Plenary Session of the 18th CPC Central Committee proposed to allow the market to play a decisive role in resource allocation and give better play to the role of the government, achieving another breakthrough in the theory and practice of the CPC. The 19th National Congress of the CPC further answered major questions, such as how to accelerate the improvement of the socialist market economy system and what the focus of economic system reform is, and offered direction to further define the relationship between the government and the market at the historical intersection of the Two Centenary Goals. It is in the continuous exploration of the relationship between the government and the market that China's economic system reform has deepened and advanced the reform in other fields.

In addition, further defining the relationship between the government and the market is the key to deepening economic system reform. Deepening economic system reform is a systematic project involving the market system, enterprise system, macro management, finance, labor and employment, social security, foreign economy, and many other aspects. Among them, the relationship between the government and the market is the key. Historic achievements have been made in China's reform, opening up, and economic development, and socialism with

Chinese characteristics has entered a new era. However, there remain outstanding problems in China's development, such as low quality and efficiency of development, weak innovation ability, shortcomings in the field of people's livelihoods, a large gap between urban and rural regional development and income distribution, and so on. Solidifying the relationship between the government and the market is key to solving the problem of unbalanced and insufficient development and to further promoting economic system reform. Only by understanding and defining the relationship between the government and the market can China comprehensively promote reforms in various other fields and solve the deep-seated problems in the economic system.

Finally, the relationship between the government and the market is also the theme of the evolution of the market economy system. Throughout the evolution and development of the market economy system in Western capitalist countries, the economic theories of state interventionism and laissez-faire dominated alternately. The classical economics school represented by Adam Smith advocates the allocation of resources through free market competition and that the government only acts as a "night watchman." However, the outbreak of the great economic crisis in the 1930s exposed the disadvantages of the free market approach. As a reflection on the complete free market, Keynesianism advocates intervention in the economy with a policy based on total demand management. However, with the emergence of serious "stagflation" in the 1970s, neoliberalism economics, which denied the role of government, rose. After the international financial crisis in 2008, the reflection on neoliberalism became the trend in economics. Therefore, in a certain sense, the history of market economy theory is a history of the debate over the relationship between the government and the market.

II. Allowing the Market to Play a Decisive Role in Resource Allocation

1. The basis for the decisive role of the market in resource allocation

The market economy is essentially an economy in which the market determines the allocation of resources. It is the general law of the market economy and the basic requirement for the law of value to play its role. The specific tenets of a market economy include the following: enterprises are the subjects of market allocation of resources and will decide what to produce, how much to produce, how to produce, and for whom to produce independently according to market needs; the price mechanism is the core of market allocation of resources, and the dominant price formation mechanism is market competition so that the price can fully reflect the supply and demand of resources; the market system is the basis for market allocation of resources, the modern market system allows enterprises to operate independently and compete fairly, consumers to choose and consume independently, and commodities and factors to flow freely and be exchanged equally; a sound market order is a guarantee for the market allocation of resources, and the government should establish fair, open, and transparent market rules and implement unified market regulation.

The market is the most efficient form of resource allocation. Economic development aims to improve the efficiency of resource allocation, produce as many products with as few resources as possible, and obtain as many benefits as possible. Both theory and practice have proven that the market is the most efficient form of resource allocation. First, the market can effectively process and transmit economic information. It offers incomparable advantages over other mechanisms in processing and transmitting a large amount of information about production and consumption and supply and demand. Second, the market can automatically coordinate the interest relationship so that the interest relationship between various economic activities can be balanced through the market so as to motivate all parties. Third, the market can effectively correct the imbalance between supply and demand, to form a long-term trend of rational distribution of social labor in each production department in proportion. In addition, the market can encourage innovation and the survival of the fittest, help improve the quality and efficiency of economic development, and promote reform in quality, efficiency, and power of economic development.

The decisive role of the market in resource allocation highlights problem orientation. Since the reform and opening-up, China's socialist market economy system has experienced a process of gradual establishment and continuous improvement. However, there are still many drawbacks that restrict the vitality of market subjects and hinder the full play of market and value laws. For example, the market order is not standardized, and the phenomenon of seeking economic benefits by improper means is widespread; the development of production factor market lags behind, factors are idle, and a large number of effective needs are not met; market rules are not unified, and there is significant departmental and local protectionism; insufficient market competition hinders the survival of the fittest and structural adjustment; and so on. If these problems are not solved, it is difficult to form a perfect socialist market economy system, and it is also difficult to change the mode of development and adjust the economic structure. Allowing the market to play a decisive role in resource allocation is conducive to promoting market-oriented reform in breadth and depth and building a modern economic system.

2. How to give play to the decisive role of the market in resource allocation

First, to give play to the decisive role of the market in resource allocation, it is required that the circulation and aggregation of market resource elements should be guided by the value law of the market, and various obstacles to the flow of market resource elements artificially set by malicious monopoly and excessive administrative regulation should be eliminated. Specifically: first, China needs to establish fair, open, and transparent market rules and implement a unified market access system in which all kinds of market subjects can equally enter the areas outside the negative list according to law. Second, it needs to implement unified market regulation, clean up and abolish various rules and practices that hinder the national unified market and fair competition, strictly prohibit and punish all kinds of illegal preferential policies, and oppose local protectionism, monopoly, and unfair competition. In addition, it is necessary to improve the mechanism that the price is mainly determined by the market; any price that can be formed by the market should be determined by the market, and the government should not intervene improperly. China should promote price reform in the fields of water, oil, natural gas, electricity, transportation, and telecommunications and liberalize prices in competitive links; the scope of government pricing is mainly limited to important public utilities, public welfare services, and network-based natural monopoly sectors so as to improve transparency and accept social supervision; and it should improve the price formation mechanism of agricultural products and pay attention to the role of the market in forming prices. Finally, it is necessary to establish a unified urban and rural construction land market; on the premise of conforming to the planning and use control, rural collective operating construction land is allowed to be sold, leased, and pooled in shares, with the same access to the market, the same right, and the same price as state-owned land so as to promote the circulation of rural land according to the market law and bring more market-oriented factors to the land price formation mechanism.

Second, to give play to the decisive role of the market in resource allocation, market subjects must meet the requirements of the market economy. State-owned enterprises are important market subjects that manufacture goods, provide services, and participate in market competition in China's socialist market economy. For a long time, although China's state-owned enterprises have undergone several rounds of market-oriented transformation, there remain problems that do not meet the requirements of the market economy. For example, most leaders of state-owned enterprises have political experience and administrative level. These unique resources of state-owned enterprises affect the requirements of market equality and fair competition. First, state-owned enterprises need to integrate with the market economy on the whole, adapt to the new situation of marketization and internationalization, and further deepen the reform of state-owned enterprises with a focus on standardizing business decisions, maintaining and increasing the value of assets, ensuring fair participation in competition, improving enterprise efficiency, enhancing enterprise vitality, and undertaking social responsibility. Second, in view of prominent problems such as the administrative background of the leaders of state-owned enterprises, China needs to improve the corporate governance structure with coordinated operation and effective checks and balances; establish a professional manager system to give better play to the role of entrepreneurs; deepen the reform of the system by which internal managers are promoted or demoted, employees enter or leave, and income increases or decreases; establish a long-term incentive and restraint mechanism and strengthen the accountability of state-owned enterprises for operation and investment; and explore and promote the disclosure of major information such as the financial budget of state-owned enterprises. State-owned enterprises should reasonably increase the proportion of market-oriented selection and employment and reasonably determine and strictly regulate the salary level, job treatment, job consumption, and business consumption of managers of state-owned enterprises.

III. Giving Better Play to the Role of Government

1. The basis for giving better play to the role of government

Giving better play to the role of government reflects the superiority of the socialist system. The market plays a decisive role in resource allocation, but it does not play all roles. On the one hand, the role of a market mechanism is conditional, including the legal system, competition rules, macro environment, social security, etc. These conditions cannot be formed by relying on the role of the market itself. On the other hand, the market economy has problems of local failure, blindness, spontaneity and lag, polarization between the rich and the poor, and economic fluctuations. The capitalist market economy is dominated by the law of surplus value, which brings about the opposition between labor and capital, resulting in profound disadvantages such as polarization between the rich and the poor, overproduction, economic virtualization, prominent ecological crisis, and so on. The socialist system is based on public ownership of the means of production and adheres to a people-centered value orientation. Scientific macro-control and effective government governance are the internal requirements for giving play to the advantages of the socialist market economy system. In the socialist market economy with Chinese characteristics, the responsibilities and functions of the government are as follows: maintaining macroeconomic stability, strengthening and optimizing public services, ensuring fair competition, strengthening market regulation, maintaining market order, promoting sustainable development, promoting common prosperity, and remedying market failure. Fundamentally speaking, to give better play to the role of the government is to strive to solve the problem of unbalanced and insufficient development on the basis of liberating and developing social productive forces, meeting people's growing needs for a better life, and constantly promoting people's comprehensive development and the common prosperity of all people.

Changing development concepts and changing government functions are key parts of giving better play to the role of the government. At present, there are still two outstanding problems in giving play to the role of the government in China. First, some regions and sectors still focus only on GDP. As a result, the plans and policies formulated are often inappropriate, unsuitable, or even contrary to the new development concept. Second, there are still problems in government functions, such as dislocation, acting beyond authority, and absence. The powers that should be delegated to the market and society have not been fully and properly delegated, and the things that should be managed have not been managed well or properly. To correctly handle the relationship between the government and the market, China must firmly grasp the two keys of changing development concepts and changing government functions. These two aspects are interrelated: if China does not establish a new development concept, there will inevitably be inaction or misconduct of the government; without changing government functions, the new development concept cannot be implemented well. Government departments at all levels should firmly establish new development concepts, strive to improve the ability and level of the overall implementation of the new development concepts, and focus their work on promoting innovative, coordinated, green, open, and shared development. At the same time, China should implement the new development concepts in the deepened reform of the economic system, strive to build a government under the rule of law and a service-oriented government, further simplify administration and delegate power, greatly reduce the direct allocation of resources by the government, and shift the focus of its work to creating a fair competitive market environment, protecting the ecological environment, and supporting innovation so as to enhance the driving force and vitality of economic development.

Adhering to the centralized and unified leadership of the CPC over economic work is the fundamental guarantee for giving better play to the role of government. The most essential characteristic of socialism with Chinese characteristics is the leadership of the CPC. The greatest advantage of the socialist system with Chinese characteristics is the leadership of the CPC. Adhering to the overall leadership of the CPC and giving full play to the leading role of the CPC in overall planning and coordinating all parties is an important feature of China's socialist market economy system. Economic work is the central task of the CPC, and the leadership of the CPC should be fully reflected in it. China must fully understand and give play to the role of CPC leadership over economic work, including grasping the direction, planning the overall situation, putting forward strategies, formulating policies, promoting legislation, creating a good environment, etc. The leadership of the CPC provides a fundamental guarantee for fully realizing the role of the government. In terms of the division of functions and work layout of Party committees and governments at all levels, the important issues involving economic and social development plans, major principles and policies, overall work arrangements, national economy, and people's livelihoods shall be collectively discussed and decided by the Party committees; for routine work, the government and its departments shall make decisions and manage according to their responsibilities and authorities. Party committees at various levels shall support the government to fully perform its responsibilities according to law.

2. The transformation of government functions

(1) Transforming government functions and clarifying the different functions of government and market

The market plays a decisive role in resource allocation, indicating that the main force of economic development is in the market, enterprises and people are the subjects of wealth creation, and the government should be the subject of creating a fair competition environment. The function of the government should turn to serving the market subjects and creating a good environment. The government should stimulate the enthusiasm of social members to create wealth and enhance the internal driving force of economic development by protecting the legitimate rights and interests of the market subjects and fair competition.

(2) Transforming government functions and strengthening government public services

The government should strive to establish a social fairness security system with fair rights, opportunities, and rules. The establishment of a fair social security system is important for giving full play to the positive functions of the government and preventing market failure. The law of the survival of the fittest in the market economy determines that the market will not only optimize the allocation of resources but also produce many losers. Even the winners of market competition sometimes encounter crises due to the influence of natural or man-made disasters. A fair security system can eliminate worries for market participants to engage in market competition; provide effective basic public services such as compulsory education, medical care, public health, public employment services, and basic social security for the majority of social members; promote the harmonious and healthy development of the market economy; and fully reflect the achievements of economic development as people's comprehensive development. Based on China's national conditions, the subject of the construction of social fairness security system is the government, which plays a key role.

(3) Transforming government functions, being oriented by the construction of a government under the rule of law, and implementing delegation, restriction, and decentralization of authority

China should adhere to the rule of law and administration by law and adhere to the integrated construction of the country, government, and society under the rule of law. It must respect the standard offset forth by the Constitution so that the government's public power acts are prohibited unless they are expressly permitted, and civil rights acts are permissible until they are shown to be prohibited by law. China should further improve the People's Congress system so that people's representatives at all levels can restrict administrative power according to law, and through institutional arrangements, allow all people to enjoy rights and perform their obligations equally according to law so as to further realize social fairness and justice. The government should further streamline administration and delegate power, deepen the reform of the administrative examination and approval system, minimize the management of micro affairs by the central government, cancel the examination and approval of all economic activities that can be effectively regulated by the market mechanism, and standardize the management of reserved administrative examination and approval matters; and improve efficiency. All economic and social matters that are directly oriented to the grassroots level, with a large number and covering a wide range, and are more conveniently and effectively managed by the local government, should be delegated to the local and grassroots level.

IV. Combining the "Invisible Hand" with the "Visible Hand" More Effectively

Allowing the market to play a decisive role in resource allocation and giving better play to the role of the government is not only an important part of the CPC's basic strategy in the new era but also an inevitable requirement for building a modern economic system. In giving play to the role of the market and the government, China should adhere to dialectics and dichotomy, strive to form a pattern of organic unity, mutual complementarity, coordination, and mutual promotion of the role of the market and the role of the government, and try to improve the CPC's ability to control the socialist market economy. In the new era, the country should continue to seek to define the relationship between the government and the market in accordance with the requirements of "building an economic system with effective market mechanism, dynamic micro subjects and moderate macro-control" proposed by the 19th National Congress of the CPC. China needs an "effective market" and a "promising government" to give full play to the advantages of both the "invisible hand" and the "visible hand" and better reflect the characteristics and advantages of the socialist market economy system.

1. Deeply understanding the unity of effective market and effective government

To allow the market to play a decisive role in resource allocation and give better play to the role of the government, the two should be organically unified and complementary rather than being separated and denied by one other. An effective market is not only an important goal of the government but also serves as an indicator of a successful and promising government. A promising government is not only an important guarantee for an effective market mechanism and the vitality of micro subjects but also essential for making up for market failure. The main reason why China has made great achievements in its reform and opening-up is that it not only gives full play to the role of the market but also upholds the leadership of the CPC and the role of the government so that the market and the government are combined organically. One can see that the backwardness of the market economy in many developing countries is not only manifested in a weak market role, imperfect market system, chaotic market order, and distorted price signal but also in a weak government role, insufficient capacity, low efficiency, and lack of authority. Only by giving full play to the advantages of the government and the market can China ensure the sustainable and healthy development of the economy.

2. Closely focusing on the organic unity of government and market to promote reform in relevant fields

China should adhere to the direction of socialist market economy reform and strive to build an economic system with an effective market mechanism, dynamic micro subjects, and moderate macro-control. On the one hand, China should further improve the modern market system by deepening the reform of the economic system, enhancing the vitality of microeconomic subjects, and giving enterprises and individuals more vitality and space to develop and create wealth. On the other hand, by deepening the reform of the economic system, China should further modernize the national governance system and governance capacity in the economic field, strengthen and improve the CPC's leadership over economic work, innovate and improve macro-control, give play to the strategic guiding role of the national development plan, improve the coordination mechanism of fiscal, monetary, industrial, and regional economic policies, and accelerate the establishment of a modern financial system, deepen market-oriented reform of interest rates and exchange rates, and improve the two-pillar regulatory framework of monetary policy and macro-prudential policy. To give better play to the role of the government, China should start with promoting social fairness and justice and improving people's well-being, step up the construction of a system that plays a major role in ensuring social fairness and justice, ensure that all people have a greater sense of gain in co-construction and sharing, and constantly promote comprehensive human development and common prosperity for all people.

3. Firmly grasping the key point of improving the property rights system and market-oriented allocation of factors

The 19th National Congress of the CPC stressed that economic system reforms must focus on improving the property rights system and market-oriented allocation of factors so as to achieve effective incentives of property rights, free flow of factors, flexible price response, fair and orderly competition, and survival of the fittest. To define the relationship between the government and the market, China must focus on improving the property rights system and the market-oriented allocation of factors now. In improving the property rights system, the government should speed up the improvement of various state-owned asset management systems and reform the authorized management system of state-owned capital; deepen the reform of state-owned enterprises and develop a mixed ownership economy; improve the property rights protection system; protect the property rights of entrepreneurs according to law; and actively guide private enterprises to use the property rights market to combine private capital. In promoting the market-oriented allocation of factors, China should deepen the reform of the commercial system, break the administrative monopoly, prevent market monopoly, and speed up the market-oriented reform of factor prices; deepen the reform of the investment and financing system and give play to the key role of investment in optimizing supply structure; and deepen the reform of the financial system and promote the healthy development of the multi-level capital market.

SECTION 3

The Operation Mechanism of the Socialist Market Economy with Chinese Characteristics

The operation mechanism of the socialist market economy with Chinese characteristics is the realization mechanism and internal function of the socialist market economy system with Chinese characteristics. It is a mechanism for regulating economic operations through the fluctuation of market prices, the pursuit of interests by socialist market subjects, and the change of market supply and demand in the continuously improved market system. It is the organic connection among and function of supply and demand, competition, price, and other elements in the body of a market economy. The operation mechanism of a socialist market economy has developed into an interactive and interconnected set of mechanisms composed of mechanisms for price, supply and demand, competition, risk and income equivalence, survival of the fittest, and so on.

I. The Generality and Particularity of the Operation Environment

The market economy is always running in and influenced by a specific institutional and market environment. Because of this, the market economies of different countries and regions of the world exemplify distinct characteristics.

The general environment for the operation of the modern market economy has the following five characteristics. First, the market system is composed of five basic markets: commodity, capital, labor, technology, and natural resources, which respectively perform the functions of commodity exchange, capital financing, labor flow, and the transformation of technological achievements. Second, in the market system, the law of value and the law of supply and demand are followed by the exchange of goods, labor services, technology, and resources, exerting the lasting effect of the principle of free exchange and contract. Third, competition has become an indispensable element for commodity value formation, effective allocation of resources, active scientific and technological innovation, and productivity development under the framework of the market system. Fourth, the market system is unified nationwide, ensuring fair competition among commodity producers and rational transfer of production factors. Fifth, the market system is open. This openness is embodied in integration into the international environment, extensive foreign trade, foreign economic and technological exchanges, and cooperation, recognition, and compliance with international value law, international practices, and international rules.

The market system, composed of the commodity market, financial market, labor market, technology market, and natural resources, provides the general environment for market operation. There are mutual restraints, interdependence, and mutual promotion among various markets within the market system. In order to give full play to the overall function of the market system, a unified, open, competitive, and orderly market must be formed.

In addition to the general characteristics of the market system, the biggest difference from the operating environment of the socialist market economy lies in the institutional environment. The socialist market economy with Chinese characteristics operates under the socialist institutional environment, and its particularity is mainly reflected in three aspects. First, the market subject of the socialist market system is composed of multiple sectors of the economy dominated by the public economy. Although both public and non-public ownership are important components of the socialist market economy, China should keep public ownership in the dominant position within the ownership structure, give play to the leading role of the state-owned economy, and constantly enhance the economic vitality, control, and influence of the state-owned economy. As a result, the nature of the market system is socialist. Second, the main economic relations in the socialist market system fully reflect the essential requirement of socialism. The essence of socialism is to liberate and develop productive forces, eliminate exploitation and polarization, and finally achieve common prosperity. This requirement determines that the commodity relations in the socialist market system are mainly the exchange relation and interest allocation relation among workers, not the capital relation, which is only a supplement. Third, the socialist market system plays its role in a particular way. The socialist market system not only gives play to the decisive role of the market mechanism in the allocation of resources but also gives full play to the role of the government in macro-control. Although the capitalist market system also gives play to the role of the market and the government, the attribute of the socialist system determines that the government macro-control in the socialist market system is very different from that in the capitalist market system in terms of the goal, content, basic mode, and role of control.

II. The Generality and Particularity of Operation Mechanisms

1. The price mechanism

The price mechanism refers to the movement of the organic connection between the change in the market price of a commodity in the market and the change in the supply-demand relationship of the commodity in the market in the process of market competition. It reflects the relation between supply and demand through market price information and regulates production and circulation through such market price information, to achieve resource allocation. Therefore, price changes and supply-demand changes are interrelated, and they restrict one other. The price mechanism is the most sensitive and effective adjusting mechanism in the market mechanism. The change in price has a very significant impact on all of the social and economic activities.

The price mechanism is at the most important position of the market mechanism, so the role of the market mechanism must be realized by the price mechanism. The price mechanism is a competitive tool for commodity producers and operators and a barometer of market supply and demand for national macro-control. At the same time, the price mechanism can solve three basic questions: what and how much society should produce, how to produce it, and for whom to produce it. Price can adjust multiple income distributions, and the price mechanism also directly affects consumers' purchase behavior. In particular, the price mechanism can spontaneously adjust the total supply and demand and realize the balance between the total supply and demand in the process of market resource allocation. On the one hand, the price mechanism can drive commodity producers to advance technological innovation and improve management by affecting the relationship of interests. It can also drive producers to adjust production orientation by affecting the interest relationship, to realize the redistribution of social labor among different departments, and then adjust the total supply structure of society. On the other hand, the price mechanism guides consumption tendency through price changes. For general commodities, the result of the price mechanism is: when the price rises, the demand decreases; and when the price falls, the demand rises. This induces fluctuation and even changes in consumption tendency. In addition, the price mechanism provides signals for national macro-control. The law and trend change of commodity price fluctuation under the action of price mechanism can provide regular information reflecting the market's supply and demand situation for the national macro-control of the market.

2. The supply and demand mechanism

The supply and demand mechanism refers to the mechanism that affects the combination of various production factors through the contradictory movement of supply and demand of commodities, labor services, and various social resources. With the market prices of various commodities formed in the unbalanced state between supply and demand, it adjusts social production and demand through market signals, such as price and market supply and demand, and finally realizes the basic balance between supply and demand. In the supply and demand mechanism, supply and demand refers to the supply and demand of a commodity or factor in the market. Supply emphasizes the use value of a certain commodity or factor provided by the market subject to the market, while demand emphasizes the demand for the use value of such commodity or factor limited by purchasing power.

There are three basic states in which the supply and demand mechanism works.

(1) When the supply of a commodity or factor is greater than the demand, the price of that commodity or factor will decline; the competition among sellers will increase, prompting the seller to reduce the production scale; the interest rate and wage will decline with the reduction of the seller's production scale. This state is beneficial to buyers, namely consumers, who can buy commodities or factors with high quality and low prices.

(2) When the supply of a commodity or factor is less than the demand, the price of the commodity or factor will rise; the competition between buyers will increase, prompting the seller to

continue to expand the production scale; the interest rate and wage will increase with the expansion of the seller's production scale. This state is beneficial to sellers, namely producers, who can not only sell more commodities or factors but also sell them at higher prices and gain more profits.

(3) When the supply of a commodity or factor is equal to the demand, the state of equilibrium of supply and demand is reached. If this state lasts for a long time, the law of supply and demand will temporarily be out of action. However, in practice, the equilibrium of supply and demand is only a fleeting state—when the supply of a commodity or factor is greater than the demand, the action of the supply and demand mechanism causes the transformation of the supply to be less than the demand, and the transformation process passes by the fleeting point of equilibrium of supply and demand. Conversely, when the supply of a certain commodity or factor is less than the demand, the action of the supply and demand mechanism causes the transformation of the supply to be greater than the demand, and the transformation process likewise passes the fleeting point of equilibrium of supply and demand. Therefore, the equilibrium of supply and demand is a transit point for the mutual transformation of the first two states, not a constant state. The imbalance between supply and demand is absolute, while the equilibrium is relative. From the imbalance to the equilibrium, and then from the new equilibrium to the new imbalance, this cycle continues to repeat.

3. The competition mechanism

Competition is a necessary condition for the operation of a socialist market economy. The determination of commodity value and the realization of value law are inseparable from competition. The essence of competition is the comparison of labor consumption among different commodity producers and operators in the process of production and operation. In the modern socialist market economy, competition is deeper and more complicated. There is competition not only among buyers and sellers but also between buyers and sellers. The main means of competition in the same production sector is price competition, which is to defeat competitors at a lower price. Between different sectors, it is mainly the inflow or outflow of funds. The funds will flow from sectors with low-profit margins to sectors with high-profit margins.

The competition mechanism is the objective requirement for market subjects to strive for profit conditions to maximize their own interests. It is the means and method for the survival of the fittest in market economic activities. Through the full play of the competition mechanism, winners and losers are decided among the traders in the market, thus promoting the spiral rise of economic quality and quantity. Therefore, the competition mechanism is one of the most important economic mechanisms of a socialist market economy, as well as an inherent law of the market economy.

The existence of the competition mechanism and the exertion of its function must meet the following conditions. First, commodity producers and operators should be independent economic entities, have the right to participate in the competition, then seize the opportunity in the competition, and determine their production and operation direction and investment scale according to the market trend. Second, the corresponding benefits obtained by commodity producers and operators in competition should be recognized. Commodity producers and operators do not compete for the sake of competition. If they cannot obtain independent benefits from competition, the competition mechanism will inevitably stagnate. Third, China should have the environment required for competition, which means the competition place or market system should be improved. Only when all kinds of markets are complete, and the market system is perfect can China give full play to the market competition mechanism and carry out orderly competition. In addition, there should be sound competition laws and regulations to ensure a fair and orderly competition environment.

The competition mechanism plays an important role in the operation and development of the socialist market economy. First, it transforms the individual value of commodities into social value. Second, it encourages producers to improve technology, management, and labor productivity. Third, it encourages producers to organize and arrange production according to market demand to adapt production to demand.

4. The risk and return equivalence mechanism

Market subjects will face the risk of profit, loss, and bankruptcy in their activities of production, exchange, distribution, and consumption. This is an inevitable law of a market economy. Under the temptation of interests, risk acts on market subjects as an external pressure at the same time. In the face of risks, there may be greater profit opportunities. Low-risk market behaviors generally result in less profit and loss; high-risk market behaviors generally result in more profit and loss. Therefore, in the process of pursuing interests in the market, people experience the game of risk and return, which tends to make the risks and returns symmetrical and balanced.

The risk mechanism restricts the market behavior. With huge pressure of loss and even bankruptcy that may be brought on by competition, risk motivates market subjects to improve the operation and management, enhance market competition strength, and improve their ability to adjust and adapt to the operation risk.

5. The "survival of the fittest" mechanism

The market competition under the market mechanism will have different outcomes for enterprises with different economic strengths, management abilities, and adaptability. The market competition mechanism will inevitably be represented by the survival of the fittest mechanism.

Market competition and the survival of the fittest are universal laws in modern economic life. The "baton" effect generated from these laws has become a powerful lever for social progress. If China does not eliminate those who are inefficient and those who lack innovation ability and adaptability, it cannot encourage those who are efficient. Thus, society cannot progress. The elimination of the inferior and inefficient will inevitably shorten the average scale of social labor time so as to improve social labor productivity and develop productive forces.

From the perspective of the law of social progress, the law of survival of the fittest can be said to exist forever. However, the institutional background of this mechanism is different, and its mode of action and the use of it by social subjects are quite different, because the evaluation basis and scale of the superior and the inferior are obviously different under different institutional backgrounds. Under the condition of a market economy based on private ownership, the survival of the fittest mechanism is actually a replica of social Darwinism. The pursuit of surplus value by capital objectively stimulates the progress of production technology. By contrast, the survival of the fittest mechanism in the socialist market economy functions based on the competitive relationship among enterprises with completely independent property rights of legal persons. It is an important part of the reform of the modern enterprise system and the overall revitalization of the state-owned economy.

SECTION 4

Accelerating the Improvement of the Socialist Market Economy

To accelerate the improvement of the socialist market economy system, China must focus on improving the property rights system and the market-oriented allocation of factors; realize the effective incentive of property rights, the free flow of factors, flexible price response, fair and orderly competition, and the survival of the fittest in enterprises; and accelerate the improvement of the modern property rights system.

The modern property rights system is the cornerstone of the socialist market economy system. Improving the modern property rights system is one of the key priorities in deepening economic system reform, as determined in the report to the 19th National Congress of the CPC. Clear ownership, clear rights and responsibilities, strict protection, and smooth circulation are the basic characteristics of the modern property rights system, and at its core is property rights protection.

To improve the modern property rights system, the basic economic system of keeping public ownership as the mainstay of the economy while allowing diverse sectors to develop side by side must be upheld and improved. This basic economic system is not only an important pillar of the socialist system with Chinese characteristics but also the foundation of the socialist market economy system. To improve the modern property rights system, China must consolidate and develop the public sector of the economy, and encourage, support, and guide the development of the non-public economy.

To improve the modern property rights system, efforts should be made to strengthen the protection of property rights. With fairness as the core principle, the government should protect the economic property rights and legitimate interests of all forms of ownership according to law, and protect the property rights of economic organizations and natural persons of all forms of ownership according to law. The property rights of the public economy are inviolable, as are the property rights of the non-public economy. China should strengthen the judicial protection of all kinds of property rights and seriously investigate and address violations of all kinds according to law. Only by consolidating this foundation can China realize the equal use of production factors and fair participation in market competition in all kinds of ownership economies according to law.

In the new era, as innovation has become the first driving force behind development, it is particularly important to improve the intellectual property system. China should not only strictly protect it according to law but also achieve a greater breakthrough in the effective incentive of property rights. It should implement a distribution policy guided by increasing the value of knowledge, explore the implementation of equity, option, and dividend incentives for scientific research personnel, and give full play to the long-term incentivizing role of intellectual property rights in scientific and technological innovation and achievement transformation.

II. Accelerating the Market-Oriented Allocation of Factors

Accelerating the construction and improvement of the factor market is another key point in deepening economic system reform. The construction of China's modern market system has made great progress, but compared with the commodity and service market, the construction of the factor market is relatively lagging, which has become one of the main obstacles restricting the free flow of factors such as labor, land, capital, technology, and information.

China should deepen the reform of the labor market and ensure equal employment opportunities according to law. The labor force is the most active factor of production, and employment is the foundation of people's livelihoods. China should deepen the reform of a registered residence system as a breakthrough and improve the employment legal system, eliminate the segmentation between urban and rural areas and between regions and industries, eliminate identity and gender discrimination, and actively comply with the development of new industries and new employment forms. Moreover, the government should citizenize permanent residents who are able to work and live in towns and cities in an orderly manner and achieve the free flow of the labor force between urban and rural areas.

China should deepen the reform of the land market and accelerate the construction of a unified urban and rural construction land market. It should adhere to the collective ownership of rural land, and strictly control, plan, and manage the use of land. The country should also improve the rights and functions of rural collective operational construction land so that it can have the same access to the market, rights, and price as urban construction land.

China should deepen the reform of the capital market and promote the healthy development of the multi-level capital market. It should standardize the development of the stock market, develop the bond market in an orderly manner, steadily develop the futures and derivatives market, and increase the proportion of direct financing. The government should also deepen the reform of the financial system, start with and be based on serving the real economy, and comprehensively improve the ability and level of financial services. It should improve the financial regulatory system, accelerate the construction of relevant laws and regulations, improve the corporate governance structure of financial institutions, strengthen the construction of macro-prudential management system, strengthen functional supervision and behavior supervision, and hold the bottom line of "no systemic financial risk."

III. Accelerating the Improvement of the Mechanism in Which Prices Are Mainly Determined by the Market

Price determination by the market is the basic requirement of a market economy and the basic approach for market allocation of resources. Only when the price signal is true, objective, and sensitive can the adjusting role of the price lever be given full play. At present, nearly 98% of China's commodity and service prices have been liberalized and are determined by the market, and the mechanism of price determination by the market has been basically established.

China should allow the market to play a decisive role in resource allocation and speed up the market-oriented reform of factor prices. It should deepen the reform of the factor price formation mechanism in the fields of resource products and monopoly industries, further eliminate various forms of natural monopoly and administrative monopoly, separate infrastructure from operation, and implement market-oriented allocation of public resources according to the characteristics of different industries such as water, oil, natural gas, electric power, transportation, and telecommunications, and liberalize the prices of competitive businesses and competitive links, to truly reflect the market supply and demand, the resource scarcity and the environmental damage cost. At the same time, China should strengthen the anti-monopoly law enforcement in the field of price and strengthen the supervision during and after the event.

The nation should deepen the market-oriented reform of the interest rate and exchange rate, steadily promote the internationalization of Renminbi (RMB), improve the internationalization level of the financial market, and realize the convertibility of RMB capital account in an orderly way.

IV. Accelerating the Improvement of the Market Environment for Fair Competition

The government of China should fully implement the market access negative list system and clean up and cancel all rules and practices that get in the way of a unified market and fair competition. Fair competition is a prerequisite for the market mechanism to work. To create a fair competition market environment, China should continue to deepen reforms that entail "streamlining administration, delegating powers, and improving regulation and services" with the commercial system as the breakthrough, accelerate the full implementation of the market access negative list system and the fair competition review system, and minimize government intervention in enterprise operation.

Improving the international competitiveness of China's economy can only be achieved through a mutual opening up between China and other countries such that all parties can benefit. Helpful attempts have been made in 11 pilot FTZs in Shanghai and other places to establish a market access negative list system. Based on the pilot experience, China should be able to accelerate the full implementation of the market access negative list system. At the same time, the government should improve the fair competition review system and strengthen the construction of law enforcement capacity. Internally, it should focus on breaking regional segmentation and industrial monopoly, removing market barriers, and speeding up the clean-up and abolition of various regulations and practices that hinder the formation of a unified market and fair competition. Externally, the government should greatly relax market access, expand the opening of the service industry to the outside world, actively and steadily globalize, promote trade and investment liberalization and facilitation, and promote economic globalization.

The market economy is an economy ruled by law, and the rule of law is the internal requirement of the socialist market economy. China should accelerate the revision of the laws against unfair competition and land management; accelerate the improvement of the legal systems related to property rights, contracts, and intellectual property rights; strictly implement the general provisions of the civil law, the anti-monopoly law, the law on the promotion of SMEs, and intellectual property laws; and strengthen the crackdown and punishment of illegal acts. The market regulatory system should be improved in accordance with the principles of unity, standardization, and effectiveness.

The social credit system should be established and improved. China should accelerate the construction and improvement of the enterprise and individual credit rating system, establish an effective credit incentive and defaulter punishment system, strengthen the credit awareness and integrity behavior of the whole society, and create a market environment of honesty, trustworthiness, and fair competition.

V. Accelerating the Establishment of the Dominant Position of Various Enterprises in the Market

China should deepen the reform of state-owned enterprises and develop a mixed-ownership economy. State-owned enterprises make up the main body of the state-owned economy and serve as the material and political basis of socialism with Chinese characteristics. They should take a clear stand to become stronger, better, and bigger. To deepen the reform of state-owned enterprises, the nation must adhere to the leadership of the CPC over state-owned enterprises, to the direction of modern enterprise system reform, and to the principle of guidance by category. The country should develop the mixed ownership economy steadily and in an orderly way, establish a mechanism of equity checks and balances, improve the corporate governance structure, stimulate the vitality and creativity of state-owned enterprises in market competition, improve the competitiveness of state-owned enterprises, and expand the influence of state-owned capital. China should also accelerate the strategic adjustment of the state-owned economy, reform the authorized operation system of state-owned capital, improve the regulatory system of state-owned assets, accelerate the reorganization and establishment of state-owned capital investment and operation companies, and realize the optimization of the layout and structural adjustment of the state-owned economy.

To support the development of private enterprises, the government should enhance service awareness, communicate closely with private enterprises, help them solve practical difficulties, and jointly build a new government-enterprise relationship with private enterprises. The government should also abolish discriminatory policies and practices, protect the property rights and business autonomy of private enterprises according to law, stimulate and protect entrepreneurship, guide private enterprises to improve their management level, and encourage private enterprises to establish a modern enterprise system.

VI. Innovating and Improving the Role of Macro-Control

The core aim of economic system reform is to properly handle the relationship between the government and the market. To accelerate the improvement of the socialist market economy system, the government must give better play to the role of the government through scientific, appropriate, and effective macro-control.

China should innovate and improve macro-control according to the law of economic and social development. Additionally, it should implement the new development concept, innovate the regulation and service model, give play to the strategic guiding role of the national development plan, and improve the coordination mechanism of fiscal, monetary, industrial, regional, and other economic policies. China should establish and improve mechanisms for major issue research, democratic decision-making, and policy evaluation and adjustment, and try to use the Internet, big data, and other means to promote the modernization of governance capacity.

The nation must respect the role of the market and the dominant position of enterprises, and fully and correctly perform government functions. It should further streamline administration and delegate power. In principle, administrative licensing should not be established for any matter that can be effectively regulated by the market mechanism, handled by social organizations, or independently decided by citizens and legal persons within the scope of the law. China should further deepen the reform of the administrative system. The government should mainly use economic, legal, technical standards, and other means to guide and regulate economic and social activities, focus on macro-control, market regulation, social management, public services, and environmental protection, and reduce administrative intervention. It should further improve the supervision mechanism and allow people to better supervise the government's administration according to the law through more open government affairs. The government should take the initiative to accept the supervision of the public, the press, and public opinion. It should improve the performance management system; strengthen the assessment and evaluation of the implementation of major decisions and arrangements, the performance of duties in accordance with the law and the actual results; and constantly improve the credibility and execution of the government.

PART THREE

Development Concepts and Building a Modern Economic System

CHAPTER SIX

Development Concepts of Socialism with Chinese Characteristics for a New Era

The vision of innovative, coordinated, green, open, and shared development put forth at the Fifth Plenary Session of the 18th CPC Central Committee is the core essence of Xi Jinping Thought on Socialism with Chinese Characteristics for a New Era.[18] It demonstrates strong consciousness relating to problem-solving and goal orientation while reflecting the Party's new understanding of developmental drivers, structure, conditions, strategies and goals, and their internal logic during the decisive stage in building a moderately prosperous society in all respects. It is another major innovation of China's theory of development and a profound change in relation to China's overall development.

SECTION 1
The Vision of Innovative, Coordinated, Green, Open, and Shared Development

"Law" is the inherent, essential, inevitable, and stable connection in the existence and development of the component parts of a given society. The law of human social development exists within the process of historical development. China needs to analyze and understand the law through the standpoint and viewpoint of dialectics and historical materialism and strive to make the subjective world consistent with the objective world so as to actively follow and grasp the laws, firmly establish the correct developmental concept, and promote economic development and social progress.

The first development premise is that scientific development follows economic laws. In terms of development, that means being "real and uncompromised," "systematic, holistic and coordinated," as well as providing "higher quality, greater benefit, better structure and full release of advantages." To achieve high-quality, efficient, and sustainable development that respects the laws of the economy, the fundamental approach should be to accelerate the transformation of the economic development mode, with the key being to deepen the strategic adjustment of the industrial structure. Supply-side reform is the main starting point for the transformation of the development mode and structural adjustment. China should move forward in the five priority tasks of cutting overcapacity, reducing excess inventory, deleveraging, lowering costs, and strengthening areas. It should take a multi-pronged approach and tackle both the symptoms and root causes of the multitudinous issues facing the Chinese economy, which will ultimately prove to be successful.

The second premise is that sustainable development follows the natural law. That means regarding the sound environment as an invaluable asset and development achieving material progress both economically and ecologically provides the best for a comprehensively richer civilization.

> We need both green mountains and clear water, and mountains of gold and silver; when it is impossible to have both, we should maintain green mountains and clear water rather than mountains of gold and silver; in addition, green mountains and clear water are as good as mountains of gold and silver.[19]

The third development premise is that inclusive development follows the laws of social governance. That means development that focuses on: "unswervingly pursuing prosperity for all,"[20] being "people-centered,"[21] catering to "people's yearning for a better life,"[22] and "giving the entire population an increased sense of shared gain."[23]

China has experienced the general trend of the times, featuring the conversion of new and old drivers of growth. Centering on the modernization of the national governance system and governance capacity, China adapts to and leads the new normal of economic development, harmoniously promotes a four-pronged comprehensive strategy,[24] and puts forward a vision of innovative, coordinated, green, open, and shared development, which is a highly strategic, programmatic, leading, and rational approach. Innovation is the primary driving force for economic and social development and is at the core of China's overall development. It not only further entrenches the role of S&T as the primary productive force but also enables innovation to enter theoretical, institutional, cultural, and other comprehensive arenas. Coordination is an inherent requirement for sustained and sound economic and social development. It aims to achieve balanced and coordinated development on all fronts and enhance its integrity in the process. "Greenness" is an important embodiment of the sustainable development of the Chinese nation and the people's pursuit of a better life. It is not only a historical summation of the experience and lessons of the development of human civilization but also a strategic plan to lead China's long-term development. Opening up is the only way for the country to prosper and develop; China's recent development is a model case study on the efficacy of reform and opening-up and demonstrates that such a process is clearly a necessary requirement for expanding the space for economic development and improving the level of the national economy. Sharing is an essential requirement of socialism with Chinese characteristics and the inevitable outcome of building a moderately prosperous society in all respects, seeing that all Chinese people have a greater sense of fulfillment as they contribute to and gain from development. The vision of innovative, coordinated, green, open, and shared development focuses on addressing such issues as the driving force of further growth, harmony between humanity and nature, internal and external integration of development, and social fairness and justice. This vision is a concentrated embodiment of development ideas, direction, and focus, and an organic whole with internal interaction, interconnection, and mutual promotion. China will utilize new development concepts to guide new practices, thus making the country's future development path all the clearer.

SECTION 2
Innovation as a Driving Force of Development

Innovation is the driving force of historical progress and the key to the development of a new era, ranking first among the five elements of the vision of innovative, coordinated, green, open, and shared development. Leading the development of the times with innovative growth will surely bring about a profound change in the overall situation of China's advancement and will provide fundamental guidance and strong impetus for building a moderately prosperous society in all respects, thus aiding in realizing the Chinese Dream of national rejuvenation.

I. Innovative Development as the Core of China's Overall Development

Innovative development should be at the core of China's overall development, allowing the nation to adapt to and lead the developmental trend of the times. Innovation, especially scientific and technological innovation, is at the critical core of national competitiveness. In today's world, economic and social development is increasingly dependent upon innovation in theory, systems, S&T, culture, and other fields, with the new advantages of international competition increasingly reflected in innovation capacity. Whoever takes the first step toward innovation can gain the initiative to lead the subsequent development. Globally, a new round of scientific and technological revolution and industrial reform is emerging, and some major disruptive technological innovations are creating new industries and new forms of business, which will have a major impact on the transformation and adjustment of the world economy. The industrial innovation, institutional innovation, and social governance transformation promoted by the rapid development of the global scientific and technological revolution have begun to profoundly affect the reordering of comprehensive national strength and the competitiveness of all countries. Domestically, although China has made great achievements in regard to S&T in recent years, its overall level of development in such fields is not high and remains incapable of supporting economic and social development sufficiently, with the contribution to economic growth far lower than that of developed countries. Innovation as the core of overall development will help us to keep abreast of and eventually catch up and lead these global trends.

Making innovative development central to China's overall development strategy will ensure that our country enjoys enduring peace and stability and sustains its development. The modern national competition is mainly about overall national strength and fundamentally about innovation capacity. Looking at history, the center of gravity of the world economy has moved several times, but the main axis of scientific and technological innovation has been continuously spinning, supporting economic development and guiding the global social trend. Some European and American countries seized great opportunities, such as the steam engine revolution, the electrical revolution, and the information technology revolution, and became world powers or increased their strength. By contrast, China, which repeatedly missed the tide of the world's technological revolutions, was reduced from being the world's largest economy to a backward and beaten semi-colonial and semi-feudal society. This is the lesson of history and the sorrow of the nation. Chinese society must fully absorb the experience and lessons of both ancient and modern times from all over the world, base itself on the new historical starting point, and face new practical challenges in order to adopt and implement an innovation-driven development strategy. Innovation has become the key to determining the destiny of China's development, enhancing its economic and national strength, and improving its international competitiveness and status. Putting innovation at the core of the overall development situation can not only help us to consolidate the achievements that have been made in the development and building a moderately prosperous society in all respects but also promote the sustained and sound development of the country and the harmonious development of the nation while boosting the confidence, determination, and ability to achieve the Two Centenary Goals (of building a moderately prosperous society in all respects, and building China into a great modern socialist power) on a better foundation and at a higher level.

Putting innovative development at the core of China's overall development will realize a new leap in understanding and promote all undertakings to a higher level. Putting innovation at the core of development will certainly bring about fundamental and long-term changes to the country's overall development. The history of human social development has seen the continuously influential existence of the law of innovation, which has come to dominate China just as elsewhere. The essence of innovation is constant reform, specifically reflected in transforming the old world and building a new one from the perspective of politics, improving the efficiency of traditional factors of production, creating new factors of production, and forming new combinations of factors so as to provide a steady stream of endogenous power for sustainable economic development, and to carry forward the essence of tradition while overcoming its drawbacks from the perspective of ideology and culture. Placing innovation at the center of the national development strategy, making it common practice nationwide, and constantly encouraging it not only theoretically but also across institutions, science, technology, and culture, will help to raise the whole Party's understanding of this law. This will enable the government to advance the understanding of the law of innovation in all walks of life, while pushing for fundamental, comprehensive, and long-term changes in China's overall development, building it initially into an economic and innovative power and ultimately into a great modern socialist power that is prosperous, strong, democratic, civilized and harmonious.

II. Innovation as the Primary Driving Force for Development

1. Determine China's development ideas, direction, and outlook

Innovation, especially comprehensive innovation, refers to the total-factor, whole-system, and all-around reform involving the relations between the superstructure and economic base and between production relations and productivity. Theoretical, institutional, scientific, and technological, as well as cultural innovation, have a profound impact on and provide a strong impetus for the overall situation of economic, social, and national development. Ideological and theoretical innovation belong to "brain-driven" innovation, which is the forerunner of social development and reform and also the ideological soul and methodological source of all kinds of innovative activities. Institutional innovation belongs to "motive power" innovation. It is the guarantee of sustainable innovation that can stimulate the vitality of all kinds of innovation and is also the key to leading economic and social development. Scientific and technological innovation belongs to "active power" innovation and is the top priority of overall innovation. Cultural innovation belongs to "soft power" innovation in essence and is the foundation of cultivating national vitality and cohesion, which provides inexhaustible intellectual impetus for all kinds of innovative activities. These four types of innovation represent the direction of China's development and will determine its future development.

2. Determine China's development speed, scale, structure, quality, and efficiency

Modern development features the utilization of less and less natural resources and more and more elements of innovation. China's economy is large in scale, but due to its large population and lower level of natural resources per capita, the traditional developmental path, which is dominated by land, labor, and capital, is no longer feasible. Only through innovation, especially scientific and technological innovation, and innovation-driven sustainable development, can the bottleneck of economic and social development be broken, thus allowing for a successful navigation of the middle-income trap. As China has entered a new normal in economic development, the fundamental way for it to move from the medium-low end to the medium-high end and create new advantages under the new normal is through innovation. Only through this can the country: fundamentally address the problems of unbalanced, uncoordinated, and unsustainable development; address such pressing problems as China's lack of impetus for development, its extensive growth[25] development model, its low industrial level, and the increasing constraints on resources and the environment; enhance China's development capacity; accelerate the formation of an economic system and development model that is mainly guided and supported by innovation; open up broad space for transforming the mode of economic development; optimize the economic structure; improve the ecological environment; raise the quality and efficiency of development; and promote the sustained and healthy development of China's economy and society.

3. Determine China's ability and strength to catch up with and surpass the current world leaders in S&T

Scientific and technological innovation is the core of national competitiveness and the most critical type of innovation. Therefore, innovation becoming the primary driving force for development depends largely on scientific and technological innovation. Whether innovation can form an efficient combination of the following factors by resolving the contradiction between unlimited demand and limited resources, as well as continuously increasing the effective supply of factors and continuously improving productivity, also depends upon scientific and technological innovation. Under the background of increasingly fierce international development competition and the transformation of China's development ability, the country must focus its development on innovation, form an institutional framework to promote innovation, and foster more innovation-driven development that fully enables first-mover advantages. This requires a reliance on innovation to pool and integrate high-end elements, foster new drivers of growth, rely on innovation to foster and develop high-end industries, and build new advantages, in order to create both a highland of innovation and new space for China's economic development. In addition, the government also needs to strengthen basic research, enhance original and integrated innovation, and promote the digestion, absorption and re-innovation of foreign innovation, establish strategic and frontier orientation, and promote major technological breakthroughs concerning the overall situation of development.[26] Moreover, it is necessary to strengthen the dominant position and leading role of enterprises in innovation, form a number of leading innovative enterprises with international competitiveness, promote cross-sector and cross-industry collaborative innovation, and accelerate deeper government-industry-university-research-application collaboration. China should also adhere to a global vision, promote openness and innovation, and provide strong support for economic transformation and upgrading.

III. The Development of Innovative Soft Power and the Cultivation of Innovative Talents

There are steps that can be taken to improve innovative soft power and cultivate innovative talents.

1. Advocating innovation, as innovation means future-driven development

In policy-making, institutional arrangement, and resource allocation, priority should be given to scientific and technological innovation as the most important strategic resources to improve the agglomeration ability and utilization efficiency of innovation resources. The government should also: fully enable financial capital leveraging; guide social resource investment in innovation; form a new pattern of multiple-input government funds, financial capital, and social capital; and expand the scale of investment in innovation and entrepreneurship. China should furthermore strengthen legal guarantees for innovation, foster a fair, open, and transparent market environment, enhance the motivation for innovation of various market entities, and create a social environment conducive to innovative development. Finally, China should abandon the ideas and practices that do not conform to innovation-driven development and use the innovative development concept to solve development problems, tap development potential, build on development advantages, and open up the development horizon.

2. Making talents the primary resource of innovative development

After all, innovation is about talent innovation and is driven by talent. Therefore, strengthening the nation through human resource development should be addressed by: speeding up the strategic adjustment of talent structure; highlighting the need to cultivate high-grade, high-precision, advanced, and scarce talents; striving to seek, cultivate and gather strategic scientists, leading talents in S&T, entrepreneurial talents, and highly skilled talents; and creating a number of world-class scientists, leading talents in S&T, engineers, and high-level innovation teams. China should implement a more open and active policy to attract innovative talent, focus on the cultivation of cutting-edge innovative talent and young scientific and technological talent, and strive to improve the scientific literacy of all people. The government should improve the talent evaluation and incentivization mechanism and empower leading innovative talent with greater control over human, financial, and property resources so that they can fully unleash their potential for innovative development.

3. Popularizing innovation in the whole society

Innovative development needs to be embraced by all to succeed. China should carry forward the culture of innovation, advocate the innovative spirit of being the first and daring to stand out, and make innovation a value orientation, a way of thinking, and a habit of life for the whole society. The government should: activate the wisdom and creativity of the people; stimulate the vitality of innovation and entrepreneurship; promote mass entrepreneurship and innovation; encourage the development of space for mass innovation, crowdsourcing, crowd support, and crowd funding; maximize the innovation potential of the whole society, to bring forth the vitality of all labor, knowledge, technologies, management, and capital, and foster a social atmosphere in which innovation is admired, desired and available to all.

SECTION 3
Remedying Unbalanced Development through Coordinated Development

The concept of coordinated development is the creative application of the Marxist theory of coordinated development[27] and the Party's comprehensive understanding of the laws governing economic and social development. It provides a fundamental basis for improving development conditions and efficiency and expanding development space.

I. Steady and Sustained Economic and Social Development through Coordinated Development

The significance of promoting coordinated development is as follows.

1. Avoiding the middle-income trap through coordinated development

Development requires coordination and linkage of all aspects and factors. To eliminate economic and social contradictions, China should not only promote development but also coordinate well to achieve comprehensive consideration and balance. Shortly after the end of World War II, many countries and regions fell into the "middle-income trap," with stagnant economic development plagued by employment difficulties, polarization between the rich and the poor, social unrest, rampant corruption, poor-quality housing, and a shortage of public services. Therefore, balanced and coordinated development has become a measure of whether a country can achieve sustainable growth. Only by establishing the concept of coordinated development and promoting coordinated and balanced development among different regions, sectors, and aspects can China overcome the "middle-income trap" and pave the way for the realization of the Two Centenary Goals and the Chinese Dream of national rejuvenation.

2. Coordinated development being paramount to building a moderately prosperous society in all respects

It is these latter three keywords, "in all respects," that make this goal particularly difficult. Achieving this important goal involves not only realizing prosperity in cities but also avoiding poverty in rural areas; not only the further development of East China but also the development of West China, Central China, and Northeast China; not only getting rich in material terms but also in spirit; not only achieving economic development but also enhancing environmental protection. The crucial "all respects" proviso is not met naturally but can only be a product of coordinated efforts. To realize coordination, China needs to follow through on its overall plans while maintaining a balance, systematizing the coordinated development process, integrating divergent local functions, and improving the weak areas and links so as to form a balanced development structure and enhance developmental potential. Only by firmly establishing the concept of coordinated development and adhering to it can society resolve the problems of the imbalance between different regions, between urban and rural areas, between material progress and cultural and ethical progress, and between economic and national defense development, while promoting the synchronous development of new industrialization, informatization, urbanization, agricultural modernization, and greening. Once this is done, it will enhance China's hard and soft power, as well as continuously augment the overall efficiency of development, thus allowing for a moderately prosperous society that satisfies the people in all respects.

3. Highlighting the law of development through coordinated development

Development must be socially inclusive in accordance with economic, natural, and social laws, and efforts must be made to make development more coordinated and balanced. This is a deepened and concrete manifestation of the Marxist law of the development of human society,[28] which supports the practical and effective concept of coordinated development in contemporary China. Further study should be undertaken to grasp the important statements on the following: coordinated development in Xi Jinping's Thought on Socialism with Chinese Characteristics; improve our ability to understand the law of development and the law of coordinated development; improve our ability to act in accordance with the law and promote the coordinated development of all undertakings.

II. Promoting Balanced and Coordinated Development and Making Joint Material, Cultural and Ethical Progress

The scope of coordination is the whole; the method of coordination is to fully enable the efficiency of a whole; the purpose of coordination is to enhance the wholeness of development. Coordinated development focuses on addressing the long-standing problem of unbalanced development in China, promoting sustained and sound economic and social development, and maximizing the function of the whole, which is a profound change that will affect the nation's overall development. Coordinated development requires coordination among different aspects and links of modernization construction, coordination between productivity and productive relations, and between the superstructure and the economic base. Combining the following doctrines—that everything has two aspects and that it also has key points—in accordance with the overall layout of the cause of socialism with Chinese characteristics will allow for a successful realization of the aforementioned four-pronged comprehensive strategy. This is the basic requirement for adhering to materialist dialectics,[29] considered here a prerequisite for sustained and sound economic and social development and an important principle for accomplishing economic and social work.

1. Adherence to coordinated development among regions and between city and countryside

Coordination requires regional balance to realize the balanced development of different regions as a whole. China has a vast territory with different natural conditions, natural resources, and historical bases in different regions. Therefore, there has long been a great gap in development among different regions. So, leadership needs to coordinate the overall development strategy of the entire nation, which entails: the development of West China, the revitalization of Northeast China, and the rise of Central China, all spearheaded by the more advanced region of East China. The government should accelerate the establishment and improvement of the mechanisms and institutions for the integrated development of urban and rural areas, improve the long-term mechanism of rural infrastructure investment, promote the extension of urban public services to the countryside, and improve the level of socialist new rural construction. New patterns of coordinated regional development should be shaped featuring: the orderly and free flow of elements, effective implementation of the functional zoning strategy, equal access to basic public services, and adequate supply of resources—bearing in mind the natural capacity of the environment, while striving to realize balanced regional development as a whole. There should be coordination and promotion of the four-pronged comprehensive strategy and the five-sphere integrated plan;[30] coordination of material progress with cultural and ethical progress; promotion of the coordinated development of the economy and society; promotion of the synchronous development of new industrialization, informatization, urbanization and agricultural modernization; enhancement of China's hard power as well as soft power; broadening of the development space during coordinated development; and bolstering of the momentum of development while strengthening weak areas so as to break new ground in coordinated and balanced development as quickly as possible.

2. Economic development kept in step with social development and integrated with national defense development

Coordination requires an overall balance in all fields, and efforts should be made to promote an overall balance between economic, social, and national defense construction. Since reform and opening-up, China's economy has developed rapidly. However, China's social construction has lagged behind and is prone to problems such as the middle-income trap—so often the Achilles heel of numerous other nations as they continued along their respective paths of development—which has led to a series of social contradictions. This requires the country to devote more energy and resources to improving education, employment, social security, medical and public health, and environmental protection while developing the economy so as to address the most immediate and practical issues of greatest concern to the people and ensure that all the people can share the development fruits. In the meantime, it must be noted that maintaining the achievements of development requires a strong national defense capability and a stable environment for development. To this end, the government should deeply root the national defense construction in the country's economic and social matrix. This entails accelerating the formation of an all-factor, multifield, and highly efficient pattern of deeply integrated military and civilian development, to enable national defense construction to gain more profound material support and development momentum from economic and social construction, and enable the latter to derive a more powerful security guarantee and technical support from national defense construction.

3. Equal importance attached to material, cultural and ethical progress

Coordination requires us to ensure balanced development of not just material progress but also cultural and ethical progress. Some local governments have been accustomed to taking GDP growth as the most important indicator, while neglecting ideological and cultural progress and the improvement of social civilization. Therefore, material cultural and ethical progress need to be advanced together, ensuring the parallel development of both hard and soft power. Leadership should stick to the orientation of an advanced socialist culture, speed up cultural reform and development, promote socialist cultural and ethical progress, and build a socialist cultural power. Our capacity for international communication should be strengthened, and Chinese culture should be promoted globally. The government should build consensus and pool strength by virtue of the Chinese Dream and core socialist values, guiding the people to strengthen our confidence in the path, theory, and system of socialism with Chinese characteristics and unite people of all ethnic groups in China to build a great modern socialist country.

SECTION 4
Creating Harmony between People and Nature through Green Development

Man is part of nature but also, due to our high level of consciousness, a potential protector or destroyer of it; we, as human beings dependent on the living ecosystem for our survival, must respect nature, follow its ways, and protect it. Only by observing the laws of nature can mankind avoid costly blunders in its exploitation. The modernization that China pursues is one characterized by harmonious coexistence between man and nature. In addition to creating more material and cultural wealth to meet people's ever-increasing needs for a better life, we also need to provide more quality ecological goods to meet people's ever-growing needs for a beautiful environment. Taking green development as an important concept of China's overall development reflects our Party's deepened understanding of the laws governing economic and social development.

I. Green Development Bears on China's Overall Development

The concept of green development is an enlightened conclusion drawn from rational reflection on the problems of the times. Due to China's recent decades of rapid economic growth, the country's carrying capacity of resources and the environment is approaching its limit. The traditional development mode characterized by high input, high consumption, and high pollution is no longer sustainable. This extensive development mode has not only overwhelmed China's energy and resources but also caused a wide range of environmental problems, such as haze, water pollution, and excessive levels of heavy metals in the soil. All these show that the biggest bottleneck for China to enter the new era is resources and protection of the environment. With the value orientation of harmony between man and nature, the main principle of green, low-carbon, and circular development, and the basic starting point of ecological civilization construction, the concept of green development embodies the Party's scientific insight into the necessary characteristics of China's economic and social development at the current stage. Taking the path of green, low-carbon, and circular development is essential for China to break through the bottleneck of resource depletion and environmental protection and also an inevitable choice for us to adjust the economic structure, change the mode of development, and realize sustainable development.

The concept of green development contains an accurate insight into the present moment. In today's world, countries have become an ecological community with a shared future of close interdependence, encapsulated in Chairman Mao's poetry—"Warm and Cold, We Share Together."[31] Over the past few years, increasingly severe global issues such as greenhouse gas emissions, ozone layer destruction, chemical pollution, excessive air pollution, and biodiversity reduction have posed unprecedented threats to global ecological security. The construction of an ecological civilization has thus become the trend of development and the consensus of more and more countries and people, with a huge bearing on the future of mankind. Therefore, the international community should join hands to enable global ecological civilizational construction. China's leadership has not only produced a systematic top-level design and specific plans for promoting the construction of an ecological civilization but also elevated it to the height of the development strategy of the Party and the country, demonstrating responsible leadership as a great power. To maintain global ecological security, the Party has actively participated in the formulation of international green economy regulations and global sustainable development goals and strengthened international exchanges in green S&T.

The concept of green development is based on a deep understanding of the law of development. To promote China's socialist modernization construction, the government should: have a clear understanding of how to transition from industrial civilization to ecological civilization; give high priority to the construction of an ecological civilization in the overall landscape of modernization; ensure green development's integration into the economic, political, cultural and social construction processes; act on the principles of prioritizing resource and environmental protection and letting nature restore itself; and develop spatial layouts, industrial structures, and ways of work and life that help conserve resources and protect the environment. With this, China can restore the serenity, harmony, and beauty of nature.

II. Promoting Green Development and Building a Beautiful China

1. Working to build a truly rich country through green development

Wealth serves as the foundation of a powerful country, and resources and the environment serve as the foundation of a rich country. Today's scientific and technological revolution is oriented toward green, low-carbon, and circular development, with broad prospects for development. In particular, the energy conservation and environmental protection industries contain many new sources of economic growth. China should therefore build a rich country through green development. Specifically, it should, in terms of the development mode, promote the transition from the extensive mode with low-cost factor input and high ecological and environmental costs to the "double wheel drive" mode of innovative and green development and, in terms of energy and resources utilization, promote the transition from low efficiency and high emissions to high efficiency, greenness, and safety. The government should rapidly boost the energy conservation and environmental protection of industry, further promote the circular economy (for example, in the green upgrading process of industrial clusters), accelerate the diffusion and application of green and smart technologies, and thus promote the rise of green manufacturing and green service industries. To implement the concept of green development and promote the building of a rich country through green development, leadership should: properly handle the relationship between economic development and environmental protection; establish the concept of an ecological civilization respecting, conforming to, and protecting nature; pursue a model of sustainable development featuring increased production, higher living standards, and healthy ecosystems; and strive to make green development strongly supportive of promoting China's prosperity.

2. Improving people's livelihoods through green development

The concept of green development takes improving people's livelihoods through green development as its basic value orientation. A sound ecological environment is the fairest and most inclusive public product. To improve the ecological environment is to improve people's livelihoods. With the dramatic economic and social development and the improvement of people's living standards since reform and opening-up, people have a higher and higher demand for the ecological environment, and its quality holds an increasingly prominent position in the happiness index. However, the current ecological environment quality in China is still not satisfactory, which has become a weak link affecting people's quality of life and may even evolve into a social and political issue. The strategy of adhering to green development and benefiting the people by providing clean water, fresh air, safe food, and a beautiful environment bears on the fundamental interests of the overwhelming majority of the people, on the long-term interests of the development of the Chinese nation, and is a scientific choice made by the Party to improve people's well-being in the new era.

3. Promoting green production

A green production mode is the basis for the concept of green development. Only by making the economy substantially greener and promoting the formation of a green production mode can Chinese society forge a bright future integrating economic growth and a healthy environment. Therefore, the government should strive to build an industrial structure with higher scientific and technological content, less resource consumption, and less environmental pollution, speed up the development of green industries, and form new growth points for economic and social development. Developing green industries means avoiding the use of harmful materials, reducing the waste of materials and energy in the production process, improving the utilization rate of resources, reducing waste emissions, strengthening waste treatment, and promoting the greening of the entire industry chain from product design, production and development to product packaging and distribution. Together, this will realize a virtuous cycle between the ecosystem and the economic system and realize the organic unity of economic, ecological, and social benefits.

4. Building a beautiful China

The concept of green development aims to build a beautiful China, which not only clarifies the important goal orientation of China's current development but also enriches the blueprint for the Chinese Dream. It is the great responsibility and mission of the Party to govern and rejuvenate the country in the new era to persist in green development and build a beautiful and sustainable China for both living and working. To this end, the leadership should: speed up the construction of a number of major ecological and environmental functional zones; establish a scientific and reasonable pattern of urbanization, agricultural development, ecological security, and maintenance of the natural shoreline; implement ecological protection and restoration projects of mountains, rivers, forests, farmland, and lakes; launch a large-scale land greening campaign; and improve the system for protecting natural forests. Efforts should be strengthened to promote the establishment of an industrial system for green, low-carbon, and circular development, promote the development of a low-carbon circular economy, and implement conservation across the board and the efficient use of resources.

III. Green Development as a Responsibility Shared by All

1. Developing a green value orientation

As a Chinese saying goes, "Green mountains and clear water are as good as mountains of gold and silver,"[32] which emphasizes that a beautiful ecological environment is both productive capacity and social wealth and highlights the important value of the ecological environment in economic and social development. This saying emphasizes that the ecological environment and economic and social development will supplement each other, that neither of them can thus be ignored, and that as a nation, China should regard the win-win situation of ecological beauty and economic growth as an important value standard for scientific development. The saying also emphasizes that green mountains and clear water are more precious than mountains of gold and silver, indicating that when the protection of the ecological environment conflicts with economic and social development, the protection of the former must receive priority. To adhere to green development, the following needs to be done: develop a green value orientation; properly handle the relationship between economic development and ecological environment protection; firmly establish the concept that protecting the ecological environment is equal to protecting and developing productive capacity; and promote green development, low-carbon development, and circular development more consciously. The ecological environment should never be sacrificed for temporary economic growth.

2. Developing the thinking mode of green development

To establish and practice the concept of green development, a green way of thinking should be developed, encompassing five areas, as follows.

First, being problem-oriented: deeply analyzing and thinking about the key issues affecting green development and striving to solve a series of outstanding problems in ecological protection and environmental governance.

Second, being innovative: using novel methods to deal with new problems in the construction of an ecological civilization and eliminating the old thinking and old approaches of "treatment after pollution" and "end-of-pipe treatment."

Third, thinking about worst-case scenarios: taking into account both the needs of this generation and those of future generations without eroding the environmental carrying capacity necessary for economic and social development.

Fourth, being law-based: thinking and acting in accordance with the law to plan for green development by guiding, regulating, promoting, and guaranteeing the construction of an ecological civilization with scientific legislation, strict law enforcement, fair administration of justice, and observance of law by all. In this regard, improvements in environmental protection legislation should be sped up and environmental laws rigorously enforced, environmental governance strengthened, and a solid barrier for ecological security built.

Fifth, thinking in a systematic way: attaching importance to the construction of ecological civilization in the five-sphere integrated plan for socialism with Chinese characteristics and considering green development as a systematic endeavor within scientific and overall planning.[33]

3. Developing a green lifestyle

A green lifestyle touches everyone's daily lives. It reflects our recognition and practice of the concept of green development and plays a fundamental and key role in the ultimate realization of green development and ecological civilization. Everyone is responsible for protecting the environment, and everyone should contribute to green development. People should advocate and practice frugal, green, low-carbon, civilized, and healthy lifestyles anandption modes. People should promote the development of a green lifestyle, giving priority to conservation, strengthening the awareness of full resource utilization, and developing a sense of conservation and full resource utilization clothing, food, housing, transportation, and tourism. People should advocate environment-friendly consumption, promote green clothing, a green diet, green housing, green transportation, and green tourism, and resist and oppose extravagance, waste, and unreasonable consumption. Green development is not only a concept but also a practice. People should not only sit down calmly to plan carefully but also stand up boldly to take positive actions. People should accelerate the building of a resource-conserving and environmentally friendly society, realizing harmony between human beings and nature, and advancing the program of building a beautiful China so as to leave green hills and clear waters to future generations and make new contributions to global ecological security.

SECTION 5

Optimizing both Domestically and Externally Oriented Development through "Open Development"

China and the world's development are mutually reinforcing. China's development under reform and opening-up laid the foundations not only for the country's own prosperity but also for the journey of the whole world to an inclusive community with a shared future for mankind. The concept of open development provides a guide to action for improving the quality of this development and the domestic and external relationship.

I. Open Development Provides Opportunity for Profound Changes

1. An advanced concept that accurately captures domestic and international development trends

In recent years, the opening-up policy has faced a new trend, with the policy's basis and condition changing deeply. From the international perspective, in the post-COVID era, the world economy is faced with deep adjustments due to the trauma caused by the pandemic. International economic cooperation and competition have changed deeply. All nations need to join hands to tackle challenges in development and economic globalization while at the same time competing with each other in advancing cutting-edge technology, integrating the global value chain, and restructuring trade rules. From the domestic perspective, the Chinese economy has adapted to the new normal at high speed. To advance the new normal and seize this vital strategic opportunity, China must promote high-quality development at a high level. This increased pace of open development is not a chance to continue with the past approaches but to pursue an open economy at a higher level via new measures and ways of thinking. This should be based on domestic realities, taking advantage of not only the resources, market, and regimen but also both domestic and international markets. China should promote reform, development, and innovation by opening up and mutually sharing the fruits with every country.

2. A scientific concept that helps us deepen our understanding of the development law

It has already been said that openness brings progress, while self-seclusion leaves one behind, which is especially true in the economic globalization era. Since the end of World War II, with the upsurge of economic globalization, manufacturing has become more internationalized than ever, and global economic ties have been getting closer and closer. From relative poverty, China has become the world's second-largest economy and the number one international trading country, owing to deepening reform and expanding openness. The power of opening up accords with the development law. In the current era, the nation can only acquire capital, technology, resources, increased markets, and opportunities on demand by opening up internationally. Only then can full use be made of comparative advantages and create more social wealth. Through open development, China is able to learn lessons from domestic and international experiences and seize the key to economic globalization, reflecting a better understanding of the laws of economic and social development.

3. Insistence on open development brings profound changes

Insisting on opening up is the only way of promoting innovation in the face of fierce international competition, developing talent, and injecting new impetus for innovative development; promoting the domestic and international economic connection and acquiring new space for coordinated development in expanding the international market; promoting better development and acquiring a new basis for shared international development. Open development is a concept, regimen, and pattern that not only advances China to deepen its reform into an export-oriented economy but also promotes mutual benefit cooperation with all nations.

II. Promoting International Cooperation and Upgrading the Open Economy

The core of open development is to promote interactions between China and the international community, and the goal is to improve the quality of opening up and to develop a higher-level open economy. Open development means pursuing a set of policies that are both active and equal, as well as comprehensive and mutually beneficial, in an effort to upgrade China's open economy on all fronts.

1. Active opening-up

China should take opening up as an intrinsic requirement and boost the opening-up process more actively. It should: insist on implementing opening up with a broader scope and depth and build up a new development pattern giving priority to domestic circulation, which is promoted by both domestic and international circulation; perfect the mechanism conducive to international trade and investment rules and mutual benefits; have a louder voice over international regimes in global economic management by participating in global governance; realize the organic unification between opening up and safeguarding economic security; and seek a higher level of overall well-being in boosting opening up. In recent years, China has made steady progress in strengthening cooperation between the G20 nations, promoting Belt and Road cooperation, and setting up the Asian Infrastructure Investment Bank (AIIB). In the post-COVID era, the global economy is recovering slowly, and international trade protectionism is on the rise. China insists on following the opening-up policy unswervingly, which demonstrates its responsibility as a major promoter of global free trade.

2. Two-way opening-up

Paying equal attention to inward and outward-oriented trade is a main feature of an open economy at a higher stage and an effective way of coordinating both domestic and international markets, resources, and rules. For inward-oriented trade, China has been accelerating the transformation of economic development and paying more attention to attracting quality capital investments. It has also been focusing on learning technological innovation from international investments, advanced management experience, and high-quality international talent. For outward-oriented trade, China has been: broadening its horizons from being a large trading nation to a nation with a deep and comprehensive integration of markets, energy resources, and investments that are directed toward investment in the outside world; providing support for Chinese entrepreneurship; boosting investment with the outside world; and promoting the outward-oriented trade process for equipment, technology, standards, and services in order to improve China's position in the global value chain. Promoting two-way opening-up requires an orderly circulation between domestic and international markets, efficient allocation of resources, and deep market merging.

3. Equal opening-up

This means creating a development atmosphere for domestic and foreign investment with fair competition. Equal opening-up should: change the past measures whereby foreign investment relied on preferential policies for providing land and revenue; provide equal and bright markets for foreign investment; make the production factors, market competition, and legal protection equal for all; implement a system of pre-established national treatment plus a negative list across the board; and significantly expand market access. All businesses registered in China will be treated equally. The policies and protection for their legal right toward foreign capital will never be changed. The direction of change will never change for providing better service for foreign capital in China and strengthening the confidence of overseas enterprises for long-term development in China.

4. All-around opening-up

Arrange new measures, contents, and space for opening up and make new ground in pursuing bidirectional opening up on all fronts. All-around opening-up reflects in measures: insisting on independence and equivalence; strengthening the outward-oriented investment strategy; accelerating the free trade zone strategy; coordinating multilateral, bilateral, and regional opening-up and cooperation; promoting Belt and Road cooperation, enabling links running eastward and westward, across land and over sea. It reflects in contents: further liberalize the general manufacturing sector; promote the orderly opening-up of the service sector and the two-way opening-up of the financial sector; promote infrastructure connectivity. It reflects in space: change the pattern that East China is faster than West China and coastland better than inland; restructure a new pattern of coastland and inland cooperation and interaction. To advance all-around opening-up, China needs to strengthen strategic mutual trust, economic and trade cooperation, and people-to-people exchanges.

5. Mutually beneficial opening-up

Strengthen international exchanges and cooperation and make economic globalization more inclusive so that its benefits are shared by all. At the beginning of 2017, faced with reverse globalization, including conservatism, populism, protectionism, and exclusivism, the world had to make a choice for its peace and development: open or close, cooperate or choose conflict, reform or conserve. President Xi Jinping delivered the keynote speeches "Shoulder Responsibility of Our Times and Promote Global Growth Together" and "Work Together to Build a Community of Shared Future for Mankind" successively at Davos and the United Nations (UN) Office in Geneva. China announced that it stands against retrogression, reverse globalization, and protectionism. He said that China would make economic globalization more inclusive so that its benefits are shared by all with the concept of building a community with a shared future for mankind, which drew widespread attention. In the post-COVID era, economic globalization has been severely hit. Upholding the opening-up policy, China calls for an open global economy and strengthening of the multilateral trade mechanism, providing enough space for world development. China advocates regional free trade as a supplement to multilateral trade rather than a blockade, making economic globalization more inclusive so that its benefits are shared by all. Open development provides a broader market and development space, which forms a new win-win pattern. Promoting win-win opening-up requires all-around multi-tiered international cooperation and boosting the converging interests of all countries and regions to achieve mutual benefits.

III. Open Development that Promotes Mutually Beneficial International Cooperation

1. Advancing Belt and Road cooperation

The Belt and Road Initiative (BRI) is a major strategic initiative of China aimed at promoting international cooperation based on the principle of consultation, contribution, and shared benefits. Under the guidance of openness, inclusiveness, and mutual learning, the BRI is people-oriented and is improving bilateral and multilateral cooperative mechanisms in order to promote pragmatic cooperation with related countries and regions in various fields. It seeks better connectivity in policy, infrastructure, trade, and financial services and closer ties between the peoples of various countries. It encourages cooperation in education, technology, culture, tourism, hygiene, and environmental protection and the joint building of financial cooperative platforms featuring openness, diversification, and mutual benefits, providing new drivers for world sustainable development and bringing true benefits for people along the route.

2. Fostering new advantages on international cooperation and competition

Forming a new system of opening up is the key to fostering new advantages. China should establish a trade facilitation system and mechanism and fully implement single-window document processing for international trade and customs clearance integration; improve the quality of free trade pilot zones and replicate them on a larger scale; make an innovative management system for foreign investment and fully implement the pre-access national treatment plus negative list management system; improve the overseas investment management system, and cancel various unreasonable restrictions toward overseas investment; accelerate the construction of an open and safe financial system, improve the foreign-related legal and regulatory system, and establish a sound risk prevention and control system. Through the comprehensive deepening of reforms, China will vigorously create a competitive and orderly market environment, a transparent and efficient government environment, a fair and just legal environment, a win-win cultural environment, and a legal and international facilitation business environment while accelerating the formation of a business environment conducive to the cultivation of new institutional arrangements for comparative competitive advantages.

3. Breaking new ground in the opening-up strategy

To improve the local impact of opening up, China should implement the idea of combining open economic development with coordinated regional development, support Chinese coastal areas to fully participate in global economic cooperation and competition, accelerate the pace of opening up of inland and border areas, and form opening up bases with different emphases.

To improve the impact of foreign trade, China should accelerate the optimization and upgrading of trade, promote the transformation of foreign trade from large import and export volumes to high-quality and high-price, and strive to build a strong trade country. To improve two-way investment while vigorously introducing foreign capital and advanced technology, China should support local enterprises to expand their overseas investment, actively build a financial service platform, and provide better financial services for international production capacity and equipment manufacturing cooperation. At the same time, leadership should pay attention to deepening the cooperation and development between the mainland and Hong Kong, Macau, and Taiwan.

4. Improving the reform of the global economic governance system

In recent years, China's concept of building a community with a shared future for mankind has become increasingly popular and widely accepted by the international community. It has been seen in many UN documents and resolutions. This concept, which is in line with the trend of the times, is extremely inclusive and forward-looking, transcends nations, countries, and ideologies, and is not only a new concept for reforming and improving global governance but also a new direction for the development of economic globalization, as well as being a boost to the world's modern economic thinking. In this interlocked world, it is impossible for any country, enterprise, or individual to deal with the challenges on the international stage alone., which requires the globe to work together to build a community with a shared future. The historical trend of shifting to a new model of globalization featuring peace and development, win-win cooperation, mutual respect, equality, and mutual benefit, and building a community with a shared future for mankind is unstoppable. China strives to promote mutually beneficial international cooperation and has become a backbone force promoting a new international economic order that advocates equality, justice, and win-win cooperation.

SECTION 6
Shared Development Enabling Social Fairness and Justice

Joint contribution and shared benefits represent the ideal state of economic and social development. In essence, the concept of sharing is a people-centered development philosophy. It reflects the requirements of gradually realizing common prosperity, the fundamental purpose of the Communist Party to serve the people wholeheartedly, the historical materialism that the people are the fundamental driving force for historical development, the essence of socialism, and the purpose of the Party, and the fundamental development concept of scientifically planning for the well-being of the people and long-term peace and stability of the country.

I. Shared Development That Lifts the Whole Nation

1. Only by promoting shared development can the promotion of national stability, ethnic unity, and advanced development be realized

The modern development concept does not come into being out of thin air but comes from the effort of summarizing, reflecting, and transcending development practices. From international experience and lessons, some countries have not shared their development equally with others. Unfortunately, throughout history, the advancements of some populations have been based on the losses or deprivation of other people, resulting in antagonism between different social groups and even social disruption and fragmentation, constant internal strife, and endless ethnic conflicts. Such internal friction has seriously hindered the development of these countries and the well-being of their people. Therefore, with the reflection on the failure of economic growth to bring about a sufficient reduction in poverty, the international community has put forward concepts such as "broad-based growth," "shared growth," "pro-poor growth," and "inclusive growth."[34] These ideas and practices have achieved certain results in improving people's living standards and promoting social fairness and justice. The concept of shared development proposed by President Xi Jinping is a reference to and transcendence of these experiences and lessons. Therefore, China should adhere to the people-oriented principle, put the people first, guide China's development with the concept of shared development, safeguard social fairness and justice, and ensure development is for the people and by the people and with its benefits shared by all the people. Only by pursuing shared development can China achieve national stability, ethnic unity, and people's satisfaction and keep up with and lead the development trend of the times.

2. Only by pursuing shared development can China achieve the Two Centenary Goals and the great rejuvenation of the Chinese nation

The development philosophy serves the respective goals, and great goals require a valid scientific concept of development to back them up. Achieving the Two Centenary Goals is today's great cause of governing and rejuvenating the country under the leadership of the Party and the people of all ethnic groups. From the perspective of the first centenary goal of building a moderately prosperous society in all respects, such a society with only satisfactory "gross value" and "per capita GDP" is not a moderately prosperous society in all respects, and the false state of some parts of the population being declared "moderately prosperous" may damage the value of such a society, compromising the actual progress. A moderately prosperous society in all respects means that the benefits are shared by all and that no one should be left behind. This is exactly where the difficulty lies and what leadership needs to tackle. To achieve this kind of society, China should plan in accordance with the concept of shared development, achieving a general improvement in people's living standards and quality, and especially helping poor areas and poor people leave poverty behind. From the perspective of the second centenary goal of building China into a great modern socialist power, China should pursue shared development and ensure that everyone has a sense of gain and a stronger sense of well-being. The universal enjoyment of the fruits of reform and development is the core principle and fundamental task of the Party and the first yardstick to judge whether the Two Centenary Goals have been achieved.

3. Only shared development can promote the Sinicization, modernization, and popularization of the Marxist Outlook on Development[35]

This development outlook should not only answer the questions of the driving force, thinking, direction, and layout of development but also answer the questions of who the development is for and who should enjoy its benefits so as to systematically grasp the law of development.

The concept of shared development clearly answers the question of who should share the benefits of development; that is, it should be shared by the people and, of course, especially the Chinese people. The nation should adhere to the idea of people-centered development, which is the fundamental position of the Marxist political economy. Shared development means insisting on improving people's well-being, promoting people's all-around development, and making steady progress toward common prosperity as both the starting point and goal of economic development. The concept of shared development is a theoretical innovation that closely combines the Marxist Outlook on Development with the reality, the trend of the times, and the expectations of the masses in today's China, as well as a theoretical innovation involving promoting social fairness and justice, which will allow us to gradually realize the common prosperity of all people. It is the adherence to and development of the Scientific Outlook on Development and further promotes the Sinicization, modernization, and popularization of that Outlook, lifting our understanding of the law of development to a new level.

II. Building a Fair Society through Shared Development

Sharing is not only an ideal but something tangible. It should be based on the premise of promoting social fairness and justice and a focus on poverty alleviation and narrowing the income gap. To achieve this, China should promote equal access to basic public services between different regions and between urban and rural areas. The purpose of sharing is to achieve common prosperity.

1. Implementing shared development requires a people-first ideology

China's goal is to put the people first and live up to the people's aspiration for a better life. In various work arrangements and development plans, leadership should adhere to the position of the Chinese people as masters of the country, adhere to the governing idea of development for the people, development by the people, and with development achievements shared by the people, while always keeping the people's suffering in mind, regarding the people's aspiration for a better life as the goal of the work of governments at all levels and constantly meeting the people's ever-growing economic, political, cultural, social, ecological and environmental needs. Only in this way can China harness the enthusiasm, initiative, and creativity of the people, draw on the efforts of the whole people to advance the cause of socialism with Chinese characteristics, make the size of the market bigger and bigger, and increase development momentum to unite the people further toward a shared goal of common prosperity.

2. Implementing shared development requires systems improvement

China should fully guarantee and fully enable the basic rights that the people should enjoy in all aspects and share out the ever-growing "pie" so as to fully demonstrate the superiority of the socialist system and give the entire population an increased sense of shared gain. Leadership should always take full employment as one of the main objectives of the government's work, implementing more proactive employment policies, striving to create more jobs, improving policies to support entrepreneurship, and encouraging job growth through the creation of new businesses. China should further improve the reform of the income distribution system, continuously increase the income of urban and rural residents, expand the middle-income group, and constantly narrow the income gap. Leadership should establish a fairer, more robust, and more sustainable social security system, promote the development of pension, medical care, unemployment, work-related injury, and maternity insurance for urban workers and urban and rural residents, and strive to achieve full coverage of the social security system. China should enhance the role of transfer payments and reform and improve the social assistance system, to make policy-based poverty alleviation and assistance more accurate, timely, effective, and reasonable.

3. Poverty alleviation and narrowing the income gap

Sharing is not about egalitarianism. To achieve sharing, a wealth gap is admitted and allowed, but the gap should be controlled within a reasonable range to prevent extreme disparity between the rich and the poor, and efforts should be made to eliminate poverty in particular. Currently, poverty alleviation has become the most arduous task in building a moderately prosperous society in all respects and the most basic requirement for promoting shared development. It was a solemn commitment made by the Party to the people to ensure that the rural population living below the current poverty standard got rid of poverty by 2020, something which was achieved.[36] On the basis of promoting poverty alleviation, China should continue to build on the current trend and narrow the income gap. If the income gap does not narrow, there will be no solid foundation for shared development. While making the pie bigger, leadership must make sure that it is well distributed so as to form a pattern of income distribution that reflects the requirements of fairness and justice and conforms to the orientation of shared development.

4. Equal access to basic public services between regions and urban and rural areas

Basic public services must adhere to the principles of inclusive, basic, equitable, and sustainable development. Strengthening and optimizing public services is an important way to promote social fairness, justice, and common prosperity. Currently, there is a large gap in the level of basic public services between East, Central, and West China and between urban and rural areas. In particular, the old revolutionary base areas, ethnic minority areas, border areas, and poor areas have relatively limited financial resources, and a relatively low level of basic public services, thus holding them back from enjoying the fruits of the nation's overall labor. Shared development should cover everyone and should start by solving the most realistic issues affecting people's immediate interests and those of the greatest concern to the people, focus on the weak areas and disadvantaged groups, improve and maximize coverage of the basic public service system so that all parts of the country are provided with basically equal access to basic public services that benefit all the people.

5. Gradual realization of common prosperity goal

Sharing means benefit sharing by broad masses of people, with the purposes of eliminating the extreme disparity between the rich and the poor and avoiding polarization in income distribution. China should, by dismantling the economic straitjacket and unlocking the growth potential, eventually achieve common prosperity for all the people. Poverty is not socialism, nor is polarization. The essence of Chinese socialism is to ensure that the people share the fruits of reform and development and achieve common prosperity. Achieving common prosperity is a long-term process that will not happen overnight.

III. Full Participation, Joint Contribution, and Shared Benefits

People contribute so that they can share the benefits, and if they want to take a share, they must make a contribution. Only by creating a sound environment in which everyone participates, contributes, and shares the benefits can the government strengthen the advantages of development, pool the strength of development, and raise the level of development. There are three tasks that must be addressed.

1. Creating a sound environment for joint contribution and benefit sharing through institutional innovation and good guidance of public opinion

Whether the impetus for joint contribution and the level of benefit sharing can be enhanced depends on how sound the social environment is. The key is to improve the institutional environment and the ideological and public opinion environment. To improve the institutional environment, China should carefully review its institutions, mechanisms, policies, and regulations in all aspects, guarantee everyone's right to participate, offer everyone the opportunity to do their part, and ensure that everyone enjoys the fruits of reform and development through institutional innovation. To improve the ideological and public opinion environment, the Party should arm the national and local leadership with theories so that they realize that shared development is crucial to the success of development, to the well-being of the people, to the ruling status of the Party, and to the long-term peace and stability of the country. The CPC should, through extensive publicity and guidance, make the masses realize that the cause of socialism with Chinese characteristics belongs to hundreds of millions of people who, of course, enjoy the benefits and have the responsibility of making due contributions. Just as the saying goes, "Where many help to gather firewood, the flames shoot high."[37] By working on public opinion guidance and institutional innovation, a sound environment for joint contribution and benefit sharing can be created, and the level of joint contribution and benefit sharing can be constantly raised.

2. Continuously improving people's well-being through quality and capacity improvement

Whether shared development can be harnessed for social and economic development and satisfy the people is a test of the governance capacity of the Party and the quality and capability of the "critical minority"—the national and local leadership. A new concept requires new actions, and new actions rely on excellent quality and ability. To promote development, national and local leadership must keep benefit sharing and the concept of the people in mind. They should resolutely do what is conducive to shared development and never do the opposite. They should strengthen investigation and study, recognize and grasp particular opportunities and situations, enhance practical experience, acquire several skills, develop new ideas and measures to promote shared development, measure and test the actual work with sharing as the benchmark, devote great energy to addressing obstacles and problems affecting shared development, make development more fair and inclusive, and endow all people with a greater sense of benefit and happiness in development.

3. Working together to promote national development with the participation and contribution of all

Without joint contribution, there can be no benefit sharing. Shared development is not only about everyone sharing the benefits but also about everyone participating and making a contribution to the development of the country, the revitalization of the nation, and the well-being of individuals. Today, although China has leaped to be the second-largest economy in the world and has greatly improved its comprehensive national strength, it is still in the primary stage of socialism. China still lags far behind developed countries in terms of per capita GDP, the level of S&T and education, and the ecological level. Even if China overtakes the US and becomes the world's largest economy in the future, its per capita GDP will remain low. Therefore, there is no room for complacency, and no one should expect to rest on their laurels. Sharing is not about profiting from other people's toil but should be based on the premise of joint contribution and efforts.

CHAPTER SEVEN

Building a Modern Economic System

In the context of implementing the new development concept and building a modern economic system, how can a broader understanding be gained of the necessary scientific connotations for such a system? Why should such a system be built, and how should it be done? These are the three major theoretical and practical problems that require serious study to be understood comprehensively.

SECTION 1

Scientific Connotation of a Modern Economic System

Building a modern economic system is a very ambitious undertaking. It is not only a major theoretical proposition but also a huge practical challenge. Such a system is an organic whole composed of the interrelation and internal connection of all links, levels, and fields of social and economic activities.

I. Building an Innovation-Led and Coordinated Industrial System

The system of industrial organization is an important component of the production links of an economic system, as well as its material basis. Modern industrial systems should be comprised of high-end, high-value-added, technological, and knowledge-intensive industries in the global value chain with international market competitiveness representing the direction of industrial upgrading and consumption structure transformation being a future goal. Although China has established a relatively complete industrial system at present, the quality and efficiency of the organic combination of elements such as human resources, capital, and technologies within that system need to be urgently improved; the trend of talent and capital being distracted from their intended purpose has not been fundamentally reversed; and the transformation from technological innovation and scientific and technological achievements to actual productivity remains stuck in a long cycle with a relatively low transformation rate. To address these problems, steps need to be taken to speed up the construction of a modern industrial system, to regard the real economy as the main body of the coordinated development of economic construction and industry, to boost industrial upgrading with scientific and technological innovation, to continuously feed the modern economic system through the financial system, to constantly improve the quality of human resources, and finally to fully improve the quality and efficiency of collaborative input of labor, capital, and technology.

II. Building a Unified and Open Market System with Orderly Competition

The core mechanism of a modern economic system is a modern market system, which is an organic unity that includes the factor market and all markets derived from it. Currently, China's socialist market economic system continues to improve, but there still exist some outstanding problems, such as non-standard market order, underdeveloped factor markets, idleness of factors, and large unmet effective needs. In addition, China's socialist market economic system remains hindered by non-uniform market rules, rampant sectoral and local protectionism, inadequate market competition, which impedes the survival of the fittest, structural adjustment, and so on. To resolve these problems, China must speed up the construction of a unified, open, and orderly competitive market system so that the market plays a decisive role in the allocation of resources. Fully implementing the negative list system for market access, sorting out and abolishing regulations and practices that impede the unified market and fair competition, breaking administrative monopolies, precluding the forming of market monopolies, speeding up the reform of market-based pricing of factors of production, removing market barriers, improving the efficiency and fairness of resource allocation should all be priorities; along with realizing smooth market access, standardized market opening and order, flexible pricing responses, sufficient, fair and orderly competition and effective protection and incentives for property rights. Speeding up the formation of a modern market system featuring independent operation and fair competition of enterprises, with business survival determined by competition, free choice, and free consumption by consumers combined with the free flow and equal exchange of commodities and various other factors should also be a central focus.

III. Building an Efficient and Fair Income Distribution System

The income distribution system is a fundamental and basic institutional arrangement for economic and social development. It is an important cornerstone of the socialist modern economic system and an endogenous driver for development. To build a modern economic system, in the distribution link, the government should realize reasonable income distribution, social fairness and justice, and common prosperity for all the people. Therefore, adherence to and improvement of the basic system of socialist distribution must be the goal, along with attaching importance to efficiency and fairness in primary distribution and redistribution, insisting on the distribution system of multiple modes of distribution in the principle of "to each according to his work." This would entail a better combination of the distribution according to one's performance, the distribution according to factors of production, and handling of the distribution relations among the government, enterprises, and residents. In addition, increasing and guaranteeing the property income of urban and rural residents, broadening the investment channels for the public to participate in the sharing of development dividends, strengthening the protection of property rights in the non-public sector and the protection of intellectual property rights and enhancing people's sense of property security must all be implemented. China should also increase the government's expenditure on people's livelihoods and promote equal access to basic public services. Efforts should also be made to promote the spirit of achieving prosperity through hard work. This would mean encouraging people to create a better life through labor, as well as to increase personal income in step with economic growth and raise labor remuneration in step with increases in labor productivity. Striving to achieve reasonable income distribution, social fairness, and common prosperity of all people and seeing that the gains of reform and development benefit the citizenry in a fair way would garner broad support for the government's economic goals.

IV. Building a System of Coordinated Urban-Rural and Regional Development to Help Local Regions Develop Their Own Strengths

Following the implementation of regional policies such as the China Western Development, the rise of Central China, and the rejuvenation of the old northeast industrial base, the central government proposed another three major national and regional development strategies, namely, coordinated development of the Beijing–Tianjin–Hebei (BTH) region, Yangtze River Economic Belt, and the Belt and Road Initiative. By giving full play to the leading role of the BRI and the Yangtze River Economic Belt, China will further promote the development of the central and western regions so as to further narrow the development gap between the various regions (East, West, Central) within China. While devoting great energy to the rejuvenation of the old northeast industrial base, the government will implement the strategy of coordinated development of the BTH region and promote the cooperation and development within the BTH region so as to narrow the development gap between the northern and the southern areas of China. The government should also adhere to the concept of coordinated development, implement the strategy of coordinated urban-rural and regional development, establish a more effective new mechanism for coordinated urban-rural and regional development, accelerate the implementation of RRS, develop a scientific and rational pattern of coordinated development between new-type urbanization and anti-urbanization, and accelerate the development of old revolutionary base areas, ethnic minority areas, border areas, and poverty stricken areas. Efforts should be made to strive to achieve benign regional interaction, integrated urban-rural development, and overall optimization of land and sea resources, to foster and leverage regional comparative strengths, to reinforce complementarity between regions, and to shape a new framework of coordinated regional development.

V. Building a Green Development System that Conserves Resources and Is Environmentally Friendly

Internationally, the industrialization process of developed Western countries has brought very profound experience and lessons of pollution before treatment. Domestically, China's extensive economic development in recent decades has also accumulated a large number of ecological and environmental problems, which have become not only a detriment to people's livelihoods but also a weak link restricting China's economic and social development in the future. A modern economic system must be a green development system that is resource-saving and environmentally friendly. Development should not only be speed-oriented but also benefit oriented. The mode of "extensive economy" should be eliminated, and a path of harmonious coexistence between humanity and nature should be taken. In addition, China should strike the best balance between development and protection, between the local benefits and the overall benefits, and between the immediate effects and the long-term effects. The path ahead must resolutely abandon the development mode and practice that damages or even destroys the ecological environment while promoting the substantial appreciation of natural capital and fostering a green development model and lifestyle. Firmly upholding the concept of green development and acting on the principles of prioritizing resource conservation and environmental protection and letting nature restore itself, developing spatial layouts, industrial structures, and ways of work and life that help conserve resources and protect the environment must also be a priority. With this, the serenity, harmony, and beauty of nature can be restored.

VI. Building a Diverse, Balanced, Secure, and Efficient System for Opening Up on All Fronts

Open development is the only pathway toward national prosperity and development. Today, China has become deeply integrated with the rest of the world. Both China's and global development provide reciprocal opportunities and conditions and are mutually reinforcing. To build a modern economic system, the government should not only balance China's economic, political, cultural, social, and ecological development but also actively lead the trend of economic globalization, promote the internal and external linkage of development, and retain the internal and external balance, meaning the balance between opening up to the outside world on all fronts while maintaining national security. The aims should be to: grasp the trend toward deeper integration of China's economy with the world by implementing the concept of open development; balance our domestic and international interests by taking the initiative in adapting to changes in the international situation. Furthermore, it should accurately identify the new requirements of domestic reform and development by ensuring better coordination in pursuing the "bringing in" and "going global" strategies with the BRI as the key focal point. This would mean following the principle of extensive consultation, joint contribution, and shared benefits while pursuing a win-win strategy of opening up and accelerating efforts to foster new advantages in international economic cooperation and competition.

Efforts should be pursued to enhance "opening up the economy wider to the world, and promote the transformation of opening up toward structural optimization, depth expansion, and efficiency improvement."

VII. Building an Economic System That Gives Full Play to the Role of the Market and the Government

The modernization of the economic system is the institutional guarantee for the construction of an up-to-date economic network, and the construction of such a system comprising an effective market mechanism, dynamic micro-level subject, and macroeconomic control is not only the goal at the large scale but also matches contemporary scientific consensus regarding these systems. Throughout nearly 40 years of hard work, China's socialist market economic system has steadily improved. In recent years, the reform of streamlining administration and delegating power, improving regulation, and upgrading services have been further deepened, which has effectively stimulated and released market vitality. In the meantime, there have been continued efforts to innovate the way in which macro-control is exercised, along with the adoption of the proper macroeconomic policies. The government has taken range-based, targeted, well-timed, and precise macro-control measures to keep the economy operating within an appropriate range. However, there are still many problems to be addressed in China's micro and macro-economic system, which still falls far short of the requirements for building a modern power and modern economic system. Therefore, steps must be taken to speed up the establishment of an economic system that matches the modern economic system while also getting rid of the path dependence on the old catch-up system in the past and boldly reforming the system and mechanism that do not meet the requirements of the development of productive forces. Adherence to the orientation of reform toward the socialist market economy should be a given, as well as giving play to the decisive role of the market in the allocation of resources, bringing the functions of government into better action, fully inspiring the vigor of the micro main body of the market, building a good institutional framework of the modern economic system, and striving to "realize effective market mechanism, dynamic micro-level subject, and macroeconomic control."[38]

SECTION 2
The Necessity and Urgency of Building a Modern Economic System

Building a modern economic system is an urgent requirement for China in order to transform its economic development pattern, optimize its economic structure, and transform its drivers of economic growth. A major decision made by the CPC Central Committee in the overall interests of the Party and the country, with a view to achieving the Two Centenary Goals and conforming to the new requirements of socialism with Chinese characteristics as it enters a new era, has thus been made. To gain a deep understanding of the necessity and urgency of building a modern economic system, well-targeted steps need to be taken in the following three dimensions.

I. The Basic Way to Build China into a Great Modern Socialist Country

The 19th National Congress of the CPC, based on the scientific analysis of the development trend of socialism with Chinese characteristics in the new era, put forward the goal of securing a decisive victory in building a moderately prosperous society in all respects, basically achieving socialist modernization by 2035 and developing China into a great modern socialist country that is prosperous, strong, democratic, culturally advanced, harmonious, and beautiful by the middle of the 21st century. Building a modern economic system is not only a major task to fully construct a modern socialist country but also the only way in which to achieve high-quality development. To achieve the Two Centenary Goals and build China into a great modern socialist country in all respects, the government must build on the basis of high-quality development. High-quality development is the catch-phrase of a new era in which the vision of innovative, coordinated, green, open, and shared development is fully implemented, with innovation as the primary driver, coordination as the endogenous characteristic, green as the universal form, openness as the only way, and sharing as the fundamental purpose. Only by achieving high-quality development can China bring about a pattern of development characterized by economic prosperity, political democracy, cultural prosperity, social equity, and sound ecology and build a great modern socialist country that meets the targets listed above.

II. Resolving the Principal Contradiction Facing Chinese Society in the New Era

To build a modern economic system is to turn people's expectations for a better life into reality, seeking more benefits for people's livelihoods, addressing their concerns, and enhancing their sense of gain, happiness, and achievement. China must advance the five-sphere integrated plan and the four-pronged comprehensive strategy in a coordinated way. The central task is to implement the new vision of development and construct a modern economic system. This includes building an innovation-led industrial system for coordinated development, raising the quality and efficiency of the supply system, and continuously providing better and newer goods and services to meet the diverse, personalized, and ever-expanding needs of the people. There are a number of steps that should be taken: Firstly, to build a green development system that is resource-conserving and environment-friendly, and gradually meet the people's yearning needs for fresh air, clean water and a sound ecological environment; Secondly, to build a system of coordinated urban-rural and regional development to help local regions develop their own strengths, gradually narrow the development gap between urban and rural areas and between different regions, and bridge the weak links of unbalanced and inadequate development; Thirdly, to build an efficient and fair income distribution system to ensure reasonable income distribution, social fairness and justice, and common prosperity; Fourthly, to build an economic system in which the market plays a decisive role in allocating resources and the role of the government is given better play to, build a comprehensively modern open market system, stimulate the vitality of innovation, creativity and development of the whole society and provide institutional guarantees for the modernization of the industrial, green development, urban-rural and regional development system and income distribution systems respectively. Therefore, the construction of a modern economic system is an important condition for promoting the resolution of the principle social contradictions in the new era.

III. Transforming the Development Mode and Achieving High-Quality Development

Only by building a modern economic system can the nation realize the transformation of the economy from quantity expansion to quality improvement, promote the growth of the manufacturing industry, and promote medium-high level development of the industrial structure; and can a positive change be affected with the main motive force of development from low-cost factor input to scientific and technological innovation and human resource quality advantages, significantly improving the total factor productivity and overall economic benefits. To cross the barrier and realize the strategic goal for China's development, reliance must be put on innovative development to accelerate the construction of a modern industrial system with high technology content, low resource consumption, and less environmental pollution, strengthen the organic integration of industrial chain and innovation chain, foster new growth and competitive advantage, and speed up the formation of a modern economic system and development mode with innovation as the main, leading and supporting force. Only by building such a modern economic system, adhering to the principle of quality and efficiency first, promoting the quality, efficiency, and driver changes of economic development, improving the total factor productivity, continuously accelerating the construction of an industrial system with the coordinated development of the real economy, scientific and technological innovation, modern finance and human resources, and speeding up the construction of an economic system with the effective market mechanism, dynamic micro-level subject, and macroeconomic control, can the necessary changes be realized. These, of course, being: the extensive development mode featuring speed and quantity preference formed under the old catch-up system, make the supply structure better adapt to the rapid change and upgrading trend of the demand structure, truly dissolve the surplus production capacity, reduce economic leverage, accelerate the revitalization of the real economy, provide a higher level and higher quality of supply, foster new drivers of growth and new growth points in the areas that meet the people's ever-growing needs for a better life, and further promote comprehensive and balanced development of people and society.

SECTION 3
How to Build a Modern Economic System

Only by speeding up the construction of a modern economic system, stepping up efforts to improve the quality and efficiency of development, and comprehensively pushing forward the five-sphere integrated plan of economic, political, cultural, social, and ecological civilization construction can China better meet people's growing needs for a better life, strive to solve the outstanding problems of inadequate and unbalanced development and achieve the Two Centenary Goals.

I. Advancing the Comprehensive Strategy in a Coordinated Manner and Deepening the Supply-Side Structural Reform

China will enter a new stage of development, which will fully respond to changes in the principle social contradictions and constantly meet the needs of the people for a better life. This will feature high-quality and more balanced and adequate development, allowing the nation to embark on a new journey to fully build a modern socialist country and march toward the second centenary goal. It will also be the stage in which China will comprehensively respond to the major changes in the world, taking into account both the overall international and domestic situations and proactively extending and shaping the period of strategic opportunities.

1. Accelerating the transition from "Made in China" to "Made by China"

Emphasis should be placed on the transition from China's speed to China's quality in order to achieve the great leap from a Large Manufacturing Country to a World Manufacturing Power. To build a modern economic system, China must focus its economic development on the real economy, give priority to improving the quality of the supply system, and significantly enhance the qualitative advantage of the Chinese economy. The key and most difficult point of the real economy lies in the manufacturing industry. In order to realize the historical leap of "Made in China," society as a whole must rely on scientific and technological innovation to realize the great leap from "Made in China" to "Made by China," from China's speed to China's quality, from Chinese products to Chinese brands, and from a Large Manufacturing Country to a World Manufacturing Power, which involves the advancement of technological innovation, quality improvement, and brand building at the strategic level. The government should promote the deep integration of the Internet, big data, AI, and the real economy, utilize new technologies and new business forms to transform and improve the traditional manufacturing industry, and strive to transform it into intelligent manufacturing. In conjunction, it should also speed up the development of advanced manufacturing and equipment manufacturing, foster world-class manufacturing clusters and other core brand forces, and promote the overall leap of Chinese products in the process of global value chain remodeling.

2. Strengthening the construction of infrastructure networks for transportation, power grids, information, and logistics

Currently, China's mileage of expressways and railways in operation ranks first in the world, with a massive scale of infrastructure construction. However, China is still faced with the problem of unbalanced and inadequate regional supply chains. Many poverty-stricken areas still seriously lag behind in infrastructure, such as irrigation and water conservancy, transportation, and communication, and are faced with an unbalanced distribution of infrastructure among regions and an insufficient utilization efficiency of facilities. To strengthen the construction of the infrastructure network, efforts should be made to balance the development pattern, strengthen the weak links, improve the infrastructure connectivity, fully realize the production efficiency of the infrastructure network, and provide more "external economy" for industrial development.

3. Giving play to the role of human capital and enhancing soft power for industrial development

The government should aim to do a number of things, which include the following: to inspire and protect the entrepreneurial spirit, to carry forward the spirit of model workers and craftsmen, and fully mobilize the production enthusiasm of entrepreneurs and backbone workers, the two key groups in economic activities It should also advocate for the spirit of cooperation and healthy competitive culture, and encourage enterprises to form innovation alliances and conduct joint R&D focusing on key generic technologies in the industry. Promoting the sharing of manufacturing resources and exploring innovative modes such as networked collaborative manufacturing and cloud manufacturing while also promoting specialized and socialized division of labor and collaboration should be undertaken. Finally, the government should improve the industrial ecosystem, promote coordinated development of large-, medium- and small-sized enterprises, encourage them to focus on areas of comparative advantage, and create more hidden champions; and finally, improve the quality of the supply system by mobilizing the enthusiasm of human capital and social cooperation.

4. Persisting in capacity reduction, de-stocking, deleveraging, cost reduction, and improvement in underdeveloped areas, optimizing the allocation of existing resources, expanding high-quality incremental supply, and achieving a dynamic balance between supply and demand

China should deepen the reform of market-based allocation of factors and focus on "breaking-through," "establishment," and "reduction." Specifically, hard work should be undertaken to achieve the following: eliminate ineffective supply, deal with the "zombie enterprises" and promote the resolution of excess capacity; foster new drivers of growth, strengthen scientific and technological innovation, promote the optimization and upgrading of traditional industries, cultivate a number of pioneering enterprises with innovative capabilities, and actively promote the in-depth development of military-civilian integration; reduce costs in the real economy, lower the cost of institutional transactions, continue to clean up the fees and charges levied on businesses, step up efforts in investigation and rectification of arbitrary charges, deepen the reform in the electric power, oil and natural gas, railway and other industries, and reduce the cost of energy use and logistics; make new progress in capacity reduction, de-stocking, deleveraging, cost reduction, and improvement in underdeveloped areas, optimize the allocation of stock resources, improve the quality of the supply system, adapt to new changes in demand, and achieve a dynamic balance between supply and demand at a higher level.

5. Adhering to the "double driver" strategy and accelerating the formation of a new development pattern where the domestic circulation is the main body and the domestic and international dual circulations promote each other

The world today is undergoing profound changes unseen in a century, and a new round of scientific and technological revolution and industrial revolution are developing in depth. Under the new international and domestic situation, and in order to maintain sustained, stable, and high-quality development of the national economy, China must foster a strong domestic market, adhere to the strategic basis of expanding domestic demand, ensure unimpeded domestic circulation, and enable the domestic and international dual circulations to promote each other, comprehensively promote consumption and expand the space for investment. It should also build a new open economic system at a higher level, open up wider to the outside world in all respects, promote the liberalization and facilitation of investment and trade, and continue to build a modern socialist country with Chinese characteristics.

II. Implementing a Developmental Vision to Become a Global Leader in Innovation

1. Strengthening the construction of a national innovation system and optimizing the overall layout of the national strategic science, technology, and innovation chain

The following should be undertaken: accelerate the implementation of the strategy of innovation-driven development, strengthen the strategic support for the modern economic system and the construction of the national innovation system respectively, enhance the strategic scientific and technological force, promote the deep integration of scientific and technological innovation and economic and social development, and foster more innovation-driven and first-mover advantages in leading development; This should be combined with a deepening reform of the S&T systems, while developing a market-oriented system for technological innovation in which enterprises are the main players and synergy is created through the joint efforts of enterprises, universities, and research institutes. Supporting innovation by small and medium-sized enterprises and encouraging the application of advances in S&T should also be a focus, along with priority given to fostering national strategic scientific and technological forces and laying out national laboratories in major innovation fields capable of breaking through technical barriers, leading the research direction and serving as an effective platform. Relying on superior innovation units and integrating national innovation resources to accomplish key scientific and technological tasks the nation should also speed up the development of large-scale national S&T infrastructures and leverage the three comprehensive national science centers in Huairou (Beijing), Zhangjiang (Shanghai) and Hefei (Anhui) to give full play to their scale advantages of clusters of large scientific equipment and gathering of world-class scientists to allow for breakthroughs in major scientific problems and bottlenecks in cutting-edge S&T. Encouraging world-class scientific talents and research teams to actively participate in or lead international science programs and projects, contributing "Chinese wisdom" to the scientific development of the world, and enhancing the openness of the national innovation system, alongside developing a market-oriented system for technological innovation in which enterprises are the main players and where synergy is created through the joint efforts of enterprises, universities, and research institutes should all take place. Finally, a focus should be placed on cultivating a group of leading innovative enterprises with core technological capabilities and good integration of innovation resources to realize the transformation and application of technological innovation at the most efficient rate.

2. Focusing on the "Three Orientations" and promoting key breakthroughs in scientific and technological innovation

China should prioritize the following: One, aim at the world's cutting-edge S&T, strengthen basic research, and achieve major breakthroughs in forward-looking basic research and leading original achievements; Two, carry out a forward-looking layout and promote scientific and technological innovation in a coordinated way focusing on the three main orientations, including "oriented toward the world's cutting-edge S&T, oriented toward the major economic battlefields and oriented toward the major national needs,"[39] so as to open up each key node in the chain of transformation from scientific and technological achievements to real productive forces. In terms of source reserve, the CPC advocates the combination of goal orientation and free exploration to strengthen both basic and applied basic research, encourage scientific researchers to enhance original innovation at the forefront of science, focus on addressing weak areas, and strive to form a number of forward-looking and leading original research results. Therefore, the focus should be aimed at these areas: One, on major national S&T projects, integration of research forces, jointly tackling key generic technologies and core technologies in key fields, and enhancing innovation capabilities in key links and key fields; Two, centering on the "S&T Innovation 2030-Major Projects," strengthening scientific research in space, deep sea, new energy, new materials, intelligent manufacturing, and other high-tech fields, and make breakthroughs and master a number of disruptive and leading cutting-edge technologies; Three, promote the tackling of key problems and demonstration application in the field of modern engineering, and strengthen development and integration of technologies and development and large-scale application of equipment in the field of marine engineering, heavy equipment, and other modern engineering.

3. Taking human resources as the primary resource to support the development of S&T and strengthening the talent team for scientific and technological innovation

The government should advocate an innovation culture, strengthen the creation, protection, and application of intellectual property rights, promote innovation education, further optimize the environment for innovation and entrepreneurship in the whole society, speed up the team building of high-end scientific and technological innovation talents, highlight the orientation of "cultivating high-grade, high-precision, advanced and scarce talents," speed up the pace of training a large number of internationally advanced strategic scientific and technological talents, leading scientific and technological talents, especially young scientific and technological talents and high-level innovation teams, focus on cultivating young scientific and technological talents with scientific research potential, pave the way for their success, and form the backbone of the future scientific and technological teams.

4. Continuing to promote the strategy of innovation-driven development and highlighting the supporting and leading role of scientific and technological innovation in implementing supply-side structural reform and fostering new growth drivers

China should focus on the following: strengthening basic applied research, expanding and implementing major national S&T projects, and highlighting key generic technologies, cutting-edge technologies, modern engineering technologies, and disruptive technological innovations so as to provide strong support for building up the nation into a power in S&T space, transportation, cyberspace—a digital China, meaning a "smart society." Focus should also be placed on emerging fields such as new-generation information networks and intelligent green manufacturing, promotion of innovation of an industrial technology system, acceleration of the deep integration of industrialization and informatization, and leading the development of emerging industrial clusters with the support of mass technological breakthroughs should take place This should be combined with attaching importance to the coordination of technological innovation and management innovation, conforming to the trend of informatization, expanding the emerging service industry based on Internet and modern logistics, and stepping up efforts to develop the digital, platform, sharing and intelligent economies respectively. Finally, optimizing the regional innovation layout, promoting the reasonable division of labor through agglomeration and flow of innovation elements, and realizing cross-regional integration of innovation elements by relying on regional innovation centers should be undertaken. For the development of East China, the focus should be placed on improving original innovation and integrated innovation capacity; for the development of Central and West China, as well as on differentiation and "leap-frog" development, the focus should be on building and improving carriers for innovation and entrepreneurship, developing low-cost, convenient and opening maker spaces and virtual innovation communities, guiding social capital to participate in the incubation and cultivation of innovative small and micro businesses, promoting the introduction of maker culture into the campus, and stimulating the creative vitality of the whole of society.

III. Implementing the RRS, Accelerating Efforts to Improve Weak Links, and Consolidating the Foundation of a Modern Economic System

Issues concerning agriculture, rural areas, and farmers are fundamental to the national welfare and people's livelihoods, and also an area of weaknesses in building a modern economic system that needs to be urgently addressed. Without agricultural and rural modernization, there will be no modernization of the country. Strong agriculture, beautiful rural areas, and rich farmers are the source of the sense of gain and happiness of hundreds of millions of farmers and determine the quality of Chinese society as a moderately prosperous society in all respects and the quality of its socialist modernization. The implementation of the RRS is an inevitable requirement to solve the contradiction between the unbalanced and inadequate development and the people's growing needs for a better life, to realize the Two Centenary Goals, to build a modern economic system and achieve coordinated development, and to realize the common prosperity for everyone. To effectively implement the concept of coordinated development, the government should implement the RRS, follow the path to rural revitalization of socialism with Chinese characteristics by adhering to the Party's leadership over rural work, prioritize development of agriculture and rural areas, allowing for the dominant role of farmers, strive for comprehensive revitalization of rural areas, integrate urban-rural development and harmonious coexistence between human and nature, take effective measures according to local conditions, and proceed in an orderly step by step way.

IV. Adhering to the New Concept of Coordinated Development and Striving to Make Regional Development More Holistic and Coordinated

It is the internal requirement of building a modern economic system to actively promote coordinated development among regions, optimize the spatial layout of the modern economic system, and implement the strategy of coordinated development among regions. Since the 18th National Congress of the CPC, the thinking and mode of China's coordinated regional development have also been further adjusted and optimized. Following the implementation of regional policies such as the China Western Development, the rise of Central China, and the rejuvenation of the old northeast industrial base, the central government proposed another three major national and regional development strategies, namely, coordinated development of the BTH region, the Yangtze River Economic Belt, and the BRI. By giving full play to the leading role of the BRI and the Yangtze River Economic Belt, the government will further promote the development of the central and western regions so as to further narrow the development gap between the eastern, central, and western parts of China. While devoting great energy to the rejuvenation of the old northeast industrial base, the government will also implement the strategy of coordinated development of the BTH region and promote cooperation and development within this region so as to narrow the development gap between North and South China. However, due to China's vast territorial size, the prominent problems of unbalanced, uncoordinated, and unsustainable development accentuated by long-term high-speed and unbalanced development have become a weakness in the construction of a modern economic system. Therefore, much attention should be paid to the concept of coordinated development and implementation of the strategy of regional coordinated development.

V. Accelerating the Improvement in the Socialist Market Economy System to Provide a Strong Institutional Guarantee for Building a Modern Economic System

To build a modern economic system and promote high-quality development and economic transformation and upgrading, the government should deepen the reform of the economic system, improve the institutional guarantee for such a system, speed up the improvement of the socialist market economy system, resolutely eliminate the shortcomings of various institutions and mechanisms, and stimulate the vitality for innovation and entrepreneurship across society writ large.

To improve the socialist market economy system, the government must pay heed to the following: build a unified and open market system with orderly competition so that the market plays a decisive role in the allocation of resources. Secondly, it should deepen economic structural reforms with a focus on improving the property rights system and market-based allocation of factors of production and resolutely remove institutional and mechanism barriers that restrict the vitality and power of development so as to realize the effective incentive of property rights, the free flow of factors, flexible price responsiveness, fair and orderly competition, and business survival determined by competition. Next, it should fully implement the system of a negative list for market access, clear up and abolish all kinds of regulations and practices that hinder the unification of the market and fair competition, break administrative monopolies, preclude the forming of market monopolies, speed up the reform of market-based pricing of factors of production, and extend the restrictions on market access in the service sector; and finally, strive to remove market barriers and improve the efficiency and fairness of resource allocation.

The government should adhere to and improve China's basic socialist economic system and system of distribution, unswervingly consolidate and develop both the public sector of the economy, and encourage, support, and guide the development of the non-public sector of the economy while stimulating the vitality of various market players. It should also address the following: further implement and improve the management system of all kinds of state-owned assets, reform the system for authorized operation of state-owned capital, develop the economy of mixed ownership, and accelerate the optimization of the distribution, structural adjustment, and strategic reorganization of the state-owned economy. The government should further support state capital in becoming stronger, doing better, and growing bigger, improve the reform plan for state-owned enterprises and capital, accelerate the transformation of the functions of state-owned capital supervising institutions with a focus on capital management, and reform the system for authorized operation of state-owned capital. A focus should also be placed on strengthening the Party's leadership and the Party building within state-owned enterprises and encouraging them to improve their modern corporate systems and corporate governance structures. This should be combined with further improving the property rights protection system, stimulating and protecting entrepreneurship, identifying and correcting property rights dispute cases with strong social responses in accordance with the law, creating a market environment for fair competition, supporting and guiding the development of the private economy, and giving full play to the advantages of the private economy in the diversified market demands. It should also actively develop the mixed ownership economy, promote the diversification of property rights, realize the cross-shareholding and two-way entry of state-owned capital and private capital through multiple channels and in multiple ways, and restructure and rebuild the micro-entities of enterprises. Finally, there should be a deepening reform of the income distribution system to ensure that the income growth of urban and rural residents is in harmony with overall economic growth, protecting the property income of urban and rural residents and expanding investment channels for people to participate in and share the dividends of development.

Furthermore, the nation should tackle the following: deepen the reform of streamlining administration and delegating power, improving regulation, and upgrading services, and the reform of the business system, fully implement the system of a negative list for market access, speed up the reform of market-based pricing of factors of production, and improve the market supervision system, This should be done in conjunction with comprehensively deepening the reform, transform government functions, giving play to the government's role in market maintenance, guidance and cultivation, truly reducing institutional transaction costs, removing obstacles to the rational flow and effective allocation of factors of production, delegating power to the market and society. Stimulating the development and innovation vitality of main market and social players, creating a market environment of fair competition, strengthening market players' confidence in future development, and stabilizing their expectations for investment and innovation should all take place. Finally, the government needs to fully implement and continuously improve the system of a negative list for market access, break the discriminatory restrictions and various hidden obstacles, and speed up the construction of a new type of cordial and clean relationship between government and business.

The following should be undertaken: innovate and improve macro-control, giving full play to the strategic guiding role of national development plans, improve mechanisms for coordination mechanism of financial, monetary, industrial, regional, consumption, investment policies and other economic policies, and deepen the reform of the financial system. A strengthening of the financial sector's ability to serve the real economy, quickly reversing the trend of finance being distracted from its intended purpose and resolving the problems such as the circulation of financial resources within the system, and the misallocation and low efficiency of said resources, to effectively prevent and control financial risks. In the meantime, steps should be taken to improve the dual-pillar regulatory framework of monetary policy and macro-prudential policy while adhering to the underlying principle of aligning stability with sustainable progress and adhering to the overall thinking of upholding the policy framework of stable macro policies, flexible micro policies, and social policies that ensure basic needs are met, and a deepening of market-oriented reform of interest rates and exchange rates. Finally, an acceleration of the improvement of the financial regulatory system and keep the bottom line of no systematic financial risk.

Finally, the government should speed up the establishment of a modern fiscal and taxation system and the establishment of a fiscal relationship between the central and local governments built upon clearly defined rights and responsibilities, with appropriate financial resource allocation and greater balance between regions. It should also establish a fully standardized, transparent, standard, scientific, and restrained budget system and take the full implementation of budget performance management. Finally, it should strive to improve the budget management system and the taxation system, establish a system with administrative power that is commensurate with expenditure responsibility, promote the establishment of a modern fiscal system, deepen the reform of the taxation system, improve the local tax system, and speed up the efforts to address the imbalance between local revenue and expenditure and land financial problems.

VI. Implementing the New Concept of Open Development and Breaking New Ground in Pursuing Opening Up on All Fronts

China and the rest of the world provide complementary development opportunities, conditions, and drivers. To build a modern economic system, the government needs to not only strike a balance between economic, political, cultural, social, and ecological development but also actively lead the trend of economic globalization, promote the internal and external linkage of development, and build a high-level, open and international modern economic system. To grasp the trend of deep integration of China into the global economy, the nation should strive to develop an open economy, improve the international competitiveness of a modern economic system, make better use of global resources and markets, continue to actively promote international exchanges and cooperation under the framework of the BRI, pay equal attention to bringing in and going global, follow the principle of extensive consultation, participate in joint contribution and shared benefits, uphold a win-win opening-up strategy, and accelerate efforts to foster new advantages in international economic cooperation and competition.

VII. Stepping Up Efforts to Develop the Real Economy to Lay a Solid Foundation for a Modern Economic System

The real economy is relative to the financial economy and is concerned with the production and sale of physical goods and services with direct, close-contact lending.

The real economy covers most areas of the primary, secondary, and tertiary industries. It serves as the guarantee of people's lives and the foundation of the national economy. Expanding and strengthening the real economy is the supporting role of building a modern industrial system and also the goal and main task of deepening supply-side structural reform. The real economy is the foundation of a country's economy, the fundamental source of wealth creation, and an important pillar of national prosperity. Focus should be put on economic development of the real economy while unswervingly striving to build Manufacturing Power, Quality Power, Cyberspace Power, and Digital China and upgrading the industrial base, modernizing industrial chains, and improving the quality and core competitiveness of the economy.

To build a modern economic system, the focus should be put on: One, expansion and strengthening of the real economy, integration, and investment in production factors such as S&T, human resources, and capital into the real economy, deepening supply-side structural reform, further optimizing the allocation of existing resources, and strive to promote economic transformation and upgrading to raise the quality and efficiency of the economy; Two, foster and expand emerging industries, accelerate the development of advanced manufacturing industry, promote the deep integration of Internet, big data and AI with the real economy, invest the various resource factors in the real economy, adopt policies and measures to better facilitate the development of the real economy and intensify our efforts to develop it so as to create a development environment and social atmosphere of down-to-earth and laborious entrepreneurship and to build up fortunes through development of industries. In terms of R&D design, green low carbon, modern supply chain, human capital services, inspection and testing, brand construction, financing leasing, e-commerce, and other key areas, steps should be taken to actively develop service-oriented manufacturing, guide and support the shift of manufacturing industry from mainly providing products to providing both products and services and achieve transformation and upgrading of manufacturing in the service-oriented direction. What is also required is a firm grasp of the main direction of intelligent manufacturing while stepping up efforts to implement intelligent manufacturing projects, support enterprises to accelerate digitalization, networking, and intelligent transformation, promote the deep integration of informatization and industrialization, promote the transformation and upgrading of the industry, and accelerate the promotion of Chinese industries toward the middle and high-end of the global value chain. To pursue progress while ensuring stability and achieve steady and sound economic development, efforts should be made to strengthen the real economy, building its solid foundations in order to make fresh progress in transforming the mode of economic development and better cope with various risks and challenges.

The Development Path and Development Strategy

PART FOUR

The Development Path and
Development Strategy

CHAPTER EIGHT

The Path of Four Modernizations in the New Era

Before reform and opening-up, China once put forward the Four Modernizations—the goal of modernizing China's industry, agriculture, national defense, and S&T. Due to historical limitations, urbanization was not mentioned at the time. Neither was the concept of information technology (IT) application, though the modernization of S&T was proposed. The road to the New Four Modernizations is thus a new path China has taken in recent years. Following the New Four Modernizations development path ("new" industrialization, application of IT, urbanization, and agricultural modernization) is an inevitable requirement for comprehensively building a modern socialist country and realizing the great rejuvenation of the Chinese nation. To promote the development of the Four Modernizations, China must firmly grasp the new characteristics of the four fronts in the new era, termed the New Four Modernizations, and identify the focus of their synchronized development.

SECTION 1
The Path of New Industrialization with Chinese Characteristics

Chinese socialism has entered a new era, with the economy having been transitioning from a phase of rapid growth to a stage of high-quality development. This is a pivotal stage for transforming China's growth model, improving the country's economic structure, and fostering new drivers of growth.

I. The Goals and Tasks of the New Industrialization Development Strategy

To pursue new industrialization, China should persist in using IT to propel industrialization. This will stimulate IT application, accelerating industrialization featuring high scientific and technological content, good economic returns, low resource consumption, little environmental pollution, and the full utilization of China's human resource advantages. This is a path based on China's current stage of development that draws on others' experiences and lessons, and it is a path that gives full play to the comparative advantages and late-comer advantages of China. The country should keep to its path of carrying out industrialization in a novel way and advancing IT application, urbanization, and agricultural modernization. The nation should promote the integration of IT application and industrialization, the interaction between industrialization and urbanization, and the coordination between urbanization and agricultural modernization, thus achieving the New Four Modernizations in a harmonized manner. Additionally, China should reach the goal of "realizing basic 'new' industrialization, and greatly improving the level of IT application" by 2035 when the goal of basically achieving socialist modernization is met.

II. The Content and Characteristics of New Industrialization

The new road to industrialization is a road of innovation and reform and opening-up. It contains the following seven elements.

(1) Pursue economic development on the basis of scientific and technological progress, offering an elevated starting point for the rapid development of industrialization
(2) Pay attention to improving the quality and efficiency of growth, optimizing the allocation of resources, and increasing economic efficiency and returns
(3) Promote advanced and practical technology to improve energy and resource utilization efficiency and remove energy and resource constraints
(4) Prevent pollution and protect the eco-environment, ensuring the economy and ecology develop in harmony
(5) Provide quality products and services that can foster consumption, meet people's needs, and increase market competitiveness
(6) Take a people-oriented approach to raising the ability of the labor force, fully utilizing China's human resources advantages, focusing on improving people's well-being, and ensuring the health of laborers
(7) Integrate IT application and industrialization while balancing industrialization, urbanization, and agricultural modernization to develop a modern service industry

New industrialization is different from traditional industrialization in the following three aspects.

First, it seizes the opportunity for a new round of scientific revolution and industrial transformation. In the traditional method of industrializing, a country mainly relies on resource and production factor endowments, fully leverages the price advantages of low-cost labor and other production factors, and takes advantage of the global industrial division to gradually upgrade from the low-end to the mid-high end of the value chain. This is how many advanced countries became industrialized. Although the time they spent on industrialization is different, these countries have all become modernized through industrialization. In the past 40 years of reform and opening-up, China has seized the historic opportunities of trade and investment, technological progress, and industrial transfer against the backdrop of economic globalization and achieved accelerated development, thus entering the ranks of middle- and high-income countries.

At present, a new global round of scientific revolution and industrial transformation has brought a huge impact on human production and life. Manufacturing has more extensively and deeply combined with the Internet, big data, and AI. Smart manufacturing and service are becoming a general trend for the transformation and upgrading of traditional industries and manufacturing around the world. The rapid development and extensive application of IT and internet technology pose a huge challenge to the traditional method of industrializing: it is increasingly difficult for a country to mainly rely on advantages in natural resources and labor resources to achieve industrialization and ultimately modernization. China has seized a very favorable time window and caught up significantly in industrialization and economic development, but it has not yet been industrialized fully. Its overall technological innovation capability is not strong enough. Neither is its international competitiveness in most sectors or its overall economic strength. It needs to further industrial upgrading in the global value chain and enhance competitiveness. Therefore, strategies like "Made in China 2025" and "Internet Plus" have been implemented. The aim is to seize the opportunities of the new round of technological revolution and industrial transformation and comprehensively promote the integration and interaction between industrialization and IT application, between technological innovation and business model innovation, and between manufacturing and service industries. This will create a shift from "Made in China" to "Created in China," from the speed of growth to the quality of development, and from Chinese products to Chinese brands, to finally complete the strategic task of making Chinese manufacturing stronger.

Second, new industrialization strives to revitalize the real economy. In order to smoothly step into the next stage of industrialization, China must speed up the building of an industrial system featuring coordinated development of the real economy with technological innovation, modern finance, and human resources. Building such an industrial system is one of the core components of building a modern economic system. It will strongly promote China's industrialization process, making it possible for China to become fully industrialized in the next 15–20 years and enter a post-industrial period.

Today, with China's economy purposefully shifting from a phase of rapid growth to a stage of quality development, the government needs to: change the outdated thinking of blindly pursuing scale and speed; give priority to improving the quality of the supply system; further supply-side structural reform; strive to improve the technological level, standard, quality, efficiency, benefits and competitiveness of industries, especially manufacturing, via advancing "new" industrialization; and enhance the economy's strength in terms of quality. These moves are key to the revitalization of the real economy.

Third, new industrialization is guided by the new development philosophy and strives to solve problems caused by unbalanced and inadequate development. As socialism with Chinese characteristics has entered a new era, the principal contradiction facing Chinese society has evolved from its earlier state. What the country now faces is the contradiction between unbalanced and inadequate development and the people's ever-growing needs for a better life. Unbalanced and inadequate development is the more prominent element. These imbalances and inadequacies also exist in the country's industrialization drive, such as: between industrial development and environmental protection; the imbalance between product supply and demand structure; within regional development; the large size of companies relative to the weakness of the industries they constitute; the inadequate abilities in innovation and system integration; and the heavy dependence on foreign countries in access to key technologies. These problems must be solved in order to forge a new path to industrialization under the guidance of the new development concept.

China should adhere to innovation-driven development and strive to promote a new type of industrialization featuring technological progress, structural optimization, and a continuous increase in total factor productivity. Industry, especially manufacturing, is the main engine for making technological progress and building a new industrial system. The primary task of new industrialization is to promote overall technological progress, accelerating breakthroughs in key technologies that have a broad application and core component production in a number of important strategic industries, reducing dependence on external sources, and enhancing the country's ability to integrate systems, support infrastructure and set standards. At present, it is particularly necessary to facilitate next-generation IT penetrating widely and deeply into traditional industrial sectors and promoting the restructuring and upgrading of traditional manufacturing so that traditional manufacturing growth can soon be mainly driven by improving labor productivity and total factor productivity. Besides, efforts should be made in advancing the development of emerging and future industries so that they can soon become pillars of support for China's medium-high economic growth and industrial upgrade to the medium-high level.

III. Specific Requirements for Advancing New Industrialization

1. Combine the optimization of the allocation of available resources with the increase of high-quality supply to improve overall industrialization

Now, the structural contradiction that has been built up in the long process of China's industrialization has become conspicuous, with overcapacity at the low end and shortages at the high-end coexisting, many industries being big but not powerful, and industrialization being of low quality. Therefore, China must accelerate the transformation of industrialization from the pursuit of scale and speed to the pursuit of quality and efficiency and strive to make breakthroughs in key links such as R&D and design, sales network, brand cultivation, and supply chain management that can effectively increase the level in the value chain. The government must accelerate the optimization and upgrading of traditional industries in line with international standards. Meanwhile, leadership should promote the development of new technologies, new models, new formats, and new industries, further expand the industrial chain, upgrade the value chain and improve the supply chain, and comprehensively improve the core competitiveness of the industry to move it up to the mid-high level.

2. Combine industrialization with IT application and use IT to propel industrialization

In recent years, a new round of technological revolution centered on mobile Internet, cloud computing, big data, the Internet of Things, and other new-generation information technologies has emerged rapidly and become a new engine driving industrialization. Unlike developed countries that have entered the stage of IT application after finishing industrialization, China has caught up with the IT wave while its industrialization has not yet been completed. In this situation, China needs to combine industrialization with IT application and use IT to propel industrialization. To this end, China should use the Internet, big data, AI, and other modern technologies to promote reform in production, management, and marketing models and lead the restructuring of the industrial value chain system. The country should use data and new platform rules to accelerate the construction of an internet-based, smart, service-oriented, and collaborative "Internet Plus" industrial ecosystem, thus strengthening the driving effect of IT on industrialization.

3. Combine manufacturing with services to realize their coordinated development

Service-oriented manufacturing is becoming a global trend in industrial development. But to develop the service economy does not mean reducing manufacturing or de-industrializing, but realizing a synergy between manufacturing and services. On the one hand, China should accelerate the development of advanced manufacturing, fostering a number of world-class advanced manufacturing clusters and quickening the pace of building China into a manufacturing power. On the other hand, the country needs to guide and support the change in the manufacturing industry from mainly providing products to providing both products and services so as to restructure and upgrade it into service-type manufacturing.

4. Combine industrialization with urbanization to ensure industrialization and urbanization go hand in hand

China's urbanization lags far behind its industrialization, which hampers the qualitative improvement of industrialization. Therefore, the country should actively and steadily advance the new type of urbanization and make overall plans for the coordinated development of urban and rural areas. It is necessary to promote the formation of an urbanization layout with city clusters as a major form and coordinate the development of large, medium, and small cities and small towns while accelerating the settlement of former agricultural populations who have migrated to the cities. Meanwhile, it is necessary to vigorously implement the rural vitalization strategy and develop a new type of relationship between industry and agriculture and between urban and rural areas. This relationship will see industry promoting agriculture, urban areas supporting rural development, agriculture and industry benefitting each other, and the integration of urban and rural development. This will ensure that industrialization and urbanization reinforce each other and advance in parallel.

5. Combine sustainable industrialization with the building of an ecological civilization

The traditional method to achieve industrialization, featuring high investment, high consumption, high pollution, and low-level quantitative expansion, is unsustainable. To promote the "new" industrialization in the new era, China must realize that lucid waters and lush mountains are invaluable assets and act on this understanding. It must: effectively integrate the construction of ecological civilization into the whole process of the industrialization drive; establish a sound economic system for green, low-carbon, and circular development; ensure mankind and nature live in harmony; and achieve sustainable industrialization with low resource consumption and less environmental pollution.

6. Combine industrialization with opening up to continuously enhance global competitiveness and China's economic influence

The country will vigorously raise the level of "going global" and take part in international economic cooperation on a broader scale, in more spheres, and at a higher level. The government will foster new advantages in international economic cooperation and competition and strive to occupy a better position in the international division of labor. The country needs to actively integrate into the international industrial chain and value chain, expand the scope of international cooperation from processing and manufacturing to high-end links such as cooperative R&D, joint design, marketing, and brand cultivation, and enhance the capacity for self-development and core competitiveness in cooperation.

SECTION 2

The Path of IT Application with Chinese Characteristics

IT application is a highly positive global development trend and an important force to promote economic and social reform. Speeding up IT application has become a common choice in all countries. Forcefully moving IT application forward is a strategic measure affecting the entire picture of the country's modernization drive.

I. The Content and Characteristics of IT Application

According to the definition in the "National Informatization Development Strategy (2006–2020),"[40] "informatization" is the historical process of fully using information technology, developing the use of information resources, stimulating information exchange and knowledge sharing, raising the quality of economic growth, and promoting the transformation of economic and social development. All of this makes informatization a new productive force. Human society has gone through approximately 10,000 years of the agricultural stage[41] and 300 years of the industrial stage[42] and is now entering an information-based stage of economic development. The use of professional knowledge and insight, especially the effective use of information, has become the main factor in the creation of wealth. The IT application has become an important part of economic and social vitality and competitiveness and a brand-new engine of productivity in addition to science & technology and management.

The information economy and industrial economy, or rather, the information society and industrial society, have very different modes of production. In the industrial stage, products are manufactured by man-operated machines. And in the information-based stage, an ever-increasing number of products are manufactured by machines controlled by electronic information equipment, while people are more dedicated to the research and production of electronic information equipment. Clearly, the information society is an important and advanced historical stage in the development of human society. IT application is now part of this historical process, in which various information technologies and various forms of information are applied to production, service, and management in all spheres of society and to different aspects of life in order to continuously promote social, economic, and technological development and improve the quality of people's lives.

IT application has gone through three development stages—digital application, networking, and smart application—which are also widely acknowledged as the three characteristics of IT application. These are explained in the "Outline of National Informatization Development Strategy"[43] as summarized below:

(1) Digital application. Digital application is the process of converting complex and varied information (including text, sound, graphics, images, and films) into measurable numbers and data, building proper digital models based on these numbers and data, and converting them into binary codes that can be processed by a computer. Digitization is the technical foundation of digital computers, multimedia, software and intelligent technology, and the information society.

(2) Networking. Networking means to use communication and computer technologies to interconnect computers and various electronic terminal devices at different locations and allow them to communicate with each other according to certain network protocols for the purpose of sharing software, hardware, and data resources among all users.

(3) Smart application. Smart application refers to the application of combined modern technologies in a certain field, such as communication & information technology, computer network technology (CNT), industrial technology, and intelligent control technology. In practice, it is now mainly reflected as the comprehensive application of computer technology, precise sensing technology, and GPS technology. Its application brings about several advantages. First, the working environment of operators is greatly improved, and work intensity is reduced. Second, the quality and efficiency of work are improved. Third, it can be used in some dangerous situations, such as on construction sites. Fourth, it's environment-friendly and energy-saving. Fifth, it allows machines to become more automated and

intelligent. Sixth, the reliability of equipment is enhanced, cutting maintenance costs. Finally, it allows for intelligent fault diagnosis to become a reality.

II. The Significance of Advancing IT Application

1. A strategic choice to seize the historic opportunities provided by the information revolution and create new advantages in international competition

Developing countries scramble for the opportunities brought by the restructuring of industrial chains, use IT to stimulate economic transformation and development, and strive to grasp the initiative in development. All countries worldwide are accelerating their strategic arrangements in cyberspace, and the competition to win key resources and formulate international norms is growing more acute and complex every day. Accelerating IT application and building digital countries have thus become a global consensus.

The world economy is accelerating the transition into one where the network & IT industry play an important part. China must seize this historic opportunity to apply IT to foster new growth drivers. This will: promote new development; enhance IT infrastructure; deeply integrate the Internet into the real economy; accelerate the application of digital and intelligent technologies in traditional industries; make the digital economy bigger and stronger; and create new space for economic development.

2. Advancing IT Application leads the new normal of economic growth and strengthens the new drivers of development

To achieve these ends, China needs to implement IT application in the entire process of China's modernization drive and unleash its huge potential. Driving modernization with IT application to build China into a cyber power is an important measure to implement the four-pronged comprehensive strategy and a logical choice to realize the Two Centenary Goals and the Chinese Dream of national rejuvenation.

3. Advancing IT Application pursues a people-oriented approach to development

China will give full play to the advantages of the Internet and carry out "Internet Plus Education," "Internet Plus Healthcare," and "Internet Plus Culture"[44] initiatives to promote equal access to basic public services. The country will give rein to the role of the Internet in boosting poverty relief and moving forward with targeted poverty assistance and poverty relief. The leadership will also: let more people in need have access to the Internet, let agricultural products be sold directly from the countryside through the Internet, let children in the mountainous areas be able to receive quality education through the Internet, and accelerate the promotion of e-governance and encourage governments at all levels to break information barriers and improve service efficiency.

4. Conducive to modernizing the national governance system and governance capacity

China needs to: develop e-governance in a holistic way; build an integrated online service platform; move forward with the construction of novel smart cities in a hierarchical and categorized manner; break down information barriers; build a national information resource-sharing system; and use IT-based means to better understand social situations, unblock communication channels and better assist scientific policymaking.

III. The Main Tasks and Priorities for Advancing China's IT Application

1. Promote in-depth IT application in the industrial circle

Centering on the requirements of promoting industrial restructuring and upgrading, the country should promote IT coverage, penetration, application, integration, and innovation in the industrial circle on all fronts and at multiple levels. There are five aspects to this:

(1) Promote IT application widely in the industrial field
(2) Promote innovation in comprehensive integrated application and business collaboration
(3) Speed up the process of making manufacturing more service-oriented
(4) Promote IT application in energy conservation and emission reduction
(5) Establish a service support system for the integration of IT application and industrialization

2. Accelerate IT application in the service sector

To meet the needs of developing the service industry and upgrading the resident consumption structure, we should deepen IT application in the service sector, actively foster new service formats, and promote the development of modern services. There are three aspects to this:

(1) Guide the sound development of e-commerce, exploring regulatory models suitable for the development of e-commerce and accelerating the establishment of a standardized and orderly e-commerce market order
(2) Improve the level of IT application in logistics, promoting the integrated development of e-commerce and IT-based logistics
(3) Improve the level of IT application in key areas of the service sector, accelerating information sharing among the banking, securities, and insurance sectors and improving its macro regulation capability and comprehensive supervision of the financial sector

3. Improve the level of IT application in SMEs

China should improve the service system to provide support and services for IT application in SMEs and further IT application in the core business links. There are two aspects to this:

(1) Deepen IT application in SMEs, supporting SMEs to participate in industry chain cooperation with leading enterprises as the core
(2) Continue to implement projects to promote IT application in SMEs, developing and perfecting the information service platform for industrial cluster and SME cluster areas to continuously improve the service system

4. Promote IT application in agriculture and rural areas

The promotion of IT application in agriculture and rural areas should be positioned prominently in the construction of a new socialist countryside to give full play to its important role in changing agricultural development models, improving farmers' lives and balancing urban and rural development, and boosting agriculture and benefit farmers. There are two aspects to this:

(1) Perfect the comprehensive information service system in rural areas
(2) Strengthen the integration of agriculture-related information resources

Leadership should promote IT application in agricultural production, operation, management, and service and make agricultural production and operation more precise, intensive, and intelligent. The country should carry out tests and demonstrations of IT application in agriculture and develop IT application models with local characteristics.

5. Deepen e-governance application on all fronts

China should strengthen the top-level design of e-governance, persist in deepening e-governance applications, improve the organizational structure of government, and improve the government's ability in public services. There are three aspects to this:

(1) Promote the in-depth integration of IT and government affairs
(2) Enhance e-governance service capacity at the grassroots, making comprehensive use of telecommunication networks, radio and television networks, and the Internet to enrich the public service capabilities of e-government
(3) Improve IT application in social management

China should establish a population information-sharing mechanism and build a comprehensive social management information system with full coverage, dynamic tracking, information sharing, and complete functions. It should also form an IT-based social management system that is led by the government, participated in by all sectors of society, and serves the overall interests of the country.

6. Improve IT application in social undertakings

Toward the goal of equal access to basic public services, China should continuously improve IT application in the fields of education, healthcare, employment, and social security and provide solid support for the modernization of social undertakings. There are three aspects to this:

(1) Improve IT application in education
(2) Accelerate IT application in medical care and public health
(3) Build an employment and social security information service system covering urban and rural residents

The government needs to promote this system to cover issues related to the employment and social security of poor rural dwellers, such as the employment of rural workers, rural endowment insurance, disaster reduction and relief, social assistance, social welfare, minimum living security, and charity. Leadership should promote the sharing of comprehensive information concerning employment and social security information for the disabled and improve the ability to provide accessible information services to them.

7. Coordinate the integrated development of urbanization and IT application

China should give rein to the important role of IT in innovating urban management models and improving urban service capabilities in order to provide strong support for solving urban development problems and realizing precise and efficient management. There are three aspects to this:

(1) Pursue smarter urban operation and management and promote the sharing and coordination of all kinds of information on city management
(2) Promote IT application in the community
(3) Improve the IT-based management of public security

China needs to deepen IT application in public security and improve the information system for public security prevention and control. The country should refine the mechanisms of information reporting and release, emergency response, and disaster relief for public emergencies.

8. Strengthen the development and utilization of information resources

China should continuously promote the sharing of governmental information, enhance the public welfare information serviceability, and improve the development and utilization of information resources. There are four aspects to this:

(1) Improve the ability to share governmental information
(2) Increase the use of public welfare information
(3) Develop an advanced web culture
(4) Grow the digital content industry by creating digital content, developing key enterprises, and encouraging innovative business models

9. Build the next-generation national comprehensive information infrastructure

China should seize the opportunity as information networks evolve and upgrade, implement the Broadband China strategy,[45] and focus on the broadband connectivity rate, speed increase, and network integration so as to accelerate the construction of a next-generation national information infrastructure that is comprehensive, secure, and ubiquitous. There are five aspects to this:

(1) Accelerate the optimization and upgrading of broadband networks and balanced development among regions
(2) Promote large-scale commercial use and deployment of the next-generation Internet
(3) Build safe and reliable IT application infrastructure
(4) Accelerate the converged development of mass telecommunication networks, radio and television networks, and next-generation Internet
(5) Optimize the layout of the international telecommunications network, accelerating the deployment of access points for overseas business and international data centers and improving the ability to provide information network services for overseas institutions and enterprises

10. Promote the intelligent transformation and upgrading of infrastructure in important areas

China should accelerate the digital, network-based, and intelligent transformation, upgrade energy, transportation, water conservancy, environmental resources, and other fields, and promote the accurate management and efficient operation of important infrastructure.

(1) Speed up the construction of smart grids
(2) Build a smarter integrated transportation system
(3) Improve the level of information management of basic resources

Specifically, China should establish and perfect the environmental resource monitoring system. The country should establish an information system featuring full-process dynamic monitoring, pollution source control, and ecological conversation for basic resources such as land, mineral resources, and forests. Additionally, China should improve early warning, decision-making, and law enforcement abilities in the field of land resources and environmental protection.

11. Enhance citizen's IT ability

China should actively carry out IT education and training and cultivate IT talents. The country should create a talent training system where school education (including basic education, tertiary education, and professional education) combines with continuous education, and government guidance and private training complement each other. Through multiple channels and methods, such as tertiary education and continuous education, China can accelerate the cultivation of innovative, technical, and skilled IT talents.

12. Strengthen the construction of a network and information security guarantee system

Efforts should be made in the following three aspects.

(1) Ensure the security of basic information networks and important information systems, strengthening cyberspace strategic early warning and active defense and enhancing abilities

in situational awareness, monitoring and early warning, emergency response, and law enforcement regarding network and information security

(2) Strengthen the foundation of information security, enhancing information security infrastructure and increasing information security supervision and law enforcement capabilities

(3) Strengthen the security management of information content, strengthening management of the basic data on the Internet, accessing the management of new technology and new businesses, and conducting security assessments of new businesses

Also, the government should strengthen the construction of key news websites, standardize the management of comprehensive commercial websites, and build a healthy and orderly network communication system.

SECTION 3
The Path of New Urbanization with Chinese Characteristics

According to the five-sphere integrated plan for building socialism with Chinese characteristics, the path of new urbanization with Chinese characteristics is the only way to build a moderately prosperous society in all respects, accelerate the socialist modernization drive, and realize the Chinese Dream of national rejuvenation.

I. New Urbanization

1. Incorporate industrialization, IT application, and agricultural modernization

Industrialization is foremost and is the driving force for development, while agricultural modernization forms an important foundation. IT application has a late-comer advantage and provides new impetus into development. Urbanization also provides development space for industrialization and IT application and propels agricultural modernization, therefore playing an irreplaceable role in the integration of the three components.

To promote urbanization, China must give rein to the role of industrialization as the driving force, agricultural modernization as the foundation, and IT application as the leader so as to achieve the New Four Modernizations integration. The country should promote the integration of IT application and industrialization, the interaction between industrialization and urbanization, and coordination between urbanization and agricultural modernization. It should promote the unification of urban development and industrial support, employment transfer, and population agglomeration. China should ensure an equal exchange of factors of production between urban and rural areas and balance the allocation of public resources between them. What the country aims to achieve is a new type of relationship between industry and agriculture and between urban and rural areas in which industry promotes agriculture, urban areas support rural development, agriculture and industry benefit each other, and there is integrated urban and rural development.

2. Balance the population, the economy, resources, and the environment

In order to meet the requirements of being "resource-efficient and environmentally friendly," China should develop industries and attract residents based on the carrying capacity of resources and the environment in cities and towns, strive to develop a low-consumption, low-carbon, and circular economy, and conserve energy and reduce emissions to protect and improve the eco-environment. It should treat and control garbage, sewage, noise, and other pollutants through city standards, increase the green areas and woodlands, highlight urban ecological construction, promote the harmonious coexistence between city and nature and between mankind and the urban environment, and build eco-friendly cities. What China aims to achieve is to guarantee the quality, efficiency, and welfare of urbanization and advance it in a sustainable way.

3. Feature the coordinated development of large, medium, and small cities and small towns

Based on the carrying capacity of resources and the environment and complete public service functions, China should rationally control the excessive expansion of large cities and accelerate the improvement of facilities and services in small and medium-sized cities. It should focus on the rational distribution of industries and the development of supporting clusters. It needs to focus on expanding and strengthening emerging industries, especially modern services, and innovating and upgrading production methods and technological processes. China should build digital, IT-based, and smart cities and towns. By guiding the gathering of population and industries, the country aims to form a reasonable and orderly development pattern of large, medium, and small cities, promote the optimization of urban geographic space and the common prosperity of central cities and satellite towns, and create an urban environment suitable for living, working and traveling.

4. Feature the coordinated development of population agglomeration, granting of urban residency, and provision of public services

It is not urbanization in the true sense to only have non-agricultural transfer and the spatial transfer of rural labor. Nor is it high-quality urbanization to only feature population agglomeration and industrial optimization, but fail to provide migrant workers in cities access to basic public services or improve the quality of life and the living environment. Therefore, China should reform the social management system of the urban population and gradually establish a unified urban and rural residence registration system so that the migrant population enjoys the same rights as the urban population in terms of medical care, education, pension, and unemployment relief, etc., and the settled migrant population fully enjoys the rights of an urban citizen.

II. The Principles for Advancing New Urbanization

1. Follow the rules and make the best use of the opportunities available

To push forward urbanization, China must base policies on the country's realities in this primary stage of socialism to be assured of success. Leadership must be practical and realistic in setting goals for urbanization. It should not rush to find quick success by issuing administrative orders, regulations, or procedures that unnecessarily burden ground-level workers. China should promote urbanization in an active, stable, and solid manner and with a clear direction, steady pace, and specific measures.

2. Improve the quality of the environment and protect it

China should put emphasis on improving the results of urbanization and steadily increase the urbanization level of the registered population. It should improve the efficiency of urban land use and the population density of urban built-up areas. It should also improve energy use efficiency and reduce energy consumption and carbon dioxide emissions. China should attach great importance to ecological safety, expand the proportion of green space, including forests, lakes, and wetlands, and enhance water conservation capacity and environmental capacity. It should continuously improve the environment, reduce the total discharge of major pollutants, control land use intensity, increase the ability to resist and mitigate natural disasters, and improve the level of protection of historical cultural relics. The country should implement eco-friendly measures in the push for green, circular, and low-carbon development, minimize interference and damage to nature, and protect and intensively use land, water, energy, and other resources. Finally, China should take special care to preserve traditional culture while developing cities and towns with historical landmarks and local or ethnic features.

3. Take a people-centered approach and promote the granting of urban residency to people moving to cities

A people-centered approach is indispensable. China should improve the educational and civilizational level of the urban population and the living standard of residents and make it a top priority to grant urban residency to those who are able to work and live in cities and towns stably in an orderly manner. In addition, an overall plan is necessary. China should build a scientific and reasonable macro layout for urbanization based on the carrying capacity of resources and the environment, take city clusters as the main form, and devise appropriate plans to ensure that large, medium, and small cities and small towns complement each other with well-defined functions for coordinated development.

4. Handle the relationship between the government as the leader and the market as the driving force

To promote urbanization, China must pay attention to handling two pairs of relations. One is the relationship between the market and the government. China should let the market play a decisive role in the allocation of resources and give full play to the government's role in creating an institutional environment, preparing development plans, building infrastructure, providing public services, strengthening social governance, etc. The other relationship is that between the central and local governments. The central government formulates major policies and makes the overall plan and strategy for urbanization, while the localities implement the overall plan based on local realities and draw up corresponding plans to creatively carry out the construction and management work.

III. The Main Tasks for the Development of New Urbanization

1. Gradually settle the agricultural populations who have migrated to the cities

China will follow two principles. One is respecting people's will and letting them make their own choices. The other is encouraging different areas to implement reform in light of their local circumstances and at their own pace. On this basis, China needs to take a holistic approach to advancing reform of the household registration system and ensuring equal access to basic public services, taking the rural population who have migrated to the cities as the core while giving consideration to graduates from universities, colleges, and technical schools, the urban population working in cities or towns away from their registered residence, and the agricultural population on the outskirts of cities and towns. This will entail three areas of focus:

(1) Promote eligible agricultural migrant population to settle in cities and towns
(2) Allow the agricultural migrant population to enjoy basic public services in cities and towns
(3) Establish a sound mechanism for promoting the urbanization of the agricultural migrant population

2. Optimize the layout and form of urbanization

As stated earlier, this requires China to foster the coordinated development of large, medium, and small cities and small towns based on major city clusters, improve the carrying capacity of the cities, and accelerate granting urban residency to people from the countryside who have moved to cities. China needs to work to improve the quality of city clusters, promote network construction in cities, and accelerate reform of the household registration system to better attract and accommodate the rural residents moving to urban areas. The sound development of characteristic towns should be guided, and the gap between urban and rural areas should be narrowed. It is necessary to accelerate the building of a scientific and reasonable pattern of urbanization, agricultural development, ecological security, and natural coastline, vigorously promote the establishment of a green and low-carbon recycling-based industrial system, increase environmental governance and build strong ecological shelter zones, and accelerate the formation of a new pattern of modernization drive and a new modern economic system in which man and nature live in harmony.

China should optimize the spatial layout of urbanization and the scale and structure of cities and towns according to the characteristics of land, water resources, atmospheric circulation, and the carrying capacity of the eco-environment. In the urbanized regions set aside in the "Main Functional Areas Planning,"[46] the government should adhere to the principles of "overall planning, reasonable distribution, well-defined functions, and cooperation" to develop city clusters with high agglomeration efficiency, a strong ability to drive the development of surrounding areas, excellent urban systems and strong complementary functions. This will make them an important platform for supporting national economic growth, balancing regional development, and participating in international competition and cooperation. China should build an urbanization strategy for the coordinated development of cities and small towns based on the "two horizontal and three vertical"[47] railways. The two horizontal railways refer to China's Land Bridge and the railway along the Yangtze River, while the three vertical ones refer to the coastal railway, Beijing–Harbin & Beijing–Guangzhou railways, and the Baotou–Kunming Passage. The city clusters and node cities on these lines are the fulcrum, and other urbanized areas are important components. Specifically, this will entail five areas of focus:

(1) Optimize and upgrade the city clusters in the eastern region
(2) Cultivate and develop city clusters in the central and western regions
(3) Establish a coordination mechanism for the development of city clusters
(4) Promote the coordinated development of various cities
(5) Strengthen the support of comprehensive transportation networks

3. Increase the sustainability of cities

China should transform the method of urban development more rapidly, optimize the spatial structure of cities, enhance the economy, infrastructure, and public services of cities and the carrying capacity of resources and the environment for the population while effectively preventing and treating urban problems, and building harmonious, livable, distinctive and vibrant modern cities. There are six specific measures:

(1) Strengthen the ability to support the labor market
(2) Optimize the spatial structure and management pattern of cities
(3) Improve basic public services
(4) Enhance urban planning and construction
(5) Build new cities
(6) Reinforce and innovate social governance in cities

4. Integrate urban and rural development

China should continue to encourage industry to support agriculture in return for agriculture's earlier contribution to its development and encourage cities to support rural areas. It should give more to farmers, take less from them, and lift restrictions on their economic activities. The country should better balance urban and rural development, boost rural development, work to narrow the gap between urban and rural areas, and promote the coordinated advancement of urbanization and the building of new rural areas. This will entail three areas of focus:

(1) Speed up improvements to institutions and mechanisms for promoting integrated urban and rural development
(2) Accelerate the process of agricultural modernization
(3) Build new socialist rural areas

5. Reform and perfect the systems and mechanisms for urbanization development

China should: strengthen the top-level design and overall planning of the institutions overseeing urbanization; respect the laws of the market; promote coordinated reform in key areas, such as population management, land management, finance, tax revenue and banking, urban housing, administrative management, and the ecological environment; and form an institutional environment conducive to the sound development of urbanization. There are five specific measures to be taken:

(1) Promote reform of the population management system
(2) Deepen reform of the land management system
(3) Innovate the fund guarantee mechanism for urbanization
(4) Perfect the urban housing system
(5) Strengthen the ecological and environmental protection system

SECTION 4

The Path of New Agricultural Modernization with Chinese Characteristics

Agricultural modernization is the basic method to solve issues relating to agriculture, rural areas, and farmers (the "Three Rural Issues"),[48] to build a moderately prosperous society in all respects, and to build a well-rounded modern socialist country. Efforts should be made to blaze a new trail of agricultural modernization with advanced production technology, moderate business scale, strong market competitiveness, and a sustainable ecological environment.

I. The Content of the Path of Agricultural Modernization with Chinese Characteristics

Generally speaking, agricultural modernization refers to the transformation process and means of moving from traditional to modern agriculture. Since the founding of the PRC, several generations of central leadership have actively explored the path of agricultural modernization with Chinese characteristics. Four major goals in this regard have been formed: the modernization of production conditions, socialization of production organizations, application of scientific production technology, and sustainability of the ecological environment. The agricultural modernization in China is carried out under a specific historical background, and so comes with its own distinctive characteristics. It is agricultural modernization implemented on the basis of small-holder farming during the transition from a planned economy to a market economy and with the wealth of farmers being relatively low to begin with. Due to the disadvantageous starting point, China still has a long way to go to achieve agricultural modernization but is certain to achieve it.

To promote agricultural modernization in the new era, China must focus on the core task of ensuring national food security and firmly follow the two basic requirements of having Chinese characteristics and being "new." Having Chinese characteristics means basing the process on

China's realities and conforming to the conditions of China's economic and social systems and the characteristics of resource endowments. Being "new" means demonstrating the underlying features of our times, closely following the new concepts and trends of world agricultural development, and putting the latest scientific and technological achievements into practice. The new path to agricultural modernization with Chinese characteristics is a process of using modern technology and management to develop rationally, allocating and using various agricultural resources, optimizing the market and the ecological environment, and achieving sustainable development under specific conditions in China. Agricultural modernization with Chinese characteristics is the process where China's traditional agriculture transforms into modern agriculture. It is the process by which the comprehensive production capacity of agriculture becomes modernized. It is a process in which agricultural laborers with modern qualities use modern agricultural production methods to produce high-quality agricultural goods that can meet the needs of the society under the specific conditions of China.

II. The Features of the Path of Agricultural Modernization with Chinese Characteristics

First, it adheres to the basic strategy of balancing urban and rural economic and social development. In reviewing the agricultural development of various countries in the world, China has found that in the process of advancing industrialization and urbanization, many countries have suffered from agricultural recessions and a depressed rural economy due to negligence. This, in turn, has taken a toll on the development and stability of the entire country. However, as agriculture's share of GDP gradually declines, this will by no means change *the status* of agriculture as the foundation of the national economy.[49] As the resolution of issues concerning agriculture, rural areas, and farmers has an overall impact on building a moderately prosperous society in all respects, leadership must always make it a top priority in the work of the whole Party.

Second, agricultural modernization implements the policy of encouraging industry to support agriculture in return for agriculture's early contribution to its development and encouraging cities to support rural areas. China's agricultural and rural development has lagged behind for too long. The fundamental reasons are that the economic and social management system derived from the urban-rural dual economic structure has not been broken, and the resulting loss of rural production factors and the apparent lack of financial and technical support for agriculture have not changed.

Third, agricultural modernization develops the public financial system and improves the transfer payment system. Any nation would find it challenging to achieve agricultural modernization by solely relying on the strength of the farmers. Establishing a public financial system, improving the transfer payment system, and forming a support and protection system for agriculture that conforms to WTO rules and has the local nation's own characteristics are common practices in countries that have achieved agricultural modernization. With the improvement of industrialization and urbanization, a permanent mechanism of industry promoting agriculture and urban areas helping rural areas is taking shape in China. Measures must be taken to comprehensively deepen rural reform, increase the coverage of public finance in rural areas, strengthen rural public services, create more jobs for farmers, increase farmers' income, and reduce their burdens. This will provide institutional guarantees for the construction of modern agriculture and a new socialist countryside.

Fourth, agricultural modernization emphasizes improving the overall agricultural production capacity, which marks the level of agricultural modernization. China ranks among the top in the world in terms of the total production of many agricultural products but still lags behind developed countries in terms of input-output rate and economic benefits.

III. The Central Tasks of the Path of Agricultural Modernization with Chinese Characteristics

1. Build an innovation-driven agricultural industry and concentrate efforts on transformation and upgrading

Innovation is the primary driving force of agricultural modernization. China must: promote innovation in the supply system, S&T research and implementation, and in agricultural systems and institutions: implement the adoption of a food crop production strategy based on farmland management and the application of technology: and foster healthier and more sustainable growth drivers. Efforts should be made in the following aspects:

(1) Promote agricultural restructuring
(2) Enhance the safety assurance capability of grains and other important agricultural produce
(3) Cultivate stronger technology and equipment and increase IT application
(4) Deepen agricultural and rural reform

2. Benefit rural communities through coordination and pursue balanced development

Coordination is the inherent requirement of agricultural modernization. China must establish a holistic and systematic view and foster industrial integration, regional coordination, and synergy among major participants. It must make sure production planning goes hand in hand with economic and social development, resource availability, and environmental tolerance, and promote agricultural modernization to develop at pace and greatly. Efforts should be made in the following aspects:

(1) Push forward integrated and harmonious development among the primary, secondary, and tertiary industries in rural areas
(2) Balance agricultural development among regions
(3) Promote the balanced development of various forms of agricultural entities

3. Vitalize agriculture with green development and seek greater sustainability

Green development is an important symbol of agricultural modernization. Guided by the conviction that lucid water and lush mountains are invaluable assets, China must pursue green agricultural development and improve the weak links in ecological construction and quality and safety. It must also achieve efficient resource utilization, stable ecosystems, a good production environment, and quality products. Efforts should be made in the following aspects:

(1) Step up resource conservation and ecological restoration
(2) Strengthen the protection of the agricultural environment
(3) Ensure the quality and safety of agricultural products

4. Facilitate agricultural development through higher-level opening up and expanded foreign cooperation

Opening up is an essential requirement to achieve agricultural modernization. China must adhere to two-way opening up, win-win cooperation, and common development; strengthening cooperation in agriculture with foreign countries; giving equal attention to markets and resources at home and abroad; and further opening up in agriculture. Efforts should be made in the following aspects:

(1) Optimize cooperation planning
(2) Upgrade overall international cooperation in agriculture
(3) Push for sound growth in agricultural trade

5. Enrich farmers through sharing and improving the livelihoods and well-being of the rural population

Sharing is an essential requirement of agricultural modernization. Adhering to the idea of development for the people and relying on the people, China must sustainably enhance farmers' income and strive to build a new agricultural development system featuring fair opportunities, equal access to services, and sharing of results so that farmers can live a more dignified life. Efforts should be made in the following aspects:

(1) Carry out targeted poverty elimination with tailored industrial development
(2) Promote agricultural development in special regions
(3) Provide equitable access to infrastructure and public services in rural and urban areas

6. Strengthen policy support with stronger efforts in strengthening agriculture, benefiting rural communities, and enriching farmers

Policy support and government support are the key to rural revitalization. Progress should be made in the following aspects:

(1) Improve fiscal support policies for agriculture
(2) Innovate financial support policies for agriculture
(3) Perfect agricultural land use policies
(4) Improve market regulation policies for agricultural products

IV. Policies and Measures That Advance the Path of Agricultural Modernization

First, agricultural infrastructure must be enhanced. China should strengthen the protection of arable land and speed up the development of high-standard farmland. China should launch farmland pollution control projects to tackle non-point source pollution and heavy metal pollution. The country should improve water conservation facilities, with different focuses in different areas. It will focus on the dredging and reconstruction of the ponds and weirs and the construction of the end canal system in the hilly and mountainous areas in the south. China will build small pumping stations and other drought-relief facilities in the main grain-producing areas in the central plains and water-saving irrigation facilities in the arid and semi-arid areas in the northwest. The country should improve rural infrastructure by upgrading rural power grids and roads and improving production and living conditions in rural areas.

Second, the scientific and technological progress in agriculture must be accelerated. China should carry out three kinds of key projects as follows:

(1) The S&T project for the high-yield seed industry. Efforts should be made to cultivate more breakthrough high-yield varieties like super-hybrid rice by increasing investment and tackling difficult problems concerning the output increase of agricultural produce.
(2) The S&T project for the model to increase grain yield. The integration of agricultural equipment and technology should be deepened on the basis of mechanization. China should tackle key problems in weak links and technological bottlenecks to integrate and assemble regional and standardized high-yield and high-efficiency technology models.
(3) The R&D project for sustainable agricultural development. China should conduct research on advanced applicable technologies and promote technologies to save land, water, pesticide, energy, and labor so as to reduce production costs and improve resource utilization efficiency.

Third, policies to support and protect agriculture should be enhanced. The agricultural subsidy policy system should be improved. China should perfect policies related to direct subsidies to farmers for growing grain and general subsidies for purchasing agricultural supplies. These should be linked to the area of contracted land by farmers that will establish a stable growth mechanism to motivate ordinary farmers to grow grain. China should set up subsidies for the scaled operation of grain, linking them to the actual grain-growing area and mainly tilting them toward large farming households, family farms, and farmers' cooperatives in order to motivate scaled agricultural entities to grow grain. In addition, a price support system should be built. China should improve the minimum purchase price policy for key grain varieties, reasonably determining and continuously increasing the minimum purchase price and maintaining a reasonable level of grain prices. The country should explore the establishment of a target price and price difference subsidy system for important agricultural products to protect farmers' income gained from farming and growing grain. China should increase the rewards and subsidies of major grain-producing counties to incentivize the main producing areas.

Fourth, new forms of business entities should be vigorously cultivated. China should enhance policies to support new agricultural entities. According to the different development stages of family farms and other new entities, the country should make support policies with different focuses. For instance, China should help solve such problems as credit guarantees, infrastructure, land transfer, and land use for facilities in the early stage of development, as well as help tackle problems involving quality, safety, and brand building in the mature stage. The country should strengthen supervision of the influx of industrial and commercial capital into the agricultural sector, resolutely prohibiting non-agricultural use of arable land and guiding non-grain use of arable land. The country should step up the cultivation of "new" professional farmers. In this regard, China should establish standards and formulate corresponding support policies to make farming an occupation with "an entry threshold, an economic return, a guaranteed income, and professional dignity." The country should also establish a mechanism to encourage high-caliber talents to return to the countryside, supporting graduates from colleges and universities and people returning to their hometowns to start businesses dedicated to modern agriculture.

Fifth, the reform of agricultural and rural systems should be deepened. Following the direction of market-oriented reform, China should seek major breakthroughs in three aspects as follows:

(1) Improve the rural land system. China should strengthen the protection of land property rights, explore the establishment of a mechanism to separate rural land contracting rights and management rights, and improve the inheritance, transfer, and withdrawal mechanisms. The country should allow rural collective construction land to enter the market for circulation. It should improve the compensation mechanism for land acquisition and reasonably determine the compensation standard.

(2) Improve the commercial service system for agriculture. China needs to deepen the reform of grassroots public service institutions for agriculture, support the development of various service organizations for agriculture, and encourage the development of various forms of agricultural production services. This will accelerate the construction of a diversified socialized service system.

(3) Deepen rural financial reform. China needs to promote innovation in rural financial organizations, build village banks and other new rural financial institutions, and support the formation of rural mutual fund organizations. The country should innovate the rural mortgage guarantee mechanism and explore the implementation of large- and medium-sized agricultural implements, rural land contractual management rights, and other mortgage loan pilot projects. China should perfect the policy-based agricultural insurance system, expanding insurance coverage and establishing a mechanism for diffusing the risk of huge catastrophes.

SECTION 5
SECTION 5
The Path of Synchronized Development of New Four Modernizations

At present, China has entered the middle and late stages of industrialization and is in the process of the in-depth development of the New Four Modernizations. Pursuing the New Four Modernizations and ensuring their synchronized development is not only a strategic task of China's socialist modernization drive but also an important driving force to accelerate the formation of a new economic and social development model and promote the sustained and sound development of the Chinese economy and society.

I. The Need for Synchronized Development of the New Four Modernizations

The path of synchronized development of the New Four Modernizations ("new" industrialization, IT application, urbanization, and agricultural modernization) features the integration between IT application and industrialization, the interaction between industrialization and urbanization, and the coordination between urbanization and agricultural modernization. As the basic method to realize China's modernization, the New Four Modernizations are mutually connected and reinforcing. Industrialization and IT application are "twin brothers" that have reached a certain development stage, and their deep integration provides the direction and driving force of industrial upgrading. Urbanization has the greatest potential to stimulate domestic demand and serves as the platform for the modernization drive. Finally, agricultural modernization is the cornerstone and an important fulcrum for China's economic and social development. In other words, what's key to synchronized development is the mutual support and mutual promotion of the New Four Modernizations, which form a synergy. Additionally, the essence of synchronized development is the interaction of the Four Modernizations, thus forming a complete system. Regarding the relations of the Four Modernizations, industrialization produces supply, and urbanization creates demand; industrialization and urbanization drive and equip agricultural modernization, which in turn provide support and guarantee for industrialization and urbanization; and IT application promotes the other three modernizations. Therefore, by promoting the synchronized and harmonized development of the Four Modernizations as they interact with each other, China can realize a leap-forward development in social productivity.

1. A strong practical pertinence

Since the outset of the new century, China's four modernizations have entered a new development phase and achieved ever-better coordination. However, there are still obvious shortcomings, such as insufficient integration of IT application and industrialization; insufficient interaction between industrialization and urbanization; weak coordination between urbanization, industrialization, and agricultural modernization; and slow agricultural modernization.

Over the years, China's IT application has developed rapidly and led the world in some areas. Furthermore, industrialization has also shown fast growth, far greater than that of urbanization and agricultural modernization. As a result, there are 260 million more permanent residents in cities and towns than the registered population there, resulting in a new dual structure inside urban areas. There are a series of problems caused by the uncoordinated, unbalanced, and inadequate development between urban and rural areas and between industrial and agricultural sectors. At present, urbanization in China is relatively lagging behind and of low quality. Besides that, the biggest challenge facing the four modernizations is agricultural modernization being left far behind, making it a weak link in China's modernization drive. Also, the poor agricultural foundation and the underdeveloped rural areas have together become the biggest constraint for building a moderately prosperous society in all respects.

The key to solving these problems is to implement the concept of coordinated development and promote the synchronized development of the New Four Modernizations. The synchronized development of the New Four Modernizations emphasizes that industrialization, IT application, urbanization, and agricultural modernization are interrelated and indivisible as a whole and become unified in the socialist modernization drive. The synchronization of the four modernizations is not only a strategic task of China's socialist modernization but also an important driving force for accelerating the formation of a new economic development mode and promoting the sustained and sound development of China's economy. To this end, General Secretary Xi pointed out, "We must promote the synchronized development of new industrialization, IT application, urbanization, and agricultural modernization, gradually increase the supporting role of strategic emerging industries and the service sector, and move our traditional industries up to the medium-high end of the value chain, and foster new growth areas by giving play to market mechanisms and relying more on innovation in industrialization."

2. Inevitability

Since reform and opening-up, a large number of surplus rural laborers have entered cities and towns and worked in non-agricultural industries as a result of the rapid development of China's industrialization. Hence, productivity has been greatly liberated and developed, leading to rapid economic growth for more than 30 years. By the end of 2011, China's urban population had reached 691 million and accounted for 51.27% of the total, which meant that China was no longer a country with a predominantly rural population and ushered in an era of the "city-based society."

However, China's working-age population has been declining year by year since reaching its peak in 2012. An undersupply of labor has thus begun to appear in some regions and industries while wage costs have kept rising. This has led to a gradual loss of the production advantages of labor-intensive products, weakened export competitiveness, and a severe overcapacity in iron & steel and other industries. All of this indicates that China has entered a new stage of medium-high economic growth.

Changes in the economic development stage and the driver of growth have provided inherent requirements and important opportunities for the synchronized development of the New Four Modernizations. To achieve quality, profitability, and sustainable economic growth and the synchronized development of the New Four Modernizations, China needs to: improve the quality of industrialization via IT application; advance urbanization to expand domestic demand; and promote agricultural modernization, which will guarantee the safety of agricultural produce following the mass migration of farmers to urban areas.

II. The Significance of Synchronized Development

1. The synchronized development of the New Four Modernizations: a major innovation in China's modernization theory and practice

The proposal and promotion of the New Four Modernizations and their synchronized development is a major innovation in China's modernization theory and practice. It is simultaneously a new achievement in the adaption of Marx's modernization theory to Chinese conditions and a new interpretation and exploration by the CPC of the development of China's modernization drive in the new era. Although each individual part is not new, the synchronized development of the New Four Modernizations emphasized by the Party and the state is a major theoretical and practical innovation.

The synchronized development of the New Four Modernizations meets the requirements of the Scientific Outlook on Development and the vision of innovative, coordinated, green, open, and shared development. It stresses increasing the quality of development and balancing economic growth and ecological protection while pursuing the harmony of people, society, and nature. The synchronized development of the New Four Modernizations will allow China to achieve greater progress in productive forces and the relations of production so as to realize scientific and harmonious development and build a moderately prosperous society in all respects.

The synchronized development of the New Four Modernizations profoundly reflects the shift in the development concept from being "material-oriented" to "people-oriented." It aims to enhance the all-around development of the people, the quality of life of the people, and ultimately the happiness index of the people. In the future, China's urbanization will focus on the urbanization of people (which means converting the rural population to urban residents), industrialization of energy conservation and environmental protection, IT application in smart cities, and agricultural modernization of food safety. All these will, at last, be at the service of the people.

Transcending the old modernization path of developed countries, the synchronized development of the New Four Modernizations represents a scientific understanding of the requirements of China's economic and social development. It is also a "golden key" for accelerating economic structural adjustment, which will surely inject a strong impetus into China's modernization drive.

2. The synchronized development of the New Four Modernizations: a major strategic decision for China's modernization drive

The proposal and promotion of the New Four Modernizations and their synchronized development provide a general way of thought for China's modernization drive. It is also a major strategic decision made by the CPC based on the overall situation, long-term consideration, and the requirements of the times.

Industrialization is a prerequisite for realizing modernization. To accelerate China's modernization drive, the country must take a new path to industrialization. IT application is a logical choice for realizing modernization. The new era requires us to use IT to propel industrialization and use industrialization to stimulate IT application, promoting the deep integration of both. Urbanization is the route China must take to realize modernization and improve people's well-being, while industrialization is the support for urbanization. So, China needs to integrate industrial development, job creation, and population agglomeration to promote the interaction between industrialization and urbanization. Agricultural modernization is the foundation for realizing modernization. There is no way to promote industrialization or urbanization under the conditions of agricultural decline, with run-down villages and poverty among poor rural dwellers. China must take the road of coordinated development of urbanization and agricultural modernization to achieve a new type of relations between industry and agriculture and between urban and rural areas. One in which industry promotes agriculture, urban areas support rural development, agriculture and industry benefit each other, and there is integrated urban and rural development.

3. The synchronized development of New Four Modernizations: an unremitting pursuit of achieving national rejuvenation

The proposal and promotion of the New Four Modernizations and their synchronized development reflect the unremitting pursuit of building China into a modern socialist country and realizing the great rejuvenation of the Chinese nation. Advancing the synchronized development of the New Four Modernizations is a strategic deployment and core requirement for economic and social development in the current times. As said at the beginning of the chapter, prior to reform and opening-up, China put forward the Four Modernizations, i.e., the goal of modernizing China's industry, agriculture, national defense, and S&T. The road to the New Four Modernizations is a new path the country has taken in recent years. The most important backdrop for it is the adoption of the reform and opening-up policy and a socialist market economy and an open economy, which greatly motivated the initiative and creativity of the people nationwide to advance modernization. Meanwhile, China has also learned from the experience and lessons of foreign countries in modernization.

The essence of the New Four Modernizations is as follows. In industrialization, China should stress fostering competitive advantages based on the optimal allocation of resources, value quality, and efficiency, and pay attention to resource conservation and environmental friendliness. In IT application, the country should emphasize that IT application and industrialization reinforce each other to provide impetus to structural adjustment and industrial upgrading. In urbanization, China should take a people-oriented approach, increasing people's development opportunities and improving people's quality of life. Finally, in agricultural modernization, the country should pay special attention to modernizing agricultural production and operation methods and farmers' way of life.

Therefore, the New Four Modernizations and their synchronized development are proposed to address the deep-seated contradictions and problems in economic and social development.

They provide not only the basic methods of achieving China's modernization but also a package solution to a series of challenges and problems that emerge in the modernization process. As President Xi pointed out, "We are also advancing the new type of industrialization, IT application, urbanization, and agricultural modernization in a coordinated way, which will help relieve 'growing pains.'"

III. Efforts to Advance Synchronized Development

1. Shore up the weak links in agricultural modernization

To strengthen agricultural modernization, China must recognize that addressing issues concerning agriculture, rural areas, and farmers have a central place on the work agenda. The country must prioritize the development of agriculture and rural areas and speed up the modernization of agriculture and villages to build rural areas with thriving businesses, pleasant living environments, social etiquette and civility, effective governance, and prosperity. China will establish industrial, production, and business operation systems for modern agriculture and improve the systems for supporting and protecting agriculture. The country will develop appropriately scaled agricultural operations of various forms, cultivate new types of agri-businesses, improve specialized agricultural services, and encourage small household farmers to become involved in modern agriculture. China needs to accelerate the advancement of agricultural supply-side structural reform. The country will adjust and optimize the product, industrial, and distribution structure in the agricultural sector, strengthen the quality of agricultural produce, and foster new driving forces for agricultural and rural development. The ultimate aim is to create a path of agricultural modernization with Chinese characteristics featuring output efficiency, product safety, resource conservation, and environment friendliness.

2. Give play to the supporting and leading role of scientific and technological innovation

Implementing an innovation-driven development strategy will determine the future of the Chinese nation. Innovation is essential for China's modernization drive and in particular scientific and technological innovation. In "new" industrialization, China must accelerate the development of a market-oriented system for technological innovation in which enterprises are the main players and synergy is created through the joint efforts of enterprises, universities, and research institutes. The country must realize major breakthroughs in scientific and technological innovation. It also must promote the shift from "Made in China" to "Created in China," from high-speed growth to high-quality development, and from Chinese products to Chinese brands. In IT application, the country should vigorously promote the innovation of network information technology. China needs to foster new growth drivers via IT application and then promote new development. In urbanization, the country should give rein to the important role of scientific and technological innovation. It is necessary to strengthen the building of smart cities and technologically innovative towns and improve the urban public service so as to attract a strong and talented workforce. In agricultural modernization, China must take the road of developing agriculture through scientific and technological progress. The country should implement the strategy of revitalizing agriculture through quality development, accelerating the transformation in orientation from output increase to quality improvement, and boosting the innovation ability, competitiveness, and total factor productivity in the agricultural sector. All of this will quicken the transition from a large agrarian country to a world-class agricultural powerhouse.

3. Meet the requirements of green development

Man and nature form a community of life. Green development is a necessary condition for sustainable development and an important manifestation of people's pursuit of a better life. To promote the synchronized development of the New Four Modernizations, China must take the path of ecological progress with low consumption of resources and low emissions. In "new" industrialization, the country will develop green industries, such as energy-saving and environmental protection industries, and clean production and clean energy industries. In IT application, China should develop green information technology for environmental protection and ecological governance and utilize information technology to boost ecosystem protection and build a beautiful China. In urbanization, the country should respect and protect nature and follow its laws. China needs to promote green, circular, and low-carbon development, minimizing interference and damage to nature and seeking compact, intensive, efficient, and green development. In agricultural modernization, the country must be committed to ensuring harmony between man and nature, to green development in rural areas, and to the systematic and coordinated stewardship of mountains, rivers, and forests, as well as farmlands, lakes, and grasslands. China should strengthen the comprehensive treatment of severe environmental problems in rural areas, establish a market-oriented diversified ecological compensation mechanism, increase the supply of ecological products and services, and achieve the unity of people's affluence and ecological beauty.

4. Promote the integrated development of the New Four Modernizations

New industrialization, IT application, urbanization, and agricultural modernization must be advanced together. First, IT application and new industrialization must be deeply integrated. Efforts should be made to foster strategic emerging industries, develop smart manufacturing and modern services, create new industries, new formats, and new business models, and build a new system for modern industrial development. Among them, China should pay particular attention to deepening the integration of the Internet and the real economy. To this end, the country will make traditional industries more digitalized and intelligent, build a bigger and stronger digital economy, and expand new space for economic development. Second, IT application and urbanization must be integrated. China should carry out "Internet Plus Education," "Internet Plus Healthcare," and "Internet Plus Culture" actions to promote equal access to basic public services. Third, IT application and agricultural modernization must be integrated. The country needs to quicken Internet construction in rural areas, expand the coverage of optical fiber networks and broadband networks there, and improve the level of intelligent agricultural production and network-based management via IT application. Fourth, "new" industrialization, urbanization, and agricultural modernization must be integrated, letting industry give full support to agriculture and urban areas to spur rural development. In this way, China aims to achieve new types of industry-agriculture and urban-rural relationships under which industry and agriculture, as well as urban and rural areas, reinforce each other and achieve comprehensive integration and common prosperity.

IV. Promoting the Deep Integration of IT Application and Industrialization

First, China should use IT to propel industrialization. It means making full use of information technology, rationally and effectively using and developing information resources, as well as using information equipment and technology to update and equip various sectors of the national economy, thereby promoting the path to industrialization. IT application mainly propels industrialization in the following aspects:

(1) The information industry promotes the transformation of the production modes of traditional industries.
(2) IT application transforms the operations and management methods of enterprises.
(3) IT application causes changes in the organizational structure of traditional enterprises.

Second, China should use industrialization to stimulate IT application. This means providing all-around support for IT application, including materials, capital, and technology, as industrialization progresses. Traditional industries are the technological and industrial basis for the development of IT application. Following this, traditional industries can open up new markets for IT application. "Made in China 2025,"[50] smart manufacturing, and "Internet Plus"[51] are concepts closely related to the integration of IT application and industrialization.

To promote the deep integration of IT application and industrialization, China should step up efforts to formulate the guidelines and planning system in the "1+X"[52] initiative around the implementation of Made in China 2025. It should also organize the launch of major projects such as the construction of the national manufacturing innovation center, develop smart manufacturing, strengthen the overall industrial base, and strive to achieve substantial breakthroughs in a number of important areas and key links.

V. Promoting Interaction between Industrialization and Urbanization

1. Synchronized evolution of industrialization and urbanization and integration of the three industries over time

Chronologically, there are different dominators and characteristics at different development stages. The first stage is the starting stage, in which industrialization is the core and cornerstone and promotes the development of urbanization. The second stage is the growth stage, during which industrialization and urbanization also reach the mid-term phase and interact most obviously. The balance of power also changes as the level of industrialization gradually lags behind that of urbanization. The third stage is the mature period, in which the influence of industrialization begins to fade while urbanization gradually becomes the center of economic development. The leading industry of urban development changes from the industry to the services sector, and the modern service industry and IT industry become the main sectors that attract the workforce.

2. Integration of industry and city and functional zoning by area

By adjusting the spatial distribution of industries, industrialization promotes the process of urbanization, the formation of functional areas, and the interactive development of industry and city. Through agglomeration economies, urbanization reduces space transaction costs, propels industrialization, and further promotes the integration of industry and city. This process is the organic unity of two agglomeration economies: one is the production-based agglomeration economy, and the other is the transaction-based agglomeration economy.

VI. Promoting Coordination between Urbanization and Agricultural Modernization

To seek the harmonized development of urbanization and agricultural modernization, China should regard urban and rural areas/residents, industry, and agriculture as a whole when making overall plans and conducting comprehensive research. The country needs to promote urban and rural integration and coordination in such fields as planning, construction, industrial development, market information, policy measures, eco-environment protection, and social programs through system reform and policy adjustments. China will change the long-standing urban-rural economic and social structure and achieve equality in policy and national treatment and complementarity in industrial development. This will ensure that farmers are entitled to enjoy the same level of civilization and benefits as urban residents and that the urban and rural economy and society develop in a comprehensive, coordinated, and sustainable manner.

CHAPTER NINE

The Implementation of the RRS

The upgrade from "New Countryside Construction" to "Rural Revitalization" represents a conceptual innovation in the Party's work related to agriculture, rural areas, and rural people. The implementation of this RRS, which aims at bringing modernization to the agricultural sector, will be a historical advance that will win a decisive victory in building a moderately prosperous society in all respects, a modern socialist country in an all-around way.

SECTION 1
The Significance of Implementing the RRS

China is a traditional agrarian country with a large rural population, a chasm separating outcomes in urban and rural areas, and pressing issues relating to agriculture, rural governance, and farmers. The "Three Rural Issues"—agriculture, rural areas, and farmers—have been a major concern to the central government and the theme of the No. 1 Central Document for 19 consecutive years since 2004 and for 24 years since China's reform and opening-up. The RRS was first proposed in the report to the 19th National Congress of the CPC. Then, in January 2018, the CPC Central Committee and the State Council issued "Opinions on the Implementation of the RRS," which indicates that China's rural revitalization will enter a new period of development.

I. The Goals and Tasks of Implementing the RRS

Implementing the RRS requires an abidance to the general requirement of building rural areas with thriving businesses, pleasant living environments, social etiquette, civility, effective governance, and prosperity. It also means that the state must put in place sound systems, mechanisms, and policies to promote integrated urban-rural development, must push forward coordinated economic, political, cultural, social, ecological, and party development in rural areas, must accelerate the modernization of rural governance systems and increase their capacity, must speed up agricultural and rural modernization, and must pursue rural revitalization in a way that is distinctive of Chinese socialism. When this happens, agriculture will become an industry with bright prospects, farming will become an appealing occupation, and rural areas will become beautiful communities in which people live and work in peace and contentment.

The "Chinese characteristics" of socialist rural revitalization are manifested in three aspects. First, resolving issues relating to agriculture, rural areas, and farmers is the number one priority for the Party and essential to the overall situation. This is a characteristic of the Chinese system. Second, rural revitalization is based on the collective ownership of land, the most important means of production in China. Such a structure of ownership helps prevent several bad outcomes: bankruptcy among farmers, rural household differentiation, and the migration of a large number of destitute smallholders to cities and towns in the course of modernization. Third, to advance agricultural supply-side structural reform, it will be necessary to establish an efficient, sustainable, and competitive industrial system to support rural revitalization. Given the current conditions prevailing in China, it is not feasible to rely solely on high levels of welfare to retain rural populations. A prosperous countryside must be achieved through the development of thriving businesses.

The RRS is a major strategy put forward by China based on a profound understanding of urban and rural dynamics, contemporary trends, and the laws of urban and rural development. The implementation of the RRS embodies a unity of past and present. It is a new driving force for rural development in the new era, an inevitable prerequisite for resolving the tension between unbalanced and inadequate development, on the one hand, and the people's ever-growing needs for a better life, on the other. Pursuing this strategy clears the way to accomplish the Two Centenary Goals and to achieve common prosperity for all the people.

II. The Significance of Implementing the RRS

The significance of the RRS can be demonstrated by reflecting on a number of factors.

(1) The RRS embodies the unity of past and present history and reality for those in rural areas pursuing the Chinese Dream. It is an impetus for rural development in the new era. Judging from the history of human civilization, rural decline is a worldwide problem, an inevitable result of urbanization and industrialization. After the founding of New China, the nation began to pursue industrialization. Through that initial period and even into the period of reform, relevant policies have always been centered on the city and industry. Undeniably, however, rural areas have made great contributions to the growth of cities and industries. Today's proposal of rural revitalization is an affirmation of the esteemed status of the countryside. The introduction of the RRS means putting the countryside on an equal

footing with the city and regarding both as an organic whole so that it becomes possible to fully leverage the industrial, ecological, cultural, and other resources in rural areas and to better motivate farmers to be catalysts of rural development, establishing a more sustainable endogenous growth mechanism.

(2) The RRS addresses a serious tension, the tension between existing development that is unbalanced and inadequate and the people's ever-growing need for a better life. Inadequate rural development and uneven urban-rural development prominently manifest this principal tension facing Chinese society. In the course of its period of rapid industrialization and urban influx, China's urban and rural areas have become economically divided, and this divide can also be seen comparing one rural area to another. At present, the two most prominent imbalances are the imbalance between urban and rural development and the imbalance within rural development. The greatest inadequacy exists in rural development, which includes inadequate development of agricultural modernization and a new socialist countryside, inadequate development of education, science, culture, and health in rural areas, and inadequate sharing of the fruits of modern social development with farmers.

(3) The RRS is an inevitable requirement for realizing the Two Centenary Goals. It helps extend China's scope of modernization from cities to rural areas. Due to historical reasons, there are many barriers that lie in the path of agricultural modernization, a new socialist countryside, and educational, technological, and cultural development for farmers. Looking ahead to the time when economic growth and income increase, both urban and rural residents have many expectations for the construction and development of rural areas. Introducing the RRS means that China will formulate and implement a special strategic plan for rural revitalization, turning the countryside into a new growth vista, a new key area for the modernization drive. The key to rural revitalization is not to turn a village into a city but to narrow and gradually eliminate the urban/rural gap in residents' working conditions, living standards, and quality of life. It is not to turn villagers into city residents but to ensure equal public welfare and equity in public services regardless of place of residency. The goal of implementing the RRS is to modernize agriculture and update rural areas.

(4) The RRS is a correction of the past miscalculation that emphasized agriculture over rural development. As the terminology changes from the discussion of "urban-rural coordination" to "urban-rural integration," emphasis is put upon the equal status of urban and rural regions, the interaction of urban and rural factors, and the integration of urban and rural space. A large rural population is a basic condition in China. Even after urbanization reaches the maturity period, there will still be about 400 million rural residents. Therefore, China cannot achieve its overall modernization without the modernization of its agriculture and countryside. At present, the biggest disparity between China and developed countries exists in the countryside instead of cities. Rural development remains a major Chinese shortcoming, as the nation is plagued by a series of problems, such as insufficient infrastructure, backward living conditions, and the loss of traditional culture.

(5) The RRS is a prerequisite to achieving the common prosperity of all people, and it further helps China's implementation of the five-sphere integrated plan in rural areas. The general

objective of the strategy (viz. to build rural areas with thriving businesses, pleasant living environments, social etiquette and civility, effective governance, and prosperity) and the five-sphere integrated plan (viz. to promote coordinated progress in the economic, political, cultural, social and eco-environmental fields) are connected with each other, as is evident from the text. "Thriving businesses and prosperity" correspond to progress in economic and social fields. A "pleasant living environment" corresponds to progress in the eco-environmental field. "Social etiquette and civility" correspond to progress in the cultural and social fields. And "effective governance" corresponds to progress in the political field.

Compared with the requirements for building a new socialist countryside (i.e., advanced production, better living standards, a civilized lifestyle, clean surroundings, and democratic management), the general objective of the RRS is a higher-level development requirement. Yet both the strategy and the initiative of building a new socialist countryside emphasize "common prosperity," which is a fundamental principle of Chinese socialism, reflecting the nature and objectives of socialism as well as the common ideal of all people.

SECTION 2

The Guiding Ideology and Development Goals for Implementing the RRS

The RRS must be based on various governmental and agricultural conditions; it must strengthen the nation's sense of responsibility, mission, and urgency, and it must promote the enhancement of agriculture, the improvement of rural areas, and the personal development of rural people in every way possible. Properly executed, the strategy will leave the Chinese people with greater determination, clearer goals, and more powerful measures and will write a new chapter in the overall story of Chinese rural competence.

I. The Guiding Philosophy and General Requirement for Implementing the RRS

The major components entailed in implementing the RRS are outlined below.

1. Take building rural areas with thriving businesses as the central task
Such building involves several tasks: fostering industrial development, facilitating the flow of factors such as capital, technology, and talents to rural areas, mobilizing the enthusiasm and creativity of farmers, forming an industrial system for modern agriculture, promoting the integrated development of primary, secondary and tertiary industries in rural areas, and maintaining the vitality of agricultural and rural economic development. Rural areas become revitalized when vitality is injected into them. And vitality comes from thriving businesses. The countryside must take on a new look, with abundant grain and livestock and deep integration of primary, secondary, and tertiary industries. China must promote the overall upgrading of

agriculture, embrace a paradigm shift from increasing production to improving quality, and promote the emergence of new industries and new business formats in rural areas.

2. The establishment of rural areas with high quality of life, involves a focus on green development

It necessitates strengthening resource and environmental protection in rural areas, vigorously improving infrastructure such as water, electricity, road, gas, housing, and communication, coordinating the protection of mountains, rivers, forests, farmlands, lakes, and grasslands, and protecting the lucid waters, lush mountains, and the refreshing and clean pastoral scenery. A beautiful China relies on beautiful countryside. The rural ecology of the countryside must be restored and improved, turning its ecological advantages into valuable assets for development.

3. Progress in culture, education, medical care, and public health

The nation should step away from outdated social mores and embrace the progress of civilization. This entails promoting China's agricultural heritage and fine traditions so that the overall quality of farmers and the level of civility in rural areas will be further improved. This task requires us to not only carry forward outstanding agricultural traditions of the past but also to guide farmers to embrace modern values and legal awareness, thus improving the general disposition of rural residents and imbuing rural society with a greater degree of civility. It is a task that cannot be finished quickly; it requires sustained effort. Therefore, local leaders should attempt to locate particularly talented individuals and encourage people from all walks of life to devote themselves to rural cultural development, establishing a new driving force in rural China.

4. The establishment of rural areas with effective leadership

The development of grassroots democracy and the rule of law must be strengthened, healthy social trends fostered, illegal activities punished, and the countryside made more harmonious, stable, and orderly. This approach requires a combination of self-governance, rule of law, rule of virtue, and innovation in rural governance mechanisms. Rural governance is the cornerstone of national governance. Chinese authorities must combine modern governance concepts and learned experience with traditional governance resources, resolving conflicts with self-governance, bringing an end to conflicts by applying the rule by law, and promoting beneficence with the rule of virtue so that people live and work in peace and the countryside becomes harmonious and stable.

5. Revitalize rural prosperity: sustainable income, modern living, and common prosperity

The goal is to significantly narrow the gap between urban and rural areas with respect to living standards and basic public services. A number of priorities emerge: opening avenues for wealth creation, increasing rural incomes in a comprehensive way, improving farmers' living standards, and improving public services in rural areas.

In order to promote rural revitalization, the overarching priority must be to vigorously develop rural productivity, support employment, encourage business startups, and open up channels to increase rural incomes. Adherence to norms of urban-rural integration and the principle of giving priority to agriculture and rural areas will be extremely advantageous. China must follow the laws of rural development and preserve the rural landscape.

II. The Development Goals of Implementing the RRS

In accordance with the strategic arrangement proposed by the 19th National Congress of the CPC, two documents were drafted that specified goals in the implementation of the RRS. These documents, the Central Rural Work Conference (Dec. 2017) and the No. 1 Central Document (2018), aimed to secure a decisive victory in building a moderately prosperous society in all aspects and achieving the second centenary goal in two stages. The goals were these:

(1) The short-term goal: By the year 2020, important progress will be made, with an institutional framework and policy system basically in place. The overall agricultural production capacity will have increased significantly, and the agricultural supply system will have improved in evident ways. Integration between primary, secondary, and tertiary industries in rural areas will be more firmly established. More channels to raise farmers' income will have opened up. Disparities in living standards between urban and rural residents will be gradually reduced. No Chinese people will live under the existing poverty line since all poverty-stricken counties in China will have been lifted out of poverty. Regional poverty will be eliminated, rural infrastructure enhanced, and rural living environments improved. Solid progress will be made in building a beautiful and livable countryside. Equitable access to basic public services will be further enhanced. A system and mechanism for urban and rural integration will be initially established. The countryside will be more attractive to talent, the rural eco-environment will be improved, and agricultural ecological serviceability will be boosted. Rural grassroots organizations with party organization at the core will be developed, and the rural governance system will be perfected. Systems and mechanisms for the Party's leadership in rural work will have further improved. The ideas and measures for promoting rural revitalization will be established in all departments and regions.

(2) The mid-term goal: By the year 2035, decisive progress will be made with basic rural and agricultural modernization. The agricultural structure will fundamentally improve, and the employment quality of farmers will increase significantly. Relative poverty will be further alleviated. Solid progress will be made toward universal prosperity. Equitable access to basic public services will be guaranteed, and the system and mechanism for urban and rural integration will be further perfected. Social etiquette and civility will reach a new height, and the rural governance system will be perfected. The rural eco-environment will be fundamentally improved, and the goal of building a beautiful and livable countryside will be basically realized.

(3) The long-term goal: By the year 2050, all-around revitalization featuring strong agriculture, beautiful countryside, and prosperous farmers will become a reality.

The time schedule of the three goals of the RRS is consistent with that set out in the report to the 19th National Congress of the CPC. "Important progress" means that systems and mechanisms for the RRS have been established and that rural civilization, social governance, and industrial development have achieved initial results. "Decisive progress" means that RRS systems and mechanisms have been further straightened out, barriers to the bidirectional flow of factors between urban and rural areas have been eliminated completely, and rural and agricultural modernization has been realized. "All-around revitalization" means that all systems, mechanisms, and policies for the RRS are quite complete: urban and rural areas interact with and reinforce each other; rural areas have strong agriculture, a beautiful countryside, and well-off farmers; and issues relating to agriculture, rural areas, and farmers have been resolved.

III. The Basic Principles of Implementing the RRS

Below are a set of basic principles at work in the implementation of the RRS:

(1) Persistence is needed in maintaining party leadership in rural work. Systems and mechanisms for the Party's governance over rural affairs must be improved, including an intra-party system of laws and regulations, to ensure the Party always provides overall leadership and coordinates the efforts of all involved, thereby providing a strong political guarantee for rural revitalization.

(2) Persistence is needed in prioritizing rural and agricultural development. Stakeholders must act in concert and be united in understanding that rural revitalization is the common will of the whole Party. Priority should be given to rural areas in areas such as official assignment, factor allocation, capital investment, and public services so that shortcomings in various rural developments can be remedied more quickly.

(3) Persistence is needed in prioritizing the status of farmers. Policymakers should mobilize the enthusiasm, initiative, and creativity of farmers, all the while respecting their wishes and helping them embody their primary role and pioneering spirit. The protection of farmers' fundamental interests and the promotion of farmers' common prosperity must be seen as a fundamental goal of the state. As this priority is made manifest in action, a continuous increase in farmers' incomes will develop, and Chinese society will continuously improve farmers' sense of fulfillment, happiness, and security.

(4) Persistence is needed in a comprehensive way. It is critical to develop a good grasp of the scientific implications of rural revitalization, to explore the various functions and values of rural areas, and to push forward coordinated economic, political, cultural, social, ecological, and party development in rural areas. With a focus on synergy and relevance, it will be possible to make coordinated progress.

(5) Persistence is needed in integrating urban and rural development. Institutional barriers should be removed, and the free flow and equal exchange of urban and rural factors should be promoted. The consistent understanding must be that the market plays the decisive role in resource allocation, the government better plays its role, and new industrialization, IT

application, urbanization, and agricultural modernization go hand in hand. Within this framework, a new type of relationship will emerge between industry and agriculture, city and countryside, a relationship within which industry and agriculture, urban and rural, mutually reinforce each other and achieve comprehensive integration and common prosperity.

(6) Persistence is needed in pursuing harmony between man and nature. Lucid waters and lush mountains are invaluable assets; the nation must realize this and act on this understanding. Systematic governance of mountains, rivers, forests, farmlands, lakes, and grasslands must be carried out in a holistic manner, acting on the principles of resource conservation and environmental protection, as well as the awareness that nature can restore itself. Red lines in ecological conservation should be strictly adhered to. Rural revitalization should be led by green development.

(7) Persistence is needed in adjusting measures to local conditions and making gradual progress. A scientific grasp of the idiosyncratic characteristics of differentiated development in rural areas is necessary, as is proficiency in top-level design. A pattern must develop employing certain steps: first, strengthening guidance in planning; then prioritizing key areas; then implementing differentiated measures; and finally, putting forward success as a paradigm for other areas. China will do everything in its capacity, avoiding the addition of new requirements at each level, eschewing the one-size-fits-all approach, and rejecting the practice of formality for formality's sake. Sustained effort will result in solid progress.

SECTION 3
Deepening Rural Reform

Deepening reform is the fundamental way to boost rural revitalization. It is a long-term and strategic institutional arrangement and an inexhaustible driving force for rural revitalization. This reform takes many forms.

I. Adherence to the Strategy of Prioritizing Agriculture and Rural Areas

Prioritizing the development of agriculture and rural areas is a strategic approach that helps China achieve the Two Centenary Goals and remedy shortcomings in agricultural and rural development. This approach entails that issues concerning agriculture, rural areas, and farmers should have a central place on the work agenda of the Party, as it embarks on a journey to fully build a modern socialist China. The industry-agriculture relationship and the urban-rural relationship must be adjusted and ameliorated. Rural areas must be prioritized in terms of factor allocation, resources, and public services. The development of the agricultural and rural economy must be quickened. Inadequacies in public services, infrastructure, and information exchange within rural areas must be addressed, in order to narrow the gap with urban areas. By doing so, agriculture may again become an industry with bright prospects, farming an appealing occupation, and rural areas beautiful communities in which people live and work in peace and contentment.

II. Advancing Reform of the Rural Land System

Rural land contracting practices will remain stable and unchanged on a long-term basis. The current round of contracts will be extended for another 30 years upon expiration, a move that will not only stabilize farmers' expectations but also leave room for further policy improvement. The implementation of Three Rights Separation (referring to ownership, contract, and management rights) is a major innovation in China's rural reform since it embodies the dialectical unity between the "changed" and the "unchanged" in land contracting and satisfies the needs of land circulation.

(1) Gather information that will inform the reform of the rural collective property rights system. This is a major step in rural reform, and it dovetails with the reform of the rural land system. Property rights system reform aims to safeguard the property rights and interests of rural people and to strengthen the collective economy. In order to implement the central government's Opinions on Steadily Advancing Reform of the Rural Collective Property Rights System, it is imperative to skillfully clear and verify rural collective assets in order to better understand the situation.

(2) Advance the reform of the rural collective property rights system by expanding its scope. The scope of pilot reform of rural collective assets shares and powers should be expanded so as to promote successful experiences and practices. Moreover, the government must invigorate rural collective assets, improve the allocation and utilization efficiency of various resource factors in rural areas, and develop/expand the collective economy through multiple channels.

III. Accelerating the Development of Modern Agriculture

Modernized agriculture is the foundation of a modern economic system. At present, China's agricultural modernization is still a weak link in the synchronized development of the Four Modernizations. Therefore, it is important to advance new development concepts, to focus on pursuing agricultural supply-side structural reform, and to work toward the goal of ensuring the effective supply of agricultural products, the sustained and rapid growth of farmers' income, and the continuance of sustainable agricultural development. The development quality, efficiency, and competitiveness of agriculture must be improved. This means taking the path of agricultural modernization with a focus on output efficiency, product safety, resource conservation, and environment friendliness. China should aim to achieve notable progress in agricultural modernization by 2020, realize basic agricultural modernization by 2035, and build China into a modern agricultural power by 2049.

This path toward modernization involves each of the following.

(1) China's control over its own food supply must be safeguarded
Given the size of the nation (over a billion people), providing sustenance to the population has always been the top priority for the country and the primary task of agricultural development.

Feeding the population involves consolidating and increasing grain production capacity, adopting a food crop production strategy based on farmland management and the application of technology, implementing the strategy of storing grain on the ground and storing grain on technology, implementing a maximally strict system for protecting farmland, building high-standard farmland on a massive scale, protecting and improving the quality of cultivated land, and increasing the application of improved varieties, machinery, technology, and IT in agriculture. China must expedite delimiting and building the functional zone for grain production and the protection zone for important agricultural products, must perfect benefit compensation mechanisms for major production areas, and must mobilize the agricultural enthusiasm of local governments in rural areas and the passion for farming and growing possessed by many residents in these areas.

(2) Three major systems for modern agriculture must be established
The industrial, production, and business operation systems are the "three pillars" of modern agriculture, and each must be encouraged:

- To accelerate the establishment of the industrial system for modern agriculture, China should promote the transformation, upgrading, and integrated development of planting, forestry, animal husbandry, fishery, agricultural product processing/circulation, and agricultural service industries.
- To accelerate the establishment of the production system for modern agriculture, China should supply agriculture with modern materials and equipment, equip farmers with modern S&T, and transform agriculture with modern production methods. There is a pressing need to push forward technological innovation and the application of results, to promote mechanization and IT application in agricultural production and operation, and to enhance overall agricultural productivity and the ability to offset risks.
- To accelerate the establishment of the business operation system for modern agriculture, China should diligently nurture new professional farmers and new business entities, improve the agricultural commercial service system, make agricultural operation more intensive, systematic, upscaled, socialized, and industrialized, and accelerate the transformation and upgrading of agriculture.

(3) Agricultural structure must be adjusted, and the integrated development of primary, secondary, and tertiary industries in rural areas must be promoted, in the process optimizing agricultural structure in products, businesses, and layout
Centralized planning can help promote a balance between basic food, cash crops, fodder crops, and various agricultural industries (forestry, animal husbandry, and fishery). It will be possible to integrate planting, breeding, processing, and sales and to promote the integrated development of primary, secondary, and tertiary industries in order to extend the industrial chain and upgrade the value chain. Stakeholders need to realize that agricultural growth is propelled by quality and branding. In this vein, it would be good to promote standardized production and full-process

supervision, to place emphasis on supplying quality, environmentally agricultural products, and to comprehensively improve the quality and safety of produce. The agricultural product processing industry deserves attention, as does the promotion of entrepreneurship and innovation in rural areas, each of which will promote the integrated development of primary, secondary, and tertiary industries.

Each of the three major sub-industries within agriculture (planting, husbandry, and fishery) deserves particular attention. To advance agricultural restructuring, one focus should be on corn, which will promote the restructuring of the planting industry. An additional focus should be on pigs and herbivorous animal husbandry, which will help promote the restructuring of the livestock industry. A third focus should be placed on fishing. Resource conservation, output reduction, and income raises can all act to promote the restructuring of the fishery industry in a sustainable way.

One priority in agricultural reform is to improve systems so that they support and protect agriculture. Such improvement involves adapting to the market-based situation, with a focus on protecting and mobilizing the enthusiasm of rural people. Efforts to reform and improve fiscal subsidy policy, to make optimal use of existing resources and increase supply, to provide stronger support to structural adjustment, to protect resources and the environment, and to advance R&D investment should be encouraged. China should establish proven interest compensation mechanisms for functional zones of food production (e.g., wheat, rice, corn) and protected areas for the production of important agricultural products (e.g., soybean, cotton, rapeseed, sugar cane, natural rubber). A more market-oriented approach is needed, which would involve deepening the reform of the grain purchase and storage systems and price formation mechanisms, reducing direct intervention in the market, and protecting the reasonable income of producers. Rural financial, insurance, and agricultural trade regulation policies must be improved in order to promote the sound development of the industry.

A thriving agriculture industry in China requires vitality, creativity, and stewardship. The nation should develop new industries and business formats—e.g., distinctive industries, leisure agriculture, rural tourism, and e-commerce—in rural areas. At the same time, green development of agriculture should be encouraged, in addition to systematic governance of natural resources (mountains, rivers, forests, farmlands, lakes, and grasslands). Chinese leadership must reinforce the prevention and control of agricultural non-point source pollution, implement water-saving actions, strengthen wetland protection and restoration, promote systems of crop rotation and fallowing, encourage grassland ecological conservation and "Grain for Green" programs, and accelerate the formation of green production modes in agriculture.

(4) Appropriately scaled agricultural operations of various forms must be strengthened, encouraging small household farmers to become involved in modern agriculture

New business entities and moderately scaled operations are the leading forces for the transformation, restructuring, and modernization of the agricultural sector. China can take a role in actively fostering new entities such as family farms, specialized farmer cooperatives, and agricultural enterprises, implementing multiple operation modes such as pooling of land as shares, land transfer, entrusted land management, and joint farming so as to raise the level of moderately scaled agricultural operations.

Meanwhile, China's national conditions have determined that ordinary farmers will remain the fundamental basis of agricultural production for a long time. As such, it is important to protect the interests of smallholders. The benefit coupling mechanism should be improved, and smallholders should be encouraged to participate in scaled operations and modern production through multiple channels so that they can share the proceeds of agricultural modernization. The national and local governments should cooperate in developing diversified agricultural productive services and should perfect the agricultural socialized service system. The government must reform the grassroots agricultural technology extension system, even as it continues to explore methods of encouraging the joint development of public services to extend agricultural technology and operational technical services.

IV. Strengthening Basic Services in Rural Communities

The Chinese countryside is remarkable for the harmony and stability it enjoys; this harmony and stability must be safeguarded. Meeting farmers' needs for a better life is the fundamental goal, supplemented by the goals of strengthening basic services in rural communities, innovating in rural social governance, and achieving the long-term stability of rural areas.

The rural governance model, which combines self-governance, the rule of law, and the rule of virtue, needs improvement. Such an integrated model brings a new paradigm to thinking about how to strengthen rural governance. Improvement cannot be accomplished all at once, however. First, it will be necessary to explore new rural governance models, giving full play to the role of grassroots party organizations as the core of leadership, and moreover to reinforce systems of community-level self-governance, make village affairs more transparent, and incorporate the role of various talented individuals, experienced consultants, and other groups into rural governance. Second, the rule of law must be strengthened in rural areas, even as steps are taken to improve rural life: the building of peaceful towns and villages, the implementation of special campaigns to address prominent public security problems, the creation of programs to help rural people grow in compliance to the law and use the law to protect their rights and interests. Third, the government will vigorously promote the development of the spiritual aspects of rural life over time. This may mean things like encouraging traditional culture and civilized customs, singing the themes of the times, cultivating new social trends, praising good deeds, championing China's underlying values, spreading positive energy, and denouncing immoral behavior in the form of village regulations, education, and punishment.

A strong work team must be formed to tackle the "Three Rural Issues." The cultivation, allocation, and use of agricultural and rural cadres is a matter of great importance and should be treated as such. China must dedicate time and resources to training professional rural service personnel who have a good knowledge of agriculture, love rural areas, and care about rural people. It must also raise awareness of the Party's policies related to the "Three Rural Issues" as well as professional training and must enhance the ability to guide services for agriculture, rural areas, and farmers. Leading cadres at all levels should be encouraged to go to the countryside and engage with farmers in their work. County and township party committees and governments must exert great efforts in work related to agriculture, rural areas, and farmers. Optimizing the structure of community-level leadership in rural areas must be a priority, even while leaders buttress the work of college graduates serving as village officials, diligently select and appoint "first secretaries," recruit more township civil servants via examination, and elect more township leading cadres from outstanding village cadres. The rural service personnel must have a profound affection for the land, for agriculture, and for farming, and they must carry forward the fine values and traditions of the nation's work.

V. Further Deepening Rural Supply-Side Reform

Under the circumstances of this new era, the major problems facing China's agriculture have changed from a lack of supply to the threat of structural contradictions, which are prominently manifested in the current coexistence of excessive demand alongside excessive supply. Therefore, pushing forward supply-side reform in the agricultural sector and increasing the sector's comprehensive benefits and competitiveness has become a major goal when formulating government policies. A necessary condition of the reform is that national food security has been ensured and that demand has been roughly coordinated with supply. The goal of the reform is to increase farmers' income and ensure the effective supply of agricultural products while ensuring supply quality. And the fundamental approach is to seek institutional reform and mechanism innovation. By optimizing industrial, production, and business operating systems and by improving land output rate, resource utilization rate, and labor productivity, China will create a paradigm shift in agricultural and rural development, moving from an over-reliance on resource consumption to the pursuit of ecological sustainability, from an emphasis on quantity to an emphasis on quality.

To advance agricultural supply-side structural reform, the supply of quality, environmentally friendly agricultural products must be increased, and the agricultural structure must be optimized. The nation will adapt to market demand and optimize product structure. It will develop moderately scaled operations and optimize the business structure. It will leverage comparative advantages and optimize the regional structure. At the same time, China will work to accomplish a variety of other imperatives: accelerating scientific and technological innovation, enhancing agricultural development momentum, promoting integrated development, and optimizing industrial structure. In the attempt to promote sustainable agricultural development, green production must be adopted, and various major problems in the agricultural environment must be addressed. The market should play a decisive role in resource allocation, and the government should guide decisions surrounding that allocation. It is time to reform the price formation mechanism for important agricultural products like grain, reform the purchase and stockpiling system, deepen reforms of the rural property rights system, reform the budget system to support agriculture, accelerate innovation in rural financial systems, and improve mechanisms for rural entrepreneurship and innovation. By deepening rural reform more quickly, the market will be invigorated, boosting the free flow of resources and stimulating market players so as to inject a strong impetus into agricultural supply-side structural reform.

Promoting the agricultural supply-side structural reform is a long-term process with many severe challenges, both in terms of handling the relationship between the government and the market and in terms of coordinating the interests of all involved. Reform should be advanced steadfastly, but not foolishly: the nation must face up to these difficulties and challenges. China must dare to endure the tumult of reform, all the while reducing its costs and actively guarding against risks. Grain production capacity must not be reduced, the momentum of farmers' rising incomes must not be reversed, and rural areas must maintain stability. Agricultural supply-side structural reform will bring a profound change to agriculture, rural areas, and rural people. The direction of reform has been clear, and the bottom line has been drawn. Success in rural reform is achieved by respecting creation at the grassroots level. This method should also be adopted to advance agricultural supply-side structural reform. Chinese leaders must respect grassroots practices, encourage farmers to create, and strive to create a relaxed atmosphere for reform and innovation.

CHAPTER TEN

Optimizing the Spatial Pattern of Economic and Coordinated Regional Development

China's long-standing basic guideline for regional economic development has involved the following imperatives: to improve the territorial space, to promote the coordinated development of regions, and to build a national territorial space layout and support system that will sustain high-quality development. The task of optimizing spatial structure is critically important to improving efficiency in regional economic development.

SECTION 1
Measures to Promote Coordinated Regional Development in the New Era

I. The Significance of Implementing the Strategy of Coordinated Regional Development

There are a number of ways in which the implementation of a strategy of coordinated regional development will be significant for China.

First, the strategy is an important way to enhance the synergy of regional development. Uneven development among various regions is a basic expectation in China due to large differences between regions. Regional development strategies are an important component of economic and social development strategy. Since 1999, China has gradually formulated a "master strategy" for regional development. This strategy aims at the development of the West, the revitalization of the Northeast, the rise of Central China, and the trailblazing development role of the East. Since the 18th National Congress of the CPC, the CPC Central Committee, with Xi at its core, has coordinated domestic and foreign affairs and has placed greater focus on the overall situation. It has proposed various approaches to promote the formation of a new pattern of nationwide interactive development: the Belt and Road Initiative, strategies for the Coordinated Development of the BTH region, and strategies for the Development of the Yangtze River Economic Belt. The main objectives in implementing the coordinated regional development strategy were introduced in the report to the 19th National Congress of the CPC. By enhancing the connectivity of regional strategies at all levels and the synergy and integrity of regional development, China will certainly break new ground in coordinated regional development.

Second, the strategy is an inherent requirement in opening up new space for regional development. With the construction of large-scale infrastructure, especially the high-speed railway network and the telecommunication network, inter-regional connectivity in China has reached an unprecedented level, which sets the stage for the formation of a new pattern of nationwide interactive development between regions. As China's urbanization accelerates, city clusters and metropolitan areas play an increasingly important role in economic and social development. The rapid growth of the marine economy, as well, has made expanding the blue economy increasingly important. Any implementation of a coordinated regional development strategy involves incorporating areas with a variety of sizes and roles into national strategies for overall planning and arrangement. The areas involved may be regions, cities, rural areas, coastland areas, and even portions of the sea. In all these locations, it is important to promote regional interaction, urban-rural linkage, and land-sea coordination. This is of great strategic significance in the effort to optimize the spatial structure and open up new space for regional development.

Third, the strategy is an important support for the creation of a modern economic system. Regional economies are cornerstones of the national economic system. At the present moment, China's economy has shifted from a stage of high-speed growth to a stage of high-quality development. In the pursuit of regional economic development, the focus must be on this development stage, which means optimizing the economic structure and efficiently switching to new drivers of growth. The coordinated regional development strategy will be implemented to draw upon the comparative advantages of each region and deepen the division of labor between regions. The free flow of factors will be promoted, improving the spatial allocation efficiency of resources. It will be possible to narrow the gap in basic public services so that the people in all regions can enjoy equitable access to basic public services. Through intentional planning, different regions will develop according to their main functions so as to promote a spatial balance between population, economy, resources, and the environment, thereby achieving more efficient, fairer, and more sustainable development with higher quality in all regions. This sort of improved regional development will play a supportive role in improving the quality and effectiveness of China's economic development and promoting the creation of a modern economic system.

Fourth, the strategy is a major measure to achieve the Two Centenary Goals. The coming years are crucial for achieving the first centenary goal and moving toward the second centenary goal. To build a moderately prosperous society in an all-around way, the focus must be on priorities, on addressing inadequacies, and on shoring up points of weakness. To implement the coordinated regional development strategy, China must focus on the priority of work which is related to contiguous poor areas as a whole and must remedy weaknesses in alleviating the poverty of the rural poor to resolutely fight the battle against poverty. By doing this, it will be possible to achieve the following goals by 2020: No rural poor population will live under the existing poverty line; all poverty-stricken counties in China will be lifted out of poverty; and regional poverty will be eliminated. This is a major strategic move that will help the people in poverty-stricken areas join other Chinese citizens as they enter a well-off society in all aspects. To build a moderately prosperous society in all aspects by 2020 and embark on a journey of building a socialist modern country in an all-around way, the coordinated regional development strategy must be continuously implemented, and modernization must be promoted in a coordinated way in all regions, as the Chinese people strive to achieve common prosperity for all.

II. Measures to Implement the Strategy

In the space below, a number of imperatives required to implement the coordinated regional development strategy are discussed:

(1) Establish a new pattern for the development and protection of territorial space. This pattern should give full play to the comparative advantages of different regions on the basis of local carrying capacity (how much population the environment can sustain) and should gradually form a spatial framework consisting of urbanized areas, main production areas for agricultural products, and production functional areas. The pattern should also optimize the distribution of major infrastructure, major productivity, and public resources.

(2) Advance coordinated regional development. The CPC has been the catalyst for a new stage of large-scale development in the Western region, impressive breakthroughs in the revitalization of Northeast China, the pursuit of high-quality development in Central China, and an increased rate of modernization in East China. Smaller areas will also receive attention, as old revolutionary base areas and ethnic minority areas are given assistance in speeding up development and as border areas receive aid in promoting prosperity and stability along the border and in improving the lives of the people there. China will advance various projects that create innovation platforms and new growth poles, including the coordinated development of the BTH region, the development of the Guangdong–Hong Kong–Macao Greater Bay Area, and the integrated development of the Yangtze River Delta.

(3) Establish the Xiong'an New Area at a high standard. The core task driving the coordinated development of the BTH region is to relieve Beijing of functions nonessential to its role as the capital, and a primary way to accomplish this is to improve the new mechanism for coordinated regional development. With this improved mechanism, it should be possible to develop a Chinese way to solve "urban diseases." The government will also expedite the building of a sub-administrative center for Beijing and form an optimized structure for the capital's core functions. Three key areas stand out as areas of potential breakthrough: transportation, ecology, and industry. China must fulfill its potential by building an integrated and modernized transportation network, expanding environmental capacity and

ecological space, and optimizing its industrial layout. These interventions will set the tone for collaborative innovation in communities in the BTH region.

(4) Persist in the overall development of land and sea, develop the "blue economy," and bolster China's standing as a maritime power. China is a major maritime country, and the ocean plays a very important role in the overall development and opening up of the country. Therefore, coordinated land and marine development must consistently be pursued in an effort to increase China's maritime stature. It is necessary to accelerate the development of the marine economy, optimize the structure of the marine industry, and grow this industry into a pillar industry so as to lay a solid foundation for building China into a maritime power. Implementation of maritime ecosystem-based comprehensive management will also be beneficial, as it increases the protection and development management of coastal zones and coastal beaches. China must safeguard and expand its maritime rights and interests in a coordinated way—moreover, safeguarding the freedom of maritime navigation and maritime passage—and a variety of methods can be developed to accomplish this.

(5) Promote new, people-centered urbanization. In coming years, China will implement an action plan for urban renewal, move forward with projects for urban ecological restoration and functional improvement, coordinate urban development (planning, construction, and management), rightsize cities (determining population, population density, and spatial structure), and enhance the coordinated development of cities and towns of various sizes. The structure of administrative divisions will be optimized, giving full play to the leading role of central cities and city clusters. Modern metropolitan areas will be built. The nation will promote the development of the Chengdu–Chongqing economic zone and will more broadly promote urbanization with a focus on county towns.

III. Promoting the Formation of a New Pattern of Integrated Urban-Rural Development

The task of integrating urban and rural development is challenging. Here are a set of ideas for a pattern that can guide such development:

(1) Networks of cities and towns will be created based on city clusters, enabling coordinated development between cities of different sizes and small towns. The city cluster is an important growth pole of China's economic development, and it is also the new hallmark of China's innovation-driven development. In accordance with the requirements of optimizing city clusters in the Eastern region and developing city clusters in the Central and Western regions, China will continue to support a number of city clusters that participate in international dynamics and that promote balanced development of territorial space alongside the coordinated development of regions. The clusters include the Yangtze River Delta, the Pearl River Delta, the BTH region, the Chengdu–Chongqing area, the middle reaches of the Yangtze River, the Central Plains, the Harbin–Changsha area, and the Beibu Gulf zone. Big cities have tremendous potential to drive the development of small and medium-sized cities, gradually

forming a development pattern featuring horizontally differentiated development combined with vertical division of labor. The government will perfect the coordination mechanism of city clusters, accelerate the construction of the inter-city rapid transit system, and promote the coordination among cities in the industrial division of labor, infrastructure, ecological protection, and environmental governance so as to enhance coordinated development between cities of all sizes and small towns.

(2) The work of granting permanent urban residency to incoming rural residents will be expedited. Such work is crucial to promoting the new type of urbanization. At the end of 2016, the percentage of the registered urban population relative to the total population and the percentage of the permanent urban population relative to the total reached 41.2% and 57.4%, an increase of 5.9% and 4.8% points, respectively, over those numbers at the end of 2012. It is necessary to deepen the reform of the household registration system, lower the threshold, and open up new channels for granting urban residency so as to ensure that the urbanization rate of the registered population in the country will increase to about 45% by 2020. The full coverage of the residence permit system must also be accelerated, encouraging local governments to expand the scope of public services for residence permit holders and to improve service standards.

IV. Establishing New, Effective Mechanisms to Ensure Coordinated Development

The following steps should be taken to ensure that effective mechanisms for coordinated development are put in place:

(1) Give full play to the role of market mechanisms. Rules and practices that hinder a unified market and fair competition have no place and should be removed. Explicit and implicit market barriers should also be removed, and the orderly and free flow of factors of production across regions should be promoted, even as efficiency and fairness of resource allocation are improved and the establishment of a unified and open market system with orderly national competition is accelerated.

(2) Innovate regional cooperation mechanisms. In accordance with the principle of leveraging complementary strengths for mutual benefit, China will support the development of multi-level, multi-form, multi-field regional cooperation. It will also back up industrial transfer across regions, support the joint construction of cooperation platforms such as industrial parks, and encourage various forms of innovation in regional cooperation mechanisms (e.g., organizational guarantee, consistency in planning, coordination of interests, incentive and constraint, fund sharing, information sharing, policy coordination, and dispute resolution).

(3) Improve regional mutual assistance mechanisms. China will improve the paired assistance system between developed and underdeveloped regions, come up with new ways to provide assistance, and strengthen assistance in education, S&T, and talent. The development ability of underdeveloped regions will be enhanced, and paired assistance will be promoted, changing it from an approach that mainly benefits one side to one that benefits both sides.

(4) Establish sound region-wide compensation mechanisms. China will establish and improve the compensation mechanism for ecological protection in the upper, middle, and lower reaches of the river basin, will develop ecological compensation demonstration areas based on localized ecological function, will perfect the benefits compensation mechanism between resource exploitation areas and resource utilization areas, and will increase transfer payments to areas of major agricultural production and key ecological function, in order to coordinate and balance inter-regional interests.

SECTION 2

Advancing the BTH Coordinated Development and the Construction of the Xiong'an New Area

I. The BTH Coordinated Development: A Major National Strategy in the New Era

Coordinated development in the BTH region meets an important need to build a new capital economic circle and promote innovation in regional development systems in the future. This development is needed in order to explore and improve the layout of city clusters and to provide models for optimized development of regional development. It is needed to explore an effective path for ecological progress and promote the balanced development of population, economy, resources, and the environment. And it is needed as a way to draw upon the complementary advantages of the BTH region, promote the development of the Bohai Economic Rim, and drive the development of the northern hinterland. As a major national strategy, BTH Coordinated Development is required not only to solve the contradictions and problems facing these three areas but also to optimize regional planning for national development, improve the spatial structure of social productive factors, create new economic growth poles, and form new economic development patterns.

II. Methods to Promote the BTH Coordinated Development

The purpose of coordinated development in the BTH region is to combine complementary strengths in pursuing mutual benefit. Thus, when leadership turns its attention to speeding this development, a scientific and sustainable path is needed. Various economic and spatial structures must be modified, a model for optimized development of densely populated areas must be explored, coordinated regional development must be promoted, and new growth poles must be created as China blazes a new trail for intensive development. Throughout the world, the functional areas of the capitals of major countries are usually under the direct jurisdiction of the central government rather than local governments. Over many years of Chinese history, the needs of Beijing's functional areas have become increasingly clear. The orderly shifting of Beijing's non-capital functions to address its "metropolitan mire" is a central facet of the strategy of BTH

Coordinated Development. The core of the strategy involves adjusting economic and spatial structures to realize the coordinated and orderly development of the three areas. The strategy undeniably manifests a vision of innovative, coordinated, green, open, and shared development, a vision that can guide the diligent construction of the capital's functional areas.

The sorts of methods that will successfully promote coordinated development in the BTH region all possess the following characteristics:

(1) An unswerving focus on moving non-capital functions away from Beijing. The capital city should not be a magnet for industries that could thrive elsewhere. A key goal, then, is to continuously relocate manufacturing industries, especially high-consumption industries (but also some tertiary industries such as regional logistics bases and specialized markets), and to relocate some public service functions (e.g., education, healthcare, and training agencies) and some administrative and institutional service organizations. Moreover, the nation should employ high-level planning in constructing the sub-administrative center for Beijing, with the aim of establishing it as a demonstration zone for a world-class city, an exemplar of the new urbanization, and a locus for the coordinated development of the BTH region. The population of downtown Beijing is expected to settle down to 400,000 to 500,000 permanent residents by 2035. The Beijing government must combine the process of phasing out non-capital functions with environmental stewardship, population control, and the enhancement of functions. This change is undertaken in order to coordinate the use of space spared, promote the restructuring of the old downtown area of Beijing, and optimize the essential functions of the capital.

(2) A level of dedication to optimizing the spatial pattern of the BTH city cluster. In accordance with the framework of "one core, two cities, three axes, four areas, and multiple nodes" determined by the Outline of the Plan for Coordinated Development of the BTH Region, the plan is to build a world-class city cluster with Beijing as the core. There are several key tasks involved. First, Beijing's role as "one core" deserves a great deal of deference, even as the government aims to strengthen the integrated and coordinated development of Beijing and Tianjin as the "two cities" that are intended to jointly lead and drive the development of surrounding areas. Second, industrial development belts and urban agglomeration axes should be built to form the main framework of regional development; they may be built along the major transportation corridors like Beijing–Tianjin, Beijing–Baoding–Shijiazhuang, and Beijing–Tangshan–Qinhuangdao. Third, it will be necessary to increase the overall carrying capacity of regional central cities and node cities, attract industries and populations in an orderly manner, and form a modern urban system featuring clear positioning, a reasonable division of labor, unencumbered functionality, and ecological sustainability, as the nation embarks on a green, low-carbon innovative urbanization path.

(3) A commitment to make breakthroughs in key tasks in a coordinated way. This commitment has many dimensions:

- Efforts will be made to build "a BTH region on the track." To this end, the Chinese government will build a more convenient and unimpeded highway network, create a "one-hour commuting circle," build modern airports and ports, and further modernize transportation organizations and services.
- Integrated environmental access and an exit mechanism will be established. Steps will be taken to strengthen the joint prevention, control, and governance of pollutants in the air and water. Energy production and consumption will be revolutionized. Meanwhile, efforts will be made to expand the regional environmental capacity and ecological space, including the promotion of the development of the Yanshan–Taihang Mountain Ecological Safety Barrier, the Ecological Transitional Zone of Beijing–Tianjin–Baoding Wetlands, and the National Park Ring.
- Supply-side structural reform will be deepened in accordance with the requirements of building a modern economic system. Leadership will straighten out the industrial development chains of the three areas and will build platforms for strategic cooperation and function transfer, such as the Caofeidian Integrated Development Zone, the Beijing New Airport Economic Zone, the Zhangjiakou–Chengdu Ecological Area, and the Tianjin Binhai New Area. In addition, advantageous industrial clusters based on regions will be created in order to service the whole country and drive the development of the world.
- The reform of all-around innovation in the BTH region will be deepened. In this regard, the construction of a national scientific and technological innovation center must be promoted with global influence in Beijing, even as progress is made to integrate three factors: Beijing's original innovation, Tianjin's transformation of R&D achievements, and Hebei's promotion and application of the first two factors. The cities will pool efforts to support the construction of a pioneer zone of innovation-driven development in the Xiong'an New Area in Hebei, forming a community of collaborative innovation.
- Stakeholders will promote the integrated reform of markets for factors of finance, land, technology, and information, even as they create a high ground for regional systems and improve mechanisms for coordinated development in public administration, infrastructure connectivity, co-environmental protection, scientific research, and technological innovation.
- Long-term mechanisms for coordinated management in border areas will be established in order to unify planning, policies, management, and control.
- Efforts will be made to improve the energy, water resources, and other infrastructure systems, including joint construction, benefit sharing, balanced development, and intensive use. These improvements will contribute to making the capital city and its surroundings a diverse and dynamic cultural system and building a public service system with quality facilities distributed evenly in both urban and rural areas.
- The commitments of Beijing and Tianjin to provide paired assistance to surrounding areas in Hebei Province, such as Zhangjiakou, Chengde, and Baoding, must be fulfilled.

III. Developing Plans and Adopting High Standards in Building the Xiong'an New Area

To deepen the strategy of BTH Coordinated Development and the planning and building of the Xiong'an New Area in Hebei Province must be seen as an important breakthrough point from which to explore new models for the optimized development of densely populated areas, seek new ways of regional development, create new growth poles for economic and social development, realize new horizons for expanded opening up, and develop a new platform for foreign cooperation.

Xiong'an is another new area of national significance, in addition to the Shenzhen Special Economic Zone and Shanghai Pudong New District. Its establishment is a strategy that will have lasting importance for the millennium to come, a significant national event. In the planning and building of Xiong'an New Area, China must persistently embody the global vision, international standards, distinctive Chinese features, and future-oriented goals, putting ecological conservation first and pursuing green development. A people-centered approach should be adopted, focusing on safeguarding and improving people's livelihoods and protecting and promoting the excellent Chinese traditional culture in its historical context so as to make this new area a major step toward the full implementation of Xi Jinping Thought on Socialism with Chinese Characteristics for a New Era.

According to the plan for the Xiong'an New Area, there are seven key tasks: building a green and smart new city, creating a beautiful ecological environment, developing high-end high-tech industries, providing high-quality public services, building a fast and efficient transport network, advancing system and mechanism reform, and expanding opening up on all fronts. The urban area that is built must be contemporary, green, eco-friendly, and livable, divided into four zones: the pioneer zone of innovation-driven development, the demonstration zone of coordinated development, the pilot zone of opening up and development, and an aspirational demonstration zone of innovation-driven development that implements the New Development Concept.

Construction objectives are as follows. By 2020, the early form of the Xiong'an New Area should take shape, with a major transportation network, the construction of basic infrastructure, and a framework for industrial distribution in place. At that time, significant progress will have been made in the comprehensive environmental management and ecological restoration of Baiyangdian Lake. By 2030, a contemporary city that is competitive and influential, a city that brings man and nature into harmony, and a city that is green, smart, livable, and business-friendly will shine.

SECTION 3
Protecting and Developing the Yangtze River Economic Belt

The Yangtze River Economic Belt spans the East, Middle, and West of China, and it has unique advantages and huge development potential. Since the reform and opening-up, it has developed into one of the regions with the greatest overall strength and strategic support in all of China.

I. The Foundation of Protection and Development for the Belt

Spanning the East, Middle, and West of China, the Yangtze River Economic Belt covers eleven provinces and municipalities, including Shanghai, Jiangsu, Zhejiang, Anhui, Jiangxi, Hubei, Hunan, Chongqing, Sichuan, Yunnan, and Guizhou. It boasts a population of 600 million and occupies an area of approximately 2.05 million square kilometers. Over thousands of years of cultivation, the Yangtze River Basin has become one of the most developed regions in China in terms of agriculture, industry, commerce, culture, education, science, and technology. It contributes 45% of the national GDP and has huge development potential because of its location, resources, industries, human resources, markets, etc. At present, the Belt faces many problems in need of resolution. Among the worst of these problems are severe problems in the ecological environment, bottlenecks in Yangtze River waterways, uneven regional development, the arduous task of industrial restructuring and upgrading, and incomplete regional cooperation mechanisms.

II. The Significance of Protecting and Developing the Belt

The protection and development of the Yangtze River Economic Belt must proceed in the direction of an eco-first, green development path so that the mother river of the Chinese nation will remain vigorous forever. The Belt will help release huge potential in domestic demand across the vast hinterland of the Yangtze's upper and middle reaches and help expand economic growth space from coastal areas to the inland region along the river. It will form a complementary, collaborative, and interactive pattern in the upper, middle, and lower reaches of the Yangtze River and will narrow the development gap between the East, Middle, and West of China. It is conducive to breaking down administrative divisions and market barriers and promoting the orderly and free flow of economic factors, the efficient allocation of resources and market integration, and the coordination of regional economic development. It helps optimize industrial structure and urbanization layout along the Yangtze River, building new corridors for two-way opening up across land and sea, fostering new competitive advantages in international economic cooperation, and promoting economic quality, efficiency, and upgrading. Finally, the Belt is of great practical significance and far-reaching historical significance as a key step toward the realization of the Two Centenary Goals and the Chinese Dream of national rejuvenation.

III. Imperatives for the Protection and Development of the Yangtze River Economic Belt

Considering how important the Yangtze River Economic Belt is, its development cannot be left to chance. The following steps must be taken.

1. Vigorously protect the ecological environment of the Yangtze River

The protection and restoration of the eco-environment of the Yangtze River must be China's first and focal priority, which means promoting well-coordinated environmental conservation and avoiding excessive development. By fully implementing the planning for main functional zones, the nation will clarify ecological function zoning, setting red lines for ecological protection, the development and utilization of water resources, and pollution intake limitation in water function zones. China will seize the opportunity to strengthen assessments of cross-border water quality, promote coordinated governance, and keep the Yangtze River clean and pure. A green ecological corridor will be built, with coordinated development of the upper, middle, and lower reaches and with harmony between man and nature.

There are four approaches that stand out in terms of safeguarding the environment of the Yangtze River:

(1) Protect and improve the water environment. This involves strict control of industrial pollution, consistent disposal of urban sewage and garbage, careful restriction of agricultural non-point source pollution, and great limit of ship pollution.

(2) Protect and restore water ecology. The key tasks here are to properly handle the relationship between rivers and lakes, to strengthen the protection of aquatic biodiversity, and to enhance the protection and ecological restoration of forests along the river.

(3) Effectively protect and rationally use water resources. This means strengthening the protection of water sources, especially drinking water sources, optimizing the allocation of water resources, building a water-saving society, and establishing a sound flood control and disaster reduction system.

(4) Use the waterfront resources of the Yangtze River in an orderly manner. Orderly use involves a rational division of shoreline functions and the disciplined use of shoreline resources.

Beyond following these approaches, it is also necessary to accelerate the formation of a new mechanism for coordinated regional development. The eco-environment protection of the Yangtze River is a systematic project involving a large number of different regions. To do it, the walls between various administrative divisions must be lowered, effective market mechanisms must be used, the role of the government must be respected, and joint control of environmental pollution must be strengthened. But additional steps are needed, as well. China should promote the establishment of ecological compensation mechanisms across regions and the upper, middle, and lower reaches of the Yangtze River and quicken its pace in the formation of a new mechanism for coordinated regional development and river basin management. The main tasks are as follows:

(1) Establish a negative list management system
(2) Strengthen joint prevention and control of environmental pollution
(3) Establish a compensation mechanism for the ecological protection of the Yangtze River
(4) Develop demonstration zones for promoting ecological progress

2. Speed up the formation of an integrated multi-dimensional transportation corridor

Accelerating the interconnection of transportation infrastructure is the first step to promoting the development of the Yangtze River Economic Belt. Efforts should be made to promote the smooth flow of the Yangtze River, turning it into a golden waterway, and to coordinate the construction of railways, highways, airlines, and pipelines. The result will be an interconnected, standardized, and intelligent three-dimensional transportation corridor, which will further improve quality and efficiency and will strengthen strategic support for the development of the Yangtze River Economic Belt. Some specific measures along these lines are:

(1) Improve its function as a golden waterway. It is important to comprehensively promote the systematic governance of arterial waterways, coordinate the construction of branch waterways, accelerate ship type standardization, and improve the intelligent service and safety guarantee system.

(2) Promote the rational distribution of ports. It is also important to strengthen the division of labor and cooperation of ports, developing modern shipping services and enhancing the construction of the collection and distribution system.

(3) Improve comprehensive traffic network. Specific measures are as follows:

- A focus will be placed on developing the Yangtze River, China's main artery, speeding up railway construction, and implementing a project to break railway bottlenecks. These railway improvements will help China form a fast and large-capacity railway passage that complements and smoothly connects with the golden waterway.

- The construction of a road system with high grade and wide coverage must be accelerated in order to effectively extend the scope of influence of the golden waterway.

- The route network will be optimized, the density of flights between major cities will be increased, and international routes will be expanded, even as efforts are made to actively develop air express. The nation will deepen the reform of low-altitude airspace management and vigorously develop general aviation.

- Overall plans and rational distributions will be made for oil and gas pipelines, speeding up the construction of trunk pipelines, building transmission systems, distribution systems, and storage facilities, and increasing the transmission proportion of crude oil and refined oil via pipelines.

(4) Vigorously develop multimodal transport. Specific measures are as follows:

- In accordance with the requirement of "seamless passenger and freight transfer," it is necessary to accelerate the construction of national comprehensive transport hubs, to develop regional transport hubs in an orderly way, to improve the operating efficiency of the integrated transport system, and to strengthen guidance for industrial layout and support for urban development.

- The development of multimodal transport must be accelerated. This involves encouraging the development of rail-water, road-water, air-rail, and other multimodal transport, increasing the proportion of rail-water transport of containers and bulk cargoes, improving the efficiency of road-water and air-rail transport, and enhancing the integration of transport services.

3. Enhance innovation-driven industrial transformation and upgrading

Innovation is an important factor in promoting industrial transformation and upgrading in the Yangtze River Economic Belt. A new era of technological revolution and industrial transformation is underway globally, and China must take advantage. It must also vigorously implement innovation-driven development strategies, strengthen supply-side structural reform, make progress in the reform, innovation, and development of new drivers, eliminate backward and excess production capacity, promote more rapid industrial transformation and upgrading, and form modern industrial corridors with high agglomeration and great international competitiveness.

Innovation-driven transformation necessitates the following actions:

(1) Improve capability for independent innovation. This means building demonstration areas for innovation, strengthening basic innovation platforms, attracting additional talent, enhancing companies' capabilities in technological innovation, and creating an ecological system of innovation and entrepreneurship.

(2) Boost industrial transformation and upgrading. This means propelling the integration and upgrading of traditional industries, building industrial clusters, pushing forward agricultural modernization, promoting the service industry, and vigorously developing a modern culture industry.

(3) Form core competitive power. This means fostering and strengthening strategic emerging industries, promoting the construction of new-generation information infrastructure, and advancing the integrated development of information and industry.

(4) Guide the orderly transfer of industries. This means mapping out priorities for industrial transfer, building platforms for such transfer, and innovating industrial transfer modes.

4. Actively promote new-type urbanization

Promoting new-type urbanization is one of the important tasks for the development of the Yangtze River Economic Belt. Given the considerable differences in the quality and sophistication of urbanization in the upper, middle, and lower reaches of the Yangtze River, coordinated development of large, medium-sized, and small cities must be customized to each location, allowing interaction of the Eastern, Middle, and Western regions to promote new-type urbanization instead of taking a "one-size-fits-all" approach.

Actively promoting new urbanization requires China to do the following:

(1) Optimize the spatial pattern of urbanization. Efforts should be put into expanding city clusters and metropolitan areas, promoting the coordinated development of various cities, and improving the construction of urban transport.

(2) Promote the transfer of the agricultural population into urban residences while also expanding opportunities for rural residents to settle in cities and innovating the urbanization mode of rural people.

(3) Advance the construction of new cities. Leadership should improve the lives of urban residents, strengthen their urban identity, increase the overall carrying capacity of cities, and innovate urban planning and management.

(4) Balance urban and rural development. Efforts should be devoted to promoting the construction of beautiful countryside, increasing development-based poverty alleviation, and improving residents' living standards.

5. Strive to take new strides in all-around opening-up

The following strides should be taken toward reform and opening-up:

(1) Strengthen the leading role of Shanghai and the Yangtze River Delta region. This means replicating and promoting the reform and innovation experience of China (Shanghai) Pilot Free Trade Zone (SHFTZ), allowing SHFTZ to be a pioneering zone for service trade innovation policies. It means encouraging Shanghai and the Yangtze River Delta region to focus on the development of high-end industries, high value-added links, and headquarters economy, fostering new competitive advantages centered on technology, brand, quality, and service, and taking the lead in creating an upgraded version of an open economy. It means promoting the efforts of the Yangtze River Delta region and the upper and middle reaches of the Yangtze River to jointly build a chain of cooperation in shipping and processing trade and finance. Finally, it means taking the lead in building a system of rules that leads the development of cross-border e-commerce and international trade.

(2) Transform Yunnan into a hub that influences South Asia and Southeast Asia. This means speeding up the promotion of connectivity with surrounding infrastructure and making cross-border transport more convenient. It means building an import and export distribution network for South Asia and Southeast Asia with Kunming as the center, and promoting the development of processing trade, bonded logistics, cross-border e-commerce, and other businesses. Finally, it means accelerating the development of the pilot zone for comprehensive financial reform in border areas of Yunnan and promoting the construction of relevant key pilot zones for development and opening up.

(3) Encourage the prosperity of open inland economies. This means promoting regional inter-active cooperation and industrial agglomeration development, building Chongqing into an important support for the development and opening up of the West, and creating inland open economies such as Chengdu, Wuhan, Changsha, Nanchang, and Hefei. And it means improving the pivot layout of ports at the middle and upper reaches, supporting the rational establishment of inspection sites to directly handle the import and export formalities of goods at major stations along the international railway freight transport routes and important inland ports, and supporting the addition of international passenger routes, freight routes, and flights at inland airports.

6. Innovate systems and mechanisms for coordinated regional development

Uneven development is a prominent problem facing the Yangtze River Economic Belt since there are clear gaps in market integration and basic public services between regions. These weak links must be shored up as the construction of an integrated market system is promoted, and the overall level of basic public services in the region improves.

(1) Push forward the construction of an integrated market system. This system should include the following three aspects: a unified procedure for entry into the market, expedited co-construction and sharing of infrastructure, and an optimized investment and financing system.

(2) Promote the cooperative development of basic public services. This type of development is an important part of the coordinated development of the Yangtze River Economic Belt. Its lynchpin is innovation in systems and mechanisms for cooperation and coordinated development. And innovation in these systems and mechanisms should be applied to all areas of basic public services. It involves accelerating educational development and cooperation, promoting the balanced development of public culture, coordinating medical care and public health, and improving the regional social security system.

SECTION 4

Pursuing Coordinated Land and Marine Development and Building China into a Maritime Power

Expanding the maritime economy (the "blue economic space") to build China into a maritime power is a natural outgrowth of China's development law and the world's developmental trends. It is an inevitable choice to achieve the Two Centenary Goals and realize the Chinese Dream of national rejuvenation. In the new era of socialism with Chinese characteristics, the socialist cause necessarily prompts the nation to adhere to the coordinated development of land and sea and to step up efforts to build China into a strong maritime country. It is important to integrate the development of maritime undertakings into the great cause of building a moderately prosperous society in all respects and comprehensively building a great modern socialist country. This integration situates China at the beginning of a new journey that will see it become a maritime power.

I. The Scientific Meaning of Building China into a Maritime Power

1. The concept of a maritime power

A "maritime power" is a country with a powerful and comprehensive ability to develop, use, protect, and control the ocean. At present, China has developed an export-oriented economy that is highly dependent on the ocean. As China becomes more reliant on marine resources and space, it also needs to safeguard and expand various maritime rights and interests outside the jurisdiction of the sea. All these need to be secured as the nation grows into a maritime power.

2. Strategies for building China into a maritime power

A number of strategies stand out as particularly important:

(1) Know the ocean. Exploring and learning about the ocean is a prerequisite for the development, utilization, and protection of ocean resources. Mankind's exploration of the ocean is endless. Only a comprehensive, accurate, and profound understanding of the ocean and its laws can provide a solid scientific basis for building maritime power. To know the ocean, China needs to strengthen marine scientific research, bolster the training of marine professionals, and broaden the whole nation's awareness of the ocean.

(2) Use the ocean. The development and scientific use of the ocean in an effort to expand the maritime economy stands as an important symbol of the progress of human civilization and an undeniable precondition for sustainable engagement with marine resources and environments. To use the ocean, China should strengthen the leading role of planning and zoning, enhance its capacity to profitably develop the ocean, and increase survey and evaluation capabilities in ocean contexts.

(3) Build an ecological ocean. The ecological progress of the ocean is an indispensable part of the ecological development of China. A beautiful China cannot be separated from a beautiful ocean. The ecological progress of the ocean must be consciously integrated into the whole process of economic, political, cultural, and social development. To build an ecological ocean, China must adhere to the overall requirements of "the planned, intensive, ecological, scientific and legal use of the sea" and promote the construction of demonstration zones for maritime ecological progress.

(4) Control the ocean. Comprehensive control of the ocean is an important guarantee that China will become a maritime power. In addition to a maritime defense force appropriate to the national conditions, a management and control pattern should be created, a pattern that features a comprehensive application of administrative, legal, economic, and other means, as well as cooperation between the central and local governments and coordination between the government's leadership and social participation. To control the ocean, China must improve marine laws and regulations, strengthen the integrated management of the ocean, and improve the ability to enforce maritime rights.

(5) Build a harmonious ocean. Although it is an arduous task to safeguard maritime rights and interests, China is still committed to creating a sea of cooperation and friendship for coastal countries. To build a harmonious ocean, China must uphold the maritime diplomacy policy of win-win cooperation, deepen and expand bilateral and regional maritime cooperation, and fully participate in international maritime affairs.

II. The Significance of Building China into a Maritime Power

The advantages that will accrue to China from taking its place as a maritime power are not inconsiderable. Building the nation into a maritime power is significant in the following ways.

1. Related to the survival and development of the Chinese nation and the country's prosperity and security

Adhering to coordinated land and sea development and solidly advancing the building of maritime power is not only about coordinating the relationship between land and sea development but, more importantly, about incorporating marine affairs into plans for overall national development. In the new era, the ocean plays an even more important role in the country's economic development pattern. It plays a more prominent role in safeguarding national sovereignty, security, and development interests. It plays a more significant role in the country's ecological progress. And it takes up a higher strategic position in international political, economic, military, and technological competitions. The development of China's marine programs helps the nation thrive and increases its security. Although China is undeniably a major country both on land and at sea, its resolute commitment to ocean affairs and to making itself a maritime power will be a significant step toward the sustained and sound development of China's economy and society, safeguarding national sovereignty, security, and development interests, achieving the goal of building a moderately prosperous society in all respects, and then realizing the great rejuvenation of the Chinese nation.

Throughout the history of human development, it can be seen that dedication to the goal of becoming a maritime power is a sure path to national prosperity and renewal. Some countries, however, merely go to the sea for colonial plunder. The trajectory of China's development path is not about plunder but about building a rich and powerful country by the sea and seeking harmony between man and ocean in various forms of mutually beneficial cooperation. The focus must be on the overall development of the cause of socialism with Chinese characteristics through practices like coordinating domestic and international situations, adhering to coordinated land and sea development, and steadily promoting the building of maritime power through peace, development, cooperation, and win-win methods.

2. Promote the rejuvenation of the great Chinese nation

The ocean contains valuable assets for the sustainable development of mankind. It is a strategic place for all countries to promote economic and social development and a place to participate in international competition.

Building China into a maritime power is an important part of the cause of socialism with Chinese characteristics. To push forward this cause, the nation must maintain focus on the development path that leads to mutual benefit. This development path involves four transformations. First, over time, the Chinese ability to develop marine resources will improve, and the maritime economy will be transformed into one based on quality and efficiency. Second, marine ecosystems will be protected as an orientation of exploitation is transformed into an orientation focused on conservation and recycling. Third, China will experience a transformation that allows it to facilitate innovation in marine S&T, making better use of ocean resources. Fourth and finally, the maritime rights and interests of China will be safeguarded, guided by a new, transformational, and holistic approach.

To promote the building of a maritime power in the new era, a focus must be placed on the "four transformations" above in an attempt to continuously improve the nation's overall capacity to develop, protect, and use the ocean, as well as its ability to uphold its maritime rights and interests. China must grow in the knowledge of, care for, and management of the ocean, setting a path for China to become a strong maritime nation far into the future.

3. Conducive to safeguarding maritime rights and benefits and maritime security and to building a cooperative, win-win partnership

Safeguarding maritime rights and benefits and maritime security is an integral component of building maritime power. Currently, China's interests in sovereignty, security, and development increasingly point the nation toward the importance of the ocean. To build a maritime power, China must continuously improve its comprehensive ability to safeguard maritime interests and protect maritime security from infringement. President Xi said that upholding the principles of peace, sovereignty, inclusiveness, and co-governance, China should develop the deep sea, polar region, outer space, and the Internet into new frontiers for cooperation among all parties rather than arenas for contest. This provides a Chinese approach for the international community to better solve maritime problems and jointly develop the oceans. Being a maritime power in the new area means continuing to make good use of the important strategic opportunity period for China's development while at the same time considering, designing, and implementing the work of maritime rights protection from the strategic perspective of China's long-term development and overall interests. It also means a deep and committed level of participation in global ocean governance, building a cooperative and mutually beneficial partnership with other countries to make the ocean shared by all countries. To safeguard maritime rights and benefits and maritime security, all countries should break the zero-sum game mentality and establish a modern concept of mutually beneficial cooperation.

III. China's Responsibilities in Developing the Marine Economy

1. Promote the transformation of the marine economy to an economy based on quality and efficiency

A developed marine economy is the material basis of maritime power. At present, China's marine economy still develops in an uneven, uncoordinated, and unsustainable way. To improve the quality of marine economic growth, it is necessary to establish a modern marine economic approach featuring comprehensive development of land and sea resources at multiple levels, shifting from a single marine industry to an open and diversified marine industry that is large enough to encompass many sub-industries. Moreover, it is necessary to tap into domestic and foreign markets to further deepen the marine supply-side structural reform, foster new drivers of marine economic development, and develop new business formats, new products, new technologies, and new services in the marine field so as to inject a strong stimulant into the development of the "21st Century Maritime Silk Road" and bring new opportunities for world development.

2. Promote the transformation of ocean development in ways that incorporate recycling

Efforts should be focused on promoting well-coordinated environmental conservation and avoiding excessive development. The government should attach equal importance to development and conservation, protecting the waters of the marine ecosystem as if protecting one's own lifeblood. The deteriorating condition of the marine eco-environment must be comprehensively reversed, even as China encourages the intensive and economical use of marine resources and establishes compensation mechanisms for marine ecology and damage to the marine ecosystem. Following the principle of prioritizing conservation and protection and focusing on natural recovery, it is of vital importance to strengthen marine environmental protection and ecological restoration, promote low-carbon industrial development, and improve marine disaster prevention and mitigation capabilities so as to enhance maritime ecological progress. The main tasks are as follows:

(1) Strengthen the protection and restoration of marine ecosystems
(2) Boost the comprehensive management of the marine environment
(3) Promote intensive and economical use of marine resources
(4) Advance the low-carbon development of the marine industry
(5) Improve marine disaster prevention and mitigation capabilities

3. Promote the transformation of marine technology in a way that prioritizes innovation

Advanced marine S&T is an important symbol of maritime power. Compared with developed countries, China still lags far behind in the development of marine S&T. Current Chinese marine technologies cannot meet the needs of marine development and security. Overall plans must be made for marine S&T innovation, knowing what can and cannot be done, and advancing major breakthroughs in deep-water, green, and safe high-tech fields. The enhancement of marine S&T innovation capabilities is a national priority, and the sharing of the accompanying resources is a national focus. Once capabilities are in place and resources are being shared, the next step is to arrange projects, bases, and talents in a coordinated way. China must strengthen the overall plan for marine S&T development, develop and master core technologies in the marine field, perfect the marine S&T innovation system, and continuously promote the commercialization of marine scientific and technological achievements. The innovation of key marine technologies must be strengthened, the supporting capacity of innovation in S&T must be enhanced, international competitiveness must be engaged, the pilot projects of marine economic innovation and development must be deepened, and systems and mechanisms innovation for marine talents must be promoted. The main tasks are as follows:

(1) Support major technological innovation in the maritime field
(2) Promote the commercialization of scientific achievements
(3) Carry out pilot projects to deepen marine economic development
(4) Innovate marine talent systems and mechanisms

4. Transform the Chinese approach from a focus on maritime rights protection to a more holistic focus

China currently faces a complicated morass of maritime rights protection and maritime security, where countries fight fiercely. It is critical to navigate these domestic and international situations skillfully, properly balancing the relationship between stability and rights protection. Under the current circumstance, China must, in accordance with the requirements of General Secretary Xi, "be well-prepared to deal with various complex situations." A powerful modern navy is needed, a navy that becomes an important force in maintaining world peace and development while maintaining maritime security and pursuing national interests. On many sensitive and major issues such as the Diaoyu Islands, the South China Sea, freedom of navigation, and historical rights, the principle of peace should guide the way, and multiple measures should be taken simultaneously to pragmatically promote joint development of the ocean, achieving steady progress while safeguarding maritime rights.

5. Optimize the layout of marine economic development

According to the national plan for marine functional zones, China will further optimize the arrangement of the three marine economic circles in the North, East, and South and engage in other forms of marine economic development. These plans will be made in accordance with the natural resource endowment, eco-environmental capacity, industrial foundation, and development potential of different regions and sea areas and will proceed under the guidance of the overall strategy for regional development and various other major strategies (the Belt and Road Initiative, the BTH Coordinated Development and the development of the Yangtze River Economic Belt). Other important steps include increasing the protection of islands and adjacent sea areas, rationally developing important islands, supporting the development of remote islands, tightening island resource protection and development management, promoting the layout of deep sea and open sea areas, accelerating the expansion of the blue economic space, and forming a new pattern of the marine economy with global presence. Key regions in need of attention include the following:

(1) The Northern Marine Economic Circle (including the coastal and marine areas of the Liaodong Peninsula, the Bohai Bay, and the Shandong Peninsula)
(2) The Eastern Marine Economic Circle (including the coastal and marine areas of Jiangsu, Shanghai, and Zhejiang)
(3) The Southern Marine Economic Circle (including the coastal and marine areas of Fujian, the Pearl River Estuary and its two wings, the Beibu Gulf of Guangxi, and the Hainan Island)

(4) Various islands in need of development and conservation (including development projects in key islands, e.g., Zhoushan Islands New Area of Zhejiang Province, Pingtan Comprehensive Experimental Zone of Fujian Province, and Hengqin Island of Guangdong Province)

(5) Deep sea and open sea ripe for spatial expansion

6. Promote the optimization and upgrading of the marine industry

Traditional marine industries in China are in need of transformation and upgrading. In the process, the nation has the opportunity to accelerate the development of emerging industries, increase the scale and sophistication of marine service industries, enhance the development of industrial clusters, standardize the marine industry, and boost its international competitiveness. The main tasks are listed below.

(1) Adjust and optimize traditional marine industries (including fishery, oil & gas, shipbuilding, transportation, salt, and chemical)

(2) Foster and expand emerging marine industries (including equipment manufacturing, pharmaceutical and biological products, seawater utilization, and renewable energy)

(3) Expand and upgrade the marine service industry (including tourism, shipping service, marine culture, offshore financial services, and public service)

(4) Facilitate the development of industrial clusters

7. Accelerate the development of marine economic cooperation

Centering on the development of the 21st Century Maritime Silk Road, China will build international and domestic maritime catalysts of strategic growth, will strengthen investment cooperation in the marine industry, will encourage international cooperation in the marine field, will establish and improve a service guarantee system for outbound investment in the marine economy, and will create new space for marine economic cooperation and development. The main tasks are as follows.

(1) Enhance maritime connectivity by promoting the construction of domestic shipping ports and advancing the construction of overseas shipping port hubs

(2) Promote the effective alignment of marine industries

(3) Propel marine economic exchanges and cooperation (including marine S&T education, marine ecosystem conservation, and marine disaster prevention/mitigation)

(4) Perfect the support system for foreign cooperation, strengthen government guidance and services, and improve market-oriented services

8. Deepen reform of the marine economic system

Such reform must give full play to the decisive role of the market in resource allocation and show deference to the government's role, promoting reform in key links of the marine economy and forming systems conducive to the development of the marine economy. Here are the main tasks.

(1) Improve the modern marine economic market system
(2) Straighten out the system and mechanism for the marine industrial development
(3) Accelerate reform of the marine economic investment and financing system
(4) Promote the sharing of marine information

SECTION 5

The Development of Agriculture in the Pursuit of All-Around Rural Revitalization

Issues concerning agriculture, rural areas, and farmers must be addressed properly. In pursuing socialist rural vitality with distinctive Chinese features, the Chinese leadership has an opportunity to fully implement an RRS, to see that the industry gives full support to agriculture, and to guarantee that urban areas help spur rural development. This cooperation will create a new relationship between industry and agriculture, between urban and rural, under which these often-opposed entities reinforce each other and achieve coordinated development and common prosperity, thus speeding up the modernization of rural areas.

I. Implementing the RRS in All Aspects

To implement the RRS comprehensively, one must realize the important position rural development has in socialist modernization. The comprehensive service capacity of counties must increase, and towns and villages must be built into regional centers to serve the needs of rural people. There must be coordinated planning and construction of county towns, with an emphasis on protecting traditional villages and rural landscapes. China must promote scientific education and methodology among farmers and must promote the revitalization of rural talents.

II. Improving the Quality, Performance, and Competitiveness of Agriculture

Ensuring food security is a bottom-line necessity, and thus the related task of improving the system to support and protect agriculture is a necessity as well. China must adhere to the strictest farmland protection system, must boost the construction of water conservancy facilities, must carry out high-standard farmland construction projects, must strengthen technology and equipment support for agriculture, and must build smart agriculture. As time passes, the nation will make agricultural development greener, make it subject to better standards, enhance supervision over the quality and safety of agricultural products, and build demonstration zones for agricultural modernization. Supply-side structural reform will be advanced, production structure and layout in the agricultural sector will be optimized, and high-quality grain projects will be promoted. Three functional zones—the zone for food production, the zone for key agricultural products, and the zone for special agricultural products—will all be strengthened. The nation will push forward the integrated development of primary, secondary, and tertiary industries in rural areas, facilitate the growth of new business models for the rural economy, and expand the space for farmers to increase their incomes.

III. Deepening Rural Reform

There are a large number of governmental actions associated with rural reform. As reform unfolds, the government will improve the mechanism for the integrated development of urban and rural areas, promote the equal exchange and two-way flow of urban and rural factors, and enhance the vitality of rural development. It will accelerate to foster new agricultural business entities such as farmers' cooperatives and family farms. It will actively explore the implementation of a system of collective construction land for commercial use entering the market. It will perfect the professional agricultural social service system, improve the unified construction land market in urban and rural areas, deepen reform of the rural collective property rights system, develop a new type of rural collective economy, and improve the rural financial service system by developing agricultural insurance.

IV. Allowing Gains in Poverty Alleviation to Help China Move toward Rural Revival

A signature indicator for the realization of the first centenary goal of building a moderately prosperous society in all aspects is lifting people out of poverty. For the rural people who have cast off poverty, the outcomes of poverty alleviation must be consolidated, which means improving the monitoring and assistance mechanisms to prevent the poor from falling back into poverty, providing follow-up support for those relocated from inhospitable areas, strengthening the management of funds for poverty alleviation projects, and promoting the sustainable development of characteristic industries. The social security and relief system in rural areas must also be perfected.

The East and the West each possess qualities needed by the other, which leaves great opportunities for mutual support. In accordance with the growth of financial resources, the Eastern region will gradually increase financial assistance for poverty-stricken areas they are paired to help. Aid funds and projects will be mainly titled to poverty-stricken villages and populations. Leadership will improve the inter-provincial aid pair-ups, implement the action of "joining hands to achieve moderate prosperity," and facilitate an improved strategy of targeted poverty alleviation. Gradient transfer of industries from the East to the West will be promoted, and industrial efforts in poverty alleviation will be boosted. China will further strengthen special support to designated poor areas and establish an assessment and evaluation mechanism to ensure that all units fulfill their responsibilities in alleviating poverty. The Chinese nation has a fine tradition of helping the poor and assisting the needy. As such, the nation must perfect the participation mechanisms for all social sectors, encouraging and supporting private enterprises, social organizations, and individuals that participate in the work of development-oriented poverty reduction, putting energetic effort into creating public-welfare brands for poverty alleviation, commending organizations and individuals that have made outstanding contributions, and motivating all sectors of society to care, support and participate in poverty alleviation even more diligently.

PART FIVE

Promoting Healthy Development of Market Entities

In a market economy, enterprises are the subject of the most basic and important market activities and the micro basis upon which market mechanisms operate. How does the government optimize the business environment, deepen enterprise reform, and cultivate the healthy development of enterprises? This is a major theoretical and practical question that a socialist political economy with Chinese characteristics must answer.

CHAPTER ELEVEN

Development of State-Owned Economy and Reform of State-Owned Enterprises

State-owned enterprises and state-owned economy are an important part of the socialist market economy with Chinese characteristics. The management system of various state-owned assets needs improvement. The authorized management system of state-owned capital should be reformed, and the optimization of the layout should be accelerated. In addition, China would benefit from the structural adjustment and strategic restructuring of the state-owned economy, promoting the preservation and appreciation of state-owned assets and making state-owned capital stronger, better, and bigger.

SECTION 1
The Role of State-Owned Economy and State-Owned Enterprises

Common prosperity is the distinguishing characteristic of socialism with Chinese characteristics and also a central goal of such socialism. The basic economic system that keeps public ownership as the mainstay of the economy and allows diverse sectors to develop side by side is not only an important pillar of the socialist system with Chinese characteristics; it is indeed the foundation of a socialist market economy. It is a fundamental imperative within Chinese socialism that the nation would pursue common prosperity by making the state-owned economy and state-owned enterprises bigger and stronger.

I. The Meaning of State-Owned Economy and State-Owned Enterprise

The "state-owned economy" (or "public sector") specifically refers to an economic type in which the means of production are owned by the state. It is an important part of a socialist public ownership economy and has often been called a socialist economy "under ownership by the whole people." The state-owned economy, as an economic sector in which assets are owned by the state, includes not only those enterprises that are wholly *owned* by the state but also the state-owned economic sectors of enterprises fully *controlled* by the state, along with relatively state-controlled enterprises and general shareholding enterprises of state-owned capital. Article 7 of the Constitution of the PRC clearly states: "The state-owned economy, namely the socialist economy under ownership by the whole people, is the leading force in the national economy. The state guarantees the consolidation and development of the state-owned economy."

"State-owned enterprises" are the enterprises that are funded by the state and whose ultimate property rights are owned by all the people. Typical state-owned enterprises include wholly state-owned enterprises and fully state-controlled enterprises. In the modern market economy, state-owned enterprises are unique in two important ways: first, state-owned enterprises play a leading role in the state-owned economy; second, state-owned enterprises are not organized in the same way other enterprises are, having their own generally applicable principles.

In China, state-owned enterprises are the major players in the state-owned economy, which includes the total economic volume formed by the state-owned enterprises and the social capital driven by these enterprises. The essential attribute of the state-owned economy and state-owned enterprises is their ownership by the whole people.

II. Classification of State-Owned Enterprises

State-owned enterprises are divided into two types: commercial state-owned enterprises and public-welfare-oriented state-owned enterprises. This division is based on the strategic positioning and developmental goals of state-owned capital, combined with the role, current situation, and needs of different state-owned enterprises in economic and social development, according to the main business and core business scope.

Commercial state-owned enterprises aim at enhancing the vitality of the public sector, amplifying the function of the state-owned capital, and preserving and increasing the value of the state-owned assets. They conduct commercial operations based on market-oriented requirements, functioning independently according to the law so as to achieve "survival of the fittest" in the context of fair and orderly market competition. Since the main business of commercial state-owned enterprises is to play a key role in situations involving national security and the lifeline of the national economy, these enterprises mainly undertake certain special tasks, focusing on the development of forward-looking strategic industries with the goal of ensuring national security and the operation of national economy so as to facilitate the organic unity of the economic, social and security benefits of state-owned enterprises.

Commercial state-owned enterprises and public-welfare-oriented state-owned enterprises are independent market entities, and their operation mechanism must meet the requirements of the market economy. In their role as state-owned enterprises under the condition of the socialist market economy, they must consciously serve the national strategy and actively fulfill their social responsibility.

Public-welfare-oriented state-owned enterprises aim to protect people's livelihoods, serve society, and provide public goods and services. Through these enterprises, the prices of necessary products or services can be regulated by the government. Moreover, public welfare-oriented enterprises are capable of responding to market mechanisms in order to improve the efficiency and capacity of public service.

III. The Role of State-Owned Economy and State-Owned Enterprises

1. The basis of production relations in China's socialist system

The basis of production relations refers to the ownership of means of production—that is, the economic relations formed by people in owning, possessing, controlling, and using the means of production. Who owns and controls the means of production not only determines the relations between people in the direct production process but also determines their relations in distribution, exchange, and consumption. As such, the basis of production relations, whatever that basis may be, determines the nature of society. If the basic means of production are in the hands of different people, the network of social relationships in a society will change, which will in turn change the nature of state and political power within that society.

The realization of common prosperity is an essential requirement of socialism, and public ownership of the means of production dominated by the state-owned economy is the foundation of socialism's capacity to eliminate exploitation, quash polarization, and finally achieve common prosperity.

2. Support of comprehensive national strength

As an emerging industrial country, China's economy ranks second in the world now, but its economy remains underdeveloped, with many industries still at the low end of the international industrial division system. State-owned enterprises play a major role in narrowing the gap in S&T. Since the founding of the PRC, China has invested a huge amount of money in both basic industries and pillar industries. These investments epitomize the comprehensive national strength of the country, and they have cultivated a large number of industry leaders and important backbone enterprises. Those backbone enterprises are a prominent way for China to flex its international muscles—the backbone force representing China's participation in international competition, wherein these enterprises constitute an important economic force that must be relied on to accelerate the process of national industrialization.

3. Ensuring the healthy development of the national economy and promoting social harmony and stability

An important task of the state-owned economy is to ensure national political, economic, and defense security. China's public sector maintains control of the military, energy, finance, communications, and other important industries and fields related to national security and the lifeblood of the Chinese economy. It is a critical safeguard for national security. Given its history and development, the state-owned economy plays a unique role in regulating the speed and direction of national economic growth from a big-picture, long-term perspective, overcoming the limitations and disadvantages of market mechanisms, supporting, guiding, and driving the sustainable development of the national economy, and safeguarding national economic security.

The state-owned economy also plays an exemplary role in promoting social harmony and stability. State-owned enterprises actively fulfill their social responsibilities: they operate in accordance with the law, communicate in an honest and trustworthy way, save resources, protect the environment, focus on the needs of people, and set an example for other enterprises. In addition, state-owned enterprises have actively participated in targeted poverty alleviation, have provided aid to Xinjiang and Tibet, and have engaged in various charitable endeavors, making positive contributions toward the construction of a harmonious society.

4. Ensuring the realization of national strategic objectives

The public sector is a major tool for implementing national strategy since it provides a strong impetus for the realization of national strategic objectives. To strengthen China's economic strength, national defense strength, and national cohesion, and to consolidate and improve the socialist system, China must consistently promote the development and growth of the state-owned economy. Against the backdrop of economic globalization, the state-owned economy sets the tone for the Chinese strategy of "going global." In terms of the development process of international operations, state-owned enterprises start earlier than private enterprises and play a leading role.

5. Providing public products and public services

By fulfilling their social responsibilities, state-owned enterprises actively participate in the construction of the public service system. They provide material basis, information feedback channels, policy implementation channels, and technical support for the construction of the public service system. Many state-owned enterprises take responsibility for the provision of public products and services. Due to the non-profit and exclusive nature of these products and services, their supply chains are dominated by state-owned enterprises and other portions of the public sector.

The basic public service facilities provided by state-owned enterprises include state-owned infrastructure facilities such as those covering water supply, power supply, heating, communications, and transportation. These services meet the daily needs of the public and are an important foundation for the development of the national economy. Moreover, the task of building infrastructure is long and time-consuming, meaning that the private sector can rarely afford it.

The Reform and Development of State-Owned Enterprises

Deepening the reform of state-owned enterprises is one of the major tasks China has in building socialism with Chinese characteristics at a new historical moment. A series of important reform proposals advanced by President Xi point in a helpful direction and provide fundamental guidance for the reform of state-owned enterprises in the new era. This section will proceed to discuss those proposals and the central tasks involved in deepening the reform of state-owned enterprises.

I. The Significance of Deepening State-Owned Enterprise Reform

State-owned enterprises are an important force to promote national modernization and protect the common interests of the people and are also an important material and political basis for the development of the Party and the country. There are several significant reasons to deepen this sort of reform.

1. Essential to the task of upholding and developing socialism with Chinese characteristics

The pursuit of socialism with Chinese characteristics is the theme of all the theories and practices of the CPC since the reform and opening-up. During this time, the economic system has kept public ownership as the mainstay of the economy and has allowed diverse sectors to develop side by side; this is an important part of the socialist system with Chinese characteristics. Deepening the reform of state-owned enterprises, improving efficiency and vitality, and developing a strong and powerful public sector are the fundamental requirements to maintain and improve the basic economic system, and they are also preconditions for upholding and developing socialism with Chinese characteristics.

China has made great progress in the reform of state-owned enterprises. The top-level design and construction of the "1+N" document have been completed, the "ten reform pilot projects" have been further promoted, and the implementation of major reform measures has been effective. The government's approach to state-owned enterprises has undergone major changes, becoming more closely integrated with the market economy, becoming stronger in terms of scale and competitiveness, and becoming significantly improved in terms of operation quality and efficiency. A number of key enterprises with core competitiveness have emerged in international and domestic market competition and have made great contributions to promoting economic and social development, ensuring people's livelihoods, improving people's prospects, opening up international markets, and enhancing China's comprehensive strength. The public sector has played a leading role in all this progress. However, state-owned enterprises are not without their problems. These problems include unbalanced reform, imperfect regulatory mechanisms and institutions, and unreasonable layout structure. The reform and development of state-owned enterprises must be pushed forward with greater determination and strength, which means forming a state-owned assets management system, a modern enterprise system, and a market-oriented operation mechanism. These interventions must be more in line with the requirements of the new era of socialism with Chinese characteristics.

2. A major task to realize the Two Centenary Goals

After building a moderately prosperous society in all aspects and achieving the first centenary goal by 2020, China will embark upon a new journey of building a more thoroughly modern socialist country as it works hard to achieve the second centenary goal. In this historical process, state-owned enterprises have played an important and irreplaceable role. They have embodied the new concept of development and have taken the lead in fulfilling their political, economic, and social responsibilities, guided by the five-sphere integrated plan and the four-pronged comprehensive strategy. They have made a number of world-class, landmark achievements in scientific and technological innovation in the fields of manned space flight, lunar exploration, deep-sea exploration, high-speed railway, commercial aircraft, Ultra-High Voltage (UHV) power transmission and transformation, and mobile communications. They have undertaken a number of major projects in infrastructure, public service engineering, and national defense technology. All these achievements and projects are a testament to China's strength and responsibility. In the new historical period, the reform and development of state-owned enterprises must resonate with the realization of the Two Centenary Goals and must advance the people's yearning for a better life. That is the glorious mission and historical responsibility that state-owned enterprises must shoulder.

3. An objective requirement to promote the sustainable and healthy development of China's economy

China is now entering a new stage of development, in which the speed, structure, and power of China's development acquire new characteristics. State-owned enterprises are the vanguard at the forefront of China's advanced productive capacity, comprehensive national strength, and international competitiveness. With a strong industrial influence, they play a leading role in adapting to, grasping, and leading the new normal of economic development and promoting supply-side structural reform. Since the 18th National Congress, state-owned enterprises have adopted a tone of seeking progress while maintaining stability. They have, moreover, insisted on highlighting the main business, even while focusing on developing the real economy, implementing much-needed supply-side structural reforms, carrying out in-depth lean operations, improving quality and efficiency, pursuing vigorous restructuring and integration, developing strategic emerging industries, resolving overcapacity, and disposing of "zombie enterprises." They have effectively promoted the transformation and upgrading of the national economy and have made positive contributions to the sustainable and healthy development of China's economy. In the new stage of development, China must further deepen the reform of state-owned enterprises by promoting the layout optimization, structural adjustment, and strategic reorganization of the state-owned economy, state-owned capital, and state-owned enterprises. Such reform also points to a future when state-owned enterprises pursue higher quality development, better efficiency, and better structure when they effectively play the leading role they are designed to play, and when they promote China's economy to achieve medium- and high-speed growth.

II. Basic Requirements for Deepening State-Owned Enterprise Reform

1. Upholding and improving the basic economic system

The basic economic system of China keeps public ownership as the mainstay of the economy and allows diverse sectors to develop side by side. It is not only an important pillar of the socialist system with Chinese characteristics but also the foundation of the socialist market economic system. In order to uphold and improve this basic economic system, it is necessary to consolidate and develop the public sector of the economy in an abiding way, encouraging, supporting, and guiding the development of an unshakable non-public economy. The dominant position of the state-owned economy must be reaffirmed, giving full play to its leading role in the broader economy and making state-owned enterprises stronger, better, and bigger. Such a dominant position is reflected in the fact that the public sector should grow in quantity and scale and form a reasonable layout with other ownership economies; it is reflected in the quality and efficiency of the state-owned economy and its competitiveness in both domestic and international markets; it is reflected in the fact that the state-owned economy has controlling power in key industries.

Some have expressed concern that deeper reform of state-owned enterprises is a recipe for large-scale withdrawal of these enterprises from competitive fields or even their disappearance. These concerns are completely unfounded. Reform is compatible with a strong state-owned sector if China adheres to the "two unshakable policies": give full play to the leading role of the state-owned economy through reform and simultaneously advance a complementary policy, the mutual promotion, and common development of various ownership economies. There must be cross-shareholding and the mutual integration of state-owned capital, collective capital, and non-public capital. It is also imperative to develop a mixed-ownership economy and move forward in a spirit of teamwork, pursuing the mutual promotion and common development of various types of ownership capital.

2. Adhering to the reform direction of the socialist market economy

The commitment to reform China's socialist market economy is a basic requirement for enhancing the vitality and competitiveness of state-owned enterprises. With the system of the market economy making continuous improvement, the market environment constantly changing, and global market competition on the rise, a particular onus is placed on state-owned enterprises to adhere to the direction of market-oriented reform. The entry of China's economy into the new normal brings about a period of trial and testing, a period that calls for the release of reform dividends, the accelerated transformation of the development mode of state-owned enterprises, the release of new development potential, the cultivation of development power, and the expansion of development space. Fierce competition with Western multinational companies in the domestic and foreign markets means that state-owned enterprises must intensify market-oriented reform, enhance their familiarity with international markets, adapt to the rules of the international market, and cultivate new advantages which will give China leverage in international cooperation and competition against the background of fierce market competition.

First and foremost, state-owned enterprises are enterprises. To deepen the reform of state-owned enterprises, these organizations must both become more vital and better regulated. In order to speed up the construction of a modern state-owned enterprise system, they must follow the law of market economy and the law of enterprise development, adhere to various forms of separation (government and enterprise, government and capital, ownership and management rights), and adhere to the unity of rights, obligations, and responsibilities. They should additionally carry out reform, development, regulation, responsibility setting, and assessment by category, even as they promote the in-depth integration of state-owned enterprises with the market economy, participate in market competition fairly with enterprises of other ownership, and truly become a legally independent, self-financing, self-risk-bearing, self-developing market entity. Meanwhile, the Chinese government must deepen the reform of the management system for state-owned assets, must effectively solve various problems in the regulation of state-owned assets (such as acting beyond authority, vacancy, and dislocation), must realize a transformation from focusing on enterprise regulation to focusing on capital regulation, and must form a state-owned assets management system, a modern enterprise system and a market-oriented operation mechanism that are more in line with the basic economic system and the requirements of the development of the socialist market economy.

3. Making state-owned enterprises stronger, better, and bigger

State-owned enterprises are owned by the whole people. They are an important force to promote national modernization and to protect the common interests of the people and are also an important material and political basis for the development of the Party and the country. Given a thorough analysis of China's national conditions and an accurate grasp of its dynamics in the wake of the primary stage of Chinese socialism, the need to unswervingly prioritize state-owned enterprises in the development of the country is obvious, as is the need to consistently make state-owned enterprises stronger, better and bigger. Such a commitment is in line with China's situation in the opening decades of the 21st century. Making state-owned enterprises stronger, better, and bigger and giving full play to the leading role of the public sector are preconditions to safeguarding the fundamental interests of the overwhelming majority of the people and are an important guarantee for building a moderately prosperous society in an all-around way.

To deepen the reform of state-owned enterprises, China must stick to the bottom line, ensure that the influence of the state-owned economy in key industries is not weakened, and protect against concerns about a loss of state-owned assets or concerns that the reform of state-owned enterprises might be an opportunity for speculators to make huge profits in the wave of reform. By comprehensively deepening the reform of state-owned enterprises, the government should drive these enterprises to achieve excellent business performance, corporate governance, corporate image, layout, and structure so as to eventually develop into world-class enterprises with international competitiveness. At the same time, it cannot be forgotten that the relationship between state-owned enterprises and enterprises of other ownership is not a negative correlation;

all these enterprises can coexist in a complementary relationship. They are mutually beneficial, they share common development, and they can be unified in the process of socialist modernization.

4. Strengthening the leadership of the CPC over state-owned enterprises

The essential characteristic of socialism with Chinese characteristics—and its greatest advantage—is the leadership of the CPC. To deepen the reform of state-owned enterprises, it is necessary to uphold and strengthen the leadership of the CPC. Through the strengthening of this leadership, state-owned enterprises can become a real force to resolutely implement the decisions and deployment of the CPC Central Committee and an important force to help the CPC overcome many obstacles in the way of a prosperous society. The party organizations in state-owned enterprises must play a leading role in both business-related and political contexts, and the Party committees or Party leadership groups in state-owned enterprises must fulfill their major responsibilities.

There is a need to strengthen the leadership of the CPC and improve corporate governance in a unified manner. This means making the legal status of party organizations in the corporate governance structure clear. It means fulfilling the responsibility to strictly manage and govern the Party. It means adhering to the principle that the Party should manage the Party and strictly govern the Party in an all-around way, building and strengthening grassroots party organizations in state-owned enterprises, continuously promoting anti-corruption work that keeps the administration clean and honest, strengthening the construction of leading groups and talent teams, and striving to cultivate a high-quality enterprise leadership team that is loyal to the Party, brave in innovation, well managed, promising and honest.

III. Key Tasks toward Deepening the Reform of State-Owned Enterprises

1. Promoting the reform of state-owned enterprises by category

Promoting the reform of state-owned enterprises by category is a necessary task that contributed to deepening the reform of state-owned enterprises. There are many state-owned enterprises in China, and they have great responsibilities. To deepen the reform of state-owned enterprises, it is necessary to accurately define the functional orientation of these different enterprises. An approach that promotes reform of state-owned enterprises by category would represent a significant step toward solving a number of problems: unclear functions; inaccurate positioning and diversified objectives of state-owned capital; weak pertinence of supervision and management; unscientific assessment and evaluation of state-owned assets; and blind decision-making and extensive expansion within some state-owned enterprises.

Commercial state-owned enterprises conduct commercial operations based on market-oriented requirements, and they are also in need of reform. Since they aim at enhancing the vitality of the state-owned economy, amplifying the function of state-owned capital, and realizing the value preservation and appreciation of state-owned assets, it is important to help these enterprises carry out production and operation activities independently according to the law, letting their fate be governed by "survival of the fittest" and allowing fair and orderly market competition. For commercial state-owned enterprises in major competitive industries and fields, there is reason, in principle, to implement reform of the corporate system and the joint stock system, even while actively introducing other state-owned capital or various non-state-owned capital to realize the diversification of equity. Enterprises should adopt flexible approaches where state-owned capital can be the absolute or relative controlling shareholder, or merely a shareholder, striving to promote their listings as a whole. For these state-owned enterprises, evaluation should be based on performance indicators, the value preservation and appreciation of state-owned assets, and the level of market competitiveness.

For commercial state-owned enterprises whose main business is in important industries and fields involving national security and economic interests and that mainly undertake major special tasks, the controlling position of state-owned capital must be maintained, and non-state-owned capital must be supported in shareholding. For natural monopoly industries, reform must maintain separations between government and enterprise and between government and capital. It also must promote franchise operations and strengthen government regulation. With a due appreciation of the unique qualities of different industries, Chinese leaders should implement a separation between network and operation, should open up competitive businesses, and should promote the marketization of public resource allocation. For the enterprises that need to be wholly owned by the state, other state-owned capital should be introduced, with diversified stock rights. Special business and competitive business should be separated effectively and operated and accounted for independently. As for state-owned enterprises, assessments should focus not only on business performance indicators and the value preservation/appreciation of state-owned assets but also should be done with a view toward serving the national strategy, ensuring national security and the operation of the national economy, developing cutting-edge strategic industries, and accomplishing special tasks.

Public-welfare-oriented state-owned enterprises are also in need of reform. As organizations that aim to protect people's livelihoods, serve society, and provide public goods and services, public-welfare-oriented state-owned enterprises introduce market mechanisms and improve the efficiency and capability of public service. Such enterprises can be wholly owned by the state, and those qualified can diversify their investors. They can also encourage non-state-owned enterprises to partner in the enterprise's operations by purchasing services, franchising, taking on the role of principal-agent, and other means. For public-welfare-oriented state-owned enterprises, China should focus on cost control, product quality, service quality, operation efficiency, and guarantee ability. According to the different characteristics of enterprises, business performance indicators, value preservation of state-owned assets, and appreciation of state-owned assets should be assessed, but social evaluation should also be incorporated into the assessment.

2. Improving the modern enterprise system
The reform direction of state-owned enterprises points toward building a modern state-owned enterprise system with Chinese characteristics. This system will be a major theoretical and practical innovation in the modern enterprise system. The path to improvement passes through at least five stages:

First, promoting the reform of the corporate system and the joint stock system. The reform of the corporate system must be strengthened at the group level. This means actively introducing various investors to realize equity diversification, vigorously promoting the restructuring and listing of state-owned enterprises, and creating conditions for the overall listing of group companies. The percentage of state-owned equity should be gradually adjusted in keeping with the functional orientation of different enterprises. An operation mechanism should be formed, a mechanism with a diversified equity structure, standardized behavior of shareholders, effective internal restraints, and efficient and flexible operations.

Second, improving the corporate governance of companies. It is imperative to promote the establishment of the board of directors, to standardize the behavior of the chairman and general manager in exercising power, and to establish and improve supervision in decision-making implementation with consistent rights and responsibilities, coordinated operation, and effective checks & balances. Full play must be given to the decision-making role of the board of directors, the supervision role of the board of supervisors, the management role of corporate managers, and the political core role of the Party organization. As such, checks and balances within the board of directors must be strengthened in order to achieve standardized corporate governance.

Third, establishing a categorized and hierarchical management system of leaders in state-owned enterprises. There is an important principle that the Party should implement the principle of supervising the performance of officials. The board of directors should be chosen in accordance with the law, the board of directors should choose business managers in accordance with the law, and business managers should exercise the power of personnel employment, promotion, and demotion in accordance with the law. This orderly procedure will innovatively develop effective methods to realize the abovementioned requirements. Personnel selection and employment will be customized so as to fit well with the different types and levels of enterprises. This may involve the implementation of a selection system, an appointment system, or an employment system. The professional manager system will be implemented, and internal training will be combined with external introduction.

Fourth, implementing an enterprise salary distribution system in line with the socialist market economy. The distribution mechanism should be improved in a way that has both incentives and restraints, stresses both efficiency and fairness, conforms to the general law of enterprises, and reflects the characteristics of state-owned enterprises. A wage determination and normal growth mechanism that is basically adapted to the labor market and linked to the economic benefits of enterprises and labor productivity should be established and improved.

Fifth, deepening the reform of the internal employment system in enterprises. The system of open recruitment and competitive employment for all kinds of enterprise management personnel should be improved, the vision for personnel selection should be broadened, and channels of employment should be expanded. China should establish a market-oriented open recruitment system for enterprise employees, build a harmonious labor relationship, standardize all kinds of employment management in accordance with the law, establish and improve the market-oriented employment system centering on contract management and based on post management, and truly form a reasonable flow mechanism in which managers can be promoted and demoted, employees hired and fired.

3. Improving the state-owned asset management system

Since the reform and opening-up, the reform of China's state-owned asset management system has steadily advanced. Nevertheless, it must be noted that there remain problems that urgently need to be resolved. According to the Decision of the CPC Central Committee on Several Significant Issues Concerning Comprehensively Deepening Reform and the relevant arrangements of the State Council, the following opinions on reforming and improving the state-owned asset management system are hereby offered.

First, focusing on capital regulation to promote the transformation of the functions of state-owned asset supervision and regulatory authority. Those in authority over state-owned asset supervision and regulation should perform the investor's functions according to law, should scientifically define the regulatory boundaries of state-owned assets investors, should establish the regulatory power list and responsibility list, and should realize a transformation from focusing on enterprise regulation to focusing on capital regulation. With respect to factors that are controllable, management should be scientific, focusing on managing the distribution of state-owned capital, standardizing capital operation, increasing capital return, and maintaining capital security; with respect to what cannot be controlled, power should be delegated according to law, and never act beyond its authority.

Second, focusing on capital regulation to reform the authorized operation system of state-owned capital. China should reorganize and establish state-owned capital investment and operation companies. It should also explore effective operation modes, define the boundary between the ownership and the operation rights of state-owned capital, and promote industrial agglomeration, transformation, and upgrading. The layout structure of state-owned capital should be optimized through investment, financing, industrial cultivation, and capital integration. The rational flow of state-owned capital should be promoted even as value preservation and appreciation are achieved through equity operation, value management, and orderly market competition.

Third, focusing on capital regulation to promote the rational flow and optimal allocation of state-owned capital. Chinese leaders should allow the market to provide direction while enterprises remain the major actors. The distribution structure of state-owned capital should be optimized, and the overall function and efficiency of the state-owned economy should be enhanced. The key investment directions of state-owned capital, moreover, should be optimized, concentrating state-owned capital in important fields, namely those related to national security, economic lifeblood, people's livelihoods, strategic emerging industries, and advantageous enterprises with core competitiveness. A great deal of attention should be given to the role of state-owned capital investment and operation companies. The state should also clean up and withdraw some state-owned enterprises, reorganize and integrate some state-owned enterprises, and innovate and develop some state-owned enterprises.

Fourth, focusing on capital regulation to promote the centralized and unified regulation of productive state-owned assets. The basic management of state-owned assets must be strengthened, and a budget management system for state-owned capital operation must be established, a system covering all state-owned enterprises with hierarchical management. This focus on capital regulation will achieve value preservation and appreciation of state-owned assets, as well as promoting the development of state-owned capital and effectively preventing the loss of state-owned assets.

4. Developing a mixed-ownership economy

The establishment of a mixed-ownership economy as a primary means of realizing the basic economic system is influenced by the change of ownership structure in China. The development of the mixed-ownership economy is conducive to improving the function, maintaining and increasing the value, and improving the competitiveness of state-owned capital. It does this by consolidating the dominant position of public ownership and enhancing the vitality, control, and influence of the public sector. This sort of development is also conducive to promoting enterprise system innovation, motivating various market competitors, and cultivating world-class enterprises with global competitiveness.

5. Strengthening supervision to prevent the loss of state-owned assets

The state-owned assets of enterprises are the common wealth of all the people. It is an inevitable requirement for building a moderately prosperous society in an all-around way and realizing the common prosperity of all the people to ensure the security of state-owned assets and to prevent their loss. Ensuring their security means the following things:

First, strengthening the internal supervision of enterprises. The internal supervision system of the enterprise needs improvement, which means clarifying the supervision responsibilities of the board of supervisors, as well as those involved in audits, discipline inspection and supervision, patrol, and legal and financial departments. Improvement of the supervision system and enhancement of the executive power of the system will also be necessary.

Second, establishing an efficient and collaborative external supervision mechanism. China must strengthen the supervision of investors, speed up the writing of laws and regulations governing the conduct of state-owned enterprises, standardize the operation process, and reinforce the supervision of key businesses, key areas of reform, and important links in the operation of state-owned capital and overseas state-owned assets.

Third, implementing information disclosure and strengthening social supervision. The information disclosure system of state-owned assets and state-owned enterprises should be improved, a unified information disclosure network platform should be established, and state-owned enterprises should become more transparent.

Fourth, strictly implementing an accountability mechanism. Leaders should establish and improve the mechanism for investigating major decision-making errors, dereliction of duty, and negligence in state-owned enterprises. They should also establish and improve the supervision and accountability mechanism of state-owned assets in enterprises.

6. Cultivating globally competitive enterprises

State-owned enterprises should be encouraged to carry out international operations in depth. This means that they would continue to strengthen open cooperation, push advantageous industries to enter into Belt and Road cooperation, distribute China's equipment manufacturing, technology, standards, and services to the world, make full use of markets (domestic and international) and resources, cultivate a variety of international business talents, and direct a number of leading enterprises in the allocation of international resources. Chinese leadership should vigorously implement the innovation-driven development strategy, should encourage state-owned enterprises to continually increase R&D investment guided by the market, should break into a number of key technologies, should cultivate various high-value-added cutting-edge products, should create a number of internationally renowned high-end brands, and should encourage enterprises which can lead the development of global industrial technology. But additional steps are needed. These steps include accelerating the promotion of industrial upgrading, moving forward to the high end of the value chain in some advantageous industries and fields, striving to occupy a favorable position in international market competition, and forming a number of leading enterprises with discourse power and influence in global industrial development.

SECTION 3
Mixed-Ownership Reform of State-Owned Enterprises

A mixed-ownership economy—that is, an economy with cross-shareholding and mutual integration of state-owned capital, collective capital, and non-public capital—is an important means of realizing the basic economic system, and it is conducive to improving the function of state-owned capital, maintaining/increasing its value, and improving its competitiveness. It is also conducive to pushing forward the complementation, mutual promotion, and common development of various types of ownership capital.

I. Connotations of the Mixed-Ownership Reform of State-Owned Enterprises

In essence, a mixed-ownership economy is a joint-stock economy in which different ownership capitals hold shares of each other. It is a dynamic and efficient form of capital organization. To develop a mixed-ownership economy, it is necessary to push forward the complementation, mutual promotion, and common development of various types of ownership capital. The development of a mixed-ownership economy by state-owned enterprises and the realization of cross-shareholding and mutual integration of various types of ownership capital can give full play to the advantages of scale, technology, and management of state-owned capital. It can also give full play to the vitality and creativity of non-state-owned capital, driving state-owned enterprises to improve the corporate governance structure, improving the investment and operation efficiency of state-owned capital, and incentivizing non-state-owned capital to use production factors equally and share operating income fairly. This is of great benefit to the liberation and development of social productive forces and to the creation of world-class enterprises with global competitiveness.

The reform of mixed ownership involves further deepening the reform of the property rights system governing state-owned enterprises. It emphasizes the cross-shareholding and mutual integration of different ownership systems, making full use of the characteristics of different types of capital to realize the complementary advantages of various ownership systems. All ownership economies exist as shareholders and operate in accordance with corporate law. Their legitimate interests are "sacred and inviolable." What the mixed ownership reform should solve is the real market-oriented problem of enterprises. It will ensure that the owners and the incentive and restraint mechanisms are in place.

Here are the ways to develop a mixed ownership economy: First, the reform of mixed ownership of state-owned enterprises should be promoted. For state-owned enterprises that have already implemented mixed ownership through the implementation of a joint-stock system and listing, efforts should be made to improve the modern enterprise system and increase the efficiency of capital operation; for state-owned enterprises that are suitable for further promoting the reform of mixed ownership, the government should give full play to the role of the market mechanism, adhere to the implementation of policies according to local conditions, industries, and enterprises, and should be independent, controlling or participating in shareholding as appropriate, without forced matching, full coverage, or fixed timetables.

Second, non-state-owned capital should be introduced and encouraged to participate in the reform of state-owned enterprises. Non-state-owned capital investors are encouraged to participate in the restructuring and reorganization of state-owned enterprises or the capital increase and share expansion of state-controlled listed companies. They are also encouraged to participate in corporate operations and management by investing in shares, purchasing shares, subscribing to convertible bonds, and engaging in stock replacement.

Third, state-owned capital should be encouraged to join non-state-owned enterprises in various ways. Full play should be given to the role of state-owned capital investment and operation companies as capital operation platforms, and equity investment should be made in non-state-owned enterprises with great development potential and strong growth through marketization, a focus on public services, advanced technology, ecological and environmental protection, and strategic industries.

Fourth, the implementation of an employee stock ownership plan (ESOP) should be explored in mixed-ownership enterprises. Through the implementation of ESOP, the long-term incentive and restraint mechanism is established, and the equity transfer and exit mechanism is established and improved to ensure openness and transparency within ESOP.

II. The Necessity of Mixed-Ownership Reform of State-Owned Enterprises

1. Upholding and improving the basic economic system

The basic economic system, which keeps public ownership as the mainstay of the economy and allows diverse sectors to develop side by side, is the foundation of the socialist market economic system. Fundamentally speaking, to uphold and improve the basic economic system just means to give full play to the advantages of various forms of ownership, to stimulate the vitality and creativity of these forms, and to promote the development of social productive forces. Through the development of a mixed-ownership economy, China can promote the cross-shareholding and mutual integration of various ownership economies. This will mean leveraging the power of the scale advantages, technical advantages, and management advantages of the public sector, giving full play to the vitality and creativity of the non-public economy, and pushing forward the complementation, mutual promotion, and common development of various ownership economies so as to promote the continuous improvement of the basic economic system.

2. Improving the operation vitality and efficiency of state-owned capital

At present, there are still some tensions and problems in the development of state-owned enterprises, and promoting the mixed-ownership reform of state-owned enterprises is exactly the right breakthrough to solve these problems. By carrying out mixed-ownership reform, it will be possible to make use of the characteristics of different types of capital, realize the complementary advantages of different ownership economies, form a corporate governance structure with effective checks and balances for various property owners, and hasten the establishment of a modern enterprise system of state-owned enterprises. It is also imperative to motivate state-owned enterprises to improve the internal management mechanism, which allows only the fittest to survive, managers to be promoted and demoted, employees to be hired and fired, and income to increase and decrease. The endogenous power of state-owned enterprises should be stimulated. Property rights should be further clarified, supervision and balance of different property owners strengthened, asset disposal of state-owned enterprises regulated more efficiently, the loss of assets prevented, and the preservation and appreciation of assets realized.

3. Improving the structure and quality of the supply

Promoting supply-side structural reform is a tested solution that will adjust the structure of the economy, changing the mode of economic development so that it aims at improving the quality of supply and meeting the needs of the people. State-owned enterprises are an important subject of China's market economy and play an important role in deepening supply-side structural reform, optimizing supply structure, and improving supply efficiency. By promoting the mixed-ownership reform of state-owned enterprises, state-owned enterprises can be assisted in capturing market demand more sensitively, finding market opportunities, organizing and allocating factor resources more efficiently and flexibly, promoting the development of new technologies, new industries, and new formats, and driving China's supply structure to leap to the middle and high-end level as a whole.

4. Improving the sustainable innovation ability of state-owned enterprises and other ownership enterprises, especially private enterprises

Promoting the mixed-ownership reform of state-owned enterprises will help to solve the problem of concentration and the long-term immobilization of state-owned capital equity. It will improve the corporate governance structure of state-owned enterprises in which all parties perform their respective duties. It will strengthen the internal incentives of enterprises, reduce the agency cost of state-owned enterprises, and form a flexible and efficient market-oriented operation mechanism that can provide institutional support for the sustainable innovation ability of state-owned enterprises. Under such reform, enterprises will assume their respective responsibilities and coordinate their operations with effective checks and balances.

An important feature of innovation activities is a long investment cycle and high risk to investors. According to the theory of corporate governance, managers are more willing than shareholders to prioritize actions that are beneficial in the short term over actions, such as innovative activities, that are beneficial in the long run. The improvement of internal governance structures in state-owned enterprises brought about by mixed-ownership reform will encourage managers of state-owned enterprises to carry out more innovative activities, stimulate the innovation vitality of state-owned enterprises, and then improve the overall innovation ability of the state-owned economy. In addition, the improvement of operation efficiency brought by the mixed-ownership reform of state-owned enterprises will improve the profitability of these enterprises and create the necessary material conditions for state-owned enterprises to increase R&D investment and improve innovation ability.

Promoting the mixed-ownership reform of state-owned enterprises also helps to stimulate the innovation of private enterprises. Generally speaking, state-owned enterprises are at their best in basic fields, public-welfare-oriented fields, cutting-edge fields, and innovation fields that reflect the strategic intentions of national development, while private enterprises have a better ability to meet the diversified needs of the market and stimulate innovation vitality. They form a complementary economic structure of the state-owned economy and the private sector. Such complementary economic structure, under the incentive of the system and mechanism provided by the mixed-ownership reform, can create conditions for the innovation interaction and integrated development of state-owned enterprises and private enterprises. This is because innovation will permeate different fields. The innovation of state-owned enterprises stimulated by mixed-ownership reform will inevitably spread from state-owned enterprises to private enterprises and improve the development level and innovation ability of private enterprises. At the same time, increased innovation from private enterprises will also spread to state-owned enterprises. The resultant dynamic will promote innovation within state-owned enterprises, realize the continuous interactive innovation between state-owned enterprises and private enterprises, improve the overall innovation level and innovation ability of China's economy, implement the innovation-driven development strategy, and provide lasting power for the sustainable and healthy development, transformation and upgrading of China's economy.

III. Achievements and Existing Problems in the Mixed-Ownership Reform of State-Owned Enterprises

At present, the mixed-ownership reform of state-owned enterprises in China has accelerated significantly and has achieved remarkable results. The main achievements are as follows: first, reform has been pushed forward level by level. According to the data of the State-owned Assets Supervision and Administration Commission of the State Council (SASAC), in 2016, the proportion of mixed-ownership enterprises at the level of central enterprises was 68.9% in 2016, an increase of 45.6% over the previous year; the mixed-ownership enterprises at the level of local state-owned enterprises accounted for 47%, an increase of 3% over the previous year; at the group level, the number of state-owned enterprises that completed mixed-ownership reform had also increased significantly. Since 2017, the above indicators have maintained a continuous and stable growth trend.

Second, reform has been pushed forward with pilot projects in key fields. At present, state-owned enterprises in the fields of telecommunications, civil aviation, railway, electric power, military industry, oil, and natural gas—all of which are related to national security and the lifeline of the national economy—have taken substantial steps forward in mixed-ownership reform.

Third, reform has been pushed forward with collaboration in the governance mechanism. At present, some state-owned enterprises not only realize the form of mixed ownership through joint-stock reform or listing but also focus on market-oriented adjustment in executive incentive, manager appointment, employee stock ownership and other aspects so as to improve the collaborative governance mechanism of mixed-ownership enterprises.

At the same time, on the road to mixed-ownership reform of state-owned enterprises at the present stage, some contradictions and problems begin to appear and need to be solved urgently, including these: there are high barriers to entry for private enterprises in monopoly industries; hidden barriers like the "glass door," the "revolving door" and the "spring door" still exist; some local governments will still intervene in the operation and development of mixed-ownership enterprises through state-owned equity; corporate governance is not transparent and standard enough; and it is difficult to integrate the corporate cultures of state-owned enterprises and non-state-owned enterprises.

IV. Key Tasks in the Mixed-Ownership Reform of State-Owned Enterprises

1. Promoting the mixed-ownership reform of state-owned enterprises by category

First, a distinction must be made between "already mixed" enterprises and those that are "suitable for mixing." For state-owned enterprises that have already implemented mixed ownership, efforts should be made to improve the modern enterprise system and improve the efficiency of capital operation. For the state-owned enterprises suitable for the continuous promotion of mixed-ownership reform, full play should be given to the role of the market mechanism, and reform should be carried out in a standardized and orderly way.

Second, a distinction must be made between commercial and public-welfare-oriented state-owned enterprises. Commercial state-owned enterprises whose main business is in fully competitive industries and fields should be oriented toward increasing economic benefits and innovating business models. They should actively introduce other state-owned capital or various types of non-state-owned capital in order to realize equity diversification by making full use of overall listing or by other means. With capital as the link, the governance structure and management mode of mixed-ownership enterprises should be improved so as to turn them into real market subjects.

For commercial state-owned enterprises whose main business is in important industries and fields, the focus should be on maintaining the controlling position of state-owned capital and facilitating the participation of non-state-owned capital in shareholding.

For naturally monopolistic industries pursuing reform, it again becomes necessary to maintain a separation between government and enterprise, a separation between government and capital. It is also necessary to promote franchise operations and strengthen government regulation. The right approach will be customized to the specific conditions of different industries. Approaches include implementing the separation between network and operation, opening up competitive businesses, and promoting the marketization of public resource allocation. At the same time, regulation by category should be strengthened in accordance with the law, and the profit model should be subject to standards. For public-welfare-oriented state-owned enterprises, it is imperative to strengthen guidance by category in keeping with the different business characteristics in different industries and fields, in the process providing public goods and services such as public utilities (water supply, electricity, gas, and heating), public transportation, and public facilities. Qualified enterprises should also be aided in diversifying investors. Non-state-owned enterprises are encouraged to participate in the operation by purchasing services, franchising, entrustment and agency, and other means.

2. Promoting the mixed-ownership reform of state-owned enterprises by level

It is important to promote mixed-ownership reform at the level of subsidiaries in an orderly way. For subsidiaries or sub-subsidiaries of state-owned group companies, China should focus on real economy enterprises (such as those engaged in R&D innovation and production services), introduce non-state-owned capital, accelerate innovation (technology, management, and business models related), reasonably limit the legal person levels, and effectively reduce management levels.

Mixed-ownership reform must also be promoted at the level of group companies. In the specific areas clearly defined by the state, the government should uphold the controlling position of state-owned capital, forming a reasonable governance structure and a market-oriented operation mechanism; in other areas, the proportion of state-owned equity should be gradually adjusted through overall listing, merger/reorganization, and the issuance of convertible bonds. All kinds of investors should be welcome so as to form a business mechanism with a diversified equity structure, standardized shareholder behavior, effective internal restraints, and efficient and flexible operation.

3. Encouraging various sorts of capital to participate in the mixed-ownership reform of state-owned enterprises

First, non-state-owned capital investors should be encouraged to participate in the restructuring and reorganization of state-owned enterprises, the capital increase and share expansion of state-controlled listed companies, and the corporate operation and management by buying stakes, purchasing shares, subscribing for convertible bonds from state-owned enterprises, and conducting share rights swaps with state-owned enterprises.

Second, collective capital should be encouraged to participate in the mixed-ownership reform of state-owned enterprises. The government should clarify the property rights of collective assets and develop economic entities with diversified equity, industrialized operation, and standardized management. Collective capital, assets, and other factors of production with confirmed property rights are allowed to join the shares at their assessed value and to participate in the mixed-ownership reform of state-owned enterprises.

Third, China should introduce foreign capital to participate in the restructuring and reorganization. This will mean forming joint ventures with state-owned enterprises, developing a mixed-ownership economy, participating in international competition and the global industrial division of labor, improving the capability of global allocation of resources, and encouraging the full use of resources and elements such as the international market, technology, and talents by overseas M&A, investment & financing cooperation, offshore finance, and other means.

Fourth, the PPP (Public Private Partnership) mode of cooperation between government and social capital must be promoted. Government investment should be facilitated, and priority should be given to projects that introduce social capital through investment subsidies, fund injection, guarantee subsidies, and loan discounts.

Fifth, in the context of market choice, state-owned capital should be encouraged to carry out equity integration, strategic cooperation, and resource integration with non-state-owned enterprises through investment, joint investment, merger, and reorganization so as to develop a mixed-ownership economy and give full play to the role of the capital operation platform for state-owned capital investment and operation companies.

Sixth, preferred stock and state special management stock should be explored and improved. When state-owned capital participates in the equity of non-state-owned enterprises or state-owned enterprises introduce non-state-owned capital, it is worth exploring the possibility of a state special management stock system in a few specific areas, a system that will allow part of the state-owned capital to be converted into preferred shares.

Seventh, the implementation of an ESOP in mixed-ownership enterprises should be explored. The principle of combining incentives with restraints can be a guide to such implementation. ESOPs can be promoted through pilot projects.

4. Establishing and improving the governance mechanism of mixed-ownership enterprises

A number of steps are needed in the attempt to improve the governance mechanism of mixed-ownership enterprises.

First, the market subject position of enterprises must be further established and ensured. The government should not interfere in the independent operation of enterprises, and shareholders should not interfere in an enterprise's daily operations. These guarantees will ensure that enterprise governance is standardized, and the incentive and restraint mechanism is in place.

Second, the corporate governance structure of mixed-ownership enterprises should be improved. This means establishing and improving the modern enterprise system, clarifying property rights, allowing the same stock to share the same rights, and protecting the rights and interests of all kinds of shareholders in accordance with the law.

Third, a professional manager system in mixed-ownership enterprises should be implemented. China should establish a number of market-oriented mechanisms (e.g., one for personnel selection and employment, another for incentive and restraint), including the hiring of professional managers who are assessed in a market-oriented way. These managers will be responsible for business management according to the law so as to smooth the channel of identity transformation between the existing managers and professional managers. Strict enforcement of the term management and performance assessment of professional managers is needed, as is acceleration in the establishment of an exit mechanism.

5. Establishing operation rules according to the law

The establishment of amenable operation rules will be in accordance with the following goals:

First, strictly standardizing the operation process and approval procedures. In accordance with relevant laws and regulations, the authorized operation of state-owned assets and property right trading should be subject to standards, and in the process, the procedures for the transfer of state-owned property rights (such as asset and capital verification, evaluation, pricing, transfer transactions, registration, and confirmation of rights) should be improved so as to prevent tunneling.

Second, improving the pricing mechanism for state-owned assets. In accordance with the principles of openness, fairness, and impartiality, the trading mode of state-owned assets should be improved, and the procedures and transactions of state-owned assets (such as registration, transfer, liquidation, and withdrawal) should be strictly regulated. Through the property rights, equity, and securities markets, China can find and reasonably determine asset prices, give play to the role of specialized intermediaries, and improve the asset pricing mechanism.

Third, effectively strengthening regulation. The regulation of the mixed-ownership reform of state-owned enterprises should be strengthened, and the trading rules and regulatory system of state-owned property rights should be improved. Give full play to the role of third-party institutions in asset and capital verification, financial audit, asset pricing, equity custody, etc. Strengthen internal supervision of the employees of enterprises. Further, disclose information and consciously accept social supervision.

6. Creating a good setting for mixed-ownership reform of state-owned enterprises

The environment for mixed-ownership reform can be improved in the following four ways:

First, strengthening the protection of property rights. It is important to protect the property and intellectual property rights of various investors of mixed ownership enterprises in accordance with applicable laws and give equal legal protection to the economic property rights and legitimate interests of various ownership systems.

Second, improving the multi-level capital market. It is important to accelerate the establishment of an over-the-counter market with unified rules and standardized transactions, to promote the equity trading of non-listed joint-stock companies and improve the trading mechanisms for equity, creditor's rights, property rights, intellectual property rights, trusts, financial leasing, industrial investment funds, and other products.

Third, revising policies so as to support the mixed-ownership reform of state-owned enterprises. It is important to further streamline administration, delegate power, and improve policies concerning industrial and commercial registration, fiscal and taxation management, land management, and financial services.

Fourth, accelerating the establishment and improvement of laws and regulations. It is important to improve laws, regulations, and rules related to the mixed-ownership economy. China must also improve the relevant legal systems related to various legal subdisciplines (contract law, property law, company law, enterprise state-owned assets law, and enterprise bankruptcy law) and speed up the formulation of laws and regulations on property rights protection, market access and exit, trading rules, and fair competition.

CHAPTER TWELVE

The Development of the Private Sector: Mass Innovation and Entrepreneurship

To comprehensively deepen the reform, it is necessary to stimulate the market and cultivate new market entities. Mass innovation and entrepreneurship are central factors in promoting the development of the private sector and realizing the harmonious development of diverse forms of ownership.

SECTION 1
The Role of the Private Sector

I. The Development History of China's Private Sector

Over the past 40 years of reform and opening-up, China's policy approach to the private sector has improved, and the private sector has played an increasingly important role in stabilizing growth, increasing employment, increasing tax revenue, and restructuring. From small to large, from weak to strong, private sector growth has progressed through four stages.

The first stage captures the period of time that saw the private sector as a "beneficial supplement" in theory while China pursued preliminary development in practice (1978–1992). Deng Xiaoping proposed in 1978 that China should encourage certain regions, enterprises, and individuals to be first in achieving prosperity through good management and honest work.[53] The 12th National Congress of the CPC proposed "encouraging and supporting the individual economy of working people as a necessary and beneficial supplement to the public sector."[54] The 13th National Congress proposed that the "private sector is also a necessary and beneficial supplement to the public sector," marking that the CPC began to realize the role of market factors in regulating economic interests and promoting economic development.[55] During this period, the government adopted a systematic and limited policy that advanced the development of the private sector.

The second stage captures a period that saw the private sector as an "important part" in theory, even as China pursued rapid development in practice (1992–2002). At this stage, China placed additional focus on ensuring and guiding the development of the non-public economy. In 1992, Deng Xiaoping put forward "three benefits" in his southern speech. The 15th National Congress established that "keeping socialist public ownership as the mainstay of the economy and allowing diverse forms of ownership to develop side by side is a basic economic system at the primary stage of socialism in China,"[56] and for the first time explicitly made the claim that the "non-public economy is an important part of the socialist market economy."[57] A series of reform measures, including the Opinions on Standardization of Joint Stock Limited Companies, were issued, injecting great vitality into the vigorous development of the private sector. A wave of entrepreneurship overtook the nation, a wave that saw an influx of workers move from the public to the private sector.

The third stage captures a stretch of time when the government advanced "unshakable policies" in theory and leapfrog development in practice (2002–2012). The 16th National Congress proposed that "it is necessary to encourage, support, and guide the development of the non-public sectors of the economy."[58] The 17th National Congress proposed that China "ensure equal protection of property rights and create a new situation in which all economic sectors compete on an equal footing and reinforce each other."[59] The 36 Articles on Non-public Economy, the Enterprise Income Tax Law, the Property Law, and other policies and regulations promoting the private sector were issued. The policy system and legal system promoting the development of the non-public economy were increasingly improved. At this stage, China's entry into the World Trade Organization (WTO) and the rise of Internet entrepreneurship created more opportunities for the private sector.

The fourth stage, which is still underway, embraces "three equalities" in theory and focuses on transformation and development in practice. The 18th National Congress proposed that "economic entities under all forms of ownership have equal access to factors of production in accordance with the law, compete on a level playing field, and are protected by the law as equals."[60] The Third Plenary Session of the 18th CPC Central Committee proposed that "we should adhere to equal rights, equal opportunities, and equal rules, abolish all forms of unreasonable regulations on the non-public economy, eliminate all hidden barriers, and formulate specific measures by which non-public enterprises may enter franchised fields."[61] The Fifth Plenary Session of the 19th CPC Central Committee proposed that "we should uphold and improve the basic socialist economic system, give full play to the decisive role of the market in the allocation of resources, give better play to government resources, promote the better combination of efficient market and promising government, stimulate the vitality of various market subjects, and encourage, support and guide the development of the non-public economy with great resolve."[62]

II. The Status of China's Private Sector

1. The private sector as an important part of the economy

After the founding of the PRC, a process that thoroughly revolutionized capitalist industry and commerce, the private sector was eliminated, only 160,000 households were left in the individual economy, and a single socialist ownership structure was established. Facts have proven that such a unified public ownership structure inhibited productivity in the primary stage of socialism and hindered the development of socially productive forces. This historical lesson is very profound. In the aftermath of learning such a profound historical lesson, China's correct understanding of the non-public economy and its status began with the individual economy. Over the course of the development of the socialist market economy, the rapid growth of the private sector and other non-public sectors, and the increasing role these sectors play in the national economy, the Party's principles and policies on non-public economy have encountered a period of rapid change.

Despite using less than 40% of China's resources, private enterprises pay more than 50% of taxes, create more than 60% of China's GDP, contribute more than 70% of technological innovation and new product development, and provide more than 80% of jobs. They have transformed into an important part of the socialist market economy and a foundation for China's economic and social development. The private economy plays an important role in upholding the national economy, expanding employment, and increasing national financial revenue. Its existence and development serve socialism and encourage the development of a socialist market economy and socialist modernization.

2. The social and political status of private entrepreneurs

Since the reform and opening-up, new changes have taken place in the composition of China's social classes, changes that have occurred alongside the development of the private sector. In his 2001 speech at the meeting celebrating the 80th anniversary of the founding of the CPC, Comrade Jiang Zemin pointed out: "Since the reform and opening-up, new changes have taken place in the composition of China's social classes, with the emergence of entrepreneurs and technicians of private S&T enterprises, managerial and technical personnel employed by foreign-funded enterprises, self-employed people, private enterprises, employees of intermediary organizations, and freelancers, who are also builders of socialism with Chinese characteristics." The term "builder" indicates the social status of non-public sector individuals, and it is a sign of the new respect being shown to individuals working in the non-public economy. Affirming the social status of "builders" in the non-public economy will help to clarify and enhance their social responsibility and guide the healthy development of this portion of the economy.

As an important part of the non-public economy, private entrepreneurs not only are builders of the cause of socialism with Chinese characteristics but also can be absorbed into the Communist Party as outstanding members. Absorbing outstanding private entrepreneurs into the CPC has a long and beneficial history. It has been shown to expand and strengthen the Party's base and to consolidate the Party's ruling position. (To consolidate its ruling position, a ruling party must have a solid class foundation and a broad base.) As the ruling party, the CPC must adapt to the changing situation, consolidate its support, expand the reach of that support, and improve the Party's social influence. To further develop the cause of building socialism with Chinese characteristics under the leadership of the CPC in a complex and dynamic international environment, China must unite as many people as possible.

In fact, the integration of outstanding individuals in the non-public sector into the CPC has become an example visible to a vast number of people in this sector. It plays an exemplary role, helping the CPC unite and guide those in the private sector so as to encourage their role as builders of socialism with Chinese characteristics. Of course, when absorbing outstanding private entrepreneurs into the CPC, the Party must adhere to the fixed standards and procedures that ensure its integrity. Standards of education for private entrepreneurs entering the Party must be strengthened and indeed must be more demanding than standards for general entrepreneurs. This will provide them with guidance that will make them a vanguard, a group of individuals who play an exemplary role among private entrepreneurs.

III. The Role of the Private Sector

The private sector is the most dynamic, innovative, and creative force in the market economy, and it is also an important force driving China's economic development. Private enterprises play a prominent role in creating jobs, raising tax revenue, and promoting economic development. As China's economy enters the new normal in recent years, private enterprises have become highlights in the field of economic development. The data show that the contribution rate of private enterprises to China's GDP is as high as 60%, providing about 80% of urban jobs, absorbing more than 70% of the rural labor force, creating about 90% of newly added jobs, and raising more than 50% of the tax revenue. Private sector influences permeate the Chinese economy, and they play the following roles.

1. The private sector's role in the development of the national economy
The private sector is still the basic force to create market vitality and stimulate economic growth. China's private sector continues to develop and expand, having become a vital force in the national economy. It is an important cause of the continuous rapid growth of the national economy. Over the past 40 years of reform and opening-up, the government's support for private enterprises has been increasing. The development of the non-public economy, including private enterprises, has stepped onto the fast track. The social wealth created by private enterprises has grown rapidly. The proportion of GDP created by the private sector has rapidly increased from 1% in the early stage of reform to more than 50% in 2015.

2. The private sector's role in financial revenue
Tax is the main pillar of national revenue, and the private sector is an important source of tax income for the government, accounting for 50% of the total tax. There is also potential for more.

In 2016, tax revenue from the private sector increased by 5.5%, 0.7% points higher than national tax growth. Among the 1,062 large enterprise groups with annual tax payments of more than 300 million yuan under the service and management of the State Administration of Taxation, the tax revenue and operating revenue of 312 private enterprises increased by 9.1% and 12.5% respectively in 2016, which were significantly higher than those of state-owned enterprises and foreign-funded enterprises. Among the national top 500 tax-paying enterprises, there are 42 private enterprises whose tax payment, operating revenue, and net profit increased by 24.4%, 38.7%, and 44.4%, respectively, in 2016, far higher than the other top 500 tax-paying enterprises. Most small and micro enterprises are private. In 2016, there were 3.67 million profitable small and micro enterprises, with a year-on-year growth of 8.12%. In 2017, the accumulated tax revenue of private enterprises was approximately 7,667 billion yuan, accounting for 52.5% of total tax revenue, an increase of 1.2% points over the same period in the previous year.

3. The private sector's role in reforming state-owned enterprises

The development of the private sector pushes reform from outside to inside the system and promotes the reform of the state-owned economy. It has caused competitive pressure on state-owned enterprises to grow gradually. The original monopoly of state-owned enterprises was broken up. Over time, this caused monopoly profits to disappear, worsening the financial situation of some state-owned enterprises, as increased losses further exposed the weaknesses of the state-owned enterprise system. The increasing pressure of market competition is an important external condition forcing state-owned enterprises to deepen reform. At the same time, private enterprises have accepted a large number of redundant or surplus personnel transferred from the reform of state-owned enterprises, a practice that greatly contributes to the reemployment of laid-off workers and goes some way toward alleviating the social contradictions caused by these layoffs. According to the 2016 Chinese Private Enterprise Survey Report, 6.3% of enterprises merged or acquired state-owned enterprises; and another 10.2% of enterprises are preparing to merge and acquire state-owned enterprises. 18.3% of the surveyed enterprises were transformed from state-owned or collective enterprises into private enterprises.

4. The private sector's role in social employment

The contribution of the private sector to the national economy is increasing and now occupies a considerable position. Private sector development can raise the level of employment in China. In the course of its rapid development, the private sector has spurred a huge demand for labor, which provides a buffer zone to ease employment pressure. It is a main channel to absorb laid-off workers, rural surplus labor, and urban new labor. In terms of enterprises above the designated size, the employment of private enterprises is obviously better than that of state-owned enterprises. As the defining characteristics of the private sector are to give full play to the role of private capital, motivate the masses to start their own businesses flexibly, and broaden the opportunities for employment, and the potential that the private sector has to solve the problem of social employment is huge.

IV. Problems in the Development of China's Private Sector

Despite the undeniable advantages possessed by the private sector, it is faced with many problems.

1. Difficult and expensive financing

For a long time, the problem of difficult and expensive financing has been an obstacle to the rapid development of the private sector. Private enterprises encounter a wide variety of problems, including high loan thresholds, complicated credit procedures, difficulty in credit enhancement, poor fund-time matching, weak loan stability, high bank loan interest rates, high third-party service fees, high bank loan renewal costs, and high private financing costs. Bank loans are the most important financing channels for private enterprises, but domestic banks often impose financial constraints and require tangible assets as collateral for loans. Small and medium-sized enterprises (SMEs) face their own unique set of problems, such as their lack of capital, the small scale of their assets, the weak ability of sustainable operations, and so on. Therefore, when the market changes, their resistance to risk is poor. High risk makes it difficult for SMEs and enterprises with light assets (such as Internet enterprises) to get loans.

In order to promote the sustainable and healthy development of the private sector, the government must urgently encourage various commercial banks to provide loan services for private enterprises and to work closely with government agencies to facilitate policy guidance, financial incentives, and other mechanisms. Banks must also receive motivation to guide private enterprises in honest and legal operations as they improve their own financing environments, help strong private enterprises speed up the pace of direct financing through listing, and ease the capital constraints of private enterprises. Therefore, it is necessary to change the assessment mechanism of financial institutions, reshape their organizational structure, and overcome the problem of information asymmetry between borrowers and lenders.

2. Struggle to be competitive

More than 90% of private enterprises in China are small, medium, or micro enterprises. Limited by market access, enterprise quality, and other conditions, most of them are engaged in traditional manufacturing, service, and other competitive industries. They rely on low-cost, low-level imitation and low-level processing to compete in the market over the long run, and their products have low technology content, sparse innovation, and lack of core competitiveness, resulting in a predictably weak showing in the market.

At present, a new era of technological revolution and industrial change is gripping the world. In the face of this revolution, China must deepen the reform of its technological system, must guide enterprises as they increase investment in R&D, must strive to master key technologies and independent intellectual property rights, must strengthen support for innovation in SMEs, and must establish an innovation system around the competitive needs of enterprises—a market-oriented system, a system that thoroughly integrates industry, university, and research deeply.

In particular, the government must see to it that technological innovation drives other forms of innovation: innovation of product, production, and business model. The government must also strive to expand the value chain to R&D, standard setting, sales, and service; it must continuously develop new technologies; it must break ground in new fields, launch new products, and lead consumption innovation through product innovation.

At the same time, private enterprises in traditional industries should be driven to carry out technological innovation and transformation, upgrading to the high end of the value chain. The integration of industrialization and informatization should be promoted, and the level of intelligent manufacturing should be improved. The focus should be placed on quality brand construction, improving manufacturing quality and enterprise competitiveness, and making use of the advantages of Chinese technology, management, and product excellence as a way to enter overseas markets. This last step can only be accomplished through the transfer of production capacity and the cooperation of investment projects, but its accomplishment would bring China greater development space and many advantages.

3. Ownership discrimination

Ownership discrimination, a practice by which state-owned enterprises are given preferential treatment in credit decisions, has always been an important factor affecting the development of the private sector. There is a widespread phenomenon of ownership discrimination in Chinese society. Almost all the policies and even public opinions concerning government management and enterprises are labeled with ownership. Every enterprise has an ownership label, which forms a deep ownership gap in the market. The "two unshakable policies" have solved the problem of private capital investment and the political status of private entrepreneurs. The CPC Central Committee and the State Council have already issued the Opinions on Improving the Property Rights Protection System for Legal Protection of Property Rights, but they are not yet fully implemented. Enterprises under different ownership systems have in fact received unequal policy treatment, and they struggle to get equal treatment in the implementation process.

In order to combat ownership discrimination, the negative list for market access should be shortened, and a great deal of red tape must be removed since it inhibits a unified market with fair competition. China should deepen commercial system reform, break administrative monopolies, prevent market monopolies, speed up the marketization reform of factor prices, relax access restrictions in the service industry, and improve the market regulatory system. The market must play a decisive role in the allocation of resources, and the government must play its role more skillfully. The Chinese approach should respect equal rights, equal opportunities, and equal rules, abolishing all forms of unreasonable regulations in the private sector of the economy, eliminating any hidden barriers, and formulating specific measures that help non-public enterprises enter franchised fields. The "three equalities" proposal reflects the determination and confidence of the Party and the country to break up monopolies and to build a unified and open market system with orderly competition and fair, open, and transparent market rules.

SECTION 2
Protecting Property Rights and Stimulating Entrepreneurship

I. The Importance of Improving the Property Rights Protection System

1. Protect the right to property

Property rights include the right to own, possess, use, control, and dispose of property. Individual enterprises and wholly foreign-owned enterprises in the private sector clearly possess property rights since they have independent control and exclusive ownership over all their properties. These enterprises can become market subjects with self-management, self-financing, self-restraint, and self-development. The property rights system is a system of rules and customs governing the definitions, operations, transactions, and means of protection for various properties and property rights, and it is arranged in a way suitable for socialized production and the modern market economy. A property right includes the legal and exclusive ownership, possession right, income right, and disposal right that a subject has with respect to a given object.

The property rights system is a cornerstone of the socialist market economy, and protecting these rights is a necessary condition for upholding the basic socialist economic system. Our ancestors believe that individuals shall have peace of mind when they possess a piece of land. The effective guarantee and realization of the property rights of economic entities are the foundation of the sustainable and sound development of the economy and society.

2. Ensure market order

The main function of property rights is to provide incentives and constraints so that economic entities participate in market economic activities, reduce uncertainty, and internalize externality. An improvement of the property rights system that makes room for all kinds of ownership economies and all kinds of property rights to be clearly defined, smoothly transferred, and strictly protected is an important guarantee that standardizes the production and operation behavior of market entities. Such an improvement would also optimize the allocation of resources, reduce market transaction costs, and form a good market order. It is a basic premise on which the effective operation of the socialist market economic system is built.

Given current economic realities, China must further consolidate the basic economic system to keep public ownership as the mainstay of the economy and to allow diverse sectors to develop side by side. This goal requires the nation to improve the property rights system covering all kinds of ownership economies, to protect all kinds of property rights according to law, to promote the fair transaction and circulation of property rights, and to consolidate the micro foundation of the socialist market economy.

3. Ensure the vitality of market entities

The pursuit of property rights and the benefits that accrue to those possessing them are fundamental driving forces that motivate various market entities to carry out production and operation activities under the condition of a market economy. A series of reform practices, such as the Household Responsibility System reform and the reform of state-owned enterprises, have proven that the establishment of a sound property rights system can effectively stimulate the vitality and creativity of market subjects. Seeing that China's economic development has now entered the new normal, a number of steps are imperative, steps that will help China effectively respond to challenges and maintain sustainable and healthy economic development. These steps include further stimulating market vitality and the spirit of innovation, stabilizing social expectations, enhancing the lasting power of economic development, and giving full play to the enthusiasm, initiative, and creativity of various market entities (especially entrepreneurs) in entrepreneurship, innovation and investment. The steps can only proceed alongside an improvement of the property rights system.

4. Ensure market expectations

There can be no meaningful social equality without an equal and fair system of property rights. Social stability, as well, relies on the stability of the property rights system. In the wake of such great improvements in material living conditions for the Chinese people, improvements that yield a continuous increase in personal property, it is particularly important to safeguard personal property. Any improvement in the property rights system that protects property rights more effectively is also a means of protecting people's honest work, honoring their yearning for a better life, and creating a fair and stable social environment. With the expansion of China's middle class and the growing number of wealthy individuals—alongside the awareness of how technological progress contributes to economic growth—a great number of entrepreneurs and technologically literate residents, among other groups, have expressed strong demands that property rights and interests be clarified and property protection be strengthened.

II. Improving the Property Rights Protection System to Develop the Private Sector

There is a strong connective fabric linking property rights protection to growth in the private sector. In order to take advantage of this connection, China must pursue the following goals.

1. Strengthen the protection of intellectual property rights in order to provide a guarantee for the innovation and development of private enterprises

There have already been successes in the area of property rights protection. The "three-in-one" intellectual property administrative department of patent, trademark, and copyright was established in the free trade zone, an accomplishment that should be set forward as an example. Moving forward, it is necessary to speed up the integration and optimization of administrative functions, integrating the administrative management and law enforcement functions of trademarks (as well as those functions of copyright) within the Intellectual Property Administration. At the same time, the construction of a comprehensive administrative law enforcement team for intellectual property rights should be accelerated, placing more emphasis on quick response, and the low cost of safeguarding rights in administrative enforcement should receive public attention. In some areas with a developed private economy, intellectual property courts should be set up to increase the number of grassroots courts with authority over intellectual property civil cases and to reduce litigation costs. Decisions should be made to hasten the establishment of a punitive compensation system for intellectual property infringement, to increase the cost of infringement, and to protect the innovation benefits of various market subjects in accordance with the law.

2. Create an atmosphere in which the whole society respects and protects property rights

Property rights protection must be considered an important part of the teaching of civics classes and must be included in company policies, regulations, and training plans. Enterprises should actively raise awareness of property rights protection, communicating the concept of the equal, comprehensive, and legal protection of private enterprises and individual property rights so that these ideas become deeply embedded into the hearts of people. A regular public disclosure system of government defaulters should be established, in-depth special governance of government defaulters should be carried out, and the defaulters should be urged to fulfill their legal obligations as soon as possible. In the case of damage to the legal property rights of private enterprises, relevant parties should be compensated, and relevant personnel should be investigated. China should actively publicize successful experiences of this sort, with the goal of motivating more individuals and enterprises to participate in entrepreneurship and innovation.

3. Improve the supporting policies and working mechanisms for the protection of property rights in the private sector

Relevant government departments should strengthen their research on the protection of private property rights and actively improve supporting policies and mechanisms. They should establish and improve the work coordination mechanism between various departments involved in property rights protection and keep abreast of new and thorny issues related to property rights. All government agencies should carry out special supervision on implementing the Opinions on Improving the Property Rights Protection System for Legal Protection of Property Rights in a timely way, should accelerate the handling of existing property rights cases, and should promptly inform the public about the handling of certain cases of property rights protection that have been resolved.

III. The Meaning and Significance of Entrepreneurship

1. The meaning of entrepreneurship

A helpful way to express what it means to be an entrepreneur is by bringing forward the three responsibilities of entrepreneurs and then explaining the functioning of the five types of spirit that characterize them.

(1) The three responsibilities

First of all, entrepreneurs should take political responsibility. Political responsibility revolves around faith and political determination. The political core and leading role of party organization deserve a great deal of respect. Entrepreneurs working in the spirit of Chinese reform must unswervingly follow the policies of the CPC, must maintain confidence in the future of China, and must not be disturbed by various lies and rumors. Only in this way can they concentrate on seizing opportunities and accelerating development.

Secondly, entrepreneurs should take economic responsibility. Entrepreneurs are the organizers, users, and controllers of production factors, and they take upon themselves the important duty of promoting China's economic development. Under the new economic normal, enterprises face new challenges, and it is an ideal time for excellent entrepreneurs to distinguish themselves. In this great era, great Chinese enterprises, great Chinese entrepreneurs, and great Chinese entrepreneurship are emerging and will continue to emerge. If they are to bear the responsibility for development, entrepreneurs must uphold the philosophy of independent innovation, independent brand, and independent capital. Moreover, they must develop the real economy by sticking to real industry, innovation, and transformation. High-quality operation of enterprises will be achieved in the context of continued innovation, the innovation that helps entrepreneurs fulfill their responsibility to accelerate the development of China's economy.

Finally, entrepreneurs should take social responsibility. Corporate social responsibility means that enterprises not only create profits and bear legal responsibilities to shareholders and employees but also bear responsibilities to consumers, communities, and the environment. Corporate social responsibility requires enterprises to go beyond the traditional idea in which profits are the only goal. Instead, it prioritizes attention to human value in the production process, and it emphasizes the enterprise's impact on the environment, consumers, and society. Corporate social responsibility includes corporate governance and moral standards, respect for social culture and the political system, compliance with existing laws, common rules, and international standards, the prevention of corruption and bribery, and diligent care for consumers and customers. It includes responsibility toward people in the form of employee safety plans, equal employment opportunities, resistance to discrimination and unfair pay, etc. It includes responsibility for the environment, including maintenance of environmental quality, use of clean energy, joint responses to climate change, protection of biodiversity, and the like. It includes contributions to social and economic welfare, which is part of the core strategy of enterprises and may manifest itself in social investment, giving to charity, or community service.

(2) The five spirits

The "entrepreneurial spirit" refers to hard work, thrift, tenacity, and courage to explore. It is not only the traditional virtue of the Chinese nation but also the basic spiritual characteristic of Chinese entrepreneurs.

The "innovative spirit" means daring to be the first, having the courage to break the rules, constantly creating, demonstrating originality, opening up new markets, realizing new values, and exploring new breakthroughs in products, management, technology, and other areas.

The "craftsman spirit" is evident in the concentration of the worker and the perfection of the work. The craftsman spirit is a guarantee of quality products that promote the good of both the public and the enterprise.

The "learning spirit" is evident whenever the Chinese people are diligent in learning and good at thinking—that is when they combine learning well with thinking well. The times are changing rapidly. A constant course of study will allow China to keep up with the pace of the times, attain commanding heights of knowledge, seize intellectual opportunities, and become strong and successful.

The "responsibility spirit" involves improving people's living conditions with a focus on morality and serving the country through industry. This spirit requires entrepreneurs to have "political direction, development ability, cultural literacy, and responsibility."

2. The significance of entrepreneurship

(1) Entrepreneurship fuels innovation

Innovation is the foundation for the survival and development of enterprises. Entrepreneurship drives product innovation, and it is the key engine for enterprises to promote the reform process. Cultivating entrepreneurship is, in its own right, a process of innovation. In the course of this process, opportunities for new products or services are recognized, created, and finally developed to generate new wealth-creation capabilities. As entrepreneurship is the driving force of enterprise innovation, it has a decisive impact on the success or failure of this innovation. When an enterprise innovates, this can help it improve its organizational form and management efficiency so that it can continuously improve efficiency and adapt to the requirements of economic development.

(2) Entrepreneurship permeates all levels of society

When one looks closely at the nature of entrepreneurship, it becomes clear that entrepreneurship permeates many different levels of society: the individual level, the organizational level, and the social level. It has a significant and far-reaching impact on all aspects of society.

Research on individual entrepreneurship is based on the entrepreneurs themselves, including the individual characteristics of entrepreneurs, the elements of individual entrepreneurship, and the way that individual entrepreneurs behave in the entrepreneurial process. Individual entrepreneurship can trigger "variability" and "transition" in the entrepreneur's behavior. It can also promote the entrepreneur's creative activities and realize the enlargement and expansion of the entrepreneur's resource endowment.

Organizational entrepreneurship focuses on the overall innovation and entrepreneurship behavior of enterprises or organizations. Organizational entrepreneurship exists within a process in which individuals or groups build a new company patterned after existing companies or restructure/reorganize existing companies. It is a process in which a series of unique resources are gathered together to look for opportunities and where research focuses on opportunities rather than the current resources. It is an important way for an organization to seek out competitive advantages in a dynamic and complex environment.

Social entrepreneurship refers to the extensive penetration of entrepreneurship throughout the whole society. Social entrepreneurship applies the entrepreneurship, innovation, and adventurousness of entrepreneurs to non-profit social organizations in order to create new value. It is not only about the individual characteristics of independent entrepreneurs but about the social impact of those characteristics. Since it is a comprehensive spiritual quality formed within certain social, economic, and cultural environments, social entrepreneurship flows out of the talents of the individual entrepreneurs, a special group of people motivated by an innovative and daring spirit.

As can be seen from these three aspects, entrepreneurship is a closely linked and unified whole. The purpose of individual entrepreneurship research is to inspire individuals to consciously acquire this spirit, which will become an important spiritual factor in motivating individual business startups. The research goal of organizational entrepreneurship is to let enterprises consciously organize and establish corporate culture, to develop a system that embodies the characteristics of entrepreneurship, and to make such entrepreneurship an important spiritual pillar to promote the sustainable and rapid development of enterprises. The research of social entrepreneurship is to fully guide the construction of entrepreneurship culture in communities, regions, countries, and even the whole society, stimulating the innovation and entrepreneurial enthusiasm of the society and maximizing the benefits of entrepreneurship in promoting economic and social development.

(3) Entrepreneurship drives social development

Entrepreneurship is an inexhaustible source of power for sustainable innovation and the development of enterprises, and it is one of the most important driving forces to promote national economic development in the 21st century. Entrepreneurship is a driving force for technological innovation and industrial structure change; it is a creator of social employment, an important source of wealth accumulation, and a driving force of institutional change. The economic impact of entrepreneurship is immeasurable. Entrepreneurship not only drives the improvement of corporate performance and economic development but also promotes the progress of the whole society.

A few of these points deserve consideration at greater length:

- Entrepreneurship is an important driving force for technological innovation. Because of their unique personal capacities, especially their keen insight and abundant experience, entrepreneurs are amazing innovators. They play an important role in advocating, encouraging, coordinating, and organizing the implementation of technological innovation.
- Entrepreneurship is the driving force of industrial structure change. The entrepreneurial spirit often finds its expression in the founding or reorganization of enterprises. Entrepreneurs have keen insight, long-term vision, and an understanding of what it takes to get enterprises off the ground. They typically have gifts in organization, management, and innovation and can rapidly intuit all the favorable opportunities in the market. Entrepreneurship encourages the industrialization of technological innovation achievements and is an important tool for the development of industrial clusters and the transformation and upgrading of industrial structures.
- Entrepreneurship creates social employment. Through an innovative and entrepreneurial spirit, entrepreneurs find inventive ways to meet people's needs, create new market demands,

and find a large number of new enterprises. The development of these enterprises involves the hiring of various employees, thus creating all kinds of development opportunities, in addition to the gains involved by the employment of the workers themselves.

- Entrepreneurship is an important source of wealth accumulation. Whether in developed or in newly industrialized economies, economic growth and prosperity are inseparable from the entrepreneurial activities of excellent entrepreneurs. Economic development has driven wealth accumulation. On the other hand, this accumulation of wealth is the natural flowering of the achievements of generations of entrepreneurs who used their talents to contribute to society, a fitting reward for the diligence of wealth creators.
- Entrepreneurship is the driving force of institutional change. Entrepreneurs who have the courage to challenge themselves will not just passively respond to changes in the outside world but will also actively attempt to change the environment. The dynamic mechanism of institutional evolution lies in entrepreneurs' innovation or arbitrage activities and in the interaction of entrepreneurs in creating or realizing potential profit opportunities.

IV. Stimulating and Protecting Entrepreneurship

As has been made evident above, the well-being of the state depends in large part upon the actions of entrepreneurs. China must encourage and protect entrepreneurship. This will mean recognizing its importance, broadening the space in which it operates, strengthening property rights, reducing its cost, placing focus on honesty and integrity, and cultivating public opinion that lines up to support it.

1. Recognizing the important role of entrepreneurship

Entrepreneurship is an important factor in production. Its unique role is irreplaceable. It is an important driving force and spiritual pillar for China to implement an innovation-driven development strategy, promote mass entrepreneurship and innovation, change the mode of development, and promote economic restructuring. To change the driving force of economic development to innovation, the leading role of entrepreneurship in fostering innovation must be recognized, and the cultivation and stimulation of entrepreneurship must be put in the core position of an innovation-driven development strategy. China should speed up the reform of the economic system, give play to the decisive role of the market in the allocation of resources, and create conditions amenable to maximizing the talents of entrepreneurs as the nation cultivates and stimulates entrepreneurship.

2. Broadening the space of entrepreneurs' innovation and entrepreneurship

A good market competition environment and broad market space is needed for the full release of entrepreneurs' innovative ability. The reform of state-owned enterprises and monopoly industries must be further accelerated, unreasonable administrative monopolies and market monopolies must be broken up, and restrictions on the scale, equity ratio, and business scope must be canceled in accordance with the principle that "entry is allowed without approval if no prohibition is imposed." It is also imperative to remove regional administrative barriers, expand the space for entrepreneurs to invest and start businesses, break the hidden access control of national and provincial large project investments, and encourage cooperation between private entrepreneurs and entrepreneurs in the public sector. This cooperation could involve the management of land or capital but could also involve the sharing of expertise, certification, and various other resources.

The government plays a key role in supporting entrepreneurship. Individuals in the private sector should accordingly give full play to the functions of the government and support a governmental role in creating a good entrepreneurial culture, improving the support policies for innovation and entrepreneurship, and supporting and encouraging entrepreneurs to actively participate in innovation and entrepreneurship activities. Leaders must strengthen the construction of the enterprise service system, prioritize key areas, encourage the opening of businesses, and support the healthy growth of entrepreneurial enterprises. The construction of a factor market system should be accelerated, and a relaxed market environment for business startups should be created. All these things will help motivate innovation and entrepreneurship in the whole society.

3. Strengthening the protection of property rights and the rights of entrepreneurs
The incentive provided by property rights is the best stimulator and propellant of entrepreneurship. The protection of property rights must further be strengthened until China is able to effectively safeguard the legitimate rights and interests of entrepreneurs. This entails a number of changes. The government must improve the legal system related to property rights protection, accelerate the compilation of the civil code, bolster legal policies related to contracts and intellectual property rights, clean up the unfair provisions of laws and regulations, and equally protect various market subjects. The promise-keeping mechanism of the government should be improved, and the construction of a government ruled by law and integrity vigorously should be promoted so that the government can truly serve the people. Efforts should be made to solve problems such as the government's failure to make administrative decisions according to law and the government's tendency to use administrative power to infringe on the property rights of enterprises and entrepreneurs in times of default or political instability. The transformation of government functions should be accelerated, giving rise to a thorough separation of government and enterprise and ensuring that enterprises can become independent entities. China must straighten out its approach to property rights, must separate property ownership from the legal property rights of enterprises, and must guarantee the entity status of enterprises as legal persons. The protection of intellectual property rights should also be strengthened, as a healthy environment where the whole society shows honor and deference to the protection of intellectual property rights is fostered. It is imperative to effectively protect the private property, the legitimate rights, and the legitimate interests of enterprises and entrepreneurs, in addition to strictly and promptly addressing illegal acts of retaliation, slander, and injury to entrepreneurs, according to law.

4. Reducing the cost of entrepreneurship and innovation
Under the market economy system, entrepreneurs are always looking for an ideal situation, a setting that can give them the greatest ability to exercise their talents and maximize wealth

creation. Complicated procedures frustrate entrepreneurs, as do high costs. Such conditions are not conducive to cultivating and stimulating entrepreneurship. The government, and especially the leading cadres, should establish a cordial and clean government/enterprise relationship with private entrepreneurs, streamlining work processes, improving the efficiency of government services, and resolutely putting an end to rent-seeking corruption and tunneling. China should speed up reform in related fields and effectively reduce the cost of logistics and energy resources. It should also improve support policies for innovation and entrepreneurship, strengthen the preferential policies on funds, talents, and land, and reduce startup costs. Tax and other preferential policies should be improved to effectively reduce the burden on startups.

5. Building a business environment of honesty and integrity

The growth of entrepreneurship in China calls for a fair, transparent, and stable environment characterized by social integrity. This environment is needed because it will strengthen the ideological and moral education of entrepreneurs and the cultivation of their sense of social responsibility, and it will strongly promote the culture and spirit of integrity in the whole society. The incentive for organizations to act in good faith should be strengthened. Responsible behaviors should be put prominently before the public eye, with honest enterprises being commended, outstanding individuals being praised, and faithless entities facing the consequences. Chinese leaders should establish and improve the joint punishment mechanism for defaulters, give full play to comprehensive regulatory effectiveness in the administrative, judicial, financial, social, and other fields, establish the inter-departmental linkage response and default restraint mechanisms, and restrict defaulters according to the law so as to truly realize Xi's goal that "dishonesty in one place [leads] to restrictions everywhere."[63] This new approach to defaults requires China to promote the formation of social restraints and disciplinary measures, improve the recording and disclosure system of default information, and restrict defaulters in various market activities. The public opinion supervision mechanism must be improved, a reward defaulter reporting system established, a reward system for whistleblowers implemented, and the legitimate rights and interests of whistleblowers protected.

Moreover, a number of credit service agencies should be developed. There should be a multi-level and all-around credit service organization system in which public credit service agencies and social credit service agencies complement each other, allowing basic credit information services and value-added services to complement each other.

6. Cultivating public opinion to promote entrepreneurship

In order to promote economic and social transformation for an improving socialist market economic system, China must raise awareness about the positive aspects of entrepreneurship, in the process creating an environment in which public opinion favorable for the growth of entrepreneurs and the cultivation of entrepreneurship flourishes. Entrepreneurs are scarce resources in society. The whole society should form a social atmosphere that respects entrepreneurs, understands them, and supports them, honoring the special labor of entrepreneurs, attaching importance to their social value, and fully affirming the contribution of entrepreneurs to China's economic and social development. It is important to conscientiously study and encapsulate the successful experience of entrepreneurs, explore the typical development pattern of entrepreneurial talent, and actively promote entrepreneurship in the whole society, especially the sort of entrepreneurship that dares to take risks and reap the rewards.

SECTION 3
Comprehensively Promoting Mass Innovation and Entrepreneurship

Innovation is the soul of social progress. Entrepreneurship is an important way to promote economic and social development and to improve people's livelihoods. Innovation and entrepreneurship coexist with one another in an interconnected way. The nation needs to further optimize the ecological context of innovation and entrepreneurship in a systematic way, strengthening policy supply, breaking through the bottleneck of development, fully releasing the potential of innovation and entrepreneurship to the whole of society, and promoting mass entrepreneurship and innovation on a broader scale, a higher level, and a deeper degree.

I. The Significance of Mass Innovation and Entrepreneurship

Mass innovation and entrepreneurship reflect the generalized patterns of human innovation and economic development. It is the best way to realize and implement an innovation-driven development strategy, and it is a major structural reform that promotes supply innovation. Such innovation and entrepreneurship is the result of summarizing the practical experience and theoretical understanding embodied by many years of domestic and foreign development and is in line with the development practice and innovation trend in the entire world.

1. An important tool for any innovation-driven development strategy
Any sensible attempt to promote innovation and development will inevitably uphold people-oriented innovation, improve the national education level, and fully mobilize and stimulate people's genetic gifts for entrepreneurship and innovation. It will advance innovation by advancing the interests of enterprises; it will strongly promote the development of startup enterprises; it will strengthen the role of enterprises as the engine of innovation. The proposal of mass entrepreneurship and innovation closely aligns entrepreneurship and innovation with people and enterprises. It not only highlights the need to build the engine of economic growth but simultaneously highlights the need to build the engine of employment and social development. It not only highlights elite entrepreneurship but also highlights grassroots entrepreneurship and practical innovation, reflecting the general requirements of "four-in-one" innovation. It pursues the development of entrepreneurship, innovation, people, and enterprises—all at the same time— vindicating a scientific approach to innovation and entrepreneurship theory and opening up a new world for this theory and the resultant practices.

Truth be told, the history of human social development is actually a history of mass entrepreneurship and innovation. For example, many important technologies in the steam engine revolution were invented by technicians. The practice since China's reform and opening-up has fully illustrated that. For example, in the early 1980s, after the reform of the Household Responsibility System, farmers were greatly motivated, and a large number of township enterprises emerged, forming numerous startups represented by Wanxiang Group today. Since then, with the reform of the economic system and the scientific and technological system, a large number of scientific researchers and employees of state-owned enterprises have gone to start their own businesses. A large number of private enterprises emerged from this exodus, forming the startups represented by Huawei, Lenovo, and Haier today. Many of them are "startups by grassroots," which are within the scope of mass innovation and entrepreneurship. Moreover, it now seems that many successful enterprises are often built by the "grassroots." Those enterprises have become first-class enterprises in China and even in the world after decades of innovation and development.

2. A key approach to innovation-driven development

If China is to pursue an innovation-driven development strategy, scientific and technological innovation must be at the center of the big picture of national development. Leaders at all levels must respect the leading role of scientific and technological innovation, realizing that scientifically competent personnel are the backbone of such innovation. They must leverage the infinite wisdom and strength of the masses to the maximum extent, forming a new horizon of mass innovation and entrepreneurship. This involves relying on the "Internet Plus" platform, gathering wisdom for innovation, laying a social foundation for technological advancement, opening up channels for scientific and technological achievement, realizing the effective linkage between innovation and the industrial chain, and creating new competitive advantages for Chinese development.

China must take its place as a global leader in education and technology. This means integrating S&T with the creativity of Chinese citizens in a way that is richer, more thorough, and more expansive. It means striving to break through in key technologies and lead the world in technological advancement. It means the transformation of scientific and technological achievements into real productive forces through mass innovation and entrepreneurship. These advancements will not proceed unless the quality of education is improved, the reform of the S&T system is accomplished, the cornerstone of talent and technology for innovation is strengthened, mass entrepreneurship and innovation are promoted, and the spirit of innovation and entrepreneurship is instilled throughout the whole society so that startups emerge and grow, building upon the entrepreneurship and innovation of new and existing enterprises. Enterprises, both new and old, will inject new force and vitality into the nation's economy, constituting a new driving force for economic development.

3. Drive the development of economic organizations

Keeping public ownership as the mainstay of the economy and allowing diverse sectors to develop side by side is the basic economic system of China. To promote the common development of diverse sectors, it is necessary to enhance the efficiency and competitiveness of enterprises, radiate entrepreneurship, meet new needs, open up new markets, create high-quality products and services that can stimulate the needs of consumers, accelerate the transformation of development momentum, and promote the vigorous development of new technologies, new industries, and new formats. The most important priority is to allow more social capital to participate in investment, fully stimulating the vitality of microeconomic entities through the reform of government systems.

As the engine of economic development, mass innovation and entrepreneurship can greatly increase effective supply, enhance microeconomic vitality, accelerate the development of emerging industries, expand employment, increase residents' incomes, motivate social vertical flow, and promote fairness and justice. In the current situation, building mass innovation and entrepreneurship should receive focus as the new engine and power of China's economic growth. Various reforms should be vigorously promoted: the reform of government regulation, investment, and financing; the reform of the S&T system; the reform of key areas such as biomedicine and health, new energy, energy conservation, environmental protection, general aviation, and cultural tourism. For example, China should focus on cultivating small and micro enterprises even while promoting innovation within large enterprises, vigorously promoting the reform of investment, financing, and capital market, and striving to solve the problems of difficult and expensive financing for enterprises.

The areas in which innovation and entrepreneurship lead the way to reform are not few. The reform of energy, electricity, logistics, and other systems deserves urgent attention, as do efforts to reduce the cost of entrepreneurship and innovation. Structural reform of the fiscal and taxation system should be encouraged, reducing the tax burden on small and micro enterprises. On the production side, leaders should open up market access in the service industry, allow more new enterprises to enter fairly, and develop emerging industry clusters (such as those related to the modern service industry), thus creating strong new engines. Entrepreneurship and innovation should be further promoted in traditional industries, and enterprises should be encouraged to actively utilize Internet Plus, big data, and other new technologies, and technological innovation should be carried out extensively in order to accelerate the pace of the traditional manufacturing industry moving toward the middle and high end. It is necessary to adapt to the current rapid development trend of new technologies, new products, and new formats, to improve the government management system, to strengthen the support of talents, technology, finance, and other elements, and to create a good ecology conducive to the continuous emergence and development of emerging enterprises and the rapid commercialization of new technologies, new products, and new formats.

II. Policies that Promote Mass Innovation and Entrepreneurship

A number of policies would go a long way toward promoting mass innovation and entrepreneurship.

1. Construct demonstration bases

There are three reasons to pursue the construction of demonstration bases.

First, regional demonstration bases typically focus on areas where entrepreneurial and innovative resources are gathered. They focus on promoting the construction of a service-oriented government, improving policies and measures for entrepreneurship and innovation, expanding the sources of venture capital, building an ecological environment for entrepreneurship and innovation, and strengthening the construction of entrepreneurship and innovation culture.

Second, demonstration bases of colleges and universities and scientific research institutes intentionally tap human and technological resources. They promote the transformation of talent advantages and scientific and technological advantages into industrial and economic advantages; they focus on improving the training and flow mechanism of entrepreneurial talents; they accelerate the transformation of scientific and technological achievements, build an entrepreneurial support system for college students, and improve the support service system for entrepreneurship and innovation.

Third, enterprise demonstration bases typically give play to the central role of leading enterprises with outstanding innovation capability, strong entrepreneurial atmospheres, and a strong resource integration capability. This allows them to focus on building enterprise management systems suitable for entrepreneurship and innovation, as well as on stimulating the creativity of enterprise employees, expanding investment and financing channels for entrepreneurship and innovation, and unlocking the resources for entrepreneurship and innovation within enterprises.

2. Strategically deploy the 14th Five-Year Plan

In the CPC Central Committee's proposal on formulating the 14th Five-Year Plan for national economic and social development, the long-term goal for 2035 indicates that China should keep the central position of innovation in the big picture while pursuing the establishment of national modernization. It should take scientific and technological self-reliance/self-improvement as strategic support for national development, setting out to produce world-class scientific research, resolve ongoing economic problems, meet the country's significant needs, and promote the health and welfare of the Chinese people. The strategy of invigorating the country through science and education should be further implemented as the country is strengthened through human resources and innovation-driven development, the national innovation system is improved, and the establishment of a strong country through S&T is accelerated.

3. Further optimize the ecological environment for innovation and entrepreneurship

In order to further promote supply-side structural reform, comprehensively implement the innovation-driven development strategy, accelerate the continuous transformation of new and old driving forces, and strive to revitalize the real economy, Chinese leadership must adhere to the principle of "integration, coordination, and sharing," and must promote the in-depth development of mass innovation and entrepreneurship. The ecological environment for innovation and entrepreneurship must be further optimized, which means striving to promote the reform of "streamlining administration, delegating powers, and improving regulation and services," but also means building a prudential regulatory mechanism for inclusive innovation and effectively promoting the transformation of government functions. It is necessary to further expand the scope of innovation and entrepreneurship, to promote more diversified innovation and entrepreneurship groups, to effectively promote the integration and development of various market subjects, and to give play to the leading role of large enterprises, scientific research institutes, and institutions of higher learning. China must also further enhance the scientific and technological reputation of innovation and entrepreneurship, strive to stimulate the creative potential of professionals in tech fields and highly skilled individuals, strengthen the organic connection between basic research and applied technology research, accelerate the transformation of scientific and technological achievements into real productivity, and promote the vigorous development of innovative enterprises in an effective manner. The development of new technologies, new formats, and new modes should be accelerated, optimizing the upgrading of industrial structures through major initiatives such as "Internet Plus," "Made in China 2025," and the integration of civil and military development. The deep integration of innovation and entrepreneurship with the real economy should be a central goal.

III. Pooling Wisdom and Strength to Promote Mass Innovation and Entrepreneurship

The promotion of mass entrepreneurship and innovation is a major reform measure that will fully stimulate the wisdom and creativity of the people and an important way to realize prosperity for the Chinese people. It is, therefore, imperative to resolutely eliminate all kinds of shackles, allowing entrepreneurship and innovation to become ubiquitous, gathering strong new momentum for economic and social development. This momentum will involve a number of new or evolving approaches:

1. Creating a healthy environment for innovation and entrepreneurship

What core factor is involved in promoting mass innovation and entrepreneurship? The key is to provide them freedom: freedom so that entrepreneurs can apply new technologies, develop new products, create new types of demand, cultivate new markets, build new formats, and inject a steady stream of power and vitality into economic development. This requires the government, enterprises, universities, scientific research institutions, and other departments to continually make efforts to form a consensus, a joint force for development, and to jointly create a healthy environment for innovation and entrepreneurship in the society as a whole.

First, the government should transform its functions, streamline administration, and delegate powers. In addition to actively creating a pro-innovation culture, publicizing success stories, and lauding entrepreneurial accomplishments, it should also allow the market to function as a multi-level capital market, establish a contact mechanism among regions, allow advanced enterprises to impart their own working methods and experiences, and encourage entrepreneurial resources such as talents, technology, and capital to flow freely among regions. Moreover, in the annual assessment, it should evaluate the innovation and entrepreneurship environment as an important performance assessment indicator, diligently fulfill governmental responsibilities, and work for the people in a down-to-earth manner.

Second, enterprises should gather and integrate innovation and entrepreneurship resources and policies, vigorously developing new entrepreneurship service institutions such as "maker space." Enterprises should have a keen sense for business; they should excel at making use of existing innovation and entrepreneurship resources; they should take advantage of existing facilities and conditions; they should maximize the integration and utilization of national independent innovation demonstration zones, national high-tech zones, university S&T parks, technology business incubators, and other resources. At the same time, they should have a savvy understanding of the relevant national and local support policies for innovation and entrepreneurship and should place an emphasis on using only the best resources so that every entrepreneur can "use their wisdom, gain their profits and create their wealth."[64]

Third, colleges and universities should accelerate the establishment of programs in innovation and entrepreneurship. This means changing the traditional concept of employment, guiding college students to form a correct understanding of that concept, formulating relevant policies, and providing corresponding facilities to help and encourage college students to start their own businesses. In particular, higher education institutions can help college students find entrepreneurial projects, grasp entrepreneurial skills, and realize their entrepreneurial dreams through the establishment of entrepreneurial salons, entrepreneurial competitions, entrepreneurial training camps, and other low-cost, convenient, and open entrepreneurship activities.

Fourth, scientific research institutes should strive to turn scientific research achievements into reality, strengthening guidance by category, revitalizing existing resources, making good use of traditional incubators, university S&T parks, and other institutions, striving to turn existing resources into physical objects, and continuing to meet the new needs of innovation and entrepreneurship.

2. Driving innovation and development with Internet Plus

Informatization is a prominent feature of the 21st century. Without informatization, any country or region will be abandoned by the whole world. Through the rapid development of informatization, the Internet now goes deep into millions of households, constantly changing our way of life. In the era of "Internet Plus," to develop the economy and change our lives better, all walks of life should integrate with the Internet actively, extensively, and deeply, creating more economic and social value in the development of "Internet Plus." "An 'Internet Plus' action plan should be advanced to promote the integration of mobile internet, cloud computing, big data, and Internet of Things (IoT) with the modern manufacturing industry, a sharing economy should be developed, and the National Big Data Strategy should be implemented."[65] Therefore, China must continue to encourage industrial innovation, must promote cross-industry integration, and must promote the continuous development, transformation, and upgrading of Chinese society through the impetus of "Internet Plus," all in an attempt to promote the livelihood of the Chinese people.

In terms of enterprise informatization, leaders should make use of Internet platform resources efficiently, letting more SMEs gain advanced experience and space for innovation and development and comprehensively improving the competitiveness of enterprises. In terms of governance, leaders should change the traditional management mode and vigorously develop the model of "Internet Plus Public Services." It is important to make use of new media and social networking platforms to build a management and service system for smart cities so that more enterprises can enjoy the benefits of "Internet Plus" and can compete and develop fairly in a free market. With these things in place, China can create a fair and just social atmosphere and constantly promote the innovation and development of China's economy and society.

3. Improving systems and mechanisms and providing policy support
First, it is necessary to create a good legal environment, policy environment, and market environment to reduce the burden on market subjects, to implement appropriate policies, and to regulate as necessary. The state must improve systems, improve service, optimize management, implement relevant incentive policies, and provide real incentives to innovators and entrepreneurs.

Second, China should improve its inclusive tax policy and accelerate the implementation of relevant preferential tax policies. The government's support mode for startups should be changed from "selective and distributed" to "inclusive and guiding." The leverage role of fiscal funds on social capital should be emphasized, which will attract "large investments" of social capital by using the "small investment" the government makes in innovation and entrepreneurship. A market-oriented pattern of innovative resource allocation must also be formed, along with a market approach prioritizing fair competition and survival of the fittest.

Third, China must strengthen the influence and credibility of its media and must strengthen policy implementation supervision. The public should be directed toward examples of excellence: great policies, excellent entrepreneurs, innovative talents, paradigmatic cases, and outstanding examples of teamwork. There must be a concerted effort to create a culture and social atmosphere where people dare to explore, where they encourage innovation and tolerate failure. At the same time, the government should organize and carry out supervision and inspection on the implementation of various policies and measures for promoting mass entrepreneurship and innovation, should establish and improve the policy implementation evaluation and notification system, and should ensure that all policy measures take root.

Macroeconomic Regulation

PART SIX

Macroeconomic Regulation

CHAPTER THIRTEEN

Macroeconomic Regulation

It is important to realize the decisive role of the market in the allocation of resources but also to appreciate the influential role of the government. China must strive to build an economic system with effective market mechanisms, dynamic micro subjects, and moderate macro-control, a system that spurs innovation and competitiveness.

SECTION 1
The Significance of Macroeconomic Regulation

When it comes to the role of the market and the government, the correct approach is to better integrate dialectical and dichotomous approaches and to make good use of both the "invisible hand" and the "visible hand," striving to form a pattern of organic unity, mutual coordination and mutual promotion between the role of the market and the role of the government. This approach will promote the sustainable and healthy development of both the economy and society.

I. The Meaning and Causes of Market Failure

One fundamental truth about market mechanisms is this: the optimal allocation of resources is a completely competitive market structure. However, a fully competitive market structure is usually only a theoretical assumption, difficult to realize in real life. In the case of incomplete markets, market failure is inevitable. Market failure refers to a lack of efficiency in the allocation of resources so that optimal allocation of resources cannot be achieved. Due to the existence of market failure, it is sometimes difficult to achieve truly efficient development through market regulation alone.

Market failure usually occurs due to one or more of the following four causes.

1. Monopoly

In the modern market structure, monopolies are everywhere. "Monopoly" is a term in economics that indicates when a capitalist enterprise manipulates commodity production and circulation in one or several sectors by means of agreement, alliance, union, or equity participation. ("Oligopoly" is a term for when several enterprises do the same). Monopolies typically have a huge amount of capital under their control with sufficient scale of production, operation, and market share so as to obtain high profits. There are several types of monopoly: economic monopoly, administrative monopoly, and natural monopoly. Economic monopoly means that the advantage producers have in setting prices is obtained through competition. In an administrative monopoly, manufacturers obtain their monopolistic advantages with the help of administrative power. Natural monopoly refers to a monopoly that makes competition impossible or hamstrings the potential for competition due to the concentration of resources. Where monopolies or oligopolies occur, they undermine the ability of market mechanisms to automatically adjust in order to achieve an optimal state of resource allocation. Manufacturers within a monopoly usually have greater market control. In order to gain abnormally high profits, the commodity prices set by these manufacturers are often higher than the general equilibrium price. When impacted by monopolies and oligopolies, the market cannot allocate resources effectively.

2. Externalities

Externalities are present when an individual's economic activities have some positive or negative effects on other members of the society, and the benefits or losses brought by such positive or negative effects are not experienced by the economic subjects themselves. When an economic subject's actions have a positive effect on others, but they themselves cannot enjoy the appropriate compensation, such an effect is called a positive externality or an external economy. Conversely, when the activities or behaviors of an economic subject have a negative impact on other members of the society, but the economic subject him/herself does not bear this cost, such an effect is called a negative externality or an external diseconomy. As externalities cannot be adjusted by market mechanisms, when externalities exist, the behavior and result of economic activity participants cannot be effectively reflected by the market price system, which affects the role of the market mechanism in optimizing resource allocation.

3. Public goods

Public goods are social goods or services necessary for the normal existence and development of society. These goods or services cannot be provided by the individual alone (whether s/he is willing or not) but must be provided by the most authoritative and influential public institutions (e.g., the government). Public goods, unlike private goods, are generally non-competitive and nonexclusive. Non-competitiveness means that when an economic subject uses public goods, other economic subjects are not prevented from using these goods at the same time. Non-exclusivity means that when public goods are produced, they are accessible to be enjoyed by everyone, not just one portion of the population—or at least that the cost of excluding them is very high. Non-governmental entities in the market do not directly bear the production and maintenance costs of public goods, but they can nevertheless enjoy public goods freely. Therefore, driven by the market mechanism to maximize profits, producers often exploit the free use of public resources, plundering that which is owned in common and then failing to allow these resources to replenish, resulting in the excessive use of public goods. Sometimes, although users understand that the protection of long-term interests requires the rational use of public resources, there is blind competition in use because the market mechanism itself cannot provide institutional norms, and they feel the need to defend themselves against the excessive use of others.

4. Information asymmetry

Information asymmetry means that in the process of market transactions, the information possessed by various economic entities is unequal, and there are certain differences in the understanding of relevant information. Some economic entities have information that other members do not, and perhaps cannot, have. In the market, there are advantaged parties with more valuable information and disadvantaged parties with less information. The former is usually in a better strategic position than the latter. The existence of information asymmetry militates against the assumption that the market mechanism can realize an optimal allocation of resources since it contributes to an imbalance of interests between different parties in market transactions and affects the efficiency of market allocations. Information asymmetry commonly causes the social economy to be inefficient. Therefore, in the case of information asymmetry, market regulation cannot produce optimal resource allocation.

II. The Necessity of Macroeconomic Regulation

Due to the various threats discussed above (e.g., the objective existence of market failure and the risks of externalities/information asymmetry), there are times when economic development should not rely on the automatic regulation function of the market alone. The market mechanism is not always able to realize an effective allocation of resources. In the case of market failure, it is particularly important for the government to implement macroeconomic regulation and control. Appropriate government intervention in the economy can correct the adverse impact of market failure on resource allocation to a considerable extent.

Looking from the perspective of the Chinese plan to reform and open to the international market economy, the establishment of an effective government macro-control system to maintain economic growth is a high priority. Scientific and effective macro-control is also a prerequisite for improving the socialist market economy system. By giving full play to the role of government macro-control, China can improve efficiency, promote fairness, and optimize the allocation of social resources. The report to the 19th National Congress of the CPC indicated that "We should give play to the decisive role of the market in the allocation of resources and give better play to the role of the government." The government should also grow in understanding the necessity of governmental macroeconomic regulation, nevertheless emphasizing that the "invisible hand" of the market plays the central role in resource allocation. In the socialist market economy, it is not only the invisible hand that matters. It is also the "visible hand": the role of government in macroeconomic regulation. Scientific approaches are needed to address market failures such as monopolies, public goods, and externalities.

In addition, the existence of internal and external risks to the Chinese economy highlights the need for macroeconomic regulation. There are many internal economic and social problems to be solved in the process of China's development. The quality and efficiency of development are not high, the income gap and the gap between urban and rural regional development still loom large, and economic risks such as excessive leverage and overcapacity (which are not conducive to the realization of common prosperity) continue to threaten. At the same time, external risks should not be underestimated. China's economy is increasingly linked with global economic development, which makes it more vulnerable to the impact of the international economic and political environment. In the five years since the 18th National Congress, the world economic recovery has been weak, local conflicts and turbulence abound, and many signs point to instability or decline. These factors create a danger to China's economic development. Although the market mechanism plays a decisive role in resource allocation, it has always been difficult to effectively solve major problems in China's economic development, such as unfair social distribution and increased economic risks at home and abroad. These factors are intertwined, highlighting the need for government macroeconomic regulation. Centralized regulation makes up for the lack of spontaneous market adjustment, playing a role needed for the good and healthy development of the market economy. The "invisible hand" works in concert with the "visible hand" to build an economic system with an effective market mechanism, dynamic micro subjects, and moderate macro-control.

The development of China's socialist market economy urgently requires the government to exert macroeconomic regulation. China's economy has evolved from a stage of high-speed growth to one of high-quality development. Building a modern economic system is an urgent requirement for this transition. Such an accomplishment also satisfies the strategic goal of China's development, but it cannot be completed by relying solely on the spontaneous regulation function of the market.

III. The Meaning of Macroeconomic Regulation

Macroeconomic regulation is premised on the belief that the market plays a decisive role in resource allocation, and it happens when the government in a socialist market economy manages the operation process of the economy by means of planning, law, and administration. This regulation exists for the main purpose of realizing the country's expected development strategy and centralized planning. Regulation occurs in three stages: expectation management, real-time management, and post-event management. (Expectation management occurs before the event, real-time management during, and post-event management after.) In terms of the sequencing of implementation, macroeconomic regulation focuses on expectation and real-time management.

Generally speaking, macroeconomic regulation has the following three characteristics.

First, macroeconomic regulation within a market economy reinforces the foundations of the market economy and composes an important part of the market economy. It does not impose upon participants in the economy in the way that microeconomic interventions might. Planned economy management, for example, manages and regulates the national economy by requiring prepared plans and guiding documents so as to realize the planned and proportional development of the economy. This process involves direct intervention by the government in microeconomic activity. In contrast, macroeconomic regulation within a market economy reinforces the market economy through the indirect regulation of economic activities by the government. Unlike planned economy management, which prompts the government to sometimes interfere with the decisions of microeconomic subjects via approval at various levels, macroeconomic regulation mainly changes the environmental parameters for corporations and individuals when they make economic decisions. This approach improves the market economy instead of hamstringing it, and allows the market to play a decisive role in resource allocation. The transformation from planned management under the planned economy system to macro-control under the market economy system means that the economic functions of the government will change from direct management and micro-management to indirect management and macro-management.

Second, the central task of macroeconomic regulation is the balancing of total economic output. Macroeconomic regulation is the regulation of total output rather than individual output. With macroeconomic regulation and control, the state maintains the basic balance between total social supply and demand to prevent two market imbalances: overproduction or economic overheating. Total social demand refers to the total quantity of products and services in a society that is bought and sold at a certain price level. It is usually the sum of consumption demand, investment demand, government purchase demand, and net export demand. Total social supply refers to the total quantity of products and services that all corporations in the economy are willing and able to provide at any price level. The total supply depends on economic resources such as labor, capital, land, management, and technology. When the total demand equals the total supply, the economy is in equilibrium; when the total demand is greater than the total supply, there will be economic overheating and inflation; when the total demand is less than the total supply, there will be overproduction and deflation. Whenever there is an imbalance between total supply and total demand, the total economic output can be adjusted through macroeconomic regulation to help balance supply with demand.

Third, macroeconomic regulation is constantly enriched and improved with the reform and development of a market economy and the optimization of government coordination and management functions. In the process of China's marketization, the Chinese government has engaged in several rounds of macroeconomic regulation, and its experience through each successive round has helped it learn and improve.

IV. The Institutional Superiority of Socialist Macroeconomic Regulation

The socialist system with Chinese characteristics determines that China's macroeconomic regulations are institutionally superior to a certain extent. This superiority of the socialist system mainly arises because of China's political and economic systems.

1. A superior political system

China's current political systems include the system of people's congress, the system of regional ethnic autonomy, the system of community-level self-governance, and the system of multi-party cooperation and political consultation under the leadership of the CPC. The system of people's congress plays a positive role in promoting democracy and encouraging the people to participate in state management. The system of regional ethnic autonomy is an organic combination of centralized leadership and local control, predicated on the interplay between territorial integrity and national unity. It enhances the cohesion of the Chinese nation, is conducive to safeguarding national unity and security, and enables people of all ethnic groups, especially ethnic minorities, to combine their deep feelings of attachment to their own group with love of their motherland, consciously shouldering the glorious responsibility of defending the unity and the frontier of the country. The system of community-level self-governance further integrates localized self-governance into the overall process of China's political construction in an organic way so that individuals can increasingly exercise certain democratic rights. The system of multi-party cooperation and political consultation under the leadership of the CPC has consolidated and expanded a patriotic and unified front, promoted the advancement of socialist democratic politics, and maintained unity and stability. Under the socialist system with Chinese characteristics, state power is quite stable, which ensures the long-term stable development of the country, further promotes reform, opening up, and socialist modernization, and provides a political platform for socialist macroeconomic regulation.

2. A superior economic system

It would be advantageous, within a socialist framework, to uphold and improve basic economic and distribution systems, to steadfastly consolidate and develop the public sector, and to encourage, support and guide the development of the private sector, giving play to the decisive role of the market in the allocation of resources. The socialist system with Chinese characteristics can give full play to the superiority of the socialist system and reflect the principle of common prosperity while absorbing social funds, alleviating employment pressure, and bolstering economic strength. It may simultaneously promote national cohesion, strengthen the military, and improve China's international status.

Public ownership of land and other important economic resources enhances the government's ability to allocate resources and gives full play to the role of macroeconomic regulation by concentrating human, material, and financial resources that can be used in major infrastructure projects or to respond to various threats and emergencies. In addition, China is in the process of transitioning from a planned economy to a market economy. Although the government's current macroeconomic regulation is a departure from the planned economic management of the past, the government retains the same ability to reorganize the national economy and reasonably distribute productive forces it had in the period of the planned economy. By developing a long-term economic plan, the state can offset the limitations of market economies, which often ignore long-term and overall interests.

SECTION 2

Objectives of Macroeconomic Regulation

The overall objective of macro-control is the sustainable, healthy, and stable development of the national economy, including the four traditional objectives: economic growth, full employment, price stability, and balance-of-payments equilibrium. Two other two core objectives are included within this overall objective: to improve living standards and to pursue high-quality economic development with Chinese characteristics and in line with China's national conditions.

I. Promoting Economic Growth

The promotion of economic growth is the primary objective of macroeconomic regulation. Economic growth refers to the growth of total GDP and per-capita output, which is mainly reflected by two factors: the expansion of economic scale and the optimization of economic structure. With the deepening of supply-side structural reform, China's economic structure has been continuously optimized, emerging industries such as the digital economy have been booming, and the construction of infrastructure such as high-speed railways, highways, bridges, ports, and airports has been accelerated. China's economy has shifted from the high-speed growth stage to the high-quality development stage and is in a key period of changing its development mode, optimizing its economic structure, and transforming its growth model. At present, China's economy maintains medium- and high-speed growth, ranking top among the major countries in the world. Its GDP has increased from 54 trillion yuan to 80 trillion yuan, ranking second in the world and contributing more than 30% of world economic growth.

At present, there are still various outstanding problems to be solved in China, such as unbalanced and insufficient development, low quality and inefficient development, and obstacles in the way of innovation. The real economy needs to operate at a higher level, and there is much progress needed toward protecting the environment. Many Chinese citizens still struggle to thrive, the task of poverty alleviation is arduous, the gap between urban and rural regional development and income distribution is still large, and people face many difficulties in employment, education, medical treatment, housing, and retirement. There is room for improvement in terms of civic mindedness. Social conflicts are often interrelated and entrenched, certain aspects of governance are not fully based in law, and the national governance system and governance capacity need to be strengthened. Ideological disputes continue, and new situations in national security arise. The rollout of some reform plans and major policies has occasionally sputtered, and many aspects of party building remain weak.

The key to solving these problems is to achieve rapid, stable, and sustainable growth of the national economy. The 19th National Congress put forward a plan to work hard during the next 15 years to build on the foundation created by the moderately prosperous society in the period from 2020 to 2035 and to basically realize socialist modernization by 2035. In order to achieve this goal, the government should adopt various macroeconomic regulation methods to expand demand, optimize structure, encourage innovation, select reasonable growth modes and objectives, ensure the quality of economic growth, and expedite such growth.

II. Increasing Employment

Employment is the foundation of an individual's livelihood and is of special significance to China, a densely populated country. Due to fluctuations in economic operations and changes in industrial structure, unemployment is inevitable in the process of economic development, but it can vary in degree and kind. Considering the large population of China, its transitioning economy, and the immature state of its labor market, the unemployment situation in China is particularly complicated, which manifests in the following three ways.

First, there is a great deal of *invisible underemployment*. This involves a situation in which a person is unable to find a job in their preferred field, leading to the choice to work at another job, one that may not provide a living wage. It is a common phenomenon in developing countries. Second, there is transitional unemployment, that is, structural unemployment caused by China's economic reform and transformation. Third, there are many factors that have nothing to do with the efficiency of workers in the labor market, such as gender, age, registered residence, etc., but which employers use to discriminate against workers, seriously hindering the employment opportunities of those who are affected.

The high unemployment rate will bring heavy costs, including the loss of human resources, the reduction of output, and the increased burdens of social assistance. These costs usher in a series of social problems that are not conducive to the long-term stability of the society. The report to the 19th National Congress indicated:

Employment is pivotal to people's well-being. We must give high priority to employment and pursue a proactive employment policy, striving to achieve fuller employment and create better quality jobs. We will launch vocational skills training programs on a big scale, give particular attention to tackling structural unemployment, and create more jobs by encouraging business startups. We will provide extensive public employment services to open more channels for college graduates and other young people, as well as migrant rural workers, to find jobs and start their own businesses. We must remove institutional barriers that block the social mobility of labor and talent and ensure that every one of our people has the chance to pursue a career through hard work.[66]

Therefore, the government should place great emphasis on the expansion of employment in economic and social development, should implement active and effective employment policies, and should support entrepreneurship and flexible employment through macroeconomic regulation so as to achieve the goal of full employment.

III. Stabilizing Prices

The stability of the overall price level is not only an important condition for the balance of the economic aggregate and the rational allocation of resources; it is also an important symbol for the implementation of monetary policy. Keeping the overall price level stable does not mean that prices remain unchanged but that the overall price level is within a range acceptable to both economic officials and residents. Only when the overall price level remains generally stable and the price signal is true and reliable can we ensure the steady growth of the market economy. When the price level rises sharply, there will be problems such as economic overheating and inflation. When the price level falls sharply, there will be problems such as soaring unemployment and deflation. In order to maintain the stable operation of the national economy, the Chinese government has always regarded keeping prices stable as the main goal of macroeconomic regulation. It actively undertakes various control measures to stabilize price expectations and keep prices from undergoing any dramatic changes.

IV. Maintaining Balance-of-Payments Equilibrium

Balance-of-payments equilibrium is an objective of macroeconomic regulation. Balance of payments refers to the systematic monetary records of all a country's foreign economic transactions during a certain period of time (usually a year). It is not only a key indicator of the country's foreign political and economic relations but also a reflection of a country's position in the world economy and how it has changed. A country is in balance-of-payments equilibrium when the total amount of its international income is equal to the total amount of its expenditures for the relevant time period. When its total international income is greater than its total expenditures, this is a trade surplus; when it is less, it is a trade deficit. A continuous surplus in the balance of payments will destroy the balance between domestic total demand and total supply so that total demand rapidly exceeds total supply, and normal economic growth is impacted. The surplus will also result in the country's loss of the right to obtain preferential loans from international financial organizations. A continuous deficit in the balance of payments will affect the country's ability to import the means of production required for economic production, will inhibit the growth of the national economy, and will lead to a huge loss of foreign exchange reserves and a shortage of domestic foreign exchange, resulting in an increase in the foreign exchange rate and a decline in the local currency exchange rate. Excessive declines in the local currency exchange rate scare away international capital flight and may even prompt a currency crisis. A continuous deficit could also plunge the country into a debt crisis.

The achievement of balance-of-payments equilibrium has an important impact on a country's steady economic development. The report to the 19th National Congress stated that:

> We will expand foreign trade, develop new models and new forms of trade, and turn China into a trader of quality. We will adopt policies to promote high-standard liberalization and facilitation of trade and investment; we will implement the system of pre-establishment national treatment plus a negative list across the board, significantly ease market access, further open the service sector, and protect the legitimate rights and interests of foreign investors.[67]

With these intentions as the backdrop, China's economy will be more open and export-oriented, and maintaining the balance-of-payments equilibrium will become more important. The Chinese government should actively regulate to address this situation, adjusting fiscal and financial policies, balancing international payments, maintaining trade stability, and promoting stable economic growth.

V. Improving People's Living Standards

China must always hold the interests of the Chinese people paramount. But what does this mean in practice? It means that the government must do each of the following: allow the fruits of reform and development to benefit all the people more fairly, make progress toward realizing common prosperity, strengthen institutions, guide expectations, improve the public service system, ensure the basic needs of the people are met, respond to popular demands for a better life, promote social fairness and justice, form effective social governance, and give a richer, more secure and more sustainable sense of access, happiness and security to the people. Improving people's living standards is the central goal of Chinese macroeconomic regulation and the crowning achievement that shows the superiority of the socialist system.

VI. Pursuing High-Quality Economic Development

At present, Chinese socialism has entered a new era, and China's social and economic development has also entered a new era. If the nation pursues speed at the expense of quality, it will not meet the basic requirements of this era. Pursuing and promoting high-quality development is a prerequisite for maintaining sustainable and healthy development. High-quality development is an essential response to the transformation of China's main social contradictions, a response that promotes a moderately prosperous society in all respects using socialist methods and that also clears a path toward continually richer economic development. The promotion of high-quality development is an important yardstick against which to measure development ideas, whether they be the formulation of economic policies or the implementation of macroeconomic regulation at present and in the future.

The improvement of people's living standards through macroeconomic regulation is mainly reflected in indicators of per-capita income and per-capita GDP among urban and rural residents. Since it began to open up, China's per-capita income and per-capita GDP among both urban and rural residents have increased rapidly. In order to achieve China's goal of building a moderately prosperous society in all respects by 2020 and doubling the per-capita income that urban and rural areas enjoyed in 2010, better macroeconomic regulation is needed, accelerating the construction of a modern economic system and modernizing the national governance system and governance capacity so that China might become a country demonstrating impressive national strength and international influence, and over time realize the common prosperity of all people. In such a circumstance, the Chinese people will enjoy a happier and healthier life, and the Chinese nation will stand with its head held high among the nations of the world.

SECTION 3
Methods and Means of Macroeconomic Regulation

Implementing macroeconomic regulation in an effective way involves continual innovation and improvement, giving play to the strategic guiding role of national development planning, focusing on indirect control, improving the coordination mechanism of fiscal, monetary, industrial, regional, and other economic policies, and using a variety of policy measures to accomplish these goals.

I. Methods of Macroeconomic Regulation

There are generally two forms of governmental macroeconomic regulation: direct regulation and indirect regulation. After 30 years of implementing and learning methods of reform, the Chinese government's thinking on macroeconomic regulation has become clearer over time. It has settled on an approach that centers around macroeconomic regulation based on indirect regulation but supplements this indirect regulation with direct regulation.

Direct regulation happens when the government directly controls production, circulation, consumption, and distribution by requiring mandatory plans and guiding documents, making decisions for micro subjects such as corporations, and carrying out mandatory management and regulation of economic activities. Direct regulation is mainly administrative, carrying with it the advantages of simple and convenient management and timeliness. Indirect regulation, in contrast, does not involve the government directly intervening in the decision-making of market subjects but instead regulates the market by formulating laws and setting policies, indirectly guiding economic activities by adjusting their parameters so that the activities of micro subjects ineluctably meet regulation objectives. Indirect regulation does not interfere with the production and operation of corporations. Corporations can make their own choices about how to accommodate the general framework of government regulation based on their own priorities and needs.

The essence of macroeconomic regulation is the government's intervention in the market. However, under the socialist market economy system, when formulating and implementing macro-control policies, the government would do best to fully respect the norms of the market and let the market play a decisive role in resource allocation. When macroeconomic regulation is dominated by indirect regulation but supplemented by direct regulation, this is conducive to maximizing the vitality of various economic subjects and promoting the efficient, stable, and sustainable development of the economy.

At the various stages of the socialist market economy system, spanning several decades of development and reform, China's ideas and means of macro-control have kept pace with the times. In recent years, China has innovated and implemented range-based, targeted, and well-timed regulation, along with timely and appropriate pre-adjustment and fine-tuning so that the foresight, pertinence, and effectiveness of regulation have been significantly strengthened, and the stable operation of the economy (including structural optimization and upgrading) has been promoted. Range-based regulation is an innovation of the Chinese government's macroeconomic regulation mode. Unlike the past, when the government only focused on certain specific numerical targets of economic growth, this new approach focuses more on observing results of the macro operation with a reasonable range. For example, the main expected goal of economic development in 2018 was to increase GDP by about 6.5%. This goal gives a floating space. In other words, whether the economic growth rate is higher or lower than 6.5%, it is in a reasonable range as long as it can ensure relatively full employment without large fluctuations. The "lower limit" of the reasonable range of economic operation is designed to stabilize growth and ensure employment; the "upper limit" is to prevent inflation. Targeted regulation aims to maintain concentration, implement comprehensive policies, make sensible adjustments using a range-based approach, grasp key areas, discern important connections, rely on methods of reform, and leverage market forces in ways that promote prosperity. Timely regulation requires the government to flexibly decide and choose which policy measures to implement in a way that is responsive to the market situation and the characteristics of various adjustment measures.

II. Means of Macroeconomic Regulation

The objectives of macroeconomic regulation are realized by means of various macroeconomic regulation mechanisms implemented by the government. These methods identify specific ways of implementing macro-control, most prominently economic means, legal means, and administrative means.

1. Economic means

Economic means are in effect when the government adjusts various economic parameters according to the laws of economics and the law of value and does so by giving a regulatory role to economic leverage so as to guide the market economy toward the goal of macroeconomic regulation. Economic means mainly include monetary policy, fiscal policy, industrial policy, income policy, land policy, and medium- and long-term economic planning.

Monetary policy involves state action by the People's Bank of China, which is able to adjust interest rates by controlling the money supply to achieve its specific economic objectives, thereby influencing investment activities and the national economy. Fiscal policy involves state action which affects and regulates total demand and then exerts an influence on employment and national income through the changes in fiscal expenditure and tax policy according to the guiding principles of fiscal work. Industrial policy involves state action, which formulates national economic plans (including mandatory and guiding plans), industrial structure adjustment plans, and industrial support plans. In addition, industrial policy implements financial investment and financing, utilizes monetary policy tools, carries out project approval to guide the direction of industrial development, promotes the upgrading of industrial structures, and coordinates the national industrial structure so as to ensure the healthy and sustainable development of the national economy. Income policy involves state action advancing measures such as price control and tax regulation to manage the growth rate of prices, money, wages, and other income. The land policy involves state action to create and enforce a code of conduct established by the state in the development, utilization, governance, protection, and management of land resources in accordance with political and economic goals in a certain period of time. It is an important regulatory means to deal with various contradictions in land relations. The introduction of land policy into macroeconomic regulation is a major innovation in China's macroeconomic regulation theory.

Medium- and long-term economic planning is a hallmark of China's socialist macroeconomic regulation and is relatively stable. China is transforming from a planned economy system to a market economy system, but this does not mean that the means of planned regulation must be abolished. Planning reflects the direction of a country's development and is the basis for macroeconomic regulation. Under the planned economy system, planned adjustment was mainly reflected in a mandatory plan that directly controlled the behaviors and decisions of various economic sectors. Under the socialist market economy system, the content of planned adjustment is biased toward guiding plans such as economic development strategy, productivity layout, and economic structure adjustment. Medium- and long-term economic planning under the socialist market economy system can help China avoid the limitations of the market economy, such as lack of foresight and unreasonable industrial layout.

Under the market economy system, economic means is the most common and widely used means of macroeconomic regulation. In economic activities, various economic means are often used together to build a clearly differentiated means system with coordinated cooperation so as to achieve the best regulation effect.

2. Legal means

Legal means of macro-regulation apply when the state formulates and applies economic regulations to restrict and standardize the behavior of market economic subjects, to coordinate the interests among economic subjects, to solve economic disputes, to crack down on criminal activity, and to maintain normal economic order so as to achieve the goal of unity, fairness, and integrity of the socialist market and the stable operation of the national economy. Legal means are characterized by restraint, compulsion, authority, and stability. A socialist market economy needs to run under the framework of a socialist legal system. A legal structure undergirding macroeconomic regulation will provide a strong guarantee of its effectiveness. Through legal means, the state can effectively safeguard various ownership economies, protect public property and personal property, allow all economic sectors to enjoy legitimate rights and interests, adjust horizontal and vertical relations among various economic organizations, ensure the reasonable order of economic operation, and maintain the market environment of fair competition. Law plays an extremely important role in ensuring the realization of the objectives of macroeconomic regulation.

3. Administrative means

Administrative means are how the government directly regulates economic activities through reliance on administrative institutions. The state may adopt mandatory administrative methods such as orders, instructions, and regulations, or it may use "visible hands" to achieve the goal of macro-control. Administrative means are mandatory, vertical, free, and efficient. The higher-level government controls the behaviors of subordinate organizations with administrative orders. Subordinate organizations must obey and execute the orders issued by the higher-level government unconditionally. Administrative intervention is a necessary means of socialist macroeconomic regulation. When faced with global economic activities, sudden economic events, or projects that must be completed in a short time, economic means often cannot provide an agile response. Better results can be achieved with administrative means.

However, administrative means also have some limitations. On the one hand, administrative intervention directly interferes with the market economy, which is likely to lead to market failure and other problems; on the other hand, administrative actions are often affected by bureaucracy, corruption, and other factors, resulting in policy distortion, improper official style, and so on. Administrative intervention is a double-edged sword. It must be employed in conformity with existing laws and cannot be abused.

III. Measures to Deepen the Reform of Macroeconomic Management

A number of measures can be taken that will deepen reform in macroeconomic regulation, particularly in the context of management systems:

1. Giving full play to the strategic guiding role of the national development plan and strengthening the pertinence and foresight of macroeconomic management

The national development plan is an important guide for macro-control, showing the strategic intention and medium- and long-term development goals of the CPC and the country. It plays a guiding and regulatory role in economic and social development. The Party and the whole society must be mobilized to promote its implementation, a mobilization that has the following components.

First, it involves letting the guidance and restriction functions play a bigger role in macroeconomic planning. There are numerous plans in existence (medium- and long-term plans, annual plans for policies such as public budget, land development, and resource allocation), and the macro guidance for these plans must be strengthened, including their overall planning and coordination functions. These improvements will allow China to achieve an organic combination of objectives and means of macro-control and improve the orientation, guidance, and restraint of the plan.

Second, it involves improving the planning system. In order to strengthen the overall management of the plan, it is necessary to build a development plan system with clear levels, clear functions, and mutual coordination, make future plans more systematic, and strengthen the degree to which the special and regional plans support overall planning, and the local plans support national planning.

Third, it involves improving the implementation mechanism of the plan. On the basis of midterm and final evaluations of the implementation of the medium- and long-term plan outline, annual monitoring and evaluation will be put into place, and the unified implementation of the national strategy will be strengthened at all levels.

2. Strengthening the supporting role of fiscal, monetary, industrial, regional, and other macroeconomic policies

Strengthening the role of various macroeconomic policies must proceed in several steps. First, it is imperative to accelerate the establishment of a modern financial system and build a national/local administrative relationship with clear powers and responsibilities, coordinated financial resources, and regional balance. A comprehensive, standardized, transparent, scientific, and binding budget system will be established, and the local tax system will be improved.

Second, monetary policy must become more adaptable and flexible. This involves deepening the reform of the financial system, enhancing the government's ability to provide financial services for the real economy, increasing the proportion of direct financing, and promoting the healthy development of a multi-level capital market. The two-pillar regulatory framework of monetary policy and macroprudential policy must be improved, and market-oriented reform of interest rates and exchange rates must be deepened. The financial regulatory system must be resilient and must hold the bottom line that there will be "no systemic financial risk."

Third, systems and mechanisms to promote consumption and enhance the fundamental role of consumption in economic development must receive additional attention. There is an opportunity to embrace the trend of consumption transformation and upgrade, striving to increase the effective supply of high-quality products and services, and a further opportunity to deepen the reform of the income distribution system and to expand middle-income groups.

Fourth, the reform of the investment and financing system must be more comprehensive and must give play to the key role of investment in optimizing the supply structure. As reform of the investment and financing system deepens, there is an opportunity to enhance the leveraging role of government funds, promote the integration of government, banks, enterprises, and society, expand effective investment, and improve the efficiency of capital use and the incremental capital-output ratio. China can and should further liberalize access, improve services, improve the environment, strengthen supervision, and stimulate the vitality of private investment.

Fifth, China must accurately implement industrial policies. A modern industrial system should be built, one that accelerates the transformation and upgrading of traditional industries, focuses on cultivating strategic emerging industries, promotes the optimization and upgrading of industrial structure, and drives industrial development with scientific and technological innovation.

Sixth, it is necessary to innovate and improve regional policies. A key aspect of this change is the implementation of the three major strategies of the Belt and Road Initiative, the coordinated development of the BTH region, and the development of the Yangtze Economic Belt. Other aspects involve promoting the development of the four major regions (Western, Northeast, Central, and Eastern regions) and the coordinated development of urban and rural areas, further promoting a new type of people-centered urbanization, giving play to the power of innovation to inspire and the role of state-level new areas to lead, and expanding new space for economic development.

3. Improving the coordination mechanism of macroeconomic policies and enhancing the compatibility of various macroeconomic policy methods

The compatibility of policy methods refers to the interdependence, mutual restriction, complementarity, and mutual substitution of various policies and methods. In the practice of macro-control, the CPC Central Committee pays special attention to the combination of scientific and effective means, comprehensively considering whether various macroeconomic management objectives are compatible. It also analyzes the compatibility between macroeconomic management objectives and policy means and aims to use combined means of macroeconomic management effectively. At present, the complicated economic situation calls for diversified policy tools to achieve diversified regulation and control objectives. Therefore, it is necessary to strengthen policy coordination and cooperation in all aspects, making coordinated use of macro-control policies with Chinese characteristics and improving the accuracy and effectiveness of these policies.

This coordination happens at three levels: First, coordination at the departmental level. By strengthening the overall planning of macroeconomic policies and strengthening the coordination of policy timing, boundary, direction, and objectives, it is possible to realize the optimal combination of fiscal, monetary, industrial, regional, and investment policies and form a joint regulatory force. Second, coordination at the central and local levels. At the central level, the Chinese government should prioritize a good top-level design, fully considering local realities and mobilizing local enthusiasm to the greatest extent; at the local level, governments should strengthen the understanding, implementation, and transmission of macroeconomic policies and should guide market actors to respond to macroeconomic policies rationally, and thus realize the intentions of these policies. Third, communication and coordination at the international level. China should adopt a global perspective, which means actively participating in the communication and coordination of international macroeconomic policies and the adjustment and construction of international economic rules and striving to create a good external economic environment.

4. Innovating macroeconomic management methods and strengthening expectation guidance

Moving forward, the government needs to innovate new methods of macro-control and promote the modernization of the national governance system and governance capacity. With the Internet, cloud computing, and other means, it is possible to accelerate the reform of statistical systems and promote the sharing of information resources. The expectation is that big-data thinking will normalize scientific decision-making, delicacy management, and accurate services, which will greatly promote the progress of the government management concept and the social governance model. It will additionally promote the construction of a law-based, innovative, clean, smart, and service-oriented government, a government that will gradually realize the modernization of governance capacity and provide support and guarantees for macro-control.

The target orientation of macroeconomic management requires innovation, a process that is already underway. Facing a complex situation at home and abroad, China has successively implemented range-based regulation, targeted regulation, and well-timed regulation. Range-based regulation focuses on stabilizing the total quantity. Effective regulation of this sort requires adherence to bottom-line thinking, seeks to achieve progress through stability, and provides clear expectations for market subjects. Targeted regulation requires applying a more innovative approach, relying more on market forces, and taking structural adjustment and mode transformation as the focus of regulation. Well-timed regulation calls for a focus on accurate thinking. It emphasizes policy reserves and response plans and attempts to promulgate policies at the right time and with the right amount of force. The combination of range-based regulation, targeted regulation, and well-timed regulation not only expands the objectives of macroeconomic management but also improves the accuracy of macroeconomic management.

Expectation guidance means that relevant government departments change the information on which market expectation is based through various forms of communication so as to influence the expectations of markets and better achieve the goal of macro-control. In the Internet age, guiding the market's expectations in this way not only has low operation cost but also can accomplish the desired goal very quickly with the help of the rapid dissemination of information so as to shorten the time lag of monetary policy.

At present, the use of expectation guidance directed toward the monetary policy of China's central bank still needs to be improved. First, communication channels between the central bank and the market need to be broadened, enriching the content of communication so as to improve the transparency of monetary policy. Second, the government needs to appropriately accelerate the transformation of monetary policy from quantitative regulation to price-based regulation and give full play to the guiding role of interest rates on expectations. Third, research advances must be made to understand how to impact market expectations. The central bank needs to learn to outstrip the market in understanding information about economic operations and trends, and it must act decisively based on this understanding. This will allow the bank to interact with the market more effectively, will improve the efficiency of expectation guidance, and will stabilize the expectation of economic and social development.

SECTION 4

Deepening Supply-Side Structural Reform

The main purposes of implementing supply-side structural reform are to adjust China's economic structure, to achieve the optimal allocation of factors, and to improve the quality and quantity of economic growth. Supply-side structural reform must remain a central task, which means comprehensively promoting the work of stabilizing growth, advancing reform, adjusting structure, benefiting people's livelihoods, preventing risks, vigorously promoting reform and opening-up, and innovating so as to improve macro-control.

I. The Background of Supply-Side Structural Reform

At present, China's supply-side problems are increasingly prominent, even while attempts to manage simple total demand face great limitations, so regulation from the supply side is needed. Under this new situation, governmental macro-control is required to coordinate the relationship between supply management and demand management. At the same time, the current focus of macroeconomic policy is to solve structural problems rather than to modify total economic output, so macro-control policy should shift from total output control to structural control. Indeed, it is evident that supply-side structural reform is becoming the main focus of China's macroeconomic policy. Supply-side structural reform should be understood as a turning point for the innovation and development of the national macroeconomic regulation system, shifting the macro-control system from one that focuses on the demand side to one that focuses on both demand-side and supply-side regulation and coordinating demand management with supply-side structural reform.

At the same time, the supply side obviously does not adapt to changes in demand structure. First, there is excessive ineffective low-end supply. Some traditional industries have serious overcapacity and low-capacity utilization. Second, the effective and medium- and high-end supply is insufficient. Supply-side adjustment obviously lags behind the upgrading of th demand structure and cannot meet the needs of people for a better life and for economic transformation. Third, institutional mechanisms have constrained the adjustment of the supply structure. Affected by the constraints of traditional systems and mechanisms, supply-side adjustment shows obvious stickiness and hysteresis, making it difficult to allocate production factors from ineffective demand fields to effective demand fields and from low-end fields to medium- and high-end fields. As of yet, the supply potential of new products and services has not been unleashed.

II. Recent Tasks in the Promotion of Supply-Side Structural Reform

The following tasks, already underway, will promote reform in this important area.

1. Cutting overcapacity and optimizing supply structure

In the current environment, many portions of the economy experience excessive capacity; individual corporations may have such overcapacity, limiting their growth space and making them "zombie enterprises." The government must cut that overcapacity and steadily resolve serious capacity problems within these corporations. At present, there is serious overcapacity in China's manufacturing industries, such as steel, coal, cement, and electrolytic aluminum, forcing the implementation of supply-side structural reform.

Overcapacity carries with it many perils. First, overcapacity has caused serious losses to various corporations, impacting overall economic vitality and efficiency. Second, overcapacity involves significant resource waste, harming intergenerational equity, long-term prosperity, and sustainable social development. Third, since the overcapacity mostly pertains to medium- and low-end products, the result is an outdated supply structure that hampers economic competitiveness. Therefore, China must eliminate outdated capacity through supply-side structural reform to make room for the development of emerging industries.

To reduce overcapacity, it is not only necessary to reduce or even eliminate excessive capacity but also to help and guide enterprises with overcapacity to adjust their approaches, developing and improving their enterprise management mechanisms. First, there must be an effective exit mechanism and elimination mechanism for excessive capacity, mechanisms that apply to stop operation, bankruptcy liquidation, mergers, and reorganizations. Such mechanisms address the situation of "zombie enterprises" that experience long-term losses and face insolvency or corporations that fail to meet environmental protection and work safety standards and lack plans to change. Second, a number of related steps are needed: reform corporations with excessive capacity, successfully address problems that plague these corporations (outdated systems, suboptimal machinery, organizational bloat, inconsistency of responsibility, blind decision-making, insider control), disentangle dysfunctional enmeshments between government and enterprise, or between ownership and management rights. The goal is to establish and improve the market-oriented corporate operation and management system. Third, in view of the structural imbalance between supply and demand caused by the upgrading of consumption structure and consumption demand, it is necessary to continuously improve the added value of products and services in the industrial chain through technological innovation so as to replace high-end imported products and consume part of production capacity. More attention should be paid to innovation that drives the optimization of industrial structure, product structure, organizational structure, institutional structure, and layout structure so as to promote industrial transformation, upgrading, and the transformation of economic development mode. Finally, it is important to steadily promote the cutting of overcapacity, to treat the assets and liabilities of enterprises appropriately, to improve fiscal and tax support (including special awards, subsidies, and other supporting work), to implement various employment and social security policies, and to effectively protect the legitimate rights and interests of corporations and their employees.

2. Destocking and removing supply redundancy

Destocking is a method used to resolve real estate inventory, especially in third- and fourth-tier cities. Destocking in the real estate market requires the application of effort on both the supply side and the demand side. Supply should be cut. The construction scale of new houses in cities and regions with high inventory should be reduced, and the probability of uncompleted projects should be reduced through M&A and restructuring. At the same time, demand should be increased. One important method to increase demand is to accelerate new urbanization construction. In order to increase the urbanization rate of registered residents and deepen the reform of the housing system, it is important to speed up migrant workers' "citizenization," expand effective demand, integrate channels of supply and demand, digest the inventory, and stabilize the real estate market. At the same time, the implementation of the registered residence system reform plan should be accelerated, allowing the rural migrant population and other non-registered residents to settle down in their place of employment so that the expectation and demand for house purchasing or long-term renting in the place of employment will be formed. In addition, there should be a deepening of reform in the housing system, including the continuing establishment of a housing system focusing on both ownership and renting, the improvement of the rental housing system (dominated by market allocation but with basic guarantees provided by the government), and support for rental housing consumption which promotes the healthy development of the rental housing market.

3. Deleveraging and preventing systemic financial risks

Deleveraging is mainly aimed at the financial field and should be both active and stable. Specifically, deleveraging aims to improve the debt structure, increase production efficiency, promote economic growth, and gradually digest the bubbles and leverage problems using both administrative intervention and market instruments in a controllable way and with a controllable rhythm.

In the short term, deleveraging involves implementing policies by category, making rational use of financial market instruments, and gradually resolving the stock debt risk of various corporations. It also involves the following steps: First, it is important to support sustainable corporations that adapt to market development but have temporary difficulties in capital flow; in this context, support means helping them reduce their debt burden by means of debt transfer or replacement. Second, there is a need to actively explore a market-oriented and law-based debt-to-equity swap implementation plan, promote corporate debt restructuring, and establish a market-oriented exit mechanism. Third, asset securitization of business entities should be promoted and existing funds revitalized. Large- and medium-sized enterprises with stable cash flow and low systemic risk should receive priority, and various steps should be taken: convert existing assets into tradable objects through structural financing arrangements, improve capital liquidity, reduce financing costs, match the maturity of assets and liabilities, and give full play to the benefits and value of assets. At the same time, Chinese leaders should further explore the market maker system, encouraging enthusiasm among market makers, improving their market-making ability, and furthermore enhancing the liquidity of the secondary market in asset securitization products.

A greater reliance on the price discovery and value regression functions of the capital market will allow securitization products to be priced by the market reasonably.

In the medium and long term, the financing channels of Chinese enterprises must gradually broaden, and the proportion of direct financing must expand. There are two simultaneous paths that China should take under the framework of macroprudential and microprudential regulation. On the one hand, commercial banks should strictly implement the capital management system, build a credit risk assessment system, and improve their anti-risk ability by adjusting the risk weight and optimizing credit structure—all the while strictly controlling the scale of shadow banks and off-balance-sheet business risks and controlling the leverage ratio of corporate departments from the source. On the other hand, it is important to actively develop and improve the multi-level capital market and increase the proportion of direct financing. Equity financing should be promoted through multiple channels, the reform of the Growth Enterprise Market (GEM) and the New OTC Market should be deepened, and the development of the regional equity market should be standardized. Meanwhile, it is important to promote the development of the bond market, help corporations optimize financing structure, reduce financing costs, resolve debt risks, standardize various financing behaviors, guide social capital so that it concentrates on high-quality enterprises, and create a good market environment for the investment in and financing of various economic entities.

4. Reducing costs and increasing corporate profit margin

Cost reduction involves identifying and removing various factors that lead to high costs within corporations, including high institutional transaction costs, high labor costs, high social security contributions, and high financing costs. An initial step is to reduce the institutional transaction costs of enterprises by doing each of the following: transforming government functions, deepening the reform of the commercial system by streamlining administration, delegating powers, improving regulation and services, implementing the negative list system, gradually liberalizing access, promoting competition, and improving supply. Second, the reform of the fiscal and taxation system must also be deepened. This means strengthening tax reduction, carrying out regulation and control with reserve requirement ratio (RRR) cuts, focusing on standardizing various fees and government funds, creating a fair tax environment, and reducing the actual tax burden of corporations. Third, an opportunity exists to help enterprises reduce financial costs and provide a good financing environment. The government therefore needs to deepen financial reform, enhance the function of the policy financing guarantee system, strengthen the linkage between local finance and financial policies, smooth the service channels of the banking system for small-, medium-sized, and micro-enterprises, streamline financial services for real economy enterprises, improve regulatory norms for new internet financial formats such as the P2P online loan platform, and give full play to the financing services of internet finance for small-, medium-sized and micro-enterprises in order to effectively prevent risks. Fourth, it is an important objective to reduce the rate of various social security contributions and reduce the burden of rising labor costs on enterprises as much as possible. Public finance, and in particular the allocation of state-owned assets and dividends from state-owned enterprises, can be used to support social security, reduce unnecessary government expenses such as the "three public expenses," and subsidize the social security fund. Fifth, the government should promote the reform of the circulation system, break up monopoly pricing in logistics, and help enterprises reduce logistical costs. Finally, it is imperative to flexibly reduce the prices of energy and resources consumed by enterprises, give full play to the market pricing mechanism, and break up monopoly pricing in some energy and resource fields.

5. Strengthening areas of weakness and expanding effective supply

There are two areas of weakness that particularly need strengthening: weakness in development and weakness in securing people's livelihoods. The weakness of development mainly refers to forms of weakness in scientific innovation, technological innovation, transportation infrastructure, and ecological response. Weakness in securing people's livelihood mainly refers to the weakness in the effective supply of public services and the need to increase the income of low-income farmers. Much needs to be done.

(1) To address the weakness in scientific and technological innovation, it is important to accelerate the formation of mass innovation, tap the potential of enterprises, stimulate the vitality of the people, and enhance the strength of innovation subjects.

(2) To address the weakness in transportation infrastructure, it will be necessary to deepen the reform of the transportation system, enhance the competitiveness of transportation services, and build a high-level integrated transportation infrastructure network and transportation service system.

(3) To address the weakness in ecological response, there must be an increased commitment to green development, promoting the construction of an ecologically responsible civilization. This means that innovation must use green S&T as a guide, and the government must handle the relationship between economic development and environmental protection appropriately, promoting green development, circular development, and low-carbon development.

(4) To address weaknesses in securing people's livelihoods, a number of steps are needed: First, the Chinese government should accelerate the improvement of the public service system, should improve the system of government purchase of services, and should address deficits in various areas: education, medical care, social security services, employment services, culture services, etc. Basic public services should become more standardized and equitable. Second, China must win the battle against poverty: it must improve the working mechanism of targeted poverty alleviation; it must clarify the supporting measures aimed at alleviating poverty; it must strengthen infrastructure construction in poor areas; and it must redirect a wide variety of resources to poor areas. Third, the government must make up for the weakness of its institutions with the spirit of reform and innovation. Deepening the reform of the Party's development system is an important goal, along with establishing a good institutional framework system and generally breaking down the old to replace it with the new, in a spirit of reform and innovation. It is not only the systems that do not meet the needs of the development that need to be cleaned up but also newer systems that

are nevertheless capable of being perfected in order to form a more mature and complete institutional system.

III. New Arrangements for Deepening Supply-Side Structural Reform

In the development stage of socialism with Chinese characteristics in the new era, the task of building a modern economic system must be centered around the real economy. It must aim at improving the quality of the supply system and significantly enhancing the competitive edge of China's economy.

This task entails several other actions. First, it is imperative to accelerate the establishment of manufacturing power, hasten the development of advanced manufacturing industries, and moreover promote the deep integration of the Internet, big data, AI, and the real economy. China must not pass up the opportunity to form new momentum in the fields of medium- and high-end consumption, innovation leadership, green energy, low carbon, the sharing economy, the modern supply chain, and human capital services. Second, the government ought to support optimization and upgrading in traditional industries, accelerate the modernization of the service industry, and raise the Chinese economic approach to the level of international standards. Third, Chinese industries must move toward the middle and high end of the global value chain and must cultivate a number of world-class advanced manufacturing clusters. Fourth, the construction of various infrastructure networks (e.g., water conservancy, railway, highway, water transportation, aviation, pipelines, power grid, information, and logistics) deserves additional support. Fifth, as discussed earlier, it is important to combat overcapacity by destocking, deleveraging, and reducing costs while strengthening areas of weakness and optimizing the allocation of existing resources by expanding high-quality incremental supply. All this aims at achieving a dynamic balance between supply and demand. Sixth, entrepreneurship should be fostered diligently, and more social subjects should be encouraged to participate in innovation and entrepreneurship. Seventh, a team of knowledgeable, skilled, and innovative workers is needed to carry forward the model worker spirit and the spirit of craftsmanship; and to create an ethic that honors labor, a professionalism that pursues excellence.

As China's economy enters a new stage of transformation and upgrading, some institutional systems have seriously lagged behind, and thus there is an urgent demand for innovative institutional supply. This demand can be summed up in one sentence: The market must play a decisive role in the allocation of resources, and the government must more judiciously choose when to assert its role. In China's current market economy, however, there are still obvious limitations to supply that hamper economic growth—limitations involving land, labor, capital, innovation, and other crucial factors. Chinese institutions, facing limitations in their structure and output, can no longer meet the ever-expanding needs of a huge number of middle-class families. These shortcomings are not conducive to unleashing the consumption potential of China.

The innovation of institutional supply should first be an innovation in the way the government manages the economy and society, an innovation that aims at a stable institutional environment. Fiscal and tax reform must be promoted. The economic relationships between government and citizens, between central and local government, must be strengthened. A standardized government financial management system must be formed. In particular, there is a need to: modify the population policy and consolidate the supply foundation; promote land system reform, releasing the untapped vitality of supply; accelerate the reform of the financial system and remove financial repression; implement an innovation-driven strategy; open up supply space; deepen the reforms that streamline administration and delegate power to promote supply quality; and, finally, build and maintain a reformed social service system.

China must make it a priority to deepen supply-side structural reform. A transformation should take place from talking about "made in China" to talking about "created in China," from the "speed of China" to the "quality of China." China should no longer simply be a "large" manufacturing country; it should be a *powerful* one. The reform of a market-oriented allocation of factors, which focuses on "breaking ineffective supply, cultivating new momentum and innovative leaders and reducing costs," will permeate the public perception of the nation. This shall occur when efforts to vigorously break up ineffective supply take effect, the government gains the focus to dispose of "zombie enterprises," and efforts to resolve excessive capacity gain a foothold. China must absolutely cultivate the new momentum evident today, strengthening scientific and technological innovation, promoting the optimization and upgrade of traditional industries, growing a number of leading enterprises with innovative ability, and actively promoting the in-depth development of military-civilian integration. High costs in the real economy must be reduced, along with institutional transaction costs. The government must continue its firm steps to stop the unauthorized levying of fees on enterprises, must strengthen the investigation and rectification of arbitrary charges, must deepen the reform of industries such as electric power, oil and gas, and railway, and must reduce the costs of energy consumption and logistics. In the effort to promote supply-side structural reform, it must accelerate the optimization and upgrading of the manufacturing industry, keep on "cutting overcapacity, destocking, deleveraging, reducing costs and strengthening areas of weakness," and deepen reform that streamlines administration, delegates power, combines power delegation with administration, and optimizes services.

CHAPTER FOURTEEN

Macroeconomic Regulation Policies

The policy orientation for China's macroeconomic regulation and control is to uphold the underlying principle of pursuing progress while ensuring stability. This entails a number of other actions. It means adhering to the unity of various objectives: stabilizing growth, adjusting structure, benefiting people's livelihoods, and preventing risks. It also means maintaining normal economic operations in accordance with the general idea that macro policies should be stable, industrial policies should be appropriate, micro policies should be flexible, reform policies should be practical, and social policies should provide basic security and support.

SECTION 1
The Principle of Pursuing Progress While Ensuring Stability

The underlying principle of pursuing progress while ensuring stability constitutes an important part of Xi Jinping Thought on Socialism with Chinese Characteristics for a New Era. It is not only an important principle in economics but also a major requirement for all fields.

I. A Scientific Approach to Pursuing Progress While Ensuring Stability

The principle of pursuing progress while ensuring stability is both an important principle of governance and a type of methodology for fulfilling economic tasks. It requires leaders to successfully navigate the balance between stability and progress, knowing how to time government interventions and how sizable these interventions should be. At present, the concept of pursuing progress while ensuring stability is not properly understood. In particular, disputes remain about basic questions such as what it means to pursue progress while ensuring stability, why China should pursue progress while ensuring stability, and how China can pursue progress while ensuring stability. Therefore, it is necessary to systematically answer the three basic questions above in theory, comprehensively and dialectically exploring the meaning of pursuing progress while ensuring stability, clearing up misunderstandings, and laying a solid cognitive foundation for the intentional implementation of this underlying principle.

Despite the questions that remain, it is clear that upholding the principle of pursuing progress while ensuring stability is an internal requirement for the development of socialism with Chinese characteristics in the new era. To uphold this principle, it is necessary to accurately grasp its rich connotations and requirements. Stability is the cornerstone of development and the backdrop of an ambitious vision. As an important principle of governing the country and a type of methodology for fulfilling economic tasks, the fundamental goal of pursuing progress while ensuring stability is to stabilize the overall situation while nevertheless making continuous progress. Stability is the cornerstone that holds the nation together, while progress is the nation's purpose and orientation.

With the foundation and premise of stability, it becomes possible to promote progress more scientifically and sustainably. But the dynamic is also reinforced in the other direction: the driving force of progress makes it possible to achieve stability more effectively and at a higher level. The relation between stability and progress is a dialectical relation according to which they restrict and encourage each other, complement each other, and promote each other. China must make good use of dialectical thinking, systematic thinking, and bottom-line thinking. It must grasp the bases of stability, find breakthrough points for effective progress, make progress in key areas on the premise of stability, pursue advancement in a measured way, and keep moving toward a new era of development. Stability is undoubtedly the priority because only economic and social stability can create a stable macro environment which leads to the new normal of economic development and deepens supply-side structural reform. Pursuing stability means stabilizing economic operations, keeping these operations within a reasonable range, and focusing on the maintenance of a number of other factors: steady and rapid economic development, the basic stability of the overall price level, the stability of the employment situation, and overarching political and social stability. These tasks involve the maintenance of stability for macro policies and the continuance of a proactive fiscal policy and prudent monetary policy. Market expectations should be stable.

For the market to be stable and the overall situation to be stable, expectations must also be stable. This creates a necessity for upholding the basic economic system, adhering to the direction of socialist market economy reform, expanding opening up, and stabilizing the confidence of private entrepreneurs. Expectation guidance must be strengthened, and the government must become more credible. The prevention and management of financial risks must become more of a priority. A better understanding of the strength of reform, the speed of development, and the degree of economic and social affordability is needed. Basic social support for the Chinese people must be provided while still holding to the bottom line, maintaining focus on top priorities, improving the system, and guiding public opinion so as to expand the people's sense of fulfillment.

II. The Significance of Pursuing Progress While Ensuring Stability

Pursuing progress while ensuring stability is a strategic requirement for achieving the Two Centenary Goals. At this point in time, China is closer to the goal of the great rejuvenation of the Chinese nation than at any time in history. However, the closer the goal becomes, the greater the resistance to progress. Building a moderately prosperous society in all aspects has entered a decisive stage, economic development has entered a new normal, and reform has entered a critical period. This is an environment of "three-period superposition," namely the shifting period of growth rate, the painful period of structural adjustment, and the digestion period of early stimulus policies. Despite the fact that it currently maintains long-term positive momentum, China's economy also faces challenges because of the existence of many tensions and the intersection of various risks and hidden dangers, with a prominent tension being that between overcapacity and the upgrading of demand structure. Problems, such as an insufficient internal driving force for economic growth, the accumulation of financial risks, and increasing difficulties in particular regions, still exist. A critical point has been reached, where the economy must climb over the barrier and tackle these problems in order to reform. China faces a complex and dynamic international political and economic environment, along with new changes in domestic economic operations. Against this backdrop, the nation should not only strengthen its confidence and determination in development but also be fully prepared to deal with risks and challenges. Only by implementing the underlying principle of pursuing progress while ensuring stability, grasping the relationship between "stability" and "progress" scientifically, maintaining strategic concentration, adhering to problem orientation and bottom-line thinking, and daily manifesting its perseverant spirit will China be able to better seize opportunities, meet challenges, reinforce its foundation, make progress, accomplish its goals, and push economic and social development to a new level.

Pursuing progress while ensuring stability is a realistic approach that can address the three major structural imbalances: the internal structural imbalance between supply and demand in the real economy, the imbalance between finance and the real economy, and the imbalance between real estate and the real economy. These three imbalances have blocked the economic cycle and reduced economic vitality, resulting in the lack of an internal driving force of economic growth and the continuous accumulation of financial risks. To rectify these imbalances, China must follow the principle and pursue progress in a stable way. If the nation blindly seeks progress, pursuing a rapid and significant recovery of short-term economic indicators, even while it lacks an internal driving force of growth, it will inevitably continue to rely on the traditional economic growth model alongside a rapid expansion of real estate investment and credit. This result will undoubtedly further increase the imbalance. "Zombie enterprises" will not be cleaned up, overcapacity will only be resolved with great difficulty, excessive financialization will not be restrained, and the pressure of financial stability and the redirection of funds from the real economy to financial markets will be further exacerbated. Moreover, the rapid rise of real estate prices in first-tier cities and some second-tier cities will continue to exist alongside the increase of real estate inventory in third- and fourth-tier cities.

The CPC's historical experience of leadership in economic development has consistently taught the following lesson: pursuing measured progress. The practice of economic intervention since the founding of the PRC shows that the blind pursuit of progress, if progress is understood as indicators and short-term changes, sets the stage over the long term for major setbacks. Conversely, the experience of upholding the principle of pursuing progress while ensuring stability has been encouraging, even when the economy has faced great difficulties. These difficulties can be overcome, with the result of good economic growth performance and additional potential for future development. From 1998 to 2002, despite being faced with a number of severe challenges (e.g., the impact of the external Asian financial crisis, the difficulties of domestic state-owned enterprises, and the large-scale exposure to financial risks), the central government upheld the principle of pursuing progress while ensuring stability, vigorously promoted the reform of state-owned enterprises, finance, housing, and other fields, expanded opening up by joining the WTO, and made remarkable progress in deepening reform, opening up, and making structural adjustments. Therefore, it not only stabilized its economic operations but also laid a solid institutional foundation for rapid economic growth from 2003 to 2007.

Pursuing progress while ensuring stability is also a strategic way of dealing with the current uncertainty at home and abroad. On the one hand, there are still many uncertain factors in the international economic and financial environment. The profound impact of the international financial crisis persists, and global economic recovery remains weak. De-globalization is on the rise, and the haze of trade and investment protectionism has not dissipated. Geopolitical conflicts emerge one after the other. The leverage ratio of non-financial sectors is still rising, the normalization of monetary policies in major economies may be impacting global financial stability, and the international economic and financial environment faces great uncertainty. On the other hand, there are still many issues to confront on the domestic front. With the in-depth promotion of supply-side structural reform, corporate expectations have improved, market confidence has been strengthened, and financial risks have been kept under control. However, economic operations still face downward pressure, the driving forces powering economic growth are as yet insufficient, and the risk of a "gray rhino" in the financial field still exists. In the face of possible negative changes in the environment at home and abroad, what is needed is bottom-line thinking, an approach that will maintain a buffer so that the economy can endure possible shocks by pursuing progress while ensuring stability. This is also an important reason why there has been room for the expected economic growth target since the reform and opening-up.

III. A Strategic Focus on Pursuing Progress While Ensuring Stability

With China's development premised on overall social stability, progress can be pursued while ensuring stability. The overall approach must be positive and enterprising so that this progress involves changes in the growth model, new breakthroughs in deepening reform, and outstanding achievements in improving people's livelihoods.

President Xi Jinping said, "As we pursue stability, we will focus on achieving steady economic performance."[68] Against the background of a period of shifting economic growth and great downward pressure on growth, the key to understanding "steady economic performance" lies in avoiding a rigid mentality that holds the status quo fixed and fails to respond to emerging indicators. Leaders must not fall into the misconception the expected economic growth targets cannot be adjusted (even adjusted downward) so as to respond to changes in domestic and foreign economic climate. Steady economic performance does not preclude the timely and appropriate lowering of growth targets and the downward fluctuation of economic indicators within a reasonable range. The lowering of expected growth targets in a timely and appropriate manner according to the objective factors—factors like the entry of economic development into the new normal—can accurately be said to pursue progress while ensuring stability. The expected growth target was lowered from about 7.5% in 2013 to about 6.5% in 2017, and actual growth was gradually reduced from 7.8% in 2013 to 6.7% in 2016. The practice has proven that steady economic performance does not require the growth rate to be rigidly maintained and mechanically stabilized and does not mean that the growth target and growth rate cannot be lowered. In the absence of major fluctuations, pursuing progress while ensuring stability means that China will move "one step back and two steps forward," sacrificing some speed in exchange for significant improvements in growth quality and efficiency.

"The focus of progress is to deepen reform, opening up, and structural adjustment."[69] "Progress" should not be myopically understood as the recovery of economic indicators in the short term but rather as the type of reform, opening up, and structural adjustment that lays the foundation for medium- and long-term economic growth. The key to understanding "progress" lies in understanding structure. The 2016 Central Economic Work Conference pointed out that "although there are cyclical and aggregate factors, the root cause of the prominent contradictions and problems faced by China's economic operation is the major structural imbalance, resulting in a rocky economic cycle." When pursuing structural adjustments, it is necessary to go beyond the microeconomic paradigm of enterprises, industries, and regions, even beyond the paradigm of demand, in order to grasp structures from a macroscopic perspective according to the economic operation mechanism, and to make clear the direction of structural adjustment. The current major structural imbalances are mainly reflected in the internal structural imbalance between supply and demand in the real economy, the imbalance between finance and the real economy, and the imbalance between finance and real estate. To pursue progress in a stable way and promote structural adjustments, Chinese leadership should focus on promoting the rebalancing of the three major structural imbalances.

IV. Strategic Support for Pursuing Progress While Ensuring Stability

Pursuing progress while ensuring stability is supported by late-development advantages. China has become the world's second-largest economy, but it is still a developing economy. There remains a clear gap between China's average level of technology/industry and the world's technological/industrial frontier. China retains strong late-development advantages and significant growth potential. Even if the rate of expansion of the world's technological and industrial frontier significantly decreases, the existence of these late-development advantages can ensure that China has the potential to maintain a relatively rapid speed of technological progress.

The existence of such advantages highlights that strong and stable leadership and the capacity to innovate with the times are prerequisites for the development of a national political party or government. By deepening reform in all areas and building a new open economic system, China will be able to ensure the continuous release of the potential contained in its late-development advantages for many decades to come. Some people worry that, unlike various smaller economies that have successfully caught up, the release of late-development advantages in super-large economies will be subject to global demand. The thinking goes that China is so big that the international market can't accommodate the full release of its late-development advantages. The view is mistaken, however. It neither recognizes that the domestic demand of big countries can constitute a huge support nor that China is committed to promoting global inclusive growth. The Belt and Road Initiative—an initiative characterized by openness and inclusiveness, an initiative that pursues mutual benefit and win-win cooperation aimed at joint consultation, joint construction, and sharing—is the centerpiece of China's efforts to achieve its own development by promoting global growth, especially including the common development of developing economies.

The imperative of pursuing progress while ensuring stability is made possible because the system is reformable. It is through continuous innovation that the system can meet the needs of economic development. Under the influence of specific interest groups, any system has a natural tendency to degenerate since the system helpful to the past development stage may not be able to adapt to a new environment.

Compared with the world's other major economies, China has shown obvious advantages in the system's reformability. This is for a number of reasons. Firstly, China has a strong awareness of reform. The reform is never completed but is always ongoing. That is the understanding of the CPC Central Committee under the leadership of Xi, and it has made a deep impression on the minds of all Chinese people. Secondly, the improvement of political ecology provides a good environment for reform. Any exploration or implementation of reform requires promising networks of officials, as well as entrepreneurs in the political field. The in-depth implementation of anti-corruption interventions and the creation of a clean and positive political environment are conducive to guiding the efforts of leaders and officials in driving institutional innovation and forming a good atmosphere for reformers. Finally, the current tensions and challenges are also helpful in building a consensus focused on reform. Reform practices at all times and in all countries show that one of the important reasons why it is difficult to form a reform consensus is the constraint of entrenched misconceptions. These deep-rooted ideas can be broken only through the evolution of practice and through practical education. With economic development entering the new normal, the disadvantages of the institutional factors affecting China's economic and social development are becoming more evident to the people, and thus the necessity and direction of reform are also evident.

The goal of pursuing progress while ensuring stability is also aided by the advantages of a large country. Firstly, global power has the capacity to offset risks. Due to their large economic volume and large internal market, global powers generally have more room to maneuver in response to external shocks and thus relatively little economic volatility. As long as there are no major mistakes in macroeconomic policies, China can effectively weather all kinds of risks and shocks. Secondly, large countries have favorable conditions for the release of late-development advantages. Such release does not involve a simple copy of foreign technology and business models; it is accompanied by a large number of innovations. In general, the innovation ecology of large nations is relatively healthy. The huge economic scale and its accompanying diversity leave more space for startups to challenge existing large enterprises and ensure the vertical social mobility of enterprises—that is, the possibility of innovative enterprises growing from small to large. Finally, great powers have more advantages in terms of the system's reformability. When the reform itself contains great risks, the vast territory of a great power provides a broad "trial and error" space for the pilot programs for various types of reform. After the pilot has concluded, leaders can review the lessons learned, incorporate successful elements of the experience, and move forward in an informed and cost-effective way. The reason why China's system is so reformable is that it has made full use of the advantages of its size, perfecting the effective management of reform risks and costs through local reform pilot projects.

SECTION 2
Proactive Fiscal Policy

Fiscal policy is an important part of macroeconomic policy. The term itself refers to a series of policies, guidelines, and measures formulated by the government according to objective economic laws, which are in place to guide fiscal work and handle fiscal relations. It is the basic means for the government to regulate economic operations, intervene in economic activities, promote stable economic growth and sustainable development, and achieve expected social and economic goals. The subjects of fiscal policy include central and local governments at all levels. The responsibilities of the central government are different, of course, from those of local governments. The central government typically engages in national resource allocation, national income distribution, the pursuit of national economic stability, and subordinate government funding; local governments undertake the functions of resource allocation, income redistribution, the pursuit of local stability, and funding for other local governments at or above the county level.

I. The Objectives and Tools of Fiscal Policy

1. Objectives of fiscal policy
The objectives of fiscal policy refer to various choices about government fiscal expenditure, tax and debt level, or government fiscal revenue for the purpose of reducing unemployment, steadying economic fluctuations, preventing inflation, and achieving stable economic growth. In other words, fiscal policy refers to policies whereby the government changes taxes and expenditures to

affect aggregate demand and thus indirectly affect employment and national income. Reforming taxes means changing the tax rate and tax rate structure. Reforming government expenditures means changing both purchasing expenditures and transfer payments for goods and services. It is one of the main policies of the state to intervene in the economy since fiscal policy is an integral part of national economic policy and is closely related to other economic policies. The formulation and implementation of fiscal policy should be coordinated with financial policy, industrial policy, income distribution policy, and other economic policies.

There are two forms of government expenditure: one is government purchasing, which refers to the government's expenditure on goods and services (e.g., purchase of military equipment, construction of roads, payment of judges' salaries, etc.), and the other is government transfer payments to increase the income of some groups (e.g., payments to the elderly or unemployed). Tax is another form of fiscal policy that affects the overall economy in two ways. First, taxes affect people's income. Second, taxes can affect goods and factors of production, so they can impact incentive mechanisms and behaviors.

2. Tools of fiscal policy

The government has many tools at its disposal to impact the economy in a positive or stabilizing way.

(1) Government expenditure

Government expenditure refers to the sum of expenditures of governments at all levels in the whole country, composed of specific expenditure items. The category of government expenditure can be divided into government purchases and government transfer payments.

Government purchases are purchases of goods and services by the government, such as the purchase of military supplies or office supplies, government employee salaries, and expenditures required for public projects. Government purchase expenditure is a major factor in determining the size of the national income, and its scale is directly related to the increase or decrease of total social demand. Purchase expenditure plays a very important role in regulating the total expenditure level of the whole society.

Government transfer payments are the portions of governmental expenditure that apply to social welfare insurance, poverty relief, and subsidies. Transfer payments cannot be counted as a component of national income. What these payments do is transfer and redistribute income among different social entities by means of government action.

(2) Government revenue

Tax is an important way for the state to participate in the distribution of social goods through the exercise of political power. It is free, mandatory, fixed, and authoritative. Tax is the most important part of government revenue. Like government purchase expenditures and transfer payments, taxes also have a multiplier effect—that is, the change in tax has a multiplier effect on the change in national income. A judicious approach to taxation can adjust the structure of industries and realize an optimal allocation of resources, using tools like the adjustment of the tax rate and redefinition of tax categories. Leaders can adjust personal income and wealth and can achieve fair distribution through a progressive personal income tax and property tax. The way to promote the realization of financial objectives through tax is to flexibly use various taxation elements: properly set up tax categories and tax items to form a reasonable tax system so as to determine the scope and level of tax regulation and achieve coordination among various taxes; determine the tax rate and define the quantitative limit of tax regulation so that taxes can play the guiding role as a policy intervention; provide for necessary tax reductions and additions.

When the government's tax revenue is insufficient to make up for government expenditure, government debt can be issued as another part of government revenue. Government debt is the debt of the government to the public (i.e., the public becomes the creditor). Different from tax, debt is a special form in which the government uses credit to raise fiscal funds, including central government debt and local government debt.

(3) Fiscal expenditure

Fiscal expenditure is the general expenditure (or current account expenditure) of the government to meet public needs. It includes purchase expenditure and transfer expenditure, each of which has different effects on the national economy.

From the perspective of end use, administrative expenditure, national defense expenditure, culture, education, science, health, and other fiscal expenditures are essential expenditures needed to guarantee public welfare. The government's investment capacity and investment direction play a key role in the adjustment of social and economic structure and economic development.

Transfer expenditure is an important tool for the government to carry out macro-control and management, and especially to adjust the balance of total social supply and demand. For example, social security expenditure and fiscal subsidies play the role of a "safety valve" and "lubricant" in modern society. When the economy is depressed and unemployment increases, the government increases both social security expenditures and fiscal subsidies in order to increase social purchasing power, which helps to restore the balance between supply and demand. Conversely, these two expenditures can be reduced to avoid excessive demand.

(4) Government bonds

Government bonds are a form of intervention in which the state raises fiscal funds according to the principle of paid credit. They are also an important means to realize macro-control and fiscal policy. The adjusting role of government bonds in the economy is mainly reflected in three effects. The first is the crowding-out effect. That is, through the issuance of government bonds, the funds of the private sector for investment or consumption will be reduced in order to adjust investment and consumption. The second is the monetary effect, which refers to the changes in money supply and demand caused by the issuance of government bonds. On the one hand, this effect may turn "potential money" into real circulating money; on the other hand, it may transfer money deposited in the private sector to the government or increase the money supply through the purchase of government bonds by the central bank. The third is the interest rate effect, which means that the market interest rate level is affected by the adjustment of the interest rate level of government bonds and the change of supply and demand in the capital market. The interest rate effect may have an expansion or contraction effect on the economy.

Under the conditions of modern credit, the market issuance of government bonds is not only the main carrier to communicate fiscal policy and monetary policy but also their coupling point. Therefore, when government bonds are implemented as tools of fiscal policy, they should not only coordinate with other tools of fiscal policy but also with monetary policy.

(5) Government investment

Government investment refers to expenditures laid out by the government for capital projects, which eventually constitute fixed assets. Government investment projects mainly occur in basic industries, public facilities, and emerging high-tech leading industries (those characterized by natural monopoly, large external effects, high industrial correlation, and the effect of demonstration and induction). This kind of investment is a driving force of economic growth and has a multiplier effect. The so-called multiplier effect of investment refers to the multiple income growth caused by every additional yuan of investment.

II. Classification of Fiscal Policy

Fiscal policies can be categorized in multiple ways. When these policies are considered from the perspective of their role in regulating the economic cycle, there are two types of fiscal policy, automatic and discretionary. When considered from the perspective of overall demand, there are three types: proactive, tight, and neutral.

1. Automatic fiscal stabilizer and discretionary fiscal policy

The division of fiscal policy into automatic stabilizer and discretionary fiscal policy is based on the role of fiscal policy in regulating the economic cycle.

(1) Automatic fiscal stabilizer means that the fiscal system itself has an internal operation mechanism that can automatically adjust the economy in response to the development of the economy and society without other intervention by the government. It is mainly reflected in two contexts: on the one hand, the use of a progressive income tax acts as an automatic stabilizer, incorporating both individual income tax and corporate income tax. During an economic downturn, the profits of individuals and enterprises will decrease, and the number of individuals and enterprises eligible for tax payments will also decrease. Therefore, the tax base will be relatively smaller, the progressive tax rate will be lowered, and taxes will automatically be reduced. As the reduction of tax revenue is greater than that of personal income and corporate profits, this reduction will produce a stimulus to prevent the excessive decline of personal consumption and corporate investment and will help hold back economic recession. During economic overheating, its mechanism is just the opposite. On the other hand, government welfare expenditure acts as an automatic stabilizer. If there is an economic recession, the number of people who meet the criteria for receiving unemployment benefits

and other benefits will increase, and thus the distribution of unemployment benefits and other benefits will tend to naturally increase as well, which will help to inhibit the continuous decline of consumer spending and prevent a further economic recession. During economic prosperity, its mechanism is just the opposite.

(2) Discretionary fiscal policy refers to the government's proactive and flexible choice of different types of contracyclical fiscal policy tools suited to the economic and social conditions at a given time. These tools aim to intervene in economic operations and achieve the objectives of fiscal policy. Discretionary fiscal policy includes a pump-priming policy and a compensatory policy. Pump-priming policy refers to a policy of public investment during an economic downturn aimed at increasing effective demand and revitalizing the economy. Compensatory policy refers to the government's conscious fiscal policy that aims to counteract worrisome changes in the current economic situation so as to achieve the purpose of stabilizing economic fluctuations. During a period of economic downturn, the government increases investment and consumption demand in order to alleviate the impact of deflation, increasing social effective demand and stimulating economic growth by increasing expenditure and reducing revenue. Conversely, during a period of economic prosperity, the government uses fiscal policies in order to curb inflation. It might increase revenue and reduce expenditure to curb excess demand and stabilize economic fluctuations.

2. Proactive fiscal policy, tight fiscal policy, and neutral fiscal policy

(1) Proactive fiscal policy is a policy that increases and stimulates total demand through fiscal distribution activities. Such measures include: reducing government bonds, reducing the tax rate, increasing government purchases, and transferring payments.

(2) Tight fiscal policy (also known as moderately tight fiscal policy) aims at reducing and restraining total demand through fiscal distribution activities. The main measures are increasing government bonds, raising the tax rate, reducing government purchases, and transferring payments.

(3) Neutral fiscal policy (also known as prudent fiscal policy) means that the impact of fiscal distribution activities on total social demand remains neutral.

III. China's Fiscal Policy in the New Era

As the economic situation facing China has changed over the last few decades, China's fiscal policies have also changed. A number of shifts are evident to the close observer.

1. A shift from focusing on aggregate issues to solving structural problems

In macroeconomic textbooks and other macroeconomic frameworks, fiscal policy is considered an aggregate variable and analyzed in the context of three factors: consumption, investment, and export. The main role of proactive fiscal policy is to expand total social demand. However, China now faces a prominent structural problem. President Xi captured this nicely when he said concerning China's economic development under the new normal: there are cyclical and aggregate problems in China's economic development, but structural problems are the most prominent, and the main contradictions are on the supply side. Therefore, the focus of China's proactive fiscal policy has become promoting supply-side structural reform and solving the problem of structural imbalance. Compared with monetary policy, fiscal policy has a stronger function of adjusting structure. China's proactive fiscal policy has shifted from focusing on aggregate issues to focusing more on solving structural problems. Therefore, the nation must stand firm in not adopting strong stimulus policies that would have had an economy-wide impact.

2. A shift from focusing on solving economic problems to implementing comprehensive policies

In the past, the implementation of proactive fiscal policy mostly focused on the macro-economy, either "pulling" the growth rate or "stabilizing" it. However, economic growth is not the only aspect of development. As a tool of national governance, it is not enough for proactive fiscal policy to focus on solving economic problems. As the situation changes and the economy and society become more closely intertwined, it is difficult to solve economic problems by focusing solely on the economy. Only by expanding the vision of proactive fiscal policy beyond the economy and focusing on comprehensive policy implementation can the nation maintain the stability of both economy and society. When the government increases investment in key areas such as people's basic livelihood security, poverty alleviation, education, culture, health, and ecological civilization, and when the government strengthens its capacity to ensure basic public services, it is actually improving the supply side of public services, and therefore implementing people-centered development thought.

From this point of view, fiscal policy is not only an economic policy but also a social policy. Through the protection of people's livelihoods and the provision of public services, fiscal policy improves workers' quality and lays a solid foundation for the implementation of the innovation-driven development strategy. It is also an indispensable source of incentives. Distribution incentives, market incentives, behavior incentives, and social incentives are all generated by means of tax, fund, subsidy, and other policy instruments. These instruments not only stimulate innovation among scientific and technological personnel and entrepreneurship among enterprises and individuals but also generate local innovation, arouse social vitality, and realize the development of both material and spiritual civilization.

3. A shift from relying on deficits to optimizing the revenue and expenditure structure

In the past, people often measured proactive fiscal policy by the deficit ratio and the government debt. In cases of insufficient total demand, raising the deficit ratio and expanding debt can effectively expand total social demand. However, when faced with structural problems, this idea will no longer work. Moreover, if the deficit ratio and debt are excessively increased, there will be more fiscal risk, not less. Structural problems must be solved by structural methods, and the fiscal policy space should be expanded through the optimization of fiscal revenue and expenditure structure.

4. A shift from macro-control to public risk management

In essence, macro-control is a short-term, emergency public risk intervention by the government. It is an important aspect of public risk management, but not the whole of it. Under the new normal of economic development, China should not only resolve public risks in a timely fashion but also improve public risk management by preventing the generation and accumulation of public risks. China's current proactive fiscal policy has escaped from the rut of traditional macro-control thinking. On the basis of fully understanding the characteristics of the new normal of China's economic development, it has incorporated fiscal policy into the national public risk management system, shifting from a focus on current risk resolution to risk management, addressing short-term risks promptly while preventing long-term and strategic risks.

5. A shift from focusing on "flow optimization" to "overall adjustment of fiscal resources"

Fiscal policy should be more proactive and effective and should assist supply-side structural reform. It should ensure that public services are inclusive. It should meet essential needs and ensure basic living standards for people in difficulty. The narrow fiscal view must be abandoned, and public finance can no longer be understood from the perspective of the "accountant" or the "cashier"; rather, it should be based on the structural characteristics and operation laws of China's economy. The perspective needed is well summarized: "Finance is the foundation and an important pillar of state governance."[70] Therefore, fiscal policy needs to shift from focusing on the "flow optimization" of fiscal revenue and expenditure to focusing on the "overall adjustment of fiscal resources." Although focusing on the fiscal revenue and expenditure flow and optimizing the revenue and expenditure structure can work to some extent, this approach will not solve the deep structural problems caused by China's current resource allocation.

Promoting the overall adjustment of public resources and solving structural contradictions is the approach needed to solve current economic problems. Firstly, the government must implement an overall adjustment of public resources, alleviate fiscal pressure, and activate economic vitality. Secondly, it should coordinate the relation between taxes and fees, improve the tax system to promote the development of the manufacturing industry and social fairness, and eliminate tax factors that inhibit industrial upgrading. Finally, it should adjust the debt structure, increase tolerance of fiscal deficits, and optimize the deficit policy.

6. A shift toward focusing on solving the problems of unbalanced and insufficient development

In Western economies, fiscal policy is regarded as a contracyclical fiscal policy tool of the government. In practice, all countries choose fiscal policies with the goal of adjusting the trend of economic growth. In the new era, China has become the second largest economy in the world, forming a complete output system, a complete infrastructure system, and a huge consumption demand system. Under these conditions, the most pressing issues no longer involve increasing the speed of growth but rather ensuring that this growth benefits everyone more fairly, building a moderately prosperous society in all aspects, fully highlighting the advantages of socialism with Chinese characteristics, and letting the broad masses of the people fully understand the necessity of reform. The rationale behind China's fiscal policy is to boost economic growth and fully amplify the economic effects of social policies by expanding consumption and public welfare investment. The orientation shift involved in proactive fiscal policy shows that the Party and the state have closely analyzed the conditions and practical requirements of the new era and are exploring the fiscal policy with a new vision, a vision in line with the law of socialist development. An important function of public finance is to provide public goods. As such, fiscal policy is the most convenient and effective tool for the government to implement social development policies. To build socialism with Chinese characteristics, full play must be given to the supporting role of fiscal policy in social development. Both an expansion of basic public service investment and structural adjustments are needed in order to drive economic development.

7. A shift to a focus on high-intensity tax and fee reduction

Building a modern economic system requires China to optimize the institutional environment. The tax system directly affects the factor allocation pattern, the market competition pattern, and the regional development pattern. Since the 18th National Congress, China has reduced taxes by more than two trillion yuan, alleviated the burden of market subjects by more than three trillion yuan, reduced taxes and fees by one trillion yuan in 2017, and maintained the same efforts to reduce taxes and fees in 2018, on a scale of more than 800 billion yuan. Such a large-scale tax and fee reduction is rare in the world. Moreover, China's tax and fee reductions were achieved through a wide-ranging reform of the tax system. This shows that high-intensity tax and fee reduction is not a simple short-term policy intervention but a long-term pattern of institutional change. The government's focus is now to create institutional conditions for building a modern economic system and fully realizing the social fairness function of the tax system. Furthermore, the immediate effect of tax and fee reduction is to reduce the burden of market subjects and leave funds to market subjects. The ultimate effect is to standardize the behavior of rising government revenue and eliminate institutional obstacles to fair competition and high-quality development.

8. An acceleration of the construction of a modern fiscal system

China's clear powers and responsibilities operate at two levels. First, according to the principle of unified leadership and hierarchical management, the respective administrative, judicial, and legislative powers of central and local governments will be refined. Based on the results of this refinement, the respective financial powers of central and local governments will be clearly defined. Second, central and local expenditure responsibilities and their realization methods will be verified scientifically according to the division of powers and the pattern of income division between central and local governments.

Financial resources coordination also includes two levels. First, central and local governments coordinate their respective income and expenditure responsibilities. Second, the total financial resources held by these governments are coordinated with expenditure responsibility. Regional balance happens when three conditions are satisfied: the inter-provincial income gap is controlled within a reasonable range for income division, the inter-provincial distribution of transfer payments from central to local is reasonable, and the income division and transfer payments within various provinces are relatively balanced.

SECTION 3
Prudent Monetary Policy

Monetary policy is one of the most important instruments of macro-control. Monetary policy refers to policy measures taken by a country's central bank or monetary authority to adjust and control money supply or interest rates in order to achieve certain macroeconomic objectives. In modern economies, the central bank carries out financial macro-control through monetary policy to achieve the purpose of the government's management of monetary stability and the stable operation of the financial system.

I. Objectives of Monetary Policy

Macroeconomic operation determines the goal of monetary policy, and the choice of the ultimate goal of monetary policy depends on various major tensions in economic and social development. Looking from the perspective of monetary policy operation globally, the goal of monetary policy is not to pursue a single goal or constant key goal in a consistent and prolonged manner but to adjust and change policy goals or priorities to suit the changing economic and financial environment, and to distinguish which steps are suitable to which economic challenges. During a period of economic expansion, central banks typically make it their goal to stabilize prices and currency. In periods of economic contraction, the focus shifts to promoting economic growth and full employment. In periods of serious disequilibrium in the balance of payments and sharp fluctuation of the exchange rate, balancing the balance of payments is typically the priority.

A closer analysis of each of the monetary policy interventions mentioned above is below.

1. Stabilizing currency and curbing inflation

The goal of China's monetary policy before 1993 was twofold. The Trial Regulations of the PRC on the Administration of Banks, promulgated in 1986, defined the currency policy as follows: "The central bank, the Agricultural Bank of China, and other financial institutions should aim at developing the economy, stabilizing the currency and increasing economic benefits." Currency stabilization is one of the dual goals of monetary policy. Influenced by the traditional pursuit of high-speed economic growth and the lack of vigilance against inflation, inflation has become more and more serious with the rapid growth of China's economy. It is, therefore, particularly important to stabilize the currency. The content of currency stabilization includes both internal currency stabilization (stabilizing domestic prices) and external currency stabilization (stabilizing the foreign exchange rate).

2. Promoting economic growth

Since the 1970s, the implementation of monetary policy in developing countries has proven the relationship between monetary policy and economic growth, and the role of monetary policy in promoting economic growth has become a focus of attention. The Law of the PRC on the People's Bank of China, implemented in 2004, once again stipulated that the goal of China's monetary policy is to "stabilize the currency and thus promote economic growth." At present, China's economy has entered the new normal, under which it is more urgent to maintain economic growth. This urgency comes from the structural transformation of economic development and also from various new objectives and requirements put forward in the decisive stage of building a moderately prosperous society in all aspects. It is particularly important to ensure sustained and stable economic growth through the regulation of monetary policy.

3. Achieving full employment

Employment is the foundation of people's livelihoods. The issue of employment is not only an economic issue but also a social and political issue. Full employment is a criterion to measure whether the resources of a country have been fully utilized and whether its economy has developed adequately. If full employment is achieved, this means that the society's resources have been effectively utilized to the greatest extent and that economic development is normal. As unemployment affects not only the efficiency of resource allocation but also the stability and well-being of citizens, all countries take full employment as an important goal of monetary policy.

4. Maintaining a balance-of-payments equilibrium

Ensuring a balance-of-payments equilibrium is an important step on the way to securing economic security and the sustained and stable growth of the national economy. Any balance-of-payments disequilibrium, whether a surplus or a deficit, will have an adverse impact on the country's economy. A very large balance-of-payments deficit may have a variety of damaging effects. It could lead to a sharp decline in the confidence of foreign exchange markets in the local currency. It could lead to a large outflow of capital or a reduction in foreign exchange reserves and substantial depreciation of the local currency. It could trigger a monetary and financial crisis. Any long-term huge surplus will lead to a large number of idle foreign exchange reserves and a waste of resources. The central bank will issue more domestic currency to buy a large amount of foreign exchange, leading to or aggravating domestic inflation.

The role of monetary policy in adjusting the balance of payments is mainly to adjust interest rates and exchange rates. Raising the exchange rate can attract international capital to flow into the country, reducing the capital account deficit or increasing its surplus; lowering it can do the inverse. Exchange rate changes mainly affect international trade. The appreciation of local currency will promote imports, inhibit exports, increase the trade deficit, or decrease surplus so as to increase the deficit or decrease the surplus of entry items; the depreciation of currency will do the opposite.

All things considered, the harm of deficit is greater than the harm of surplus. Therefore, countries adjust the balance-of-payments disequilibrium mainly to reduce or even eliminate the international trade deficit and achieve the goal of balance-of-payments equilibrium through the coordination of local and foreign currencies.

II. The Tools of Monetary Policy

A monetary policy tool is a means used by the central bank to achieve a monetary policy goal. Monetary policy tools are divided into general tools and selective tools.

1. Reserve requirements

China began to implement the reserve requirement system in 1984, which was also the beginning of the People's Bank of China's formal functioning as the central bank. The reserve requirement is one of the central bank's monetary policy tools. The RRR determines the excess reserve level of financial institutions, and the excess reserve level represents the liquidity of the financial market. Its main contents include the adjustment of the RRR, the provisions on the types of institutions that pay the required reserve, the types of liabilities, the types of reserve assets, the accrual method of the required reserve, and the relevant penalties for violating the reserve payment system. The functions of the reserve requirement system are twofold: first, regulating the liquidity of the financial system; second, alleviating the volatility of short-term interest rates in the money market.

The reserve requirement policy tool is mainly aimed at regulating market liquidity: when the market liquidity is tight, the central bank releases liquidity by lowering the RRR; when the liquidity is loose, the central bank tightens liquidity by raising the RRR. The advantage of the reserve requirement is that it has a quick and direct effect on the market, without bias, while its main disadvantage is the fact that it lacks flexibility and can have too strong an impact on the market. Therefore, the reserve requirement is considered the most violent monetary policy tool.

2. Refinancing

Refinancing happens when the central bank, as a "bank of banks," lends money to commercial banks. By controlling the amount of loans to commercial banks, the central bank can control and adjust the money supply and credit scale.

Since the reform, the refinancing powers of China's central bank have been an important monetary policy tool supporting the management of credit scale. According to the length of the refinancing period, refinancing from the central bank of China can be categorized into three types: annual loan, seasonal loan, and daily loan. In order to improve the flexibility and effectiveness of its refinancing policy, the central bank has focused refinancing on seasonal and daily loans. In 2004, the People's Bank of China issued a decision to implement a floating interest rate system of refinancing as of March 25, 2004. The implementation of the floating interest rate system was another important step in steadily promoting the marketization of the interest rate, an action that improves the interest rate formation mechanism of the central bank and gradually improves the ability of the central bank to guide the market interest rate. Interest rate marketization is also conducive to straightening out the capital interest rate relationship between the central bank and the borrower, improving the precision, effectiveness, and transparency of refinancing management, and gradually transitioning the refinancing interest rate system to the international practice.

3. Rediscount operations

Rediscounting describes the process when financial institutions transfer unexpired discounted commercial bills to the central bank in the form of discounts in order to obtain funds. It is a monetary policy tool of the central bank. The adjustment of the rediscount policy can affect not only the amount of money in the market but also the interest rate level of the market. This means that it has a significant impact on the economy. After 1995, China began to use rediscounting as a monetary policy tool, helping the nation control the money supply and stabilize currency by transmitting monetary signals through rediscounts. The function of rediscounting is twofold: first, as the last "valve" for financial institutions to obtain liquidity, rediscounting plays an important role in the whole financial system; second, the adjustment of the rediscount interest rate is also a signal of monetary policy tightness, with a strong alert effect.

"Rediscounting" generally refers to the rediscount and various loan instruments from the central bank to commercial banks and other financial institutions. Generally, it includes the adjustment of the rediscount rate and the qualification to apply to the central bank for the rediscount and loan. Adjusting the rediscount interest rate is more flexible and focuses on the short term. In a mature market economy, the central bank can adjust the interest rate at any time according to the capital supply and demand of the market and can adjust the capital supply and demand in the market by affecting the behavior of commercial banks. In other words, the central bank is able to indirectly adjust the supply and demand of market funds through commercial banks. The bills requiring rediscount, as well as the relevant loan types and application institutions, focus on the long-term and change the flow of funds with the effect of inhibition or support.

4. Open market operations

In most developed countries, open market operation is the main monetary policy tool for the central bank to increase or decrease the base currency and regulate market liquidity. Through securities and foreign exchange transactions between the central bank and designated dealers, the monetary policy control goal is realized. China's open market operations include RMB operations and foreign exchange operations. In March 1994, with the implementation of the reform of China's foreign exchange management system and the online launch of the foreign exchange trading center, foreign exchange open market operation was officially launched in China. By participating in the inter-bank foreign exchange market, the People's Bank of China adjusted the domestic foreign exchange supply and demand in timely ways and stabilized the RMB exchange rate, which has played an important role in ensuring the smooth implementation of the foreign exchange system reform characterized by the settlement and sale of foreign exchange.

The People's Bank of China officially launched RMB open market operation on April 9, 1996, and established the technical network system for operation in a preliminary way, formulating relevant trading procedures and measures. A primary dealer system was implemented to facilitate China's open market business. 2004 was a year of great significance in the development of open market operations within the People's Bank of China. In light of newfound liquidity changes, such as the rapid growth of funds outstanding for foreign exchange and the large fluctuation of financial funds, stress was placed on strengthening the establishment of the liquidity management system throughout the year. The open market operation system was further improved, innovation of open market operation was promoted, and a relatively active situation in liquidity management of the banking system came up. Since then, the foresight of open market operation has been enhanced, and transparency has been further improved. The central bank's bill issuance system is becoming more and more mature. It plays an increasingly prominent role in macro-control and market development.

5. Interest rate policy

The interest rate is the ratio of the amount of interest to loan funds in a certain period. It is usually categorized into three kinds: annual interest rate, monthly interest rate, and daily interest rate. According to the type of borrower and lender, and the length of the loan term, interest rates can be differentiated in a more granular way: legal interest rate versus market interest rate, short-term interest rate versus medium- or long-term interest rate, fixed interest rate versus floating interest rate, nominal interest rate versus real interest rate.

Interest rate policy is not only an important part of China's monetary policy but also one of the main means by which monetary policy is implemented. Based on the needs of the moment, the People's Bank of China uses interest rate tools to adjust the interest rate level and interest rate structure in a timely way. This indirectly impacts the supply and demand of funds and thereby achieves the established objectives of monetary policy. The interest rate tools used by the People's Bank of China mainly include the following:

(1) Adjusting the benchmark interest rate of the central bank, including the following rates: the refinancing interest rate, which refers to the interest rate used for the loans offered by the People's Bank of China to financial institutions; the rediscount interest rate, which refers to the interest rate used for the rediscount of discounted bills held by financial institutions to the People's Bank of China; the deposit reserve rate, which refers to the rate of interest paid by the People's Bank of China on the required reserve deposited by financial institutions; the interest rate on excess reserve, which refers to the rate of interest paid by the central bank for that portion of a financial institution's reserve that exceeds the required reserve
(2) Adjusting the required reserve rate for financial institutions
(3) Developing the floating range of the deposit and loan rates of financial institutions
(4) Formulating relevant policies and adjusting the structure and levels of various interest rates

Since the reform and opening-up, the People's Bank of China has strengthened the use of interest rate instruments. The interest rate regulation mode has been more flexible, and the regulation mechanism has consistently improved. By adjusting the interest rate level/structure and by reforming the interest rate management system, the bank has gradually turned the interest rate into an important lever. In the new era, China should accelerate the market-oriented reform of interest rates. This involves launching certificates of deposit for enterprises and individuals in a timely way, expanding the scope of liability products and market-oriented pricing in financial institutions, strengthening the construction of a benchmark interest rate system in the financial market, and improving the market-oriented interest rate system and interest rate transmission mechanism. At the same time, it is necessary to improve the interest rate regulation system of the central bank, to enhance the ability of the central bank to regulate interest rates, and to bolster the effectiveness of macro-control. With the gradual advancement of the market-oriented reform of interest rates, the interest rate policy will stop relying wholly on direct regulation of rates and move toward indirect regulation. As an effective economic lever, interest rates will play a more important role in the national macro-control system for many decades.

6. Foreign exchange rate policy

Exchange rate policy refers to the policy instrument adopted by a national (or regional) government to maintain the exchange rate between its own currency and foreign currency at an appropriate level through the promulgation of financial laws and regulations and the implementation of policy provisions. Exchange rate policy includes objectives and tools.

The objectives of the exchange rate policy are as follows:

(1) To maintain export competitiveness, to achieve balance-of-payments equilibrium, and to advance economic growth
(2) To stabilize prices
(3) To prevent excessive exchange rate fluctuations so as to ensure the stability of the financial system

Exchange rate policy tools include the choice of exchange rate systems, the determination of the exchange rate level, and the adjustment of the exchange rate level. The choice of exchange rate system provides the most leverage to the government. It refers to a series of arrangements and regulations made by a national government on the determination of the exchange rate level of its own currency and on the way that the exchange rate changes. Traditionally, there are two main types of exchange rate systems: a fixed exchange rate system and a floating exchange rate system.

In the new era, the market-oriented formation mechanism of the RMB exchange rate must be continually improved, and the convertibility of capital accounts must be steadily promoted, including the orderly improvement of the convertibility of transactions under personal capital. China must launch the pilot for qualified domestic individual investors, establish a foreign debt management system under the macroprudential framework, and improve the cross-border capital flow monitoring system under unified national online management. It will continue to strengthen the determination of market supply and demand, all the while enhancing the floating flexibility of the RMB exchange rate and striving to internationalize the RMB.

7. Standing lending facility

Drawing on international experience, the People's Bank of China established a standing lending facility in 2013. It is a normal liquidity supply channel of the People's Bank of China, and its main function is to meet the vital long-term liquidity demands of financial institutions. It works mainly with policy banks and national commercial banks, offering loans that mature in 1-3 months. The interest rate level is determined comprehensively according to the needs of monetary policy regulation and the guiding market interest rate. A standing loan is issued in the form of a mortgage, and qualified collateral includes bond assets with high credit ratings and high-quality credit assets. On February 11, 2015, the People's Bank of China announced its intention to expand branches of the standing lending facility across the country to provide short-term liquidity support for qualified small- and medium-sized financial institutions.

III. China's Monetary Policy in the New Era

China's monetary policy in the new era must first of all enhance the capacity of finance to serve the real economy. It must moreover improve the two-pillar regulatory framework of monetary policy and macroprudential policy, deepening the market-oriented reform of interest rates and exchange rates. Finally, it must strengthen the financial regulatory system and hold to the standard that there will be "no systemic financial risk."

1. Combining monetary policy and macro prudence for financial stability

The main objectives of monetary policy are to maintain price stability and promote economic growth. Considering such objectives, along with the need to prevent financial risks and maintain financial stability, the pillar of macro prudence is required. This need can be clearly seen from the experience and lessons of the US subprime mortgage crisis in 2007 and the collapse of Lehman Brothers in 2008. A set of considerations are involved in the practice of macro prudence, which involves keeping the overall economic situation in mind at all times. Leaders must consider counter-cyclical adjustment, cross-market regulatory risks, and the overall leverage ratio. They must also consider how to have a macroprudential parameter in each economic cycle so that enterprises and financial institutions can prevent such risks in advance at different stages of the economic cycle and thus be able to issue warnings about (or even prevent) possible problems.

2. Advocating neutral prudent monetary policy

"Prudent" monetary policy has been implemented for many years since 2011 and has achieved remarkable results on the whole. However, for many reasons—such as the great downward pressure on the economy and the large fluctuations in the financial market—the implementation of monetary policy in some periods might be prudent but slightly loose. The general tone of monetary policy in 2017 was still prudence, but the need to remain "prudent and neutral" was emphasized. This was a significant change made on the basis of an in-depth analysis of the current internal and external situation and its challenges. It pointed the direction for grasping the strength and rhythm of monetary policy regulation and balancing the relations among various objectives.

At present, China's economic structural contradictions remain prominent. The overexpansion of total demand may further solidify structural distortions and imbalances. In addition, with the rise of inflation expectations, asset bubbles in some areas have become more serious. Under the open macro structure, China will be faced with the "hard constraints" and "sharp contrast" of asset prices.

3. Stabilizing total quantity: leveraging price-quantity tools and macroeprudential policies

In recent years, the mode of the money supply has changed a lot. From the perspective of base money, the supply of money adjusts passively to demand through the channel of funds outstanding for foreign exchange in the past and is changed to the active supply by the central bank. From the perspective of broad money, money has historically been supplied mainly through credit and funds outstanding for foreign exchange, but now, with the change of foreign exchange channels, money is more often supplied through securities investment and interbank channels. China needs to adapt to the changes in money supply mode, paying close attention to the possible impact of domestic and foreign situations on liquidity and flexibly using a combination of various monetary policy tools (both those related to quantity and to price) to keep liquidity basically stable. At the same time, monetary policy in the new era should more comprehensively include counter-cyclical adjustments of social financing activities, should promote the steady operation of the banking system, and should integrate internet financial innovation into macroprudential regulation in a timely way so as to enhance the foresight and effectiveness of financial macro-control and maintain financial stability.

4. Balancing prudent monetary policy: a call for neutrality and tightness

China must manage the total money supply, maintain reasonable growth in the scale of broad money (M2), increase the money and credit supply at an appropriate pace, expand aggregate financing for the economy by an appropriate amount, maintain reasonable and stable liquidity, and increase the proportion of direct financing, especially equity financing. Leaders should also smooth the transmission channels of monetary policy, make good use of differentiated reserves, differentiated credit, and other policies, and guide more funds to invest in underappreciated endeavors (small and micro enterprises, "agriculture, rural areas and farmers," and poor areas) so as to serve the real economy better. In the process of economic restructuring, monetary policy should be prudent and stable. Total demand should be moderately expanded, and the economy should be prevented from falling too fast in a short period. But even in such cases, it is wise to avoid injecting excessive liquidity so as to prevent the risk of leverage and asset bubbles due to an excessive supply of money.

The relationship among various objectives, such as steady growth, structural adjustment, bubble suppression, and risk prevention, needs to be coordinated. However, in reality, all parties have the same goal: a loosening of monetary policy. Once financial risks emerge, they hope that the central bank can help deal with these risks by issuing more money. Trade-offs between various objectives increase the difficulty of monetary policy operation significantly. "Stability" is multifaceted. It first applies to the task of stabilizing the total amount of monetary and credit supply, adapting to various changes in the mode of money supply in order to maintain the basic stability of liquidity. But stability also applies to the financial system as a whole, which is stabilized when the government promotes a basic balance of international payments and keeps the RMB exchange rate steady at a reasonable and balanced level, maintaining a focus on the prevention and control of asset bubbles, improving the regulatory capacity, and holding the bottom line of no systemic financial risk.

On the premise of stability, China should strive to achieve "progress" in key areas, to further improve the quality and efficiency of financial services to the real economy, to prevent being diverted out of the real economy, and to solve the imbalance between finance and the real economy. Financial reform should be deepened, the transmission channels and mechanisms of monetary policy should be eased, and financial resources should be allocated more efficiently.

5. Enhancing financial reforms and streamlining monetary policy transmission

At present, with the rapid development of the financial market and financial innovation, the role of interest rates in adjusting capital supply and demand and in impacting the behavior of economic subjects is more obvious. This means that the requirements for accelerating the transformation of the monetary policy regulation framework and further improving the interest rate transmission mechanism are raised. The price regulation and transmission efficiency of China's monetary policy need to be enhanced. In particular, the transmission to the credit market is not smooth enough. China should further promote the market-oriented reform of interest rates, should urge financial institutions to enhance their independent, reasonable pricing ability and their risk management level, should strive to cultivate market benchmark interest rates and yield curves, and should enhance the central bank's ability to regulate interest rates. The interest rate corridor should be further improved, along with the efficiency of standing lending facilities. Moreover, it is necessary to effectively give play to the role of the upper limit of the interest rate corridor, improve the RMB exchange rate formation mechanism, enhance the flexibility of the RMB rate, and keep the RMB rate stable at a reasonable and balanced level. Meanwhile, the government must further improve the macroprudential policy framework for capital flows, carry out counter-cyclical adjustments of capital flows, and prevent major currency mismatches and large-scale capital flows caused by "herd behavior" from impacting the real economy. In an open macroeconomic pattern, the role of the automatic stabilizer of the exchange rate deserves more attention. A set of additional tasks remain: strengthening macroprudential management, improving the coordination of domestic and foreign currency policies, accelerating the improvement of the RMB exchange rate formation mechanism, enhancing exchange rate flexibility, strengthening macroprudential management, and striving to guide expectations in a reasonable way.

6. Preventing and resolving financial risks effectively, pursuant to the bottom-line goal of no systemic risk

The prevention and control of financial risks must have a more prominent place in policy. Stabilizing total quantity and optimizing structure help prevent risks on a macro level. China should further improve its macroprudential policy framework, strengthening counter-cyclical liquidity management and guiding rational credit growth. It should prevent the "sick expansion" of institutions and eliminate various conditions that enable the generation and accumulation of risks. To prevent financial speculation and unreasonable leverage, investment guidance for institutions using central bank funds should be strengthened, encouraging banks to direct these funds in support of the real economy. It is important to improve the process of expectation management and to give full play to the role of the prices of basic financial assets, namely interest and exchange rates, in managing and adjusting expectations. Prices should be determined by the market to the greatest extent possible. Every effort should be made, moreover, to prevent excessive fluctuations and expectation divergence in interest and exchange rates so as to maintain the basic stability of the financial market. Since financial markets are flush with risks, systems should be established to address these risks, systems that can operate under the existing framework. In the current environment, it is more critical than ever that China further studies the reform of the financial regulation system, that it makes financial regulation more pertinent and effective, and that it optimizes and improves various institutional arrangements for financial risk prevention and treatment.

SECTION 4
Precise Industrial Policy

Industrial policy is a policy that is formulated by the state to guide the direction of national industrial development, to guide and promote the upgrading of industrial structure, to coordinate the structure of national industries, and to achieve the healthy and sustainable development of the national economy. National industrial policy is the sum of various policies by which the government intervenes in the formation and development of industry to achieve certain economic and social goals. Intervention includes planning, guidance, promotion, adjustment, protection, support, and restriction.

I. The Scope and Function of Industrial Policy

Industrial policy includes industrial organization policy, industrial structure policy, industrial technology policy, industrial layout policy, and other policies and regulations that have a significant impact on industrial development. Various industrial policies interrelate with one another and coalesce to form an organic policy system. Industrial policy functions as an important means for the state to strengthen macro-control, curb the excessive growth of fixed-asset investments, prevent the vicious expansion of some industries, promote the development of emerging industries, adjust and optimize industrial structure, improve industrial quality, enhance the international competitiveness of industries, and maintain the sustainable, rapid, and healthy development of the national economy.

Industrial policy is mainly realized by formulating national economic plans (including the mandatory plan, the guiding plan, industrial structure adjustment plans, and industrial support plans), implementing financial investment and financing, using monetary means, and carrying out project approval. Both socialist countries and capitalist countries have formulated industrial policies, but the objectives, contents, instruments, and methods of realizing industrial policy are different in different types of countries. Industrial policy in socialist countries aims to guide and promote the upgrading of industrial structure, forming new economic growth points to sustain economic development and improve living standards, and avoiding the "middle-income trap" of developing countries. As a kind of symmetrical regulation, it is mainly realized by state-owned enterprises' completion of mandatory and guiding plans, national industrial structure adjustment plans, industrial support plans, proactive fiscal policies, and project approval policies. Such policy is always characterized by the establishment of norms and the application of foresight. The content of industrial policy in capitalist countries is the balance of supply and demand, aimed at correcting the imbalance of supply and demand through government intervention in the case of economic crisis. As a kind of balance regulation, it is mainly realized through monetary policy, characterized by periodicity and lag. Therefore, the formulation and realization of industrial policy in socialist countries would be properly understood as a form of macro-control, while the formulation and realization of industrial policy in capitalist countries would be better characterized as government intervention in the economy.

Implementation of industrial policy is a necessary condition for the sustainable development of the social economy, a manifestation of the superiority of the socialist system, and an essential characteristic of the socialist market economy. This implementation is led by state-owned enterprises, guides fiscal investment and financing, and plays a critical role in the macro-economy. The government is the macroeconomic entity of the socialist market economy. It is not external to the market system but rather part of the system. The goal of its conscious industrial macro-control is not to intervene in the market economy nor to establish a planned economy but to provide a necessary link for the normal operation of the market economy, the upgrading of industrial structure, and the sustainable development of the economy.

II. The Classification and Significance of Industrial Policy

Industrial policy means can be categorized into the following four types: direct intervention support, direct intervention restriction, indirect guiding support, and indirect guiding restriction. A variety of instruments can be used to implement an industrial policy, including law, rules, regulation, public finance, tax incentives, and financial management. China is a socialist market economy country. The economic means represented by public finance, tax, money, and banking should be the main means for the implementation of China's industrial policy. The effects of industrial policy usually last a long time since they focus on medium- and long-term economic development planning and guidance. Legal means, in particular, have high authority and relative stability. Therefore, it is also very important to implement industrial policy by legal means.

1. Policy

Government departments should issue policies to encourage industrial development. An excellent example is the in-depth implementation of "Made in China 2025," which accelerated the application of big data, cloud computing, and the Internet of Things. In accordance with examples like that, China should work toward replacing traditional industrial production, management, and marketing modes with new technologies, new formats, and new models. The nation should focus on the development of intelligent manufacturing, advance the construction of a national intelligent manufacturing demonstration zone and manufacturing innovation center, implement a project of strengthening industrial development at the grassroots level, advance various special projects involving major equipment, develop advanced manufacturing industry, and help Chinese manufacturing to move toward medium- and high-end.

2. Regulation and control

Certain government departments occasionally issue policies to restrict and eliminate some industries and production capacity. For example, in February 2016, the State Council issued the Opinions on Resolving Overcapacity in the Coal Industry to Achieve Poverty Alleviation and Development, as well as the Opinions on Resolving Overcapacity in the Iron and Steel Industry to Achieve Poverty Alleviation and Development. This latter document required the industry to cut crude steel production capacity by 100-150 million tons in five years, withdraw about 500 million tons of coal production capacity in 3–5 years, and reduce and restructure about 500 million tons of coal production capacity. Subsequently, the state set up 100 billion yuan in special funds for incentives and subsidies to encourage the steel and coal industry to cut overcapacity by market-oriented means. Such interventions are not confined to the national government. Each local government, considering its own reality, formulates detailed operation plans, cuts overcapacity, and takes action according to its own internally developed road map.

3. Industry

Government departments issue policies to set some industry access thresholds and enact various industry management measures aimed at standardizing the development of the industry. For example, on March 27, 2018, the Ministry of Industry and Information Technology issued the Key Points for the Standardization of New Energy Vehicles in 2018 and the Key Points for the Standardization of Intelligent Connected Vehicles in 2018, which put forward the overall objectives for automotive materials, vehicle development, key system components for vehicles, charging infrastructure, standard system optimization, etc. The Ministry stated that international exchanges and coordination will be further accelerated to promote the internationalization of Chinese standards.

4. Economic hot spots

Government departments issue some policies in response to certain urgent economic needs, such as the Opinions on Implementation of Further Promoting the Agricultural Supply-side Structural Reform issued by the National Development and Reform Commission on March 8, 2017.

5. Industrial structural adjustment

Industrial structure adjustment is defined as the execution of changes in industrial composition. The Guiding Catalogue for Industrial Structure Adjustment, issued by the National Development and Reform Commission from time to time, is a programmatic document for China's industrial structure adjustment in different periods.

6. Industrial development sequencing

Industrial development sequencing is the basis for various sectors and regions to implement industrial policies and the guiding goal of various economic policies. Since the situation of the same industry in various fields of social reproduction is often different, different policies are needed. Therefore, the industrial development sequence should be arranged in accordance with the different fields of social reproduction. The development sequence of major industries is shown below.

(1) Industries and products in fields that focus on production, the products with strict restrictions on production, and the products for which production is stopped
(2) Industries and products in fields that focus on capital construction, and the industries and products regarding which the capital construction is stopped or strictly restricted
(3) Industries and products for which technological transformation is encouraged
(4) Products and services for which export or import is encouraged or restricted in foreign trade

III. Precise Industrial Policy in the New Era

To build a modern industrial system, there must be an industrial policy, which is a new requirement for deepening supply-side structural reform. This policy will aim to accelerate the construction of an innovative China with a modern economic system, to implement the RRS, and to realize the regional coordinated development strategy. The importance of industrial policy can be expressed in three points.

1. An important tool to promote economic development

The formulation and implementation of industrial policy is a practice in countries all over the world. Industrial policy becomes prominent in various periods of development in market economies. Although different countries use industrial policy differently and on different occasions, no economy can completely ignore industrial policy. From the response to the Great Depression to the full recovery after World War II, the boundary of American industrial policy was greatly expanded, and a large number of codes and acts related to industrial policy were passed, such as the Agricultural Adjustment Act and the National Industrial Recovery Act. After entering the 21st century, in order to maintain its position as a global innovation leader and to improve corporate competitiveness, the US made extensive use of industrial technology policies and industrial organization policies. In 2015, R&D expenditure at the federal government level alone reached $132.3 billion.

Industrial policy is an important means by which countries guide economic development. It can intervene in the process of social reproduction in a more targeted way than other economic policies. As an important means for the government to regulate the economy, the industrial policy does not only play the role of making up for market failure and flattening the economic cycle; it also promotes scientific and technological innovation and industrial structure upgrading, and it helps the economy develop in a more efficient, quality-driven, and sustainable way. Take Germany's "Industry 4.0" program as an example. As an important part of Germany's High-Tech Strategy 2020, the Industry 4.0 program integrates the research and innovation resources of government, industry, university, research, and social organizations to the greatest extent. By promoting the deep integration of manufacturing industries with information and communications technologies, the intelligent level of industry has reached a new level, acting as a catalyst for the evolution of production technology and production organization mode. The implementation of the Industry 4.0 program has not only promoted the comprehensive intelligence of Germany's national economic system but also maintained and improved Germany's existing industrial competitive advantage. It has guaranteed Germany a place in the new global scientific and technological revolution, which involves the transformation of industries.

In the background of any story of one economy catching up to and surpassing the others, there will always be the support of industrial policy. In the history of world economic development, whether Britain overtook the Netherlands or the US overtook Britain, whether Japan and Western Europe quickly completed economic reconstruction after World War II, or whether a number of developing countries achieved rapid economic development after getting rid of colonial rule, the impact of industrial policy is always apparent. Due to certain backward initial conditions, it is difficult to complete the catch-up task faced by late developing countries through spontaneous evolution. The government needs to use industrial policy to accelerate the accumulation of domestic capital and to promote the rapid expansion of key sectors and enterprises so as to establish a world-class production capacity as soon as possible.

2. An important support for China's economic development

Since the reform and opening-up, China has changed from a poor and backward country to the world's second-largest economy and its largest manufacturing country. This change remarkably happened in less than forty years. Numerous industries, including aerospace, railway, electric power, and communication, have become among the world's most competitive, people's living standards have been significantly improved, and international competitiveness has been continuously enhanced. These historical changes have all been supported by industrial policy. The effective formulation and application of industrial policy is not only a driving force behind China's national conditions but also the concentrated embodiment of the institutional superiority of China.

China is a large developing country. The realization of national modernization necessitates the guidance of industrial policy. As a developing country, China will be in the primary stage of socialism for a long time, pursuing the historical task of overtaking developed countries and building a modern socialist power. Nevertheless, China's task of accelerating the improvement of the socialist market economy system remains quite arduous. No matter what theory or practice one subscribes to, the spontaneous force of the market, unaided by policy, is insufficient to complete the two historical tasks of national modernization and market-oriented reform in a short period of time. While the role of the market must be given full play, it is also necessary to rely on an effective national strategy for guidance and organizational regulation. Industrial policy is an important tool for that.

Take the equipment manufacturing industry as an example. For a period of time, China's high-end equipment manufacturing was contained by developed countries and became a bottleneck restricting China's economic development. As a large developing socialist country, China can't achieve modernization with money and markets alone but must also have independent R&D and independent manufacturing of major technical equipment. Since 2005, China has implemented the industrial policy of revitalizing the equipment manufacturing industry and has made special plans for the development of major technical equipment and major industrial technology. The industries supported by that policy in 2005 have now reached an internationally advanced level and become "Chinese symbols" in the equipment manufacturing industry. Among their number are included dozens of categories such as nuclear power units at the level of a million KW, UHV AC/DC transmission, complete sets of large sheet cold and hot rolling equipment, large container ships, and high-speed trains. By promoting this type of progress, industrial policy has effectively improved the overall level of China's manufacturing industry.

China is a socialist country. To realize people-centered development, the guarantee of industrial policy is needed. Beneficial forms of development must be suited to the nature of the social system. Under capitalist systems, people's production and life are subject to the rule of spontaneous market forces, and economic development is completely controlled by capital. China is a socialist country, however. Economic development in a socialist state cannot simply pursue profit maximization but should reflect people-centered development thought, though focused on concepts like innovation, coordination, greenness, openness, and sharing. To implement these thoughts and ideas, it is not enough to focus on fiscal policy, monetary policy, and other aggregate policies. Structural policies must also be implemented at the meso level in order to ensure the long-term and fundamental interests of the people, which are the fundamental direction of industrial development in a socialist setting.

3. Implementing precise industrial policy

Industrial policy is the "weather vane" that points in the right direction to shape, reform, and develop industrial structures. With the aid of such an agile form of direction, industrial policy has promoted China's economic development and structural upgrading. It is undeniable that there have been some immature industrial policies in China, which brought with them many negative effects. These problems are inevitable growing pains in the process of building a modern industrial system in China. The lessons are learned, and the nation will adjust to them. If the formulation of industrial policy is divorced from specific national conditions and violates the law of economic development, it may fail to play the role of rational allocation of resources and optimization of industrial structure. It may even hinder the modernization process of a country.

Social Security Policy That Provides Basic Support

Social security policy refers to the sum of a series of strategies, decrees, measures, and regulations on social insurance, social assistance, social welfare, and social preferential treatment and resettlement formulated by the government under the guidance of some social value concept to achieve certain social goals and expectations, aiming at intervening in the life risks of individuals and groups in the life cycle and providing social security support.

I. Different Types of Social Security Policy

Due to differences in economic and social development levels, systems, and culture, social security systems look different in different places. Having been adapted from the practical experience of Western countries and the design of the social security system framework by the International Labor Organization, in combination with the basic national conditions and the practical operation of social security in China, China's social security system mainly includes the following contents.

1. Social insurance policy

The social insurance policy is a policy formulated by the government to ensure that workers can still enjoy the basic right to life when their income is interrupted, reduced, or even lost due to permanent injury or loss of the ability to work. The policy might be responsive to conditions like old age, disease, disability, childbirth, death, and unemployment. Social insurance is the basic pillar of the social security system. Social insurance policies should provide insurance to as many members of society as possible and should at least ensure that the vast majority of workers get the protection of social insurance. As a form of security, social insurance should follow the principle of universality, a principle that insists upon sharing the risks of the minority with those in the powerful majority. This feature will help Chinese leaders solve the basic living needs of workers, give play to the public welfare function of insurance, and promote social stability.

In China, social insurance policy includes five parts: maternity insurance, medical insurance, unemployment insurance, employment injury insurance, and pension insurance.

2. Social assistance policy

The social assistance policy is a social security policy formulated by the government to maintain a minimum living standard among citizens. In accordance with legal standards and procedures, the state provides citizens with social assistance (including material assistance, monetary assistance, and labor services) to meet their minimum living needs when they are unable to maintain a minimum living standard for various reasons. Social assistance is the lowest level of social security. It is an effective means to provide the most basic standard of living security for Chinese residents who have fallen into poverty. On the one hand, the implementation of social assistance aims at eliminating poverty and embodies the principle of fairness in the operation of the modern market economy; on the other hand, it also recognizes the right to survival while advancing the development of social members who would otherwise lack basic living security. Today's social assistance is different from past charity and poverty relief. It is motivated by a combination of poverty alleviation, mutual assistance, and self-help.

China's social assistance policy includes poverty alleviation, development policy, minimum living security, disaster assistance, medical assistance, legal aid, and special personnel assistance.

3. Social welfare policy

Social welfare policy is a social security policy formulated by the state to improve the national quality of life. The welfare system belongs to a higher level of social security, and its purpose is to promote the general improvement of people's well-being. In a broad sense, social welfare refers to various subsidies, public facilities, and social services provided by the state for citizens to improve their material and cultural living conditions. In a narrow sense, social welfare describes social insurance and social assistance projects adopted to solve existing social problems, reduce social pathology, and keep some citizens from falling into a vicious cycle of deterioration.

China's social welfare policy includes public welfare, labor welfare, welfare for the elderly, welfare for the disabled, welfare for children, welfare for women, and welfare for soldiers.

4. Social preferential treatment policy

The social preferential treatment policy is a special social security policy of praise and preferential treatment, which requires the state to provide funds and services to ensure a certain living standard for those picked out for legal preferential treatment according to the law. Social preferential treatment is a special social security that meets the basic needs of highly respected soldiers and their family members, as well as those whose lives or health are damaged for safeguarding national or social interests and engaging in official activities.

II. The Function of Social Security Policies

The "function" of social security policy picks out the impact and role of social security policy on society. Robert King Merton once made the distinction between explicit and implicit functions.[71] Social security policy can solve social problems, meet the needs of residents, and protect existing systems; these are its explicit functions. Social security policy is also a tool for the ruling class to achieve class rule and protect those with vested interests; this is its implicit function. At this moment in Chinese history, the positive functions of social security policy are:

1. A basic guarantee for accelerating China's economic development and social progress

The effective implementation of social security policy helps realize a social "safety net" with provisions for the elderly, medical treatment for the sick, insurance for the injured, relief for the unemployed, resettlement for the disabled, and support for those in poverty. The goals of social security policy are to ensure people's basic livelihood, relieve the worries of residents, resolve various social contradictions that may occur, and create a stable social environment for economic development. At the same time, as a means of redistribution, social security policy is the "adjuster" of income redistribution for different social groups. It realizes social fairness by ensuring people's basic living needs.

2. An important part of the socialist market economy system

A healthy socialist market economy system is an economic structure that allocates social resources based on the market mechanism. It not only calls for market entities who operate independently and bear responsibility for their own profits and losses, a unified and orderly market system, a macro-control mechanism dominated by indirect means, and a relatively complete system of laws and regulations. It also requires a sound and optimal social security system to support it. From this perspective, establishing and improving the social security system through social policies is an essential part of the socialist market economy.

3. Providing the necessary conditions for the reform of state-owned units

In China, the reform of state-owned units, including state-owned enterprises and state-owned institutions, has always been the most important part of reforming the whole system. It is undeniably related to the success or failure of that reform. As the reform of the social security system struggles to gain a foothold, and the social safety net remains imperfect, the reform of China's state-owned units, especially state-owned enterprises, is also restricted. Only by constantly improving the social security policy and perfecting the social security system can the government speed up the reform of state-owned enterprises.

III. The Principle That Social Policies Provide Basic Support

"Social policy should provide basic support" actually contains the basis for an important law of social construction and social welfare: a good social policy must be inclusive, lasting, and effective.

"Inclusive" means that the policy allows the fruits of development to benefit everyone, being oriented toward the road of common prosperity and the guarantee of a social safety net. Despite the fact that everyone has different gifts, abilities, accomplishments, and opportunities, which means that their salaries and living standards may be different, society should provide basic living security. This conviction is based not only on the principle of meeting basic living needs but also on the principle of ensuring individuals the right to survival and the right to development.

"Lasting" means that the supply level of social welfare should be commensurate with the actual development level. The government should do its best with the resources at its disposal. A party that rules for a long time should have a plan for long-term stability. It should not unrealistically make commitments of lofty social welfare in order to pander to the population, as some irresponsible political parties abroad do. There must be a recognition of the tension between the cyclical fluctuation of economic development and the sustained growth of welfare. Economic growth happens in fits and starts; in contrast, the level of welfare benefits is difficult to rein in once it has grown. Lessons can be drawn from the excessive expansion of social welfare, which other countries have difficulty supporting. These lessons will help China avoid embarking on the road of high debt, financial crisis, political dishonesty, and governmental collapse.

"Effective" means that the provision of social security and social welfare should be compatible with mechanisms that encourage "getting rich and improving life through hard work." Socialism is not egalitarianism. It is not a "big pot" that provides plenty for everyone. It is not a means of punishing diligence and rewarding laziness. A profound lesson has been learned in this regard. If a society is to be full of vitality, it must establish a social vertical flow mechanism of fair competition so that everyone has the opportunity to change their own life by virtue of their hard work, honesty, wisdom, and talent. As President of the PRC Xi Jinping said, individuals should be encouraged to work hard and become rich through diligence, and a social environment with equal rights, fair opportunities, and fair rules should be created and maintained so that everyone can have a chance to succeed through hard work.

IV. Implications of Social Policies Providing Basic Support

Social policy should provide basic support for the following four aspects: security and improvement of people's livelihoods, building a moderately prosperous society in all aspects, social harmony and stability, and the transformation of economic development.

1. Providing basic support for the security and improvement of people's livelihoods

Social policy should provide basic security in compulsory education, medical care, and retirement pension and should meet people's basic needs for survival and development. Special assistance should be provided for people with special difficulties to help them make ends meet. Support should be provided for people in urgent need of assistance to help them tide over various difficulties they encounter unexpectedly in life. "Help people in need more and do less useless work."[72]

The goal of economic development is to improve people's livelihoods, which means that social policy must be combined with economic policy. The government should study the difficulties and problems of various groups in a targeted way, establishing a social security system and effectively supporting people's livelihood security. China should strengthen the construction of the social security system in the following five ways: first, implementing the national insurance plan; second, realizing the national overall planning of endowment insurance in a timely way; third, improving the unified basic medical insurance system and serious disease insurance system for urban and rural residents; fourth, coordinating the urban and rural social assistance system even while improving the minimum living security; fifth, insisting that housing is for living in, not for speculation, and speeding up the implementation of a housing system with support for both rental and purchase, a housing system with multiple sources of supply and multiple channels of support so that all people can have a place to live.

2. Providing basic support for building a moderately prosperous society in all aspects

Building a moderately prosperous society in all aspects is a major task for China during the 13th Five-Year Plan period. China has put forward five development concepts guiding the building of a moderately prosperous society in all aspects, and the concept of sharing is one of these five. Sharing means that all social members of society can participate in the development process and share the achievements of development. Socialism with Chinese characteristics has entered a new era. The main tension in Chinese society has become the tension between the people's growing need for a better life and the reality of unbalanced and insufficient development. Sharing is one of the key ways to adjust to the unbalanced and insufficient development of society.

3. Providing basic support for social harmony and stability

The Engel coefficient of urban and rural residents in China decreased from 57.5% (urban) and 67.7% (rural) in 1978 to 29.3% (urban) and 32.2% (rural) in 2016, and people's living standards have improved. At the same time, China's social differentiation and inequality are also gradually expanding. The development of social welfare is unbalanced in many different contexts: between urban and rural areas, between different geographical regions, and between different populations or occupations. These imbalances lead to an increase and deepening of social tensions, resulting in a serious negative impact on social harmony. Given these realities, China must use the strengthening and security-providing role of social policy to harmonize and stabilize relationships between social groups, easing tension and resentment.

4. Providing basic support for the transformation of economic development

As China enters the new normal, the developing economic situation will inevitably be accompanied by new social problems. The government must not remain mired in a pure but naïve economic vision but must instead combine social policy with economic policy, consider the problems arising from economic development from a broader perspective, realize the positive security-providing role of social policy in the transformation of economic development mode, and achieve the coordinated development of the economy and people's livelihood security.

V. Implementing a More Proactive Social Policy in the New Era

A number of tasks stand between the status quo and the creation of more proactive social policies. Some of these tasks are listed below:

1. Dedicating attention to social arrangements that improve people's livelihoods

In the final analysis, the institutional superiority of socialism with Chinese characteristics should be reflected in the continuous enhancement of the country's comprehensive strength and the rapid improvement of people's livelihoods. Improving people's livelihoods involves many factors. Employment is a fundamental issue affecting individual well-being, so efforts should be made to increase jobs. Income is also associated with livelihood, which puts a premium on the growth of labor remuneration as labor productivity improves. Additional issues affecting well-being are education, social security, and poverty eradication. With respect to education, China should strive to provide education in a way that meets the people's needs. Social security should be inclusive and protective of citizens, and a more fair and sustainable social security system should be established.

When it comes to poverty eradication, the government should pay special attention to people with great difficulty.

The goal of improving social arrangements is, on the one hand, to promote things like social stability, development, and social justice, creating a favorable environment for long-term and stable economic growth by ensuring that all people have basic social and economic security and meeting people's basic needs for survival; on the other hand, it can not only reduce risk in social work by developing and releasing human potential but also directly promote the improvement of productivity.

2. Consolidating the foundation of urban and rural community construction

An important change in China's social structure is the transformation of the organizational form of social life from "unit" to "community." At present, in order to achieve both vitality and order in social life, China must invigorate the construction of grassroots communities. Chinese President Xi Jinping indicated that "the focus of social governance must fall on the urban and rural communities, and the foundation of social governance will be solid if community service and management capabilities are strong."[73] "The resources, services, and management should be put at the grassroots level as far as possible."[74] Employment is the foundation of people's livelihoods. It could hardly be any more important, then, in the grand scheme of things. As such, an employment priority strategy should be urgently implemented, the promotion of employment in the objectives of economic and social development should be prioritized, an economic and social development strategy conducive to expanding employment should be chosen, and more employment opportunities should be created.

3. Giving more play to the role of social forces

In terms of innovating social governance, the core problem China faces is the question of how to handle the relationship between government and society. Chinese President Xi Jinping pointed out that the relationship between government and society should be handled well. This means giving play to the role of social forces in the management of social affairs. Some affairs that are not suitable for the government to manage can be managed by the masses according to the law. At the same time, it is also necessary to strengthen the standardization and guidance of various social organizations.

4. Innovating social governance by conforming to the law

The approach of "believing in petition instead of law" in society is inappropriate. It increases administrative costs and makes some common problems difficult to solve for a long time. A rule-of-law approach to governance is needed, whereby the authority of the rule of law is strengthened, supervision according to law becomes the norm, and Party members and government officials gain motivation to think and act according to law. In particular, the government should provide a strong legal guarantee allowing people to live and work in peace and contentment, should improve the system that plays an important role in safeguarding the vital interests of the people, should strengthen the authoritative position of the law in resolving contradictions, and should allow the people to feel from the bottom of their hearts that their rights are protected, and their interests are safeguarded. A new approach to social governance requires new ideas. After solving the problem of food and clothing, people demand peace. Innovative social governance should be based on ensuring that people live and work in peace and contentment, in a society that is stable and orderly. If a society can't even experience peace, how can it ensure happiness?

5. Basing the provision of basic support on proactive social policy

Under the conditions of modern society, social policy aims at supporting and protecting people in need so that they can live their chosen way of life. In this way, modern social policy is not only remedial but also developmental. When looked at from this perspective, a proactive, protective social policy is characterized by remedy, timeliness, effectiveness, humanism, and development. This social policy should pay attention to the following four aspects. Firstly, the policy should be aimed at the appropriate individuals. In particular, groups facing difficulties in surviving and thriving due to economic structural adjustments and the slowdown of economic growth should be targeted. Secondly, the policy should help them effectively. The methodology is of the essence. When it comes to the difficulties in employment and survival encountered by the above groups, help should not only focus on addressing their difficulties through assistance but also on empowering them and helping them achieve self-reliance and self-improvement. Thirdly, the policy should be people-oriented. The key to assistance is to provide care, which does not mean charity. Care incorporates the perspective of others, whereas charity does not. When providing security, the government should pay attention to enhancing the reality of humanistic care. Only when the recipients feel care can they feel more happiness and experience better social and economic lives. Finally, attention should be paid to the development of social policy. China's economic transformation faces the challenge of unemployment. In addition to providing more jobs, proactive social policy should also focus on cultivating the abilities of the unemployed so that the unemployed can enhance their ability to do the job and cope with difficulties, and the structural unemployment figures can be reduced.

PART SEVEN

Building a Community with a Shared Future for Mankind alongside an Open Economy

CHAPTER FIFTEEN

Global Cooperation toward a Shared Future for Mankind

Economic globalization refers to the set of interdependent and interconnected cross-border economic activities that form an organic integrated economy on a global scale. Globalization involves foreign trade, capital flow, technology transfer, and provision of services. It is a flow of production factors, including commodities, technology, information, service, currency, talent, capital, and management experience across countries or regions. Globalization represents one of the major characteristics of the contemporary world economy and is an important trend in world economic growth. In today's world, globalization has transcended the economic dimension, expanding into a wide range of areas, such as politics, finance, social customs, ecological response, culture, science, and technology. Therefore, globalization in the new era is not merely about economic globalization but about a broader range of issues.

SECTION 1
New Trends and Features of Globalization

After the end of the Cold War, globalization has become a major engine of world economic growth that has driven global development and progress. According to the statistics of the UN, the number of people living in extreme poverty in the world fell from 1.9 billion in 1990 to 836 million in 2015, better than the expected goal of halving that number. The improved situation of those facing moderate or severe financial difficulty in the context of globalization shows that economic globalization is beneficial to the world in general. With the rapid expansion of global wealth, international cooperation has improved to an unprecedented level. In 1992, the Maastricht

Treaty was officially signed to promote the free flow of capital and establish a single European market. In 1999, Europe's single currency, the Euro, was launched. In 1995, the WTO, which governs trade in goods, services, and intellectual property, was officially established to replace the General Agreement on Tariffs and Trade (GATT). From 1995 to now, with the acceleration of cross-regional economic cooperation, the number of global free trade agreements has increased from 38 to 282.

Historically, economic globalization promotes the development of social productivity and leads to the inevitable result of scientific and technological progress. It does so much more effectively than plans created by certain individuals or countries. Globalization has boosted world economic growth and promoted the flow of commodities and capital, along with the progress of technology, development, the transmission of ideas and values, and people-to-people exchanges. However, it is evident that economic globalization is a double-edged sword. At a time when the world economy is in a downturn, the global economy faces significant challenges to growth, which highlight the tensions between growth and distribution, between capital and labor, and between efficiency and equity. Under such circumstances, both developed and developing countries will experience significant pressure.

Globalization in the new era has seen some new trends and features. The voice of anti-globalization and the isolationist approach—a direct competitor to globalization—reflect the inadequacy of a simplistic approach to economic globalization. This situation deserves much attention and reflection.

I. New Trends in Globalization and Global Trade

Global trade and economic development have been hard hit by the spread of the COVID-19 pandemic since the end of 2019. To effectively cope with the impact of the pandemic on their own economies, countries around the world have generally taken measures of lockdown and strict restrictions on the international movement of people and goods. Objectively, this has had a strong impact on international trade and exchange, leading to a significant slowdown in economic globalization. A parallel development has been the growth of trade protectionism. Multilateral international trade cooperation under the WTO framework is facing severe challenges, and unilateral and regional economic cooperation seems to be taking its place.

Holding high the banner of trade protectionism with the slogan "America First," former US President Donald Trump has become a leading figure in this new wave of anti-globalization. According to the 2017 US trade agenda announced by the Office of the US Trade Representative (USTR), the US will no longer strictly follow WTO rules but will instead use trade policy to defend its sovereignty, as evidenced by the fact that the "strict implementation of the US trade law" was named the top priority among the four priorities of the US government. As the world's largest economy, the US has adopted more than 1,200 trade protection measures from 2009 to 2017, accounting for 15.4 % of the world's total of 7,833. This trend became increasingly obvious after Trump took office. In the first half of 2017 alone, 65 trade protection measures were taken by the Trump administration. According to a WTO statistical report, 309 trade protection measures took place around the world in the first half of 2017, of which 256 were taken by G20 members. Trade protectionism has brought uncertainty to the smooth development of globalization.

II. A Globalization Trend that Anti-globalization Cannot Quell

As stated above, there is a rising tide of anti-globalization in the West, from Brexit to Trump's ascendency to the rise of the French right-wing party. These developments highlight the intensified internal contradictions experienced by Western developed countries and the ensuing spillover effects against the backdrop of sluggish world economic growth. A good understanding of anti-globalization is of great significance to anyone who wants to enhance China's international status and global governance capabilities by pursuing globalization, drawing on its advantages while steering clear of its disadvantages.

As an inevitable trend in the development of human society, globalization points to the direction the world will be headed for. There is nothing wrong with globalization itself. The root cause of anti-globalization is the ineffectiveness of the existing global governance mechanism, not globalism as such. The current rules-based international system is unable to effectively manage global affairs or address global challenges, resulting in the continuous accumulation of global issues and an unbalanced world order. The evolution of globalization is accompanied by an increasingly obvious power shift, deepened interdependence between countries, and a growing number of global challenges. Many new issues and situations need to be addressed through new methods and ideas. However, the existing global governance system and its corresponding institutional arrangements are seriously outdated. If old approaches to international relations are used to address new issues of global governance, the outcome is more often than not ineffective. It is a Band Aid on a gaping wound.

In his 2017 keynote speech at the World Economic Forum in Davos, Switzerland, Chinese President Xi Jinping said, "Economic globalization has become the Pandora's Box in the eyes of many, but it could not be blamed for every problem. We need to adapt to and guide economic globalization and cushion its negative impact so as to deliver its benefits to all." Globalization is the overriding trend, but anti-globalization is a phenomenon that coexists alongside globalization and challenges it. It is impossible to tackle emerging challenges such as terrorism, climate change, the energy crisis, and cybersecurity simply by relying on any individual country. The key to addressing these challenges is good leadership, the ability to turn disadvantages into advantages, an improved global governance system, and the establishment of a new type of international relations based on win-win cooperation.

Amid the rising tide of anti-globalization, globalization is experiencing some adjustments, but its main direction remains unchanged. From a trade perspective alone, despite a great deal of uncertainty in the global economic environment between the second half of 2016 to the first half of 2017, anti-globalization was not as acute as previously predicted. Globalization forged ahead against the headwind. In this period, macroeconomic affairs on a global level, as well as trade situations, continued to improve, with a restoration of imports and exports in major economies and a recovery in global trade volume. Although some countries suffered a decline in exports and investments, the situation of global trade gradually improved, thanks to the consolidation and reinforcement of globalization and the curbs on anti-globalization. However, various economies are now faced with severe challenges due to the current trade barriers and protectionism worldwide. The growing number of global trade protection measures and trade disputes all suggest that anti-globalization retains a great deal of momentum.

Opposition to globalization has indeed posed a challenge to existing globalist systems, but it also brings new opportunities for the international community to reshape rules and standards. From an optimistic perspective, anti-globalization reflects the fact that there are problems with some of the current rules and institutions. For example, the fruitful results of globalization have not been distributed appropriately; benefits are mostly shared among developed countries, while underdeveloped countries and their citizens have no access to such benefits. Consequently, the wealth gap continues to widen, and one adverse impact of globalization expands. Anti-globalization signals the objective requirement for rule adjustment and reshaping that is embedded In economic development. It can be a strong force that drives the world into a new framework for cooperation. Anti-globalization has also brought opportunities for a new round of development and growth. It is a driving force behind a dynamic response to globalization, which may then transform into "re-globalization" and ultimately into a "new globalization."

The trend of globalization is also affected by political, cultural, and ethnic factors, as well as many other factors. Cross-border population mobility, immigration issues, and nationalism are among the reasons for the increased opposition to globalization. Former United Kingdom (UK) Prime Minister Theresa May said that a hard Brexit is designed to better serve the globalization of Britain and to seek a new solution to the current predicament. What anti-globalists really oppose is not globalization itself, but a series of problems brought about by globalization. When a fast-growing economy hits a bottleneck, and the economic slowdown dampens momentum, countries often sour on the sustained expansion of globalization. Since the trend of economic globalization is irreversible, problems associated with globalization must be handled properly so as to allow the world to share the development dividend and truly achieve globalization.

III. Addressing Problems Concerning the Future of Globalization

At the present time, the world economy has been mired in a long-term downturn. The wealth gap and the North-South gap have become increasingly obvious, which results in the emergence of ideas and developments that threaten globalization. As of now, no effective solutions are apparent to the following three major tensions in the economic field—at least no solutions that clearly address the core issues involved.

First of all, global growth momentum is not sufficient to sustain world economic growth. The world economy is now growing at its slowest speed in seven years, and global trade growth continues to be lower than economic growth. Short-term incentives turn out to be less effective than long-term incentives, and in-depth structural reform is still underway. The world economy is being transformed. Unfortunately, the traditional economic growth engine has become less powerful. New technologies, such as AI and 3D printing, continue to emerge, but until new sources of growth are found, the world economy will not be able to blaze a trail forward.

Second, global economic governance needs to improve its efficiency in adapting to changes in the world economy. Emerging markets and developing countries (such as China, India, and Brazil) have contributed up to 80% of global economic growth. In the past few decades, the composition of international economic power has evolved profoundly, but the global governance system is not representative and inclusive enough to reflect the new pattern. Although the global industrial layout keeps adjusting, and new industrial, value, and supply chains are taking shape, trade and investment rules fail to keep up with the new situation since closed mechanisms and fragmented rules are in place. The global financial market needs to enhance its capacity to resist risks, but the global financial governance mechanism cannot yet adapt to the new requirements. It is exceptionally hard to solve such problems in an international financial market that has experienced frequent turmoil and a series of asset bubbles.

Third, unbalanced global development makes it difficult to meet people's expectations for a better life. The ongoing Fourth Industrial Revolution will have an extremely wide and profound impact on the global political and economic landscape. For instance, inequality will be exacerbated. In particular, the gap between capital return and labor return may widen. The wealthiest 1% of the world's population will possess more wealth than the remaining 99%. Inequality of income distribution and imbalance of development space are concerning. More than 700 million people in the world still live in extreme poverty. For many families, having a warm home, enough food, and a stable job is still a pipe dream. Unbalanced global development is the biggest challenge facing the world and a major cause of social unrest in some countries.

The above three examples show that there is an urgent need to solve certain problems raised by existing trends of economic growth, governance, and development. Although the current waves of the rising tide of anti-globalization are not as high as predicted, this wave will have a worse impact on world economic development compared to other possible approaches to de-globalization and re-globalization. In the face of these developments, globalization has to make some adjustments, although it will not cease to be dominant. Going forward, a new and improved type of globalization should better promote mutually beneficial cooperation, thereby reshaping global political, economic, and commercial structures.

There are steps that must be taken to embrace this new globalization:

First, a dynamic growth model must be created, driven by innovation. The fundamental challenge to the world economy is a shortage of growth momentum. Innovation is the primary driving force of development. Compared with the previous rounds of the industrial revolution, the Fourth Industrial Revolution is advancing at an exponential rather than a linear rate. Only by making bold changes and innovations can solutions be found to tackle the bottleneck of global economic growth and development. At the G20 Hangzhou Summit, leaders reached a consensus on the following steps:

[The G20 agrees to] take innovation as a key driver and foster new driving forces of growth for both individual countries and the global economy. We should develop a new development philosophy and rise above the debate about whether there should be more fiscal stimulus or more monetary easing. We should adopt a multipronged approach to address both the symptoms and the underlying problems. We should adopt new policy instruments and advance structural reform to create more space for growth and sustain its momentum. We should develop new growth models and seize opportunities presented by the new round of industrial revolution and digital economy. We should meet the challenges of climate change and the aging population. We should address the negative impact of IT application and automation on jobs. When cultivating new industries and new forms models of business models, we should create new jobs and restore confidence and hope to our people.[75]

Second, an open and interconnected cooperation model must be created, a model that can deliver win-win results. Everyone on the globe now lives in a community with a shared future. We depend on each other, and our interests are highly integrated. Every country has the right to develop, but it needs to consider its own interests at a broader level and never harm the interests of other countries. The people of the world must show tremendous commitment to developing an open global economy to share opportunities and interests and to achieve mutual benefit. Significant efforts should be made to develop global connectivity so as to enable differing countries to achieve interconnected growth and common prosperity. Global free trade and investment must be grown by promoting trade/investment liberalization and facilitation in a business-friendly environment and by clearly opposing protectionism.

Third, it is important to advance with the times and create an equitable and rational governance model. The international community has an increasingly urgent need for reform of the global economic governance system. As long as it adapts to the new requirements of the international economic landscape, the global governance system will likely provide a strong guarantee for the global economy. All countries, big or small, strong or weak, rich or poor, are equal members of the international community, and they should be allowed to participate in decision-making, enjoy rights and fulfill obligations on an equal footing. The global community must increase the representation and strengthen the voice of emerging market countries and developing countries; it must champion multilateralism and safeguard the authority and effectiveness of multilateral institutions; it must live up to its commitments and follow the rules instead of making whatever choices seem advantageous at the time.

Fourth, a fair, inclusive, and balanced development model that benefits all must be created. The purpose of development is to benefit the people. In order to promote more balanced development and create equal opportunities to ensure benefits are shared by all, improved concepts and models are needed, concepts and models that will achieve development in a fairer, more effective, and more coordinated manner. An "innovative, dynamic, interconnected, and inclusive world economy" is needed to breathe new life into globalization. This advance will help the world create a social atmosphere in which diligence and entrepreneurship are encouraged, and everyone's labor is respected. It will help the world address issues such as poverty, unemployment, and the income gap, taking care of the disadvantaged in order to promote social equity and justice. It will help the world protect the environment and promote the coordinated development of the economy, society, and environment, achieving harmony between human and nature and between human and society. It is important to implement the UN 2030 Agenda for Sustainable Development in order to pursue balanced development on a global scale.

SECTION 2

A New Type of International Relations with Mutually Beneficial Economic and Trade Ties

In the face of the new trends and problems in globalization, we must work toward a new type of international relations featuring mutual respect, fairness, justice, and win-win cooperation. In economic and trade fields, China will build mutually beneficial economic and trade relations to promote the sustained and sound development of the world economy.

I. The Implications and Background of a New Type of International Relations

1. The implications of a new type of international relations

Mutual respect is the basis for building a new type of international relations. Mutual respect means respecting the rights of the people of all countries to choose their own development path. All countries, big or small, rich or poor, strong or weak, advanced or backward, should be committed to mutual respect and equal consultation on the basis of the Five Principles of Peaceful Coexistence and should resolutely reject the traditional law of the jungle. A new type of international relations emphasizes that all countries in the world are equal and resolutely opposes the choices of the big, the strong, and the rich to bully the small, the weak, and the poor. Concerning the principle of sovereignty, the sovereignty and territorial integrity of another country should be inviolable. No country should intervene in the domestic affairs of other countries; on the contrary, the right of all countries to independently choose their own social system and development path should be defended, and respect should be shown to each country's approach to promoting economic and social development and improving people's lives. In major power relations, a premium should be placed on avoiding conflicts while promoting mutual respect and mutual benefit; in the relations between major powers and small countries, each party should treat one another as equals, upholding justice while pursuing shared interests. China's actions are consistent with its words, so it has received extensive appreciation from people around the world. Mutual respect guarantees peace and prosperity in the world and lays the foundation for building a new type of international relations.

Fairness and justice provide a platform on which to build this new type of international relations. Democracy should be championed in international relations, and hegemonism and power politics should be opposed. Just nations should boycott the practice of rich countries exploiting poor countries. They should follow the principle of achieving shared growth through discussion and collaboration in engaging in global governance, transforming the irrational aspects of the international economic and political system, and solving global issues in accordance with principles of fairness and justice. The world situation after the end of the Cold War is still embroiled in various kinds of tension and conflict, with the persistence of hegemonism and power politics. After all, some Western countries still believe in the Western superiority theory and European centralism and disregard international fairness and justice. Since the global financial crisis, the developed countries in Europe and the Americas, long-time leaders of global development, have encountered one crisis after another. In response, they have taken measures in international politics, the economy, military preparedness, and other fields to shift their burdens onto others, driven by their native capitalist ideology. Fueled by globalization, issues such as unbalanced development, inadequate governance, the digital divide, and the wealth gap have become increasingly acute, making the international and domestic situations of small and weak countries gradually worse. Against this backdrop, China proposes the initiative to build a new type of international relations. In addition to opposing other countries' engagement in power politics and hegemonism, China will never seek hegemony or expansion, no matter how strong it has become.

Win-win cooperation between a wide variety of countries is the goal of building a new type of international relations. Based on this core concept, cooperation must be deepened with other countries. The goal should be to uphold justice while pursuing shared interests, jointly meet challenges, share opportunities, develop global partnerships, and advocate state-to-state relations based on partnerships instead of alliances. The leaders of nations must address global issues and achieve common development and prosperity through international cooperation. In the context of globalization, the interests of all countries in the world are increasingly integrated. Despite the differences in the political systems, economic development levels, and cultural beliefs, win-win cooperation can be expanded based on what we all have in common. Neither opposition, pressure, nor confrontation are solutions to global challenges.

To foster a new type of international relations featuring win-win cooperation, nations must be guided by the concept of building a community with a shared future for mankind. They must implement the idea of mutually beneficial cooperation in all aspects of foreign cooperation, including politics, economy, security, culture, and ecology. As such, it is clearly China's message that nations should build partnerships in which countries treat each other as equals, engaging in mutual consultation and showing mutual understanding; that they foster a security paradigm featuring fairness, justice, joint contribution, and shared benefits; that they promote open, innovative, and inclusive development that benefits all; that they increase inter-civilization exchanges to promote harmony, inclusiveness, and respect for differences; and that they build an ecosystem that puts Mother Nature and green development first.

Obviously, the new type of international relations envisioned here transcends the model of international relations led by Western countries. Modern models of international relations have been built under the leadership of Western countries, and these models reflect the interests of these countries as well as their narrow-minded values and international behavior patterns. Driven by such ideas as "the law of the jungle," "the strong bullying the weak," and "winner takes all," strength, alliance, and war have become tools for them to implement national policies. This means countenancing all kinds of unfair and unjust acts, such as aggression and expansion, colonization and plunder, and the bullying of the weak by the strong. Such acts of aggression have become basic components of the international relations model for many decades now. One of its inevitable results is escalating international conflicts and even large-scale international wars, including two World Wars and the Cold War. Faced with profound changes in the international situation and the objective demand for solidarity, all countries should jointly promote the establishment of a new type of international relations featuring win-win cooperation, and people all over the world should work together to defend world peace and promote common development.

2. The background to proposing a new type of international relations

Building a new type of international relations is in line with the times. The world is undergoing major developments, transformation, and adjustment. The trends of global multi-polarity, economic globalization, IT application, and cultural diversity are surging forward, and changes in the global governance system and the international order are accelerating. And yet, as a world, we face growing uncertainties and destabilizing factors. Global economic growth lacks energy; the gap between rich and poor continues to widen; certain regions are regularly embroiled in conflict; non-traditional security threats like terrorism, cybersecurity, major infectious diseases, and climate change continue to spread. As human beings, we have many common challenges to face. It has been demonstrated that the global expansion of unilateralism and a zero-sum game, even if it can bring about temporary benefits, cannot possibly resist the "periodic law" of historical rise and fall. No country can address the many challenges facing mankind on its own; no country can afford to retreat into self-isolation.

China's advocacy for building a new type of international relations is also based on its own experience, tradition, strength, and need. The advocacy reflects an ideology of "harmony" and "pursuing a just cause for the common good," a traditional culture in which "the strong does not oppress the weak and the rich do not bully the poor," and the constantly rising ability China has to shape the international system. After the Opium War of 1840, China became a semi-colonial and semi-feudal society and was plunged into the darkness of domestic turmoil and foreign aggression. Its people, ravaged by war, saw their homeland torn apart. They lived in poverty and despair.

Unlike many countries that have grown stronger by colonization and military expansion over the centuries, China has reached where it is today by wholly peaceful means. The pacific nature of China's rise is unprecedented in the history of human development. It is epoch-making. Once the Chinese nation makes the leap from merely standing to growing to its full stature and exerting its full influence, it will be more convincing and credible when it proposes a new type of international relations, when it advocates democracy in international relations, when it insists on the equality of all countries, big or small, strong or weak, rich or poor, when it advocates for equal treatment and consultation regardless of race and nationality to prevent the historical tragedy caused by the law of the jungle. The 19th National Congress of the CPC explicitly states that China will never seek hegemony or engage in expansion, no matter what stage of development it reaches. Promoting the construction of a new approach to international relations is not only the embodiment of China's role as a great power and its sense of responsibility in international affairs but also in line with China's fundamental interests and long-term development interests.

Building a new type of international relations is the mission of the CPC. In the past, the globalization process led by developed countries and the West has made great achievements in promoting industrial and technological innovation and in shaping the "civilization highlands" dominated by Western countries. However, it has also brought about an ideological trend of "reverse globalization." This trend is driven by a mixture of nationalism, extremism, and the like, along with the serious imbalance in benefit distribution between countries and social classes in this process. The pursuit of peace and prosperity around the world has suffered a setback. What is wrong with the world and what should be done? This is a commonly voiced question in the international community. The CPC has made explicit its mission in the report to the 19th National Congress, stating, "The CPC strives for both the well-being of the Chinese people and human progress. To make new and greater contributions for mankind is our Party's abiding mission." This declaration highlights the Party's historical consciousness, global vision, and concern for the world. The approach the CPC takes distinguishes it from other political parties and mirrors its international image.

International and domestic development offers a greater opportunity to build a new type of international relations. Globally, peace and development remain primary objectives for this era. They remain, moreover, irreversible trends. Countries are becoming increasingly interconnected and interdependent, and relative international forces are becoming more balanced. Adhering to the path of peaceful development and building a community with a shared future for mankind transcends the differences of countries, parties, and institutions. This is reflected in the universal aspirations of the international majority since peaceful development serves the common interests of the international community. Domestically, as the world's second-largest economy, China continuously serves as a powerhouse in world economic growth, with a contribution rate of about 30%. It is making its way toward the central stage of the world, enjoying a more prestigious international status and being able to make greater contributions. Chinese planning can provide a new modernization path for developing countries, Chinese solutions, a route to exploring better social systems, and Chinese wisdom a way to address the challenges facing mankind.

3. Basic thoughts on fostering a new type of international relations

To build a new type of international relations with mutually beneficial cooperation at the core, it is necessary to uphold the fine traditions of Chinese diplomacy, conform to the development trends of the times, rethink the traditional theory of international relations, and follow the purposes and principles of the UN Charter on sovereign equality, the peaceful settlement of international disputes, and the promotion of international cooperation. Below are some basic thoughts on how to foster this cooperation.

Establishing a community with a shared future is the common goal of handling international relations. Over the last 500 years, colonialism, imperialism, and hegemonism invariably led to confrontation and division, which has taken a heavy toll on human society. In building a new type of international relations featuring win-win cooperation, Chinese leadership has looked closely into the direction of human society based on insights into the international situation and world developmental trends. Working on this preliminary investigation, China has put forward an overall plan and general path in five aspects:

> Build partnerships in which countries treat each other as equals, engage in mutual consultation, and show mutual understanding; create a security architecture featuring fairness, justice, joint contribution, and shared benefits; promote open, innovative, and inclusive development that benefits all; increase inter-civilization exchanges to promote harmony, inclusiveness, and respect for differences; and build an ecosystem that puts mother nature and green development first.[76]

Such practices demonstrate China's intentions and its sense of responsibility as a big power to share with other countries a common destiny and open up new prospects for the international community to achieve lasting peace and common prosperity.

Common interests should be considered an important basis for handling international relations. In today's world, countries are interconnected and interdependent, and their interests are profoundly intertwined. The practical need and political will to create a peaceful and stable environment and to seek common development and prosperity become more critical as each year passes. In building a new type of international relations featuring win-win cooperation, the Chinese leadership has adopted a holistic perspective from which to approach international relations, calling upon every country to safeguard and promote the common interests of mankind while protecting its own national interests. The Chinese leaders emphasized that "the interests to be considered should be the interests of all"[77] and advocated that all countries should respect each other and treat each other as equals with the basic orientation of seeking common ground while reserving differences. Moreover, they recommended countries constantly consolidate and expand common interests and achieve peaceful and harmonious coexistence among nations with different social systems, different development paths, and different cultural traditions. Such practices grasp the pulse of the times and lay a solid foundation for the long-term, stable, and sound development of international relations.

We should regard win-win, mutually beneficial situations as the basic paradigm for handling international relations. In the Western theory of international relations, the law of the jungle is regarded as the standard, and all-or-nothing, winner-takes-all competition is taken for granted. In fostering a new type of international relations featuring win-win cooperation, the Chinese leadership has rid itself of the old concepts of zero-sum games and a Cold War mentality. They believe that "a single flower does not make a spring," and they advocate that all should respect the social system and development road independently chosen by each country in international relations, adhering to an approach to justice and interests that take into account the interests of all parties while protecting one's own. Such an approach will enhance common growth during self-development and set a standard for the international community to pursue win-win or all-win results. Such practices conform to the general expectations of the international community and provide new ideas to bring about a more just and equitable international order.

Cooperation must be the main approach used to handle international relations. In the context of the major developments, transformations, and adjustments being experienced by the international community, there are unprecedented opportunities. These opportunities are brought about by a reduced risk in rivalries between great powers and by the rapid advancement of S&T and the burgeoning of regional cooperation. Meanwhile, there are increasing global challenges, including terrorism, climate change, energy security, and so on. Not a single country can maintain security with its own efforts. Nor can it find a way out via the beggar-thy-neighbor strategy or by pursuing alliances that make confrontations with other nations more likely. The best choice for dealing with inter-state relations is to stick together through thick and thin, sharing opportunities and rising up to challenges together. In building a new type of international relations featuring mutually beneficial cooperation, the Chinese leadership has viewed international relations from the strategic height of world peace and development; it has advocated that nations replace opposition and confrontation with dialogue and cooperation; it has called upon all nations to effectively cope with the increasing global challenges, working together to resolve major issues related to world development through the continuous expansion of mutually beneficial cooperation. Such practices point out the correct path for the development of international relations in the present situation and inject a strong impetus for the international community to expand exchanges and cooperation and to avoid conflicts.

II. Building Mutually Beneficial Economic and Trade Ties

The establishment of mutually beneficial economic and trade ties is an important part of fostering a new type of international relations. China has consistently pursued the principle of mutual benefit in the process of opening up to the outside world. It now has become the largest trading nation and the second-largest economy in the world. But that position is precarious, and it comes with responsibilities. The pursuit of win-win cooperation is not simply about obtaining the benefits of division of labor based on comparative advantage; more importantly, it is about taking into account not only China's interests but also the interests of other nations. Comparative advantages should undeniably be capitalized on in the task of integrating into the global division of labor system, but more care should be taken to mitigate any possible adverse impacts of free trade on other countries. While utilizing industry and trade development as a vehicle to serve national interests, China should leave room for industrial development and job creation in other countries, thus promoting mutually beneficial competition and cooperation. This principle must be followed in Chinese participation in the global division of labor and trade, as the nation establishes genuine interdependence with other nations under the division of labor system of the global value chain. Developing economic and trade ties should adhere to base on practical cooperation and mutual benefit with all countries, no matter how big or small, rich or poor. Mutual benefits can be established in a number of contexts.

1. Mutually beneficial ties between China and developed countries

China enjoys steady growth in its trade with developed countries and enjoys complementary advantages as well as reciprocity and mutual benefit. The European Union (EU) is one of China's major economic and trade partners. Since the official establishment of diplomatic relations between China and the European Community (the predecessor of the EU in May 1975, bilateral relations have undergone different stages of exploration, integration, and deepening understanding and have generally been making good progress. In recent years, China's trade with the EU has entered a new stage featuring mutual reliance and the deep integration of interests. With the implementation of its "going global" strategy, China has also made certain progress in investing more in EU members. In addition to traditional fields such as trade, shipping, and banking, industrial investment led by corporate champions like Huawei, ZTE, TCL, and Haier has grown. With the ever-closer economic and trade exchanges between the two sides, Sino-European trade friction also increases year by year.

Over the past few years, the EU has introduced a series of trade protection measures, including technical trade barriers, anti-dumping, and special safeguard clauses, unveiling an increasing tendency toward trade protectionism. There has, moreover, been no significant progress in two bottlenecks, the EU arms embargo against China and its recognition of China's market economy status. However, it should be noted that the heart of the China-EU economic and trade partnership is still healthy and sound. China's overall income from economic and trade cooperation with Europe is higher than that obtained from the US or Japan. It is quite natural and inevitable to encounter challenges and contradictions at a time when bilateral cooperation in the economic and trade sectors has been increasingly expanded, intensified, and deepened. Therefore, in the future, China should continue to attach great importance to diplomatic strategy toward Europe in the fields of economics and trade, should carry out economic and trade cooperation with European countries in an active and pragmatic manner, and should deepen understanding on the basis of existing cooperative mechanisms, in order to achieve the goal of mutual benefit and win-win results.

Mutual benefit is at the heart of Sino-US economic and trade ties, as well. As the largest developing country and the largest developed country in the world, respectively, China and the US are highly complementary in their natural endowments, human resources, markets, capital, technology, and so on. The stable and sound development of such a partnership is in the common interests of both sides. China is at the lower end of the global value chain. It is the world's biggest manufacturer, with its output value accounting for 25% of the global total. Among the 500 major types of industrial products, China ranks first worldwide in terms of output in 220 categories. Moreover, it has the largest, most comprehensive, and lowest-cost labor force. The US is, in contrast, at the higher end of the global value chain. It leads the world in technology and boasts a highly developed and comprehensive service sector whose output value accounted for 79.5% of GDP in 2016. Trade between China and the US has a solid development base. China exports a large variety of consumer goods to meet the demands of American consumers while satisfying its own need for development by constantly expanding US imports of electronic, aerospace, biological, medical, agricultural products, and service trade items. In the long run, the Sino-US trade cooperation is promising.

Due to the differences in development level, industrial structure, resources, and comparative advantages, however, trade deficits and small frictions will inevitably occur in trade between the two economies. Both China and the US have the responsibility and obligation to gradually eliminate the trade deficit and optimize the trade structure between them. If good fortune prevails, the decision-makers of Beijing and Washington will conduct full and patient consultations, properly handle differences with wisdom and courage, and dispel the cloud of uncertainty for their economic and trade partnership, creating a new situation of considerable mutual benefit.

China and Japan are adjacent to each other, and this is an advantage in bilateral trade. Sino-Japanese trade promotes continuous cooperation and progress in the industry while spurring the development of regional economic comparative advantages and cooperation in East Asia. China's trade and investment cooperation with developed countries such as Canada, Australia, Switzerland, and New Zealand also maintain a good momentum of development.

2. Mutually beneficial ties between China and emerging markets/developing countries

China's trade with emerging economies and developing countries is experiencing robust growth and has huge development potential. With the comprehensive implementation of the China-ASEAN Free Trade Agreement in 2010, tariffs have been canceled for 90% of commodities, vigorously promoting the rapid growth of bilateral trade between China and ASEAN. Trade between China and South Korea is growing at a steady pace. Bilateral investment and economic cooperation also present appealing prospects. China's trade with the other BRICS countries has enjoyed rapid growth in recent years, which promotes the development of member countries' particular industrial strengths and shows the broad development prospects of emerging markets. In recent years, China has seen relatively fast growth in its trade with other developing countries, further development of trade with its historical trading partners in the Arab world, broadening areas of economic and trade cooperation with Latin American countries, and progress in bilateral trade with African countries. In all of these cases, these trade arrangements give full play to the complementary advantages of the two sides' resources and economic structures.

Commodity trade with developing countries, as an important aspect of South-South cooperation, has become an integral part of China's all-around opening-up strategy. Its scale has expanded rapidly, forming a situation ideal for economic cooperation. In the 1950s, China mainly traded with the Soviet Union and Eastern European countries. Since the 1960s, it has opened up to the group of industrialized countries. By the end of the 1980s, trade with developed countries accounted for about 90% of its total trade volume, whereas trade with developing countries measured less than 10%. In order to diversify foreign trade risks and expand the foreign trade market, the country has implemented the strategy of "market diversification" in foreign trade since the 1980s and received undeniable results. With the gradual increase of their economic development levels and capacity in mutual supply and demand, China and developing countries will gradually cement the trade ties between them.

3. Mutually beneficial bilateral and regional ties

China attaches great importance to bilateral and regional economic and trade cooperation. Currently, most countries and regions in the world have signed agreements on bilateral trade or economic cooperation with China. China has established and maintains high-level economic dialogue mechanisms with the US, Europe, Japan, Great Britain, Russia, and various other major economies. China proactively participates in the Asia-Pacific Economic Cooperation (APEC), ASEAN, the China-Japan-South Korea (10+3) Leaders Meetings, the East Asia Summit, the Forum on China-Africa Cooperation, the Greater Mekong Subregion Economic Cooperation Committee, the Central Asia Regional Economic Cooperation Committee, the Greater Tumen Initiative, and other regional and sub-regional economic cooperation mechanisms. China adheres to the principle of "good neighborly friendship and partnership" in establishing and developing various forms of cross-border economic and trade cooperation.

China takes the initiative to participate in and promote regional economic integration. As of 2017, China has signed 16 free trade agreements with 24 countries and regions on four continents, including Asia, Oceania, America, and Europe. The trade and investment amount between China and its free trade partners accounted for 25%, 51%, and 67% of China's trade in goods, trade in services, and two-way investment, respectively. And some free trade agreement talks are also underway. China has actively participated in and promoted the WTO's Doha Round, which strive to safeguard the authority of the multilateral trading system. China stresses that the negotiations should be conducive to the implementation of the principle of fairness and justice in the multilateral trading system and reflects the goal of the Doha Round as a development round. In promoting the Doha Round, China repeatedly expressed its wish to make constructive contributions suited to its level of development.

When it comes to settling disputes with its trading partners, China gives consideration to the interests of all parties and seeks common ground while putting aside differences. Since China's entry into the WTO, as its imports and exports have continually grown, the number of trade disputes and frictions between China and its trading partners has increased. These cases have mainly involved products like textiles, shoes, tires, car parts and components, and steel and chemical products. They have also covered issues like intellectual property rights, trade balance, fair trade, food safety, environmental protection, and other areas of concern. China has always preferred dialogue to confrontation and cooperation to pressure. When possible, Chinese leaders choose to settle disputes between trading partners through consultation and negotiation. China commits to give consideration to and balance the interests of all parties, settling disputes through dialogue, consultation, and negotiation. Throughout this process, it utilizes bilateral and multilateral channels and follows the rules and framework of the WTO. In recent years, China has adopted various measures to further open up its market, protect intellectual property rights, promote trade balance, reform the exchange rate formation mechanism of the RMB, and standardize the operational order of imports and exports. These and other related actions fully take into account the concerns of its trading partners. When consultations fail to settle a dispute, China appropriately handles the issue with its trading partners through the WTO dispute settlement mechanism in order to maintain the stability of the multilateral trading system.

In May 2017, President Xi announced at the Belt and Road Forum for International Cooperation that China would hold the China International Import Expo in 2018. Hosting the Expo is an important step the country is taking to firmly support free trade and economic globalization and to take the initiative in opening its market to the world. It helps promote cooperation by all countries in forming and maintaining exchanges, it helps enhance global trade and world economic growth, and it helps advance the development of an open world economy.

SECTION 3
Building a Community with a Shared Future for Mankind

The establishment of a community with a shared future for mankind, alongside a new type of international relations, is a key component of Xi Jinping Thought on Socialism with Chinese Characteristics for a New Era and also an important ideological and theoretical contribution to contemporary China is making to the world. The community with a shared future for mankind is an ideological foundation for fostering a new type of international relations, a type that sees win-win cooperation as its main feature, and a type that takes community building as its essential role. At present, the concept of building a community of common destiny proposed by President Xi has gained widespread attention and a positive response from the international community. This proposal has become a distinctive banner behind which China can march as a global leader, shaping the direction of human civilization and the transformation of global economic governance.

I. The Implications of Building a Community with a Shared Future for Mankind

Since the 18th National Congress of the CPC, President Xi has expounded upon the concept of a community with a shared future for mankind on many diplomatic occasions, showcasing China's image as a responsible power and delivering China's hope of pursuing peaceful development. Promoting the establishment of such a community is now and will continue to be the highest goal and ideal of a Chinese nation that strives to improve global governance far into the future. It is vital to China's efforts to create a favorable external environment for the realization of the Chinese Dream by actively participating in global governance, safeguarding world peace, and promoting sustainable development. It has transcended the traditional Western international relations theory and marked a major achievement: the innovation of a theory of great power diplomacy with Chinese characteristics.

1. The historical and contemporary rationale behind building a community with a shared future for mankind

We all live in the same "global village." A global consensus has formed that countries with different civilizations, different religious beliefs, different social systems, and different development levels can nevertheless form an interdependent community. The concept of a community with a shared future for mankind arose against the background of globalization and directly followed a series of events such as the Asian financial crisis in 1997, the September 11 Attacks in 2001, the Global Financial Crisis in 2008, and the outbreak of the Ebola virus in West African countries in 2014. Through the experience of responding to these disasters and the shockwaves that rippled out after the disasters, the world has gained a deeper understanding of the interdependence of countries different in regimes, cultures, and locations.

In the context of globalization, a crisis in one country can quickly spread to the whole world, endangering the entire international community through the influence of globalization. It is certainly imaginable that if countries do not cooperate with each other—if they seek benefits at the expense of neighbors, or if they shift crises onto others—these crises may cause serious turmoil and even wars, bringing disasters to human society just like what happened in the 1930s and 1940s. In response to various crises, the international community must stand together to overcome difficulties. When the Asian financial crisis occurred in 1997, China refused to depreciate the RMB and actively assisted ASEAN countries and regions in their hour of need, successfully preventing the expansion and spread of the crisis. After the Global Financial Crisis in 2008, there appeared the G20, the BRICs, and other coordination mechanisms to address crises, which brought aid in reforming the global governance system and achieved positive results.

Xi points out that the reform of the global governance system is inseparable from ideological guidance. The world today is full of complex challenges that overstep the boundaries of traditional governance and the framework of the current international system. In order to meet these challenges, the global governance system must be speedily improved, and a new type of international relations must be built, featuring equality, cooperation, and mutual benefit in a global community of common destiny. Although strengthening global governance and advancing the reform of the global governance system represents the general trend, the Cold War zero-sum mentality of opposition persists in the international sphere, along with the existence of hegemonic logic and an arrogant "End of History" mindset. Therefore, there must be a new concept, a new way of thinking, and a new consensus that will take the lead in the construction of a new-type international relations architecture. Shortly after the birth of the G20, China proposed replacing the old, zero-sum thinking of international relations with a new concept featuring win-win cooperation and pulling together in times of trouble.

In May 2010 and September 2011, Chinese leadership put forward the idea of a "community of common destiny" in the second round of the China-US Strategic and Economic Dialogue and in a discussion on promoting China-EU cooperation. This idea was the seed of the concept of a "community with a shared future for mankind." In November 2012, the following words were written in the report to the 18th National Congress of the CPC:

> It is a world where countries are connected to and dependent on one another at a level never seen before. Mankind, by living in the same global village within the same time and space where history and reality meet, has increasingly emerged as a community of common destiny in which everyone has in him- or herself a little bit of others.[78]

This was the first time that the advanced concept of a community with a shared future for mankind had been included in the important documents of the CPC. This concept became an important guiding ideology for the Party to govern and rejuvenate the country. The proposal of the concept gives full expression to China's concern for the future and destiny of mankind and the spirit of struggle for the pursuit of world harmony of the CPC as a Marxist party. It also fully reflects China's sense of responsibility as a world power.

In March 2013, during his speech at the Moscow State Institute of International Relations, President Xi conveyed to the world for the first time the Chinese judgment on the direction of human civilization:

> As the trends of world multi-polarity and economic globalization deepen and those of upholding cultural diversity and applying information technology in social life continue to make progress, mankind has never been better blessed for taking strides toward peace and development. And win-win cooperation provides the only practical way to achieve such a goal.[79]

In September 2013, when visiting the US, President Xi clearly explained to US leaders that the Chinese Dream "connects with the beautiful dreams of the people of the world, including the American dream." In September 2015, at the General Debate of the 70th Session of the UN General Assembly, he stated, "We should renew our commitment to the purposes and principles of the UN Charter, build a new type of international relations featuring win-win cooperation, and create a community of shared future for mankind." In January 2017, he delivered a keynote speech entitled Work Together to Build a Community with a Shared Future for Mankind at the Palais des Nations in Geneva. There he proposed that "actions hold the key to building a community of shared future for mankind."

Over four years, then, Xi talked about the community of common destiny on dozens of occasions. From an international "community of common destiny" to a regional "community of shared future" to a "community with a shared future for mankind," this new concept of global governance transcends the nation-state, transcends ideology, and expresses China's desire to pursue peaceful development. It reflects China's pursuit of mutually beneficial cooperation with others. By elaborating on this concept repeatedly, Xi has grasped the relevance of human interests and values, consistently searching out the highest common factor in international relations. With this concept in mind, President Xi has made the voice of China heard on different diplomatic occasions concerning the world's most important topics, including politics, economy, security, humanities, global governance, environment, development, counter-terrorism, non-proliferation, peacekeeping, women's issues, and disaster response. In this way, China has strengthened its voice in debates about international issues and discussions about international rules, has enhanced its policy transparency and predictability, and has won international acclaim.

At the G20 Hangzhou Summit, President Xi made a number of other suggestions for improving global economic governance with the spirit of "opening up, cooperation and sharing":

(1) Insist on openness, rejecting exclusive arrangements, preventing closed governance mechanisms, and avoiding fragmented rules and regulations

(2) Adhere to cooperation, working together to make rules, build mechanisms, and meet the challenge

(3) Aim for sharing and advocating so that everyone participates and everyone benefits

The Chinese nation has embraced a philosophy of peace and harmony for generations. Under the guidance of socialist ideology and this philosophy of peace, it can be expected that the global governance concept advocated by China will become a widely endorsed international consensus.

2. The implications of building a community with a shared future for mankind

What does it mean to build a community with a shared future for mankind? The implications are rich and profound. Its essence was summed by the report to the 19th National Congress of the CPC: it is about "building an open, inclusive, clean, and beautiful world that enjoys lasting peace, universal security, and common prosperity." The establishment of such a community can be understood and promoted on a number of different fronts, whether political, security-focused, economic, cultural, or ecological.

(1) Politically, nations should respect each other, discuss issues as equals, reject the Cold War mentality and power politics, and take a new approach to developing state-to-state relations, an approach focused on communication, not confrontation; on partnership, not alliance. In human history, there have been numerous wars and untold suffering caused by them. Many of these wars began when great powers sought hegemony. The lessons are profound and bitter. In light of these lessons, people of all nations have a simple and sincere desire: to pursue peace and development and to oppose poverty and war. The foundation for building a world of lasting peace is that all nations establish partnerships in which they treat each other as equals, engage in mutual consultation, and show mutual understanding. Great powers are often the decisive factors that set the tone for war or peace, and they therefore bear more responsibility for regional and world peace and development. These powers must respect each other's core interests and concerns, and they must manage tensions and differences, all the while striving to build a new type of relations with values that stand against conflict and confrontation and for mutual respect and mutually beneficial cooperation. Big countries should treat small countries as equals, avoiding any overweening manner and never playing the bully. Inter-state conflicts and differences should be handled through equal consultation and dialogue with the utmost sincerity and patience. Only when all countries follow the path of peaceful development can common growth and peaceful coexistence be realized.

(2) In terms of security, all nations should commit to settling disputes through dialogue, resolving differences through discussion, coordinating responses to conventional and unconventional threats, and opposing terrorism in all its forms. At present, the international security situation is turbulent and complex. Conventional and unconventional security threats are interwoven, as the meaning and implications of security now go well beyond

a single region or time period. At the same time, the interests of mankind have converged to a considerable degree as countries become increasingly interdependent. Under this new situation, a Cold War mentality, military alliances, and the pursuit of absolute security are no longer feasible. True security for an individual nation requires security for the wider world, as well. All parties should foster a new vision of common, comprehensive, cooperative, and sustainable security. No matter whether it is big or small, strong or weak, rich or poor, no matter what sort of historical or cultural traditions it has, and no matter its social system, a country should be respected and accommodated when it seeks to express its legitimate security concerns. All people should abide by the basic norms of international relations, such as respect for sovereignty, independence and territorial integrity, and non-interference in each other's internal affairs. Both traditional and non-traditional security should be maintained in an all-around way. All countries have the right to participate in regional security affairs on an equal footing, and they also bear the responsibility to maintain regional safety. They should solve security problems through dialogue, consultation, and mutually beneficial cooperation.

(3) Economically, China should stick together through thick and thin, promoting trade and investment liberalization and making economic globalization more open, inclusive, and balanced so that its benefits are shared by all. Development is a top priority for all countries, and common development is a prime aim of the community with a shared future. Specifically, China calls on all countries to: enhance their development capability. All in all, a country needs to rely on itself to develop and formulate development strategies that best suit its national conditions in accordance with its own characteristics; improve the environment for international development. All countries should jointly safeguard world peace, promoting development through peace and consolidating peace through development; create a favorable institutional environment, strengthening global economic governance and improving methods for coordinating the development, stepping up macroeconomic policy coordination in all countries, especially major economies; uphold WTO rules, supporting an open, transparent, inclusive, and non-discriminatory multilateral trading regime and building an open world economy; and optimize and develop partnerships, attempting to address the development imbalance between the North and the South (as well as development imbalances within each region) so that all the people can share more fruits of development and the world economy is fueled for overall sustainable growth.

(4) Culturally, it is imperative that all countries respect the diversity of civilizations, replacing estrangement with exchange, clashes with mutual learning, and cultural superiority with cultural coexistence. The diversity of human civilizations not only defines our world but also drives the progress of mankind. Diversity brings exchanges; exchanges set the ground for integration; integration leads to progress. Each civilization represents the unique vision and contribution of its people, and no civilization is superior to the others. The diversity of civilizations should be an engine driving the advance of human civilizations instead of a bone of contention. Cross-cultural exchange and dialogue should be increased in order to promote harmony, inclusiveness, and respect for differences. Different cultures should learn from

each other in competition and comparison and should grow together in mutual exchange and learning so that inter-civilization communication can serve as a bridge to enhance the friendship between peoples, a source of aspiration for the progress of human society, and a bond that keeps the world at peace.

(5) Ecologically, each nation should be good friends to the environment, cooperating to tackle climate change and protecting our planet for the sake of human survival. Human beings may utilize nature and even try to transform it. But as a part of nature, we should care for it and not place ourselves above it. Building a sound ecology is vital for mankind's future. Industrial development should be reconciled with nature as human beings pursue harmony between humanity and nature to achieve the sustainable development of the world and the all-around development of human beings. An attitude of respect toward nature is important. Human beings should follow nature's ways and protect nature, upholding the conviction that lucid waters and lush mountains are invaluable assets. The international community should steadfastly pursue green, low-carbon, circular, and sustainable development, should advance the 2030 Agenda for Sustainable Development in a balanced manner, should take action to address climate change and other new challenges, and should continue to explore a model of sound development that leads to increased production, better lives, and a good environment. These actions will be concrete steps to create a global ecosystem that puts Mother Nature and green development first.

3. The logical connection between realizing the Chinese Dream and building a community with a shared future for mankind

The most prominent feature of the Chinese Dream of national rejuvenation is to take the state, nation, and people as a community of shared future, closely linking the interests of the three parts together. The economic development of the world is inseparable from China, and China also needs the world for continued prosperity. Similarly, the Chinese Dream cannot be achieved without the establishment of a cooperative international community. But the realization of the Chinese Dream is not just about China. It will bring dividends to the whole world, and it matters for human development.

First of all, China's development is inseparable from that of the world. Since the reform and opening-up, China has become a part of economic globalization that is both broad and deep. Due to its unswerving efforts in advancing the globalization process, China became the world's largest manufacturing country in 2009. It then became the world's largest trading country in goods in 2013; its service trade volume increased from $71.9 billion in 2001 to $607 billion in 2014, rising from 13th to second in the world. In the past 40+ years of reform and opening-up, China has demonstrated through its rapid development that developing countries can benefit from globalization and can experience rapid economic growth. Its rapid development in the past half-century has been owed to the reform and opening-up, as well as to the policies of "going global" and "bringing in." From the perspective of sustainable and green development, China must continue to open up in the future, further integrating into the world economic system, giving full play to Chinese advantages in capital and production capacity, coordinating domestic and international resources and markets, exploring new space and striving to achieve win-win cooperation. To pursue development, China should adhere to the new development philosophy featuring openness, inclusiveness, and cooperation that yields mutual benefit. To this end, leaders must strive to combine the pursuit of Chinese interests with the pursuit of the common interests of others, accommodating their legitimate concerns while pursuing one's own interests and thereby expanding the convergence of common interests of all parties.

Secondly, the world needs China for continued prosperity. As it actively blends into the world, China has also shouldered its share of the burden in terms of global economic and social development. China has played an increasingly important and irreplaceable role. Its progress brings hope to the entire world. Between 1950 and 2016, China provided foreign countries with over 400 billion yuan in aid, and it will continue to increase assistance to other countries as its ability permits. Since the outbreak of the international financial crisis, China has contributed to over 30% of global growth each year on average.

China's development is an opportunity for the world. China's growth based on transformation and greater domestic demand will become a major driver of world economic growth in the coming years. In the next five years, China's annual imports will reach $1.6–1.8 trillion, and it will become the largest trading partner of 140–150 countries and regions. China will make $150–200 billion of outbound investment every year. China will complete an annual turnover of $180–200 billion in foreign contracted projects. Chinese tourists will make 140–170 million outbound visits each year with $110–130 billion of outbound consumption. The number of students studying abroad every year will be 600,000 to 800,000, and the number of foreign students studying in China will reach 400,000 to 500,000. Every 1% increase in China's urbanization rate will bring about approximately seven trillion yuan worth of market demand, which will provide a vast market with opportunities for countries all over the world to participate.

China's economic growth in the future will be mainly driven by strategic emerging industries and modern services. It will shift from an extensive mode dependent on resource input to one that relies on technological innovation. Such a change will further promote the optimization and upgrading of global industrial structures and will bring opportunities for participation and cooperation to developed countries or economies with an edge in sci-tech and services. China will continue to pursue a win-win strategy of opening up, share its own development opportunities with other countries, and welcome them to board its express train of development.

Thirdly, China's future is closely bound to the future of the world. A community with a shared future for mankind and the Chinese Dream are mingled, interdependent, and complementary. The Chinese Dream is a dream of peace, development, and win-win cooperation. But it does not benefit China alone. And the process of bringing it into reality will inject more vitality into the development of all countries in the world. China will do well only when the world does well, and vice versa. The realization of the Chinese Dream is closely interrelated with world peace and development. What we pursue is not only the well-being of the Chinese people but also the common good of all people around the world. In the era of a global village, where all countries are interdependent and share a common future, the way to move in the right direction and achieve mutual benefit is by fostering a sense of community and moving in concert with other nations. China's opening of the BRI and introduction of the AIIB are moves to achieve a win-win situation and share the benefits of development.

II. The Significance and Direction of Building a Community with a Shared Future for Mankind

1. The great significance of building a community with a shared future for mankind

The idea of building a community with a shared future for mankind has been a component of important diplomatic thoughts and propositions at different periods of New China. Since the founding of the PRC, especially after the reform and opening-up, Chinese communists have attached great importance to the establishment of peaceful, stable, fair, and reasonable international relations and order. They have accordingly proposed a series of important diplomatic concepts, including the Five Principles of Peaceful Coexistence, the establishment of a new international political and economic order, the path of peaceful development, the building of a harmonious world, etc. Since the 18th National Congress, the CPC Central Committee, with Xi at its core, has actively promoted innovations in diplomatic theories and practices on the basis of developing these important diplomatic thoughts, thoughts that are rooted in history. The CPC Committee put forward a series of new concepts and propositions, such as the Belt and Road Initiative, the Concept of Global Governance, the New Security Concept, the Scientific Outlook on Development, Upholding Justice While Pursuing Shared Interests, and Outlook on Globalization, forming General Secretary Xi's "Thought on Diplomacy" in the great practice of making new progress in major-country diplomacy with Chinese characteristics. As the core and quintessence of Xi's Thought on Diplomacy, the idea of building a community with a shared future for mankind has become a diplomatic strategy for adhering to and developing socialism with Chinese characteristics in the new era. It has demonstrated the Party's confidence in the path of socialism with Chinese characteristics, a socialism manifest in Chinese theories, the Chinese system, and Chinese culture. It has also embodied China's global vision and sense of responsibility as a major country as it integrates its own development with the development of the world.

The idea of building a community with a shared future for mankind reflects the common values pursued by all mankind, which include peace, development, equity, justice, democracy, and freedom. Since modern times, human beings have been striving to build a fair and reasonable international order, safeguard world peace, and realize common prosperity. After the victory of the World Anti-Fascist War, under the impetus of China and other forces of justice, the UN Charter and other important documents established basic norms governing international relations. These norms reflect the lofty ideals of the international community as it pursues lasting peace, fairness, and justice. The norms include sovereign equality, non-interference in internal affairs, and the peaceful settlement of international disputes. As economic globalization deepens and global challenges become increasingly prominent, the interests of countries that were once very different have begun to converge. In a globalized world, that which threatens one may threaten all. Therefore, the awareness of a community of shared futures is growing and becoming a powerful positive force in promoting international coordination and cooperation. Chinese traditional culture upholds the ideology of harmony, advocates creating a world truly shared by all, and deems that if different countries or cultures "represent themselves with diversity and integrity, the world will be blessed with harmony and unity." These factors demonstrate that the traditional culture has the DNA of a community with a shared future for mankind.

The idea of building a community with a shared future for mankind is adapted to the historical changes in the relationship between China and the world in the new era. China and the rest of the world are currently positioned at a new historical starting point. This is, first of all, because China and the world are increasingly inseparable from one another. In 2016, China's contribution to world economic growth exceeded 30%, and its total import and export volume reached $3.69 trillion, accounting for more than 30% of GDP. China has become a country that is highly reliant on global trade. Facts prove that China will do well only when the world does well, and vice versa. The realization of the Chinese Dream of national rejuvenation is closely linked to the beautiful dreams of many other people around the world, and it is inseparable from the world dream of lasting peace and common prosperity. In addition, China's great achievements in reform and opening-up cannot be disentangled from their history in the support and cooperation of the world. This is one reason that rising China has the responsibility and capability to share development opportunities with other countries. The better China develops, the more capable it will be to influence the world and make more significant contributions to the international community. The idea of building such a community confirms Chinese wisdom and Chinese approaches to global governance.

The idea of building a community with a shared future for mankind points the direction for the development of the world. At present, global development is facing great challenges. Economic globalization is pushing against a headwind; the world economy is noticeably sluggish; development gaps widen; regional conflicts occur frequently; global challenges such as terrorism and refugee flows emerge one after another; and various social and political trends of thought are mingling and clashing. The core of building a community of a shared future is to pursue peace, development, and win-win cooperation, oppose war, eliminate poverty, avoid confrontation, and avoid zero-sum games. This idea encounters the most important issues in the world head-on, offering solutions to the questions that baffle many.

2. The direction of building a community with a shared future for mankind

China should stay committed to building a world of lasting peace through dialogue and consultation. When countries enjoy peace, so will the world; when countries fight, the world suffers. From the Peloponnesian War in the 15th century BC to the two World Wars and the Cold War that lasted more than four decades, the human race has learned painful and profound lessons. After the Second World War, the UN was established, winning more than 70 years of relative peace for the world. The UN ought to continually play a central role in tasks that require the attention of all nations: for instance, improving mechanisms to resolve disputes more effectively, reducing international tension, and putting an end to wars and conflicts.

Countries should foster partnerships based on dialogue, non-confrontation, and non-alliance. Major powers should respect each other's core interests and concerns, keep their differences under control, and build the new model of relations outlined above. As long as different nations maintain honest communication and treat each other with respect, Thucydides's trap can be avoided. Big countries must treat smaller ones as equals instead of acting as a hegemon imposing their will on others. No country should open a Pandora's Box by willfully waging wars or undermining the international rule of law. Guided by the principle of peace, sovereignty, inclusiveness, and shared governance, the international community should turn the deep sea, the polar regions, outer space, and the Internet into new frontiers for cooperation rather than a wrestling ground for competition.

It is necessary to build a world of common security for all, and this must be done through a joint effort. No country in the world can enjoy absolute security. One country cannot have security while others are in turmoil since threats facing other countries may come back to bite the first country. All countries should pursue common, comprehensive, cooperative, and sustainable security.

Terrorism is the common enemy of mankind. Fighting terrorism is the shared responsibility of all countries. In fighting terror, it is important not just to treat the symptoms; root causes must also be addressed. Enhanced coordination is needed in order to build a united global front against terrorism so as to create an umbrella of security for people around the world. As terrorism and refugee crises are closely linked to geopolitical conflicts, resolving these conflicts provides the fundamental solution to such problems. Parties directly involved should return to the negotiating table, other parties should work to facilitate talks for peace, and all nations should respect the role the UN plays as the main channel for mediation. Pandemic diseases such as COVID-19, bird flu, Ebola, and Zika have sounded the alarm for international health security. The World Health Organization (WHO) should play a leadership role in strengthening epidemic monitoring and the sharing of information, practices, and technologies. Moreover, the international community should step up support and assistance for public health in African countries and other developing countries.

A world of common prosperity must be built through mutually beneficial cooperation. Development is the top priority for all countries. Instead of beggaring thy neighbor, countries should stick together like passengers in the same boat. All countries, and major economies in particular, should strengthen macro policy coordination, pursuing both current and long-term interests and focusing on resolving deep-seated problems. Nations should seize the historic opportunity presented by new rounds of technological revolution and industrial transformation; they should shift growth models; they should drive growth through innovation, unleashing great amounts of productivity and creativity. They should uphold WTO rules while supporting an open, transparent, inclusive, and non-discriminatory multilateral trading regime oriented toward an open world economy. Trade protectionism and self-isolation will benefit no one. Economic globalization, on the other hand, has greatly facilitated trade, investment, the flow of people, and technological advancement. In September 2017, the G20 Summit in Hangzhou focused on global economic governance and other major issues. It adopted the Blueprint on Innovative Growth, which put development for the first time in a global macro policy framework and formulated an action plan.

An open and inclusive world must be built through mutual exchange and mutual learning. The diversity of human civilizations not only defines our world but also drives the progress of mankind. There are more than 200 countries and regions, over 2,500 ethnic groups, and hundreds of religions in our world. Different histories, national conditions, ethnic groups, and customs give birth to different civilizations and make our world vibrant and colorful. There is no such thing as a superior or inferior civilization; civilizations are different only in identity and location. The diversity of civilizations should not be a source of global conflict; rather, it should be an engine driving the advance of human civilizations. Every civilization, with its own appeal and its own history, is a human treasure. Diverse civilizations should draw on each other to achieve common progress. Exchanges among civilizations must become a source of inspiration for advancing human society, a bond that keeps the world at peace.

It is critical to make our world clean and beautiful by pursuing green and low-carbon development. Humans coexist with nature, which means that any harm to nature will eventually come back to haunt us. We hardly notice natural resources such as air, water, soil, and blue sky when we have them. But we cannot survive without them. Industrialization has created material wealth never seen before, but it has also been the source of irreparable damage to the environment. Nations must maintain harmony between humanity and nature, pursuing sustainable development. Green, low-carbon, circular, and sustainable means of maintaining life and production are necessities for a common future. The international community must advance the 2030 Agenda for Sustainable Development in a balanced manner and must explore a model of sound development that ensures growth, better lives, and a good environment. The Paris Agreement is a milestone in the history of climate governance—a milestone that must not be derailed. All parties should work together to implement this agreement. China will continue to take steps to tackle climate change and fully honor its obligations.

III. China's Efforts in Building a Community with a Shared Future for Mankind

1. Follow the path of peaceful development and forge a new form of international relations featuring mutual respect, fairness, justice, and win-win cooperation

China should not give up on dreams because reality is too complicated; it should not stop pursuing Chinese ideals because they seem out of reach. Facing a world full of both hope and challenges, China remains firm in its commitment to a new form of international relations and laying a solid foundation for building a community with a shared future for mankind. China will continue to hold high the banner of peace, development, cooperation, and mutual benefit, to uphold its fundamental foreign policy goal of preserving world peace and promoting common development, and to unswervingly strengthen friendship and cooperation with other countries on the basis of the Five Principles of Peaceful Coexistence. The Chinese state endeavors to uphold international fairness and justice and reject hegemonism and power politics. It resolutely defends national interests and will never seek hegemony or engage in expansion.

2. Pursue all-around diplomacy, developing a global network of partnerships

China will fully advance its friendly relations with other countries, with neighboring countries and major economies at the center of the network of partnerships. Other developing countries will serve as the network's foundation and multilateral settings as its platform. China will deepen practical cooperation, enhance mutual political trust, garner popular support, and improve institution-building for this endeavor. It will continuously improve its diplomatic agenda in a comprehensive, multilevel, multifaceted way. China will simultaneously promote coordination and cooperation with other major countries and work to build a framework for relationships between these elite nations, featuring overall stability and balanced development. China will deepen relations with its neighbors in accordance with the values of amity, sincerity, mutual benefit, and inclusiveness. A policy of forging friendships and partnerships with its neighbors will suffuse this endeavor. Guided by the principle of upholding justice while pursuing shared interests and a focus on sincerity, real results, affinity, and good faith, China will steadfastly work to strengthen solidarity and cooperation with other developing countries.

3. Promote the construction of the Belt and Road Initiative and further deepen all-around opening-up

China will adhere to the fundamental national policy of opening up and pursuing development with its doors open wide. It will closely integrate the BRI with the task of building a community with a shared future for mankind and with the implementation of the 2030 Agenda for Sustainable Development. It will build a new platform for international cooperation to create new drivers of shared development. During this entire process, the principle of achieving shared growth through discussion and collaboration will take the lead as Chinese leaders engage in global governance and carry forward the Silk Road spirit—a spirit of peace and cooperation, openness and tolerance, mutual learning, and mutual benefit—and focus on policy coordination, infrastructure connectivity, unimpeded trade, financial integration, and closer people-to-people ties with countries along the route. The Belt and Road Initiative will become a road of peace, prosperity, openness, innovation, and civilization.

4. Participate deeply in global governance, actively guiding the direction of the reform of the international order

China will follow the principle of achieving shared growth through discussion and collaboration in global governance and will actively participate in the reform and construction of the global governance system. It will resolutely maintain the international order and international system with the purposes and principles of the UN Charter as the core. It will advance democracy in international relations and support efforts to increase the representation of developing countries in international affairs. It will take a constructive part in the settlement process of international and regional hotspot issues, actively responding to various global challenges and maintaining international and regional peace and stability. By actively maintaining the status of multilateral trade arrangements, promoting the liberalization and facilitation of international trade and investment, and opposing all forms of protectionism, China will continue to play its part as a powerful yet responsible country. Chinese wisdom and strength will continue to play a leading role in the improvement of global governance.

5. Strengthen the Party's centralized and unified leadership in external work

It is necessary to study and implement Xi's Thought on Diplomacy in a thorough, ongoing way. This will mean enhancing confidence in the path, theories, system, and culture of socialism with distinctive Chinese features. It will mean strengthening the awareness of the need to maintain political integrity. It will mean thinking in terms of the big picture, following the path put forward by Party leadership, and improving top-level design, strategic planning, and coordination on external affairs. These changes will ensure the effective implementation of the CPC Central Committee's foreign policy and strategic deployment. China has advanced institutional reforms on external work and increased the overall coordination of the efforts of various fields and departments. It will continue to carry out exchanges and will cooperate with the political parties and organizations of other countries, encouraging the people's congress, CPPCC national committees, the military, local governments, and people's organizations to engage in exchanges with other countries. It will strengthen the ranks of officials for external work, cultivating a large number of competent and versatile talents with a good knowledge of both domestic and foreign affairs.

6. Provide the world with public goods that improve global economic governance

The reform of the global economic governance system is a long-term and complex process. Leaders and beneficiaries of the old system will not automatically withdraw from this stage of history, and new leaders with new approaches are not able to transition into having decisive influences on world economic governance right away. In such a long process of transition from old to new, the world urgently needs new global public goods to make up for the shortcomings and deficiencies of existing governance systems.

CHAPTER SIXTEEN

Developing a More Advanced Open Economy

The opening of the Chinese economy must be pursued on a larger scale, in more regions, and at a deeper level. There is an opportunity to build new institutions for a more advanced and open economy. This opportunity can be seized as China promotes the development of the impressive BRI and as it actively participates in reforming the global governance system.

SECTION 1
Building a New Institution of Open Economy

It is imperative to seize hold of the historic opportunities presented by the peaceful development period. If the Chinese believe that it is possible to institute a new and open economy, thereby realizing the Chinese Dream of national rejuvenation, they must actively participate in the rapid development of economic globalization and expansion.

I. New Requirements, Characteristics, and Trends for Building a New Institution of Open Economy

In this portion of the chapter, several requirements for open development will be considered, along with several recent changes regarding such development and several trends that can be observed unfolding at the present moment.

1. New requirements for open development in the new era

As work proceeds toward a new economy, there are a number of requirements for open development in the new era.

(1) Opening up proactively. The imperative of an open economy centrally considers openness as an inherent requirement of development and thus proactively works toward openness as a goal. China's opening up forty years ago was passive. Due to its backward and weak economy at the time, the country had no choice but to open the door and participate in the international division of labor in the hope of getting out of its predicament. Today, however, China's economy has undergone tremendous changes, both qualitative and quantitative changes. China no longer participates in the same mode of economic growth as it once did. It no longer has the same types of businesses. It no longer has the same growth momentum. The current opening up must be entirely proactive, and it must be innovation-driven under the new normal in order to reap the benefits of continuous optimization and upgrading of economic structure. Those who lead this work must pay special attention to seizing the initiative and must emphasize active participation in the top-level design of international economic organizations.

(2) Opening up on all fronts. The imperative of an open economy calls for a wider space. China must develop an open economy with higher standards and a more comprehensive and broad vision. China must strive to improve its institutional voice in global economic governance. In particular, China must not only further lift restrictions on general manufacturing in the course of open development but also promote openness in the service sector: healthcare, education, finance, etc. Reform of the international financial system is also needed, along with an increase of Chinese influence in existing multilateral financial institutions and the creation of new platforms such as the AIIB, the BRICS Bank, and the Silk Road Fund.

(3) Opening up fairly. The imperative of an open economy focuses on the establishment of a level playing field for domestic and foreign investment. It requires a movement away from the practice of attracting investment by relying on land and tax policy support. It encourages China to provide foreign-funded enterprises with a fair, transparent, and predictable market environment by strengthening the rule of law. This level playing field ensures that enterprises of all types enjoy equal access to each of the following: factors of production in accordance with the law, fair participation in market competition, and equal legal protection. Opening up fairly entails that China will not change its policy on foreign investment or its protection of the legitimate rights and interests of foreign-invested enterprises. This will surely further strengthen the confidence of foreign corporations who are engaged in long-term development in China.

(4) Opening up in a mutually beneficial way. The imperative of an open economy values international cooperation and makes economic globalization more open and inclusive so that its benefits are shared by all. In contrast with an approach that sees economic growth as coming at the expense of foreign nations, a mutually beneficial win-win approach stresses the convergence of interests of these nations. It thus paves the way for interconnected

development, shared opportunities, and a shared future. Regional free trade arrangements serve as a useful supplement to the multilateral trading system by creating a vaster market and development space for all countries. Such approaches foster a new pattern of win-win cooperation in which the growth of one country reinforces and complements the growth of another.

2. New changes regarding open development in the new era

The following recent changes play a critical role in our understanding of current realities:

(1) China's status in the international division of labor has greatly improved. It has changed from an unimportant trading nation that relies on the export of primary products to a major exporter of manufactured goods. Today, China is the world's largest exporter, the second largest importer of goods, and the largest recipient of foreign direct investment (FDI). In the global trading system, China has become an increasingly important economy with ever-increasing influence on the global economy. In the years since the international financial crisis, China has made a great contribution to global economic growth.

(2) The transnational mobility of factors of production continues to increase. At present, China's open development has shifted its focus from the liberalization of trade in goods to the free flow of high-end factors of production. New competitive strength can only be achieved by harnessing various factors of production toward innovation. Any attempt to create an environment more conducive to the free flow of high-end factors must let the market mechanism of "survival of the fittest" play a decisive role in the allocation of factors of production. To do this, a unified, open, orderly, and competitive market system must be established.

(3) Standards for rules of international trade and investment are becoming more demanding. The deep integration of the global economy calls for a more complete, standardized, fair, and transparent market economy system, which inevitably ushers in high standards for rules of international trade and investment. Only by proactively adapting to the high-standard rules of the global market economy can China integrate into the mainstream of the world economy. Countries and regions that fail to meet these standards may be marginalized. Therefore, we should reinforce reform by opening up to enhance the rule of law and actively adapt to global economic and trade rules that demonstrate high standards. This is key to China's higher-level open development.

(4) The international environment for open development is becoming more perilous. Corresponding to the new normal in China is accelerated and exclusive regional economic integration on an international scale. The US intends to regain dominance over the system of global trade rules and to maintain predominance in the new economic order through regional economic cooperation centered on itself. The EU is also constantly improving its integrated institutional arrangements, with its penchant for protectionism shifting from straightforward trade protection to comprehensive economic protection covering investment, finance, intellectual property, and new industries. Due to the increased economic protectionism

displayed by developed countries, the relatively free and loose trade environment for China has become highly uncertain. At the same time, sluggish demand in the international market has led to increasingly fierce economic competition, which makes it impossible for China to win at the lower end of global industry with its low-cost advantage. As a result, China must develop advantages at the higher end of the value chain via new breakthroughs in technological innovation to regain dominance in the manufacturing industry.

3. New trends in open development in the new era

These recent trends in economic thinking must also shape attitudes toward future development:

(1) There is a shift from a focus on "enhancing current benefits" to a focus on "building a community of shared interests." In the past, one of the important guidelines for China's open development was to enhance the current benefits of international cooperation. Under the new normal, however, China's approach is more far-sighted and strategic. The country is shifting its focus on international cooperation from the goal of obtaining current benefits to the goals of promoting international infrastructure connectivity, smooth and stable industrial supply chains, the mutual exchange of talents, and the formation of an integrated production network.

(2) There is a shift from the idea of simply "opening to the outside world" to the idea of "combining domestic development *and* opening to the outside world." To carry out open development, we must take into account both domestic and international situations, which involves seeking development opportunities from the changing international situation and formulating foreign strategies from the transformation of domestic advantages. First, it is necessary to balance domestic development and international openness, the domestic and international markets and resources, the domestic industrial development and international division of labor, and the improvement of the socialist market economy and participation in the formulation of international economic and trade rules. We should make good use of China's comprehensive advantages to expand the market space and provide lasting and reliable resource guarantees. Second, it is necessary to coordinate domestic and foreign trade policies, better integrating the "bring in" and "go global" strategies. Third, it is necessary to combine opening up with the economic structural adjustment, shifting from mainly relying on investment and export to relying on a balance of consumption, investment, and export.

(3) There is also a shift from "eliminating external border barriers" to "eliminating domestic barriers." Under the new division model of the global value chain (GVC), certain features are essential. These include a global flow of intermediate goods and factors of production such as knowledge, technology, capital, personnel, and services, and an optimized combination of these entities. Such global integration in production naturally requires the consistency of market rules and the compatibility of standards among various countries. This consistency and compatibility *between* countries will be most effective once it is applied to standards *within* the country, as well. Therefore, China's policies of open development will inevitably

show a tendency to eliminate not only "border barriers" to the flow of goods and factors of production but also "domestic barriers."

(4) We are moving from a focus on "following international trends" to a focus on "influencing the international environment." With the growth of the total economic output and the rise of its international status, China will shift its role from a pure follower of international trends to an influencer and game-changer on the international scene. Working from the concept of "actively participating in global economic governance and the supply of public goods and increasing its institutional voice in global economic governance,"[80] China will assume more responsibilities and obligations in international affairs and will play a more constructive role in trends within international development.

4. New opportunities and challenges for open development in the new era

In the context of all these trends, there are difficult challenges that raise important questions. Each of these challenges can also be seen as an opportunity.

(1) A question arises about how to replace old growth drivers with new ones, a key progression in the recovery of the world economy. The impact of the international financial crisis continues to hamstring a return to prosperity: global economic recovery has been difficult and bumpy; the growth rate of global trade has been slower than that of the world economy; transnational investment has not yet returned to pre-crisis levels. Nevertheless, there are recent encouraging developments: global trade and investment have picked up; the international financial market has been generally stable; new industries, new technologies, and new business formats have emerged one after another. Despite all this, the world economy has not yet stepped out of an adjustment period characterized by unhealthy markets and sluggish growth. There are deep-seated structural contradictions not effectively resolved, new growth drivers, not yet formed, and the potential growth rate is stubbornly in decline. Great uncertainties remain. China must seize the opportunities and resolve the challenges inevitably involved in any movement toward openness in a complex global economic situation.

(2) International power is becoming more balanced, but China's role in this development is as yet unclear. The world economic structure has experienced a profound adjustment as emerging markets and developing countries find their fortunes improving simultaneously. There is an apparent shift in the global balance of power: from West to East, from North to South. In the past five years, China has been responsible for over 30% of global economic growth. Its institutional voice in the global economic governance system has become significantly louder, which is conducive to safeguarding its development interests. At the same time, as China moves closer to the center of the world stage, the international community hopes that China can play a greater role in international affairs and assume more responsibilities in addressing global challenges. The challenge is for China to effectively play an international role commensurate with its current development stage and take on the appropriate global responsibilities.

(3) The path to in-depth development on a global scale is not simple and straightforward; instead, it is characterized by twists and turns. Economic globalization in the form of liberalized trade and investment has promoted world peace, stability, and prosperity, is in the common interests of all countries in the world, and represents the direction of the development of human civilizations. But it is not smooth sailing. In recent years, a number of things have cast a shadow over the development of the world economy and trade: a sluggish world economy, development disparity, governance dilemma, equity deficit, a surging anti-globalization trend, protectionism, and the growth of inward-looking tendencies within nations. Economic globalization, however, is an irreversible trend. In-depth development is also irreversible, though it may in the future proceed at a slower pace, have new drivers, and adopt different rules. China, in concert with the rest of the world, is challenged to adapt to and guide economic globalization skillfully, making it open, inclusive, balanced, and beneficial to all.

(4) In recent years, China has shown new competitive strength as its economy opens, but the growth of this strength is sluggish; it must grow faster. China's economic development is entering a new normal. Labor costs continue to rise; resource constraints tighten; the carrying capacity of the environment approaches its upper limit. The traditional competitive advantage of the open economy has been weakened, and its traditional development model has encountered bottlenecks. In response to a threatening environment at home and abroad, China's processing trade has experienced rapid transformation and upgrading; service trade has grown rapidly; new products, new formats, and new models of foreign trade constantly emerge; the capacity of enterprises in international operation has been enhanced; and China's position in the international division of labor has gradually improved. As such, the main direction of work in opening up should be to make the best of the current situation. This means to accelerate the transformation from being a factor-driven open economy with an emphasis on scale, growth rate, and cost/price advantage into being an innovation-driven economy that focuses on quality and efficiency and has a comprehensive competitive advantage. This comprehensive advantage puts service at the core, and it extends to technology, standards, brand, and quality. Following in this direction helps China drive economic development and helps China approach new horizons in quality and efficiency.

II. Moving toward the Construction of a Higher-Level Open Economy

1. The overall objective of building a new and open economic system

As stated above, the objective of the Chinese economy must be to build a new and open economic system. This objective includes the following imperatives: to accelerate efforts to foster new advantages in international cooperation and competition; to more actively promote the balance of internal and external demand, of import and export, of foreign capital introduction and outbound investment; to gradually achieve a basic balance in international payments; to modernize governance systems capabilities for an open economy; to uphold justice while pursuing shared interests; to safeguard national interests and ensure national security; to promote the shared development of China and other nations; and to build in a way that is mutually beneficial, diversified, balanced, safe and efficient.

The following three objectives stand out in the task of building a new open economic system:

(1) To establish a new mechanism for market allocation of resources. This can be done by promoting the orderly and free flow of international and domestic factors of production, the efficient global allocation of resources, and the deep integration of the international and domestic markets; by accelerating the reform of systems and mechanisms related to the open economy; and by establishing a fair, open, orderly and competitive market system.

(2) To form a new mode of economic operation and management. In accordance with the requirements of international standards and the rule of law, this new mode will necessitate a good legal environment, allowing China to open up in accordance with the law. Skilled attorneys will establish management methods that are consistent with international high-standard investment and trade rules, form a mechanism for participating in international macroeconomic policy coordination, and improve the international economic governance structure. Finally, they will strengthen the rule of law in government behavior and market-based economic behavior, establish and improve a management mechanism such that corporations can perform their main responsibilities, the government can supervise in accordance with the law, and the public can participate extensively, improving systems and mechanisms for effectively safeguarding national interests and security in opening up.

(3) To foster new advantages in international cooperation and competition. The new system must both consolidate and expand traditional advantages, and it must accelerate the cultivation of new competitive advantages. Oriented by innovation and centering on quality and efficiency, stakeholders in the Chinese economy will create a competitive and orderly market environment, a transparent and efficient government environment, a fair and just legal environment, and a cultural environment characterized by win-win cooperation. These environments will foster comprehensive competitive advantages (involving industries, locations, business environment, rules, standards, etc.), continuously enhance innovation capabilities, comprehensively enhance our position in GVC, and promote industrial transformation and upgrading.

2. Innovation in the foreign investment management system

There is a need to improve the investment environment, expand market access for the service industry, further open up the manufacturing industry, stabilize the scale and speed of foreign investment, and improve the quality of foreign investment. In addition, the following changes are imperative:

(1) Reform the administration of foreign investment approval and industrial guidance by unifying laws and regulations for domestic and foreign-funded enterprises

(2) Shift to a management system of combining pre-establishment national treatment and the negative list

(3) Promote the institutional innovation, transformation, and upgrading of the development zone by improving the foreign investment supervision system

3. The establishment of a new system to promote the strategy of going global

It is important to implement the national strategy of going global and to strengthen overall planning and guidance. It is, moreover, imperative to establish the role of enterprises and individuals as the main entities of outbound investment, to strive to improve the quality and efficiency of foreign investment, and to promote infrastructure interconnection. A significant goal here is that industries go out, cooperate in advanced technologies, enhance the international operation capabilities of Chinese enterprises, avoid vicious competition, and safeguard the rights and interests of overseas investment. Specifically, the national strategy of going global must expand into the new era, promoting overseas investment facilitation, innovating in the methods of overseas investment cooperation, improving the service guarantee system for going global, and moving toward a synergistic dynamic of resources flowing inward and outward.

4. The establishment of a new mechanism for sustainable development of foreign trade

It is furthermore critical to foster new competitive advantages while maintaining the traditional advantages of foreign trade and strive to solve the major problems that restrict the sustainable development, transformation, and upgrade of foreign trade. This involves comprehensively enhancing the competitiveness of foreign trade, increasing the level of trade facilitation, improving the import and export promotion system, perfecting the mechanism for dealing with trade frictions, vigorously developing trade in services, and facilitating the upgrade of quality- and benefit-oriented foreign trade.

5. The optimization of the regional layout of opening up

The creation of FTZs will help drive balanced economic development by improving quality and efficiency in regional opening up. These FTZs should be based on coordinated development of the East, Middle, and West of China, across land and over sea. They will ease cooperation between the Mainland and Hong Kong, Macao, and Taiwan, and make new ground in pursuing opening up on all fronts. In terms of the construction of FTZs, the reform and opening-up of the Shanghai Pilot Free Zone can be deepened, thereby expanding the opening up of service and advanced manufacturing industries, forming a policy support system that promotes investment and innovation, and extending some opening up measures to Pudong New District. It is also important to timely sum up the reform experience of pilot areas and replicate it throughout the country. Ultimate goals include improving the new mechanism for inland opening up, cultivating new fulcrums for opening up in border areas, creating new highlands for opening up in the coastal areas, and expanding opening up to Hong Kong, Macao, and Taiwan.

6. The acceleration of BRI strategy implementation

An important goal of the BRI strategy is to achieve policy coordination, infrastructure connectivity, unimpeded trade, financial integration, and closer interpersonal connections. This cannot be done without all-around cooperation with countries along the route, building a community with shared interests, a shared future, and shared responsibility. A deep, multi-level economic and trade relationship with these countries will enhance the development of China's border and inland regions.

7. The expansion into new space for international economic cooperation

It is imperative to consolidate and strengthen the multilateral trading system, accelerate the implementation of the FTA strategy, actively participate in global economic governance, play the role of a participant and leader in making international economic and trade rules, expand international cooperation and exchanges, and strive to develop a deeply integrated and mutually beneficial network. Specific moves include upholding the rules of the world trading system; establishing a network of free trade agreements with high standards; breaking new ground in the pursuit of bilateral and multilateral economic cooperation; and establishing a new mechanism for international economic and trade negotiations.

8. The establishment of an open and safe financial system

A precondition for healthy development is the existence of a system that is open and safe. Toward that end:

Firstly, one must promote the opening up of financial sectors. This means increasing the prevalence of international operations in financial institutions, encouraging financial institutions to prudently conduct cross-border mergers and acquisitions (M&A), improving the network of overseas branches, strengthening financial services, and bolstering international cooperation in the fields of payment and market infrastructure.

Secondly, one must promote the mutual and orderly opening up of capital markets, actively and steadily promoting the convertibility of RMB capital accounts.

Thirdly, one must establish a financial support system for going global. This will be a system for overseas investment that combines policy-based finance and commercial finance, established to promote the joint globalization of financial capital and industrial capital.

Fourthly, one must expand the cross-border use of RMB. The following measures can be taken:

(1) Promote cooperation in currency swaps, further expand the scale of RMB settlement for current accounts, and support multinationals to carry out centralized operations of RMB funds
(2) Speed up the construction of a cross-border RMB payment system, further improving the global clearing system for RMB
(3) Further broaden RMB export channels and encourage the use of RMB to make loans and investments abroad
(4) Build a regional RMB bond market to further facilitate foreign institutions investing in the domestic bond market, support overseas institutions issuing RMB debt financing instruments in China, and steadily encourage domestic financial institutions and enterprises to issue RMB bonds abroad

(5) Support the innovation of RMB-denominated financial products in the offshore market, accelerate the construction of the RMB offshore market, and expand the overseas circulation of RMB

(6) Finally, improve the exchange rate formation mechanism and foreign exchange management system, which involves the expansion of the floating range of the RMB exchange rate in an orderly manner and an enhancement of the flexibility of the floating RMB exchange rate regime

Deeper reform of the foreign exchange management system is needed, further facilitating the use of foreign exchange by market players and promoting reform in the management of foreign exchange capital settlements of foreign-invested enterprises following negative list management. This entails the use of foreign exchange reserves in an innovative manner and the broadening of channels for diversified use.

9. The maintenance of a stable, fair, transparent, and predictable business environment

Progress requires a stable and predictable business environment. To this end, action in the following areas will be beneficial:

(1) Strengthen the rule of law in the open economy, following the trend of wider reform that improves laws and regulations related to foreign affairs.

(2) Foster open market entities. It is necessary to help domestic enterprises absorb advanced factors of production and develop internationally famous brands. The development of such brands, creating a group of multinational corporations with international influence, will make participation in the GVC both wider and deeper. Meanwhile—and no less critically— domestic superior enterprises will establish production and comprehensive service systems overseas in order to allocate resources and expand markets on a global scale.

(3) Optimize the environment of competitive markets, establishing a unified, open, and orderly market system with observed regulatory rules.

(4) Improve the environment for technological innovation. Through the accelerated implementation of an innovation-driven development strategy, actively integrated into the global innovation network, it is possible to comprehensively improve the level of international cooperation in China's scientific and technological innovation and utilize global innovation resources more frequently and better.

(5) Give full play to the role of industry associations and chambers of commerce, especially in formulating technical standards, standardizing industrial order, expanding international markets, and addressing trade frictions while improving their abilities in organization, coordination, and self-regulation of the industry.

10. Strengthening the construction of support and guarantee mechanisms

It will be worthwhile to cultivate individuals' talents insofar as they promote the new open economic system. Cultivating talents in this way will improve external communication channels, solidify efforts to build interpersonal rapport, improve cultural exchange and external publicity, and further improve support and guarantee measures.

11. The establishment and improvement of the guarantee system

The opening of the Chinese economy must be safeguarded by the use of guarantees. While opening wider to the outside world, China must safeguard core interests and establish a systematic, scientific, and efficient guarantee system to keep the economy open. Such safeguarding necessitates improved institutional mechanisms to manage risk and enhancements to our ability to maintain national security. Several practical steps can be taken: improving the national security review mechanism for foreign investment; establishing a risk prevention and control system for going global; building a guarantee system for the security of economy and trade; and improving the financial risk prevention and control system.

SECTION 2

Shaping a New "Dual Circulation" Pattern

A new development pattern, with domestic circulation as the mainstay, is already underway in China. Accelerating this pattern is a strategic decision made in accordance with changes in the development stage, environment, and condition of the nation, a decision that allows domestic and global circulation to reinforce one another. It is a systematic and profound change that matters to the whole picture.

There are a number of reasons that make it imperative to accelerate the growth of this "dual circulation" pattern.

I. Building a New Development Pattern as a Precondition of High-Quality Economic Development in China

The new development pattern accords with changes in China's development stage, environment, and condition. The Chinese economy has entered a stage of high-quality development. Nevertheless, Chinese society faces a contradiction: despite unbalanced and inadequate development, the Chinese people have ever-growing needs for a better life. The per capita GDP has reached $10,000, and the urbanization rate has exceeded 60%. More than 400 million Chinese people qualify as middle-income. To adapt to the new needs experienced by a society facing this central contradiction, the new development pattern emphasizes preparation for the expansion of domestic demand, which will help better meet people's needs for a better life.

II. Building a New Development Pattern to Meet the Needs of Expanding Domestic Demand

Building a new development pattern recognizes the importance of expanding domestic demand. Instead of simply repeating previous measures, it requires us to change the development mode, adjust economic structure, rely on scientific and technological innovation, foster new economic growth drivers, form new growth poles, and improve the quality and efficiency of development so that the fruits of development will benefit the people more. This development can only be achieved with care. On the one hand, China should continue to pursue supply-side structural reform as our main task, overcoming the obstacles and bottlenecks of the domestic economic cycle. On the other hand, China should also keep a firm hold on the strategic base of expanding domestic demand so as to make production, distribution, circulation, and consumption more dependent on the domestic market, to meet people's needs for a better life, to improve the adaptability of the supply system to domestic demand, to form a higher level of dynamic balance in which demand drives supply and supply creates demand, and to support the new development pattern in a sustainable, safe, efficient and stable manner.

III. Building a New Development Pattern to Improve the Quality of China's Industrial Chain and Maintain Economic Security

The Politburo meeting emphasized "building greater synergy among scale, speed, quality, structure, efficiency, and security of development." Economic security is prominently reflected in the security of the industrial chain and supply chain system. For a long time, China has been at the middle or low end of the GVC. Chinese products did not add value; Chinese brands were not sufficiently recognizable. Certain high-tech products and technologies are highly dependent on the supply chain, putting themselves at risk of being cut off at any time. All these have threatened Chinese industrial and economic security. To build a new development pattern, therefore, we must develop an independent, safe, and controllable industrial chain and supply chain.

IV. Building a New Development Pattern to Meet the Need for Technological Innovation

In an era of rapidly changing technologies, the concept of innovative development becomes critical as a way to build China's strength in S&T. It is important to strengthen collaboration in technological innovation, to improve guarantee capabilities in key links, areas, and products, and to accelerate various transformations: from Original Equipment Manufacturer (OEM) to R&D, from imitation to innovation, and from "Made in China" to "Intelligently Manufactured in China" and "Created in China." In addition, it is necessary to carry out projects of industrial infrastructure re-engineering and industrial chain upgrading at a faster pace. While consolidating the advantages of traditional industries and strengthening the leading position of superior industries, China must quicken the pace of its foray into strategic emerging industries and future industries. It must also make the industrial infrastructure more advanced and the industrial chain further modernized. In particular, Chinese leaders should leverage the unique advantages of China: the world's most complete industrial support system and China's ultra-large market, which serves as a "stabilizer" for the global industrial chain and supply chain.

V. Building a New Development Pattern to Open Doors to High Standards Instead of Shutting Them

Development that "keeps the doors closed," creating an internal loop, must eventually end in deterioration. The new development pattern emphasizes a smooth connection between domestic and international circulation, with the two circulations equally important and mutually reinforcing. It is an arrangement for higher-level open development that promotes competition and stimulates new momentum in a new situation. The competition and cooperation brought about by opening up crucially bring new vigor to domestic circulation, maintaining its vitality and competitiveness. To connect internal and external circulation is to integrate China's innovation chain, industrial chain, and supply chain on a global scale, making them indispensable.

By promoting a positive interplay between domestic and international circulation, it is possible to optimize the cross-border allocation of factors of production. Such interplay will also expand the import of high-quality goods and services so that they meet domestic production and consumption needs and will make the domestic cycle run more smoothly and effectively. To this end, China will benefit from participating more actively in the international division of labor and cooperation, from putting equal emphasis on imports and exports, from coordinating the use of foreign capital and outbound investment, and from strengthening cohesion between these two markets and their resources. This will involve a gradual transition from an opening up featuring the flow of commodities and factors to an opening of institutions, fostering improved investment and trade facilitation, a continuously optimized business environment, and international cooperation and exchange.

VI. Building a New Development Pattern to Effectively Address the Uncertainties of the Global Economy

The world today is undergoing complex and profound changes. The layout of industrial chains, supply chains, and value chains brought by global division of labor faces severe challenges, hampered by the global economic slowdown, the backlash against globalization, and the impact of COVID-19. In the face of this uncertainty, it is advisable to engage in advance planning, planning that transforms challenges into opportunities and turmoil into progress, in order to create a new development pattern. The key is to approach these challenges responsibly and deal with external contingencies with steadiness of purpose aimed at reform and opening-up. By creating a new development pattern, China can release the potential of domestic demand to not only achieve high-quality economic development but also bring newfound certainty to economic globalization, making it more open, inclusive, balanced, and mutually beneficial. This is the approach that can build a community with a shared future for mankind and result in mutually beneficial cooperation.

VII. Building a New Development Pattern to Actively Shape and Extend a Period of Strategic Opportunity

China is now in a period of strategic opportunity for development and will remain so for some time. But there are new opportunities and challenges. China's previous periods of strategic opportunity were exogenous since they were, objectively speaking, quite dependent on favorable changes in the external environment. As it becomes the world's second-largest economy, gradually transforming from a follower and learner to a leader, and sees an increase in its competitiveness and influence, China needs to be more self-reliant in striving for and creating development opportunities. As such, full play should be given to China's advantage in a combination of comprehensive industrial capacity and ultra-large-scale market. Harnessing this advantage will accelerate the establishment of a system of rules that is more fair, just, inclusive, and mutually beneficial in the new development pattern with dual circulation. It will also amplify China's voice in making international rules and will create more opportunities for economic development shared by China and other countries in the world.

In the past few decades, China has seen a miracle happen in the growth of its economy. This miracle involved an export-oriented development model that fully leveraged the advantages of low-price factors. With the changes in the external environment and the domestic factor endowments in recent years, market and resource, the two drivers of international circulation, have been significantly weakened, limiting the development space. Domestic circulation, in contrast, becomes increasingly vigorous and vital with the release of additional domestic demand potential, laying a solid foundation for the creation of the new development pattern. In fact, since the 2008 international financial crisis, China's economy has been shifting to a pattern dominated by the internal cycle. What is needed is efficient adaptation to the change in circumstances in the form of an accelerated creation of a new development pattern. This pattern will give full play to the advantages of a domestic super-large-scale market and will add a strong impetus to the economic development of China and the world at large through the prosperity of the domestic economy.

SECTION 3
The Belt and Road Initiative and a New Openness

The implementation of the BRI is a novel tool for actively adapting to the new development pattern and creating a new model for all-around opening up and win-win international cooperation.

I. The Glorious Course of BRI from an Idea to a Reality

The Belt and Road Initiative is the abbreviation of the Silk Road Economic Belt and the 21st Century Maritime Silk Road Initiative. During visits to Kazakhstan and Indonesia in 2013, President Xi introduced an initiative to jointly build the Silk Road Economic Belt and the 21st Century Maritime Silk Road, which collectively came to be known as the Belt and Road Initiative.

1. Continuing the legend of the Silk Road together

For thousands of years, the ancient silk routes spanning thousands of miles witnessed bustling scenes of trade and travel over land and sea. "Countries with differences in race, beliefs and cultural backgrounds can absolutely share peace and development as long as they persist in unity and mutual trust, equality and mutual benefit, mutual tolerance and learning from each other, as well as cooperation and the principle of win-win," said President Xi during his visit to Kazakhstan in September 2013. The achievement of shared growth through discussion and collaboration has become the basic principle for advancing the Belt & Road construction. Five years on, over 100 countries and international organizations have supported and participated in this initiative. Important resolutions passed by the UN General Assembly and Security Council contain references to it. The vision of the BRI is becoming a reality and bearing rich fruit.

2. Seeking connectivity in five areas via the BRI

Connectivity has been a yearning of mankind since ancient times. In 2013, President Xi proposed to jointly build the Silk Road Economic Belt in Kazakhstan, a country sitting on the ancient silk routes, and emphasized that they must start with work in five individual areas: "stepping up policy coordination, improving road connectivity, promoting unimpeded trade, enhancing monetary circulation, and increasing understanding between the two peoples." At this point, China has signed cooperation agreements with over 40 countries and international organizations and carried out framework cooperation on production capacity with more than 30 countries. It has invested more than $50 billion in B&R countries. The AIIB has provided $1.7 billion of loans for nine projects in B&R participating countries, and the Silk Road Fund has made $4 billion of investment. Over five years, the achievements of the BRI have exceeded expectations. The construction of economic corridors has steadily advanced; the connectivity network has gradually formed; trade and investment have grown substantially; and cooperation in important projects has been implemented steadily. Region-wide cooperation is gradually taking shape.

3. Building a community with a shared future for mankind

A community with a shared future relates to the concept of the "Society of Great Harmony." It stresses the importance of "combin[ing] China's development with the development of B&R countries and combin[ing] the Chinese Dream with the dreams of the people of these countries to provide new contents to the ancient silk routes" by cooperating in the BRI. In November 2016, the 71st session of the UN General Assembly adopted a resolution that incorporated the BRI based on the principle of achieving shared growth through discussion and collaboration, guided by the

Silk Road spirit of peace and cooperation, openness and inclusivity, mutual learning and mutual benefit, aiming at building a community with shared destiny and interests. The resolution was unanimously endorsed by all 193 member states. Three months later, the 55th session of the UN Commission for Social Development passed a resolution unanimously, in which the concept of "building a community with a shared future for mankind" was included for the first time.

II. The Content and Implications of the BRI

1. The content of the BRI

Since its inception, the BRI has continuously expanded contexts for cooperation and explored new cooperation models for self-enrichment and self-development, but its original intention and principles have remained unchanged. This is the key to understanding the BRI. It is a way to encourage win-win cooperation that promotes common development and prosperity. It is a road toward peace and friendship through the enhancement of mutual understanding and trust and the all-around strengthening of exchanges. The Belt and Road runs through the continents of Asia, Europe, and Africa, connecting the vibrant East Asia economic circle at one end with the developed European economic circle at the other and encompassing many countries with huge potential for economic development. The Silk Road Economic Belt focuses on bringing together China, Central Asia, Russia, and Europe (via the Baltic Sea), linking China with the Persian Gulf and the Mediterranean Sea through Central and West Asia, and connecting China with Southeast Asia, South Asia and the Indian Ocean. The 21st Century Maritime Silk Road is designed to go from China's coast to Europe through the South China Sea and the Indian Ocean in one route and from China's coast through the South China Sea to the South Pacific in the other.

On land, the initiative will focus on jointly building a new Eurasian Land Bridge and developing the following economic corridors: China–Mongolia–Russia, China–Central Asia–West Asia and China–Indochina Peninsula. These corridors take advantage of international transport routes, relying on core cities along the Belt and Road and using key economic industrial parks as cooperation platforms. At sea, the initiative will focus on jointly building smooth, secure and efficient transport routes connecting major sea ports along the Belt and Road. The China–Pakistan Economic Corridor and the Bangladesh-China-India-Myanmar Economic Corridor are closely related to the Belt and Road Initiative, and therefore require closer cooperation. The Initiative is an ambitious economic vision that involves opening up the countries along the Belt and Road through a cooperative economic venture. Countries must work in concert and move toward objectives of mutual benefit and common security. To be specific, they need: to improve the region's infrastructure, putting in place a secure and efficient network of land, sea, and air passages, lifting their connectivity to a higher level; to further enhance trade and investment facilitation by establishing a network of free trade areas that meet high standards, maintain close economic ties, and deepen political trust; to enhance cultural exchanges; to encourage different civilizations to learn from each other and flourish together; and to promote mutual understanding, peace, and friendship among people of all countries.

There are hundreds of features of the BRI that cement its appeal. Here are several:

(1) It is an open and inclusive initiative for regional cooperation, not an exclusionary or closed Chinese bloc. The 21st century is more interconnected than any past period. Openness brings progress, while isolation leads to regression. China believes in opening up because this is the only way to discover opportunities, seize them, make good use of them, and then take the initiative to create new opportunities and ultimately achieve national goals. The BRI is meant to turn the world's opportunities into China's opportunities and vice versa. Based on this recognition and oriented toward opening up, the BRI will promote the orderly and free flow of economic factors, highly efficient allocation of resources, and deep integration of markets. It will require broader and more in-depth regional cooperation with higher standards, and it will spur open, inclusive, and balanced regional economic cooperation architecture that benefits all by enhancing connectivity in transportation, energy, internet, and other infrastructure so as to address the issues of economic growth and balance. This means the BRI is diversified, open, inclusive, and cooperative. Being open and inclusive is an outstanding characteristic that distinguishes it from other regional economic initiatives.

(2) It is a platform for pragmatic cooperation, not a geopolitical instrument of China. The BRI captures the spirit of the Silk Road. It has strengthened exchanges and cooperation among relevant countries on all fronts and at multiple levels, fully exploring and leveraging the development potential and comparative strengths of these countries, and thus creating a mutually beneficial regional community of shared interests, futures, and responsibilities. In this dynamic, each country is an equal participant, contributor, and beneficiary. Therefore, the BRI is characterized by equality and peace from the very beginning. Equality is an important international norm China adheres to, and it is also a key foundation for the BRI. Only when it is based on equality can cooperation be lasting and mutually beneficial. The equality and inclusiveness of the BRI have eased resistance to its advancement, improved the efficiency of joint construction, and helped international cooperation truly take root. Indeed, without peaceful and stable international and regional environments, it would be impossible to pursue the BRI. Peace is an essential attribute of the BRI and a factor indispensable for its smooth progress. As such, the BRI should not be reduced to an instrument for political contests among major powers. In pursuing it, we will not resort to the old geopolitical maneuvering.

(3) It is a joint development initiative based on extensive consultation, joint contribution, and shared benefits, not a foreign aid project of China. The BRI is promoted through specific projects on the basis of bilateral or multilateral collaboration, and it is developed after adequate policy coordination, strategic complementation, and market-based operation. In May 2017, the Joint Communiqué of the Leaders Roundtable of the Belt and Road Forum for International Cooperation emphasized the basic principles for pursuing the BRI, one of which is market-based operation: recognizing the role of the market and that of business as key players, while ensuring that the government performs its proper role. This emphasis highlighted the importance of open, transparent, and non-discriminatory procurement procedures. Thus, it can be seen that the central player in the BRI is not the government but the enterprise. The fundamental method is to follow the laws of the market and realize the interests of all parties involved through the market-oriented operation. And the government

should play a directional and service-oriented function, such as building a platform, establishing mechanisms, guiding policies, etc.

(4) It is a complement to existing mechanisms, not a replacement. B&R countries have complementary strengths in resources. Some countries are rich in energy resources but short on exploitation capacity; some have abundant labor but not enough jobs; some have a large market space but a weak industrial base; and some have a strong demand for infrastructure construction but lack of money. As the world's second-largest economy and the world's leader in foreign exchange reserves, China boasts comprehensive advantages in capital, technology, talent, and management due to its increasing number of successful industries, its rich experience in infrastructure construction, and its strong equipment-manufacturing capabilities. This provides a realistic need and a great opportunity for China and other B&R parties to complement industries by leveraging their comparative strengths. Therefore, the core content of the BRI is to promote infrastructure construction and interconnection and strengthen complementarity between the Belt and Road Initiative and the national policies and development strategies of countries involved so as to deepen practical cooperation, enhance coordinated development, and achieve common prosperity. Obviously, it is not a substitute for existing regional cooperation mechanisms but a complement to these mechanisms. In fact, the BRI has realized cooperation and coordination with the policy initiatives of many relevant countries, such as the Eurasian Economic Union of Russia, the Global Maritime Fulcrum of Indonesia, the Bright Road initiative of Kazakhstan, the Steppe Road Initiative of Mongolia, the Investment Plan for Europe of the EU, and the Suez Canal Corridor Development Project of Egypt. Moreover, it has resulted in the formation of a number of landmark projects, including the Sino-Kazakhstan Logistics Cooperation Base in China's eastern port city Lianyungang. As one of the achievements of the New Eurasian Continental Bridge Economic Corridor, this logistics base has begun to realize the seamless connection of deep-water ports, ocean trunk lines, China-Europe rail service, and logistics stations. The project is fully compatible with Kazakhstan's Bright Road development strategy. Azat Turlybekuly Peruashev, chairman of the Ak Zhol Democratic Party of Kazakhstan, complimented the new economic policy "Nurly Zhol" ("Bright Road") by saying that the BRI has effectively promoted the economic development of Kazakhstan and even the entire Central Asia region, opening up vast space and creating more opportunities for wide cooperation among countries in economic, cultural and other fields.

(5) It is a bridge for cultural exchanges, not a trigger for the clash of civilizations. The BRI spans different regions, different cultures, and different religious beliefs. It brings about exchanges and mutual learning between civilizations rather than conflicts. In addition to infrastructure development and industrial cooperation and connectivity in development strategies, closer interpersonal ties are another priority in pursuing the BRI. Guided by the Silk Road spirit, BRI participating countries have engaged in efforts to build the educational Silk Road and health Silk Road and moreover participated in other forms of exchange, including the exchange of science, education, culture, health, and friendship. Such cooperation helps lay a solid popular and social foundation for pursuing the BRI. In pursuing the BRI, participating countries

ensure that when it comes to different civilizations, exchange will replace estrangement, mutual learning will replace conflict, and coexistence will replace a sense of superiority. The initiative will build a new bridge for the people of participating countries to strengthen communication and understanding, develop new ties between cultures, and strengthen dialogue, exchange, and mutual learning. This will boost understanding, respect, and trust on an international scale.

2. The implications of the BRI

The scope of cooperation in the BRI has continued to expand. It not only brings tangible cooperation dividends to all parties involved; it also spreads wisdom, strengthening countries to address challenges, create opportunities, and boost confidence. The BRI is a blueprint for the new century, a blueprint with an ancient origin. It is a coordinated plan for land and sea, a global vision.

The initiative has already accomplished a great deal, including the following:

(1) It has provided a new path and direction for global governance. In today's world, challenges are ubiquitous, and risks are on the rise. Global economic growth lacks energy; the impact of the financial crisis endures; development gaps continue to widen; "black swan" events occur frequently; trade protectionism and anti-globalization gain in popularity; regional turmoil continues; and terrorism is rampant. A concerning deficit of peace, development, and governance is faced by all mankind. There are structural problems in the existing global governance system, and there is an urgent need to find new solutions and countermeasures. As an emerging superpower, China has the ability, willingness, and responsibility to contribute wisdom and strength to improving the global governance system. In the face of such emerging challenges, China's global governance plan is: to build a community with a shared future for mankind and achieve mutual benefits. The BRI is an effort toward this goal. It emphasizes equal participation, inclusiveness, and benefits shared by all. It advocates working together to meet the challenges facing the world economy, creating new opportunities for development, seeking new drivers of development, and expanding new development space—and all these things as a way of moving toward a community of shared destiny. Based on such principles and ideas in pursuing the BRI, China has established AIIB, the BRICS New Development Bank, the Silk Road Fund, and other new international mechanisms as well as multi-form and multi-channel platforms for exchange and cooperation. All these have been established to address practical problems in the development of various countries and shortcomings of the governance system. In this way, the BRI can alleviate the dilemma that current global governance mechanisms face in meeting the actual need for being representative, effective, and timely. It can also reverse the insufficient supply of public goods to a certain extent and boost the morale of the international community participating in global governance. Meanwhile, it can meet the realistic requirements of developing countries, especially those with emerging market economies, by reforming the global governance mechanism and

thereby greatly increasing the say of emerging and developing countries. The BRI is a major breakthrough in making a more just and reasonable global governance system.

(2) It has offered a Chinese approach to win-win cooperation in the new era. Countries at different stages of development and with different forms of government have different strategic demands and different priorities, but they invariably anticipate development and prosperity. This fact offers a clue in determining the greatest common denominator among the interests of different countries. How can one country's development plan interact with the strategies of other countries in order to best utilize the strengths of each country? This is the key question one must ask in order to understand how to achieve a win-win situation. The BRI is a platform for cooperation that is formed with the goal of respecting the development path choices of all participating nations to meet their needs in seeking development opportunities. Based on the basic norms governing international relations of equality, mutual benefit, and mutual respect, the initiative focuses on the realities and needs of each country and strives to make their development strategies complementary. In addition to worldwide recognition and praise, the BRI has also achieved an increasingly remarkable early harvest, bringing tangible benefits to participating countries and boosting confidence in the potential to achieve an inclusive, balanced, sustainable, and prosperous world. One example of the BRI invigorating cooperative action between nations has occurred on the African continent. The first electrified railway in Africa, the Yaji Railway (Addis Ababa to Djibouti), opened in October 2016, and the Mombasa-Nairobi Railway opened in May 2017. These two highly influential 21st-century projects were undertaken by China. They have been praised by many African countries as the "Road of Friendship and Cooperation" and the "Road of Prosperity and Development." It can be seen from the example of China-Africa cooperation that the Belt and Road is a road of cooperation, a road of hope, and mutual benefit.

(3) It has provided a new driver and new platform for balanced, sustainable global development. The BRI covers both developing and developed countries, and it realizes the unification of South-South and North-South cooperation, which will help promote balanced and sustainable global development. Based on infrastructure construction, the initiative has promoted the orderly and free flow of economic factors and macro-policy coordination between China and relevant countries. For the developing countries participating in the BRI, the initiative is a historic opportunity to board the express train of China's economic development in order to realize their own industrialization and modernization. It has not only vigorously advanced South-South cooperation but also enhanced North-South dialogue and promoted the in-depth development of North-South cooperation. Moreover, the direction of the BRI is quite compatible with the UN 2030 Agenda for Sustainable Development. UN Secretary-General Antonio Guterres stated that both documents aim at sustainable development, attempt to provide the same things (opportunities, global public goods, win-win cooperation), and are committed to deepening national and regional ties. In order for relevant countries to fully benefit from the potential of closer relations, it is essential to strengthen the connectivity between the BRI and the 2030 Agenda for Sustainable Development, he stressed. In this regard, the BRI assists in the smooth realization of the 2030 Agenda.

(4) It is a major move for wider opening up and the top-level design of economic diplomacy. Openness brings progress, while isolation makes a person fall behind. In the long-term practice of revolution, construction, and reform, our Party has continuously deepened its understanding of the law of opening up. As Chinese socialism enters a new era, the conditions of an open economy have greatly changed, and its foundation has become more secure. The interaction between China and the world has also undergone a historical evolution. To pursue the BRI, the Communist Party has intentionally pursued domestic development planning against the backdrop of globalization. Such an approach marks a great historical change in the Party's understanding of pursuing greater openness: instead of the Chinese government controlling the entire process of opening, China instead takes leadership as mutual choices to flourish throughout the world. This new approach manifests great confidence in the path, theory, system, and culture of Chinese socialism.

III. Cooperation Priorities and Mechanisms for the BRI

Cooperation does not occur without planning. In this section, the reader will find a number of priorities that should be pursued as a part of the Belt and Road Initiative and a number of mechanisms that will promote the goals of this initiative.

1. Cooperation priorities

Countries along the Belt and Road have their own resource advantages and economies that are mutually complementary. These qualities create great potential for cooperation. Efforts should be made to promote policy coordination, infrastructure connectivity, unimpeded trade, financial integration, and closer interpersonal ties.

(1) Policy coordination

Enhancing policy coordination is an important element in implementing the initiative. Policy coordination may take the form of increased intergovernmental cooperation, the establishment of a multilevel mechanism for intergovernmental macro policy exchange and communication, the expansion of shared interests, the enhancement of mutual trust, and the promotion of efforts to create cooperative consensus. B&R countries will coordinate economic development strategies and policies, work out plans and measures for regional cooperation, negotiate the resolution of thorny issues, and jointly provide policy support for the implementation of large-scale projects.

(2) Infrastructure connectivity

Infrastructure connectivity is a priority area for implementing the initiative. With the goal of respecting each other's sovereignty and security concerns, countries along the Belt and Road must improve the connectivity of their infrastructure construction plans and technical standard systems, must jointly push forward the construction of international trunk passageways, and must form an infrastructure network connecting all sub-regions in Asia, and connecting Asia with Europe and Africa. At the same time, efforts should be made to promote green and low-carbon infrastructure construction and operation management, taking into full account the impact of climate change on the construction.

With regard to the construction of transportation infrastructure, partners in the initiative should focus on the passageways, junctions, and projects. They should give priority to linking up unconnected road sections, removing transport bottlenecks, updating road safety/traffic management facilities and equipment, and improving road network connectivity. Participating nations should also do the following: build a unified coordination mechanism for whole-course transportation; increase connectivity of customs clearance, reloading, and multi-modal transport between countries; gradually standardize amenable transport rules; push forward port infrastructure construction; build smooth land-water transportation channels with advanced port cooperation; increase sea routes and the number of voyages; and enhance information technology cooperation in maritime logistics. An additional two steps relate to air travel: the expansion of platforms for comprehensive civil aviation cooperation and a commitment to improve aviation infrastructure at a quicker pace.

The connectivity of energy infrastructure also deserves attention. China and its partners must work in concert to ensure the security of oil and gas pipelines and other transport routes. They must also build cross-border power supply networks and power transmission routes and cooperate in regional power grid upgrades and transformation. Joint advancements in the construction of cross-border optical cables and other communications trunk line networks are needed, as well as improvements in international communications connectivity: the creation of an Information Silk Road. There is a need for building bilateral cross-border optical cable networks at a quicker pace, planning transcontinental submarine optical cable projects, and improving spatial (satellite) information passageways to expand information sharing.

(3) Unimpeded trade

Investment and trade cooperation is a major task in building the Belt and Road. A key objective must be to improve investment and trade facilitation, removing barriers that stand in the way of creating a sound business environment within the region. What is needed are frank international discussions about how to open free trade areas and thus unleash the potential for expanded cooperation.

Countries along the Belt and Road should enhance customs cooperation as manifested in information exchange, mutual recognition of regulations, and mutual assistance in law enforcement. They should improve bilateral and multilateral cooperation in the fields of inspection and quarantine, certification and accreditation, standard measurement, and statistical information. They should work to ensure that the WTO Trade Facilitation Agreement takes effect and is implemented. It is also necessary to improve the customs clearance facilities at border ports, establish a "single window" at these ports, reduce customs clearance costs, and improve customs clearance capability. Increased cooperation in supply chain safety and convenience will be beneficial, as will the improvement of the coordination of cross-border supervision procedures, promotion of online checking of inspection and quarantine certificates, and facilitation of the mutual recognition of Authorized Economic Operators (AEOs). Nations must lower non-tariff barriers, jointly improve the transparency of technical trade measures, and enhance trade liberalization and facilitation.

But that is not all. Expanding trading areas, improving trade structure, exploring new growth areas of trade, promoting trade balance—all of these changes matter. Countries must innovate in their forms of trade and develop cross-border e-commerce models and other modern business models. A service trade support system should be set up to consolidate and expand conventional trade; efforts to develop modern service trade should be strengthened. The net result will be integrated investment and trade and the promotion of trade through investment.

A future shaped by the BRI will be characterized by expedited investment facilitation, the elimination of investment barriers, and the advancement of negotiations on agreements to protect the lawful rights and interests of investors (e.g., bilateral investment protection agreements and double-taxation avoidance agreements). It will further include mutual investment areas, deepening cooperation in various agricultural industries (traditional agriculture, forestry, animal husbandry, fisheries, agricultural machinery manufacturing, farm produce processing), and will promote cooperation in marine-product farming, deep-sea fishing, aquatic product processing, seawater desalination, marine biopharmacy, ocean engineering technology, environmental protection industries, marine tourism, and other fields. This cooperation will extend into the exploration and development of coal, oil, gas, metal minerals, and other conventional energy sources; into advanced cooperation in hydropower, nuclear power, wind power, solar power, and other clean, renewable energy sources; into cooperation in the processing and conversion of energy and resources at or near places where they are exploited so as to create an integrated industrial chain of energy and resource cooperation. It is important to enhance cooperation in deep-processing technology, equipment, and engineering services in energy-related fields and push forward cooperation in emerging industries. In accordance with the principles of mutual complementarity and mutual benefit, a historical level of profound cooperation between countries along the Belt and Road can be established, accompanying advances in information technology, biotechnology, new energy technology, new materials, and the like, and promoting entrepreneurial and investment cooperation mechanisms.

The division of labor and distribution of industrial chains should be improved by encouraging the entire industrial chain and related industries to develop in concert. This involves establishing R&D, production, and marketing systems and improving industrial supporting capacity and the overall competitiveness of regional industries. Countries will also benefit as they make service industries more open to each other to accelerate the development of regional service industries. There can be a new mode of investment cooperation, working together to build all forms of industrial parks—for instance, overseas economic and trade cooperation zones and cross-border economic cooperation zones—and to promote industrial cluster development. Ecological progress in conducting investment and trade should be promoted, cooperation in conserving the eco-environment increased, biodiversity protected, and climate change addressed as different nations join hands to make the new Silk Road an environment-friendly one.

(4) Financial integration

Financial integration underpins the implementation of the Belt and Road Initiative. In addition to deepening financial cooperation, more efforts in building a currency stability system in Asia must be made, as well as efforts addressing the investment and financing system and credit information system. The region should expand the scope and scale of bilateral currency swaps and settlements with other B&R countries, open and develop the bond market in Asia, make joint efforts to establish the AIIB and BRICS New Development Bank, conduct negotiation among related parties in establishing the Shanghai Cooperation Organization (SCO) financing institution, and make the Silk Road Fund operational as early as possible. Practical cooperation between the China-ASEAN Interbank Association and the SCO Interbank Association should be strengthened, as interested parties carry out multilateral financial cooperation in the form of syndicated loans and bank credit. We will support the efforts of governments of the countries along the Belt and Road and their companies and financial institutions with good credit ratings to issue RMB bonds in China. Qualified Chinese financial institutions and companies are encouraged to issue bonds in both RMB and foreign currencies outside China and use the funds thus collected in B&R countries.

China would be well-advised to strengthen cooperation in financial regulation, encourage the signing of MoUs on cooperation in bilateral financial regulation, and establish an efficient regulation coordination mechanism in the region. These steps should additionally include enhancing the system for risk response and crisis management, building a regional early-warning system for financial risks, and creating an exchange and cooperation mechanism to address cross-border risks and crises. Cross-border exchange should be encouraged, as should cooperation between credit investigation regulators, credit investigation agencies, and credit rating agencies. China should give full play to the role of the Silk Road Fund and that of sovereign wealth funds in countries along the Belt and Road and should encourage commercial equity investment funds and private funds to participate in the construction of key projects of the initiative.

(5) Closer interpersonal ties

Closer people-to-people ties lay the groundwork for public support for implementing the initiative. The spirit of friendly cooperation of the Silk Road must be carried forward through the promotion of extensive cultural and academic exchanges, personnel exchanges, media cooperation, youth and women exchanges, and volunteer services so as to win public support for deepening bilateral and multilateral cooperation.

Belt and Road countries should send more students to each other's countries and should promote cooperation in jointly running schools. China provides 10,000 government scholarships to countries along the Belt and Road every year. Various forms of cultural connection should be encouraged: culture years, arts festivals, film festivals, TV weeks, and book fairs in each other's countries. There should be cooperation in the production and translation of fine films, radio programs, and TV shows; there should be joint applications for World Cultural Heritage sites and joint protection of existing sites. Cooperation should extend to the workplace, expanding opportunities for personnel exchange and cooperation between Belt and Road countries.

Tourism can be a site of interpersonal cooperation, especially as tourism increases in scale. Tourism promotion weeks and publicity months can be created in each other's countries; competitive international tourist routes can be built, incorporating products with Silk Road features; applications for tourist visas in B&R countries can be expedited. The government should push forward cooperation on the 21st Century Maritime Silk Road cruise tourism program and should also carry out sports exchanges while supporting countries along the route in their bid to host major international sports events.

Significant progress must be made in cooperation within the disciplines of medicine, science, and technology. This means further cementing ties with neighboring countries on epidemic information sharing, facilitating the exchange of treatments and preventatives, investing in the training of medical professionals, and improving the region's capability to jointly address public health emergencies. It means providing medical assistance and emergency medical aid to countries in need, and it means taking strides in maternal and child health, disability rehabilitation, and major infectious diseases, including AIDS, tuberculosis, and malaria.

In terms of science, the needed progress will involve things like the establishment of joint labs (or research centers), international technology transfer centers, and maritime cooperation centers. China needs to promote sci-tech personnel exchanges, cooperate in tackling key sci-tech problems, and work together to improve sci-tech innovation capability. This is the right time to focus existing resources on the goal of expanding practical cooperation between countries along the Belt and Road in areas like youth employment, entrepreneurship training, vocational skill development, social security management, public administration and management, and other areas of common interest.

Political parties and parliaments must seize the opportunity to communicate, creating friendly exchanges between legislative bodies and between major political parties and political organizations within B&R countries. This communication may become a bridge. The government ought to carry out exchanges and cooperation among cities, encourage major cities in B&R countries to become sister cities, focus on promoting cultural and people-to-people exchanges, and create more lively examples of cooperation. Think tanks should be welcome to jointly conduct research and hold forums in B&R countries.

There should be an increase in exchanges and cooperation between nongovernmental organizations of B&R countries, with organized public interest activities surrounding the areas of education, healthcare, poverty reduction, biodiversity, and ecological protection for the benefit of the general public. These changes will be essential to improve the living conditions of those in poverty-stricken areas along the Belt and Road and to increase their productivity. Further advances along these lines will come as cultural and media cooperation flourishes and as China leverages the positive role of internet technologies to promote a harmonious and friendly cultural environment and to shape public opinion.

2. Cooperation mechanisms

Bilateral cooperation is essential for countries within the Belt and Road. It should be strengthened, and comprehensive development of bilateral relations through multilevel and multichannel communication should be promoted. An increased number of cooperation MoUs or plans need to be signed, even as countries work toward the development of bilateral cooperation pilot projects. Bilateral joint working mechanisms should be improved, and implementation plans (i.e., road maps) for advancing the BRI should be drawn up. Meanwhile, existing bilateral mechanisms—joint committees, mixed committees, coordinating committees, steering committees, and management committees—must be given a wider berth to coordinate and promote the implementation of cooperation projects.

A number of multilateral cooperation mechanisms currently exist, including the SCO, ASEAN Plus China (10+1), APEC, Asia-Europe Meeting (ASEM), Asia Cooperation Dialogue (ACD), the Conference on Interaction and Confidence-Building Measures in Asia (CICA), the China-Arab States Cooperation Forum (CASCF), China-Gulf Cooperation Council Strategic Dialogue, Greater Mekong Subregion (GMS) Economic Cooperation, and Central Asia Regional Economic Cooperation (CAREC). The role of these entities should be enhanced in order to strengthen communication with relevant countries and attract more countries and regions to participate in the BRI.

A number of international forums and exhibitions at regional and sub-regional levels are also hosted by B&R countries, including the Boao Forum for Asia, the China-ASEAN Expo, the China-Eurasia Expo, the Euro-Asia Economic Forum, the China International Fair for Investment and Trade, the China-South Asia Expo, the China-Arab States Expo, the West China International Fair, the China-Russia Expo, and the Qianhai Cooperation Forum. There are also art-related meetings, including the Silk Road (Dunhuang) International Culture Expo, the Silk Road International Film Festival, and the Silk Road International Book Fair. All these forums and exhibitions play a constructive role and ought to be encouraged. It can increasingly be observed that authorities and citizens in countries along the Belt and Road are exploring the historical and cultural heritage of the Belt and Road, making joint investments, and cooperating in trade and cultural exchange. For example, China recently set up the Belt and Road Forum for International Cooperation, which is held every two years. Forums for cooperation of this sort deserve a great deal of support.

IV. Comprehensively Enhancing the Level of Open Economy through the BRI

In advancing the BRI, China will fully leverage the comparative advantages of its various regions, adopt a proactive strategy of further opening up, strengthen interaction and cooperation among the eastern, western, and central regions, and comprehensively improve the openness of the Chinese economy.

1. Northern region

Xinjiang has certain geographic advantages that allow it to serve as a window of westward opening up to deepen communication and cooperation with Central, Southern, and Western Asian countries. This makes it a key transportation, trade, logistics, culture, science, and education center and a core area on the Silk Road Economic Belt. China must seize upon these advantages.

China must also give full scope to the economic and cultural strengths of the Shaanxi and Gansu provinces and the ethnic and cultural advantages of the Ningxia Hui autonomous region and the Qinghai Province. It must build Xi'an into a new focus of reform and opening-up in China's interior. It must speed up the development of cities, such as Lanzhou and Xining, and advance the establishment of the Ningxia Inland Opening Up Pilot Economic Zone with the goal of creating strategic channels, trade and logistics hubs, and key bases for industrial and cultural exchanges as the region seeks greater openness with Central, South, and West Asian countries.

It would be beneficial to give full play to Inner Mongolia's proximity to Mongolia and Russia and additionally to improve the railway links connecting Heilongjiang Province with Russia and the regional railway network, to strengthen cooperation on sea-land multi-modal transport between China's Heilongjiang, Jilin, and Liaoning provinces and Russia's Far East region, and to advance the construction of an Eurasian high-speed transport corridor linking Beijing and Moscow, with the goal of building bridges with the north.

2. Southwestern region

In the southwest, the Guangxi Zhuang autonomous region has the unique advantage of being a neighbor of ASEAN countries, an advantage that China must lean into. The region should focus on expediting the development of the Beibu Gulf Economic Zone and the Pearl River-Xijiang Economic Zone, building an international corridor opening to the ASEAN region, creating new strategic anchors for the opening up in the southwest and mid-south regions of China, and forming an important gateway connecting the Silk Road Economic Belt and the 21st Century Maritime Silk Road.

The government must make good use of the geographical advantages of the Yunnan Province. It must also advance the construction of an international transport corridor connecting China with neighboring countries, develop a new focus of economic cooperation in the Greater Mekong Subregion, and make the region a pivot upon which China can open up more broadly to South and Southeast Asia. Border trade and tourism should be promoted, along with cultural cooperation between the Tibet autonomous region and neighboring countries such as Nepal.

3. Coastal regions, and Hong Kong, Macao, and Taiwan

There are currently a number of coastal regions with economic zones boasting a high level of openness, robust economic strength, and proven dynamism. These regions include the Yangtze River Delta, the Pearl River Delta, the west coast of the Taiwan Straits, and the Bohai Rim, among others. The strength of these regions should be leveraged moving forward, even as other developing regions—such as the SHFTZ—receive assistance in development. It is imperative to support Fujian Province in becoming a core area of the 21st Century Maritime Silk Road. Various other coastal regions should be given full scope to grow into greater openness and cooperation, regions like Qianhai (Shenzhen), Nansha (Guangzhou), Hengqin (Zhuhai), and Pingtan (Fujian). These areas have the opportunity to deepen their cooperation with Hong Kong, Macao, and Taiwan and help to build the Guangdong–Hong Kong–Macao Big Bay Area.

The Chinese government should promote the development of the Zhejiang Marine Economy Development Demonstration Zone, the Fujian Marine Economic Pilot Zone, and the Zhoushan Archipelago New Area and should further open Hainan Province as an international tourist destination. It should strengthen the port construction of coastal cities such as Shanghai, Tianjin, Ningbo-Zhoushan, Guangzhou, Shenzhen, Zhanjiang, Shantou, Qingdao, Yantai, Dalian, Fuzhou, Xiamen, Quanzhou, Haikou, and Sanya. It should enhance the role of international hub airports such as Shanghai and Guangzhou. The imperative of opening up can motivate these areas to carry out deeper reform, creating new systems and mechanisms of open economy, stepping up scientific and technological innovation, and developing new advantages for participating in and leading international cooperation and competition. Through all these steps, China can become the pacesetter and driving force in the Belt and Road Initiative, particularly the building of the 21st Century Maritime Silk Road.

The unique role of overseas Chinese and the Hong Kong and Macao Special Administrative Regions can be leveraged, encouraging them to participate in and contribute to the Belt and Road Initiative. Proper arrangements for the Taiwan region to be part of this effort should also be made.

4. Inland regions

Inland regions of China have their own unique advantages, including vast tracts of land, rich human resources, and a strong industrial foundation. These advantages, too, ought to be capitalized on. A special focus should be placed on such key regions as the city clusters along the middle reaches of the Yangtze River, on the environs of Chengdu and Chongqing as well those of Hohhot, Baotou, Erdos, and Yulin, on central Henan Province, and on the regions around Harbin and Changchun. Such a focus will propel regional interaction, cooperation, and industrial concentration. Chongqing should be built into an important pivot for developing and opening up the western region, even as Chengdu, Zhengzhou, Wuhan, Changsha, Nanchang, and Hefei are developed into leading areas of opening up in the inland regions.

In addition to the above, it is advisable to accelerate cooperation between regions on the upper and middle reaches of the Yangtze River and their counterparts along Russia's Volga River. China should set up coordination mechanisms to accommodate railway transport and port customs clearance for the China–Europe corridor, cultivate the brand of "China–Europe freight trains," and construct a cross-border transport corridor connecting the eastern, central, and western regions. Inland cities such as Zhengzhou and Xi'an also deserve support in building airports and international land ports. Customs clearance cooperation between inland ports and ports in the coastal and border regions should be strengthened, and pilot e-commerce services for cross-border trade should be launched. It is the right time to optimize the layout of special customs oversight areas and develop new models of processing trade.

SECTION 4
International Free Trade Agreements and the Construction of Free Trade Areas

International free trade agreements and free trade areas (FTAs) are important forms of regional economic integration and global trade liberalization. They are also an important part of China's opening up since they enhance the development of foreign economic relations. Speeding up negotiations on free trade agreements and spurring free trade area construction will help China break new ground in pursuing opening up on all fronts and will bring more opening-up-related dividends to Chinese enterprises and Chinese people.

I. International Free Trade Agreements and the Construction of Domestic FTZs

A free trade agreement is a legally binding pact between two or more nations to reduce trade barriers, allowing products and services to flow freely across international borders and promoting economic integration.

A free trade area (FTA) has two definitions. Broadly defined by the WTO, it refers to a region in which a group of countries has signed a free trade agreement to further open their markets, phase out tariff or non-tariff barriers on the vast majority of the goods, improve market access in the service sector, and realize the liberalization of trade and investment by treating those within the agreement as most-favored-nations (MFN). As such, a free trade area promotes the free flow of goods, services, and production factors like capital, technology, and labor. The North American Free Trade Area (NAFTA) and China-Japan-ROK FTA are two examples. Some FTAs only implement free trade for certain commodities, such as the European Free Trade Association (EFTA), which limits commodities to industrial products and excludes agricultural products. Some free trade areas implement free trade for all commodities, such as the Asociación Latinoamericana de Libre Comercio (ALALC) and NAFTA, which exempt all industrial and agricultural products from tariffs and quantitative restrictions.

A narrower category is the free trade zone (FTZ), defined by the World Customs Organization (WCO) as a special economic zone established in a country that is outside the jurisdiction of customs and implements free trade and investment policies. One example is the SHFTZ. FTZs follow the policy of "inside the territory while outside customs" rather than the "inside the territory and customs" rule in the bonded areas.

Since the WTO approved the suspension of the Doha Round in July 2006, various regional and bilateral FTAs have been negotiated around the world. With the launch of negotiations on FTAs involving major economies in different regions, the competition of the world's major economies in FTAs in the field of global trade has become an important trend in the world economy. Such FTA negotiations include the Trans-Pacific Partnership (TPP), the EU-Japan Economic Partnership Agreement (EPA), the US-EU Transatlantic Trade and Investment Partnership (TTIP), and the Regional Comprehensive Economic Partnership (RCEP), an FTA strongly advocated by China. These negotiations will not only shape the future pattern of world trade but will also affect the economic and even political standing of the participating nations. According to WTO statistics, as of 2017, a total of 647 regional trade agreements (RTAs) have been notified to the WTO, and 433 have entered into force. Among these, only 124 were reached during the GATT period in 1948–1994; the other 400-plus have been reached since the formal establishment of the WTO in 1995. As of July 2013, the number of RTAs notified to the WTO was 575. Of all RTAs taking effect after 2000, bilateral FTAs account for over 90%.

Against such a backdrop, countries have set up one FTZ after another. At present, there are about 1,200 domestic FTZs in the world. They have become an important instrument for the countries and regions where they are located to develop free trade and implement trade policies. Of all nations, the US owns the largest number of FTZs in the world, with about 260 located in its major port cities.

Since it entered Asia-Pacific Economic Cooperation (APEC) in 1991 and signed an FTA with ASEAN in 2002, China has joined regional economic cooperation organizations of various sorts and has made great strides in regional economic cooperation. In 2007, the goal of "implement[ing] the strategy of building FTAs" was written into the report to the 17th National Congress of the CPC, and it was officially upgraded to a national strategy. In 2012, the report to the 18th National Congress of the CPC promised to "accelerate the implementation of the strategy of building FTAs" and to construct a standard FTA network. In 2013, the Third Plenary Session of the 18th CPC Central Committee emphasized the need to "accelerate the construction of FTAs." In 2015, the State Council issued Several Opinions on Accelerating the Implementation of the Strategy of Building FTAs. By the end of 2017, China had signed sixteen free trade agreements, fifteen of which have already come into effect, involving 24 countries and regions and covering more than 8,000 tariff-free imported goods.

In August 2013, the State Council formally approved the establishment of the SHFTZ, and on September 29 of the same year, the SHFTZ was formally established. On December 28, 2014, the Standing Committee of the National People's Congress (NPC) authorized the State Council to expand the SHFTZ to cover 120.72 square kilometers. As a new test field for China's economy, the SHFTZ carries out various reforms that aim to transform government functions, financial systems, trade services, foreign investment policies, and taxation policies. It will vigorously promote the development of Shanghai's re-export and offshore business.

On April 20, 2015, the State Council decided to expand the scope of implementation for the SHFTZ. On the same day, it approved the establishment of three pilot FTZs located in Guangdong, Tianjin, and Fujian. Then, on March 31, 2017, it approved the establishment of seven additional pilot FTZs, located in Liaoning, Zhejiang, Henan, Hubei, Chongqing, Sichuan, and Shaanxi.

At present, a "1+3+7" FTZs structure has formed in China, covering the eastern, central, and western regions. In the process of building FTZs, it is essential to achieve the correct strategic positioning, giving play to the geographical advantages of different regions as well as FTZs, and to realize diversified functional divisions. On this basis, it is necessary to closely link the FTZs with the FTAs so as to expand foreign trade and enhance its level of openness. For instance, an important open maritime gateway can be built through the FTZs in the eastern region, and FTZs in the central and western regions can be developed into important hubs for interconnection under the BRI and an important fulcrum of the strategy of central and western development.

II. Competition in International Free Trade Agreements and Free Trade Areas

When the Doha Round failed to provide the global public goods of a new multilateral free trade system, it became a trend for major economies to conclude regional FTAs on their own terms. It is easier to negotiate agreements in regional and bilateral free trade than in global multilateral trade. Ideally speaking, if the major FTAs can be mutually inclusive and open to each other such that they integrate regional and bilateral FTAs, it will be possible to overcome the impasse which concluded the Doha Round to a significant degree and allow for the promotion of in-depth development of global free trade despite the lack of global multilateral talks.

After the 2008 financial crisis, traditional FTA competition has seen a new development trend. Certain patterns have emerged:

(1) East Asia is becoming a new center for FTA negotiations. In view of the growth potential of the region, along with its economic vitality, both the US and the EU have formally regarded East Asia as the focus of their FTA strategies and have formulated ambitious plans to negotiate agreements there. In the context of competition between China and Japan, the region has become a hotly contested place for future FTAs among major countries.

(2) FTA negotiations are converging among developed economies. Four major economies in the world, including the EU, the US, China, and Japan, have signed a large number of self-centered FTAs, but have not yet reached any FTAs between themselves. Driven by various factors, substantive FTA negotiations have been conducted between the US and the EU, the US and Japan, and Japan and the EU. There are also FTAs under negotiation between the three and other advanced economies in OECD. As of 2013, the EU had 28 FTAs of various forms in force and had completed negotiations on another nine; the US had twenty FTAs in force; Japan had thirteen FTAs in force. By comparison, China had fifteen FTAs in force as of 2017. Against this backdrop, it is striking that the above-mentioned four major economies have not yet reached an FTA.

(3) FTA competition is quite fierce. On the one hand, major economies are trying their best to avoid being left out; on the other hand, they are also actively seeking to reduce, check, and even eliminate the economic, political, and security advantages that other economies have gained from FTAs. For example, the EU and Japan not only signed an FTA with Mexico, the third largest trading partner of the US, but are also trying to negotiate FTAs with Canada, the US' largest trading partner. The US has reached FTAs with South Korea, an important trading partner of China, and is also actively conducting FTA talks with the EU, ASEAN, and Japan, the largest, third-largest, and fourth-largest trading partner of China, respectively. Incorporating a competitor's important trading partners into its own FTA network is a practice that will greatly reduce the potential negative impact of the competitor's own FTAs.

(4) Standards in FTA negotiation rules vary to a great degree, but higher standards are the trend. FTAs vary from one another in terms of entry threshold, rules, clauses, and requirements. Some employ high standards that apply to many clauses, such as those regarding all-around openness, labor practices, environmental protection, and intellectual property protection. And some are lenient with a practical step-by-step approach, aiming for early harvest. Such lack of parity has led to disputes in both ideology and competitive strategy. Some economies emphasize the superiority and rationality of their own standards and devalue other FTA standards. Some deliberately raise the bar to exclude those that fail to meet it at this stage from their FTA talks, while others expect to reduce difficulties in FTA negotiations through loose standards.

(5) Different countries approach FTA competition quite differently. If the Doha Round is any indication of the typical approach of WTO member states moving forward, current rounds of competitive FTA negotiation will be characterized by idiosyncratic preferences that each country chooses in accordance with its own national conditions and specific principles. There is a huge difference in priorities between major economies in selecting FTA negotiating partners, manifesting differences in terms of geography, objective, and demand. The EU's approach to FTA competition is to pursue regional stability via political expansion eastward and the promotion of the model of regional integration.

The EU has mainly executed FTAs with southern Mediterranean countries, central and eastern European states, and some regional cooperation organizations. This approach reflects the strategic considerations of the EU in its efforts to strengthen trade ties with other regional organizations, exert economic influence, and eventually repurpose the model of regional integration at the global level.

The US adopts an allies-first, security-oriented approach in pursuit of regional influence. Almost all FTA negotiating partners, Canada and Mexico included, are its political or military allies. Such a selection is closely related to considerations of deepening alliances, safeguarding national security, and consolidating its influence in its own backyard. The work of FTA negotiations, though led by the USTR, has in fact become an integral part of US diplomacy and serves the national security strategy of the State Department and the Department of Defense.

Japan's approach is to focus on the Asia-Pacific region, counterbalancing China and implementing agricultural protection. The Japan-ASEAN FTA was concluded under the influence of the China-ASEAN FTA. In addition, the Japan-India FTA in force and the Japan-Mongolia FTA under negotiation are also partly aimed at balancing China's influence in the neighborhood.

China's approach to FTA competition is to strengthen unification, enhance East Asia integration, and expand connections with new regions. Among China's FTAs currently in force, the mainland's two Closer Economic Partnership Arrangements (CEPAs) with Hong Kong and Macao and the Economic Cooperation Framework Agreement (ECFA) with Taiwan are the three FTAs under the "One China" political framework. These are different from those among WTO members since they aim to promote unification through market availability and increasing trade. In addition, China has paid special attention to negotiations with East Asian countries.

For example, China has concluded its first FTA ("10+1") with ASEAN. It is also pushing forward negotiations in the bilateral China-ROK FTA, the trilateral China-Japan-ROK FTA, and the "10+3" FTA. These FTA talks with nations in East Asia are mainly undertaken to advance the process of East Asian economic integration and to deepen regional economic cooperation. In addition, China's FTA strategy is characterized by regional presence, with partners including New Zealand in Oceania, Costa Rica in Central America, Chile in South America, Pakistan in South Asia, and Iceland in Europe. These countries can be regarded as China's demonstration sites, gateways for future FTAs in specific regions.

Despite differences in the specific approaches to FTAs of major countries, there are also some commonalities. For example, large countries often reach FTAs with small countries rather than their economic peers. If one were aiming at economic benefits alone, however, small nations are not the ideal partners. The truth is that economic factors are not the most critical aims of most FTAs. Based on their geographic locations and diplomatic strategies, most major countries hope to utilize FTAs to keep a stable neighborhood, consolidate relations with allies, and expand regional influence.

In summary, the FTA, an initially supplementary option to the WTO's Doha Round, has demonstrated itself to be an agile means of addressing changes in the global economic power structure and the uneven distribution of economic welfare gains. Major economies see it as a trade policy instrument. By entering into regional and bilateral FTAs, they try to obtain more institutional competitive advantages while restricting the institutional space of competitors. It is worth noting that competition in global FTAs mainly exists among economic powers. In light of such competition, some medium- and small-sized economies of economic or geographic importance will be fought over. For example, the national capitals of Mexico, South Korea, Singapore, Chile and Peru, etc., have all completed FTAs with major economies and have become the main beneficiaries of such competition.

III. The Global Layout of China's FTAs and the Construction of High-Level FTZs

Turning to questions specific to China, there are two basic imperatives moving forward.

1. Improve competency in building domestic FTZs

In this regard, the following measures are needed:

(1) Deepen reform in the pilot free trade zone continuously. The solutions to certain difficult issues in the negotiation of foreign FTAs may become clearer through the experience of pilot FTZs like SHFTZ, which offer information about optimal opening modes and provide a practice basis for foreign negotiation.

(2) Perfect laws and regulations on foreign investment. The management mode of national treatment should be executed before access is added to the negative list, and foreign investment policies should be kept stable.

(3) Further develop a basic system for supervision during and after the event. Strengthen progress supervision and follow-up management after the "tolerant entry" of a market entity.

(4) Continuously execute trade relief work with competence. This involves carrying out trade remedy investigations by law and maintaining the rights and interests of industries at home.

(5) Study the trade adjustment aid mechanism and build on it. With the goal of reducing policy distortion and standardizing industrial support policies, provide aid to the industries, enterprises, and individuals that are impacted by tariff concession, promote their competitiveness, and promote industry.

(6) Perfect the third-party evaluation system of FTZ negotiation and moreover strengthen talent support to the construction of FTZs so as to build a talent team for management and negotiation that is familiar to domestic industry and proficient in international trading rules. These employees should be of good political caliber, have strong overall awareness, a high foreign language level, and excellent negotiation skills.

2. Accelerate institutional arrangements for a bilateral and multilateral trade framework for international cooperation

With regard to FTA construction, the following moves can be considered:

(1) Accelerate the establishment of neighboring FTAs. Strive to build FTAs with all adjacent countries and districts and deepen economic and trade relationships continuously, in the process of building a cooperative and mutually beneficial neighborhood market.

(2) Actively promote FTAs along the Belt and Road. FTAs established with B&R countries will help form the B&R market so as to make the Belt and Road into an open road where trade may flourish in an unrestricted way.

(3) Gradually contribute to the global FTA network. Strive to build large markets for BRICS, emerging economies, and developing countries, and strive to establish FTAs with most emerging economies, developing countries, regional economic groups in major areas, and some developed countries.

(4) Improve the opening up level of trade in goods. Negotiate tariff and non-tariff barrier concessions together with the free trade partners and open up the trade market in goods that will foster mutual benefit and win-win results.

(5) Expand the opening up of service industries. Promote greater openness in finance, education, culture, medical treatment, and other service industries, and open up access restrictions to foreign investment in various service industries such as nursing, construction design, and accounting auditing. Promote negotiations that proceed in negative list mode, negotiations based on consistent negotiation with free trade partners.

(6) Relax investment access. This involves promoting the opening up of investment markets, engaging in thorough foreign management system reform, and further optimizing the foreign investment environment. Improve the bilateral investment access between our country and free trade partners materially. Carry forward RMB capital projects in cross-

border investment and financing actively and prudently. Strengthen cooperation in currency with free trade partners, promoting trade and investment facilitation.

(7) Encourage rules negotiation. Actively participate in the negotiation of FTAs in ways that conform to China's needs. With awareness of common international rules and development trends, combined with an understanding of the development level and governance capacity of our country, accelerate negotiations concerning new topics such as IP protection, e-commerce, competitive policies, and governmental procurement.

(8) Upgrade the facilitation level of trade. Strengthen management on place of origin and implement an approved autonomous declaration system certifying the origin of goods based on a principle of self-certification. Reform customs supervision, inspection, quarantine, and other management systems, strengthen cooperation in customs inspection and other fields, and achieve one-package service for international trade.

(9) Carry forward regulation cooperation. This will require strengthening information exchange regarding supervision systems with the free trade partners, promoting moderate integration in supervision systems, procedures, methods, and standards, reducing trade costs, and increasing trade efficiency.

(10) Facilitate the movement of persons. Provide more amenable conditions for the personnel of Chinese enterprises investing overseas, especially with respect to exit and entry.

(11) Strengthen economic and technical cooperation. Include industrial cooperation, development cooperation, GVC, and other economic cooperation topics suitably so as to encourage cooperation with free trade partners.

SECTION 5
Ensuring National Economic Security in Opening Up

Openness and security are interdependent, and the vision of this independence sets the tone for the new era. China has no choice but to pursue security dynamically in the context of opening up. This involves following the trend of the world and embarking on a path of economic security, albeit with a distinctively Chinese approach. In a period of globalization, China must handle the relationship between opening up and economic security, and indeed strengthen economic security in opening up, in order to increase its own economic power and raise its position in international competition.

I. The Significance of Maintaining National Economic Security in Opening Up

National economic security refers to the degree to which a country's economic development and economic interests are not fundamentally threatened by external forces. It is mainly reflected in the maintenance of a country's economic sovereignty, its control over key economic resources, and its comprehensive ability to resist the impact of turbulence in the international market and beyond. Whether a country can win and maintain a favorable international position depends to a large extent on the overall security of its economy. Given that economic interests play a guiding and central role in the national security strategy, economic security has become a central basis, support, and objective of political and military security. At present, national economic security has received increasing attention from the governments of various countries. Since the 1990s, countries including the US, Japan, Russia, and France have successively identified it as one of the strategic objectives of national security and have developed corresponding policies and initiatives to ensure the sustainable and secure development of their economic interests.

As a large developing country, China faces various significant constraints. China lags far behind developed countries in economy, technology, culture, etc. It will be at a disadvantage in the international division of labor and international competition for a long time. Meanwhile, China is a socialist country that possesses a basic economic system with public ownership as the mainstay. Certain international forces have always been hostile to China's socialist system, with remarks about "China Threat Theory" cropping up everywhere. As such, China's economic security will naturally be impacted by particular features and requirements endemic to its basic economic system.

China is now in the middle stage of industrialization. Some branches of China's equipment industry are categorized as competitive industries according to the standards of developed countries, but they are strategic or quasi-strategic industries during this middle phase of Chinese industrialization. This particularity makes it impossible for China to have the same understanding of the contents of strategic industries as Western developed nations. The resulting threat of foreign M&A is naturally different from what the threat to developed countries was when they were at the mid-stage of industrialization. In addition to the severe constraints of the international market mentioned above, tightening environmental and resource constraints make it necessary for China to realize a new type of industrialization. However, China is still in the initial stage of building a country of innovators. The "market for technology" strategy does not work well, and many core technologies are still at the mercy of others. After joining the WTO, China is more dependent on foreign trade. Bulk resource products such as oil and iron ore rely on the international market supply. As the market for labor-intensive export products becomes highly competitive, China will be subject to ever-increasing fluctuations. China's financial market has continued to open up, making it vulnerable to the impact of the international financial crisis and debt crisis. The financial system has become one of the most sensitive areas of national economic security. Moreover, factors including inefficient use of foreign capital, rampant commercial espionage, increasing trade frictions against China, disempowerment in international economic relations, and weak control over foreign investment risks have all increased China's economic security risks.

In the new era, China's economy has shifted from a phase of rapid growth to a phase of high-quality development. The objective to open up needs to transform accordingly, with a focus on the introduction of foreign funds and product exports, switching to a focus on forming new global competitive advantages. The Chinese must make full use of their resources—along with international and domestic markets—to engage both competitively and cooperatively in the global economy, an engagement that is both broad in scope and sophisticated in approach so as to obtain maximal benefits from economic globalization. Even so, China will struggle in international competition for a long time since it is vulnerable to external threats, so the new phase of opening up needs greater economic security. What is needed is a vision of national economic security featuring development, openness, cooperation, and risk prevention. China must do its best to maintain these qualities by applying international rules, carrying out the strategy of "going global," comprehensively improving the efficiency of foreign capital utilization, strengthening financial supervision, and continuously enhancing national capacity in independent innovation.

II. The Basic Ideas of Maintaining Economic Security

As stated above, economic security is of paramount importance. Here are some approaches tied to the pursuit of that security.

1. Regard development as the top priority

The economic security of a country is subject to its economic strength. Being poor and weak is the archenemy of national economic security. But development is its lifeblood. Only by excelling in domestic affairs, economic development, and foreign relations is it possible to reduce the cost of ensuring economic security and effectively resist external risks. Economic power provides not only a prerequisite for a country to address national security-related issues by economic means but also a guarantee that such means will promote national interests. An increase in national economic strength and competitiveness is essential to safeguarding national economic security, a fact which is reflected in both the National Security Strategy of the US of America and the National Economic Security Strategy (Basic Principles) of the Russian Federation. Developing countries can do little more than continuously improve national competitiveness to break through the technological blockade, change the increasingly unfavorable terms of trade, and bypass the hierarchy in the international division of labor, thus winning a relatively suitable external environment and creating a level, fair, and reasonable economic order. For China, economic development is currently the biggest challenge to security. Therefore, development must be the top priority. China's economic strength is an important symbol and a precondition of national economic security as the country further develops.

2. Seek security in opening-up

Against the backdrop of globalization, isolation means backwardness. The surest way to safeguard economic security is by further opening up. If the nation turns away from globalization now, with the stated reason of protecting economic security, it will face more severe economic risks, not less severe ones. After 40 years of opening up, China's national economic security is stronger than ever before. The nation must always adhere to the grand strategy of opening up. Wavering in this regard is most dangerous. It is quite impossible to think systematically about China's economic security against any other background than this one: opening makes China safer. This should become the basic method adopted to pursue analysis and address concerns about economic security.

China's strategic industries in advancing globalization should be identified. The state should encourage the normal influx of foreign capital and the participation of Chinese corporations in the process of globalization. Economic security does not mean "self-sufficiency," nor does it advocate a narrow nationalism. There is no tension between economic security and reform; the way to maintain security is to deepen reform and opening-up, to advance globalization. National economic security is actually about how to achieve higher returns from opening up while avoiding risks. China should grasp the trend of economic globalization, actively join the global economic integration system, keep a firm hold of the initiative in global competition, and resolve the risks brought by economic globalization.

3. Pursue international cooperation

The rapid and free allocation of factors of production across borders has brought the economy of various countries closer together than ever. This interdependent economic relationship expands the space for common interests. As various negative impacts of economic globalization are increasingly revealed, conflicts emerge between North and South, others emerge between South and South, and regional economic and financial crises that have long plagued international economic development continue to crop up; all these conflicts can only be resolved through cooperation. When dealing with foreign economic relations, strengthening mutually beneficial cooperation is the only way to coexistence and prosperity; vicious competition and unilateral sanctions will inevitably lead to a loss on both sides. One of the characteristics of China's opening up in a new phase is to shift from emphasizing China's uniqueness (opening up should be done according to its own schedule) to emphasizing what it shares with other countries (opening up proceeds through consultation with members of the international community). There is a need for cooperative security, emphasizing the general security of all countries in the interest of pursuing common security interests. One must take into account global diversity, promoting coordination and cooperation in various fields and creating a favorable international security environment that seeks out common ground while setting aside differences. From the standpoint of national autonomy, it is key to strategically handle the relationship between national economic sovereignty and international cooperation and expand common ground by reciprocal and fair sovereign transfer and restriction. A new type of economic partnership is possible, which casts a broader net, forming a wide-ranging, multi-form consultation and cooperation mechanism. This will allow China to solve common economic problems, improve its ability to apply checks and balances in international economic affairs, and create a new ecology of international economic security. In an economically interdependent situation, economic and trade confrontation and retaliation becomes a double-edged sword. A higher-level interdependence will bring certain risks to national economic security, but it will also provide opportunities for achieving and maintaining that security at a higher level and on a larger scale.

4. Emphasize risk prevention

Proactively managing risks is much more important than responding to them reactively. The sooner a risk is addressed, the more it is capable of being handled. In an open environment, there will be more and more complex factors that endanger China's economic interests, such as the impact of external funds or financial means on China's banking and financial system and the theft of China's commercial secrets, economic information, and important technologies by industrial and commercial espionage. A passive response would only imagine countermeasures to combat problems that have already been revealed. To maintain national economic security, a proactive response is needed: one must take precautions against problems before they occur, find out problems in time, and eliminate potential hazards. It is necessary to integrate research and decision-making to effectively assess national economic risks, and to establish national economic security prevention, early warning, and response mechanisms (such mechanisms include the national important strategic material reserve system, the market emergency response mechanism, the rapid response mechanism to foreign economic emergencies, various reasonable protection mechanisms for domestic industries and markets, diversified sources of imports, and so on). It is necessary to give full play to the government's functions in macro adjustment and economic management. Medium- and long-term countermeasures to national economic security issues should be formulated. The national economic security situation should be predicted and monitored with a global perspective, making dynamic adjustments based on changes in the situation to keep a balance between deepening reforms, expanding opening up, and safeguarding national economic security. Of course, the governmental intervention must not go too far. And the act of government can by no means replace market competition.

III. Pursuing a Holistic Approach to National Security and Safeguarding China's Economic Security

China is a large developing country, but not a powerful one. The development strategy most suitable for China will be one that takes economic development as the central task and focuses on opening up and maintaining economic security so as to maintain the sound, stable, and orderly development of China's economy in the course of opening up. Economic security should be maintained as a necessary condition of overall national security. In what follows, a number of factors of this holistic approach are outlined.

1. Accurately understand a holistic view of national security

A holistic view of national security must be maintained, taking the people's security as the ultimate goal, political security as the fundamental task, and economic security as the foundation, with military, cultural, and public security as means of guaranteeing the above. The attempt to promote international security is the most effective support for establishing a national security system with Chinese characteristics.

(1) Take the people's safety as the ultimate goal. The people's safety is a foundational requirement of historical materialism and an important manifestation of the Party's nature and purpose. The CPC is a proletarian party that always represents the interests of the masses. Its fundamental goal is to serve the people wholeheartedly. Therefore, the fundamental purpose

of safeguarding national security is to ensure the safety of people's lives and property, to guarantee the basic conditions for people's survival and development, and to promote the free and all-around development of people. To this end, we must follow the principle of *people first*, and we must insist that everything done for national security is for the sake of the people, should rely on the people, and should have the support of the people.

(2) Take political security as the fundamental task. Political security refers to the degree to which a country's territorial sovereignty, political system, ideology, etc., are protected from invasions, interference, threats, and harms of all forms. The core of politics is state power, so political security is directly related to the stability of state power. Therefore, political security takes a central role at the highest level of the national security system, and it is of fundamental strategic significance. Being a socialist country under the leadership of the CPC, China's political security includes not only territorial integrity and sovereign independence but also adherence to the nature of the people's democratic dictatorship, to the distinctively Chinese socialist system, to the unshakable dominance of Marxist ideology, and most importantly, to the absolute leadership and ruling position of the CPC. In this regard, we must give political security pride of place and maintain it with a high degree of sensitivity and consciousness. It provides a fundamental political guarantee for national security.

(3) Take economic security as the foundation. As worldwide competition shifted from a focus on military prowess to a focus on economic prosperity and technological advancement since the end of the Cold War, the status of economic factors in international relations has risen continuously. Economic globalization accelerates the liberalization of global trade, investment, and finance. The economic interdependence of countries has deepened. Economic problems in one country or region may quickly become a worldwide economic risk. A ready example is the financial crisis of the US and its huge impact on the international economy. In this regard, there is not only a need to ensure China's own security from various economic influences but also to have countermeasures in place to respond to possible external economic shocks.

(4) Military, cultural, and social security are means of guarantee. Military security is directly related to national, territorial, and sovereign integrity and, as such, is related to the survival of the country, making it an indispensable guarantee for security in other sectors. Despite major achievements in economic and social development and increased non-military options for safeguarding national security, military means have always been a guarantee to effectively deter and resist foreign aggression and subversion. Cultural security is an important spiritual support for the independence and dignity of a nation. As culture plays a greater role in international competition, especially in an information age where diverse cultures interact on the Internet, it is more difficult to safeguard cultural security and more urgent to enhance the soft power of China and the influence of Chinese culture. Social security directly affects people's living standards, so it is a matter which impacts national security and stability. Therefore, in this regard, the government must make efforts to study new situations and problems in the area of social security, follow the CPC's rule-based approach, and establish and improve various countermeasures to strengthen the foundation of social security and reduce risks, thereby erecting an important shield for national security.

(5) Promotion of international security is the support. The world today is becoming a global village. No country can exist and develop in isolation, and countries have never been as interconnected as they are today. National security is not isolated, zero-sum, or absolute. It can by no means be achieved in a vacuum. Changes in the international environment are an important variable. In recent years, China has grown closer to the outside world in politics, economy, culture, and military. Many security issues are increasingly universal and inseparable from the international environment. In this regard, the country must unswervingly follow the path of peaceful development, safeguard international security while protecting national security interests, and promote the building of a harmonious world of lasting peace and common prosperity.

2. Implement the holistic approach to national security with effective measures
The following measures are needed:

(1) Establish a systematic, dialectical, and holistic approach to national security
The big picture of national security must be understood through systematic, dialectical, and worst-case-scenario thinking. This will ensure both internal and external security, homeland and public security, traditional and non-traditional security, and national and international security. Meanwhile, such short-sighted behaviors as valuing personal or partial interests while ignoring national security, valuing economic benefits while ignoring ecology, and valuing immediate benefits while ignoring long-term development must be overcome. In this way, it is possible to continuously deepen security awareness to adjust to a world in constant change and achieve success in work related to national security.

(2) Improve a centralized, integrated, efficient, and authoritative national security system
The Third Plenary Session of the 18th CPC Central Committee decided to establish the National Security Commission (NSC). The aim of its establishment is to better handle new developments and tasks in the realm of national security and build a national security system that is centralized, integrated, highly efficient, and authoritative so as to improve leadership over the work of national security. In order to implement a holistic approach to national security, it is necessary to strengthen the top-level design, further establish and improve the national security systems, effectively integrate forces, and coordinate resources of all aspects. These advances will ensure that all departments assume responsibilities and cooperate closely, establishing conditions for the overall planning for national security and bringing into existence a strong joint force to maintain security and social stability.

(3) Enhance capacity-building for national security that provides comprehensive governance and effective response
It is vitally important to enhance comprehensive national power. Economic strength is the foundation of this power. As such, top priority must be given to economic and social development, raising social productivity to a higher level. Scientific and technological strength is a strong

support to economic and social development and, by extension, to national security. Chinese leadership must vigorously improve China's ability to innovate independently, promote leapfrog development in S&T, and accelerate the transformation of knowledge and technology into practical productive forces.

The military force is a staunch force for safeguarding national security and world peace. China must strengthen national defense and the armed forces, deepen military reforms, and continuously improve our military's ability to fight and win. The people are a fount of wisdom and strength for national security. National security education for the people must be strengthened, and national security awareness among the public must be raised. The public must have a visceral understanding of their role in consciously safeguarding national security.

(4) Enhance economic strength to ensure safety

National prosperity is the fundamental guarantee of economic security. Throughout world history, powerful countries have been open. Chinese history also shows that openness leads to prosperity, and isolation leaves one behind. The Ming and Qing dynasties were closed to the outside world. When society was forced open after the Opium War, the people were in a passive and oppressed situation. This is a hard lesson that teaches the consequences of being closed off. Openness boosts national strength. With strength, a country will be relatively safe. Countries that choose not to open up for safety reasons are in fact *less* secure. What China needs is an effective and efficient opening up that can truly enhance its overall economic strength, sustainable development potential, and international competitiveness.

Development is the essence of national security. Self-reliance, independence, and self-discipline are the three essential factors that comprise the foundation of economic security.

- Self-reliance means strengthening soft and hard power to maintain economic security. National power undergirds economic security. China should continue to pursue development as the top priority and strengthen its capability in independent innovation to enhance its hard power; meanwhile, it should deepen reforms and improve the legal system to enhance soft power.
- Independence means grasping the initiative in opening up. This is a critical task. Some international proposals do harm to developing countries because they are made without considering the national conditions of the countries involved. For example, the IMF's austerity prescriptions didn't alleviate the financial crises in Latin America and Southeast Asia; they aggravated them. Therefore, China should independently decide upon reform policies and prioritize in accordance with domestic needs rather than blindly bowing to external pressure so as to safeguard the country's fundamental interests. Sometimes, independent but not reciprocal opening up, such as the SHFTZ, is necessary and beneficial.
- Self-discipline means cooperating with and contributing to international rules. Peace and harmony are the external guarantees of China's economic security. As China's international status rises, some major countries and neighboring countries have concerns that are of a dual nature. On the one hand, they hope to contain China and show evidence of jealousy;

on the other hand, they express mutual adjustment and acceptance. The wrestling between China and the outside world is a dynamic process. Whether the end result is to meet halfway and interact constructively or to fight endlessly and enter a downward spiral depends on both the external environment and the choices China makes.

In fact, these Chinese choices play an increasingly big role. Given the right choices, China's strategy opportunity period will continue longer. In general, China has volunteered to join the Western-dominated international economic system, but it is still regarded as a main beneficiary, which indicates that taking the initiative does not necessarily mean having dominant power. As such, China should abide by the existing international economic rules, actively participate in the formulation and improvement of the rules, and build a more just and reasonable international economic order with gradual and non-revolutionary measures. In this way, the nation can strive to provide global public goods and advocate rational patriotism, balancing this patriotism with global citizenship, in order to create a relaxed and safe external environment.

(5) Strengthen financial supervision and maintain financial security

With the deepening of reform and opening-up in the financial sector, the entry of RMB into the SDR, the cooperation in BRI, and the smooth operation of the AIIB, China's financial system, financial market, financial supervision, and control systems have consistently been improving, and financial institutions are growing in strength. The overall financial condition in China is optimistic, and current risks are controllable. However, it should also be noted that as China's economy shifts from high-speed growth to medium-to-high growth, some structural contradictions and institutional problems concealed by the high growth are gradually exposed, and certain financial risks become apparent. Financial security cannot be ignored. From a global perspective, the world economic recovery is weak; political and social crises triggered by financial and debt crises are spreading around the world; "Black Swan" events are frequent; a large number of international financial risks still exist; and the spillover of financial crises is prominent. China may be subject to various external shocks leaking from the monetary and fiscal policy adjustment of some countries.

From a historical point of view, many countries have encountered financial crises after a period of rapid economic growth. Some even had to stop the pace of economic growth due to the crisis; they have fallen partway along the ascendant road, their dreams of development broken. At present, China's financial industry is large in scale but not strong. It lags far behind developed countries in terms of the safety and effectiveness of the financial system, the abundance of financial products, and the degree to which financial services satisfy the needs of the real economy and the public. Moreover, China's financial supervision has not yet been able to provide what is needed for greater openness. There is still a large gap in resources: the requirements of modern financial supervision require much in terms of organization, talent, technology, and systems. China's economy is now in a critical period of transformation and upgrade. The risk of "being unrealistic" in economic life should not be underestimated. And economic development requires strong financial support. At the same time, China faces many international financial risks, such as external shocks leaking from the monetary and fiscal policy adjustment of some countries. Therefore, preventing and resolving financial risk is fundamental to the maintenance of stable and sound economic development, which calls for unswerving commitment. Even as China sustains its commitment to avoiding systemic and regional financial risks, it must work hard to create a good financial environment and provide quality financial services for the development of the real economy.

The best way to maintain financial security and promote the sound and sustainable development of the financial industry is to deepen financial reforms, thereby improving the financial system. Here are some ways to do so:

- Further optimize the environment for the development of the financial sector through reforms. This involves building a sound financial legal system, good accounting standards, sufficient transparency, and an effective financial market system.
- Advance the reform of corporate governance in the financial sector, strengthen a management philosophy based on prudence and compliance and reinforce internal restraint mechanisms within the financial industry.
- Accelerate improvement of the corporate governance structure and internal risk control mechanisms of financial institutions, hasten the establishment of a regulatory system for compliant operations, encourage financial institutions to effectively assume risk management responsibilities, improve market rules, and build violation resolution mechanisms based on markets and ruled by law.
- Strengthen the external supervision and restraint mechanism of the financial sector. In particular, improvement of the financial governance system is needed at four levels, namely, macro-prudential supervision and governance, internal governance of financial institutions, industrial self-discipline, public supervision, and the construction and management of financial agencies.
- Improve the overall quality of employees in financial institutions. It is important to train a large number of financial professionals in operations and risk management with international vision and experience.
- Further enhance the international competitiveness of financial institutions. Through market selection and government cultivation, a number of strong multinational financial institutions can be built that only take on controllable risks and demonstrate international competitiveness. Financial institutions should be encouraged to prudently conduct cross-border M&As, improve their networks of overseas branches, and raise the level of financial services.
- On the basis of continuous assessment, improve prudential supervision and effective risk management, gradually expanding openness in the financial sector to form an open, safe, fair, orderly, and positive financial ecology.

The tasks of maintaining financial security and promoting the return of finance to the real economy are naturally inseparable from efforts in financial supervision. With the development of information technology, financial risks become characterized by wide coverage, strong relevance, and intricate transmission and diffusion. This change has tended to inhibit the quality of supervisory personnel, rule-making, and supervisory coordination. Only by strengthening supervision can the occurrence of major risks, especially systemic risks, be avoided. A holistic and strategic approach to top-level design for financial development and maintenance of financial security is needed. Systematic and specific principles and goals for financial reform and development are also needed, paving the way for financial opening up and security. The past strategy of crossing the river by feeling the stones is no longer workable; the way to get the best results at a relatively low cost is to pursue a more purposeful and systematic reform. This means that China must learn from the useful experience of foreign countries, but not that it should copy blindly. Instead, a realistic approach should be adopted based on the present conditions of the nation and based on an understanding of the characteristics and laws of financial development. Therefore, China must firmly adhere to Chinese values in line with Chinese interests, proceeding in a way that does not disrupt the pace of China's financial reform, not even in order to cater to or meet the requirements of certain countries or international financial institutions.

Financial reform and development, opening up, and financial security: there are principled reasons to believe these are of equal importance, and it is possible to pursue them at the same time. The imperatives are these: adhere to the essential requirements of finance in support of the real economy; adhere to a market-based, world-class reform guideline governed by a sound legal framework; adhere to a development approach that balances innovation and supervision; adhere to an independent, gradual, secure and mutually beneficial opening-up policy; and adhere to the principles of "reforming and improving the system before opening up," "pilot test before promotion" and "opening to the domestic market before opening to the outside world." Under the guidance of these principles, China will be empowered to effectively allocate financial resources under an inclusive, open, mutually beneficial, and market-oriented strategy, with financial security guaranteed. All these represent top-level design concepts and principles for maintaining financial security.

In summary, in the context of economic globalization and China's economic development, as well as its quickened pace in opening up, China is faced with greater challenges in economic security. Drawing upon the past experience, it is imperative to establish a correct view of security. As the unswerving pursuit of opening up continues, there is an opportunity to plan China's long-term development with a global strategic vision, improving counter policies and measures and comprehensively deepening reform and development so as to earnestly safeguard national economic security.

Notes

1. Fandom, "Opium Wars," https://military-history.fandom.com/wiki/Opium_Wars.
2. "Xi's 'Socialism Only Way' Remarks Get Mixed Reaction at Home," *South China Morning Post*, accessed April 2, 2014, https://www.scmp.com/news/china/article/1463096/xis-socialism-only-way-remarks-get-mixed-reaction-home.
3. "On the People's Democratic Dictatorship," in *Selected Works of Mao Tse-tung*, accessed June 30, 1949, https://www.marxists.org/reference/archive/mao/selected-works/volume-4/mswv4_65.htm.
4. "Red Papers 8: China Advances on the Socialist Road: The Gang of Four, Revolution in the US, and the Split in the Revolutionary Communist Party," *Encyclopedia of Anti-Revisionism On-Line*, https://www.marxists.org/history/erol/ncm-5/rp-8/class.htm.
5. Tim Clutton-Brock et al. "The Evolution of Society," *Philosophical Transactions of the Royal Society B: Biological Sciences* 364, no.1533 (2009): 3127–3133.
6. "Xi's Explanation of Resolution on Major Achievements and Historical Experience of CPC over the Past Century," Xinhuanet, accessed November 16, 2021, http://en.qstheory.cn/2021-11/16/c_682069.htm.
7. Bernard Z. Keo, "Crossing the River by Feeling the Stones: Deng Xiaoping in the Making of Modern China," *Education About ASIA* 25, no. 2 (2020): 33–41.
8. Warren Breckman and Peter E. Gordon, eds., *The Cambridge History of Modern European Thought: Volume 1: The 19th Century* (London: Cambridge University Press, 2019).
9. Francis Fukuyama, *The End of History and the Last Man* (New York: Simon and Schuster, 2006).
10. Shao Zongwei, "Principle of Democracy Stressed," *China Daily*, September 2000.
11. Wiki 2, "Beidaihe Conference (1958)," https://wiki2.org/en/Beidaihe_Conference_(1958).
12. Anthony Garavente, "The Long March," *The China Quarterly* 22 (1965): 89–124.
13. "Chapter 1: The Transition from Capitalism to Communism," accessed May 3, 1982, https://fifthinternational.org/content/chapter-1-transition-capitalism-communism?q=content/chapter-1-transition-capitalism-communism.

14. "In Everything We Do We Must Proceed from the Realities of the Primary Stage of Socialism," accessed August 29, 1987, https://dengxiaopingworks.wordpress.com/2013/03/18/in-everything-we-do-we-must-proceed-from-the-realities-of-the-primary-stage-of-socialism/.

15. Shigeru Ishikawa, "China's Economic Growth Since 1949—An Assessment," *The China Quarterly* 94 (1983): 242–281.

16. "Lenin Collected Works: Volume 43," https://www.marxists.org/archive/lenin/works/cw/volume43.htm.

17. "Constitution of the People's Republic of China," http://www.npc.gov.cn/zgrdw/englishnpc/Constitution/2007-11/15/content_1372963.htm.

18. "Feature: Green Is Gold—Xi Jinping Innovates Fight against Climate Change," Xinhuanet, accessed April 22, 2021, http://www.xinhuanet.com/english/2021-04/22/c_139898299.htm.

19. "Feature: Green Is Gold—Xi Jinping Innovates Fight against Climate Change," Xinhuanet, accessed April 22, 2021, http://www.xinhuanet.com/english/2021-04/22/c_139898299.htm.

20. "Resolution of the CPC Central Committee on the Major Achievements and Historical Experience of the Party over the Past Century," Xinhuanet, https://language.chinadaily.com.cn/a/202111/18/WS6195aa45a310cdd39bc75fe0.html.

21. "Report on the Work of the Government: Delivered at the Fifth Session of the 13th National People's Congress of the People's Republic of China on March 5, 2022," Xinhuanet, https://language.chinadaily.com.cn/ a/202203/12/WS62344f4ca310fd2b29e51d59.html.

22. Ibid.

23. "China: Democracy That Works," Xinhuanet, https://language.chinadaily.com.cn/a/202112/07/WS61aefdb1a310cdd39bc79e03.html.

24. "The Four-Pronged Comprehensive Strategy," http://www.china.org.cn/english/china_key_words/2018-10/29/content_68862177.htm.

25. "From Extensive to Intensive Growth," *China Daily*, accessed August 30, 2016, http://www.chinadaily.com.cn/opinion/2016-08/30/content_26636117.htm.

26. "China Becoming a Major Innovation Power: Research and Development Capabilities Approaching Those of Developed Countries," https://www.rieti.go.jp/en/china/16120501.html#note1.

27. Han Ruyu, "The Enlightenment of Marx's Economic Thought on China's Economic Reform and Construction," *Open Access Library Journal* 5, no. 9 (2018): 1–6.

28. "Marxism and Development of Human Society," https://www.marxists.org/archive/shibdas-ghosh/1960/06/18.htm.

29. "The ABC of Materialist Dialectics," https://www.marxists.org/archive/trotsky/1939/12/abc.htm.

30. "The Five-Sphere Integrated Plan," http://www.china.org.cn/english/china_key_words/2018-10/29/content_68862031.htm.

31. Huan Chiu-chih, "Chairman Mao Is the Red Sun in the Hearts of the People of the World," *Peking Review* 30 (1966): 6–9.

32. "Green Is Gold: Clear Waters and Green Mountains are as Good as Mountains of Gold and Silver," https://chiculture.org.hk/en/china-today/1345.

33. "The White Paper of China's Practice in Poverty Alleviation," https://language.chinadaily.com.cn/a/202104/06/WS606bffe7a31024ad0bab3c43_4.html.

34. K. Alexander, "Inclusive Growth: Topic Guide" (Birmingham, UK: GSDRC, University of Birmingham, 2015).

35. "Karl Marx Theory of Economic Development," https://www.economicsdiscussion.net/economic-development/karl-marx-theory-of-economic-development/4554.

36. Zhao Hong, "Graphics: Explaining China's Poverty Alleviation Efforts," https://news.cgtn.com/news/2021-04-06/Graphics-Explaining-China-s-poverty-alleviation-efforts-ZexkKqf3Gw/index.html.

37. Ren Lixuan, "Pursuing Shared Development: The Fifth Interpretation of the 'Five Development Concepts,'" *People's Daily*, accessed December 24, 2015, http://opinion.people.com.cn/n1/2015/1224/c1003-27968566.html

38. Li Xiong, "Making Macro Regulation More Powerful, Measured, and Effective," *Economic Daily*. December 2017.

39. Xi Jinping, "Facing the Frontiers of S&T in the World and the Main Economic Battlefield, Facing the Country's Major Needs and the People's Life and Health, and Continuously Advancing in the Breadth and Depth of S&T," *People's Daily*, accessed September 20, 2020, http://cpc.people.com.cn/n1/2020/0912/c64094-31858846.html.

40. "2006–2020 National Informatization Development Strategy," https://chinacopyrightandmedia.wordpress.com/2006/03/19/2006-2020-national-informatization-development-strategy/.

41. R. Adam Dastrup, MA, GISP, *Introduction to Human Geography* (2019).

42. "Industrial Revolution," https://www.history.com/topics/industrial-revolution/industrial-revolution.

43. "Outline of the National Informatization Development Strategy," https://chinacopyrightandmedia.wordpress.com/2016/07/27/outline-of-the-national-informatization-development-strategy/.

44. "Speech at the Work Conference for Cybersecurity and Informatization," https://chinacopyrightandmedia.worldpress.com/2016/04/19/speech-at-the-work-conference-for-cybersecurity-and-informatization/.

45. "'Broadband China's Strategy to Speed Up Network," http://www.chinadaily.com.cn/business/2013-08/19/content_16903838.htm.

46. Xia Han et al, "Assessment on China's Urbanization after the Implementation of Main Functional Areas Planning," *Journal of Environmental Management* 264 (2020): 1–10.

47. Galileo Galilei Italian Institute, "Urbanisation in China and the Chongqing-Chengdu City Cluster," accessed September 17, 2019, http://www.galileiinstitute.it/urbanisation-in-china-and-the-chongqing-chengdu-city-cluster/.

48. Bao Chuanjian. "China's Rural Work Embodies People-Centered Development Philosophy," *Global Times*, March 2022.

49. "Li Keqiang Visited the Ministry of Agriculture and Rural Affairs and Hosted a Forum to Emphasize Do Not Miss the Farming Time to Grasp the Spring Management and Spring Plowing to Ensure Food Security, and Provide Solid Support for the Stability of Economic and Social Development in General," accessed March 25, 2022, http://www.moa.gov.cn/xw/zwdt/202203/t20220325_6393893.htm.

50. "Made in China 2025," https://www.csis.org/analysis/made-china-2025.

51. "Internet Plus," https://govt.chinadaily.com.cn/s/201908/16/WS5d5652dc498ebcb1905787f5/internet-plus.html.

52. "Joint Efforts to Implement Made in China 2025," http://english.www.gov.cn/premier/news/2017/02/15/content_281475568073500.htm.

53. "Deng Xiaoping: Encourage Some People to Become Well-Off First," *News of the Communist Party of China*, http://cpc.people.com.cn/GB/34136/2569304.html.

54. The 12th National Congress of the CPC, "Creating a New Situation in All Fields of Socialist Modernization," accessed September 1982, http://www.gov.cn/test/2007-08/28/content_729792.htm.

55. Zheng Wujing, "Exploration of the Basic Economic System and the Road to Common Wealth (Monograph on the Celebration of the 100th Anniversary of the Founding of the CPC)," accessed November 4, 2021, http://theory.people.com.cn/n1/2021/1104/c40531-32273032.html.

56. The 15th National Congress of the CPC, "Hold High the Great Banner of Deng Xiaoping Theory for an All-Around Advancement of the Cause of Building Socialism with Chinese Characteristics to the 21st Century," accessed September 1997, http://academics.wellesley.edu/Polisci/wj/308S/Readings/jzm15CCP.htm.

57. The 15th National Congress of the CPC, "Hold High the Great Banner of Deng Xiaoping Theory for an All-Around Advancement of the Cause of Building Socialism with Chinese Characteristics to the 21st Century," accessed September 1997, http://academics.wellesley.edu/Polisci/wj/308S/Readings/jzm15CCP.htm.

58. The 16th National Congress of the CPC. "Build a Well-Off Society in an All-Around Way and Create a New Situation in Building Socialism with Chinese Characteristics," accessed November 2002, https://www.mfa.gov.cn/ce/cegv//eng/zgbd/zgbdxw/t85779.htm.

59. The 17th National Congress of the CPC, "Hold High the Great Banner of Socialism with Chinese Characteristics and Strive for New Victories in Building a Moderately Prosperous Society in all Respects," accessed October 2007, http://www.china.org.cn/english/congress/229611.htm.

60. The 18th National Congress of the CPC, "Firmly March on the Path of Socialism with Chinese Characteristics and Strive to Complete the Building of a Moderately Prosperous Society in All Respects," accessed November 2012, https://www.mfa.gov.cn/ce/ceus/eng/zt/18th_CPC_National_Congress_Eng/t992917.htm.

61. "Decision of the CCCPC on Some Major Issues Concerning Comprehensively Deepening the Reform," Third Plenary Session of the 18th CPC Central Committee, accessed November 2013, http://www.gov.cn/jrzg/2013-11/15/content_2528179.htm.

62. "(Authorized release) Communiqué of the Fifth Plenary Session of the 19th CPC Central Committee," accessed October 29, 2020, http://www.xinhuanet.com/2020-10/29/c_1126674147.htm.

63. Xi Jinping, "Notice of the General Office of the National Development and Reform Commission and the General Office of the People's Bank of China on Issuing the List of the First Group of Cities Demonstrating the Development of Social Credit System," accessed December 28, 2017, http://www.lawinfochina.com/display.aspx?id=27246&lib=law.

64. The State Council of the PRC, "Leading the Vigorous Development of Mass Innovation and Entrepreneurship with Institutional Supply," accessed November 6, 2006, http://www.gov.cn/xinwen/2016-06/06/content_5079895.htm.

65. The State Council of the PRC: General Office of the CPC Central Committee, General Office of the State Council, "Outline of the National Strategy for the Development of Information Technology," acccessed July 27, 2016, http://www.gov.cn/zhengce/2016-07/27/content_5095336.htm.

66. Xi Jinping, "Secure a Decisive Victory in Building a Moderately Prosperous Society in All Respects and Strive for the Great Success of Socialism with Chinese Characteristics for a New Era," accessed October 18, 2017, http://www.gov.cn/zhuanti/2017-10/27/content_5234876.htm.

67. Xi Jinping, "Secure a Decisive Victory in Building a Moderately Prosperous Society in All Respects and Strive for the Great Success of Socialism with Chinese Characteristics for a New Era," accessed October 18, 2017, http://www.gov.cn/zhuanti/2017-10/27/content_5234876.htm.

68. "Making Progress While Maintaining Stability as the Guideline for the Work of the Government," accessed December 3, 2018, http://keywords.china.org.cn/2018-12/03/content_74235019.htm.

69. "Making Progress While Maintaining Stability as the Guideline for the Work of the Government," accessed December 3, 2018, http://keywords.china.org.cn/2018-12/03/content_74235019.htm.

70. "Decision of the CCCPC on Some Major Issues Concerning Comprehensively Deepening the Reform," http://www.china.org.cn/chinese/2014-01/17/content_31226494.htm.

71. Robert K. Merton, *Social Theory and Social Structure* (New York: The Free Press, 1968).

72. "Xi Jinping Thought on Socialism with Chinese Characteristics Learning Q&A," *People's Daily*, accessed September 7, 2021, https://www.12371.cn/2021/09/07/ARTI1630968878679500.shtml.

73. The Ministry of Civil Affairs in China, "Strengthening and Improving Urban and Rural Community Governance to Consolidate the Foundation of the Modernization of National Governance," accessed July 3, 2017, http://www.gov.cn/xinwen/2017-07/03/content_5207481.htm.

74. "Efforts to support grassroots governance," *Tibet Daily*, accessed November 13, 2020, https://mzzt.mca.gov.cn/article/zt_20wzqh/jdpl/202011/20201100030547.shtml.

75. "Jointly Shoulder Responsibility of Our Times, Promote Global Growth," accessed January 17, 2017, https://language.chinadaily.com.cn/2017xuexi/2017-01/18/content_29848990.htm.

76. "Working Together to Forge a New Partnership of Win-win Cooperation and Create a Community of Shared Future for Mankind," accessed September 29, 2015, https://www.fmprc.gov.cn/mfa_eng/topics_665678/2015zt/xjpdmgjxgsfwbcxlhgcl70znxlfh/201510/t20151012_705405.html.

77. "Speech by Chinese President Xi Jinping to Indonesian Parliament," accessed October 3, 2013, http://www.asean-china-center.org/english/2013-10/03/c_133062675.htm.

78. "Constitution of Communist Party of China," acessed November 14, 2012, http://www.china.org.cn/china/18th_cpc_congress/2012-11/16/content_27138030.htm.

79. "Xi Jinping Strives to Build a 'Community of Human Destiny,'" accessed October 7, 2018, http://dangshi.people.com.cn/n1/2018/1007/c85037-30326484.html.

80. "Episode 8: Adhere to Open Development and Build a Broad Community of Interests," accessed November 17, 2015, http://dangjian.people.com.cn/n/2015/1117/c399958-27825704.html.

References

BOOKS

Alexander, K. *Inclusive Growth: Topic Guide.* Birmingham, UK: GSDRC, University of Birmingham, 2015.

Bian, Zhicun, Mao Zesheng, and Xu Licheng. *The Choice of Fiscal and Monetary Policy Regime from a Macroprudential Perspective.* Beijing: China Financial Publishing House, 2015.

Breckman, Warren, and Peter E. Gordon, eds. *The Cambridge History of Modern European Thought: Volume 1: The 19th Century.* London: Cambridge University Press, 2019.

Chen, Bogeng, et al. *The Socialist Political Economy with Chinese Characteristics.* Beijing: Higher Education Press, 2016.

Chen, Jiagui, Huang Qunhui, and Zhong Hongwu. *The Report on Chinese Industrialization.* Beijing: China Social Science Press, 2007.

Chen, Jian, Li Dongfang, and Liu Zhixin. *Historical Change: The Five Years in China.* Beijing: China Yan Shi Press; Hebei Fine Arts Publishing House, 2017.

Chen, Lu. *Hebei Development Blue Book: Annual Report on the Coordinated Development of Beijing–Tianjin–Hebei (2018).* Beijing: Social Sciences Academic Press (China), 2018.

Dastrup, R. Adam. *Introduction to Human Geography.* Creative Commons License. Accessed October 2013. https://www.opengeography.org/human-geography.html.

Fukuyama, Francis. *The End of History and the Last Man.* New York: Simon and Schuster, 2006.

Gao, Hucheng. "Actively Promoting International Cooperation under the Belt and Road Initiative." In *The Guiding Materials for the Report to the 19th National Congress of the CPC*, 406–412. Beijing: People's Publishing House, 2017.

Gu, Chaolin, Yu Taofang, and Li Ping. *Human Geography Studies.* Shanghai: Higher Education Press, 2008.

Hebei Office for Philosophy and Social Sciences. *The Blue Book on Coordinated Development of Beijing–Tianjin–Hebei: An Analysis and Forecast of Beijing–Tianjin–Hebei Coordinated Development from 2014 to 2015.* Hebei: Hebei Publishing & Media, 2015.

Li, Binglong, and Xue Xingli. *Agricultural Economics*. Beijing: China Agricultural University Press, 2009.

Li, Guorong, and Peng Jiansong. *Introduction to the Chinese Non-State Sector*. Beijing: Peking University Press, 2008.

Li, Yuncai, Liu Weiping, and Chen Xuhua. *Research on Rural Modernization in China*. Hunan: Hunan People's Publishing House, 2004.

Liu, Wei, et al. *Research on China's Monetary Policy System and Conduction Mechanism*. Beijing: Economic Science Press, 2015.

Merton, Robert K. *Social Theory and Social Structure*. New York: The Free Press, 1968.

Research Group on Sustainable Development Strategy of Chinese Academy of Sciences. *2005 Strategic Report: China's Sustainable Development*. Beijing: Science Press, 2005.

Ru, Xin, and Fu Chonglan. *Blue Book on Urban-Rural Integration: Annual Report on China's Urban-Rural Integration (2013)*. Beijing: Social Sciences Academic Press (China), 2013.

Shi, Jinchuan. *Development Report on China's Private Sector (2015–2016)*. Beijing: Economic Science Press, 2016.

Song, Tao. *Political Economics*. Beijing: China Renmin University Press, 2017.

Su, Ming. *Fiscal Theory and Fiscal Policy*. Beijing: Economic Science Press, 2003.

Teaching and Research Department of Economics, National Academy of Governance. *New Orientation of China's Economy*. Beijing: People's Publishing House, 2017.

Wang, Lisheng. *Research Report on Socialist Political Economy with Chinese Characteristics*. Jinan: Jinan Press, 2017.

Wu, Chuanqing. *Research on Marxist Theory of Regional Economy*. Beijing: Economic Science Press, 2006.

Xi, Jieren. *Encyclopedia of the Scientific Outlook on Development*. Shanghai: Shanghai Lexicographical Publishing House, 2007.

Xu, Chongzheng. *Development of Private Economy and Institutional Environment*. Beijing: Economic Press China, 2008.

Yan, Kun, and Zhang Peng. *The Analysis of China's Macroeconomic Situation and Fiscal Policy*. Beijing: China Social Sciences Press, 2010.

Yu, Jianrong, He Qin, and Tang Yiyong. *Socialist Political Economy with Chinese Characteristics*. Beijing: National Academy of Governance Press, 2017.

Zhang, Hui, and Huang Zehua. *Research on the Mechanism of Monetary and Fiscal Policy Conduction and Macro-Control in China*. Beijing: Peking University Press, 2016.

Zhang, Peigang. *Development Economics*. Beijing: Peking University Press, 2009.

Zhou, Libin, Han Manling, Wang Xiyan, and Lin Yang. *Research on Regional Economic Theory under Neo-Marxism*. Beijing: Economic Science Press, 2017.

JOURNALS AND MAGAZINES

An, Qinian. "The New Stage of the Sinicization of Marxism and Marxist Philosophy in China." *Journal of Beijing Administration Institute* 2 (2017): 57–63.

Cao, Xiaoying. "Research Review of Agricultural Modernization." *Northern Economy* 19 (2012): 25–27.

Chen, Quanguo. "Sending the Warm Care of the Party and the Government to People of All Ethnic Groups in China—Earnestly Studying and Implementing General Secretary Xi Jinping's Important Exposition on Ensuring and Improving People's Livelihoods." *Qiushi* 7 (2015): 15–17.

Chen, Xiwen. "Take the Path of Agricultural Modernization with Chinese Characteristics." *Qiushi* 22 (2007): 25–28.

Cheng, Zhanheng, and Chen Yan. "Theoretical Study on the Positive Interaction between Industrialization and Urbanization." *Journal of Chengdu Institute of Public Administration* 2 (2013): 50–53.

Clutton-Brock, Tim, et al. "The Evolution of Society." *Philosophical Transactions of the Royal Society B: Biological Sciences* 364, no.1533 (2009): 3127–3133.

Deng, Ling. "Socialist Market Economy Theory Is a Major Innovation." *Theory Guide* 3 (2015): 8–9.

Dong, Yan, and Ding Yanming. "New Trends in Trade and Globalization." *China Forex* 15 (2017).

Fang, Jianzhong. "Grasping the New Connotation, New Changes and New Trends of Open Development under the New Normal." *The Masses* 6 (2016): 10–11.

Garavente, Anthony. "The Long March." *The China Quarterly* 22 (1965): 89–124.

Gu, Hailiang. "Research on the Development of Socialist Political Economy with Chinese Characteristics in the New Era." *Seeker* 12 (2017): 4–13.

Guo, Fei. "Rethinking the Principle of Distributing Production Factors according to Contribution and Engagement." *Studies on Marxism* 2 (2005): 26–31.

Han, Ruyu. "The Enlightenment of Marx's Economic Thought on China's Economic Reform and Construction." *Open Access Library Journal* 5, no. 9 (2018): 1–6.

Hou, Yajing, and Luo Yuhui. "The Inevitability and Necessity of China Adhering to the Collective Ownership of Rural Land." *Journal of Economics of Shanghai School* 2 (2017): 76–87.

Hou, Yanfeng, and Yang Wenxuan. "Scientific Connotation and Basic Characteristics of the New Industrialization Road in China." *Productivity Research* 6 (2013): 127–130, 141.

Hu, Angang, and Wu Qungang. "Agricultural Commercialization: An Important Approach to Rural Modernization in China." *Issues in Agricultural Economy* 1 (2001): 9–21.

Hu, Angang, Yan Yilong, Tang Xiao, and Liu Shenglong. "China by 2050: Comprehensive Modernization of the People-Centered Socialism." *Journal of CAG* 5 (2017): 15–20, 144.

Hua, Xingshun. "Promoting the Interactive and Coordinated Development of New Urbanization and Agricultural Modernization." *Theory Research* 4 (2013): 51, 70–73.

Huan, Chiu-chih. "Chairman Mao Is the Red Sun in the Hearts of the People of the World." *Peking Review* 30 (1966): 6–9.

Ishikawa, Shigeru. "China's Economic Growth since 1949—An Assessment." *The China Quarterly* 94 (1983): 242–281.

Huang, Kunming. "Deeply Understanding the Significance of the Four-Pronged Comprehensive Strategy.'" *Qiushi* 13 (2015): 7–11.

Jing, Puqiu and Zhang Fuming. "A Preliminary Study on the Theoretical Model of Interactive Development between Industrialization and Urbanization." *Economic Perspectives* 8 (2004): 63–66.

Kang, Airong, and Yu Fawen. "An Interpretation of Agricultural Modernization in China." *Gansu Social Sciences* 1 (2005): 188–191.

Keo, Bernard Z. "Crossing the River by Feeling the Stones: Deng Xiaoping in the Making of Modern China." *Education About ASIA* 25, no. 2 (2020): 33–41.

Li, Yanqiu. "Evolution and Enlightenment of the Socialist Ownership Structure with Chinese Characteristics." *Studies on Socialism with Chinese Characteristics* 2 (2014): 36–43.

Li, Yinghui. "Enlightenment to Henan from the Coordinated Development of Urbanization and Agricultural Modernization at Home and Abroad." *Country Agriculture Farmers (Version B)* 9 (2014): 38–40.

Li, Yining. "Comprehensively Deepening Reform and Opening-Up to Promote Sustainable and Healthy Economic Development—Notes on Studying and Implementing the Spirit of the 18th National Congress of the CPC (II): The Reform of Income Distribution System Should Give Priority to Primary Distribution." *Economic Research Journal* 3 (2013): 4–6.

Li, Yu, and Zhan Yi. "Research on Interactive Development of Industrialization and Urbanization in China." *Seeker* 10 (2013): 26–28.

Liu, Hailong. "Promoting the Interactive Development of Industrialization and Urbanization in China." *Macroeconomic Management* 6 (2016): 72–76.

Liu, Haitao. "Scientific Socialism and Socialism with Chinese Characteristics." *Truths and Facts* 3 (2016): 27–30.

Liu, He. "Dividends on the Decline—Seeking a New Balance in China (Preface)." *Information for Deciders* 5 (2017): 18–19.

Liu, Wei. "Developing Socialist Political Economy with Chinese Characteristics in the Combination of Marxism and Chinese Practices." *Economic Research Journal* 5 (2016): 4–13, 71.

Liu, Yu. "The Relations between Agricultural Modernization and Urbanization." *Urban Studies* 6 (2007): 37–40.

Liu, Yuansheng, and Yu Qianshu. "Upholding and Improving the Superior System of Collective Ownership of Rural Land." *Red Flag Manuscript* 23 (2017): 21–23.

Lu, Junhai, and Lyu Huan. "On the Characteristics of China's Modernization and Its Implications to the World." *Times of Economy & Trade* 32 (2011): 1–2, 11.

Luo, Yuhui, and Hou Yajing. "Why Should China Adhere to the Collective Ownership of Rural Land?" *Contemporary Economic Research* 2 (2017): 22–28.

Mo, Zhibin, Qin Weiguo, and Xu Jian. "From Industrialization to the Modernization Drive of Building China into a Prosperous, Strong, Democratic, Culturally Advanced and Harmonious Country—A Study on the Evolution of the Strategic Goals of the CPC's Modernization Drive after 1949." *Social Sciences in Guangxi* 4 (2007): 48–52.

Nie, Zhihong. "On Safeguarding China's Economic Security in Opening to the Outside World." *Theory Monthly* 1 (2010): 76–79.

Niu, Ruofeng. "What Path Will China Take in Agricultural Modernization?" *Chinese Rural Economy* 1 (2001): 4–11.

Peng, Shuang, and Ye Xiaodong. "Study on the Evolution, Status Quo and Adjustment of China's National Income Distribution Structure since 1978." *Economic Review* 2 (2008): 73–80.

Ren, Jie. "The Foundation of Confidence in the Socialist Road with Chinese Characteristics." *Qianxian Monthly* 6 (2017): 53–58.

Research Group of the Institute for Social Development, National Development and Reform Commission. "Study on China's National Income Distribution Structure." *Review of Economic Research* 21 (2012): 34–82.

Shi, Jianxun. "The Financial Signal in Xi Jinping Thought on Socialism with Chinese Characteristics for a New Era." *Exploration and Free Views* 12 (2017): 22–26.

———. "Four Distinctive Features of the System of Socialism with Chinese Characteristics." *Theory Study* 2 (2017): 40.

———. "Global Institutional Crisis and the Contribution of China's Reform Attempts to the World." *Journal of Xinjiang Normal University (Edition of Philosophy and Social Sciences)* 38, no. 5 (2017): 14–20.

———. "What Can the Idea of Building a Global Community of Shared Future Contribute to the World?" *People's Tribune* 28 (2017): 36–39.

Shi, Jianxun, and Wang Panpan. "Three Steps: How to Achieve Historical Leapfrog Development in China's Manufacturing Transformation and Upgrading." *Red Flag Digest* 8 (2017).

Shi, Jianxun, Zhang Kaiwen, and Li Zhaoyu. "Scientific Connotation and Construction Focus of a Modern Economic System." *Research on Financial and Economic Issues* 2 (2018): 22–31.

Shou, Sihua. "Observation on the Marxist View of Cities and Urbanization in China." *Reformation & Strategy* 30, no. 2 (2014): 89–95.

Song, Guoyou. "Global Free Trade Agreement Competition and China's Strategic Choice." *Contemporary International Relations* 5 (2013): 30–35.

Sun, Hu, and Qiao Biao. "Study on Promoting the Interactive Development between New Industrialization and New Urbanization in China." *Areal Research and Development* 33, no. 4 (2014): 64–68.

Tai, Ping. "The Model of China's Opening to the Outside World." *China Review of Political Economy* 1 (2018): 51–69.

Tang, Zhouyan. "The National Goal of Building China into a Prosperous, Strong, Democratic, Culturally Advanced and Harmonious Country." *Outlook* Z1 (2010): 66–69.

Wang, Sibin. "On the Social Policies Covering People's Basic Needs under the New Normal of Economic Development." *Dongyue Tribune* 36, no. 3 (2015): 5–9.

———. "Social Policies Covering People's Basic Needs and Their Construction." *Social Sciences in China* 6 (2017): 81–90.

Wang, Tianyi, and Wang Rui. "The Theory of Socialist Ownership and the Innovation of Chinese Ownership Structure." *Scientific Socialism* 5 (2009): 13–17.

Wang, Zhengwu. "To Develop People-Centered Socialist Political Economy with Chinese Characteristics—Review of the 10th China Seminar on Economics of Human Development." *Reformation & Strategy* 33, no. 10 (2017): 34–40, 81.

Wei, Zhong, and Wang Qiong. "The Evolution of the Distribution According to Work Principle in China: A Perspective of History of Economic Thoughts." *Economic Research Journal* 11 (2016): 4–12.

Wu, Wenqiang. "People Are the Foundation for Economic Development and Economy Should Ultimately Serve the People—Also on the Academic Principles of the People-Centered Socialist Political Economy with Chinese Characteristics." *Reformation & Strategy* 32, no. 10 (2016): 1–5.

———. "The People-Centered Social Relations of Production are Crucial to Socialism with Chinese Characteristics—Part of the Research Series on the People-Centered Socialist Political Economy with Chinese Characteristics." *Reformation & Strategy* 33, no. 6 (2017): 16–24.

Wu, Zhenxing. "An International Comparative Study on Agricultural Modernization in China." *Chinese Journal of Tropical Agriculture* 2 (2003): 10–20, 26.

Xia, Han, et al. "Assessment on China's Urbanization after the Implementation of Main Functional Areas Planning." *Journal of Environmental Management* 264 (2020): 1–10.

Yan, Shuhan. "On the Position of Socialism with Chinese Characteristics in the Development History of Scientific Socialism." *Contemporary World* 3 (2015): 2–5.

Yang, Xinming, and Sun Kuilai. "On the Essence of Socialism and Its Development." *Study & Exploration* 2 (2015): 108–111.

Yu, Jincheng. "Distribution According to Work and Its Four Interpretations in the History of Marxist Development." *Journal of Socialist Theory Guide* 3 (2016): 17–28.

Yu, Jinfu. "Marx's Theory of Distribution According to Work and China's Current Socialist Distribution System." *Contemporary Economic Research* 135, no. 11 (2006): 41–44.

Yue, Jinglun. "The Changing Role of the State in Welfare Provision: Sixty Years of Social Policy Developments in China." *Chinese Public Policy Review* 4 (2010): 39–69.

Zeng, Guoan, Li Shaowei, and Hu Jingjing. "Several Issues about the Fairness of National Income Redistribution." *Fujian Tribune (The Humanities & Social Sciences Monthly)* 12 (2008): 4–10.

Zhang, Huiming. "Exploration of the Localization of Marxism in China and Development of Economic Theory with Chinese Characteristics." *Academics* 11 (2017): 18–35.

Zhang, Yu. "Developing the Socialist Political Economy with Chinese Characteristics." *Journal of Theoretical Reference* 6 (2016): 6.

———. "The Historical Evolution of the Socialist Political Economy—Also On the Historical Contribution of the Socialist Political Economy with Chinese Characteristics." *Studies on Socialism with Chinese Characteristics* 1 (2016): 35–41.

———. "The Scientific Connotation of the Socialist Political Economy with Chinese Characteristics." *Economic Research Journal* 5 (2017): 17–19.

Zhao, Hong. "Promoting the Coordinated Development of Urbanization and Agricultural Modernization." *China Co-operation Economy* 12 (2012): 15–16.

Zhou, Xincheng. "The Basic Principle of Scientific Socialism Is the Source and Root of Socialism with Chinese Characteristics." *Red Flag Manuscript* 23 (2015): 1, 7–10.

NEWSPAPER

Ba, Fazhong. "The Profound Connotation and Significance of the 'Four Greats.'" *Chinese Social Sciences Today*, November 30, 2017.

Bao, Chuanjian. "China's Rural Work Embodies People-Centered Development Philosophy." *Global Times*, March 2022.

Bao, Xinjian. "How to Understand and Grasp the Essence of the Four-Pronged Comprehensive Strategy." *Guangming Daily*, January 20, 2016.

Chen, Jianqi. "Chinese Approach to Global Economic Governance." *Economic Information Daily*, September 28, 2017.

Chen, Long. "Local Government Debt Risk in China Is Generally Controllable." *People's Daily*, January 9, 2018.

Cheng, Enfu. "Latest Achievements in the Socialist Political Economy with Chinese Characteristics." *Guangming Daily*, January 4, 2018.

Ding, Shouhai. "Concept Differentiation and Analysis: Townization, Urbanization and New Urbanization." *Chinese Social Sciences Today*, May 30, 2014.

Dong, Yuping. "Taking Comprehensive Measures to Reduce Enterprise Cost." *Economic Daily*, February 19, 2016.

Fan, Hengshan. "Grasping the Key Points in Promoting the Mixed Ownership Reform of State-Owned Enterprises." *Economic Daily*, March 25, 2017.

Fang, Shinan. "Grasping the Main Dimensions of the Profound Connotation of Developing a Great Modern Socialist Country." *Liaoning Daily*, November 14, 2017.

———. "What Makes a Great Modern Socialist Country?" *Suzhou Daily*, January 6, 2018.

Gao, Fei. "Discovering a National Security Path with Chinese Characteristics." *People's Daily*, November 16, 2016.

Gao, Peiyong. "Major Economic Issues Faced by China in the New Era." *People's Daily*, January 8, 2018.

Gao, Shangquan. "Let the Market Play a Decisive Role in Resource Allocation." *China Reform Data*, August 17, 2015.

Gao, Yuncai, Zhu Jun, and Wang Hao. "Rural Revitalization Meets the New Expectations of Hundreds of Millions of Chinese Farmers—Policy Interpretation of the Spirit of the Central Rural Work Conference by Han Jun, Director of the Office of Central Leading Group for Rural Work." *People's Daily*, January 14, 2018.

Gu, Shengzu, and Han Longyan. "China's Private Economy Enters a New Historical Stage." www.cpcnews.cn, April 1, 2017.

Guan, Xinping. "What Basic Living Needs Should Social Policies Meet?" *Beijing Daily*, July 11, 2016.

Han, Baojiang. "Building the People-Centered Socialist Political Economy with Chinese Characteristics." *Study Times*, May 24, 2017.

Han, Qingxiang, and Yantao Zhang. "The 'Four Greats' Are an Organic Unity." *People's Tribune*, March 1, 2014.

He, Guangshun. "Historic Opportunities for China to Grow into a Maritime Power." *People's Daily*, February 11, 2018.

Huang, Qunhui. "Shifting from High-Speed Industrialization to High-Quality Industrialization." *People's Daily*, November 26, 2017.

Ji, Xiaonan. "Major Innovation of State-Owned Enterprise Reform Theory." *People's Daily*, November 10, 2017.

Lan, Haitao, and Chen Liangbao. "Strengthening Top-Level Design for Coordinated Development of Urbanization and Agricultural Modernization." *Farmers' Daily*, August 2, 2014.

Li, Peng. "Adhering to the People-Centered Economic Research Orientation." *Chinese Social Sciences Today*, June 22, 2016.

Li, Yizhong. "The Connotation and Basic Characteristics of the New Industrialization Road with Chinese Characteristics." *Entrepreneurs' Daily*, June 8, 2013.

Lian, Ping. "Rationality and Resilience Are Necessary for Deleveraging." *People's Daily*, August 4, 2017.

Lin, Limin. "Promoting a New Model of International Relations." *PLA Daily*, November 22, 2017.

Liu, Shijin. "Establishing a Fair, Open and Transparent Market Rules." *Economic Daily*, November 28, 2013.

Liu, Wei, and Chen Yanbin. "Six New Ideas on Macro-Control since the 18th National Congress of the CPC." *People's Daily*, March 1, 2017.

Liu, Wei. "Interpretation of the Essential Requirements for Socialism in the New Era." *People's Daily*, December 29, 2016.

Luo, Laijun. "The Boundary and Focus of the Supply-Side Structural Reform." *Guangming Daily*, March 30, 2016.

Ma, Sheng. "Further Promoting the Mixed Ownership Reform of State-Owned Enterprises." *Guangming Daily*, December 19, 2017.

Ma, Xuejiao. "Deleveraging in an Active and Prudent Manner." *People's Daily*, August 24, 2016.

Mei, Songwu. "Improving the 'New Four Modernizations' through Interaction—On the Multi-Point and Multi-Polar Support Strategy from the Lens of Building a Moderately Prosperous Society in All Respects." *Sichuan Daily*, February 18, 2013.

Miao, Xu. "Reform and Opening-Up Is a Powerful Driving Force for the Approach to New Industrialization—Taking a Closer Look at Comrade Xi Jinping's Important Exposition on Comprehensively Deepening Reform." *People's Daily*, March 11, 2014.

Mu, Hong. "Accelerating the Perfection of the Socialist Market Economy System." *People's Daily*, December 12, 2017.

Ping, Yan. "Active and Prudent Efforts in Deleveraging." *Economic Daily*, December 25, 2015.

Qi, Weiping. "New Achievements Must Be Made in Building 'Great Projects' in the New Era." *Guangming Daily*, January 9, 2018.

Qiu, Haiping. "The Realistic Guiding Significance of Marxist Political Economy for the Supply-Side Structural Reform." *Red Flag Manuscript*, February 5, 2016.

Qiu, Shi. "On Correctly Handling the Relationship between Government and Market." *Qiushi*, January 15, 2018.

Ren Lixuan. "Pursuing Shared Development: The Fifth Interpretation of the 'Five Development Concepts.'" *People's Daily*, December 2015.

Ren, Lixuan. "Adhering to Open Development—the Fourth Interpretation of the Five Development Concepts." *People's Daily*, December 23, 2015.

Shao Zongwei. "Principle of Democracy Stressed." *China Daily*, September 2000.

Shi, Jianxun. "A New Expression of Correctly Understanding the Change of Social Principal Contradiction." *Jiefang Daily*, November 23, 2017.

Shi, Jianxun. "Advancing the Belt and Road Initiative with Renewed Efforts." *Wenhui Daily*, March 22, 2017.

———. "Advancing the Great Process of Building a Global Community of Shared Future." *Economic Daily*, April 21, 2017.

———. "Building a Community of Shared Future Needs a Chinese Approach." *Jiefang Daily*, March 7, 2017.

———. "Building a Global Community of Shared Future to Boost the World Economy." *People's Daily Overseas Edition*, January 24, 2017.

———. "Charting a Blueprint and Creating a Better Future through Actions." *People's Daily Overseas Edition*, March 7, 2017.

———. "Comprehensively Understanding the Profound Connotation of Shaping a New Development Pattern." *Guangming Daily*, September 21, 2020.

———. "Creating High-Quality Life through High-Quality Development." *Wenhui Daily*, January 12, 2017.

———. "Eight Policies Are Needed to Make the New Economy Bigger and Stronger." *Economic Daily*, June 2, 2017.

———. "Grasping the General Trends and Plotting the Overall Situation." *Economic Daily*, January 6, 2017.

———. "High-Quality Development Is Key to a Better Life." *People's Daily Overseas Edition*, December 23, 2017.

———. "How to Build Up a Modern Economic System?" *Jiefang Daily*, January 30, 2018.

——. "How to Drive High-Quality Economic Development?" *Jiefang Daily*, January 2, 2018.

——. "Identifying and Embracing the Principal Contradiction in the New Era." *People's Daily Overseas Edition*, October 20, 2017.

——. "Identifying the Principal Contradiction to Tackle Development Challenges." *Economic Daily*, December 8, 2017.

——. "Implementing New Ideas to Lead New Development." *Economic Daily*, January 13, 2017.

——. "The New Era Calls for High-Quality Development." *People's Daily Overseas Edition*, December 19, 2017.

——. "Understanding and Grasping the New Leap in the Law of Development." *Wenhui Daily*, 2February 4, 2017.

——. "Unswervingly Promoting High-Quality Development." *Wenhui Daily*, December 22, 2017.

——. "Where Is a Better Way Out amid the Global Institutional Crisis?" *Jiefang Daily*, January 10, 2017.

Shi, Zhihong. "The Theoretical and Practical Significance of the Important Generalizations of the 'Four Greats.'" *Beijing Daily*, August 7, 2017.

Sun, Dahai. "Staying Committed to the People-Centered Value Orientation." *People's Daily*, October 23, 2017.

Wan, Adrian. "Xi's 'Socialism Only Way' Remarks Get Mixed Reaction at Home." *South China Morning Post*, April 2014.

Wang, Dongjing. "The Latest Theoretical Achievements of the Localization of Marxist Political Economy in China—Learning Xi Jinping Thought on Socialism with Chinese Characteristics for a New Era." *Guangming Daily*, January 9, 2018.

Wang, Hong. "Building China into a Maritime Power to Help Realize the Chinese Dream." *People's Daily*, November 20, 2017.

Wang, Keqiang. "Informatization: The Key to the Synchronous Development of the 'New Four Modernizations.'" *People's Daily*, March 24, 2013.

Wang, Qingshan. "Addressing the Vulnerabilities of the Intra-Party System with the Spirit of Reform and Innovation." *Guangming Daily*, April 22, 2016.

Wang, Xi. "Let State-Owned Enterprises Play the Leading Role in the Implementation of 'Quality First, Benefit Priority' Requirements." *Xinhua News Agency*, December 13, 2017.

Wang, Yi. "Building a New Model of International Relations of Win-Win Cooperation." *Study Times*, June 20, 2016.

Wang, Yiming, Chen Changsheng, and Li Chengjian. "Correctly Understanding the Supply-Side Structural Reform." *People's Daily*, March 29, 2016.

Xi, Jinping. "Facing the Frontiers of S&T in the World and the Main Economic Battlefield, Facing the Country's Major Needs and the People's Life and Health, and Continuously Advancing in the Breadth and Depth of S&T." *People's Daily*, September 2020.

Xia, Baolong. "Continue to Lead the Way in Promoting the Development of Private Economy." *People's Daily*, April 26, 2016.

Xiao, Minghui. "Ideas and Methods for China's Macroeconomic Regulation and Control." *Guangming Daily*, October 30, 2016.

Xiao, Yaqing. "Deepening the Reform of State-Owned Enterprises." *People's Daily*, December 13, 2017.

Xie, Dibin. "Upholding the People's Position is a Political Guarantee for Staying True to the Original Aspiration and Moving on." *Nanfang Daily*, August 15, 2016.

Xiong, Li. "Making Macro Regulation More Powerful, Measured and Effective." *Economic Daily*, December 2017.

Xu, Shaoshi. "Innovation and Perfection of Macroeconomic Regulation and Control." *People's Daily*, December 19, 2017.

Yang, Peiqing. "The Connotation and Development Path of New Urbanization." *Guangming Daily*, August 19, 2015.

Yang, Weiming. "Interpretating the Two Centenary Goals: Economic Development Has Shifted to a Stage of High-Quality Development." cctv.com, October 26, 2017.

Yang, Yiyong. "Xi Jinping's Economic Thought Opens a New Chapter for China's Economy." people. cn, December 19, 2017.

Ye, Mancheng. "Mixed Ownership Reform Stimulates Vitality of Innovation." *People's Daily*, June 12, 2017.

Yin, Chengjie. "Coordinating Urbanization and Agricultural Modernization." *Farmers' Daily*, November 14, 2012.

Yin, Peng. "Hotspot Analysis: Promoting the Joint Development of State-Owned Enterprises and Private Enterprises." *People's Daily*, January 26, 2018.

Yu, Xin'an. "What Is 'New' about the New Urbanization?" *China Youth Daily*, April 15, 2013.

Zeng, Xiankui. "Dual Characteristics of State-Owned Enterprises and the Mixed Ownership Reform." *Red Flag Manuscript*, December 24, 2015.

Zhang, Liqun. "Speeding up to Balance the Relationship between Government and Market, Tackling the Core Problem in the Economic Structural Reform." *Economic Daily*, June 9, 2017.

Zhang, Xin. "The Belt and Road Initiative: A New Model for International Cooperation." *Chinese Social Sciences Today*, August 27, 2015.

Zhang, Youkui. "What Is a Great Modern Socialist Country?" *Dazhong Daily*, January 25, 2018.

Zhao, Zhanhui, and Gu Zhongyang. "How to Reduce Cost with Policy Package?" *People's Daily*, January 4, 2016.

Zhao, Zhongyuan. "Breaking New Ground in Scientific Socialism Development—Significant Contribution of the CPC Central Committee with Comrade Xi Jinping at Its Core to the Localization of Marxism in China." *People's Daily*, February 7, 2017.

Zheng, Guangkui. "Upholding the Party's Leadership and Promoting High-Quality Development." *China Discipline Inspection Daily*, December 25, 2017.

Zhong, Jingwen. "Breaking New Ground for Great Cause through Innovation in Theory and Practice." *Economic Daily*, October 17, 2017.

Zhou, Yuehui. "Leading China's High-Quality Economic Development by the Supply-Side Structural Reform." *Liaoning Daily*, December 27, 2017.

Zhu, Kexin. "Striving to Realize the Chinese Dream of National Rejuvenation." *Study Times*, June 5, 2017.

WEBSITES

Academy of Chinese Studies. "Green Is Gold: Clear Waters and Green Mountains are as Good as Mountains of Gold and Silver." Accessed July 25, 2022. https://chiculture.org.hk/en/china-today/1345.

ASEAN-China Center. "Speech by Chinese President Xi Jinping to Indonesian Parliament." Accessed October 3, 2013. http://www.asean-china-center.org/english/2013-10/03/c_133062675.htm.

Cai, Rupeng. "An All-Around Introduction of the Xiong'an New Area for the First Time." Accessed October 13, 2017. http://www.inewsweek.cn/news/ cover/1775.html.

Che, Yuming, and Dong Jun. "The Central Rural Work Conference was Held in Beijing to Make an Overall Plan for the Agricultural and Rural Work in 2008." Accessed December 23, 2014. http://www.farmer.com.cn/newzt/nlh/hhg/201412/t20141223_1002844.htm.

Chen, Nanyue. "The Status of the Yangtze River Economic Belt and the Sustainable Development in the Yangtze River Basin." Accessed August 31, 2004. http://www.eedu.org.cn/Article/es/envir/edevelopment/200408/2338.html.

Chi, Hung KWAN. "China Becoming a Major Innovation Power: Research and Development Capabilities Approaching Those of Developed Countries." Accessed July 25, 2022. https://www.rieti.go.jp/en/china/16120501.html#note1.

China Copyright and Media. "2006–2020 National Informatization Development Strategy." Accessed July 25, 2022. https://chinacopyrightandmedia.wordpress.com/2006/03/19/2006-2020-national-informatization-development-strategy/.

———. "Outline of the National Informatization Development Strategy." Accessed July 25, 2022. https://chinacopyrightandmedia.wordpress.com/2016/07/27/outline-of-the-national-informatization-development-strategy/.

———. "Speech at the Work Conference for Cybersecurity and Informatization." Accessed July 25, 2022. https://chinacopyrightandmedia.wordpress.com/2016/04/19/speech-at-the-work-conference-for-cybersecurity-and-informatization/.

China Daily. "'Broadband China' Strategy to Speed Up Network." Accessed July 25, 2022. http://www.chinadaily.com.cn/business/2013-08/19/content_16903838.htm.

———. "From Extensive to Intensive Growth." Accessed July 25, 2022. http://www.chinadaily.com.cn/opinion/2016-08/30/content_26636117.htm.

———. "Internet Plus." Accessed July 25, 2022. https://govt.chinadaily.com.cn/s/201908/16/WS5d5652dc498ebcb1905787f5/internet-plus.html.

———. "Jointly Shoulder Responsibility of Our Times, Promote Global Growth."Accessed January 17, 2017. https://language.chinadaily.com.cn/2017xuexi/2017-01/18/content_29848990.htm.

China.org.cn. "Constitution of Communist Party of China (Adopted on Nov. 14, 2012)." Accessed November 14, 2012. http://www.china.org.cn/china/18th_cpc_congress/2012-11/16/content_271 38030.htm.

———. "Decision of the CCCPC on Some Major Issues Concerning Comprehensively Deepening the Reform." Accessed July 25, 2022. http://www.china.org.cn/chinese/2014-01/17/content_31226494.htm.

———. "The Five-Sphere Integrated Plan." Accessed July 25, 2022. http://www.china.org.cn/english/china_key_words/2018-10/29/content_68862031.htm.

———. "The Four-Pronged Comprehensive Strategy." Accessed July 25, 2022. http://www.china.org.cn/english/china_key_words/2018-10/29/content_68862177.htm. "The white paper of China's Practice in Poverty Alleviation." https://language.chinadaily.com.cn/a/202104/06/WS606bffe7a31 024ad0bab3c43_4.html. Accessed 25 July 2022.

———. "Making Progress While Maintaining Stability as the Guideline for the Work of the Government." Accessed December 3, 2018. http://keywords.china.org.cn/2018-12/03/content_74235019.htm.

Cui, Xia, and Zhang Yan. "Building a Global S&T Innovation Center in the Guangdong–Hong Kong–Macao Greater Bay Area." Accessed March 30, 2018. http://news.sina.com.cn/o/2018-03-10/doc-ifyscqxy8706784.shtml.

Deng, Qi, Jin Yu, and Rao Pei. "The Guidelines for the Coordinated Development of Beijing–Tianjin–Hebei Region Was Approved." Accessed May 1, 2015. http://politics.people.com.cn/n/2015/0501/c1001-26935006.html.

Dong, Jun, and Wang Libin. "President Xi Jinping Made an Important Speech at the Central Rural Work Conference Held in Beijing." Accessed December 29, 2017. http://www.xinhuanet.com/politics/2017-12/29/c_1122187923.htm.

Du, Shangze, Song Yu, and Qu Song. "Xi Jinping Strives to Build a 'Community of Human Destiny,'" people.cn. Accessed October 7, 2018. http://dangshi.people.com.cn/n1/2018/1007/c85037-30326484.html.

Economics Discussion. "Karl Marx Theory of Economic Development." Accessed July 25, 2022. https://www.economicsdiscussion.net/economic-development/karl-marx-theory-of-economic-development/4554.

English.gov.cn. "Joint Efforts to Implement Made in China 2025." Accessed July 25, 2022. http://english.www.gov.cn/premier/news/2017/02/15/content_281475568073500.htm.

Fan, Yi. "Rural Revitalization Strategy: A New Rural-Urban Relationship from the Report to the 19th National Congress of the CPC." Accessed October 20, 2017. http://opinion.caixin.com/2017-10-20/101158844.html.

Fandom. "Opium War 1839–1842." Accessed July 25, 2022. https://military-history.fandom.com/wiki/Opium_Wars.

Galileo Galilei Italian Institute. "Urbanisation in China and the Chongqing-Chengdu City Cluster." Accessed September 17, 2019. http://www.galileiinstitute.it/urbanisation-in-china-and-the-chongqing-chengdu-city-cluster/.

Gao, Yuncai. "Empowering Agricultural Modernization (Looking Ahead to the 13th Five-Year Plan Period)." Accessed April 12, 2016. http://news.163.com/16/0412/03/BKE0UGRR00014AED.html.

Hai, Pi. "Interpretation of and Suggestions on the Rural Revitalization Strategy Launched at the 19th National Congress of the CPC." Accessed December 6, 2017. http://www.thepaper.cn/newsDetail_forward_1890821.

History. "Industrial Revolution." Accessed July 25, 2022. https://www.history.com/topics/industrial-revolution/industrial-revolution

Hong, Tao. "The Year 2018 Marks the Further Advancement of the Rural Revitalization Strategy." Accessed January 3, 2018. https://news.qq.com/a/20180103/013669.htm.

Hu, Angang. "What Goals Does China Want to Achieve by 2050?" Accessed June 18, 2017. http://www.xinhuanet.com/2017-06/18/c_1121162695.htm.

Huang, Jin, and Qin Hua. "Zhou Haijiang Talks about Entrepreneurship: Taking On Three Responsibilities and Carrying Forward Five Spirits." Accessed September 29, 2017. http://dangjian.people.com.cn.

Huo, Xiaoguang, Zhang Xudong, Wang Min, Cao Guochang, and Li Yahong. "Revealing the Whole Decision-Making Process for the Xiong'an New Area." Accessed April 13, 2017. http://finance.sina.com.cn/wm/2017-04-13/doc-ifyeifqx5665248.shtml.

Kennedy, Scott. "Made in China 2025." Accessed July 25, 2022. https://www.csis.org/analysis/made-china-2025.

Kong, Linggang. "Promoting the Modernization of Agriculture and Rural Areas through the Rural Revitalization Strategy." Accessed November 2, 2017. http://www.rmlt.com.cn/2017/1102/501778.shtml?bsh_bid=1858445538.

League for the Fifth international. "Chapter 1: The Transition from Capitalism to Communism." Accessed July 25, 2022. https://fifthinternational.org/content/chapter-1-transition-capitalism-communism?q=content/chapter-1-transition-capitalism-communism.

Liu, Lu. "Interpretation of 'Implementing the Rural Revitalization Strategy' by Han Jun, Director of the Office of Central Leading Group for Rural Work." Accessed October 23, 2017. http://country.cnr.cn/focus/20171023/t20171023_523997051.shtml.

Liu, Lu, and Shen Jingwen. "Implementing the Rural Revitalization Strategy Is an Inevitable Trend of the Times." Accessed November 8, 2017. http://news.cnr.cn/theory/gc/20171108/t20171108_524016440.shtml.

Marxists Internet Archive. "The ABC of Materialist Dialectics." Accessed July 25, 2022. https://www.marxists.org/archive/trotsky/1939/12/abc.htm.

———. "Lenin Collected Works: Volume 43." Accessed July 25, 2022. https://www.marxists.org/archive/lenin/works/cw/volume43.htm.

———. "Marxism and Development of Human Society." Accessed July 25, 2022. https://www.marxists.org/archive/shibdas-ghosh/1960/06/18.htm.

Marxists Internet Archive. "On the People's Democratic Dictatorship." Accessed July25, 2022. https://www.marxists.org/reference/archive/mao/selected-works/volume-4/mswv4_65.htm.

———. "Red Papers 8: China Advances on the Socialist Road: The Gang of Four, Revolution in the US, and the Split in the Revolutionary Communist Party." Accessed July 25, 2022. https://www.marxists.org/history/erol/ncm-5/rp-8/class.htm.

Ministry of Agriculture and Rural Affairs of the PRC. "Li Keqiang Visited the Ministry of Agriculture and Rural Affairs and Hosted a Forum to Emphasize Do Not Miss the Farming Time to Grasp the Spring Management and Spring Plowing to Ensure Food Security, and Provide Solid Support for the Stability of Economic and Social Development in General." Accessed March 25, 2022. http://www.moa.gov.cn/xw/zwdt/202203/t20220325_6393893.htm.

News of the CPC. "Deng Xiaoping: Encourage Some People to Become Well-Off First." Accessed July 25, 2022. http://cpc.people.com.cn/GB/34136/2569304.html.

———. "Episode 8: Adhere to Open Development and Build a Broad Community of Interests." Accessed November 17, 2015. http://dangjian.people.com.cn/n/2015/1117/c399958-27825704.html.

Ouyang, Song. "New Era and New Thought." Accessed November 15, 2017. http://www.qstheory.cn/dukan/qs/2017-11/15/c_1121947899.htm.

People's Daily. "Xi Jinping Thought on Socialism with Chinese Characteristics Learning Q&A." Accessed September 7, 2021, https://www.12371.cn/2021/09/07/ARTI1630968878679500.shtml.

Qiao, Jinliang. "'Modernization of Agriculture and Rural Areas' Puts Forward Higher Requirements for the Work Related to Agriculture, Rural Areas and Farmers." Accessed January 9, 2018. http://views.ce.cn/view/ent/201803/09/t20180309_28403525.shtml.

Qiao, Ruiqing. "Emphasis on the Promoting Effect of Counter-Urbanization to Urbanization." Accessed March 9, 2018. http://views.ce.cn/view/ent/201803/09/t20180309_28403525.shtml.

Qin, Zhongchun. "The Significance and Priorities of Pursuing the Rural Revitalization Strategy." Accessed November 15, 2017. http://www.cet.com.cn/ycpd/sdyd/1977923.shtml.

South China Morning Post. "Xi's 'Socialism Only Way' Remarks Get Mixed Reaction at Home." Accessed April 2, 2014. https://www.scmp.com/news/china/article/1463096/xis-socialism-only-way-remarks-get-mixed-reaction-home.

The 12th National Congress of the CPC. "Creating a New Situation in All Fields of Socialist Modernization." Accessed September 1982. http://www.gov.cn/test/200708/28/content_729792.htm.

The 15th National Congress of the CPC. "Hold High the Great Banner of Deng Xiaoping Theory for an All-Around Advancement of the Cause of Building Socialism with Chinese Characteristics to the 21st Century." Accessed September 1997. http://academics.wellesley.edu/Polisci/wj/308S/Readings/jzm15CCP.htm.

The 16th National Congress of the CPC. "Build a Well-Off Society in an All-Around Way and Create a New Situation in Building Socialism with Chinese Characteristics." Accessed November 2002. https://www.mfa.gov.cn/ce/cegv//eng/zgbd/zgbdxw/t85779.htm.

The 18th National Congress of the CPC. "Firmly March on the Path of Socialism with Chinese Characteristics and Strive to Complete the Building of a Moderately Prosperous Society in All Respects." Accessed November 2012. https://www.mfa.gov.cn/ce/ceus/eng/zt/18th_CPC_National_Congress_Eng/t992917.htm.

The Ministry of Civil Affairs in China. "Strengthening and Improving Urban and Rural Community Governance to Consolidate the Foundation of the Modernization of National Governance." Accessed July 3, 2017. http://www.gov.cn/xinwen/2017-07/03/content_5207481.htm.

The National People's Congress of the PRC. "Constitution of the PRC." Accessed July 25, 2022. http://www.npc.gov.cn/zgrdw/englishnpc/Constitution/2007-11/15/content_1372963.htm.

The State Council of the PRC. "Leading the Vigorous Development of Mass Innovation and Entrepreneurship with Institutional Supply." Accessed November 6, 2006. http://www.gov.cn/xinwen/2016-06/06/content_5079895.htm.

——, General Office of the CPC Central Committee, and General Office of the State Council. "Outline of the National Strategy for the Development of Information Technology." Accessed July 27, 2016. http://www.gov.cn/zhengce/2016-07/27/content_5095336.htm.

Tibet Daily. "Efforts to Support Grassroots Governance." Accessed November 13, 2020. https://mzzt.mca.gov.cn/article/zt_20wzqh/jdpl/202011/20201100030547.shtml.

Wang, Lei. "Solid Advancing the Strategy of Rural Revitalization to Deliver People a Better Life." Accessed March 17, 2018. http://news.cnr.cn/native/gd/20180317/t20180317_524168456.shtml.

Wei, Houkai. "Unswervingly Implementing the Rural Revitalization Strategy." Accessed November 3, 2017. http://ex.cssn.cn/zx/yw/201711/t20171103_3692639.shtml.

Wiki2. "Beidaihe Conference (1958)." Accessed July 25, 2022. https://wiki2.org/en/Beidaihe_Conference_(1958).

WordPress. "In Everything We Do We Must Proceed from the Realities of the Primary Stage of Socialism." Accessed July 25, 2022. https://dengxiaopingworks.wordpress.com/2013/03/18/in-everything-we-do-we-must-proceed-from-the-realities-of-the-primary-stage-of-socialism/.

Wu, Wei. "What's 'New' about the Xiong'an New Area?" Accessed July 9, 2017. http://epaper.bjnews.com.cn/html/2017-07/09/content_687764.htm.

Xi, Jinping. "Notice of the General Office of the National Development and Reform Commission and the General Office of the People's Bank of China on Issuing the List of the First Group of Cities

Demonstrating the Development of Social Credit System." Accessed December 28, 2017. http://www.lawinfochina.com/display.aspx?id=27246&lib=law.

———. "Secure a Decisive Victory in Building a Moderately Prosperous Society in All Respects and Strive for the Great Success of Socialism with Chinese Characteristics for a New Era." Accessed October 18, 2017. http://www.gov.cn/zhuanti/2017-10/27/content_5234876.htm.

———. "Working Together to Forge a New Partnership of Win-win Cooperation and Create a Community of Shared Future for Mankind." Accessed September 29, 2015. https://www.fmprc.gov.cn/mfa_eng/topics_665678/2015zt/xjpdmgjxgsfwbcxlhgcl70znxlfh/201510/t20151012_705405.html.

Xinhuanet. "(Authorized release) Communiqué of the Fifth Plenary Session of the 19th CPC Central Committee." Accessed October 29, 2020. http://www.xinhuanet.com/2020-10/29/c_1126674147.htm.

———. "China: Democracy that Works." Accessed July 25, 2022. https://language.chinadaily.com.cn/a/202112/07/WS61aefdb1a310cdd39bc79e03.html.

———. "Feature: Green Is Gold—Xi Jinping Innovates Fight against Climate Change." Accessed July 25, 2022. http://www.xinhuanet.com/english/2021-04/22/c_139898299.htm.

———. "Full Text: Resolution of the CPC Central Committee on the Major Achievements and Historical Experience of the Party over the Past Century." Accessed July 25, 2022. https://english.www.gov.cn/policies/latestreleases/202111/16/content_WS6193a935c6d0df57f98e50b0.html.

———. "Never Limit Ourselves to Our Own Little World—Xi Jinping Puts Forward Seven Requirements for the Beijing–Tianjin–Hebei Coordinated Development." Accessed February 27, 2014. http://www.xinhuanet.com/politics/2014-02/27/c_119538131.htm.

———. "Report on the Work of the Government: Delivered at the Fifth Session of the 13th National People's Congress of the People's Republic of China on March 5, 2022." Accessed July 25, 2022, https://language.chinadaily.com.cn/a/202203/12/WS62344f4ca310fd2b29e51d59.html.

———. "Resolution of the CPC Central Committee on the Major Achievements and Historical Experience of the Party over the Past Century." Accessed July 25, 2022. https://language.chinadaily.com.cn/a/202111/18/WS6195aa45a310cdd39bc75fe0.html.

———. "Xi's Explanation of Resolution on Major Achievements and Historical Experience of CPC over Past Century." Accessed July 25, 2022. http://en.qstheory.cn/2021-11/16/c_682069.htm.

Xiong, Ruoyu. "Promoting the Synchronous Development of the 'New Four Modernizations.'" Accessed February 15, 2016. http://theory.gmw.cn/2016-02/15/content_18880816.htm.

Yao, Ling. "China Is Marching toward a Strong Maritime Country in the New Era." Accessed October 20, 2017. http://www.sohu.com/a/199143757_115376.

Ye, Xingqing. "Taking the Path of New Agricultural Modernization with Chinese Characteristics." Accessed February 26, 2015. http://news.163.com/15/0226/17/AJD7MOM300014SEH.html.

Zhang, Houming. "The Enlightenment from the Integration of Urban and Rural Development in South Korea." Accessed June 25, 2014. http://intl.ce.cn/sjjj/qy/201406/25/t20140625_3040304.shtml.

Zhang, Junbiao, and Zhang Lu. "How to View and Implement the Rural Revitalization Strategy?" Accessed November 14, 2017. http://ex.cssn.cn/glx/glx_xzlt/201711/t20171114_3741598.shtml.

Zhang, Li. "Interpretation of the 'Made in China 2025' Plan." Accessed July 15, 2015. http://www.chinatoday.com.cn/chinese/economy/fxb/201507/t20150715_800035214.html.

Zhang, Yitian. "Significant Opportunities from the Synchronous Development of the New Four Modernizations—An Interview with Liu Shijin, Deputy Director of the Development Research

Center of the State Council." Accessed March 25, 2013. http://theory.people.com.cn/n/2013/0325/c40531-20900531.html.

———. "The Synchronization Development of the New Four Modernizations is a Grand Thought on the Modernization Drive—An Interview with Han Jun, Deputy Director of the Development Research Center of the State Council)." Accessed April 21, 2013. http://politics.people.com.cn/n/2013/0421/c1001-21216998.html.

Zhao, Chao, An Bei, Wang Xi, and Zhang Xinxin. "Historic Achievements and Changes—A Commentary on How Xi Jinping's Thought on Socialist Economy with Chinese Characteristics for a New Era Steers Chinese Economy and Society Ahead." Accessed December 26, 2017. http://www.xinhuanet.com/2017-12/25/c_1122164583.htm.

Zhao, Hong. "Graphics: Explaining China's Poverty Alleviation Efforts." Accessed July 25, 2022. https://news.cgtn.com/news/2021-04-06/Graphics-Explaining-China-s-poverty-alleviation-efforts-ZexkKqf3Gw/index.html.

Zheng, Wujing. "Exploration of the Basic Economic System and the Road to Common Wealth (Monograph on the Celebration of the 100th Anniversary of the Founding of the Communist Party of China)." Accessed November 4, 2021. http://theory.people.com.cn/n1/2021/1104/c40531-32273032.html.

Index

ABOUT THE AUTHOR

JIANXUN SHI is a professor of economics at the School of Economics and Management at Tongji University, China. He has two additional positions at the university: the director of the school's Institute of Finance and Economics and the deputy dean and chief expert of its National Institute of Innovation and Development. Professor Shi is also the chief expert for major projects at the National Social Science Foundation of China, the deputy chairman of the Shanghai Society of Finance, and the deputy chairman of the Shanghai Society of World Economics. Professor Shi's research focuses on political economy, macroeconomics, and international finance. His research has won many awards, including first prize in the outstanding achievement award for philosophy and social sciences in China, the prize in the outstanding achievement award for philosophy and social sciences in Shanghai, and many others. Professor Shi has published over one hundred articles in various newspapers and magazines and has published 22 academic books and textbooks.

ABOUT THE TRANSLATOR

BOYING LI is an associate professor in the School of Political Science and International Relations at Tongji University, China, and is also an adjunct research fellow of the Institute of China and World Studies at Tongji University. Professor Li completed her doctoral degree in economics from the Antai College of Economics and Management at Shanghai Jiao Tong University and a master's degree in agricultural economics from the Department of Agricultural and Resource Economics, University of California, Davis, after having completed her bachelor's degree in economics at the School of Economics at Zhejiang University in China. Professor Li's research interests are political economy, international trade, environmental politics and policy, energy economics and policy, and empirical research methods. Professor Li has published one academic monograph called *A Study of Improving the Enforcement of Environmental Regulation through Strengthening Bureaucratic Accountability*. Professor Li's recent work has appeared in many prestigious Chinese and English academic journals, including *Resources, Recycling and Conservation, Economic Systems, Journal of Cleaner Production*, and many others. Professor Li has also chaired the research programs of the National Natural Science Foundation of China, the National Social Science Foundation of China and hosted several provincial and ministerial research projects. Professor Li has been honored as a Shanghai Chenguang Scholar.